INTERNATIONAL COURTS AND TRIBUNALS SERIES

General Editors
RUTH MACKENZIE
CESARE P. R. ROMANO
MIKAEL RASK MADSEN

The Performance of Africa's International Courts

INTERNATIONAL COURTS AND TRIBUNALS SERIES

A distinctive feature of modern international society is the increase in the number of international judicial bodies and dispute settlement and implementation control bodies; in their case-loads; and in the range and importance of the issues that are called upon to address. These factors reflect a new stage in the delivery of international justice. The International Courts and Tribunals series has been established to encourage the publication of independent and scholarly works which address, in critical and analytical fashion, the legal and policy aspects of the functioning of international courts and tribunals, including their institutional, substantive, and procedural aspects.

The Performance of Africa's International Courts

Using Litigation for Political, Legal, and Social Change

Edited by

JAMES THUO GATHII

OXFORD
UNIVERSITY PRESS

Great Clarendon Street, Oxford, OX2 6DP,
United Kingdom

Oxford University Press is a department of the University of Oxford.
It furthers the University's objective of excellence in research, scholarship,
and education by publishing worldwide. Oxford is a registered trade mark of
Oxford University Press in the UK and in certain other countries

First Edition published in 2020

Impression: 1

Published in the United States of America by Oxford University Press
198 Madison Avenue, New York, NY 10016, United States of America

British Library Cataloguing in Publication Data

Data available

Library of Congress Control Number: 2020940026

ISBN 978–0–19–886847–7

DOI: 10.1093/oso/9780198868477.001.0001

Printed and bound by
CPI Group (UK) Ltd, Croydon, CR0 4YY

Series Editor's Preface

Of all regions of the globe, Africa is home to the largest number of international courts and tribunals, making it one of the most interesting fields of study for scholars of international adjudication. In the African continent, one can find one international court with potentially continent-wide jurisdiction—the African Court on Human and Peoples' Rights—and almost a dozen sub-regional international courts and tribunals.

The African Court on Human and Peoples' Rights started operating at the end of 2006 and over the past decade it has taken its first tentative steps, receiving more than 250 cases from individuals, non-governmental organizations and the African Commission, and deciding on the merits of a few dozen of them. In 2014, the African Union adopted the so-called Malabo Protocol to merge the African Court on Human and Peoples' Rights with a future African Court of Justice, with the intent to create an African Court of Justice and Human and Peoples' Rights, a chimeric international court, with broad subject-matter jurisdiction including human rights, international criminal law, and the interpretation and application of all African Union treaties and subsidiary legal instruments. Because of its many flaws and overly ambitious scope, the African Court of Justice and Human and Peoples' Rights might never come into existence and the African Court on Human and Peoples' Rights might continue operating in its current form. However, the very fact that it was conceived is a testament to the entrepreneurial spirit that animates the African international adjudicative landscape.

Indeed, over the years, African states have also created, or attempted to create, about a dozen sub-regional international adjudicative bodies to support regional economic integration agreements. These include the Arab Maghreb Union Judicial Authority (AMU); the Court of Justice of the Common Market of Eastern and Southern Africa (COMESA); the East Africa Court of Justice (EACJ); ; the Court of Justice of the Economic and Monetary Community of Central Africa (CEMAC); the Economic Community for West African States (ECOWAS) Court of Justice (ECCJ); the Common Court of Justice and Arbitration (CCJA) of the Organization for the Harmonization of African Business Law (OHADA); the Southern African Development Community (SADC) Tribunal; and the Court of Justice of the West African Economic and Monetary Union (WAEMU). To these, one could also add the Arab Court of Human Rights (ACHR), whose statute was adopted in 2014. If it ever starts operating, it has potentially jurisdiction over Arab League members in North Africa.

Africa has also been a fertile ground for experiments in international criminal justice. Indeed, most investigations and trials of the International Criminal Court to date have focused on Africa. Moreover, between the 1990s and the early part of the twenty-first century, the continent was home to the International Criminal Tribunal for Rwanda, to the Special Court for Sierra Leone (a hybrid international criminal court; a few more were at least considered for other crises, such as Burundi), and saw the former Chadian dictator, Hissène Habré, tried in front of the Extraordinary African Chambers in the Senegalese court system.

While Africa has the highest international courts and tribunals 'fertility rate', it also has the highest 'mortality rate'. Most international adjudicative bodies in Africa have either been nonstarters, floundered after a few years, or are languishing with a paltry docket. Only a few have managed to leave a mark on African politics and relations, causing many observers, including myself, *mea culpa*, to be rather pessimistic in their assessment of the African experiments.

This excellent volume edited by James Gathii focuses on four of the most active African international courts: the EACJ; the ECOWAS Court of Justice; the SADC Tribunal; and the African Court on Human and Peoples' Rights. It tells a story of international adjudication in Africa and its impact that is much more nuanced than the usual push/pull accounts of the effectiveness of international adjudication. It rejects simplistic assessments of the effectiveness of international adjudication that rely on crude measurements of compliance with rulings (push). It also skirts more sophisticated appraisals of the effectiveness of international courts that are made by looking for signs of movement in the direction indicated by the decisions (pull). Instead, as Gathii writes in the Preface, this book argues that "... these courts have broader impacts beyond those that the measures of compliance and effectiveness focus on. The central claim made ... is that Africa's international courts have important impacts that have so far been underemphasized or entirely ignored ... ". In particular, this book shines a powerful light on the role of Africa's international courts and tribunals in the promotion of and defense of political pluralism and freedom.

Gloomy views of the African international adjudicative landscape are often the result of conscious or unconscious comparisons with peers in Europe and the Americas. However, those comparisons are both unfair and incorrect. First, they tend not to take into account that international judicialization reached Africa only in the late 1990s and 2000s, decades after it started in Europe and in the Americas. International adjudicative bodies need time to establish themselves and increase their actual and perceived legitimacy. Second, African international courts and tribunals do not seem to struggle more, or face more pushback, than most of their peers, particularly those in the Americas. Third, compared to areas of the globe that are barren of international judicialization, such as Asia and the Pacific, Africa stands out as a vibrant laboratory. Finally, and obviously, context matters. The political, historical, economic, and social context in which African courts operate is profoundly different from the context in which international courts operate in the Americas and Europe, making cross-continent comparisons of limited use.

Scholars of international adjudication have turned their gaze to Africa only relatively recently. This volume is a major step towards building a deeper understanding of international judicialization and the many challenges it faces both in Africa and in the world.

Cesare P.R. Romano
Loyola Law School Los Angeles
June 2020

Preface

This book has been more than five years in the making. When I hosted an authors' workshop in Chicago in 2016, the premise of the project was that there were impacts of Africa's international courts that were not adequately captured in the first wave of scholarship on these courts. This book captures several ways that advance our understanding of the utility and performance of these courts. For example, as the Introduction to this book more extensively shows, cases filed in these courts promote goals beyond seeking compliance. These courts provide important advantages for human rights claimants, civil society groups that advance causes related to the environment and the rule of law, opposition politicians facing authoritarian repression, among others. Litigating in Africa's international courts provides these litigants several advantages such as giving credibility and legitimacy to their cause(s); communicating and advancing their agenda of social, political, or legal change by engaging their governments in a forum they do not control; and mobilizing press reports, thereby creating public awareness of government excesses. This book examines these possibilities and their downsides in eight compelling chapters and an extensive Introduction to the book.

I thank the authors for their patience and collaboration as these themes emerged in our back and forth discussions over the last couple of years. I am particularly grateful to have a majority of authors based in Africa or from Africa who have an extensive record of research on Africa's international courts. Some, like Solomon Ebobrah, are among the pioneering set of scholars of Africa's international courts and he brings a lot of hands-on, first-hand experience of their functioning.

Many thanks too to Loyola University of Chicago School of Law and in particular to Dean Michael Kaufman for his support of this book and my many scholarly projects. Thanks also to my faculty assistants Christine Nemes and Evelyn Gonzalez for their invaluable assistance. Many research assistants over the five years this project was in progress were very helpful, perhaps too many to name. In particular, thanks to Alison Davis, Abdulkareem Yusuf, and Harrison Mbori for their outstanding research assistance. Julienne Grant, the International Law Reference Librarian at Loyola University of the Chicago School of Law, provided excellent research support for all the materials that were not easy to trace.

I also thank Laurence R. Helfer for providing me with the French language cases from the Economic Community for West African States (ECOWAS) Community Court of Justice that formed the basis of Olabisi Akinkugbe's chapter on megapolitical disputes. Ousseni Illy facilitated access to cases from the West African Economic and Monetary Union (WAEMU) and Court of Justice of the Central

African Economic and Monetary Community (CEMAC) Courts of Justice, and those will continue to inform my future work.

The Blue Book referencing of this book was undertaken by Loan Tran, an incredible third-year law student and the Managing Editor of the *Loyola University Chicago Law Journal*. I am very grateful to her for doing this together with a couple of Law Review students that she supervised. I also thank Caitlin Chenus, Audrey Mallinak, Romina Nemaei, and Brendon Pashia for their research assistance.

This book would not have been possible were it not for the very important work being done by African international court judges as well as by African international lawyers. Although this book refers to these international lawyers as activists, that is by no means to reduce the significance of their work. I am in particular grateful to Donald Deya, Chief Executive Officer of the Pan-African Lawyers Union, and Selemani Kinyunyu, Senior Policy Officer for Political and Legal Matters at African Union Advisory Board on Corruption. My friendship and admiration of many of Africa's international court judges including Isaac Lenaola and Hon. Dr. Emmanuel Ugirashebuja, Judge-President of the East African Court of Justice, were inspirational. Their willingness to support this writing project helped it to become what it is.

Last but not least, I want to thank Caroline Muthoni Mwangi-Thuo, my wife for her incredible support for my work and for her encouragement. This book is dedicated to her. Thanks too to my children, Michael, Ethan, and Rebecca for their inquisitiveness about my work.

James Thuo Gathii
Evanston IL
February 29, 2020

Table of Contents

Table of Cases

COMESA COURT OF JUSTICE

ECOWAS COURT OF JUSTICE

EAST AFRICAN COURT OF JUSTICE

Table of Treaties

Table of Legislation

List of Abbreviations

ACHPR	African Commission on Human and Peoples' Rights
ACJHPR	African Court of Justice and Human and Peoples' Rights
ACtHPR	African Court on Human and People's Rights
AEC	African Economic Community
AG	Attorney General
AHRS	African Human Rights System
AMU	Arab Maghreb Union
APC	All Progressives Congress
APDH	Actions pour la Protection des Droits de l'Homme
AU	African Union
Banjul Charter	African Charter on Human and Peoples' Rights
BEAC	*Banque des États de l'Afrique Centrale*
CCM	Chama Cha Mapinduzi (Party of the Revolution)
CDHRDA	Centre for Defence of Human Rights and Democracy in Africa
CDP	Congrès pour la Démocratie et le Progrès
CEMAC	Court of Justice of the Central African Economic and Monetary Community (*Communauté Économique et Monétaire de l'Afrique Centrale*)
CEMACCJ	The Court of Justice of the Central African Economic and Monetary Community
CHADEMA	Chama cha Demokrasia na Maendeleo
CJEU	Court of Justice of the European Union
CNDD-FDD	National Council for the Defense of Democracy-Forces for the Defense of Democracy
COBAC	Banking Commission of Central Africa
CoM	Committee of Ministers
COMESA	Common Market for Eastern and Southern Africa
CP	civil/political
CSO	Civil Society Organization
CUF	Civic United Front
DP	Democratic Party
EAC	East African Community
EACJ	East African Court of Justice
EACSOF	East African Civil Society Organisations' Forum
EALA	East African Legislative Assembly
ECCJ	ECOWAS Community Court of Justice
ECOWAS	Economic Community for West African States
EDS	Together for Democracy and Sovereignty

ES	economic/social
FDC	Forum for Democratic Change
FDU-INKINGI	United Democratic Forces of Rwanda
FIDH	International Federation of Human Rights
FORD-P	Forum for the Restoration of Democracy-People
FPR	Rwandan Patriotic Front
FREPR	Fundamental Rights Enforcement Procedure Rules
FRODEBU	Front for Democracy in Burundi
FRODEBU-Nyakuri	Front for Democracy in Burundi-Nyakuri
GATT	General Agreement on Tariffs and Trade
IACHR	Inter American Court of Human Rights
IC	International Court
ICC	International Criminal Court
ICCPR	International Covenant on Civil and Political Rights
ICJ	International Court of Justice
ICs	International Courts
IEC	Independent Electoral Commission
INEC	Independent National Electoral Commission
KANU	Kenya African National Union
LDP	Liberal Democratic Party
LP	Liberal Party
LSK	Law Society of Kenya
NAK	National Alliance Party of Kenya
NARC	National Rainbow Coalition
NCP	National Congress Party
NGO	non-governmental organization
NRM	National Resistance Movement
OAS	Organization of American States
OAU	Organization of African Unity
ODM	Orange Democratic Movement
OHADA	Organization for the Harmonization of Business Law in Africa
OHADA CCJA	The Organization for the Harmonization of Business Law in Africa Common Court Justice and Arbitration
PALU	Pan African Lawyers Union
PDP	People's Democratic Party
PNU	Party of National Unity
PS	Permanent Secretariat
PSD	Social Democratic Party
RECs	Regional Economic Communities
RPF	Rwandan Patriotic Front
RTNB	Burundi National Television and Radio
SADC	South Africa Development Community
SADCT	Southern African Development Community Tribunal
SERAP	Socio-Economic Rights Accountability Project
SG	Secretary General

SPLM-DC	Sudan People's Liberation Movement-Democratic Change
TLP	Tanzania Labour Party
TNCs	Transnational Corporations
TREMF	trade-related, market-friendly
UA	Uniform Acts
UAM	Uniform Act on Mediation
UDHR	Universal Declaration of Human Rights
UN	United Nations
UPRONA	Union pour le Progrès National
URP	United Republican Party
WAEMU	West African Economic and Monetary Union
WAEMUCJ	West African Economic and Monetary Union Court of Justice

List of Contributors

Olabisi D. Akinkugbe, Assistant Professor, Schulich School of Law, Dalhousie University, Halifax, N.S., Canada. Ph.D. (University of Ottawa); LLM (University of Toronto), LLB (Hons) (University of Lagos, Nigeria), BL (Hons) (Nigerian Law School, Abuja)

Karen J. Alter is Lady Board of Managers of the Colombian Exposition Professor of Political Science and Law at Northwestern University and a permanent visiting professor at the iCourts Center for Excellence, University of Copenhagen, Faculty of Law

Solomon T. Ebobrah CHR, University of Pretoria & Faculty of Law, Niger Delta University, Nigeria

Okechukwu J. Effoduh is Vanier Scholar and Doctoral Candidate, Osgoode Hall Law School; LLM (Osgoode); MSt in International Human Rights Law (Oxford University, U.K.), LLB (Hons) (University of Abuja, Nigeria)

James Thuo Gathii is Professor of Law and Wing-Tat Lee Chair of International Law at Loyola University of Chicago School of Law

Andrew Heinrich is a JD Candidate at Harvard Law School

Laurence R. Helfer is Harry R. Chadwick, Sr. Professor of Law at Duke Law School, a permanent visiting professor at the iCourts Center for Excellence, University of Copenhagen Faculty of Law

Victor Lando, Managing Partner, Kamau, Lando & Associates LLP/ Lecturer, Riara Law School, Nairobi LLD, LL.M University of Pretoria, LL.B, University of Nairobi, Kenya

Jacquelene Wangui Mwangi is SJD Candidate, Graduate Program Fellow and LL.M Advisor at Harvard Law School

Obiora C. Okafor is Professor and York Research Chair in International and Transnational Legal Studies at the Osgoode Hall Law School, York University, Toronto, Canada, and the United Nations Independent Expert on Human Rights and International Solidarity, Geneva, Switzerland; Ph.D, LL.M (University of British Columbia, Vancouver, Canada)

Harrison Otieno Mbori is an SJD Candidate at Loyola University of Chicago School of Law (on leave from Strathmore Law School where he teaches)

Introduction

The Performance of Africa's International Courts

James Thuo Gathii

This book challenges and makes the case for displacing the widespread pessimism that pervades assessments of Africa's relatively new international courts. These gloomy assessments raise an important and largely unexamined question. By what standards, goals, or benchmarks should the impact of these international courts be assessed? This question is of particular importance for two reasons. First, there is no consensus about how best to measure the effectiveness and impact of international courts.[1] Second, Africa's international courts operate in different legal and political contexts from their European cousins which are often the unstated benchmark for assessing the performance of Africa's international courts. In seeking to answer this question, this book focuses on four of the most active African international courts: the East African Court of Justice (EACJ); the Economic Community of West African Community Court of Justice (ECOWAS) Court of Justice; the Southern African Development Community (SADC) Tribunal; and the African Court on Human and Peoples' Rights. These courts, together with the rest of Africa's international courts, are more fully introduced in a reference guide by James T. Gathii and Harrison O. Mbori in Chapter 8.[2]

---

[1] Yuval Shany, *Assessing the Effectiveness of International Courts: A Goal Based Approach*, 106 Am. J. Int'l L. 229 (2012) (arguing that what is therefore "needed is a richer understanding of the concept of international court effectiveness—one that moves beyond the notions of compliance inducement, usage rates, and impact").

[2] The other African international courts are the Common Market for Eastern and Southern African (COMESA) Court of Justice, the Central African Economic and Monetary Community (CEMAC) Court of Justice, and the Court of Justice of the West African Economic and Monetary Union (WAEMU). These courts have not had active dockets particularly on human rights cases such as those that are the subject of this book. Another African international court oversees the supranational corporate, commercial, and business laws of the Organization for the Harmonization of Business Law in Africa (OHADA). The OHADA Common Court of Justice & Arbitration is the highest judicial body charged with their enforcement and monitoring of compliance with OHADA Uniform Acts. Finally, the Arab Maghreb Union Judicial Organ which has not been operational is discussed in the Reference Guide in Chapter 8 with a discussion on why judicialization has been weak in North Africa. The Reference Guide also discusses the African Commission on Human and Peoples' Rights and its relationship with the African Court on Human and Peoples' Rights. These are, however, not all the courts and quasi-judicial institutions in Africa. In the Reference Guide we have focused only on judicial institutions (except the African Commission on Human and Peoples' Rights) and operational institutions (except the AMU Judicial Organ). There are present in Africa other quasi-judicial institutions such as the African Committee of Experts on the Rights and Welfare of the Child (ACERWC), the High

James Thuo Gathii, *Introduction* In: *The Performance of Africa's International Courts*. Edited by: James Thuo Gathii, Oxford University Press (2020). © The Several Contributors. DOI: 10.1093/oso/9780198868477.003.0001.

Compliance and effectiveness have come to define how the impacts of international courts are assessed. Both approaches gauge the impacts of international courts based on the compliance rates of their decisions, their usage rates, as well as their overall success or lack thereof. Assessments of compliance and effectiveness of international courts fall into two broad categories.

The first approach prioritizes measuring government compliance with legal rulings.[3] Proceeding from this view, Eric Posner and John Yoo argue that a tribunal is "effective if states comply with its judgments."[4] For them, the easiest way to measure the compliance rate for a particular court is the "the number of complied-with judgments divided by the total number of judgments."[5] From this view, international courts are less likely to be effective in getting compliance with their decisions when they ignore the interests of states and decide cases based on moral ideas and interests of individuals and interest groups.[6] If judicial decisions of international courts are mostly ignored, then there is no compliance.[7] Those influenced by this approach emphasize the sheer difficulty, financially as well as politically, of enforcing human rights rules particularly through international courts.[8]

Commission of Appeal of the African Intellectual Property Organization (AIPO), and the Board of Appeal of the African Regional Industrial Property Organization (ARIPO). In addition, there are some international courts that are not yet operational. These include the African Economic Community Court of Justice (AECCJ), the Arbitration Tribunal of the Economic Community of West African States, the Economic Community of Central African States (ECCAS) Court of Justice, and the Dispute Settlement Mechanism of the African Continental Free Trade Agreement (AfCFTA).

   [3] Eric Posner & John C. Yoo, *Judicial Independence in International Tribunals*, 93 CALIF. L. REV. 1 (2005)
   [4] *Id.* at 28. Another very similar approach to compliance measures the *de facto* authority of international courts by focusing on two preconditions by a state actor (for the court to be regarded as having *de facto* authority), "(1) recognizing an obligation to comply with court rulings and (2) engaging in meaningful action pushing toward giving full effect to those rulings." *See* Karen J. Alter et al., *How Context Shapes the Authority of International Courts*, 79 L. & CONTEMP. PROBS. 7 (2016).
   [5] Posner & Yoo, *supra* note 3, at 28.
   [6] *Id.* at 1, 7.
   [7] Posner and Yoo do acknowledge that there are a variety of problems of accurately measuring compliance including temporality and selection effects. Quite importantly for this book, they do acknowledge that the limitations of their approach at measuring compliance and effectiveness of international courts cannot easily be identified independent from competing explanatory variables. *Id.* at 28–29. In other words, where there are changes in or impacts on government policy even following a decision by an international court, if this do not constitute compliance as Posner and Yoo define it, international courts are only one variable that may have resulted in such changes and impacts may be traceable to the conduct of non-state actors in multiple venues beyond an international court.
   [8] *See, e.g.*, ERIC A. POSNER, THE TWILIGHT OF HUMAN RIGHTS LAW (1st ed., 2014) (arguing that international human rights treaties (and courts) are "too ambitious, even utopian and too ambiguous," and there is little evidence that these laws have improved people's well-being). He notes that in many countries that have signed human rights treaties, political repression and human rights violations remain. He argues that enforcing human rights laws particularly in developing countries is expensive, both financially and politically, and further that bureaucracies and courts are corrupt, slow, and ineffectual. This critique is summarized as follows: international human rights law and courts are not effective because, first, there are violations despite human rights ratifications; second, human rights treaties are ambiguous and vague; and third, there has been an overexpansion of rights and conflicting values. *See also* Lucyline Nkatha Murungi & Jacques Gallinetti, *The Role of Sub-Regional Courts in the African Human Rights System*, 7 INT'L J. HUM. RTS. 129 (2010) (noting that sub-regional courts are not

Frans Viljoen's influential work on human rights in Africa notes the lack of political will to impose sanctions to enforce international court human rights judgments particularly in the ECOWAS Community Court of Justice and the SADC Tribunal.[9] A skeptical analysis of the effectiveness of Africa's international courts that proceeded from this first approach did however acknowledge that its case-specific analysis did "not capture every possible way in which an [international court] might be effective."[10]

A second approach to measuring the effectiveness and impact of international courts prioritizes examining whether or not there is movement in the direction indicated by legal rulings or the law.[11] Where there is a greater movement in the direction of the ruling, through "observable, desired changes in behavior"[12] there is greater effectiveness and vice versa. For these theorists, compliance by itself may not provide a good yardstick to measure the different roles international courts serve.[13] Further, there may be ambiguity about which goals should form the benchmark for assessing the performance of an international court.[14] Among the

---

well equipped financially nor do they have adequate personnel to fulfill their duties as courts of justice with both human rights and other jurisdiction).

[9] FRANS VILJOEN, INTERNATIONAL HUMAN RIGHTS LAW IN AFRICA 469–516 (2nd ed., 2012) (noting that the ECOWAS Court of Justice has the power to employ sanctions against states that do not comply but has failed to do so (e.g. in the Gambian case—*Manneh* case, *id.* at 497–98), Further, he notes that the SADC Tribunal had the chance to impose sanctions against Zimbabwe in the *Campbell* case but failed to do so despite making several threats; *id.* at 498). *See also* Stacy-Ann Elvy, *Theories of State Compliance with International Law: Assessing the African Union's Ability to Ensure State Compliance with the African Charter and Constitutive Act*, 41 GA. J. INT'L & COMP. L. 75 (2012–13) (noting lack of political will among African Union Member States to enforce the findings of the African Court on Human and Peoples' Rights).

[10] Daniel Abebe, *International Human Rights Law in Africa: Are Courts Effective?*, 56 VA. J. INT'L L. 537 (2017) (measuring the following variables: court structure, volume of cases, compliance rate and funding, and independence). It is notable that there is a legitimate basis for being skeptical of the implementation of the decisions of the African Court on Human and Peoples' Rights. On compliance, *see, e.g.*, Oliver Windridge, *Guest Post: 2014 at The African Court on Human and Peoples Rights—A Year in Review*, OPINIOJURIS (Oct. 1, 2015), http://opiniojuris.org/2015/01/10/guest-post-2014-african-court-human-peoples-rights-year-review/;

[11] Kal Raustiala, *Compliance and Effectiveness in International Regulatory Cooperation*, 32 CASE WESTERN RESERVE J. INT'L L. 393 (2000) (defining effectiveness as "the degree to which a legal rule or standard induces desired changes in behavior that furthers the goals of the rule; the degree to which a rule improves the state of the underlying problem; or the degree to which a rule achieves its inherent objectives").

[12] *Id.* at 393–94; *see also* Laurence Helfer, *The Effectiveness of International Adjudicators*, in OXFORD HANDBOOK OF INTERNATIONAL ADJUDICATION 464 (Karen Alter et al. eds., 2014) (identifying at least four methodological approaches to measuring the effectiveness of international courts: (i) case-specific effectiveness (under which a state changes behavior as a result of a ruling by an international court); (ii) *erga omnes* effectiveness (which measures the effectiveness of international court rulings on a broad range of constituencies); (iii) embeddedness effectiveness (under which international court adjudication is unnecessary because domestic courts are sufficient); and (iv) norm-development effectiveness (under which effectiveness is measured by how an international court helps to build a body of jurisprudence)).

[13] Laurence Helfer & Anne-Marie Slaughter, *Why States Create International Tribunals: A Response to Professors Posner and Yoo*, 93 CALIF. L. REV. 899, 918 (2005).

[14] Yuval Shany, *Assessing the Effectiveness of International Courts: A Goal Based Approach*, 106 AM. J. INT'L L. 233 (2012).

additional roles and goals that international courts serve beyond compliance, include vindicating rights and the grappling with the validity of transitional justice processes.[15] The emphasis here is that judicial decisions matter beyond compliance because quantitative measurements do not measure how such decisions create normative consequences and ripples. Scholars who use effectiveness as a measure of court performance have extended their analysis beyond European courts and found that establishing international courts in developing country contexts does not necessarily hinder the efficacy of international adjudication.[16]

This book has more in common with scholars who measure the performance of international courts by examining their effectiveness. However, as many of the chapters in this book show both compliance and effectiveness do not adequately account for the types of impact of Africa's international courts.[17] This is because there is more utility to Africa's international courts beyond whether or not their decisions have been complied with or the extent to which their decisions encourage states to move in the direction that Africa's international courts nudge them towards. In other words, this book argues and shows that these courts have broader impacts beyond those that the measures of compliance and effectiveness focus on. The central claim made in this book is that Africa's international courts have important impacts that have so far been underemphasized or entirely ignored.[18] For example, opposition politicians and parties bring strategic litigation to Africa's international courts as one venue, among others, for mobilizing support for the

[15] Tom Gerald Daly, *The Alchemists: Courts as Democracy Builders in Contemporary Thought*, 6 GLOB. CONST. 101, 108 (2017).

[16] KAREN J. ALTER & LAURENCE HELFER, TRANSPLANTING INTERNATIONAL COURTS: THE LAW AND POLITICS OF THE ANDEAN TRIBUNAL OF JUSTICE, (1st ed., 2017).

[17] This book does not seek to resolve the unsettled and contested evaluative tools and methodologies for measuring international courts. It is notable that these evaluative tools for measuring the performance of international courts proceed from theories developed to measure the performance of courts in North America and Europe. These theories therefore reflect the particular historical and institutional legacies from which they were developed. On the unsettled methodological approaches to the measurement of effectiveness of international courts, *see* Yuval Shany, *Assessing the Effectiveness of International Courts: A Goal Based Approach*, 106 AM. J. INT'L L. 229 (2012) (noting that the "current literature's lack of clear, persuasive criteria for assessing the effectiveness of international adjudication bodies, coupled with the theoretical and methodological difficulties associated with actually measuring such criteria, generates unsatisfying results as well as mis-understandings about the effectiveness of international courts"). Examples of some of the limits of measurement include the fact that the approaches emphasize quantitative measurements of international court compliance which may not be suitable to credibly and clearly demonstrate causation. *Id.* Further, there are difficulties associated with tracing the effectiveness of international courts through judicial enforcement of ideals of human rights. *Id.*

[18] In this sense, this book follows scholarship that argues in favor of exploring a broader range of objectives and theories for evaluating the performance of international courts. *See, e.g.,* Yuval Shany, *Assessing the Effectiveness of International Courts*, 2015 EUR. Y.B. INT'L ECON. L. 423 (2015), https://link.springer.com/chapter/10.1007%2F978-3-662-46748-0_19. *See also* Laurence R. Helfer, *The Effectiveness of International Adjudicators, in* THE OXFORD HANDBOOK OF INTERNATIONAL ADJUDICATION (Karen J. Alter et al. eds., 2013) (arguing in favor of four types of impacts of international courts underemphasized in the literature. These are case-specific effectiveness; *erga omnes* effectiveness, embeddedness effectiveness, and norm-development effectiveness. In so doing, this book pushes back against analysis that designate African sub-regional courts as failures).

promotion of and defense of political freedom.[19] By filing cases in international courts, opposition parties, politicians, and litigants articulate their grievances and in so doing preserve oppositional norms and values in countries where political opposition survival faces repressive control by authoritarian states. In so doing, these opposition politicians and political parties seek to build, maintain, and defend social and political movements.

In this book, this role of Africa's international courts in the promotion of and defense of political freedom is illustrated by showing how they serve as coordination points for opposition political parties in a manner that influences national politics. For example, James Thuo Gathii's chapter (Chapter 1) on the EACJ shows how cases challenging the electoral malpractices of dominant parties in the EACJ from four of the six Member States of the East African Community, facilitates opposition mobilization against those malpractices. When opposition parties win those cases, they use their judicial success to further mobilize their supporters against their government. These cases are a window into the types of electoral manipulations dominant parties engage in, but more importantly the type of effects on the democratization processes that are not readily measurable by theories based on compliance and effectiveness. By naming election violations as treaty breaches, the EACJ gives opposition political parties and politicians opportunities to rally their supporters in favor of their cause and a platform to campaign against dominant parties in their home countries. Even though many of these cases are overtly political, litigants before international courts have nearly perfected into an art how to discipline and shape their claims into legal claims that are justiciable and consistent with the law of these international courts.

As Olabisi Akinkugbe's shows in Chapter 4, cases challenging national election malpractices such as exclusionary constitutional rules on electoral candidacy in the ECOWAS Community Court of Justice become a springboard for the mobilization of opposition politics. Although cases challenging national electoral malpractices are matters of domestic rather than international jurisdiction, the ECOWAS Community Court of Justice has uniformly rejected applications to dismiss those cases on jurisdictional grounds. Thus in both East and West Africa, opposition parties and politicians use international courts among other mechanisms in their quest to structure an environment of open political competition and limited government.[20] The aim of these opposition political parties and politicians is not necessarily to prevail in the courtroom, but rather to use the opportunity or

---

[19] By emphasizing non-compliance metrics of Africa's sub-regional court performance this book foregrounds the utility of these non-European courts not merely as contexts of reception of transplanted norms, but as contexts of production as well.

[20] As Daly, *supra* note 15, at 124, argues, "[t]here is clear need for greater exploration and conceptualization of how domestic and regional courts interact as democracy builders, and how the democratization context shapes this interaction." *Id.* Daly also notes that the African Court of Human and Peoples' Rights has taken a "strong stance on violations of the African Charter regarding exclusionary constitutional rules on electoral candidacy." *Id.*

foothold an international court provides to create an additional leverage point in their quest to build and maintain movements to open political competition and to safeguard limited government in their home country. The types of impacts this book therefore focuses on are not based on "litigation as an exclusive end in it-self."[21] In this sense, this book brings to the scholarship on international courts, the social legal literature on the role of cause lawyering.[22]

In both East and West Africa, international court judges are drawn into these political strategies because opposition politicians and parties frame their cases as raising questions of treaty violations. International courts, fully aware of the limited political space they occupy adopt a variety of strategies. For example, in Chapter 5 Solomon Ebobrah and Victor Lando's show how the EACJ has turned to issuing declaratory rather than mandatory decisions. Adopting such a strategy lowers the possibility of direct confrontation with East African governments. Repeat litigants before the EACJ have leveraged its willingness to issue declaratory judgments. They have been undeterred by the fact that they are unlikely to get mandatory orders. Unlike mandatory orders, declaratory orders do not create the type of direct conflicts that mandatory orders do because they require governments to do certain things. Declaratory orders leave the governments with wiggle room about how to respond to the orders of the EACJ. It is in this context then that it becomes clear why these international courts decline the invitation by governments to readily dismiss politically sensitive human rights cases on the ground that such cases are not justiciable or because they fall within the exclusive jurisdiction of domestic courts. Because of the judicial strategy international court judges adopt, they can entertain cases as long as they raise a possible treaty violation that falls within their jurisdiction even if the factual background of such cases revolve around a political dispute. This and similar judicial approaches allow these international courts to accept and decide cases that raise questions about the structure of political competition without overstepping what is politically feasible. In so doing, international courts open pathways for opposition parties and politicians to mobilize their constituencies during the litigation and afterwards. By contrast, where international courts overstep their boundaries, as the Southern Africa Development Community (SADC) Tribunal did by ruling against the government of Zimbabwe, they risk a backlash against them. In addition, as discussed in Chapter 6 by James Gathii and Jacquelene Mwangi and further below, some African countries have withdrawn from the optional declaration under Article 34(6) of the Protocol to the African

---

[21] Michael McCann & Helena Silversten, *Rethinking Law's "Allurements": A Relational Analysis of Social Movement Lawyers in the United States*, in AUSTIN SARAT & STUART SCHEINGOLD, CAUSE LAWYERING: POLITICAL COMMITMENTS AND PROFESSIONAL RESPONSIBILITIES 269 (Keith Hawkins et al. eds.,1998).

[22] *See, e.g.*, CAUSE LAWYERS AND SOCIAL MOVEMENTS (Austin Sarat & Stuart Scheingold eds., 2006); JOEL F. HANDLER, SOCIAL MOVEMENTS AND THE LEGAL SYSTEM: A THEORY OF LAW REFORM AND SOCIAL CHANGE (1978).

Charter on the Establishment of the African Court on Human and Peoples' Rights allowing individuals and non-governmental organizations (NGOs) direct access to the court after adverse rulings against them.

A primary reason for the misalignment between the roles of African international courts such as those described earlier and measurements of their performance based on compliance and effectiveness, is because they have been developed on the basis of European and developed country experiences.[23] The fact that Africa's international courts serve roles other than those contemplated by theories of compliance and effectiveness does not mean that these African international courts are flawed or indeed failures, but rather they are an independent and legitimate type of legalization.[24] It is particularly notable how the timing of the establishment of the human rights jurisdiction of Africa's international courts has been a factor in the path these courts have followed.[25] The EACJ established its human rights cause of action in 2005, the same year that the jurisdiction of the ECOWAS Community Court of Justice was expanded to include human rights. In both East and West Africa, very active bar associations were readily at hand to mobilize these new courts. When the SADC Tribunal decided the controversial *Campbell* case against Zimbabwe in 2007, the Tribunal's jurisdiction was invoked not by civil society groups who had carefully considered their litigation strategy. Rather it was by individual litigants who did not consider the implications their politically explosive case would have on the continued availability of the Tribunal for other litigants in the future. Thus, judicialization of Zimbabwe's explosive land politics in the SADC Tribunal reflects a classic dilemma faced by movement activists about the best litigation strategies to pursue—how to capitalize on strategic litigation in a manner that does not jeopardize future access.[26] Herein lies the dilemma, while civil society groups are more likely not to bring cases that result in backlash, individual litigants who want justice for their cases may not.

In short, in the mid-2000s the role of human rights and constitutional principle in African politics had become very prominent as many African countries had renewed their commitment to constitutionalism and individual rights in the

---

[23] Indeed as Daly, *supra* note 15, at 123, notes, "the insights provided by scholarship centered on Europe will have limited relevance to regions outside Europe."

[24] *See* Alter & Helfer, *supra* note 16, at 274 (arguing that international courts outside Europe "deploy strategies that diverge from those of European tribunals in response to the distinctive legal and political contexts that these emerging courts face"). See also Sungjoon Cho & Jürgen Kurtz, *Legalizing the ASEAN Way: Adapting and Reimagining the ASEAN Investment Regime*, 66 AM. J. COMP. L. 233–66 (2018).

[25] James Gathii, *The COMESA Court of Justice*, in THE LEGITIMACY OF INTERNATIONAL TRADE COURTS AND TRIBUNALS, 314–48 (R. Howse, H. Ruiz-Fabri, G. Ulfstein, & M. Zang, eds., 2018).

[26] MARK TUSHNET, THE NAACP'S LEGAL STRATEGY AGAINST SEGREGATED EDUCATION, 1925–1958, at 138 (1987) (discussing the ideological and strategic differences among lawyers litigating to end racial segregation in the United States); William B. Rubenstein, *Divided We Litigate: Addressing Disputes Among Group Members and Lawyers in Civil Rights*, 106 YALE L. J. 1623 (1997) (examining how tactical differences and disagreements arise between group-oriented versus individual-based models of social movement litigation).

context of the third wave of democratization of the post-Cold War period. In this context, activists, opposition parties, and politicians began looking for new venues such as international courts to begin securing fidelity to commitments to human rights and the rule of law embodied in the constitutive treaties of these new courts. However, the strategies of these actors diverged and these differences have been consequential for the fate of these international courts.[27] Thus, the strategies of the lone-litigants before the SADC Tribunal diverged from the group-oriented litigation strategy of the East African Law Society before the EACJ. This book argues this context within which these international courts were established and the choices and strategies deployed by litigants should be a crucial starting point for understanding their performance and impact. The availability of regional and sub-regional human rights norms that could be judicialized in international courts created new opportunities for norm entrepreneurs such as human rights victims and their advocates in civil society and opposition parties. International courts, particularly in East and West Africa positioned themselves as friendly venues for these new norm entrepreneurs.[28] While these judges of Africa's international courts came to see it as their role to hold states true to the commitments they voluntarily entered into, the use of these courts to enforce these commitments created the potential that states would oppose the use of these courts when they extended their roles beyond what the states could accept.[29]

Major Insights Developed in the Book

Drawing on a rich interdisciplinary scholarship and in-depth case-studies, a major insight at the heart of this book therefore is that focusing only on the low compliance rates of Africa's international court decisions as proxies for measuring their impacts only tells one dimension of a multi-dimensional story for at least four important reasons.

First, measuring the compliance and effectiveness or effectiveness of international courts focuses too much on the behavior of states as well as state-based and state-driven compliance processes and in so doing ignores or underplays the roles non-state actors and judges play in shaping and using litigation processes both inside and outside of the courtroom. Thus compliance and effectiveness inadequately

---

[27] By contrast, consider the establishment of the COMESA Court of Justice in the late 1990s and located in Lusaka, Zambia, both factors that have directed it away from deciding human rights cases. For more, see Gathii, *supra* note 25, at 314–48.

[28] On the East African Court of Justice, see James Gathii, *Mission Creep or a Search for Relevance: The East African Court of Justice's Human Rights Strategy*, 24 DUKE J. COMP. & INT'L L. 249–96 (2013); for the ECOWAS Court of Justice, see Karen J. Alter et al., *A New International Human Rights Court for West Africa: The ECOWAS Community Court of Justice*, 107 AM. J. INT'L L. 737–79 (2013).

[29] See, e.g., Sebalu v. Secretary General of the East African Community, Ref. No. 1 of 2010, First Instance Div., at 42 (June 30, 2010).

measure the impact of international courts in Africa. By moving away from the emphasis on coercive capabilities of the state embedded in accounts of compliance and effectiveness, this book shows that filing cases in Africa's international courts is often a strategic decision by interest groups, litigants, and opposition political parties and politicians. These actors seek to enforce treaty commitments relating to human rights, the rule of law, and democracy in a way that those in control of dominant and authoritarian party regimes would rather they give up and betray. Even further, by bringing a domestic political dispute to an international court, they achieve another significant goal—they internationalize their dispute. In so doing, they mobilize law and capitalize on the litigation process to advance and promote their commitment to their ideals—such as the defense and promotion of political freedom. This mobilization in turn enables them to advance their social, political, and legal causes in their national jurisdictions.[30] International courts provide opposition political parties and politicians, particularly those who reject any form of compromise with dominant and authoritarian regimes in their home countries, a venue to peacefully channel political conflicts that arise from the systematic obstruction of their political activity imposed by incumbent political parties. In this sense, Africa's international courts are not only deciding and affirming the rights of these litigants and their supporters in their decisions, but also draw these international courts into national democratic politics and processes. Quite often, these cases are a strategy of pressuring and triggering domestic institutions and processes to engage with these litigants. International courts are therefore one among other pressure points opposition parties resort to defend themselves against repressive and restrictive authoritarian political practices as well as to mobilize against such practices. International courts can be particularly important venues to channel political conflict where intractable conflicts are incapable of being channeled through domestic institutions. International courts are important for opposition parties, in part because they realize they cannot realistically contend for political power in their home countries. For example, as Andrew Heinrich illustrates in Chapter 2, the EACJ has played this role for Burundi. This was particularly so when an incumbent government seeking a third term in violation of its Constitution made it impossible for opposition parties, politicians, and civil society groups to resort to domestic institutions to resolve the conflict with a highly authoritarian president. Although the EACJ cannot resolve the contentious and often violent politics of repressive governments like that of Burundi, its availability provided those opposed to the third-term bid by an authoritarian president an opportunity to collectively mobilize, protest, and seek external support and validation. The chapter by James

---

[30] From these perspectives, these litigants "believe in the ideals and values embodied in [these] norms or ideas because they believe in the ideals and values embodied in the norms, even though the pursuit of the norms may have no effect on their well-being." Martha Finnemore & Kathryn Sikkink, *International Norm Dynamics and Political Change*, 52 INT'L ORG. 897 (1998).

Thuo Gathii and Jacquelene Mwangi on the African Court on Human and Peoples' Rights (Chapter 6) shows how a broad range of actors, including political prisoners, took advantage of a favorable legal opportunity structure to advance their causes. The legal opportunity structure the, African Court on Human and Peoples' Rights, arose from the fact that once states had agreed to allow individuals to file cases in the court, its rules governing standing, jurisdiction, and admissibility are interpreted permissively, and further that the rules relating to costs do not burden potential litigants. As a result, the chapter discusses how political dissidents like Ingabire Victoire Umuhoza from Rwanda and the Tanzanian politician, the late Christopher Mtikila used litigation to advance their causes since they had run out of options within their domestic political and judicial systems. As the chapter shows, Ingabire successfully used litigation in the court in a way that we believe resulted in her release from prison. Her release was, however, a mixed blessing because not too long after that, the government of Rwanda decided to withdraw its optional declaration under Article 34(6) of the Protocol to the African Charter on the Establishment of the African Court on Human and Peoples' Rights allowing individuals and NGOs direct access to the court.

In addition, as James Thuo Gathii's chapter (Chapter 1) on elections to the East African Legislative Assembly shows, Burundi opposition parties and leaders resorted to the East African Legislative Assembly to condemn the ongoing violations of human rights in Burundi. This was in addition to resorting to the EACJ to seek its intervention against the incumbent President's bid to extend his term. Thus, resorting to an international court may advance the agenda of opposition parties, politicians and other litigants as one in a number of alternative forums or pressure points they can turn to in their multi-dimensional struggle against incumbent political parties. This is particularly true where their goal is to put pressure on the incumbent party from many different angles. However, as I note more fully later in the discussion of the backlash against the SADC Tribunal, resorting to an international court could also result in the types of setbacks for these opposition parties, such as increased repression, that characterize processes of democratization in Africa.

Second, contrary to assumptions embedded in compliance analysis that the primary reason for bringing cases to these courts is to seek compliance with favorable rulings, a primary reason that litigants and opposition politicians bring cases in Africa's international courts is to involve them in their controversies both with their government as well as with dominant political parties.[31] While they would

---

[31] In so doing, this book takes seriously the important role that local and regional norms and actors play in calling attention to government misconduct and authoritarian practices using the language of human rights and the rule of law and sub-regional courts in Africa as the site for naming these abuses and practices while seeking greater political and civic space for opposition parties and civil society actors in their quest to democratize their states. In so doing these litigants challenge what Finnemore and Sikkink referred to as the "existing logics of appropriateness." *See id.* at 898.

hope for a favorable ruling, activists, litigants, and opposition parties and politicians fully well understand that non-compliance with favorable rulings is a very
likely outcome. The chapters in this book show that these litigants fully understand
this. What is more, they have goals that go beyond whether or not governments
will comply with those rulings when and if they prevail.[32] For these litigants, filing
cases before Africa's international courts helps them in a variety of ways including
exposing the misdeeds of their governments. As Solomon Ebobrah and Victor
Lando show in their chapter (Chapter 5), the availability of international courts at
about the turn of the millennium provided a new opportunity for litigants to flag
human rights violations once they filed cases before international courts. These
cases served as a warning system, a role that cannot be underestimated, particularly where cases come from a country with ineffective domestic human rights
monitoring and protection institutions and systems. They give the example of how
the *Plaxeda Rugumba* case from Rwanda, in the EACJ publicly exposed the arrest and detention incommunicado of an individual whose family had no other
viable forums to prompt the Rwandese government to disclose his whereabouts.
In responding to the case, the government of Rwanda disclosed that Ms. Plaxeda
Rugumba was in military custody and that he had been brought before a military
tribunal. It was filing the case in the EACJ that prompted the Rwandese government to disclose they were holding him and to seek a military tribunal's order to
"regularize" his detention in accordance with Rwandese law. The cases also help
these litigants because they play a role in generating disapproval or stigma of government conduct.[33] Quite significantly, this strategy of exposing governmental
misdeeds and generating disapproval or stigma, or praise where there is obedience,
does not depend on the availability of explicit incentives or enforcement mechanisms where a judicial decision is not conformed with.[34]

The value of bringing such a case, particularly against very repressive governments, for example, the Gambian government in the case of the journalist *Chief
Ebrimah Manneh* in the ECOWAS Community Court of Justice, can set in motion a chain of events that embolden an international court. By the time the court

---

[32] Indeed as Michael Lipsky in Michael Lipsky, *Protest as a Political Resource*, 62 AM. POL. SCI. REV.
1153 (1968) argues the goal of political protest is "activating third parties to participate in controversy in
ways favorable to protest goals." *Id.*

[33] In this sense, the litigants are norm entrepreneurs who bring cases before these courts to convince others about the appropriateness or inappropriateness of their cause. On this, *see* Finnemore and
Sikkink, *supra* note 30, at 892.

[34] Compliance based approaches to evaluating the performance of international courts proceed from
a coercion-based account of law. From this perspective, coercion is an essential if not a natural requirement for a legal system. *See* H.L.A. HART, THE CONCEPT OF LAW 198 (3rd ed., 2012). According to Hart,
sanctions are necessary "as a guarantee that those who would voluntarily obey shall not be sacrificed
to those who would not." This is the approach adopted in JACK L. GOLDSMITH & ERIC A. POSNER, THE
LIMITS OF INTERNATIONAL LAW (1st ed., 2005). It is beyond the scope of this book to examine whether
there can be law without the use of coercion; for that *see* FREDERICK SCHAUER, THE FORCE OF LAW
(2015).

announced that the detention of the journalist was illegal and that his family was owed damages, his family and journalist organizations around the world had used the opportunity provided by litigating the case to condemn the repressive governance of the Gambian regime. They were also able to expose its disregard for human rights in a way that was not otherwise possible, particularly in Gambia. In the subsequent *Saidykhan* case, that involved another journalist, the Gambian government decided to appear before the ECOWAS Court of Justice to defend itself for illegal detention and torture, something it had decided not to do in the *Manneh* case. As Eboborah and Lando show in their chapter, when *Saidykhan* won his case against Gambia, there was further international outcry as well as a debate within the ECOWAS Parliament seeking an explanation of Gambia's record of human rights violations. The Gambian government resisted both cases by limiting the jurisdiction of the ECOWAS Court of Justice. That bid to clip the wings of the Court catapulted a process that resulted in treaty reforms that formally granted the Court jurisdiction over human rights.[35]

Third, foregrounding compliance inaccurately presupposes litigation is being pursued in these non-European courts because litigants see them as primary change agents. Such an assumption is based on the experience of structural reform litigation in North America and Latin America.[36] This assumption is further fortified by theoretical priorities that are based on experiences that have no direct relevance to non-European courts. Yet, as the chapters in this book show, there is no assumption by users of Africa's international courts that they are structural reformers.[37] Further as alluded to already, compliance-centric analysis do not also capture how litigating cases in international courts gives litigants opportunities to engage in political mobilization that would otherwise be difficult if not be impossible in the absence of such litigation.

In short, international courts in Africa create opportunities for political mobilization as well as for naming and shaming that would otherwise not exist.[38] Thus, whether a case is won or lost, once it is filed in an international court, it becomes a focal point to galvanize, publicize, and mobilize organizational support as well as fund-raising. When a case is lost, litigants use it to appeal to sympathetic

---

[35]   *See* Karen J. Alter, Laurence Helfer, & Jacqueline R. McAllister, *A New International Human Rights Court for West Africa: The ECOWAS Community Court of Justice*, 107 AM. J. INT'L L. 737–79 (2013).

[36]   *See* Alexandra Huneeus, *Reforming the State from Afar: Structural Reform Litigation at the Human Rights Courts*, 40 YALE J. INT'L L. 1 (2015).

[37]   In this sense, these litigants and activists intuitively know that judicial orders reduce complicated questions of governance and rights to narrowly drawn legal questions in addition to having limited remedies. In fact, they recognize that on the whole courts lack the institutional authority and capacity to enforce their own rulings. One of the classic critiques of courts as reformers is explored in GERALD ROSENBERG, THE HOLLOW HOPE: CAN COURTS BRING ABOUT SOCIAL CHANGE? (1st ed., 1991).

[38]   On how international human rights treaties create litigation opportunities, *see* BETH A. SIMMONS, MOBILIZING FOR HUMAN RIGHTS: INTERNATIONAL LAW IN DOMESTIC POLITICS (2009) (noting the treaties signal to domestic groups that there may be some people in government that may support their causes which increases their probability of prevailing than in the absence of such treaties).

individuals and groups by highlighting the injustices they face. As such these non-European international courts are not independent actors isolated from other sites of political, social, and legal contestation. From this perspective, international courts are one venue in a multi-dimensional and multi-pronged strategy that includes other venues and pressure points.

To illustrate how litigants and activists who file cases before Africa's international courts pursue goals beyond those that are contemplated by compliance and effectiveness analysis, the chapters in this book put the users of international courts and their broader strategies at the center of their analysis. A key backdrop against which the impacts analyzed in this book arise is that a dominant and often authoritarian political party in power has restricted political space for civil society and opposition politics at the national level.[39] As Gathii's chapter on cases filed challenging elections to the East African Legislative Assembly (Chapter 1) shows, the relative strength of organizational rights across the six East African member States is highly predictive of whether or not cases challenging electoral malpractices will be filed. Thus there are few to no cases challenging electoral violations arising from countries with low levels of organizational rights, such as those of assembly and association, from Burundi and Rwanda. By contrast, in countries with stronger organizational rights and a relatively autonomous legal profession like Kenya, Uganda, and Tanzania, going to an international court adds a point of contestation for civil society actors, opposition parties, and litigants to challenge electoral manipulations by a dominant party. The experience using domestic courts to advance opposition goals in these relatively more open countries is in turn diffused or strategically borrowed in countries with constricted organizational rights. For example, the East African Law Society files cases on behalf of litigants against the repressive governments of Burundi and Rwanda because of the high personal risks and costs lawyers and litigants from those countries face if they filed cases in an international court.

Fourth, measuring the performance of Africa's international courts solely on compliance and effectiveness presupposes that there is a set of universal benchmarks that must necessarily form the benchmark for assessing the efficacy of international courts everywhere.[40] Since compliance and effectiveness reflect the priorities and concerns developed in academic circles in the West, using these as the only measurements to establish the impact of international courts in Africa invariably marginalizes and trivializes the international law and other impacts

---

[39] The impacts examined in this book do not depend on a centralized enforcement mechanism that constraints state behavior. Yet, this book does not aim to and does not argue that these courts are effective as understood in the literature on effectiveness and compliance.

[40] I make this argument in <<<REFO:WBLN>>>James T. Gathii, *The Promise of International Law: A Third World View,* 2020 American Society for International Law Grotius Lecture (July 2020), forthcoming, Am. Univ. Int'l L. Rev. (2020), https://papers.ssrn.com/sol3/papers.cfm?abstract_id=3635509<<<REFC>>>.

of these and other non-European international courts. This book therefore also seeks to demarginalize the theoretical and doctrinal contributions of Africa's international courts.[41] In so doing, this book joins with scholars studying Africa's international courts such as Obiora Okafor and Rachel Murray,who have pushed back against the often too-ready dismissal and neglect of Africa's international courts. Okafor and Murray remind us that this dismissal and neglect of Africa's international courts, and in particular, its human rights system, is predicated on the view that it is outside of the "ruling" or "dominant Western and European States."[42]

This too-ready dismissal of the significance of Africa's human rights system has also been observed by Adamantia Rachovitsa.[43] Rachovitsa discusses a stream of scholarship that argues that the African Court on Human and Peoples' Rights threatens jurisprudential chaos.[44] One of the causes of such jurisprudential chaos was that the court exercises too vast a jurisdiction over violations not only of regional, but also of sub-regional and global human rights treaties. Particular anxiety is expressed in this literature about the court expanding its scope of focus beyond the interpretation and application of the African Charter on Human and Peoples' Rights to incorporate United Nations human rights treaties. As in Rachovitsa's account, this book pushes back against this Eurocentric accounts of international law that argue against Africa's international courts being on an equal footing with international courts elsewhere.

Impacts Beyond Compliance and Effectiveness

To appreciate the impacts of cases litigated in African international courts, this book proceeds from the view that one has to look at, but also beyond the traditional yardsticks of compliance and effectiveness as a measure of their performance. By going beyond compliance and effectiveness, it becomes possible to see what these yardsticks miss out and ignore. From this perspective, a view of African international courts that is primarily concerned with whether governments complied with court rulings by changing their policies and practices to mirror those rulings,[45] says little about how litigation achieves other objectives sought by activists

---

[41] *Id.*

[42] *See generally* <<<REFO:BK>>>THE AFRICAN COURT OF JUSTICE AND HUMAN AND PEOPLES' RIGHTS IN CONTEXT (Charles Jalloh, Kamari Clarke, & Vincent Nmehielle eds., 2019)<<<REFC>>>.

[43] <<<REFO:JART>>>Adamantia Rachovitsa, *On the New Judicial Animals: The Curious Case of an African Court with Material Jurisdiction of a Global Scope*, 19 HUM. RTS. L. REV. 255–89 (2019)<<<REFC>>>.

[44] *Id.*

[45] In the sense challenged in this book, compliance is defined as "a state of conformity or identity between an actor's behavior and a specified rule." ROGER FISHER, IMPROVING COMPLIANCE WITH INTERNATIONAL LAW 10 (1981); RONALD MITCHELL, INTERNATIONAL OIL POLLUTION AT SEA: ENVIRONMENTAL POLICY AND TREATY COMPLIANCE 30 (1994). Compliance measurements are also concerned with usage rates of a court (i.e. number of cases brought before a court) as well as whether a court is fulfilling the mandate set out in its constitutive charter, *see Evaluating the Performance*

and litigants including opposition political parties and politicians. These additional goals include the role of these courts as coordination points for opposition
political parties who use litigation in these international courts not only to name
and shame dominant political parties and governments, but to also publicize their
causes and to mobilize their supporters.[46] Furthermore, decisions of African international courts amplify political contestation between activists and litigants, on the
one hand, and their governments, on the other, in ways that may not be possible
in other forums exclusively controlled by their governments. This is because once
governments begin participating in proceedings before these international courts,
they become drawn into the struggles that brought the litigants to the Court in the
first place. Litigants and activists involved in these cases do not wait for the final judicial decision. Instead, these litigants and activists use their ongoing participation
in the proceedings to educate the public about their cause, to build their movement
and to seek legal validation of their cause. Sometimes, judicial decisions of these
international courts challenge the status quo in favor of the litigants and activists. This in turn helps them to build political momentum for their causes.[47] Thus
evaluating the effectiveness of African international courts only from victories in
decided cases or based on whether there has been compliance with such decisions
ignores other goals that activists and litigants before African international courts
pursue.

While litigation in African international courts may have compliance as one
goal, this book emphasizes litigation as a type or form of political, legal and social action that in addition has direct and indirect impacts that involve legal and
political mobilization as described in the paragraph above and explained further
in this introduction.[48] This book therefore contributes to expanding the literature

---

of International Courts and Tribunals, BRANDEIS INST. INT'L JUDGES (2016), https://www.brandeis.edu/
ethics/pdfs/internationaljustice/biij/Performance_BIIJ2016.pdf

[46] See, e.g., Robert Howse & Ruti Teitel, Beyond Compliance: Rethinking Why International Law
Really Matters, 1 GLOB. POL'Y 127, 130 (2010) ("In the Balkans, resolving the conflict, and building
post-conflict societies, somehow became identified with the prosecution of crimes against humanity
at the International Criminal Tribunal for the former Yugoslavia (ICTY). The role that international
criminal law could play in achieving these goals was arguably exaggerated, leading to a relative neglect
of other processes, such as local truth commissions, the building of grass-roots democratic institutions
and the reconstruction of civil society.").

[47] In this sense, the chapters in this book in part respond to critiques of Africa's sub-regional courts
and the activist groups that litigate in them and national courts as being too remote and removed from
the actual struggles of oppressed people in African countries. See, e.g., Joe Oloka-Oyango, Who Owns
the East African Community?, HUM. RTS. & PEACE CTR. OCCASIONAL PAPER SERIES No. 1, 5 (2005),
http://huripec.mak.ac.ug/wp-content/uploads/Docs/Publications/Occasional_series_1.pdf   (noting
the distance of the East African Court of Justice from "ordinary people" as well as its limited treaty
jurisdiction as a conscious design choice to limit using it in ways inconsistent with the wishes of East
African Community governments); see generally MAKAU MUTUA, HUMAN RIGHTS NGOS IN EAST
AFRICA: POLITICAL AND NORMATIVE TENSIONS (1st ed., 2009).

[48] On the view that litigation is a form of political action, see Nathan Hakman, Political Trials in the
Legal Order: A Political Scientist's Perspective, 21 J. PUB. L., 73–126 (1971); A.F. Ginger, Law as a Form of
Political Action, 9 WAYNE ST. UNIV. L. REV. 458–83 (1963).

about how best to understand the impact of international courts, beyond two of the leading approaches to the measurements of the impact of international courts—compliance and effectiveness.[49] The chapters in this book do not assume that litigation is either a strong or weak strategy for attaining goals of litigants and activists in Africa's international courts. Indeed, as Michael McCann argues, 'how law matters for social movements is infinitely more complex, mixed, variable, and contingent than can be captured in simple position statements.'[50]

In-Depth Case Study and Thick-Description Approach

This book expands the aperture for examining the work of international courts by looking at the roles Africa's international courts play beyond measuring compliance and effectiveness.[51] To demonstrate how these courts facilitate this role, the chapters in this book adopt an in-depth case-study approach that emphasizes thick description and analysis about how these cases filed in these courts enable, spur, and embolden political and legal mobilization. By foregrounding thick description, this approach differs from those whose starting point is to measure the impact of courts based on a set of defined and discrete variables such as data-sets of litigated cases isolated from the particular and localized contexts where these cases sprang from and were litigated. This approach is consistent with leading Africanist scholars Mahmood Mamdani, Thandika Mkandawire, and Wamba-dia Wamba, who encourage scholars of Africa to study social movements, urging them not to merely focus on the state.[52] According to these scholars, social movements "underline actual forms of organization and participation" of the type of popular movements that this book argues are at the very center of the performance of Africa's international courts.[53] Studies of compliance with international court decisions tend to exclusively focus on the role of the state in a way that those who study the organized social forces in Africa argue is defied by the reality.

---

[49] In fact, scholars have before alluded to the fact that increasing compliance is not the only way that international courts influence international politics (and in the context of this book) national politics. *See, e.g.*, Karen J. Alter, *Do International Courts Enhance Compliance with International Law*, 25 REV. ASIAN & PAC. STUD. 53 (2006).

[50] Michael McCann, *Law and Social Movements: Contemporary Perspectives*, 2 ANN. REV. L. & SOC. SCI. 17, 19 (2006); *see also* LITIGATING HEALTH RIGHTS: CAN COURTS BRING MORE JUSTICE TO HEALTH? (Alicia Ely Yamin & Siri Gloppen eds., 2011); COURTS AND SOCIAL TRANSFORMATION IN NEW DEMOCRACIES: AN INSTITUTIONAL VOICE FOR THE POOR? (Roberto Gargarella, Pilar Domingo, & Theunis Roux eds., 2006); COURTING SOCIAL JUSTICE: JUDICIAL ENFORCEMENT OF SOCIAL AND ECONOMIC RIGHTS IN THE DEVELOPING WORLD (Varun Gauri & Daniel M. Brinks eds., 2008).

[51] For recent calls for additional ways of measuring the impact of international human rights and courts, *see* Geoff Dancy & Christopher Fariss, *Rescuing Human Rights Law From International Legal Realism and its Critics*, 39 HUM. RTS. Q. 39 (2017).

[52] Mahmood Mamdani, Thandika Mkandawire, & Wamba-dia Wamba, *Social Movements, Social Transformation and Struggle for Democracy in Africa*, 23 ECON. & POL. WKLY. 973 (1988).

[53] *Id.* at 980.

This book does not also take comparisons such as with European supra-national institutions as a baseline for evaluating the performance of Africa's international courts.[54] The approach preferred in this book is consistent with the nature of political and legal mobilization which "unfolds over long periods of time and does not follow simple linear trends" that cannot be easily modeled empirically.[55] Further, a case-study approach as used in this book has the advantage of illuminating causal processes in a manner that is sometimes difficult in empirical accounts.[56] In addition, unlike statistical accounts, a case-study approach of similarly situated international courts in Africa has the advantage of bringing to life the names of individuals, their commitments, places, and groups they associate with in a way that statistical analysis do not usually do.[57] This book takes seriously Carsten Stahn's cautions against exclusively quantitative understandings of impact in the related context of international criminal tribunals, noting that "the power of international courts and tribunals lies not so much in their quantitative record as in their role in setting a moral or legal example or shaping discourse."[58] This more contextualized study of international courts is finally gaining attention.[59]

This does not mean dismissing empirical approaches out of hand or insisting on viewing Africa in terms of its unique specificities. Rather it is to recognize that the analytical framework adopted here offers a different starting point that better suits the primary objective of this book than that adopted in other analytical frameworks. However, the framework adopted here is not an end in itself. By foregrounding thick description, this book uses these descriptions as a springboard for further analysis and to ask further questions. Some of the questions that arise from thick description differ from those methodologies that foreground measuring compliance and effectiveness.[60] Examples of the types of questions that

[54] PATRICK CHABAL, CULTURE TROUBLES: POLITICS AND THE INTERPRETATION OF MEANING 222–23 (Jean-Pascal Daloz ed., 2006) (arguing in favor of analysis of culture that privileges thick description rather than abstract models, that privileges local knowledge over universal assumptions). International law scholar, Andrew Guzman, has noted that a highly contextualized study of one international court can produce an accurate portrait even though it may not produce generalizable findings; see Andrew T. Guzman, International Tribunals: A Rational Choice Analysis, 157 U. PA. L. REV. 177 (2008).

[55] Dancy & Fariss, supra note 51, at 26.

[56] ZACHARY ELKINS, TOM GINSBURG, & JAMES MELTON, THE ENDURANCE OF NATIONAL CONSTITUTIONS (2009).

[57] RETHINKING SOCIAL INQUIRY: DIVERSE TOOLS, SHARED STANDARDS (Henry E. Brady & David Collier eds., 2004) (noting the richness of micro- and macro-level case research in understanding social phenomena).

[58] Carsten Stahn, Between "Faith" and "Facts": By What Standards Should We Assess International Criminal Justice?, 25 LEIDEN J. INT'L L. 251–82 (2012).

[59] INTERNATIONAL COURT AUTHORITY (Karen J. Alter, Laurence R. Helfer, & Mikael Rask Madsen eds., 2018); Karen J. Alter, Laurence R. Helfer, & Mikael Rask Madsen, International Court Authority (112 iCourts Working Paper Series 1, 12, 2017).

[60] Although the authors in this book do not proceed from the kind of predictive or even abstract models that use compliance and effectiveness as measures of the performance of international courts, they too aim to explain how Africa's sub-regional courts affect legal and political processes. In addition, the thick-description approach used in this book does have its instrumental usefulness by revealing these processes.

this book sets to answer and which a thick-description approach is more likely to yield answers than other approaches include: why litigants go to these international courts when they know they might lose? Why is victory and ultimately compliance not the only goal these litigants are pursuing? What types of benefits do these litigants see, and eventually get, in these international courts? Why do litigants invest their time and energy to bring cases that are unlikely to be complied with? What prompts litigants to use international courts as forums to air and argue their grievances with their governments? Why do litigants see African international courts as forums of political protest and debate than merely as authoritative law-deciders? What are the risks that arise when Africa's international courts are used for purposes beyond advancing the compliance and effectiveness of their decisions? Ultimately, the thick-description approach adds to and complements other approaches that assess the performance of international courts such as those that measure compliance and effectiveness.

For example, the chapters in this book show how litigation in Africa's international courts influences and often propels political and legal mobilization, which is made possible because the authors put the context within which these courts and their interlocutors operate at the center of their analysis. In so doing, what is distinctive about the role of these courts in their specific context, rather than as generalizable or universal phenomenon, is more readily captured. As noted above, the chapter on election disputes relating to the East African Legislative Assembly shows how the EACJ has been drawn into the mediating disputes between dominant and opposition parties, in ways that give voice and ultimately protection to opposition parties in these elections. These validations of the rights of opposition parties that began in 2006 subsequently radiated outwards to almost all the other East African countries in several cases that followed. This example illustrates how international courts decisions become part of national, international, and regional legal, political, and social struggles.[61] Indeed, such litigation is often used as a shield against rights abuse rather than to achieve other substantive goals.[62] Thus a major insight developed in this book is how litigation before international courts has often been crucial in mobilizing law in opposition to the exercise of arbitrary power and military rulers and in exposing dehumanizing conditions.[63] While legal victory and compliance are clearly desirable objectives for litigants and opposition parties, they are not the only goals

---

[61] This book proceeds from the view that sub-regional courts are only one venue in which political, legal, and economic change is sought—as such attributing direct or indeed indirect impacts on the role of sub-regional courts alone is necessarily tracing a complex causal chain in which other pressure points and factors provide some of the explanation for the change.

[62] See Richard Abel, Speaking Law to Power: Occasions for Cause Lawyering, in CAUSE LAWYERING: POLITICAL COMMITMENTS AND PROFESSIONALS RESPONSIBILITIES 69 (Austin Sarat & Stuart Scheingold eds.,1998) (making a similar point).

[63] OBIORA CHINEDU OKAFOR, LEGITIMIZING HUMAN RIGHTS NGOS: LESSONS FROM NIGERIA 71, 80 (2006).

being pursued by activists and litigants who file cases in African international courts.

The chapters in this book therefore locate the case-law of African international courts as a new and increasingly important venue for waging political, social, and legal struggles. Many African countries have weak democratic institutions, and African international courts provide an additional venue—among a variety of options at the domestic level—through which citizens can wage their political, social, and legal struggles.[64] Often unable to reform interpretations and understandings of their rights within their domestic legal systems, these activists are increasingly turning to African international courts. As such, many of these activists and litigants are not engaged in one-off struggles confined to litigation in African international courts, but rather are using litigation in African international courts as one strategy of contesting their governments that is part of a broader set of strategies in a variety of venues.[65]

The Mobilizational Advantages of Litigating in African International Courts

The materials in this book show that reliance on traditional compliance and effectiveness approaches to measure the work of African international courts misses out locally meaningful "impacts" of their collective case-law. Focusing on the human rights case-law from a bottom-up approach that examines the motivations and strategies of the litigators and activists who bring these cases to court expands the set of tools the field can deploy to measure the significance of the human rights case-law of Africa's international courts. The role of non-state actors and the value they attach to ideals like human rights in their litigation in Africa's international courts form the basis for examining the "political and constitutive potential of the law."[66] This is because the cases filed in African international courts are part of a

---

[64] This is because there are limits to what courts can do to directly achieve social transformation, but yet courts are an important partner and catalyst when activists and litigants use them as part of a multidimensional strategy of seeking such change. *See, e.g.,* William Forbath et al., *Cultural Transformation, Deep Institutional Reform, and ESR Practice: South Africa's Treatment Action Campaign, in* STONES OF HOPE: HOW AFRICAN ACTIVISTS RECLAIM HUMAN RIGHTS TO CHALLENGE GLOBAL POVERTY 67 (Jeremy Perelman & Lucie E. White eds., 2011); Douglas NeJaime, *Winning Through Losing,* 96 IOWA L. REV. 947 (2011). Notably, litigants and activists using sub-regional courts often have little power and ability to attain their objectives through direct political means. For a view on this in another context, *see* R.C. Cortner, *Strategies and Tactics of Litigants in Constitutional Cases,* 17 J. PUB. L. 287–307 (1968).

[65] This book discusses at least three possible outcomes in cases that come before African sub-regional courts as discussed more fully in this Introduction. First, there are cases that litigants and activists bring and indeed win and sometimes there is compliance. The Ebobrah and Lando chapter that examines the East African Court of Justice makes a compelling case study of this. Second, there are cases that activists and litigants win but for which there is only a symbolic victory, for example, through an authoritative validation of claim or in building movement support and creating awareness of the issues raised in the case. Third, there are cases that are brought and lost but which catapult a counter-mobilization agenda.

[66] NeJaime, *supra* note 64, at 945.

broader strategy of spreading human rights consciousness and advocating for social, political, and legal reform consistent with human rights commitments. Those bringing these cases know full well the purpose of bringing these cases to court is not to produce immediate observable compliance and change. Activists and opposition political parties use these courts to promote new norms and ideas about rights, but also to undermine justifications of authoritarian rule inconsistent with the observance and respect for rights.[67] Obiora Okafor and Okechukwu Effoduh's chapter (Chapter 3) in this volume is a good example of this strategy. They argue that activist forces in ECOWAS engage in local to international trans-judicial communication in the ECOWAS Community Court of Justice to decide pro-poor human rights cases which in turn contribute to altering thinking and behavior with regard to the social conditions of the poor. According to them, the benefits of advancing a pro-poor agenda through clarification of treaty texts and provisions increases awareness of these interpretations that then radiates outwards among human rights activists, judges in national courts, and government officials. For example, they use the ECOWAS Community Court of Justice *Basic Education* decision that found consistent and widespread corruption, stealing, and embezzlement of public funds in the Nigerian education sector was inconsistent with the right to basic education, to illustrate the kind of normative resources—in this case, the recognition of a pro-poor anti-corruption norm—that these cases produce for those interested in advancing the cause of the poor in other forums.

In short, the goals of activists and litigants pursuing litigation in an African international courts goes beyond merely seeking victory or loss. They regard litigating in an international court as politically and legally subversive—subversive because they know that states regard being sued in international courts as a transgression of their sovereignty. In fact, African States oppose these courts having jurisdiction over them in the early stages of cases filed against them because they would rather not litigate the cases. These objections come through preliminary objections, as well as challenges to jurisdiction and admissibility. There are examples of more disruptive state responses. As the chapter by Karen J. Alter, James Thuo Gathii, and Laurence R. Helfer (Chapter 7) shows, the SADC Tribunal was suspended and its jurisdiction to receive cases from individuals removed when it decided cases to which Zimbabwe strenuously objected. In the EACJ, the treaty was amended to create an Appellate Division as one strategy of taming what Kenya in particular thought was an activist court. A unifying basis for these objections

---

[67] In fact, African scholars have recognized the importance of indirect impact forms of international law norms. *See* Frans Viljoen & Lirette Louw, *State Compliance with the Recommendations of the African Commission on Human and Peoples' Rights 1994–2004*, 101 AM. J. INT'L L. 1 (2007) (notably, indirect impact is defined by Viljoen and Louw as incremental change occurring over time); Victor Oluwasina Ayeni, *Introduction, in* IMPACT OF THE AFRICAN CHARTER AND WOMEN'S PROTOCOL IN SELECTED AFRICAN STATES 1, 7 (Victor Oluwasina Ayeni ed., 2016) (defining indirect influence to include awareness and use by civil society, national human rights institutions reference to the Women's Protocol in law school curricular and academic writings).

is that by assuming jurisdiction, international courts would undermine or assume the roles of national legislatures, executives, and even courts. The fact that states object to having to litigate these cases indicates their potential to prompt counter-movements and strategies to defend the status quo.[68] These cases also have transgressive effects[69] and are exogenous in their nature.[70] Transgressive not only because these cases are brought over the objections of states, but also for two other important reasons. First, because when a government defends a case in an international court, it is often required to provide information about the contested legal question, such as where and why a detainee without trial is detained, which in turn allows challengers to engage in a robust contestation of the government's case, both inside and outside the courtroom. The importance of litigation providing information to litigants in political settings where governance is not transparent is a significant benefit that would unlikely be realized without such litigation. Second, activist lawyers pile on multiple claims in one suit because they want to force their governments to defend the litigation over a pro-longed period. By keeping their issues in the spotlight, particularly in the media and in public debate and discussions, the government in question can figure out how best to respond to the law suits and the issues raised both inside and outside of the court room.

This strategy of engaging governments in international courts has further benefits for activists in a variety of ways.[71] First, when governments appear in court to defend themselves, this lends credibility and legitimacy to the cause(s) of the litigants. Second, it helps litigants to construct an organizational identity among like-minded actors interested in communicating and advancing their agenda of social, political, or legal change. Third, it facilitates the mobilization of outraged constituencies who share in a cause, creating a new mechanism of political expression that is disruptive of ordinary democratic politics based at the national level. Fourth, it lays a basis for appealing to other sympathetic actors through repeated international litigation and in essence builds broader support for their cause. Fifth, it helps to appeal to donors, particularly in the foreign aid community to support their cause. Sixth, it contributes to mobilizing press reports, thereby creating public

---

[68] *See* Reva B. Siegal, *Constitutional Culture, Social Movement Conflict and Constitutional Change: The Case of the De Facto ERA*, 94 Calif. L. Rev. 1362–63 (2006) (arguing that "when a movement advances transformative claims about constitutional meaning that are sufficiently persuasive that they are candidates for official ratification, movement advocacy often prompts the organization of a counter-movement dedicated to defending the status quo. At just the point that a movement for social change begins to elicit public response, it is likely to elicit this energetic defense of the status quo").

[69] For further discussion about how cause lawyering puts lawyers in tension with conventional values and practices, *see* Stuart Scheingold & Anne Bloom, *Transgressive Cause Lawyering: Practice Sites and the Politicization of the Professional*, 5 Int'l J. Legal Prof. 254 (1998).

[70] Exogenous because the bringing of the cases sets the agenda and forces the government to take a stand on something that is potentially embarrassing. At an interview at the Attorney General's office A, on July 13, 2013, Nairobi, Kenya, strong reservations were expressed about the East African Court of Justice meddling in Kenya's political affairs and in decisions made on national security grounds.

[71] A major influence here is Michael McCann, Rights at Work: Pay Equity Reform and the Politics of Legal Mobilization (1994).

awareness of government excesses. Activists hope such awareness will translate to increased rights consciousness and support for their cause of improving respect for rights. Seventh, it seeks to convince international court judges to accelerate political, social, and legal change through significant interpretive affirmations of human rights treaty provisions. Last, but not least, by nudging international courts to decide cases against a government's wishes, these courts raise the costs of non-compliance for the government that is being sued. This litigation has the potential to raise costs because of the reputational losses involved in naming and shaming governments for rights violations as well as the amount of time and resources that governments have to spend to defend themselves in these international courts.[72] The chapters in this book do not however find much evidence that reputation focused theories of compliance provide an explanatory account of why cases are filed in Africa's international courts.[73] Further, there is insufficient evidence to conclude that states calculate the cost of non-compliance when faced with a decision of an international court. This is consistent with the sanguine proposition in the literature on reputation-based theories of compliance that it is unclear whether or, if so, how states value each instance of non-compliance.[74]

In light of the foregoing potential benefits of filing cases in Africa's international courts, winning cases or seeking compliance is only one, but certainly not a primary end of those bringing cases to these courts.[75] To fully appreciate this view of African international courts, this book shows it is mistaken to regard them as independent actors isolated from other sites of political, social, and legal contestation and change.[76] Rather, this book shows that they are one option for activist and litigant action within a broader set of institutions including domestic courts.[77] As

---

[72]   Clearly there are governments that may not care to suffer any reputational loss because the stakes raised by a particular case may go beyond whether the government will suffer reputational loss. The *Nyong'o* case discussed in Chapter 1 is a good example.

[73]   On reputation-based theories of compliance, *see* ANDREW T. GUZMAN, HOW INTERNATIONAL LAW WORKS: A RATIONAL CHOICE ACCOUNT (2007).

[74]   Rachel Brewster, *The Limits of Reputation on Compliance*, 1 INT'L THEORY 323, 328–30 (2009); Rachel Brewster, *Unpacking the State's Reputation*, 50 HARV. INT'L L. J. 231, 244 (2009).

[75]   Here I agree with Howse in Howse, *supra* note 46, at 127–36, 128, when they argue that "looking at the aspirations of international law through the lens of rule compliance leads to inadequate scrutiny and understanding of the diverse complex purposes and projects that multiple actors impose and transpose on international legality, and especially a tendency to oversimplify if not distort the relation of international law to politics."

[76]   Other sites of contestation at the domestic level include legislatures, government agencies, national judiciaries, and the media. They also include donor agencies, foreign NGOs as well as foreign governments. Thus activists and litigants engaged in grassroots mobilization, engage national institutions and in doing so combine forces with international support. *See* James Thuo Gathii, *Saving the Serengeti: Africa's New International Judicial Environmentalism*, 16 CHI. J. INT'L L. 386 (2016) (discussing how domestic activism and international action combined to stop the building of a road through the Serengeti National Park in Tanzania is one illustration of this theme).

[77]   In this sense, the legal strategies pursued in sub-regional court litigation do not proceed from the assumption that law and courts are not the exclusive domain of transformative politics. *See* GERALD N. ROSENBERG, THE HOLLOW HOPE: CAN COURTS BRING ABOUT SOCIAL CHANGE 341 (1st ed., 1991); *see also* DERRICK BELL, FACES AT THE BOTTOM OF THE WELL: THE PERMANENCE OF RACISM (1992) (noting that civil rights litigation in the United States neglected economic aspects of racial inequality).

such, litigation in these courts from filing to resolution is shaped by events at other levels in a dynamic multi-dimensional context. Further, litigation loss or defeat is neither demobilizing nor unproductive—court decisions should not be considered in isolation of this broader context since they are one layer within multi-layered strategies adopted by activists and litigants.[78]

The chapters in this book also show how activists use litigation in African international courts as forums for having a public debate about policy choices and as a platform to campaign for desired political, social, and legal change. This theme is under-explored in the literature on African international courts. By appealing to the rights protected in regional trade treaties and in the African Charter of Human and Peoples' Rights and elsewhere, activists using African international courts have advanced the validation of the values and interests that are often foreclosed or are not as easily realized at the domestic level. Activists have done so by confronting these African international courts with cases on issues such as slavery, the arrest of parliamentarians within the precincts of parliament, or government seizures of land. By bringing such cases, these activists and lawyers have helped to unlock new understandings of rights that can subsequently become part of domestic law.[79] Litigating and mobilizing African international courts therefore contributes to creating new legal norms and contributes to facilitating conversations in the discourse of rights that is often foreclosed in domestic legal systems.[80]

Litigants and activists who repeatedly bring human rights cases to international courts do not bring them because their primary goal is to make governments comply with these particular decisions.[81] By bringing these cases, lawyers and activists force governments to defend their practices and policies vis-à-vis human rights guarantees. By questioning these practices and policies before African international courts, these cases contribute to destabilizing justifications advanced by governments to keep policies and practices inconsistent with rights in place.

In addition, these cases are brought before African international courts, not only to name and shame governments for human rights violations as alluded to earlier,

---

[78] From this perspective, litigation, and in fact litigation loss is "part of a multidimensional approach to social movement advocacy." *See* NeJaime, *supra* note 64; *see also* Ben Depoorter, *The Upside of Losing*, 113 COLUM. L. REV. 817 (2013).

[79] These efforts help activists to shape new constitutional understandings of rights not through the ballot box at home but through international courts and outside the typical process of constitutional amendments with the hope that these new understandings will be eventually adopted in their national jurisdictions. *See* Eric Agrikoliansky, *Cause Lawyering*, *in* THE WILEY BLACKWELL ENCYCLOPEDIA OF SOCIAL AND POLITICAL MOVEMENTS 172 (David A. Snow et al. eds., 2013) (noting that "the emergence of international legal bodies … may provide additional opportunities for action against authoritarian regimes outside of national space").

[80] *See* Sally Falk Moore, *When Transnational Authority is Contingent: Three African Instances*, *in* AUTHORITY IN TRANSNATIONAL LEGAL THEORY: THEORISING ACROSS DISCIPLINES (Roger Cotterrell & Maksymilian Del Mar eds., 2016) (noting the emergence of regional law in Africa).

[81] These activists realize that many of these governments are unlikely to comply with decisions of sub-regional courts they do not like, but this has not deterred activists from bringing these cases to court.

but also to acknowledge that a wrong has been done to those brought to court.[82] Among the active African international courts, only the ECOWAS Community Court of Justice has jurisdiction to order financial damages. Therefore recovering financial damages has not been a major motivation for bringing cases to African courts. In other words, as Okafor and Effoduh's chapter argues, these human rights cases should be evaluated, not necessarily or exclusively on whether or not they produce observable change on those bound by the rulings, but also on indirect material or symbolic effects such as through naming and framing injustices in rights language as well as becoming "leverage points for breaking institutional inertia and prompting the government into action."[83] From their quasi-constructivist approach, Okafor and Effudoh argue that these cases therefore illustrate how the process of local rights creation and diffusion is a bottom-up process, rather than a top-down one.

Unlike African international courts, national courts in many African countries are overwhelmingly conservative and committed to the status quo. They are often out of touch with social realities because they are not independent and are therefore unwilling to challenge powerful executive branches—even if only on paper. For example, national judiciaries are often reluctant to undermine legislative preferences and to interpret constitutional provisions in ways that would be inconsistent with the wishes of powerful executives. National courts therefore face the dilemma of demands of justice within unjust political and social systems and often hide behind formalistic rationales as a way of deference and acquiescence to those demands.

Although Africa's international courts are not appellate courts from decisions arising in national jurisdictions, litigants often raise treaty violations that fall within their jurisdiction, sometimes at the same time they are challenging their governments under domestic law in domestic courts. Activists and litigants turn to African international courts as a new and additional forum for channeling resistance to and protest against their governments. They seize on their inability to achieve political, legislative, or other reform initiatives at the national level as a justification for pursuing judicial intervention in an African international court. These courts help them to further expose and elevate claims that had little or no salience with benefits such as media coverage before the cases were filed. They also help to inspire movements to take more direct action such as protests that may force political concessions. Take the discussion of the 2015 *Congrès pour la Démocratie et le Progrès (CDP) & others vs. The State of Burkina Faso* case before the ECOWAS Court of Justice discussed in Akinkugbe's chapter. The opposition

---

[82]   Emilie M. Hafner-Burton, *Sticks and Stones: Naming and Shaming the Human Rights Enforcement Problem*, 62 INT'L ORG. 689–716 (2008).

[83]   CESAR RODRIGUEZ-GARAVITO & DIANA RODRIGUEZ-FRANCO, RADICAL DEPRIVATION ON TRIAL: THE IMPACT OF JUDICIAL ACTIVISM ON SOCIOECONOMIC RIGHTS IN THE GLOBAL SOUTH 22 (2015).

that had been excluded from participating in the elections used their victory in that case to mobilize their supporters. They pegged their grievances against the government on the basis of the ECOWAS Court of Justice decision that their exclusion from the elections denied them their right to participate in the elections. In so doing, a case before an international court helped the litigants to sustain resistance and to defend fragile rights in their home country in a new venue beyond the reach of an authoritarian state.

While pursuing remedies in an international court that is more likely than a national court to interpret treaty provisions expansively makes sense, there is a trade-off. Although international courts offer litigants a neutral judicial forum, recalcitrant governments can easily ignore them.[84] In addition, an international court may not fully appreciate the specificities of the local context in the same way a national judge would. Neutrality is therefore a leading virtue that makes an international court attractive. This arises because unlike domestic courts, these international courts are by and large insulated from direct political accountability to national political leadership as the backlash chapter by Alter, Gathii, and Helfer demonstrates. Litigation in an international court offers not only a higher likelihood of success, but also quite importantly an additional lever in advancing the political, legal, and social agendas activists seek to promote. In this sense, activists and litigants combine change strategies aimed at judicial and non-judicial actors at the national and international level—and when national courts refuse to order change, activists and litigants pursue other venues with responsibility for reform. By arguing that national courts had failed to act, activists used international courts and argued they had to order relief. When relief was granted, activists and litigants then used the orders to seek national legislative and executive action. The decisions embodied in grants of judicial relief and the associated activism were then used to galvanize support for those decisions which in turn created opportunities to pressure officials to adopt changes. In this way, court battles are shifted into the domain of politics.[85]

Even Judicial Losses are Good for Legal, Political, and Social Mobilization

Since victory is only one goal of this litigation, activists and litigants use defeat as an opportunity to organize their supporters, encourage fundraising as well as to

---

[84] But see Solomon Ebobrah, *Litigating Human Rights Before Africa's Sub-Regional Courts: Prospects and Challenges*, 17 Afr. J. Int'l & Comp. L. 87 (2009) (arguing that "sub-regional courts are closer to applicants in the given sub-region and therefore it is relatively cheaper to access these institutions").

[85] In this sense, these African sub-regional courts are part of what Alter calls "new style international courts" that have distinctive political agendas and effects; *see* Karen J. Alter, The New Terrain of International Law: Courts, Politics, Rights (2014).

frame these defeats as symbols or symptoms of state oppression. Activists frame such losses as unfair and unjust—an indication of how international courts are controlled by states. In short, legal defeats may serve the same purpose as legal victories.[86] Alter, Gathii, and Helfer's chapter in this book shows the disbandment of the SADC Tribunal and the removal of individual access was a major loss for activist litigants who use African international courts, yet it was followed by activism across a wide range of alternative forums to challenge the disbandment. The disbandment made it possible for activists to frame their disappointments not only vis-à-vis the government of Zimbabwe, which led the disbandment campaign, but also against the entirety of the SADC as an international institution. Hence, rather than demobilizing activists, the disbandment presented an opportunity to mobilize popular support for the revival of the SADC Tribunal with individual access still available. At least three proceedings—in the African Court and African Commission on Human and Peoples' Rights as well as in an investor challenge under a SADC Protocol—were initiated alleging that the suspension of the SADC Tribunal and the removal of individual access violated national and international law. In addition, two constitutional challenges were successful in national courts in South Africa and Tanzania on the theory that the involvement of these governments in the suspension of the SADC Tribunal constituted a violation of a right of access to justice.[87]

Critics point to the fact that some types of litigation are unproductive and even counter-productive because the disbandment of the SADC Tribunal was sparked off by a series of cases and decisions that the government of Zimbabwe strongly protested. Perhaps therefore rather than pursue a confrontational path, the litigants and judges of the SADC Tribunal may have instead decided cases that would have given it the opportunity to develop and gain legitimacy before taking on mega-political cases like the explosive land issue in Zimbabwe.[88] This is true. There are indeed costs to litigating in Africa's international courts. As noted earlier, Rwanda withdrew its declaration allowing individuals and NGOs to file cases in the African Court after a spate of cases raising political questions that the Rwandese government preferred not to litigate. In addition, Tanzania also recently withdrew its

---

[86] As McCann, *supra* note 71, shows, the pay equity litigation strategy of the 1970s and 1980s provided empowering, identity-constituting experiences for the pay-equity social movement even when it failed to produce top-down changes in public policy.

[87] The Law Society of South Africa v. The President of the Republic of South Africa 2018 (2) All SA 806 (HC); In the Matter of Constitution of the United Republic of Tanzania; In the Matter of the Basic Rights and Duties Enforcement Act; In the Matter of a Petition to Challenge the Suspension of the SADC Tribunal; In the Matter of a Petition to Challenge the Unconstitutional Act of the Government of the United Tanzania to Vote in Favor of the Suspension of the SADC Tribunal between Tanganyika Law Society Versus Ministry of Foreign Affairs and International Cooperation of the United Republic of Tanzania and the A.G. of the United Republic of Tanganyika, Miscellaneous Civil Cause No. 23 of 2014, Judgment of 4th June 2019.

[88] Erika De Wet, The Rise and Fall of the Tribunal of the Southern African Development Community: Implications for Dispute Settlement in Southern Africa, 28 ICSID REV. 45–63 (2013).

declaration allowing individuals and NGOs to file cases against it in the African Court on Human and Peoples Rights.[89] Indeed this is a major take-away of the backlash chapter (Chapter 7) in this book, which demonstrates three potential outcomes that may occur when governments are pushed beyond what they are willing to accept.

Yet, what is interesting to note in the SADC context is that the finding that the South African government acted unconstitutionally may very well have generated the domestic political pressure necessary for convincing the South African government to withdraw its signature from the new 2014 SADC Protocol that removed individual access. This is reflected in the fact that in August 2019, President Cyril Ramaposa announced at a SADC Summit that South Africa was withdrawing its signature to the 2014 Protocol.[90] It remains to be seen if South Africa will lobby other SADC governments to reinstate a SADC Tribunal with an individual complaints procedure. The communiqué of the 2019 SADC meeting provided that the "[s]ummit noted the withdrawal of South Africa's signature from the Protocol on the Tribunal in the SADC of 2014 in compliance with a Constitutional Court ruling."[91]

Therefore the claim that young courts should take time to gain legitimacy and acceptance before taking on mega-political cases is persuasive, but supporting this claim is not straightforward. This is because it is difficult to know if a young court takes time that it will gain legitimacy. This is particularly the case where acceptance of judicial review at the national level is also a work in progress. One thing is clear though—gaining legitimacy and acceptance is very conditional to the context.[92] This book makes the case that a better approach to understand what the decisions of Africa's international courts is that they risk short-term failure, but seek to contribute to long-term gains in building democracy and a broad range of creative solutions to make democratic gains plausible as perhaps the South African example with reference to the SADC Tribunal shows. Hence, consider the disbandment of the SADC Tribunal from this alternative perspective advanced in this book. In South Africa there is no treaty or domestic rules designed to facilitate the national recognition and enforcement of the decisions of the SADC Tribunal. In the absence of such rules, SADC Tribunal decisions cannot be enforced in domestic courts. To fill this gap, South African courts creatively used the common law as

---

[89] Nicole De Silva, *Individual and NGO Access to the African Court on Human and Peoples' Rights: The Latest Blow from Tanzania*, EJIL TALK! BLOG (Dec. 9, 2019), https://www.ejiltalk.org/individual-and-ngo-access-to-the-african-court-on-human-and-peoples-rights-the-latest-blow-from-tanzania/#more-17746.

[90] Nthakoana   Ngatane,   *Ramaphosa   Withdraws   SA   From   Controversial   SADC Tribunal   Protocol*,   EYEWITNESS   NEWS   (Aug.   19,   2019),   https://ewn.co.za/2019/08/18/ramaphosa-withdraws-sa-from-controversial-sadc-tribunal-protocol.)

[91] SADC, *Communiqué of the 39TH SADC Summit of Heads of State and Government, Dar es Salaam, United Republic of Tanzania* para. 10 (Aug. 17–18, 2019), https://www.sadc.int/files/1915/6614/8772/Communique_of_the_39th_SADC_Summit-English.pdf.

[92] *See* NUNO GAROUPA & TOM GINSBURG, JUDICIAL REPUTATION: A COMPARATIVE THEORY (2015).

the avenue through which to find domestic legal grounding for the enforcement of SADC court decisions in South African domestic law. The use of the common law as a tool for giving domestic effect to the decisions of the SADC Tribunal in South Africa was spurred by efforts to enforce the decisions of the SADC Tribunal in South African courts. The use of the common law to facilitate the recognition and enforcement of international court decisions in national courts is a development that can now be emulated to enforce decisions of international courts in the do-mestic legal systems of other African countries.[93]

In addition, the SADC disbandment has mobilized new constituencies who found creative ways to enforce its rulings elsewhere including in South African courts, in the African Commission and African Court of Human and Peoples' Rights as well as in an investment tribunal set up under the SADC Finance Protocol. From this perspective, the utility of the SADC Tribunal did not merely lie in its availability to remedy the thousands of violations in its region. In fact, the *Campbell* and *Flick* cases that were the signature cases of the SADC Tribunal were brought not by civil society groups but by aggrieved farmers such as Campbell who doggedly pursued their case in a national political climate in Zimbabwe hostile to judicial review. As already alluded to earlier, these farmers pursued an inter-national court remedy without reference to what implications the outcome they wanted may have had on the future availability of the Tribunal for other litigants.[94] Yet, Campbell's victory at the same time came to represent the availability of re-medial options outside of national law that presented activists and litigants with an otherwise unavailable venue. This book therefore proceeds from the view that international court victories and losses have indirect effects—serving as a coordin-ation or focal point, raising consciousness, mobilizing support for democratic and human rights causes, fundraising, legitimizing a cause, and influencing other state actors sometimes in ways that may or may not undermine the future trajectory of Africa's international courts.

In short, a compliance or enforcement approach of measuring international court performance does not fully capture how the litigation process influences the evolution of the law, but most importantly how such cases help to frame political

---

[93] This common law solution that South African courts found to enforce SADC Tribunal decisions where treaty and statutory law do not recognize sub-regional court judgments, for purposes of enforce-ment, is not reflected in the practice of other African countries. For example, the Ghanaian Supreme Court has declined to enforce orders of international courts, including of the ECOWAS Court of Justice, in the absence of legislative incorporation of the provisions of the underlying treaty establishing the court even if Ghana had ratified the treaty. *See* Amidu No.3 v. A-G, Waterville Holdings(BVI) & Woyome (No.2) 1 SCGLR 606 (2013–2014); through the African Court on Human & Peoples' Rights, Woyome v. Ghana, No. 001/2017, (ACtHPR, Nov. 24, 2017); Amidu v. Atty. Gen., Waterville Holdings (BVI), Woyome (Sup. Ct. of Ghana, Nov. 28, 2017). For a discussion, *see* Victor Essien, *Sovereignty and Subsidiarity: The Ghana Judiciary as the Bulwark Against Incipient Judicial Imperialism by African Regional Courts*, FORDHAM L. LEGAL STUD. RES. PAPER (2018), http://dx.doi.org/10.2139/ssrn.3159268.

[94] Interview with a human rights advocate in Arusha, Tanzania (May 2013) (noting that the filing of the *Campbell* case in the SADC Tribunal was a mistake).

and legal mobilization outside the court room. Further, such mobilization may happen at different points in a litigated case. For example, an unsuccessful jurisdictional or admissibility challenge by a state may galvanize public interest groups to reevaluate and return with a case that is better framed to avoid another unsuccessful challenge much the same way that a successful admissibility challenge would help catalyze such groups. In fact the experience of repeat litigation in these courts shows mobilized groups are not easily dissuaded by losses. Thus an interim decision that does not resolve the underlying dispute can provide an impetus for mobilization. Further, as the Eboborah and Lando chapter argues, where activists and litigants have an opening through a victory, the victory provides a new opportunity for them to bring new cases and pile pressure on their governments on issues of concern.

Further, courts intervene not merely or only in their final decisions, but also "through intermediate decisions that may not entirely resolve a case."[95] In fact, such interim decisions characterize decision-making in many African international courts. For example, the unprecedented decision of the First Instance Division of the EACJ imposing a permanent injunction not to build a road across the Serengeti National Park was issued as an interim decision that in turn generated an appeal before the case could be heard on the merits.[96] The possibility of such interim decisions that have a quick turnaround make African international courts viable options for activists to seek vindication of human rights and to protect individual and environmental rights. This fact suggests a further reason to be skeptical of assessing the success or failure of these courts only by reference to the number of cases litigated or exclusively on the basis of win/loss ratios.[97] Focusing only on the final outcome of cases obscures how the litigation process is used as a springboard to mobilize social and political movements in a multi-faceted process that influences not only the development of the law, but advancing legal, political, and social struggles at various points in the litigation process as well as in other venues outside these courts.[98] The struggles that predate judicial vindication including mobilizing constituencies such as bar associations, the media, and the public for political and legal change are invisible using a compliance lens. After all "published interpretations in litigated cases capture only a small part of what goes on with regard to

---

[95] Catherine Albiston, *The Rule of Law and the Litigation Process: The Paradox of Losing by Winning*, 33 L. & Soc'y Rev. 869, 871 (1999).

[96] See James Gathii, *The Court of Justice, in* THE LEGITIMACY OF INTERNATIONAL TRADE COURTS AND TRIBUNALS, 314–48 (R. Howse, H. Ruiz-Fabri, G. Ulfstein, & M. Zang eds., 2018).

[97] *See* Harold Hongju Koh, *The Haiti Paradigm in United States Human Rights Policy*, 103 YALE L. J. 2391, 2399 (1994) (arguing that transnational public law litigation is a "development whose success should be measured not by favorable judgments, but by practical results: the norms declared, the political pressure generated, the government practices abated, and the lives saved").

[98] For a related argument in the African context, see Lucy Claridge, *Litigation as a Tool for Community Empowerment: The Case of Kenya's Ogiek*, 11 ERASMUS L. REV. (2018), https://ssrn.com/abstract=3174696.

a new law."[99] In addition, repeat players who "expect to experience similar disputes in the future, generally have low stakes in the outcome of any one case, and often have the resources to pursue long-run interests."[100] This insight is consistent with looking beyond compliance and instead examining how law is used to shift disputes into alternative processes and decision-making forums.[101]

Africa's International Courts as Forums of Protest and Debate that Validate Human Rights Values

Finally, another important lens through which African international courts must be seen is as forums of protest[102] and deliberation. These courts give those who bring cases before them an opportunity to present their viewpoints, and for states who are sued to respond to those claims. From this perspective African international courts are not only merely adjudicators of private disputes or institutions that implement social reform as already alluded to earlier, but as forums through which legal, political, and social movements communicate and construct their legal, political, and social values and agendas. In so doing, litigants seek validation of the values embodied in the treaty texts of their rights, and challenging repressive governance practices. From this perspective, African international courts should not be seen as instruments of immediate political, social, and legal change.[103] Rather, litigants, activists, and opposition parties use these international courts for a variety of reasons: to articulate the legal political theories upon which their movement's goals are based; to give publicity and draw and promote public attention to mobilize aggrieved constituencies; to educate the public about a general problem of public policy; to expose conflict between aspiration of legal guarantees and the lived reality; and to put public pressure on governments and others to take their movements and concerns seriously.[104]

International courts are therefore forums where "grievances can be aired and argued"[105] and not merely authoritative law decision-makers. Seeing African international courts as forums of political protest and debate accurately captures how activist lawyers regard and use them. The focus is not too narrowly limited to the roles of judges and courts in isolation, but rather demonstrates there is a

---

[99] Albiston, *supra* note 95, at 872.

[100] *Id.* at 873.

[101] *See* Howse, *supra* note 46, at 127–36.

[102] *See, e.g.*, Jules Lobel, *Courts as Forums of Protest*, 52 UCLA L. REV. 477 (2004).

[103] In fact, the International Covenant on Social and Economic Rights makes realization of social and economic rights progressive and subject to availability of resources. National Constitutions that protect social and economic rights also have similar limitations.

[104] For an example of such a strategy in an African national context, *see* JAMES THUO GATHII, THE CONTESTED EMPOWERMENT OF KENYA'S JUDICIARY, 2010–2015: A HISTORICAL INSTITUTIONAL ANALYSIS 83–103 (2016).

[105] Lobel, *supra* note 102, at 490.

broader context in which these activists see these courts and their decisions.[106] This includes how litigation opens up sometimes often foreclosed public debate and furthers it. In so doing, litigation in African international courts opens up and expands spaces for civil society actors, citizens, and political opposition parties and contributes to shaping public opinion particularly on matters of important public concern. This means the emphasis is not always on how well cases are crafted to conform to procedural and substantive rules, but rather how the cases are framed to meet the broader goals sought by litgants and activists. Many of the rights and guarantees—such as the rule of law, democracy, and equality—that litgants and activists invoke in sub-regional and regional treaties are open-ended and vague. This means that they are ripe and open to contestation between activists and litigants, on the one hand, and governments in suits before international courts, on the other. This indeterminacy provides wiggle room for activists to file suits making broad claims and assertions against states as one part of a multi-pronged strategy for advancing their social, political, or legal goals.

For example, in both Kenya and Uganda, parliamentary rules on the election of members of the East African Legislative Assembly were changed to conform to the Treaty for the Establishment of the East African Community as a result of a series of decisions of the EACJ. These cases were brought by opposition politicians who had failed in their efforts to change these election rules without the additional weight of the decisions of the EACJ. As Gathii's chapter on election disputes to the East African Legislative Assembly shows, these election cases before the EACJ in Uganda and Kenya were part of a much larger set of conflicts between opposition and governing parties in each of the countries that were being waged in multiple other forums, including in their respective national courts, in the press, in parliament, as well as in political rallies and protests. Once the decisions of the EACJ were handed down, they became part of the contestation and were helpful in advancing the cause of the marginalized opposition parties.

In short, this book emphasizes the symbolic importance of law and its utility for organizing political and social movements.[107] From this lens, we can see how both victories and losses in African international courts encourage other litigants to sue. To counter the possibility of such wins in African international courts, African states have adopted a strategy of trying to torpedo cases at an early stage through preliminary objections or admissibility and jurisdictional challenges. In doing so, states send a signal to discourage litigants to sue. Litigation in African international courts, whether successful or not, is used by activists to mobilize constituencies, influence decision-makers, and convince the public to support their

---

[106] Perhaps it is not surprising that it is in West and East Africa where there are robust civil society groups using courts for similar purposes that we see this phenomenon. The experience of cause lawyers in Nigeria, for West Africa, and Kenya for East Africa, then become regionalized over time.

[107] *See* Michael McCann, *Legal Mobilization and Social Movements: Notes on Theory and Its Applications*, 11 STUD. L., POL., & SOC'Y 225 (1991).

cause. This is because much of the litigation in African international courts involves lawyer activists working with non-lawyers in multi-dimensional advocacy in which they pursue strategies across a number of institutional contexts at the national and international level.

Conclusions

A first generation of scholarship on Africa's international courts has assessed the origins of these courts as well as how they became human rights courts in the last two decades. A central agenda of this first generation scholarship has been to closely track the interpretations and elaborations of the rights and the rule of law in the case-law of these international courts. At the center of this scholarship therefore has been tracing the extent to which these normative commitments of human rights and the rule of law have been protected and promoted. It is fair to say that this scholarship has overwhelmingly treated these international courts as a type of constitutional court that polices violations of constitutional rules embodied in treaty law. This scholarship also focused on how international courts that were established to enforce trade rules became human rights courts. By its very nature, this scholarship focused on the important and often arcane details of legal doctrine since one of its primary purposes was to elaborate on how international courts had become enforcers of human rights norms. Further, the design of these courts as human rights courts has been a primary concern in its first wave of scholarship. Hence, scholars have expressed concern that by deciding human rights cases, these international courts were undermining and not complementing the human rights mechanisms at the regional level—the African Court of Human and Peoples' Rights as well as the African Commission on Human and Peoples' Rights.[108] These scholars have therefore been concerned about how best Africa's international courts have performed as mechanisms for transferring and socializing international human rights norms to local contexts.[109]

---

[108] *See, e.g.*, Frans Viljoen, *Courts for Africa: Considering the co-existence of the African Court on Human and Peoples' Rights and the African Court of Justice*, 22 NETH. Q. HUM. RTS. 241 (2004); Frans Viljoen, *Human Rights in Africa: Normative, Institutional and Functional Complementarity and Distinctiveness*, 18 S. AFR. J. INT'L AFF. 191 (2011); Rachel Murray, *The African Charter on Human and Peoples' Right 1987-2000: An Overview of Its Progress and Problems*, 1 AFR. HUM. RTS. L. J. 1 (2001).

[109] Murungi & Gallinetti, *supra* note 8, at 119, 130 (arguing that there is a lack of cohesiveness among the different international courts in Africa and that this raises the potential for conflicting interpretations of the same treaty provisions). *See, e.g.*, Frans Viljoen, *Regional Institutional and Remedial Arrangements for the Judicial Enforcement of Economic, Social and Cultural Rights in Africa*, in THE PROTECTION OF ECONOMIC, SOCIAL AND CULTURAL RIGHTS IN AFRICA: INTERNATIONAL, REGIONAL AND NATIONAL PERSPECTIVES 252–53 (Danwood Mzikenge Chirwa & Lilian Chenwi eds., 2016) (noting that the risks of fragmentation and law-making (creating new rights that are not in the law) by sub-regional courts). Further noting the duplication of efforts in two of Africa's international courts, the ECOWAS Court of Justice and the African Human Rights Court that has resulted in different interpretations of the same human rights clauses because of the status of both courts as final courts. *Id.* at 269–70. *See* Mia Swart, *Alternative fora for Human Rights Protection? An Evaluation of the Human*

This book takes that scholarship a step further through in-depth case studies of how litigation in these international courts impacts political, legal, and social mobilization. In so doing, it goes beyond arcane details of doctrine into the messy world of legal and political mobilization and the organizational choices made by activists, litigants, and opposition parties who bring litigation before these international courts. By focusing on political mobilization, this book departs from and expands the rights-based orientation of the first generation scholarship on Africa's international courts. In doing so, it joins scholarship on other regional courts where litigation is associated with " 'empowering groups that were previously invisible."[110] The chapters in this book show the importance of international courts beyond whether or not there is compliance with their decisions. For example, some chapters discuss their role as focal points for examining how political power gets mobilized and organized within national political systems where these cases arise. While the literature on international courts have emphasized their role in providing cooperative solutions between and among states through coordination[111] or collaboration.[112] This book by contrast emphasizes the role of international courts in resolving coordination and mobilization problems between and among opposition parties, politicians, civil society groups, and other politicians.

Other chapters focus on the role of these courts in flagging violations and serving as deliberative as well as protest forums. Thus unlike in the first generation scholarship that primarily focused on how international courts contribute to the elaboration of rights and how these relate to human rights institutions at the continental level, this book focuses on how the cases filed in international courts spring from organized political movements. These movements include political parties that mobilize and institutionalize the protections of rights in regional and sub-regional charters to achieve their goals. Thus, when groups such as opposition parties and civil society groups file cases in international courts, they are not merely seeking to

---

Rights Mandates of the African Sub-regional Courts, J. S. AFR. L. 437 (2013) (arguing that Africa's human rights courts create uncoordinated human rights jurisprudence and that forum shopping which will become an even bigger problem as these courts become more active. She also argues that the lack of a formal hierarchical relationship between sub-regional courts, on the one hand, and the African Court of Human and Peoples Rights and the African Commission on Human Rights, on the other, makes sub-regional courts more vulnerable to being ineffective); *see also*, Abdi Jibril Ali, *The Admissibility of Subregional Courts' Decisions Before the African Commission or African Court*, 6 MIZAN L. REV. 243 (2012) (noting the "divergent conclusions on the same issues, duplication of efforts, and inefficient allocation and use of scarce resources, particularly when different courts have jurisdiction over the same case," created by sub-regional courts); *see also* Murungi, *id.* at 135 (noting the danger of inconsistent interpretations of the same treaty provisions among sub-regional courts).

[110] Marcia Nina Bernardes, *Inter-American Human Rights System as a Transnational Public Sphere: Legal and Political Aspects of the Implementation of International Decisions*, 8 SUR INT'L J. HUM. RTS. 131, 146 (2011).

[111] Arthur A. Stein, *Coordination and Collaboration: Regimes in an Anarchic World*, *in* INT'L REGIMES 115 (Stephen D. Krasner ed., 1983).

[112] LESLIE JOHNS, STRENGTHENING INTERNATIONAL COURTS: THE HIDDEN COSTS OF LEGALIZATION (1st ed., 2015).

enforce the rights of a solitary individual, but rather as groups, they are leveraging their membership as organized political actors to contest with all too often a dominant political party in their country. In short, a primary insight of this book is showing how international courts act as a focal point for mobilizing and organizing political actors, including opposition parties competing for political power or contesting the use of political power by its wielders in their home country. A major contribution of this book therefore is to encourage scholars studying Africa's international courts, and indeed other international courts, to turn to insights from scholars who use the tools of social movement studies such as the effects of mobilizing law to serve legal, social, and political goals.[113] Such a move, as this book shows, opens up a more fuller and richer account of previously under-appreciated impacts of international courts beyond those in Africa.

---

[113] The literature that has influenced my approach and that of many of the other authors in this book includes: McCann, *supra* note 71; Steven E. Barkan, *Political Trials and Resource Mobilization: Towards an Understanding of Social Movement Litigation*, 58 Soc. FORCES 944 (1980); Paul Bernstein, *Legal Mobilization as a Social Movement Tactic: The Struggle for Equal Employment Opportunity*, 96 AM. J. Soc. 1201 (1991).

1

International Courts as Coordination Devices for Opposition Parties

The Case of the East African Court of Justice

James Thuo Gathii*

Introduction

Opposition political parties and politicians in countries with a dominant political party face many coordination barriers in their quest to organize against repressive governments. The repressive practices of dominant political parties weaken and undermine opposition politics through a variety of strategies including harassing and imprisoning their leaders, obstructing their opposition activities and in some instances actively encouraging divisions within and among opposition parties. Lack of funding also means they have low levels of grassroots organization, a factor that also increases the susceptibility of their leaders to be co-opted by a dominant party. Coordination is also difficult because opposition political parties and citizens may be afraid to challenge a dominant party in courts and institutions that it controls.[1] They may also not know if they challenge State repression, other citizens and groups will join them. This is significant because public support is important for resisting oppressive governance.[2] The combination of the repressive practices of

---

* Thanks to Abdulkareem Yusuf for his research assistance. Thanks also to Laurence Helfer, Tom Ginsburg, Spencer Waller, Juan Perea, Richard Steinberg, Yang Liu, and Margaret Moses for their comments on earlier drafts of this chapter.

[1] Tom Ginsburg, *Courts and New Democracies: Recent Works* (Univ. of Chicago Pub. L & Legal Theory, Working Paper No. 388, 2012), http://chicagounbound.uchicago.edu/cgi/viewcontent.cgi?article=1078&context=public_law_and_legal_theory. On the literature exploring how dominant parties make it difficult for smaller unstable opposition political parties to organize, *see* Daniel Young, *Party Dominance in Africa's Multiparty Elections* (WGAPE, UCLA Dept of Pol. Sci. Working Draft, June 4–5, 2004).

[2] *See* JAMES DENARDO, POWER IN NUMBERS: THE POLITICAL STRATEGY OF PROTEST AND REBELLION (1985). Resistance movements are particularly successful when they legitimize defections from security forces previously sympathetic with the government and when a repressive regime could no longer maintain economic solvency, get the church or powerful foreign states and institutions to back it. *See* Amado Mendoza, *"People Power" in the Philippines, 1983–86, in* CIVIL RESISTANCE AND POWER POLITICS: THE EXPERIENCE OF NONVIOLENT ACTION FROM GANDHI TO THE PRESENT (Adam Roberts, Timothy Garton Ash, & Robert Davies eds., 2009); KURT SCHOCK, UNARMED INSURRECTIONS: PEOPLE POWER IN NON-DEMOCRACIES (2004).

James Thuo Gathii, *International Courts as Coordination Devices for Opposition Parties* In: *The Performance of Africa's International Courts*. Edited by: James Thuo Gathii, Oxford University Press (2020). © The Several Contributors. DOI: 10.1093/oso/9780198868477.003.0002.

dominant parties together with the lack of information about whether "citizens will join in an effort" against the repressive conduct of a dominant party places many coordination barriers on opposition political parties and their leader.[3] Repressive practices disable opposition political parties from campaigning effectively in electoral campaigns as well as in the traditional role of being a check against executive abuse of power. Party dominance in African countries comes with large legislative majorities, which according to one study exceeds Latin American and Asian party dominance.[4] It is therefore not surprising that political party dominance in East Africa comes alongside small and unstable opposition political parties.

As I discuss in more detail in Part One, coordination in this chapter refers to the fact that an international court, the East African Court of Justice (EACJ), has made a particular outcome salient—i.e. that an election to the East African Legislative Assembly (EALA) conducted in a particular way is now acceptable to dominant and often authoritarian regimes.[5] In so doing, this outcome has largely removed uncertainty about whether dominant political parties will comply. This has in turn created a focal point because it is now clear in the six East African Community (EAC) Member States that when a dispute regarding elections to the EALA arises, the solution offered by the case-law of the EACJ will be followed. In this sense, the role of the EACJ provides an adjudicative signal that allows bargaining in the shadow of the law to opposition parties confronting dominant political party manipulation of elections to the EALA.

Because opportunities to confront party dominance are often limited or closed down at the national level, opposition political parties in the East African region have gravitated around the EACJ as a focal point around which they have mobilized against repression by dominant political parties in their home countries.[6] By providing a forum for opposition political parties, the EACJ has partially resolved the coordination problem because of the existence of a treaty-based cause of action for violation of elections to a regional parliament, the EALA. The EACJ has entertained eight cases and issued at least twenty interim decisions, arising from four of

---

[3] Ginsburg, *supra* note 1.

[4] Young, *supra* note 1.

[5] The use of coordination in this chapter is not based on game theory and extensions of its application, such as in Richard H. McAdams, *The Expressive Power of Adjudication*, 2005 U. ILL. L. REV. 1043 (2005); Tom Ginsburg & Richard H. McAdams, *Adjudicating in Anarchy: An Expressive Theory of International Dispute Resolution*, 45 WM. & MARY L. REV. 1229 (2004). However, this chapter has in common with game theoretic applications of coordination the fact that an international court has made a particular outcome salient—i.e. that an election to the EALA conducted in a particular way is now acceptable to dominant and often authoritarian regimes.

[6] Indeed, as Thomas Schelling in his book, THOMAS SCHELLING, THE STRATEGY OF CONFLICT 67 (1960), argues, coordination requires focal points to overcome their collective action problems. Similarly, in Barry Weingast, *Political Foundations of Democracy and the Rule of Law*, 91 AM. POL. SCI. REV. 245, 261 (1997) Weingast refers to constitutional rights as focal points around which citizens organize against state repression. When judicial decisions create such focal points, they may help circumvent collective action and limited public space for open dissent. On this, *see* TAMIR MOUSTAFA & TOM GINSBURG, RULE BY LAW: THE POLITICS OF COURTS IN AUTHORITARIAN REGIMES (1988).

the six EAC states testing the legality of these elections to the East African Court Legislative Assembly.[7]

This chapter argues that the enforcement of the treaty remedy by the EACJ for violations of election rules of the EALA has partly resolved a coordination problem that opposition parties face. This coordination problem arises because dominant parties in East Africa do not conduct elections to the EALA in a manner that gives opposition parties meaningful opportunities to compete. Cases challenging the electoral malpractices of dominant parties in the EACJ give opposition parties opportunities to mobilize against those malpractices not only in the Court but also in the press and in other forums. These cases are therefore windows into the types of electoral manipulations dominant parties engage in and the concerted actions opposition parties engage in as a response.

The decisions of the EACJ naming election violations as treaty breaches gives opposition political parties opportunities to rally their supporters in favor of their cause against dominant parties. Because the EACJ has been consistent in affirming that elections rather than appointments are the only permissible mode of electing members of the East African Legislative, the Court has created knowledge about when a treaty violation has occurred. This has in turn helped opposition political parties to know when they have a factual basis with a likelihood of success so that they could bring cases against dominant political parties in the EACJ. Thus in 2017, South Sudan withdrew appointees to the EALA when it was sued in the EACJ because appointments are inconsistent with the requirements of the Treaty for the Establishment of the East African Community (EAC Treaty) for electing its members. In its settlement, South Sudan agreed to conduct an election that met the requirements of the Treaty.

In addition, when opposition political parties have prevailed in having the court annul treaty inconsistent elections, they have used their judicial success to coordinate their activities against incumbent political parties thereby raising the costs of a dominant party to engage in repression against opposition political parties and politicians. Quite remarkably, the decisions of the EACJ declaring elections carried out inconsistently with treaty requirements have been complied, even when they have been sources of backlash against the Court. As I note in this chapter, the EACJ has declined to expansively interpret its jurisdiction to determine whether or not an election was treaty-compliant. Even though the Court has adopted a formalistic interpretation of this electoral jurisdiction, it has been far from acquiescent. It has not hesitated to invalidate an election even within the narrow construction of the

---

[7] *See infra* Table 1.2 at the end of this chapter for a list of all the case and interim applications. These elections take place within each of the East African national parliaments every five years. Under the Treaty for the Establishment of the East African Community, members of the EALA have to be selected in an election, rather than by other processes such as by party appointment. This case-law has established the rule that any other mode of putting in place of members of EALA other than through an election violates the treaty and the Court is empowered to remedy such a treaty breach.

Treaty that it has adopted. This consistency in upholding what constitutes a treaty-inconsistent election has contributed to the government of Sudan settling a case filed before the Court because proceeding to defend it would more likely than not has resulted in an embarrassing loss.

By providing a focal point for opposition parties to file cases against dominant and authoritarian political parties, the EACJ has become susceptible to political backlash. That is what happened when the Court decided its first case involving elections to the EALA when it reversed the election of Kenyan members to that body in 2006 for having conducted inconsistently with the Treaty for the Establishment of the East African Community. That reversal was met with stiff opposition from the ruling party in Kenya and it triggered a series of reprisals against the Court. The Court survived the backlash, but not before its jurisdiction was restricted by a two-year requirement within which cases must be filed, among other reforms aimed at making it more difficult for it to continue providing an audience to opposition political parties and other litigants. These reforms included the creation of a new Appellate Court designed to check the activist First Instance Division.[8]

This chapter makes two significant contributions to the understanding of the role of international courts. First, it shows how litigation in African sub-regional courts legitimates regime opposition in East Africa, particularly by serving as co-ordination points for these opposition parties. Using an international court galvanizes opposition parties and raises the costs of repression even for a regime with dominance in its national parliament. Second, the chapter also shows how limited organizational rights in countries like Burundi and Rwanda where the governments engage in unprecedented degrees of opposition oppression and expend large resources on policing and intelligence operations, disables and demobilizes opposition parties and civil society groups from bringing cases before international courts and engaging in other oppositional activity. This insight coincides with the recent work emphasizing the importance of organizational rights relative to individual rights. For example, Adam Chilton and Mila Versteeg show that in some contexts, organizational rights are more likely to provide better rights protection than individual rights because they create and foster independent organizations. These independent organizations in turn enforce these rights and protect them from government encroachment.[9] By contrast, individual rights depend on individuals to enforce them against governments. Further organizational rights

---

[8] Karen Alter, James Gathii, & Laurence Helfer, *Backlash against International Courts in West, East, and Southern Africa*, 27 Eur. J. Int'l L. 293 (2016).

[9] Adam Chilton & Mila Versteeg, From Parchment to Barriers: How Constitutional Rights Can Make a Difference, Ch. 1 (2019); Adam S. Chilton & Mila Versteeg, *Do Constitutional Rights Make a Difference?*, 60 Am. J. Pol. Sci. 575 (2016). Notably of course, organizational rights already exist in the Constitutions of East African States. The argument therefore is not that organizational rights are created by these textual guarantees, rather it is that there is a broader set of political and other constraints that opposition political parties are subjected to in each of the EAC Member States that in turn determines the relative scope of organizational freedom these parties enjoy.

facilitate and catalyze coordination efforts by groups[10] and in so doing help to over-come collective action problems created by social and political cleavages. For these reasons, the constitutionalization of organizational rights is more likely than not to make it difficult for governments to renege on the protection of this right.[11]

This analysis shows how in authoritarian States lawyers and litigants face risks such as imprisonment or worse. This in turn constrains and constricts organiza-tional patterns for opposition politics. The fact that opposition parties in Burundi and Rwanda have not filed cases challenging the dominant parties in their home countries in the EACJ shows the calculations that opposition politicians make when they face deliberate and institutionalized repression. Such repression not only makes filing of challenges in an international court difficult, but also severely constrains open protest. In short, high levels of repression shapes the strategic decision-making of opposition political parties. Burundi and Rwanda are illustra-tive of the manner in which governments constrain collective action by opposition groups as part of a larger strategy of maintaining political control.

Kenya, Uganda, and Tanzania differ from Burundi and Rwanda because in the former group of countries, opposition parties and civil society groups enjoy rela-tively more organizational space, a generation of radical lawyers transferred their skills litigating in national courts to litigating in the EACJ. The newest member of the EAC, South Sudan has also faced a suit in the EACJ. The fact that this case was subsequently settled shows how a particularly weak opposition political party took advantage of regime weakening during a civil war as well as the crystallization of the norm of a free election for membership in the EAC to score a victory in an international court. The cases filed in the EACJ from these countries have therefore become an additional catalyst for the mobilization of resistance against authori-tarian governance. In short, the scope of organizational rights enjoyed by oppos-ition political parties in East Africa is central to understanding anti-authoritarian mobilization in international courts. This chapter shows that even though oppos-ition parties have asymmetric relationships with dominant parties, opposition par-ties in countries where organizational rights are relatively strong, collective action including through filing cases in international courts against the dominant party is more likely than in countries where organizational rights are repressed. These themes coincide with those covered by Olabisi Akinkugbe's chapter (Chapter 4) on the judicialization of mega-political disputes in the ECOWAS Community Court of Justice.

---

[10] *See* Tom Ginsburg et al., *When to Overthrow Your Government: The Right to Resist in the World's Constitutions*, 60 UCLA L. Rev. 1184 (2013).

[11] Adam S. Chilton & Mila Versteeg, *Do Constitutional Rights Make a Difference?*, 60 Am. J. of Pol. Sci. 575 (2016). Indeed as Darryl Levinson argues, "some political arrangements [such as political com-mitment devices such as institutions] organize or empower interest groups or other political constitu-encies with a stake in maintaining these arrangements." Daryl J. Levinson, *Parchment and Politics: The Positive Puzzle of Constitutional Commitment*, 124 Harv. L. Rev. 657, 687 (2011).

This chapter proceeds as follows. Part One introduces my use of the term coordination in this chapter. It then gives a brief overview of the EACJ and EALA, before discussing the landmark *Nyong'o* decision that inaugurated access to the Court challenging treaty-inconsistent EALA elections. Part Two discusses how party dominance in Uganda, Tanzania, South Sudan, as well as in Burundi and Rwanda shape whether or not cases against treaty-inconsistent elections from those countries are filed. That part ends with a reflection of the theoretical implications this project raises.

Part One: The East African Court of Justice's Role in Coordinating East African Legislative Assembly Elections
What Do I Mean by Coordination?

I borrow from Barry Weingast[12] and John Fearon who argue that preventing a government from violating democratic rights requires coordination among citizens. For Fearon, leaders are more likely to follow electoral rules where citizens can coordinate on mass protest or rebellion against those who leaders who do not follow pre-agreed rules.[13] He argues whether or not citizens will cooperate in protesting or rebelling against electoral fraud is a coordination game.[14] Quite significantly and consistently supported in this chapter, Fearon argues that "publicly understood rules for regular elections" is a possible solution for citizens to coordinate rebellion against the performance of their leaders.[15] For Weingast, policing violations of democratic rights requires citizens to coordinate their responses—this in turn requires a coordination device to coordinate citizen reactions in defending their democratic rights.[16]

Where citizens coordinate their behavior to prevent violations of democratic rights, they can protest the abuse of electoral rules. This is particularly so when there is consensus among citizens about the permissible or legitimate scope of electoral behavior in elections. Weingast in addition argues that for electoral rules to be enforceable as such, it is in the interest of the government to comply with these rules instead of subverting them to prevent opposition political parties from assuming office into the future.[17] Where opposition political party members and their leaders are unwilling to defend these boundaries, governments can violate

---

[12] Barry Weingast, *The Political Foundations of Democracy and the Rule of Law*, 91 AM. POL. SCI. REV. 245–63 (1997).

[13] James D. Fearon, "Self-Enforcing Democracy," 126 Q. J. ECONS. 1661–708 (2011).

[14] *Id.* at 1692–93.

[15] *Id.* at 1662.

[16] Weingast, *supra* note 12, at 245, 251.

[17] *Id.* at 245, 255.

these boundaries—especially where they are able to retain public support in the face of violations.

The mere existence of a consensus on the scope of legitimate boundaries of permissible behavior is not self-enforcing in the absence of coordinating mechanisms to enforce violations.[18] In addition, the mere existence of information about the violation of these boundaries is insufficient for citizens to coordinate their support or protest against a government violating these boundaries.[19] A coordinating mechanism or device is necessary for citizens to challenge and enforce violations. Without a coordinating mechanism, the most likely outcome is a coordination failure. This is particularly so in East Africa where domestic courts are often beholden to dominant political parties. By contrast, the EACJ—a court outside the immediate political control of such dominant parties—provides an opening and opportunity to challenge electoral violations. Over the years, the case-law of the EACJ has provided a focal solution to violations of electoral rules that opposition political parties and their leaders can use to challenge the violations of the legitimate boundaries of permissible electoral behavior. In turn, opposition politicians and their members use the opportunity to litigate as an opportunity to galvanize and mobilize support against the violating government in other forums. Ultimately, these opposition politicians and their supporters engage in multidimensional struggles against their governments using litigation in the EACJ both as a galvanizing and mobilizational opportunity, but also as a focal point for coordinating those opposed to violating national electoral rules.

Coordination by opposition political parties and their leaders in this chapter therefore proceeds from the following premises. First, that citizens, and opposition political party leaders and their members, understand the permissible scope of the electoral behavior of East African governments in elections to the EALA. Second, that opposition political party members and their leaders are more likely to challenge governments that violate the permissible scope of electoral behavior in elections to the EALA because of the existence of the EACJ as a coordinating mechanism that facilitates these governments being answerable for violations of these rules. The existence of the EACJ as a coordinating mechanism helps to overcome collective action problems such as lack of consensus on the permissible scope of electoral behavior generated by ethnic divisions and the lack of domestic

---

[18] As Weingast argues in Weingast, *supra* note 12, at 245, 251, "[c]itizens are unlikely to achieve coordination in a wholly decentralized manner. Typically, differential circumstances imply there is no natural focal solution to their problem." *Id.* Notably, Adam Przeworski argues that a democratic Constitution was self-enforcing, where an incumbent steps down after an electoral loss, instead of staying on by force in violation of the Constitution because s/he expects to be better off; *see* ADAM PRZEWORSKI, DEMOCRACY AND THE MARKET: POLITICAL AND ECONOMIC REFORMS IN EASTERN EUROPE AND LATIN AMERICA (1991).

[19] Andrew T. Little, Joshua A. Tucker, & Tom LaGatta, *Elections, Protest, and Alternation of Power* (Dec. 2013), http://www.andrewtlittle.com/papers/protestalternation_web.pdf.

institutions such as courts that can independently adjudicate electoral violations.[20] Third, that the willingness of opposition politicians and their supporters to challenge violations of electoral behavior in the EACJ creates potential opportunities for them to prevent the violation of these rules in other forums outside the EACJ. Fourth, where opposition political party members and their leaders are unwilling to enforce these limits on acceptable electoral behavior in elections, governments can get away with having to comply with these rules.

To coordinate effectively, opposition political parties and their leaders require coordination goods,[21] such as the freedom to organize political parties without interference as well as freedoms of expression, assembly, and association. To communicate and coordinate with their supporters, press freedom is also important. By failing to supply these coordination goods, autocratic governments raise the cost of political coordination for opposition parties, their leaders, and supporters. The lack of coordination goods and the political repression that accompanies such denial creates very high uncertainty that opposition parties, their leaders and supporters would be willing to challenge an autocratic government both in their national institutions as well as in an international court.[22]

Some autocratic governments like Burundi restrict the supply of coordination goods as well as public goods—such as infrastructure, schools, and healthcare. Others, like Rwanda restrict the supply of coordination goods without restricting the supply of public goods. This in turn creates a weakened opposition, and an elite that benefits from the supply of public goods and any accompanying economic growth that insulates an autocratic government from challenge.

This chapter also exemplifies another form of coordination—that opposition political parties in the different countries in the EAC have signaled to each other the availability of the EACJ when they go there to complain about electoral malfeasance. In doing so, this chapter shows that how opposition political parties in East Africa succeeded in persuading the EACJ to crystalize a rule against manipulating elections to the EALA that is now widely observed in practice by four of the six members of the EAC Member States. As a result, the EACJ has provided a coordination point for opposition political parties in a meaningful way. One sign that this

---

[20] In Weingast, *supra* note 12, at 245, 257, Weingast notes, "The solution to the coordination problem is accomplished through a variety of institutional means, such as the form of electoral system, the decentralization of political power to more homogeneous political units, and the imposition of explicit limits on majorities at the national level." *Id.*

[21] On coordination goods, *see* Bruce Bueno De Mesquita & George W. Downs, *Richer But Not Freer,* FOREIGN AFF (Sept./Oct. 2005).

[22] In this chapter, Burundi and Rwanda's autocratic regimes are described as "(1) both the formal and the effective degree of the separation of powers is low, (2) the degree of corruption is high, and (3) the government leader that transgresses against constitutional rules for the sake of some allegedly higher goal—like protecting the nation against external or internal enemies or creating some glorious empire or the like—is highly popular." *See* Thomas Apolte, *A Theory of Autocratic Transition: Prerequisites to Self-Enforcing Democracy* (Center for Interdisciplinary Economics, University of Münster, Discussion Paper No. 1/2018, 2018).

rule against manipulating elections to the EALA is now very well established is that when South Sudan was sued for manipulating such an election, it agreed to conduct the election in accordance with the Treaty for the Establishment of the EAC and settled the suit. By settling the case, South Sudan was in effect acknowledging that there was an established rule against manipulating elections to the EALA.[23]

The East African Court of Justice

The EACJ is established under the Treaty for the Establishment of the East African Community.[24] Since it decided its first case in 2005 until January 2018, the EACJ has delivered eighty-five judgments, issued sixty-one interim orders, two advisory opinions, and twenty-four taxation rulings. In its original structure, the Court had one chamber.[25] However, amendments to the EAC Treaty that came into effect in March 2007 created an Appellate Division, making the Court a two-chamber court.[26] The entire court is comprised of eleven judges,[27] two from each from five of the EAC Member States and one from South Sudan.[28] The Appellate Division is comprised of five judges[29] one from each of the Member States except South Sudan. The First Instance Division is comprised of six judges from each of the six Member States of the EAC.[30] Judges hold office for a seven-year period[31] and must retire at seventy years of age.[32]

---

[23]   As I argue in this chapter, particularly in Part Two when I discuss South Sudan's decision to hold an election, consistent with the rules established by the EACJ, to which dominant political parties in East Africa have accepted or acquiesced. There is no evidence of other explanations, such as to please donors, of acceptance of this rule and its widespread compliance.

[24]   The EAC was re-established in 1999. *See* JAMES THUO GATHII, AFRICAN REGIONAL TRADE AGREEMENTS AS LEGAL REGIMES 181 (2011). The original EAC was disbanded in 1977 following major differences among the three original members: Kenya, Uganda, and Tanzania. *See id.* at 43 (discussing Kenya's dissatisfaction as a primary factor leading to dissolution); *id.* at 181 (stating the original members of the EAC were Kenya, Tanzania, and Uganda); *id.* at 268.

[25]   EAST AFRICAN COURT OF JUSTICE USER GUIDE 11 (2014), https://www.eacj.org/?page_id=3835.

[26]   Treaty for the Establishment of the East African Community, art. 24, Nov. 30, 1999, 2144 U.N.T.S. 255 (hereinafter "EAC Establishment Treaty"). The EAC Establishment Treaty provides that the Court "shall consist of a First Instance and an Appellate Division." *Id.* at art. 23(2). These amendments were made following a decision of the EACJ to which the government of Kenya strongly objected. For more on the circumstances leading to the amendments, *see* Gathii, *supra* note 24, at 268–71.

[27]   *Id.* at art. 24(2) (providing that the First Instance Division shall not comprise of more than ten judges).

[28]   *Id.* at art. 24(1)(a) (providing that no more than two judges can be appointed from the same EAC Partner State).

[29]   *Id.* at art. 24(2) (providing that the Appellate Division shall not comprise of more than five judges). This seems to be the reason that South Sudan does not have a judge on the Appellate Division. Hence unless the Treaty is amended to provide for more judges on the Appellate Division, South Sudan will have to work out a system of rotating one seat on the Appellate Division. *See* Marc Nkwame, *Juba to Appoint Judge for EACJ*, DAILY NEWS (Mar. 20, 2017), https://www.dailynews.co.tz/news/juba-to-appoint-judge-for-eacj.aspx.

[30]   EAC Establishment Treaty, *supra* note 26, at art. 24(1)(b).

[31]   *Id.* at art. 25(1).

[32]   *Id.* at art. 25(2). As a matter of practice, judicial appointments are staggered to prevent all the judges' terms coming to an end at the same time. In the first appointment round, judges are appointed

In terms of jurisdiction, the EACJ is empowered hear cases "over the interpretation and application" of the EAC Establishment Treaty.[33] The EAC Establishment Treaty then provides that the EACJ "shall have such other original, appellate, human rights and other jurisdiction *as will be determined* by the Council at a suitable subsequent date."[34] At the 15th Ordinary Summit of the EAC's Heads of State, a decision was made to defer giving the EACJ jurisdiction over human rights and to instead consult with the African Union on the matter.[35] The Summit did, however, extend the Court's jurisdiction over trade and investment cases as well as cases arising under the EAC's Monetary Union treaty.[36] The Court also has jurisdiction over disputes between the EAC and its employees;[37] arbitral disputes arising from commercial contracts between private parties; and agreements to which the EAC, any of its institutions, or EAC Member States are parties if an arbitration clause in such a contract or agreement confers such jurisdiction.[38]

Any person residing in the EAC can bring cases to the EACJ.[39] Such suit can only be filed against one of the EAC Member States or an institution of the EAC for a declaration that its conduct is inconsistent with an EAC Treaty.[40] Employees of the EAC may sue regarding the terms and conditions of their service to the EAC.[41]

---

for seven years. In the second appointment round, judges are appointed for five years. The cycle is then repeated with each subsequent appointment round. Interview with Justice Butasi, Principal Judge of the EACJ First Division, in Arusha, Tanzania (June 25, 2014).

[33] EAC Establishment Treaty, *supra* note 26, at art. 27(1). In addition, the EAC Establishment Treaty provides that the role of the Court shall be "to ensure the adherence to law in the interpretation and application of and compliance with this Treaty." *Id.* at art. 23(1).

[34] *Id.* at art. 27(2) (emphasis added).

[35] *See* EAC, Communiqué of the 15th Ordinary Summit of the EAC Heads of State 16 (Nov. 13, 2013), http://repository.eac.int/bitstream/handle/11671/546/Annex%20VI-COMMUNIQUE%20 OF%20THE%2015TH%20ORDINARY%20SUMMIT%20OF%20HEADS%20OF%20STATE. pdf?sequence=1&isAllowed=y (extending the jurisdiction of the EACJ to include commercial, investment, and monetary matters, but deciding to work with the African Union (rather than the EACJ) on matters relating to human rights and crimes against humanity).

[36] EAC, Communiqué of the 16th Ordinary Summit of the East African Community Heads of State 9 (Feb. 20, 2015), http://repository.eac.int/bitstream/handle/11671/547/COMMUNIQUE%2016TH%20 ORDINARY%20EAC%20HEADS%20OF%20STATE%20SUMMIT%2018TH%20FEB%202015-1.pdf ?sequence=1&isAllowed=y.; EAC, EACJ Gets New Judges and Deputy Principal Judge (Jan. 27, 2015), http://eacj.org/?p=1754. (noting that "[t]he Summit approved the Council recommendation to extend the jurisdiction of the [EACJ] to cover trade and investment as well as matters associated with the East African Monetary Union. On Human Rights matters as well as crimes against humanity, the Summit directed the Council of Ministers to work with the African Union on this matter").

[37] EAC Establishment Treaty, *supra* note 26, at art. 31.

[38] *Id.* at art. 32.

[39] *Id.* at art. 30(1).

[40] *Id.* at art. 30 (providing that in such a case the Court could be asked to determine "the legality of any Act, regulation, directive, decision or action of a Partner State or an institution of the EAC on grounds that such Act, regulation, directive, decision or action is unlawful or is an infringement of the provisions of this Treaty"). A carve-out in art. 30(3) provides that the Court shall have no jurisdiction "where an Act, regulation, directive, decision or action has been reserved under this Treaty to an institution of a Partner State." *Id.* at art. 30(3).

[41] *Id.* at art. 31.

In the period when the EACJ was created, national courts in East Africa had lost public confidence and the confidence of opposition parties as capable of serving as guardians of their rights when they were infringed by a dominant party. National courts are often not trusted because of corruption, incompetence, or political inclination.[42] As the EACJ became the go-to Court for opposition political parties, this in turn strengthened and helped it to survive the backlash from dominant political parties.

Before proceeding to discuss the cases challenging elections to the EALA, the next section of the chapter provides information about the Assembly.

The East African Legislative Assembly

Unlike sub-regional parliament in the Southern African Development Community (SADC), the EALA is more than a talk shop. It has legislative powers, budgetary approval authority as well as oversight responsibilities. The Treaty for the Establishment of the EAC recognizes it as the legislative organ of the EAC.[43] As a representative institution, it brings the voice of East African citizens to the regional integration process. The EALA is also financially and politically independent from the Member States. Its roles include approving the Community budget as well as making recommendations to the Council of Ministers for the implementation of the Community's objectives.[44] Another of its very significant powers is passage of community legislation, a power that it shares with the EAC Council of Ministers.

The EALA has exercised its power to legislate with diligence since its inauguration in 2001.[45] Since its inauguration, the Assembly has passed legislation on a

---

[42] Notably, national courts in Africa do not always serve regime interests, they often also provide room for opposition elites to bring cases that undermine regime interests. *See, e.g.,* TAMIR MOUSTAFA, THE STRUGGLE FOR CONSTITUTIONAL POWER LAW, POLITICS, AND ECONOMIC DEVELOPMENT IN EGYPT (2007); Mary L. Dudziak, *Who Cares about Courts? Creating a Constituency for Judicial Independence in Africa,* 101 MICH. L. REV. 1622 (2003).

[43] *See* EAC Establishment Treaty, *supra* note 26, at art. 49 (which provides for the functions of the EALA). Declaration and Treaty of the Southern African Development Community art. 9(1), Aug. 17, 1992 (which establishes SADC institutions, does not mention the Forum). *But see* Bookie Monica Kethusegile v. SADC Parliamentary Forum (2009) Case No. SADC 02 (asserting that a SADC Summit decision elevated the Forum to a SADC institution); *see also* Stephen Kingah, *EU's Engagement with African Sub-Regional Parliaments of ECOWAS, SADC, EAC and AU* (U.N. Univ. Inst. on Comp. Regional Integration Stud. Working Papers W-2012/8, 2012), at 9, http://cris.unu.edu/sites/cris.unu.edu/files/W-2012-8.pdf.

[44] The Council of Ministers is required to submit to the EALA budgetary proposals each financial year. *See* EAC Establishment Treaty, *supra* note 26, at art. 132.

[45] *See* EAC Establishment Treaty, *supra* note 26, at art. 62, providing for the EALA to exercise legislative powers to enact community law. In its strategic plan for the period 2013–2018, the EALA makes its major strategic issues to include—enhancing institutional status, administrative as well as achieving full administrative autonomy, capacity and efficiency so that it could become an even more vibrant and dynamic body. It also identifies as major objectives negotiations for the Community's integration pillars and building capacity in regional parliamentary practices. *See* East African Legislative Assembly, Strategic Plan 2013–2018 (2013) http://www.eala.org/documents/view/eala-strategic-plan-2013-2018.

broad range of EAC subjects that have become domesticated by Member States in their national legislation or that have been ratified as community law.[46] For this reason, it is not a "rubber stamp" parliament. When in 2005 the Council of Ministers sought to interfere with this legislative authority, the EALA legislative authority successfully sued the Council in the EACJ.[47] The Court stopped the Council from encroaching on its legislative mandate.[48] Since then, the EALA has asserted its power to legislate in co-decision with the Council of Ministers. As of May 2018, the Assembly had passed over seventy pieces of legislation.[49]

Another of the roles of the EALA is oversight over the EAC's organs and institutions.[50] This oversight extends to monitoring the progress made by the Community in developing its foreign and security policies.[51] The EALA engages and consults with national parliaments and East African citizens, which means its members frequently travel around the EAC. Its roles have expanded quite quickly and now include monitoring national elections within the EAC.[52]

The intense nature of lobbying to be elected[53] and the propensity of a dominant party to engage in electoral manipulation is the backdrop against which the EACJ

---

[46] *See* JAMES GATHII, SOURCES OF EAST AFRICAN COMMUNITY LAW (forthcoming 2020).

[47] Mwatela v. East African Community, App. No. 1, Judgment, East African Court of Justice (Oct. 1, 2006), https://africanlii.org/sites/default/files/Andrew%20v.%20East%20African%20Community%2C%20Ruling%2C%20Appl.%20No.%201%20of%202005%20%28EACJ%2C%20Oct.%2001%2C%202006%29_0.pdf.

[48] *See* James Gathii, *Mission Creep or a Search for Relevance: The East African Court of Justice's Human Rights Strategy*, 24 DUKE J. COMP. & INT'L L. 249 (2013).

[49] *See EALA Joins Push for Legislative Powers at ECOWAS Parliament*, EAC INTERNATIONAL (May 29, 2018), https://www.eac.int/press-releases/558-973-592-eala-joins-push-for-legislative-powers-at-ecowas-parliament.

[50] EAC Establishment Treaty, *supra* note 26, at art. 49 (requires the Council of Ministers to submit to the EALA reports on the activities of the Community, annual audit reports of the Audit Commission, and any other reports referred to it).

[51] *See* EAC Establishment Treaty, *supra* note 26, at art. 123.

[52] The budget of the EALA has grown as its membership has grown as well as its range of activities from a mere US$6,476,163 in the 2001–2002 financial year to US$533,133,909 in the 2012–2013 financial year. This represents a more than 90 percent increase in the budgetary allocations that the EALA over a ten-year period. *See* EAST AFRICAN LEGISLATIVE ASSEMBLY, STRATEGIC PLAN 2013-2018, 57 (2013) http://www.eala.org/documents/view/eala-strategic-plan-2013-2018.

[53] Being elected to the EALA comes with very desirable perks, such as salaries and allowances paid in U.S. dollars. The expanding roles the EALA in such as election monitoring adds to the per diems and allowances paid to these members. The pay and perks that come with being a member of the EALA increases the lobbying within political parties by individuals to be on the list of those to be elected. Any of those who seek to be elected to the EALA are former members of their national parliaments who lost their seats in prior elections and do not therefore have any gainful public employment that provided a livelihood and social status. In July 2014, EALA members became the highest paid in the region, and perhaps some of the highest paid on the African continent. *See Shs53m a month: Why EALA seat is a big deal for our politicians*, MATOOKE REPUBLIC (Feb. 9, 2017), http://matookerepublic.com/2017/02/09/shs53m-a-month-why-eala-seat-is-a-big-deal-for-our-politicians/. The best information I could get shows that the basic salary and sitting allowance of an EALA MP could be as high $14,908 per month, tax-free. This does not include medical and travel insurance that is also covered. *See* Dicta Asiimwe, *Uganda MPs vote for Status Quo in EALA election*, THE EAST AFRICAN (Mar. 6, 2017), https://allafrica.com/stories/201703070320.html. Such a large compensation package is therefore a huge factor in opening up splits within individual opposition parties as they lobby to elected, a factor that plays into the hands of a dominant party.

is invited to decide whether electoral outcomes are consistent with the treaty requirement of an election. In this sense then the EACJ has served as a coordination device that provides opposition parties opportunities to mobilize against the electoral manipulation for seats in the EALA engaged in by dominant parties in their respective national legislative bodies.[54]

The Treaty for the Establishment of the EAC makes provision for the election to the EALA. Each of the six Member States of the EAC is entitled to elect nine EALA members every five years. The Treaty for the Establishment of the EAC provides for elections to the EALA, the legislative arm of the EAC, as follows:

> The National Assembly of each Partner State shall elect, not from among its members, nine members of the Assembly, who shall represent as much as it is feasible, the various political parties represented in the National Assembly, shades of opinion, gender, and other special interest groups in that Partner State, in accordance with such procedure as the National Assembly of each Partner State may determine.[55]

Five of the six EAC Member States, Uganda, Kenya, Tanzania, Burundi, and South Sudan elect all nine members through their national Parliaments. Rwanda elects its EALA members who do not represent political parties through a primary system at the constituency level.[56] This means Rwandese citizens have a voice and vote in determining EALA members who represent these special interest groups—the youth, women, and persons with disabilities. Rwanda's National Electoral Commission is responsible for conducting elections for these special interest groups. However, Rwanda like all other five EAC Member States elects those members who

---

[54] The divisions that occur within individual opposition parties in the lobbying for seats in the East African Legislative Assembly do not in of themselves lend themselves to the kind of coordination through suits filed in the East African Court of Justice. These divisions may reflect ideological or personal differences within a party and are often an indication of opposition party weakness. But when these divisions play into the hands of a dominant party that prefers one side of a split within an opposition party, (a factor that strengthens the leverage of a dominant party over an opposition party), the ensuing electoral disagreements form the basis of suits in the East African Court of Justice as examined more closely in Part One and Two of this chapter. To illustrate the large interest in serving in the East African Legislative Assembly is apparent from the number of individuals who seek nomination to be elected. In 2012, for example 119 candidates applied to be nominated by the opposition Orange Democratic Movement (ODM) party. The Party eventually presented 63 to be considered for election. *See East Africa: Race for East Africa Legislative Seats*, TRADEMARK EAST AFRICA (Feb. 21, 2007), https://www.trademarkea.com/news/east-africa-race-for-east-african-legislative-assembly-seats/. *Ugandan Lawmakers Pick Nine From 47 Candidates Vying for EALA Seats*, THE EAST AFRICAN (Feb. 28, 2017), https://allafrica.com/stories/201702280497.html.

[55] EAC Establishment Treaty, *supra* note 26, at art. 50(1).

[56] Robert Mbaraga, *Rwanda Picks Nine Members of EALA*, THE EAST AFRICAN (May 19, 2017), http://www.theeastafrican.co.ke/news/2558-3934000-984qs8z/index.html; Peter Nyanzi, *EALA Elections a Missed Opportunity*, THE INDEPENDENT (June 15, 2012), https://www.independent.co.ug/eala-elections-missed-opportunity/.

represent political parties in its national assembly as required by the Treaty for the Establishment of the EAC.[57]

Although there are definite financial spoils that incentives individuals to lobby for election to the EALA, once elected, Legislative Assembly members exercise considerable independence. Although their legislative, oversight, and budget approval authority is restricted to EAC matters, members have often pushed back against the preferences of their governments. For example, while the EAC Council of Ministers has so far effectively blocked an East African human rights treaty, in 2011 the Legal Rules and Privileges Committee of the Assembly drafted a Human Rights Bill that the Assembly subsequently passed.[58] The primary sponsor of the Bill was a Burundi Assembly member from an opposition political party. Notably, this member of the Assembly was among four other Assembly members elected from opposition parties in Burundi who were re-called by their government for opposing the extension of the President's tenure beyond that allowed by the Constitution of Burundi. In a further example of the assertion of its independence, discussed further in Part Three later, the Assembly passed a strongly worded resolution noting that the recall was "tantamount to a raid on the independence and integrity of the Assembly."[59]

The Council of Ministers ultimately prevailed in ensuring the Human Rights Bill was not ratified by the Member State, but the discussion around its adoption contributed to increasing a sub-regional consciousness on the significance of the promotion and protection of human rights.[60] In addition, the Assembly through the Legal Rules and Privileges Committee has conducted good governance

[57] EAC Establishment Treaty, *supra* note 26, at art. 50(2) provides that: "(2) A person shall be qualified to be elected a member of the Assembly by the National Assembly of a Partner State in accordance with paragraph 1 of this Article if such a person: (a) is a citizen of that Partner State; (b) is qualified to be elected a member of the National Assembly of that Partner State under its Constitution; (c) is not holding office as a Minister in that Partner State; (d) is not an officer in the service of the Community; and (e) has proven experience or interest in consolidating and furthering the aims and objectives of the Community."

[58] *Bill on Human Rights is Passed by EALA*, EAST AFRICAN LEGISLATIVE ASSEMBLY (2012), http://www.eala.org/media/view/bill-on-human-rights-is-passed-by-eala.

[59] Zephania Ubwani, *EALA Rejects Burundi's Recall of Representatives*, THE CITIZEN (Nov. 27, 2015), https://www.thecitizen.co.tz/News/1840340-2974940-xqk8ijz/index.html. *See also EALA Members Tenure of Office under Threat—Assembly Member moves Urgent Motion for Resolution*, EAC INTERNATIONAL, https://www.eac.int/press-releases/283-311-155-eala-members-tenure-of-office-under-threat-assembly-member-moves-urgent-motion-for-resolution. *See also Report of the Committee on Legal Rules, Rules and Privileges on the Consideration of a Resolution Moved Under Rule 30(J) of the Assembly Rules of Procedure on a Matter of Privilege Arising From a Threat if Tenure of Office of Four Members of the East African Legislative Assembly* (Jan. 27 and Feb. 3, 2016), EAST AFRICAN COMMUNITY, http://www.eala.org/uploads/Legal_Report.pdf; *Motion for a Resolutions of the Assembly Under Rule 30(J) of the Assembly Rules of Procedure on a Matter of Privilege Arising From a Threat of Tenure of Office*, EAST AFRICAN LEGISLATIVE ASSEMBLY, http://www.eala.org/uploads/RESOLUTION_MOVED_UNDER_RULE_30_J.pdf. The recall of Burundi EALA members is discussed in more detail later in Part Three.

[60] Victor Lando, *The Domestic Effect of the East African Community's Human Rights Practice* (unpublished LL.D. thesis, University of Pretoria) (2017).

assessments of the EAC Member States under the East African Community's Protocol on Good Governance.[61]

Further, the Assembly has used its power to pass resolutions to assert its independence, while bringing attention to good governance and human rights issues in individual EAC Member States. For example, when the Council of Ministers sought to restrict private members from introducing Bills in the Assembly through a treaty amendment, the Assembly passed a resolution opposing it because if it prevailed, it would impinge on its legislative and representative function.[62] The Assembly has also passed a resolution encouraging Member States to adopt the African Charter on Democracy and Human Rights,[63] and urging Member States to expand democratic space in their national politics as required by the Charter.[64]

One particularly salient resolution condemned the murders of political leaders and in particular of one who was then a member of the EALA from Burundi.[65] A special sitting was convened to discuss that murder and to honor their fallen colleague. The Assembly debate and resolution condemned the use of "assassinations or murder as a tool to settle political differences is not only myopic, cowardly, and despicable but also has no place in the political dispensation of the modern world of democracy, freedom of expression and association."[66] The Assembly in its resolution called upon the East African Council of Ministers to invoke Chapter Seven of the United Nations Charter and as such to invite the United Nations to investigate what was going on in Burundi. When the question of inviting a UN investigation was raised in the debate, a Minister from the government of Burundi strongly opposed it. A Ugandan member of the Assembly who was elected from an opposition party strongly supported the inclusion of the recommendation for a UN investigation. At the time, the government of Burundi had declined repeated requests pursuant to United Nations Security Resolutions to send a team to monitor the crisis. The government has also rejected a request from the African Union's Peace and Security Council to send a peace mission to the country. In these contexts, EALA resolutions serve as an advocacy tool that links the legislators with advocates for

---

[61] *See, e.g.*, Report on the Assessment of Good Governance in Partner States From 1st to 5th October 2012, EALA Legal Rules Committee, http://www.eala.org/uploads/LRC%20-%20Report%20on%20the%20Assessment%20of%20Good%20Governance%20in%20Partner%20States%20-%20October%202012.pdf.

[62] Resolution of the Assembly on the Proposal to Amend Article 59 of the Treaty—Private Members Bill, East African Community (Mar. 4, 2012), http://www.eala.org/uploads/Scan_20160815_(26).pdf.

[63] A Resolution of the Assembly Urging EAC Partner States to Adopt the African Charter on Democracy and Human Rights, East African Legislative Assembly (Jan. 29, 2015), http://www.eala.org/uploads/Scan_20160801_(3).pdf.

[64] *Id.*

[65] Peter Mathuki, Resolution to Condemn the Killing of and paying Tribute to Hon. Hafsa Mossi, East African Legislative Assembly (Mar. 5, 2016) http://www.eala.org/uploads/EALA-RES-3-05-2016_-_Resolution_to_condemn_the_killing_of_Hon._Hafsa_Mossi_(FINAL).pdf.

[66] *Id.*

the promotion of human rights in the region. This also provides opportunities for cross-country collaborations among EAC legislators and human rights activists.

Another example demonstrating the Assembly's independence relates to resignations of Celestin Kabahizi, an EALA member from Rwanda before the expiry of his term because he opposed the extension of Presidential term limits in that country beyond what was then constitutionally permitted.[67] Kabahizi was elected to the EALA as a representative of one of Rwanda's opposition parties, the Social Democratic Party.[68] Like in the Burundi as discussed above, the Kagame government of Rwanda brooks no political opposition in its national politics. The Rwandese government orchestrated his resignation because of his opposition to a constitutional amendment that would have allowed President Kagame to remain in power beyond the two-term constitutional term limit.[69] There are additional examples of politicians who resigned from the EALA from Rwandese opposition parties for similar reasons.[70]

An EALA member from Rwanda resigned his position at about the same time he decided to run against President Kagame for the leadership of the ruling party in Rwanda.[71] This example is highly suggestive of the fact that membership in this

[67] Sam Learner, *Rwanda: Term Limit Controversy Masks Real Issues*, ATLANTIC COUNCIL (Oct. 15, 2015), http://www.atlanticcouncil.org/blogs/africasource/rwanda-term-limit-controversy-masks-real-issues.

[68] Notably, Celestin Kahabizi wrote his Masters of Arts thesis in Development Management on opposition politics. It was titled, "Opposition Political Parties and Democracy Consolidation Nexus: An Appraisal of Malawi's Opposition Politics from 2004–2011," and written at the Institute of Development Research and Development Policy of the Ruhr-University, Bochum. *See* Celestin Kahabizi, *Opposition Political Parties and Democracy Consolidation Nexus: Appraisal of Malawi's Opposition Politics from 2004–2011* (unpublished MA thesis).

[69] There were also two "resignations" from Rwanda's Parliament by MPs who were opposed to the constitutional amendment extending President Kagame's presidential term. *See Vocal RPF MP Resigns after Alleged "Questioning"*, THE EAST AFRICAN (June 13, 2015), http://www.theeastafrican.co.ke/news/Vocal-RPF-MP-resigns-after-alleged--questioning-/2558-2750320-format-sitemap-12vm4b4z/index.html.

[70] Ludovica Iaccino, *Rwanda: Changing the Constitution to Allow President Kagame Third Term "Will Undermine Peace and Democracy"*, INTERNATIONAL BUSINESS TIMES (June 17, 2015), https://www.ibtimes.co.uk/rwanda-changing-constitution-allow-president-kagame-third-term-will-undermine-peace-democracy-1506587. In February 2015, another EALA member, Abdul Karim Harelimana, this time a member of the ruling party of Rwanda, resigned. *See* James Karuhanga, *MP Harelimana Resigns from EALA*, THE NEW TIMES (Feb. 5, 2015), http://www.newtimes.co.rw/section/read/185652. As a member of the EALA Harelimana was very concerned about good governance in the EAC and may have been asked to resign his EALA seat for exercising independence from the Rwandese ruling party. For a question he asked as an EALA member on the status of the East African Good Governance Protocol, *see, e.g.*, his contributions in the 5th Meeting of the Session of the East African Legislative Assembly, Kigali, Rwanda 12th–26th April 2013, Priority Questions for Oral Answers, East African Legislative Assembly, http://www.eala.org/uploads/EALA%20Priority%20questions%2012%20-26%20April%202013.pdf. *See also* Placide Kayitare, *Making sense out of MP Bwiza's resignation*, INYENYERE NEWS (June 9, 2015), http://www.inyenyerinews.org/justice-and-reconciliation/making-sense-out-of-mp-bwizas-resignation/; Ludovica Laccino, *Rwanda: Changing constitution to allow President Kagame third term 'will undermine peace and democracy*, INTERNATIONAL BUSINESS TIMES (June 17, 2015), https://www.ibtimes.co.uk/rwanda-changing-constitution-allow-president-kagame-third-term-will-undermine-peace-democracy-1506587; John Mugambo, *Rwanda: Two More MPs Resign*, ALLAFRICA (June 10, 2015), http://allafrica.com/stories/201506100524.html.

[71] Kagame Re-elected RPF Chairperson, The New Paradise (Dec. 16, 2013), https://gilbertmahomed.wordpress.com/2013/12/16/kagame-re-elected-rpf-chairperson/ (noting that Abdul Karim Harlimana

sub-regional legislative assembly carves some independence for members to challenge a very well entrenched political leader, even one who uses repressive means to stay in power. His resignation from the Assembly, which was likely forced by President Kagame, also perhaps illustrates the simultaneous vulnerability such members face.

Committees of the EALA have also pushed back against authoritarian governance. In 2015, the Committee on Regional Affairs and Conflict Resolution conducted election monitoring in Burundi. It concluded that the 2015 Presidential elections held in Burundi was characterized by shrunken democratic space, repression of the opposition and as such "fell short of the principles and standards for holding free, fair and peaceful, transparent and credible elections as stipulated in various international, continental as well as the EAC principles on Election Observation and Evaluation."[72]

The Committee on Regional Affairs and Conflict Resolution also held hearings on the human rights and governance situation in Burundi in 2016 following a massive crackdown on dissidents following a failed coup attempt in that country upon a request by the Arusha based Pan-African Lawyers Union.[73] During the two-week hearing, the Committee heard from opposition politicians, their political parties and human rights groups, as well as from the government of Burundi. Evidence was presented in the hearings that there were rapes, extra-judicial killings, assassinations, detentions, and unexplained disappearances. In addition, evidence that there were mass graves and gruesome pictures of mutilations were put on record. After the hearings, the EALA adopted a report concluding that there were serious and sufficient grounds showing gross human rights violations occurred and continued in Burundi unabated.[74] This illustrates the convening power of the EALA.

By holding these hearings, the Assembly gave those in the political opposition in Burundi to get the word out of Burundi about the repressive measures undertaken by the government. The government had to publicly respond to the assertions made against it. In an interim report, the Committee recommended that the Summit had a duty "to affirm that the Community has a duty of care and responsibility to

---

discussed earlier resigned from the EALA at about the same time he was running against President Kagame as leader of ruling party).

[72] The East African Community Election Observation Mission to Legislative Assembly to the Presidential Election to the Republic of Burundi, 21 July 2015: Preliminary Report, EAST AFRICAN COMMUNITY (Jul. 23, 2015), https://www.fidh.org/IMG/pdf/eac_election_observer_mission_to_burundi_presidential_election_2015_-_preliminary_statement.pdf.

[73] Article 35 of the Rules of Procedure of the East African Legislative Assembly authorizes any member to bring a resolution to the Assembly floor. For the request, see Report of the EALA Committee on Regional Affairs and Conflict Resolution on: The Public Hearing on the Petition by Pan-African Lawyers Union (PALU) on the Deteriorating Human Rights and Humanitarian Situation in the Republic of Burundi, EAST AFRICAN LEGISLATIVE ASSEMBLY (Feb. 11, 2016), http://www.eala.org/uploads/REPORT_O_THE_PETITION_BY_PAN_AFRICAN_LAWYERS.PDF.

[74] EALA Concerned about Republic of Burundi, EALA, https://www.eac.int/press-releases/356-387-916-eala-concerned-about-republic-of-burundi.

protect the people of Burundi from violence and guarantee the safety and security of all citizens and persons in Burundi."[75] It is notable that the Burundi citizen petition was being pursued simultaneously with a case before the EACJ that sought to prevent the President of Burundi from running for a third term.[76] Thus both the EACJ and the EALA gave groups inside and outside Burundi concerned about the deteriorating human rights situation there, an opportunity to raise their concerns in highly visible regional venues. These two examples show how regional and sub-regional human rights civil society groups coordinate at a sub-regional level to mobilize against repression of opposition parties, politicians and domestic human rights groups in repressive regimes like Burundi.

The *Nyong'o* Case: Establishing a Precedent for Opposition Litigation Against EAC Governments in EALA Elections

The first case challenging the election of EALA members arose in Kenya in 2006. Some background context is important to understand how the dispute arose. A coalition of political parties that had swept the independence party out of power in 2002 was quickly disintegrating ahead of a presidential election in 2007. Although this coalition, the National Alliance Rainbow Coalition (NARC), had a substantial parliamentary majority having won the 2002 presidential election with 62.21 percent of the votes cast, fissures within it diminished its parliamentary strength.[77] An enduring source of tension was that one of the constituent parties of the NARC, the Liberal Democratic Party (LDP), had been sidelined in the sharing of cabinet positions inconsistently with a Memorandum of Understanding signed before the NARC election victory in 2002.[78] By favoring the appointment of cabinet members from his National Alliance Party of Kenya wing of the NARC coalition, President Mwai Kibaki angered LDP politicians who had supported him to victory in 2002.[79]

---

[75] *Id.*

[76] East African Civil Society Organisations' Forum (EACSOF) v. Attorney General of Burundi and 2 Others, Application No. 5 of 2015 (arising from Reference No. 2 of 2015), Ruling, East African Court of Justice (Jul. 29, 2015), http://eacsof.net/EACSOF/wp-content/uploads/2016/07/REASONED-RULING-in-EACJ-Appli...OF-vs-AG-Burundi-Others.pdf.

[77] *See* Jeffrey Stevens, *Presidential Succession in Kenya: The Transition from Moi to Kibaki*, 22 COMMONWEALTH & COMP. POL. 224 (2007) (noting that President Kibaki's electoral victory was "a political earthquake as Kibaki and NARC thrashed Kenyatta and KANU").

[78] CHARLES HORNSBY, KENYA: A HISTORY SINCE INDEPENDENCE 737 (2013).

[79] NARC was formed to oppose retiring President Daniel Arap Moi's succession plan to have Uhuru Kenyatta succeed him as President. On the LDP side of the NARC was Raila Odinga, Musalia Mudavadi, Kalonzo Musyoka, Ronald Ngala, and George Saitoti. On the National Alliance of Kenya side were Kijana Wamalwa and Kibaki. Kibaki angered the LDP side by failing to appoint the eleven nominees LDP's leaders submitted to Kibaki. Kibaki appointed only nine from the list that LDP submitted to him. Of those nine appointments, two were not from the list that LDP submitted to him. Thus, Kibaki's side of the coalition, NAK, had thirteen instead of eleven cabinet appointments, a betrayal that laid the foundation to the unraveling of NARC. Stevens, *supra* note 77, at 229–30.

As a result, the process of electing members to the EALA became embroiled in this standoff within the ruling party. Each side of the ruling party submitted its own list of nominees for slots to the EALA. To complicate matters, the burgeoning opposition parties, including those that had been part of NARC on its road to the 2002 election victory also submitted their own lists. The LDP side of the NARC government teamed up with the opposition against Kibaki's government for re-neging on its pre-election commitment to put in place a new Constitution within 100 days of its victory. That deal would have secured a prime minister position for one of the politicians on the LDP side of NARC. After a failed referendum on a new Constitution in late 2005 and with momentum building against the NARC govern-ment because of massive corruption, President Kibaki reconstituted his cabinet in 2006. The growing opposition against the government as well as within the LDP side of the ruling NARC party was the context in which Kenya's dominant NARC party found itself ahead of the 2006 EALA elections.

The immediate reason for the Kenya's opposition and the LDP wing of the ruling coalition to go to the EACJ arose from the manipulation of the dominant party, the NARC. The list of EALA nominees from the dominant wing of the ruling NARC party, the National Alliance Party of Kenya (NAK) was adopted by the Parliamentary Business Committee as the official list of nominees to be adopted by Parliament. The list from the LDP wing of the ruling NARC party was excluded. Officials of the LDP and the LDP opposition that was beginning to coalesce into the Orange Democratic Movement, (ODM), brought a case in the EACJ alleging that the EALA members from Kenya had not been lawfully elected as required by Article 50 of the Treaty for the Establishment of the EAC.[80]

In an unprecedented decision issued a few days before the swearing in of the members of the EALA, the EACJ issued an injunction ordering the Secretary General of the EAC and the Clerk of the EALA not to swear in Kenya's slate of elected members. The Court ordered that these members not been sworn in until

---

[80] Notably, the East African Court of Justice noted that the fact that there were two lists presented to the House Business Committee by the ruling NARC party and that one list had been preferred over the other did not in itself disclose a cause of action under Article 50 of the Treaty for the Establishment of the East African Community. What disclosed a cause of action was the mode of the decision—the fact that there had been no election as required by Article 50. As the Court noted, "it is argued that the fact of the election is not disputable, and that the substantive dispute arises from the two lists of nominees submitted by NARC's party leader and party whip, respectively .... That dispute is not within the ambit of Article 30. Basically, it is a dispute on who should have submitted the NARC party nominees, which dispute should have been solved through the internal party mechanism." Nyong'o v. Attorney Gen. of Kenya, Ref. No. 1 of 2006, Decision, East African Court of Justice, at 19 (Mar. 30, 2007). Notably, the Court notes that the core and material question of whether the decision about who would be Kenya's EALA members had been made consistently with Article 50 of the Treaty for the Establishment of the East African Legislative Assembly was only pleaded as "an after thought," but this did not in the Court's "considered opinion" amount to an abuse of court process which the Government of Kenya had argued; id. at 20.

the case had been heard on the merits.[81] That decision set off a swift backlash from the Kibaki Government.

In its decision on the merits, the Court found that Article 50(1) of the Treaty for the Establishment of the EAC requires each EAC member of Parliament to constitute itself into an electoral college for purposes of electing members of the EALA.[82] In contrast, the Court found that Kenya's Parliament had followed an appointment process. According to the Court, the requirement of holding an election under the Treaty for the Establishment of the EAC, is an "express, unambiguous and mandatory" requirement that could not be substituted by a decision to appoint these members instead.[83] The Court therefore rejected the Kenyan government's argument made by the government of Kenya that the Treaty for the Establishment of the EAC left unfettered discretion in each National Assembly to follow a process other than voting in electing members of the EALA. According to the Court, it "would lead to unnecessary uncertainty, if not absurdity, if Article 50 were construed to mean that the parties to the Treaty intended to attach no meaning to the words 'election' and 'to elect' used in article 50."[84] The Court interpreted Article 50 to require an election through voting that could:

> be accomplished using diverse procedures such as secret ballot, show of hands or acclamation. The electoral process may or may not involve such preliminaries as campaigns, primaries and/or nominations. An election may be contested or uncontested. In our considered view, the bottom line for compliance with Article 50 is the decision to elect is a decision of and by the National Assembly.[85]

Because Kenya's Parliament had decided the members of the EALA by ' "an appointment' by the Government controlled House Business Committee,"[86] the Court found that Kenya's rules were inconsistent with Article 50.[87] As alluded earlier, the fact that Kenya's rules did not make any provision "to cater for gender and other interest groups" as required by Article 50 was found by the Court to constitute a "significant degree of non-compliance."[88] The Court further rejected Kenya's argument that it could invoke its domestic law to justify a violation of a

---

[81] Nyong'o v. Attorney Gen. of Kenya, Ref. No. 1 of 2006, Decision, East African Court of Justice, at 3 (Nov. 27, 2006), http://www.saflii.org/ea/cases/EACJ/2006/3.pdf. >

[82] Nyong'o v. Attorney Gen. of Kenya, Ref. No. 1 of 2006, Decision, East African Court of Justice, at 29 (Mar. 30, 2007).

[83] *Id.*

[84] *Id.* at 32.

[85] *Id.* at 34.

[86] *Id.* at 23.

[87] The Court added that Kenya's Parliament had adopted an appointment rather than an electoral system "irrespective of the awareness of the possibility that the rules were an infringement of Article 50." *Id.* at 42.

[88] *Id.* at 37.

treaty obligation.[89] According to the Court, Kenya had held a "fictitious election in lieu of a real election."[90] As a result of the Court's intervention, the opening of the EALA was delayed by more than six months.

Finally, the Court in *obiter dicta* comments noted that it was a matter of concern that there was lack of uniformity in the application of Community law. According to the Court, the Member States are required to "harmonize all their national laws appertaining to the Community."[91] The Court noted that the case "demonstrated amply the urgent need for such harmonization."[92] This harmonization is particularly important in the context of elections to the EALA and underlies the ability of opposition parties to coordinate against dominant political parties. In the course of the hearing in the *Nyong'o* case against Kenya, the Court concluded that there was at the time a "glaring lack of uniformity in the application of Article 50" in the then three EAC Member States.[93] The *Nyong'o* case therefore laid the foundation for subsequent cases from other EAC Member States seeking a uniform application of Article 50 in the election of members of the EALA.[94]

That said, in the *Nyong'o* case, the EACJ interpreted Article 50 quite flexibly in two respects. First, the Court defined an election quite expansively—no vote needs takes place, a show of hands or acclamation could suffice. In fact, even campaigns, nominations, or a contested election are not necessary for an election to take place

---

[89] Nyong'o, *supra* note 82, at 41 (citing the Vienna Convention of the Law of Treaties, art. 27, May 23, 1969).

[90] Nyong'o, Ref. No. 1 of 2006, at 43. Interview with Judge C of the EACJ First Instance Division, Nairobi, Kenya (Aug. 2, 2013) (asserting that the EACJ was aware that its decision would delay the EALA's opening).

[91] Nyong'o, *supra* note 82, at 43. *See also* Legal Brains Trust Limited v. Uganda, Ref. No. 10 of 2011, East African Court of Justice (Mar. 30, 2012). This case raised a question on term limits of EALA members. The First Instance Division "strongly" advised "any Attorney General or official of any Partner State of the Community [who] makes a decision or does such an act, he or she should always warn himself or herself of the ramification of the real possibility of five different interpretations of an Article of the Treaty (from the five Partner States. We therefore find it imperative to remind Partner States particularly Attorneys General that the need for consistency in interpretation of Treaty provisions should make it imperative for them to refer questions of interpretation of the Treaty to the East African Court of Justice (EACJ), the organ established, inter alia, for that purpose." *Id.* at para. 4.7 (Resolution of Issue No. 2 by the Court).

[92] Nyong'o, *supra* note 82, at 43. To justify its jurisdictional supremacy to decide questions of interpretation of provisions of EAC treaties over national courts, the Court was explicitly granted in Article 34 of the Treaty for the Establishment of the EAC. According to the Court, this provision together with those of Article 33 was "obviously to ensure uniform interpretation and avoid possible conflicting decisions and uncertainty in the interpretation of the same provisions of the Treaty." *Id.* at 21.

[93] Nyong'o, *supra* note 82, at 27.

[94] The significance of this case also lies with the fact that since it was among its first contentious cases to decide, the Court used it to announce two additional important findings that have become foundational in subsequent litigation before the court. These are first, the Court's interpretation of the EAC Treaties binds national courts and second that standing and exhaustion of domestic remedies doctrines do not bar the court from hearing suits from private litigants. Nyong'o, *supra* note 82, at 21 (where the Court found that "Article 30 of the EAC Treaty "confers on a litigant resident in any Partner State the right of direct access to the Court for determination of the issues set out therein." As such it did "not agree with the notion that before bringing a reference under Article 30, a litigant has to 'exhaust the local remedy.' In our view there no local remedy to exhaust.".

for purposes of Article 50. Thus, the second aspect of flexibility in Article 50 as interpreted by the Court is that it gives the dominant party in parliament discretion to decide the procedure to be followed in electing members of the EALA. This discretion includes deciding how best to elect representatives to fulfill the requirements of special groups identified in Article 50. As interpreted by the EACJ, Article 50 does not therefore give iron-clad protection from dominant party electoral manipulation. In future cases, opposition parties sought to expand the scope of protection under Article 50 in a variety of ways that will be the subject of the next part of this chapter.

As I noted earlier, when the EACJ issued its decision restraining the swearing in of Kenyan members to the EALA, Kenya's President Kibaki was outraged. He initially sought to kill the Court for tipping its hat in favor of the opposition and a dissident faction of his ruling coalition. When that failed, he sent his Attorney General to the seat of the Court in Arusha to intimidate the two Kenyan judges on the Court to reverse their decision. That failed too and Kenya pursued a third strategy of clipping the powers of the Court.

Kenya succeeded in persuading the other Member States to amend the Treaty for the Establishment of the EAC to limit the future ability of the Court intrude into what Kenya argued were matters that should be left to the Member States. First, the Treaty was amended to establish an Appellate Division that most observers noted was created as a check on the "activist" First Instance Division. Second, the Treaty was amended to provide that cases had to be filed within two months after the cause of action arises. Third, the Treaty was amended to provide that where a Partner State or its institutions was charged with a responsibility under the Treaty that would preclude the Court from deciding such a question.[95] Notably, notwithstanding Kenya's initial rejection of the Court's decision, its Parliament eventually amended its rules to conform them to the Court's decision and conducted elections as contemplated by Article 50 of the Treaty for the Establishment of the EAC.[96]

The fact that the Kenyan government was so enraged by the EACJ played into the hands of the opposition and civil society groups in the country. They used the case to further mobilize against the Government in editorials in the newspapers, on radio, in political rallies, and elsewhere. They also brought a case in the EACJ challenging the legality of the Treaty amendments that the *Nyong'o* case sparked.

[95] For an exhaustive overview of this backlash, *see* Karen Alter, James Gathii, & Laurence Helfer, *Backlash Against International Courts in West, East and Southern Africa: Causes* and Consequences, 27 EUR. J. INT'L L. 293 (2016).

[96] East African Community (Election of Members of Assembly) Rules, 2007 adopted by the Parliament of Kenya on May 23, 2007. Elections under these rules were held on May 29, 2007. Election of Members of the EALA, Kenya Gazetter Notice No. 4873 (vol. CIX No. 37) (May 31, 2007). In subsequent disputes involving elections to the sub-regional parliament, the EACJ has continued to issue injunctions against election procedures that violate the EAC Treaty. *See, e.g.,* Democratic Party v. EAC Sec'y Gen., Ref. No. 6 of 2011, Judgment, 1st Inst. Div, East African Court of Justice (May 10, 2012), https://www.eacj.org//wp-content/uploads/2012/10/REF-NO.-6-OF-2011.pdf (hereinafter 'Democratic Party').

This pattern of using cases filed in the EACJ by opposition political parties to mobilize their supporters and challenge the government has become a pattern in other EAC Member States when treaty-inconsistent elections are successfully challenged in the EACJ as will be discussed further in Part Two.

Part Two: Party Dominance as a Factor in Electoral Contests for Seats in the EALA

All six EAC Member States have varying degrees of a dominant or authoritarian party. Elections to the EALA are conducted under conditions imposed by the dominant party in the respective country. The undue influence of dominant parties in electing members of the EALA in East African Member States often raises questions of compliance with the treaty requirement of an election. Electoral manipulation by dominant parties is common across these East African countries. Dominant parties engage in this manipulation because they want to have as many seats in the EALA as a reward for their loyal supporters. Those who get elected to the EALA are therefore well-connected politicians.[97] In Uganda, the ruling National Resistance Movement party's lead organ clears contestants for East African Legislative seats and often holds those elections at State House Kampala in the presence of the President.[98]

When dominant parties decline to concede more seats to opposition political parties, the division of seats designated for opposition parties often opens up battle lines among opposition parties about how many seats each opposition party would be entitled to.[99] Intra-opposition political party negotiations are complicated further by the increased numbers of independent Members of Parliament that want

---

[97] *See, e.g.,* in 2011, Rwanda elected Christophe Bazivamo to the East African Legislative Assembly. He was a career politician who had occupied several cabinet positions including Minister for Internal Security, Agriculture, Land, Environment, Forestry and Water and Mines. In addition since 2002, he had been the vice chairperson of the ruling Rwanda Patriotic Front (RPF). *See Former EALA Member, Hon Christophe Bazivamo Assumes Office as DSG*, EAST AFRICAN LEGISLATIVE ASSEMBLY (Sept. 16, 2016), http://www.eala.org/media/view/former-eala-member-hon-christophe-bazivamo-assumes-office-as-dsg#:~:text=Hon%20Bazivamo%20was%20elected%20to%20EALA%20in%202011,he%20was%20replaced%20by%20Rt%20Hon%20Anastase%20Murekezi.

[98] *See, e.g., CEC Clears All 43 NRM Aspirants to Contest for EALA Places*, THE INDEPENDENT (Feb. 5, 2017), https://www.independent.co.ug/cec-clears-43-nrm-aspirants-contest-eala-places/. *See also* Dickens Okello, *NRM Finally Elect 6 for EALA*, CHIMREPORTS (Feb. 8, 2017), http://chimpreports.com/nrm-finally-elect-6-for-eala/(indicating voting for EALA members within the party took place at State House).

[99] Lack of coordination among opposition political parties opens them up to manipulation by dominant political parties. For example, in two successive EALA elections in the Ugandan Parliament, the refusal by the ruling party, National Resistance Movement, to allow the opposition more seats resulted in feuding between the opposition parties on how to allocate the seats between themselves. *See* Nobert Mao, *EALA Elections Have Exposed Uganda's Political Battle Lines*, THE DAILY MONITOR (Feb. 12, 2007), http://www.monitor.co.ug/OpEd/Commentary/Eala-elections-have-exposed-Uganda-s-political-battle-lines/689364-3809092-lijxnsz/index.html.

representation in the EALA. In addition, dominant political parties often seek to influence or to frustrate who among opposition candidates gets elected to the EALA.[100]

Thus in Uganda, for example, the largest opposition party has twice failed to have its member elected to the EALA because smaller opposition parties have decided to vote with the ruling National Resistance Movement party.[101] Beyond seeking to influence how many seats to the EALA each political party would have, the dominant party in each of the six EAC Member State Parliaments controls the day-to-day parliamentary calendar. As such, a dominant party will only allow an election for members of the EALA to proceed only when there is a guarantee of the outcome it prefers.[102] For these reasons, the seating of the EALA has been de-layed a number of times because there was no agreement on the slate of candidates representing each party to be elected to the EALA.[103] Since considerations such a gender and regional and ethnic balance are taken into account in composing the national list of candidates to be elected, this not only complicates political party ne-gotiations on a final list, but it also gives the dominant party additional negotiating leverage to influence the outcomes on the pretext of balancing these competing considerations.

This part begins with judicial challenges of EALA elections from Uganda before proceeding to Tanzania, and then South Sudan. It ends with examining why there are no cases from Burundi and Rwanda.

Challenges of EALA Elections from Uganda

Uganda's ruling National Resistance Movement well illustrates party dominance in elections for EALA. Uganda held its first multi-party elections in 2006. The ruling National Resistance Movement won an overwhelming 213 seats in Parliament.

---

[100] Lack of internal party democracy as well as internal power struggles, leadership rivalry, ethnic and regional divisions, and factionalism within opposition parties makes them vulnerable to manipula-tion by dominant political parties. For example, in 2012 for example, a rift within the Democratic Party in Uganda's elections to the EALA arose on whether to present one or two candidates. The Democratic Party had decided to nominate only one candidate without undergoing a party primary. Thereafter, a party official presented a second candidate to Parliament without the authority of the Party, in a move that suggested the National Resistance Movement had influenced a party official to act inconsistently with its electoral chances to win a slot to the EALA.

[101] John Semakula, *Mbidde blames FDC for losing EALA bid*, NEW VISION (Mar. 2, 2017) https://www.newvision.co.ug/new_vision/news/1447609/-mbidde-blames-fdc-losing-eala-bid.

[102] Clearly opposition parties do hold up agreement on the full slate of candidates presented for elec-tion, but the disagreement in which opposition parties engage is because dominant parties leave them with few choices other than to oppose dominant party tactics.

[103] For example, Kenya has delayed sending its 2017 slate of EALA elected members in part because of lack of agreement between Kenya's political parties about the number of slots to which each is en-titled. *See* Samuel Owino, *House Approves Team to Pick EALA Representatives*, DAILY NATION (Nov. 9, 2017), http://www.nation.co.ke/news/Kenya-Eala-representatives-to-be-picked-/1056-4179350-13iujv1/index.html.

Its closest rival had a mere thirty-seven seats. Table 1.1 in this chapter summarizes these national election results. Uganda's 2006 presidential elections were particularly contentious because they came following a controversial constitutional amendment that allowed President Yoweri Museveni to seek a third term under Uganda's 1995 Constitution. Uganda therefore exhibits not merely a case of party dominance, but also a highly personalistic leadership style in which a strong Presidency engages in range of repressive practices against the opposition, Parliament, and the judiciary.

For example, to procure the amendment removing term limits in 2005, President Museveni used bribery and coercion. This included sending a para-military squad to arrest opposition politicians who had been granted bail within the precincts of the High Court of Uganda. That arrest at the height of President Museveni's heavy-handed crackdown in 2006 was brought to the EACJ in *Katabazi v Uganda*.[104] In *Katabazi*, the EACJ inaugurated a cause of action for violation of human rights when it announced that it could not abdicate its obligation to protect human rights. That case filed in 2007, became the first of many cases that litigants filed in the EACJ to vindicate their rights.[105]

That same year, 2007, Uganda's Parliament designated its slate of East African Legislative Assembly members by an announcement by the National Assembly Speaker that the members nominated by political parties had been duly elected. A challenge to those elections was filed in the Ugandan Constitutional Court in the *Oulunyah* case. That case was brought a candidate who had contested in that national election as an independent candidate for Member of Parliament in Uganda. After losing that election he sought to contest for a seat in the EALA but he was barred from contesting by the Ugandan government. His exclusion was based on the fact that he did not belong to a political party. He made two primary arguments. First, that his exclusion from that election was a violation of his rights under the Ugandan Constitution. Second, that his exclusion was also inconsistent with Article 50 of the Treaty for the Establishment of the EAC as interpreted in *Nyong'o* by the EACJ. Citing the *Nyong'o* case, he argued no election had been conducted in Uganda's Parliament.[106]

Agreeing with him, the Ugandan Constitutional Court held that the Ugandan Parliament had acted in violation of the requirement of holding an election as

---

[104] Katabazi & 21 Others v. Secretary General of the EAC & Another, Ref. No. 1 of 2007, Judgment, East African Court of Justice (Nov. 1, 2007). *See also* Simon Mutiya, *East Africa: EA Court Summons Govt Over Black Mamba Siege*, THE MONITOR (Jan. 25, 2007), http://allafrica.com/stories/200701241066.html.

[105] For a full analysis of this case, *see* James Gathii, *Mission Creep or a Search for Relevance: The East African Court of Justice's Human Rights Strategy*, 24 DUKE J. COMP. & INT'L L. 249 (2013).

[106] In particular, Jacob Oulanyah argued that the rules followed by the Ugandan Parliament did not provide for a mode of election as required by Article 50 of the Treaty for the Establishment of the EAC. The Ugandan Constitutional Court agreed with this argument. *See* Judgment of Okello Judge of Appeal in Jacob Oulanyah v. Attorney General, Constitutional Petition No. 28 of 2006 of the Constitutional Court of Uganda (unreported).

Table 1.1 Parliamentary Election Results from National Elections in East Africa

Country	Year	Party	Seats won (indirect seats)[a]
Uganda	2006	National Resistance Movement (NRM)	213 (14)
	2011		37
	2016	Forum for Democratic Change (FDC)	8[b]
		Democratic Party (DP)	263
		National Resistance Movement (NRM)	34
		Forum for Democratic Change (FDC).	12[c]
		Democratic Party (DP).	298
		National Resistance Movement (NRM).	36
		Forum for Democratic Change (FDC).	15[d]
		Democratic Party (DP).	
Tanzania	2000	Chama Cha Mapinduzi (CCM).	258
	2005	Civic United Front (CUF).	22
	2010	Tanzania Labour Party (TLP)	5[e].
	2015	Chama Cha Mapinduzi (CCM)	275
		Civic United Front (CUF).	31
		Chama Cha Demokrasia na Maendeleo (CHADEMA)	11[f]
		Chama Cha Mapinduzi (CCM)	259
		Chama cha Demokrasia na Maendeleo (CHADEMA)	48
		Civic United Front (CUF)	36[g]
		Chama Cha Mapinduzi (CCM)	253
		Chama Cha Demokrasia na Maendeleo (CHADEMA)	70
		Civic United Front (CUF)	42[h]

Table 1.1 *Continued*

Country	Year	Party	Seats won (indirect seats)[a]
Rwanda	2003	Rwandan Patriotic Front (FPR)-led Coalition.	40
	2008	Social Democratic Party (PSD)	7
	2013	Liberal Party (PL)	6[i]
		Rwandan Patriotic Front (FPR)-led Coalition	42
		Social Democratic Party (PSD)	7
		Liberal Party (PL)	4[j]
		Rwandan Patriotic Front (RPF)	41
		Social Democratic Party (PSD)	7
		Liberal Party (PL)	5[k]
South Sudan	2010	Sudan People's Liberation Movement (SPLM)	160
		Sudan People's Liberation Movement-Democratic Change (SPLM-DC)	2
		National Congress Party (NCP)	1[l]
Burundi	1993	Front for Democracy in Burundi (FRODEBU)	165
	2010	Union for National Progress (UPRONA)	16[m]
	2015	National Council for the Defense of Democracy-Forces for the Defense of Democracy (CNDD-FDD)	81
		Union for National Progress (UPRONA)	17
		Front for Democracy in Burundi-Nyakuri (FRODEBU-Nyakuri)	5[n]
		National Council for the Defense of Democracy-Forces for the Defense of Democracy (CNDD-FDD)	77
		Independents for Hope	21
		Union for National Progress (UPRONA)	2[o]

Continued

Table 1.1 *Continued*

Country	Year	Party	Seats won (indirect seats)[a]
Kenya	2002	National Rainbow Coalition (NARC)	132
	2007		68
	2013	Kenya African National Union (KANU)	15[p]
			102
		Forum for the Restoration of Democracy-People (FORD-P)	78
			16[q]
		Orange Democratic Movement (ODM) & Allies	93
			86
		Party of National Unity (PNU) & Allies	72[r]
		Orange Democratic Movement-Kenya (ODM-K)	
		Orange Democratic Movement	
		National/Jubilee Alliance.	
		United Republican Party	

[a] Indirect seats include: (a) five Youth Representatives; (b) five Representatives of disabled persons; and (c) five Workers' Representatives—at least one member of each category must be a woman. In addition, there are thirteen ex-officio members and ten members representing the Uganda People's Defence Forces.

[b] Uganda Parliament, *Elections in 2006*, INTER-PARLIAMENTARY UNION, http://www.ipu.org/parline-e/reports/arc/2329_06.htm.

[c] *Id.*

[d] *Id.*

[e] Elections *in Tanzania*, AFRICAN ELECTIONS DATABASE, http://africanelections.tripod.com/tz.html#2000_National_Assembly_Election.

[f] *Id.*

[g] *Id.*

[h] United Republic of Tanzania, *Last Elections*, INTER-PARLIAMENTARY UNION, http://www.ipu.org/parline-e/reports/2337_E.htm.

[i] Elections *in Rwanda*, AFRICA ELECTIONS DATABASE RWANDA, http://africanelections.tripod.com/rw.html.

[j] *Id.*

[k] *Rwanda*, INTER-PARLIAMENTARY UNION, http://www.ipu.org/parline-e/reports/2265_E.htm.

[l] *Elections in South Sudan*, AFRICAN ELECTIONS DATABASE, http://africanelections.tripod.com/ssd.html.

[m] Elections *in Burundi*, AFRICAN ELECTIONS DATABASE. http://africanelections.tripod.com/bi.html#1993_Presidential_Election.

[n] *Id.*

[o] https://web.archive.org/web/20150714023212/http:/www.ceniburundi.bi/IMG/pdf/deputes_national_2015-2.pdf.

[p] Elections *in Kenya*, AFRICAN ELECTIONS DATABASE, http://africanelections.tripod.com/ke.html#2002_National_Assembly_Election.

[q] *Id.*

[r] *4th March 2013 General Election Data*, THE INDEPENDENT ELECTORAL AND BOUNDARIES COMMISSION, https://www.iebc.or.ke/uploads/resources/EIqEo3LuiB.pdf.

required by Article 50 of the Treaty for the Establishment of the EAC.[107] The Court held that the Ugandan Parliament had failed to turn itself into an electoral college as the EACJ found was necessary for a valid election to be held under Article 50 of the Treaty for the Establishment of the EAC. To support its conclusion, the Ugandan Constitutional Court relied on the EACJ in the *Nyong'o* case. Further, the Constitutional Court held that the rules for election to the EALA were unconstitutional for excluding independent candidates from contesting. Finally, the Constitutional Court held that the clause "other shades of opinion" in Article 50 of the EAC Treaty includes independent candidates.

The *Oulunyah* case from the Constitutional Court in Uganda shows how a decision of an international court, the EACJ in *Nyong'o*, became part of the claim about how a dominant party had conducted elections to the EALA within one of the EAC Member States.[108] This migration of the principle in *Nyong'o* from an international to a domestic court shows how politicians who were not members of a dominant party used it to buttress their case once they were excluded from participating in EALA elections. The Ugandan government did not contest the principle laid down in the *Nyong'o* case that elections to the EALA must not be substituted by an appointment or nomination process and that Parliament had to sit as an electoral college to elect these members. Rather, it argued that it was aware that its election rules were in violation of the Article 50 of the Treaty for the Establishment of the EAC and that Parliament had commenced the process of amending the election rules.

The government lost the *Oulanyah* case in the Ugandan Constitutional Court. As the Constitutional Court noted, "[t]he argument of numerical strength is also anomalous and prejudicial against the independents who numbered 37 in the House like Forum for Democratic Change (FDC) which similarly numbered 37 and was qualified to elect whereas independents could not."[109] The Constitutional Court held that independent members of Parliament were being unconstitutionally discriminated against by being excluded from participating in East African Legislative elections because these independent candidates did not conform to the political ideologies of the existing parties.[110]

After losing the *Oulanyah* case in 2006, the National Resistance Movement dominated Parliament dragged its feet in amending the rules for EALA elections. To preempt the 2011 elections to the EALA being held under the rules that the Ugandan Constitutional Court had already found to be in violation of Article 50 of

[107] *Id.*

[108] *Id.* at 31 (where the court noted pursuant to the *Nyong'o* case, "here was earnest need to apply the provisions of the Treaty uniformly throughout the EAC, harmonize all national laws appertaining to the Community otherwise lack of uniformity would weaken the community").

[109] *Id.* at 27.

[110] *Id.* at 30. In particular, the Constitutional Court found that the exclusion of independents violated their freedom to associate in vying for seats to the EALA.

the Treaty for the Establishment of the EAC, the opposition Democratic Party of Uganda filed a challenge against the rules in the EACJ.[111]

Some important background is necessary to understand the context within which this case in the EACJ was filed. The Democratic Party had finished a distant third in the February 2011 general elections in Uganda with twelve Parliamentary seats. In that election, the ruling National Resistance Party had increased its legislative dominance having won 263 Parliamentary seats, an increase of fifty seats from the 2006 Parliamentary elections. The second largest party in Parliament, the Forum for Democratic Change reduced its seats from thirty-seven to thirty-four.

It was in large part because of the legislative dominance of the National Resistance Movement that the Democratic Party brought the case to forestall their exclusion from participating in the EALA elections of 2011. Even more, in the period immediately before filing the case in 2011, the Ugandan government had engaged in a widespread and massive clampdown of opposition political parties and their activities who were protesting President Museveni's re-election in the February 2011 general elections. As noted earlier, in those election, President Museveni's National Resistance Party won an overwhelming number of Parliamentary seats. While it is not surprising that a ruling party with such mobilizational and organizational strength could turn out those numbers, its repressive practices particularly against opposition presidential candidate Kizza Besigye for leading protests against the government were a continuation of a legacy of intolerance against the opposition.[112]

In seeking an injunction to prevent the EALA elections from being conducted under the unamended rules, the Democratic Party argued that if the Ugandan Parliament followed its rules, it would have locked them out of contesting in the EALA elections. The EACJ agreed that it was a matter of concern that under those rules, seats to the EALA would be determined on the basis of the numerical strength of parliamentary parties, rather than through an election.[113] The EACJ, like in the *Nyong'o* case first issued an injunction preventing the Ugandan parliament from conducting elections under rules that were in violation of the Treaty for the Establishment of the EAC.[114]

The Democratic Party's arguments in this case confirms the major claim in this chapter that the underlying reason for bringing the case was because Parliament had divested itself of its obligation under Article 50 of the Treaty for the

---

[111] Democratic Party, *supra* note 96.

[112] Besigye's allies took his case alleging violation of his rights to the East African Court of Justice in East Africa Law Society v. Uganda, App. No. 12, East African Court of Justice (2012), https://www.eacj.org//wp-content/uploads/2013/09/Application-no-12-of-2012.pdf.

[113] Democratic Party, *supra* note 96, at 29. The court in granting an injunction noted the harm done by allowing an election under the unamended rules would be that "there will be improperly elected Representatives of the EALA and the credibility of the EALA would be questionable ... no amount of damages would ever be able to adequately compensate the Applicants for that kind of injury." *Id.* at 35.

[114] *Id.*

Establishment of the EAC and bestowed it on the National Resistance Movement. In other words, that Parliament had abdicated its role and delegated it to the National Resistance Movement which now assumed the role of Parliament in elections to the EALA. By filing its case in the EACJ, the Democratic Party forced the Ugandan Attorney General to travel to Arusha, Tanzania at the seat of the Court. The stated reason for the Ugandan Attorney General to travel to Arusha during the hearing of the case was to seek the Court's guidance and interpretation of how the Ugandan Parliament should elect members to represent the country to the East Africa Legislative Assembly.[115] The Court must have thought that the Attorney General's request was merely face-saving. Perhaps it was aware of the reality in Uganda—that senior members of the National Resistance Movement objected to changing the rules in a way that would give opposition parties an opportunity to be elected to the EALA.[116] The Court did in fact refer to the fact that the Attorney General had never sought any interpretation from the Court notwithstanding the fact that Speaker of the Ugandan Parliament had requested him to do as much in two cases that were filed against Uganda following the 2012 EALA elections.[117] The fact that the Ugandan Attorney General personally decided to go to Court to request guidance is precisely why opposition politicians in East African go to the EACJ. The Court helps them to engage government officials in ways that are not always possible in their home countries.

Indeed were it not for the intervention of the EACJ, the attention this got in the media and the way that the opposition leveraged it in many other fora in and outside of Uganda, Parliament may never have amended those rules.[118] The Ugandan

---

[115] Sheila Naturinda, *Nyombi Seeks Court counsel on representatives to EALA*, THE MONITOR (Apr. 5, 2012), https://www.monitor.co.ug/News/National/688334-1380464-9ibkr3z/index.html.

[116] Sheila Naturinda, *Uganda Parliament Stuck on Make-up of Arusha Assembly*, DAILY MONITOR (Mar. 23, 2012), http://www.monitor.co.ug/News/World/688340-1371538-gv33kuz/index.html. *See also* Agather Atuhaire, *Local Politics goes to East Africa*, THE INDEPENDENT (May 27, 2012), https://www.independent.co.ug/local-politics-goes-east-africa/ (noting the National Resistance Movement wanted most if not all seats reserved for its party members).

[117] Democratic Party, *supra* note 96; Among Anita v. Attorney General of Uganda and Secretary General, Ref. No. 6, East African Court of Justice, at 4–5 (2012), http://eacj.org/?cases=among-a-anita-vs-attorney-general-of-uganda-and-the-secretary-general-of-the-east-african-community [*hereinafter* "Among Anita"]; Abdu Katuntu v. Attorney General of Uganda and Secretary General of EAC, Ref. No. 5, East African Court of Justice, at 4 (2012), http://eacj.org/?cases=abdu-katuntu-vs-the-attorney-general-of-uganda-and-the-secretary-general-east-african-community [hereinafter "Abdu Katuntu"].

[118] *EA Court of Justice to Hear Cases on Uganda, Deliver Judgement on Kenya Constitution Case*, AFRICAN PRESS ORGANIZATION (Sept. 23, 2011), https://appablog.wordpress.com/2011/09/23/ea-court-of-justice-to-hear-cases-on-uganda-deliver-judgement-on-kenya-constitution-case-court-to-also-deliver-ruling-on-terminal-benefits-for-staff-of-defunct-eac/; Agather Atuhaire, *Opposition Shoots Self in Foot*, THE INDEPENDENT (June 4, 2012), https://www.independent.co.ug/opposition-shoots-self-foot/; *Court Dismisses Call for Election*, THE CITIZEN (Nov. 27, 2013), http://www.thecitizen.co.tz/News/EA-court-dismisses-call-for-election-review/1840360-2090304-oavkj3/index.html; Ruth Mubiri, *Parliament Fails to Decide on EALA Representation*, UGANDA RADIO NETWORK (Mar. 16, 2012) https://ugandaradionetwork.com/story/parliament-fails-to-decide-on-eala-representation; Anthony Wasaka, *Regional Court Dismisses EALA Elections Case*, THE CITIZEN (Nov. 28, 2013), http://www.thecitizen.co.tz/News/Regional-court-dismisses-Eala-elections-case/1840360-2091652-5sdm2bz/index.html.

Parliament amended these rules on May 18, 2012, ten days after the EACJ found them to be inconsistent with the Treaty for the Establishment of the EAC. In a subsequent decision of November 25, 2013, the EACJ found that the new rules mirrored the requirements of Article 50 of the Treaty.[119] Although Uganda had conformed to its rules to the Treaty, minority political parties led by the shadow Attorney General Abdu Katuntu, brought suit in the EACJ arguing that the Ugandan Parliament had nevertheless violated Article 50 because in conducting the election, not all six political parties in Uganda's Parliament got seats in the EALA. According to these minority opposition political parties, the Treaty for the Establishment of the EAC should be construed to require that political parties to be represented in the EALA, irrespective of their numerical strength. In other words, since representation in the EALA was not based on numerical strength, opposition parties ought to be elected to the EALA alongside their colleagues from a dominant party.[120] The EACJ disagreed with these opposition parties noting that the "very nature of an election would necessitate that no candidate is assured of election merely because he is supported by a particular political party."[121]

In yet another decision challenging Uganda's EALA elections of 2012, in the EACJ, the litigants argued that those elections were inconsistent with the guarantees for representation of women contained in Article 5(3) of the Treaty for the Establishment of the EAC.[122] In essence, the challenge was based on the *Katabazi* doctrine under which the Court had declared it would not abdicate in its responsibility to adjudicate human rights cases. The Court dodged answering this particular question and instead focused in particular on whether Article 50 required all interest groups mentioned in Article 50 (women, youth, and people with disability) being represented in the slate of those elected to the EALA. In disagreeing with the litigants, the Court held that Article 50 of the Treaty for the Establishment of the EAC does not impose a mandatory requirement that women or the other groupings (youth and persons with disabilities) it mentions to be elected.[123] The Court held that the feasibility of the extent of such representation was at the discretion of each Member State Parliament. Further, the Court observed since some EAC Member States had more than a dozen political parties, the Treaty could not be interpreted to require each political party or grouping mentioned in Article 50 must be represented among those elected to serve in the EALA.[124]

Even though Uganda has amended its election rules to conform to Article 50 of the Treaty for the Establishment of the EAC, the dominance of the National Resistance Movement has not waned. Thus in the 2017 elections, the four

---

[119] Abdu Katuntu, *supra* note 117, at 31, 40.
[120] *Id.* at 34.
[121] *Id.* at 40.
[122] Among Anita, *supra* note 117, at 4–5.
[123] *Id.* at 28.
[124] *Id.* at 29.

opposition candidates who won seats in the EALA were all approved by President Museveni and the National Resistance Movement.[125] To improve their chances of being elected to the EALA, many politicians cross from smaller parties to the dominant and ruling.[126] This is also the case in Tanzania where the ruling party, Chama Cha Mapinduzi (CCM) has used its legislative dominance to control elections to the EALA.[127] I will turn next to Tanzania.

Challenges to EALA Elections From Tanzania

Tanzania's CCM ruling party has been in power since independence. It has enjoyed legislative dominance since the introduction of multi-party politics in 1992. In the 2015 general elections, for example, CCM won 253 parliamentary seats. The opposition party with the highest number of seats in that election was seventy. So dominant is CCM that it also controls the Presidency and legislature of its Union partner, Zanzibar as well as all local councils in the country. Although Tanzania allows opposition political parties, opposition party weakness effectively makes it a one-party state. While in Uganda the National Resistance Movement banks on its claim to ending a vicious civil war, in Tanzania CCM's legitimacy stems from its appeal as founding nationalist party that has for the most part had more internal democracy than its rival opposition parties.[128] Like other dominant parties, CCM has the enormous advantage of the incumbency as well as extensive executive powers of the presidency. The opposition's limited access to resources, and the low legitimacy of opposition politics in Tanzania, as in most of the rest of East Africa, has given CCM a big advantage over opposition political parties.

CCM has however faced increased electoral competition from opposition parties. In their campaigns, these opposition parties have campaigned against corruption among senior CCM politicians. In addition, CCM has used election violence against opposition politicians. Although Tanzanian courts are relatively independent, CCM controls all the administrative apparatus of the state and so law enforcement against corrupt officials is negligible. Press freedom is undermined by periodic attacks on journalists and their newspapers from the government. Harassment of opposition politicians is common. Perhaps because CCM controls

---

[125] Mike Ssegawa, *EALA Election: Museveni dismantles opposition in 9:0 show of political domination*, WATCHDOG NEWS (Mar. 1, 2017), https://www.watchdoguganda.com/news/20170301/14408/eala-elections-museveni-dismantles-opposition-in-90-show-of-political-dominion.html.

[126] *200 Defect to NRM is Ssembabule*, NEW VISION (Nov. 3, 2009), http://www.newvision.co.ug/new_vision/news/1202338/200-defect-nrm-ssembabule.

[127] Aly Salehe, *Why EALA is a blot on Tanzania*, ALLAFRICA (Apr. 9, 2017), http://allafrica.com/stories/201704100078.html.

[128] Mohabe Nyirabu, *The Multiparty Reform Process in Tanzania: The Dominance of the Ruling Party*, 7 AFR. J. POL. SCI. 99 (2002).

all the resources of the state, opposition politicians often defect to CCM further weakening opposition politics in Tanzania.[129]

The most significant challenge to Tanzanian elections to the EALA arose in 2012 when a member of the opposition Chama Cha Demokrasia na Maendeleo (CHADEMA) challenged the April 2012 elections.[130] The politician argued that the rules under which those elections were conducted was inconsistent with Article 50 of the Treaty for the Establishment of the EAC. The basis of the claim was the claim that although CHADEMA has 14 percent of the parliamentary seats in Tanzania, it had been unable to secure a seat in the EALA elections. In other words, CHADEMA argued that Article 50 required proportional representation among the parliamentary political parties among those elected to the EALA.[131]

The EACJ, citing its previous cases, held Article 50 did not guarantee a seat in the EALA for any political party or contestant. However, the Court nevertheless found that to the extent the election rules in Tanzania only permitted political party candidates to nominate candidates, they were inconsistent with Article 50 because they made no mention of the youth and persons with disabilities as special interest groups.[132] According to the Court:

> the National Assembly of Tanzania did not adhere to the expectation in Article 50(1) that each category of representation should as much as feasible be a separate and distinct category from each other. To lump all categories under "any political party which is entitled to sponsor candidates" and then grant that one category the preserve to bring candidates for other categories, so that ultimately every candidate and eventual representative would be affiliated to a political party, whether or not represented in the National Assembly, as opposed to say shades of opinion, gender and other interest groups, would be a clear violation of Article 50(1).[133]

This quote illustrates the Court's formalist approach in its Article 50 cases. This approach effectively gives dominant parties discretion to comply with Article 50 in a political context where expansive interpretations would likely trigger a backlash. For example, opposition political party politicians have failed to convince the Court to interpret Article 50 to require proportional representation of opposition parties in EALA elections. These opposition politicians have argued that any other system than proportional representation of opposition parties is a "winner takes all

---

[129] *Tanzania: Analysts Tout Soul Searching As Defections Rock Opposition Camp*, ALLAFRICA (Nov. 22, 2017), http://allafrica.com/stories/201711220791.html.

[130] Anthony Calist Komu v. Attorney General of Tanzania, Ref. No. 7, East African Court of Justice (2012), https://www.eacj.org/?cases=antony-calist-komu-vs-attorney-general-united-republic-tanzania [hereinafter "Komu"].

[131] *Id.* at 51–62.

[132] *Id.* at 62–63.

[133] *Id.* at 65.

system."[134] Rather than take a bold purposive approach to directly confront dominant party behavior in EALA elections, the Court has emphasized instead that Article 50 does not contemplate proportional representation but merely that there "is an equal opportunity to become a candidate, full participation and competition for specified groupings and at the end of the process, their effective representation in the EALA."[135]

In this particular case, the Court appeared to go out of its way not to anger Tanzania in at least three ways. First, when Tanzania refused to appear when the case was filed, the Court declined to proceed with the case until Tanzania made an application to file a response to the case way out of the time permitted under the rules. The Court went out of its way to justify its decision to accept Tanzania's late submission of its response to the case. According to the Court, since the manner of electing members of the EALA was of "paramount importance" and while it have otherwise hesitated to dismiss the application with costs, it held that "due to the public importance of the matter at hand … the justice of the case would demand that the United Republic of Tanzania is afforded an opportunity to present its side of the story so that the Court is assisted in making an informed decision."[136]

Second, the although the Court found that the rules used by Tanzania were inconsistent with Article 50 for excluding interest groups other than political parties, and for allowing political parties not represented in parliament, it did not unlike in prior cases proceed to declare those elections invalid under the Treaty. It was a victory in principle for the opposition CHADEMA party but CCM was not required to do anything as a result. The Court avoided a bold or expansive interpretation and instead took the opportunity to restate its interpretation of Article 50 first announced several years before in the *Nyong'o* case.

Third, the Court in this case emphasized its findings in prior cases that its jurisdiction is only triggered when the requirements of Article 50 are not complied with. This means that as long as an election meets the prerequisites of Article 50, when other questions arise such as whether or not there was a proper election, any dispute thereafter must be determined by the national courts of the country where the election took place.[137] For example in *Christopher Mtikila v Tanzania*,[138] where the applicant sought to annul the October 2006 EALA elections in Tanzania, the Court declined to entertain the case because although the case related to membership to the Assembly, it did not challenge the validity of

---

[134] *See, e.g.*, Komu, *supra* note 130.

[135] *Id.* at 69, citing Abdu Katuntu, *supra* note 117, at 27.

[136] Komu, *supra* note 130.

[137] *Id.* at 81.

[138] Christopher Mtikila v. Tanzania, Ref. No. 2, East African Court of Justice (2007), https://www.eacj.org/?cases=christopher-mtikila-vs-attorney-general-of-tanzania-and-others [hereinafter "Christopher Mtikila"]. When the applicant sought to have the Court review its dismissal of the case, it declined emphasizing that as long as the question before it was not the consistency of the election under Article 50, then it had no jurisdiction to hear and determine the case.

the election.[139] Thus, the EACJ has carefully circumscribed its role so that the sovereignty jealous Member States do not perceive it as intruding too much into their domestic affairs.[140]

South Sudan opts to Settle rather than Litigate an Election Challenge: Confirming Article 50 is now an Established Rule

Nothing better perhaps illustrates the broad acceptance of the Court's interpretation of Article 50 than the case of South Sudan. Although South Sudan is a recent addition to the EAC, it too has a dominant political party, the Sudanese Peoples' Liberation Movement. In the 2010 elections, it won a whopping 160 legislative seats. Two opposition political parties won a total of three seats. President Salva Kiir won the Presidency with 93 percent of the vote. The country soon thereafter fell apart in ethnically charged violence.

After South Sudan joined the EAC, President Kiir, appointed nine persons by decree to represent the country in the EALA.[141] According to the Speaker of the Transitional Legislative Assembly, Anthony Lino Makana, the representatives were selected in accordance with the provisions of the 2015 peace agreement and on the basis of their academic qualifications and political awareness.[142] What is quite clear though is that the appointments reflect the concentration of political power in the

---

[139] Instead, the applicant in the case argued that the 2006 Assembly election in Tanzania should have elected seven instead of nine members because two of the members who had served in the previous assembly had not exhausted their terms. The Court noted that this was a question that fell within the scope of Article 51(1) of the Treaty for the Establishment of the EAC which confers jurisdiction on such questions to the courts of the Member States. See Christopher Mtikila, *supra* note 138, at 4–12. See also Legal Brains Trust Limited v. Uganda, Appeal 4 of 2012, Judgment, East African Court of Justice (May 19, 2012). In this case, the Appellate Division held that where an election had not yet been called or any candidates refused or stopped from contesting and an applicant nevertheless invoked the jurisdiction of the court, it would decline to adjudicate such a case in part because the question raised was "clearly hypothetical, academic, abstract, conjectural and speculative." *Id.* at 16.

[140] A good example of how giving discretion to Parliament to decide how to conduct an election gives a dominant party the opportunity to engage electoral manipulation against the opposition comes from Uganda. In early 2017, Uganda removed the requirement of consensus and consultation among political parties on the slate of candidates to be presented for election. This gave the Speaker of the National Assembly great sway in decide who got elected. The rules also changed the rule requiring that two slots ne reserved for the opposition to one so that the other one now goes to special interest groups. This has in effect opened a three way fight—between opposition political parties, the dominant party and against interest groups. See Moses Kyeyune, *Special Interest Groups to be Represented in EALA*, THE MONITOR (Jan. 20, 2017), http://www.monitor.co.ug/News/National/Parliament--consensus--EALA--elections-interest-groups/688334-3620248-8bud3mz/index.html.

[141] *Attorney General and Speaker of the Transitional Assembly of South Sudan revoke the Nomination of Nine Members to EALA*, EAST AFRICAN COURT OF JUSTICE (July 16, 2017), https://www.eac.int/press-releases/153-legal-judicial-affairs/796-attorney-general-and-speaker-of-the-transitional-assembly-of-south-sudan-revoke-the-nomination-of-nine-members-to-eala.

[142] *South Sudan Parliament Approves EALA MPs*, SUDAN TRIBUNE (Mar. 14, 2017), http://www.sudantribune.com/spip.php?article61883.

Presidency. The President has powers of appointment, supervision, and dismissal of all state officers including judges, as well as State governors. He also has powers to suspend the country's Transitional Legislative Assembly.[143]

A South Sudanese citizen challenged the appointment decision in the EACJ as inconsistent with Article 50.[144] The applicant however withdrew the case after entering a consent agreement with representatives of the Attorney General of South Sudan and the Speaker of the Transitional Legislative Assembly of South Sudan. Under the consent agreement, the appointments of the nine members to EALA were withdrawn and a commitment was made to hold elections that would meet the requirements of Article 50 of the Treaty for the Establishment of the EAC. To enable South Sudan to meet the requirements of an Article 50 election, the Secretary General of the EAC agreed to provide a concise legal opinion to South Sudan.[145]

This settlement was arrived at just prior to the commencement of the hearing of the case. The Court already had issues *ex-parte* orders restraining administering the oath of office, or otherwise recognizing nominees from the Republic of South Sudan who had been appointed by President Kiir.[146] This settlement illustrates bargaining behind the shadow of the law.[147] Once South Sudan was sued in the Court, its officials realized it was foolhardy to defend the case because the outcome was quite clear because of the weight of precedent. Thus, the head of the Committee of Legal Affairs in the National Transitional Legislative Assembly in Juba, Dengtiel Ayuen, brought a motion in the South Sudanese Parliament to withdraw parliamentary approval of President Kiir's appointees.[148] The Attorney General of the Republic of South Sudan and the Speaker of the Parliament of South Sudan admitted that the appointment and consequent confirmation violated Article 50

---

[143] *See* Transitional Constitution of South Sudan 2011, § 101. Notably these powers are in issue in yet another case before the EACJ after President Kiir in a decree sacked all the judges in the country. *See* Hon. Justice Malek v. Minister of Justice of South Sudan and Secretary General of the East African Community, Ref. No. 7, East African Court of Justice (2017). *See also* Zephania Obwani, *South Sudan dragged to EAC's Arusha Court after Firing Judges*, THE CITIZEN (Nov. 13, 2017), http://www.thecitizen. co.tz/News/S-Sudan-dragged-to-EAC-s-Arusha-court-after-firing-judges/1840340-4184510-i5rva9z/ index.html.

[144] Silvia Nankya, *Hearing due against South Sudan EALA nominations*, UGANDA RADIO NETWORK (June 14, 2017), http://ugandaradionetwork.com.dedi3883.your-server.de/story/hearing-resumes-against-s-sudan-east-african-legislators.

[145] Santino Jada v. Attorney General of the Republic of South Sudan, Speaker of the Parliament of South Sudan and Secretary General of the East African Community, App. No. 5, East African Court of Justice (2017) (within Ref. No. 5 of 2017).

[146] Santino Jada v. Attorney General of the Republic of South Sudan, Speaker of the Parliament of South Sudan and Secretary General of the East African Community, App. No. 8, East African Court of Justice (2017).

[147] Robert H. Mnookin & Lewis Kornhauser, *Bargaining in the Shadow of the Law: The Case of Divorce*, 88 YALE L. J. 956 (1979).

[148] Joseph Oduha, *South Sudan Revokes EALA Nominations*, THE EAST AFRICAN (June 14, 2017), http://www.theeastafrican.co.ke/news/South-Sudan-revokes-EALA-nominations/2558-3970178-116scdmz/index.html. *See also* Zephania Ubwani, *New Twist on South Sudan EALA Representatives Election*, THE CITIZEN (June 16, 2017), http://www.thecitizen.co.tz/News/New-twist-on-South-Sudan-EALA-representatives--election/1840340-3973202-2gds47/index.html.

of the Treaty for the Establishment of the EAC.[149] Finally on August 2, 2017, the South Sudan Parliament finally elected representatives for the EALA in an election that the requirements of Article 50. Twenty-nine candidates contested for the nine slots. Three women were elected unopposed.[150]

Part Three: Explaining the Lack of Cases From Burundi and Rwanda and the Theoretical Implications of this Chapter

Why have no cases been filed challenging EALA elections from Burundi and Rwanda? The only cases to have been filed relating to the EALA from Rwanda, is not about a challenged election, but rather a challenge of a serving member of the EALA from a minority party that was recalled after he fell out with the ruling party in Rwanda. This case hints at an explanation why there are no cases from Burundi and Rwanda.

I argue the disproportionately high electoral dominance of the ruling parties in Rwanda and Burundi together with their particular history of prolonged presidential reigns is a very high predictor of the absence of challenges of elections to the EALA in the EACJ.

Let me begin with Burundi. Burundi's March 2005 Constitution was the outcome of a peace agreement known as the Arusha Peace and Reconciliation Agreement of August 2000. This negotiated peace agreement is widely regarded as the "political and institutional roadmap for post-conflict Burundi"[151] since it ended the country's twelve-year civil war. That agreement introduced a power-sharing deal between the Hutu and Tutsi ethnic groups in Burundi.[152] Under the deal, the Tutsi who comprise 14 percent of the population were guaranteed 40 percent membership in the National Assembly and 50 percent in the Senate. Burundi also has a proportional representation system with a closed list under which political parties cannot nominate more than two thirds of candidates from the same ethnic group.[153] President Pierre Nkurunziza was first elected by Burundi's two-chamber

---

[149] Deus Ngowi, *South Sudan Nominees for EALA Post Revoked*, ALL AFRICA (June 16, 2017), https://allafrica.com/stories/201706160206.html.

[150] Deus Ngowi, *South Sudan Nominees for EALA Post Revoked*, DAILY NEWS (June 16, 2017), https://webcache.googleusercontent.com/search?q=cache:I2pkdQJMjoYJ:https://www.dailynews.co.tz/news/south-sudan-nominees-for-eala-post-revoked-2.aspx+&cd=1&hl=en&ct=clnk&gl=us; *South Sudan Elects EALA MPs, 3 Females Unopposed*, THE SPEAR NEWS (Aug. 2, 2017), http://thespearnews.blogspot.com/2017/08/south-sudan-elects-eala-mps-3-females.html.

[151] Stef Vandeginste, *Briefing: Burundi's Electoral Crisis—Back to Power-Sharing Politics as Usual?* 114 AFR. AFFAIRS 623 (2015).

[152] The Twa minority group was incorporated in the deal in some respects as well. *See* Stef Vandeginste, *Political Representation of Minorities as Collateral Damage of Gain: The Batwa in Burundi and Rwanda*, 49 AFR. SPECTRUM 1 (2014).

[153] The Constitution also requires a 50/50 split in the military and an 80 percent super-majority in the National Assembly and two-thirds in the Senate to amend the Constitution.

Parliament as required by the Arusha Peace and Reconciliation Agreement. In 2010, he was re-elected this time through universal suffrage under the March 2005 Constitution. A coalition of opposition parties boycotted the second round in that election. While some in the opposition were really doing the government's bidding, those that did not, including civil society groups and protestors, were arrested and imprisoned. The 2005 Constitution provided for a two-term Presidential limit. There was a constitutional and legal disagreement regarding whether or not President Nkurunziza could run for a third term. The opposition argued that he could not be elected for a third term because he had been elected twice, once under the Arusha Peace and Reconciliation Agreement, and then again under the March 2005 Constitution in 2010.

President Nkurunziza eventually prevailed in getting a third term after violently putting down protests and imprisoning thousands who protested his third-term bid. He used a failed coup attempt to justify his continued repression particularly against those opposed to him. Although the main opposition parties boycotted the June 29, 2015 elections, they nevertheless legitimized President Nkurunziza's third term. Those elections were characterized by voter intimidation and bribery.

The dominant party in Burundi, the National Council for the Defense of Democracy-Forces for the Defense of Democracy (CNDD-FDD), has a strong demographic (Hutu) ethnic majority. By repressing minority groups who comprise the political opposition, the CNDD-FDD engaged in a strategy of undermining if not ending the power sharing agreement which it conceded to at a temporary moment of weakness during post-conflict peace negotiations. The CNDD-FDD has sought to regain its full strength through elections and by undermining the power sharing. In so doing, President Nkurunziza has in effect ruled Burundi as a one-party state.[154] Ending such a power sharing agreement could likely plunge the country into mass murders, or at worst genocide, between Burundi's Hutu and Tutsi communities—a prospect that has an unfortunate historical legacy in that country and neighboring Rwanda.

Thus in Burundi, a power sharing arrangement initially crafted as a conflict resolution framework, has been transformed into how those contending for political power "share control of the state among elite actors and their networks."[155] For these elites, pursuing peace is about pursuing the "equilibrium in the allocation of power, state resources, and privilege" among themselves.[156] Since elections are seen as opportunities for making a claim to scare national resources, they invariably come with the risk of upsetting the previous equilibrium.

The legislative majorities the CNDD-FDD holds in Burundi, and its control of opposition parties, is reflected with the ease with the overwhelming majorities

---

[154] Vandeginste, *supra* note 152.
[155] Vandeginste, *supra* note 151, at 634.
[156] *Id.*

contestants are elected to the EALA get easily elected. In 2012 for example, eighty-five out of eighty-five members of the Legislative Assembly voted to approve the list of EALA nominees.[157] As an illustration of the dominance of the CNDD-FDD has twice recalled members elected to the EALA. In the EALA's second session that ran from June 5, 2007 to June 4, 2012, Burundi recalled two of its members in the EALA before they could complete their terms because of their differences with CNDD-FDD.[158] Similarly, in 2015 CNDD-FDD recalled four of Burundi's members to the EALA because they opposed President Nkurunziza's bid for a third term.[159] Jeremie Ngendakumana, one of the recalled MPs was among fifty members of ruling CNDD-FDD who were earlier that year expelled from the party after petitioning President Nkurunziza not to run for a third term.[160] The political clout of the CNDD-FDD accounts for the recall of the other three members. The CNDD-FDD-allied UPRONA opposition party argued that the reasons for recalling one of their members was because he had failed to support the party during campaigns and electoral activities.[161] However, the particular member who was being recalled was in a faction of the UPRONA party that did not support the ruling CNDD-FDD. The fourth MP, Yves Nsabimana, belonged to yet another small opposition political party FRODEBU that has no representation in the Burundian parliament, and was among fifteen other small parties which boycotted the July 2015 presidential elections that legitimized President Nkuruniza's third term.[162]

The Speaker of the EALA, with the support of the rest of the Assembly membership, however declined to grant this request. They argued that recalling members was inconsistent with the Assembly as well as Community law.[163] This successful pushback against President Nkurunziza and the CNDD-FDD indicated that the EALA had become a resilient institution. More importantly for the purposes of this chapter this pushback indicates as I will note later the very limited organizational space for opposition political parties in Burundi.

Although there have been no cases from Burundi challenging EALA elections, the EACJ has been drawn into a dispute between the CNDD-FDD-allied UPRONA opposition party, on the one hand, and a faction of the UPRONA party opposed to President Nkurunziza and the CNDD-FDD. In a 2014 case the EACJ was invited by a faction of the UPRONA opposition political party, opposed to President Nkrunziza and the CNDD-FDD. This faction of the UPRONA opposition party

---

[157] *Election of Burundian Members of the East African Legislative Assembly (EALA)*, NATIONAL ASSEMBLY OF BURUNDI (Apr. 25, 2012), https://www.assemblee.bi/spip.php?article475.
[158] Christabel Ligami, *East Africa: EALA Rejects Burundi Bid to Recall Four Members*, ALLAFRICA (Nov. 28, 2015), http://allafrica.com/stories/201511302068.html.
[159] *Id.*
[160] *Id.*
[161] *Id.*
[162] *Id.*
[163] *Id.*

asked the EACJ to order Burundi to allow it to convene and conduct its party meet-ings. Those meetings had been barred by orders of the Minister of Home Affairs and enforced by armed policemen on orders from the Ministry for Security.[164] The EACJ granted orders that UPRONA's central committee was authorized to convene and hold its meetings as in accordance with Constitution and laws of Burundi had already been permitted by the Supreme Court of Burundi.[165] Notably, in its defense in this case, the Government of Burundi did not challenge UPRONA's entitlement to convene and hold meeting as long as they did so "in accordance with the law."[166]

As the foregoing case indicates, organizational rights for opposition political parties are tenuous at best. This restrictive organizational space also extends to rights of expression for opposition political parties and journalists. Journalists crit-ical of the government have often been charged with trumped up charges.[167] It is estimated that over 100 journalists have fled Burundi because some of their col-leagues face constant harassment from the state while some been murdered.[168] As of October 5, 2016, the Office of the High Commissioner for Human Rights had documented 558 cases of state-sponsored torture and mistreatment of individuals accused of participating in the 2015 attempted coup and subsequent events. The government often uses torture against opposition politicians to extract informa-tion or as punishment for opposing the government.[169]

Since the beginning of the political crisis in 2015, Burundi has also clamped down on human rights non-governmental organizations (NGOs). It has frozen their accounts and those of their leadership. Some human rights NGOs have been suspended or dissolved by the government.[170] Government-owned and operated *Le Renouveau*, the only daily newspaper in the country, and the Burundi National Television and Radio (RTNB), are some of the extremely few television and radio stations with national coverage that are allowed to operate in the country. The editor-in-chief of the country's last independent newspaper, the French-language *Iwacu*, fled the country in 2015. Three radio stations forcibly closed in the aftermath

---

[164] Bonaventure Gasutwa & 2 Ors v. Attorney General of The Republic of Burundi, App. No. 18 (2014), https://www.eacj.org//wp-content/uploads/2014/12/Ruling-on-Application-No.18-of-2014-arising-from-Reference-No.13-of-2014.pdf.

[165] *Id.* at 10.

[166] *Id.* at 8, 18. Burundi argued that "[w]e are not saying that they cannot meet, they can meet in ac-cordance with the law." *Id.*

[167] U.N. General Assembly, *Summary of Stakeholders' Submissions on Burundi*, U.N. Doc. A/HRC/WG.6/29/BDI/3, at 3 (Jan. 2018); Cheyenne Wright, *Burundi: Civil Society in Jeopardy*, GLOBAL PROSPERITY (Feb. 10, 2016), https://globalprosperity.wordpress.com/2016/02/10/burundi-civil-society-in-jeopardy/; EACSOF Breakfast Meeting Report on "Analysis of the Environment for Civic Space in Burundi," EAST AFRICAN CIVIL SOCIETY ORGANIZATIONS' FORUM, http://eacsof.net/upload/REPORTS/Analysis%20Civic%20Space/BURUNDI%20CIVIC%20SPACE%20ANALYSIS.pdf.

[168] U.N. General Assembly, *Summary of stakeholders' submissions on Burundi*, U.N. Doc. A/HRC/WG.6/29/BDI/3, at 3 (Jan. 2018).

[169] *Id.*

[170] *Id.*

of the May 2015 failed coup remained closed. The law prohibits political parties, labor unions, and foreign NGOs from owning media outlets.[171]

Rwanda has not fared any better on any of these scores than Burundi. While Rwanda is certainly a much more stable country, it has a dominant political party with a powerful president who has also extended term limits beyond the two term limit provided for in the 2003 Constitution. President Paul Kagame has been in power since 1994 when he helped end the genocide in that country. Like the other five EAC Member States, Rwanda elects the members of the EALA in Parliament. However, there is a crucial difference. Unlike in the rest of East Africa, Rwanda allows its citizens to elect the special interest group (i.e. women, youth, and people with disabilities), members of the EALA. Those elections are conducted by the government-controlled Rwandese National Electoral Commission.[172]

However, the Rwandese Parliament elects EALA members who represent political parties. The ruling Rwanda Patriotic Front and its coalition parties win national elections by over 90 percent of the votes cast. Thus Rwanda is "is a clear case of hegemonic authoritarianism, where regular seemingly multi-party elections serve only to consolidate dictatorship."[173] This hegemony is illustrated by the fact that President Kagame is a Tutsi, a community that is just about 10 percent of the population. President Kagame justifies Tutsi dominance over 90 percent of Rwanda's Hutu population by keeping alive the fear of Hutu genocidal revenge.[174]

President Kagame has legislated against what he calls "genocide ideology" and "divisionism" thereby effectively criminalizing dissent against his government. The law also prohibits the propagation of ideas based on "ethnic, regional, racial, religious, language, or other divisive characteristics." Conviction of public incitement to "genocide ideology" or "divisionism," including discrimination and sectarianism, is punishable by imprisonment of up to five to nine years and fines of 100,000 to 1 million Rwandan francs (US$123–1,234). These laws, in addition to a repressive media law passed in 2009, are broadly applied to silence political dissent and to shut down investigative journalism.[175] These laws preserve Tutsi dominance by reducing the Rwandese genocide of 1994 to a narrative of Tutsi victimhood and Hutus as perpetrators. In so doing, the Kagame government propagates its own version of the truth while narrowing down political space for dissent and criticism.[176]

---

[171] *Id.*
[172] Robert Mbaraga, *Rwanda Picks Nine Members of EALA*, THE EAST AFRICAN (May 19, 2017), http://www.theeastafrican.co.ke/news/2558-3934000-984qs8z/index.html; Peter Nyanzi, *EALA Elections a Missed Opportunity*, THE INDEPENDENT (June 15, 2012), https://www.independent.co.ug/eala-elections-missed-opportunity/.
[173] Filip Reyntjens, *Rwanda: Progress or Powder Keg?*, 26 J. DEMOCRACY 24 (2015).
[174] *Id.* at 27.
[175] U.S. Department of State, Human Rights Report 17 (2016).
[176] Ingrid Samset, *Building a Repressive Peace: The Case of Post-Genocide Rwanda*, 5 J. INTERVENTION & STATEBUILDING 265 (2011).

By criminalizing dissent, President Kagame has transformed Rwanda into a hegemonic Tutsi country in which a narrow Tutsi military and political elite controls the government.[177] Even further, the government through its military and security apparatus engages in the murder of opposition political figures critical of him. These murders are pursued in and out of the country.[178] President Kagame does not tolerate any dissent. In effect, there has been no viable political opposition since Rwanda permitted multi-party politics in 1991. Like in Burundi, press freedom is heavily restricted.[179]

Opposition political parties that want to organize meetings and demonstrations face insuperable demanding requirements. For example, Article 36 of the Rwandan Constitution and Law 33/91 make excessive demands in terms of prior authorization for demonstrations. Furthermore, appeals against the denial of permission must, according to the law, be lodged before an administrative authority, which lacks institutional independence from the ruling Rwanda Patriotic Front. The disproportionate penalties imposed, and the liability of organizers for any unlawful behavior of participants, have a chilling effect on those who want to hold peaceful demonstrations.[180] The high penalties imposed, and the liability that is meted out to organizers for any unlawful behavior of participants, have a chilling effect on those who want to hold peaceful demonstrations.[181]

To maintain political power among his small group of elite ethnic Tutsi, President Kagame has made sure there is a very weak regime of organizational rights in Rwanda. This way, his narrow leadership group can keep the narrow ruling elite happy and limit the potential of "mass movements and mass opposition" becoming quickly uncontrollable.[182] Weakened organizational rights have meant that legal consciousness in Rwanda has not grown. This in addition to repression of opposition political activity has meant that there has been little scope for broad-based organized protests and civil resistance against the Rwandese government.

---

[177] Danielle Beswick, *Managing Dissent in a Post-genocide Environment: The Challenge of Political Space in Rwanda*, 41 DEV'T AND CHANGE 225 (2010).

[178] For example, Patrick Karegeya, the co-founder of opposition group Rwanda National Congress, was murdered in a hotel in South Africa on January 1, 2014. Filip Reyntjens, *Rwanda: Progress or Powder Keg?*, 26 J. OF DEMOCRACY 25 (2015) ("Several Rwandan senior officials came close to admitting that the murder was perpetrated by a government hit squad.").

[179] Individual Submission to the Universal Periodic Review of Rwanda, at 1, (Mar. 23, 2015), https://www.upr-info.org/sites/default/files/document/rwanda/session_23_-_november_2015/article_19_upr23_rwa_e_main.pdf; *CSO Sustainability Index for Sub-Saharan Africa*, USAID FROM THE AMERICAN PEOPLE (2016), https://www.usaid.gov/sites/default/files/documents/1866/2016_Africa_CSOSI_-_508.pdf.

[180] Individual Submission, *supra* note 179.

[181] *The Situation of Human Rights Defenders in Rwanda*, INTERNATIONAL SERVICE FOR HUMAN RIGHTS (2015), https://www.upr-info.org/sites/default/files/document/rwanda/session_23_-_november_2015/ishr_upr23_rwa_e_main.pdf.

[182] Christine HACKENESCH, THE EU AND CHINA IN AFRICAN AUTHORITARIAN REGIMES: GOVERNANCE AND LIMITED STATEHOOD (2018).

Checks from NGOs on government conduct are also limited. This is because rules regulating NGOs are frequently used to interfere and undermine the activities of NGOs and to freeze their assets. For example, the former Chairman of the Rwandan League for the Promotion and Defense of Human Rights, one of the few remaining independent human rights NGOs, Laurent Munyandilikirwa—was forced to renounce his job before fleeing from Rwanda for his own safety.[183] NGOs suffer from excessive and onerous bureaucratic requirements and difficulties in obtaining registration. Applications require a "collaboration letter" from the government. In addition, regulations severely limit the independence and effectiveness of NGOs. International NGOs have also had limitations imposed on the use of their budget and are prevented from obtaining the five years registration granted to national NGOs.

Ultimately, given the pattern of repression, harassment, arrests, detentions, as well as murders of opposition party leaders, activists, and journalists, it is not surprising that there are no cases arising from Rwanda to challenge elections to the EALA. Bringing a case challenging Rwanda's elections to EALA in the EACJ would be a direct affront to President Kagame.

When activists successfully brought a case against Rwanda on a different question in a different African international court, the African Court of Human and Peoples' Rights, the government of Rwanda promptly withdrew its ratification of the instrument that allowed individuals and NGOs to bring suit against it in that Court.[184] Therefore although opposition leaders in Rwanda have publicly expressed their interest in filing cases against Rwanda in that Court as well as the EACJ,[185] the Government of Rwanda does not seem to have much regard for international courts.

Theoretical Implications Arising from the Chapter

This chapter argues that EACJ serves as a coordination device for opposition political parties confronting dominant political parties in their home countries. An important factor that makes this coordination possible are the organizational capabilities of opposition political parties in bringing suit against their governments in the EACJ. For opposition political parties, the EACJ is one among other venues of contestation against the dominant party in their home country. Thus organizational rights and capabilities are of opposition parties are an important factor that

---

[183] *Id.*

[184] Catherine Ageno, *Rwanda will not rescind decision on African Court*, THE EAST AFRICAN (Oct. 21, 2017), https://allafrica.com/stories/201710240281.html.

[185] Peter Clottey, *Rwanda Opposition Leader Continues Fight on Constitution*, VOA NEWS (Oct. 11, 2015), https://www.voanews.com/a/rwanda-opposition-leader-continues-fight-on-constitution/3001309.html.

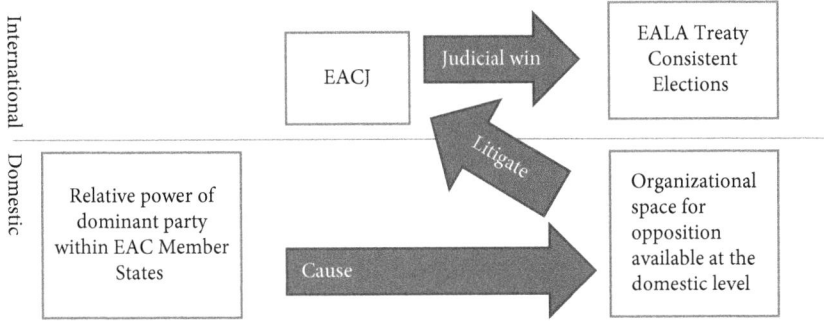

Figure 1.1 Role of EACJ

needs further exploration in future work. The findings in this chapter coincide with those in a new book by Adam Chilton and Mila Versteeg who argue that organizational rights such as those relating to the formation of political parties "are well equipped to coordinate their members' actions and organize protests, orchestrate acts of civil disobedience, mobilize the political opposition, or initiate litigation. Such actions impose costs upon the government and can render these rights self-enforcing."[186] Figure 1.1 captures how the EACJ plays its coordination role as described earlier.

While it is a truism that organizational rights are more likely to be effective when there are organizations capable of mobilizing to defend these rights, this chapter shows that there are many factors that affect the ability of opposition parties and civil society groups to effectively organize and mobilize. Thus although civil society groups and opposition political parties are legally allowed to operate in all EAC Member States, Burundi and Rwanda impose insuperable restrictions on organizational rights that make it difficult for the emergence of a resistance movement, including strong opposition parties, that can disrupt the status quo in those countries. Lack of organizational rights is compounded by the inability of weakened opposition parties to plan and coordinate their anti-regime activities. Thus while Kenya, Uganda, and Tanzania have relatively more robust organizational rights protection and where oppositional political parties can coordinate their protests and other opposition activities, the same is not true in Burundi and Rwanda. It is this extremely limited political space to engage in civic mobilization and coalition building that also accounts for the fact that opposition political parties are less likely they can bring suit against their governments in the EACJ. In other words, the absence of cases challenging electoral manipulation to the EACJ in Burundi and Rwanda illustrate the relative weakness of organizational rights among

---

[186] Adam Chilton & Mila Versteeg, From Parchment to Barriers: How Constitutional Rights Can Make a Difference, Ch. 1 (2019).

opposition parties in those countries.[187] A further point to note here is that organizational rights are much more restricted in the more hegemonic dominant political parties in Rwanda and Burundi. By contrast, in Kenya, Tanzania, and Uganda opposition parties have more organizational space to organize and as such there are more cases challenging electoral manipulation of EALA elections from these countries. These countries also have less hegemonic dominant political party systems. In addition, opposition political parties in Uganda and Kenya, and perhaps less so in Tanzania, are able to engage in a broader range of coordinated political actions such as national strikes, marches, strategic litigation, boycotts, and mass demonstrations to pressure governments towards greater democratization and respect for rights. In Burundi and Rwanda, the particularly violent and often lethal crackdowns of the governments including police surveillance of anti-regime individuals and activities discourages trust among those in the opposition and those sympathetic to them. This in turn undermines the possibility of collective action and makes opposition activity weak, localized particularly in urban areas and generally lacking in widespread support. Mass opposition political activity is further repressed by restrictions on communication technology, restrictions on NGOs including their ability to get foreign funding as well as laws that restrict civil society movements. Without the space for preparation and coordination of opposition activities and extremely limited support to opposition parties from other countries including donors, civil resistance to the highly authoritarian regimes in Burundi and Rwanda is curtailed. One of the alternative sites for opposition activity particularly in Burundi has been in the EALA where, as discussed in Part One has provided a venue for debating and expressing concern about the adverse human rights conditions in that country.

Yet, even though there have been no cases challenging elections to the EALA from Burundi, there has been a case filed by the East African Law Society in the EACJ challenging the amendment to extend presidential term limits. Even though that case was eventually dismissed, it provided civil society groups from East Africa who brought a citizen petition to the EALA an opportunity to express their opposition to repressiveness of the Government of Burundi. The repressiveness of the Governments in Burundi and Rwanda has discouraged lawyers to play a dual role as cause lawyers and core activists in the democratization processes in those countries. The reverse has been true in Kenya, Uganda, and Tanzania. A classic example is that of two-term Ugandan EALA member Mukasa Mbidde who is one of the leaders of an opposition party in Uganda and has been instrumental in bringing and litigating cases on democratization and human rights in

---

[187] As the case-studies from the various East African countries in this chapter show, opposition weaknesses stem from many factors including Lack of coordination among opposition political parties opens them up to manipulation by dominant political parties. Lack of internal party democracy as well as internal power struggles as well as leadership rivalry, ethnic and regional divisions and factionalism within opposition parties makes them vulnerable to manipulation by dominant political parties.

the EACJ.[188] However, while lawyer activists from countries with relatively lower levels of repression were able to capitalize on the extrajudicial effects of their EACJ-centered tactics, their membership in the sub-regional bar association, the East African Law Society, and the Pan-African Lawyers Union, provided a platform for bringing cases on behalf of their colleagues from Burundi and Rwanda.[189]

Another critical implication of the repressiveness of Burundi and Rwanda particularly in preventing and dissuading opposition political parties and civil society groups from pursuing cases at the EACJ to contest electoral manipulation of East African Legislative Elections demonstrates that repression is also a type of coordination game when the potential for abuses is greatest.[190] In other words, while the EACJ has served as a coordination device for opposition political parties contesting electoral manipulation for seats in the EALA, repression to quell civil society and opposition party dissension by governments serves as a deterrent. The upshot here is that the relative power of incumbent leaders of dominant and opposition party leaders shapes whether or not there will be litigation over EALA elections. This chapter shows that EAC Member States are on a spectrum in the degree to which there is organizational freedom to make it likely that opposition political leaders would consider resorting to the EACJ to contest illegal elections.

This chapter also contributes to understanding coordination among civil society actors and opposition parties with regard to how they strategize in using international courts as a lever in their struggles with their governments. In so doing, the chapter usefully complements work done on coordination between governments in the context of international courts.[191] Finally and related to the importance of organizational rights, this chapter shows repressive governments fear active and sustained broad-based civil resistance movements because they pose a direct threat to their survival. In fact, even though opposition political parties in East Africa generally receive less than a third of the total vote in presidential elections, incumbents take the threat of electoral loss seriously. Incumbents in these party dominant regimes therefore see the opposition as a threat to their long-term survival and therefore as a threat that has to be controlled and managed.[192] The fact that

---

[188] See, e.g., Democratic Party, supra note 96; Mbidde Foundation Ltd & Hon. Margaret Zziwa v. Secretary General of the East African Community & Attorney General of Uganda, Ref. Nos. 3 and 5, East African Court of Justice (2014).

[189] See, e.g., East Africa Law Society v. Burundi, Ref. No. 1, East African Court of Justice (2014), https://www.eacj.org/?cases=east-africa-law-society-vs-the-attorney-general-of-the-republic-of-burundi.

[190] Tiberiu Dragu & Yonatan Lupu, Collective Action and Constraints on Repression at the Endgame (2017), https://ssrn.com/abstract=2992622.

[191] See, e.g., Karen Alter, Do International Courts Enhance Compliance with International Law, 25 REV. OF ASIAN AND PAC. STUDIES 51 (2006) (showing how scholars who are influenced by realism as well as those who were not, agree that coordination problems might lead to effective compliance without elaborate enforcement systems).

[192] In Uganda, for example, President Museveni succeeded in having Parliament amend the Constitution to guarantee that he can run for yet another term because he was otherwise age-limited. There is even more repression and threat of coercion as strategies of maintaining power in the more repressive regimes in Burundi and Rwanda.

opposition political parties and broad-based resistance movements pose threats even to incumbents within dominant political regimes shows how the visibility of non-violent campaigns can contribute to building broad-based social movements that can under certain conditions topple undemocratic regimes, in ways that violent opposition may not.[193] Civil resistance movements embolden broad-based participation and in turn facilitates coordination and bridge building across divisions that helps to overcome the collective action problems that make building solidarity against repression difficult. Ultimately collective action is more likely to be successful in toppling a repressive regime when it denies such a repressive regime the sources of its power, particularly where there is unified mass mobilization which in turn trigger loyalty shifts by regime supporters in favor of the civil resistance.

Conclusions

An examination of cases filed against elections to the EALA, shows that cases have been filed from four of the six EAC Member States. Even though Burundi and Rwanda have opposition political parties, their activities are coercively repressed which in turn limits their freedom of action particularly in contesting elections to the EALA. For Burundi and Rwanda, the EACJ has not helped to overcome the coordination problem the opposition parties in this country face. This chapter argues that the lack of cases from Burundi and Rwanda demonstrates the high barriers put in place by extremely authoritarian states on opposition politicians and political parties to file cases against their governments both in their home judiciaries as well as in international courts. These barriers include the heavy-handed repression of organizational rights as well as other civil and political rights. Thus, even when coordination challenges are resolved by the availability of a remedial forum in the EACJ, this does not level opportunities for all opposition political parties in all East African countries to bring suit against dominant political parties. This is because the more authoritarian and determined a dominant political party and its leadership is, the higher the likelihood that its ability to subdue opposition political parties and politicians from taking steps to challenge it, even in a sub-regional court. Dominant parties in Rwanda and Burundi restrict electoral competition and close off the ability of these parties to rely on external pressures, such as the EACJ, as leverage points to check their authoritarian governance.

---

[193] ERICA CHENOWETH & MARIA J. STEPHAN, WHY CIVIL RESISTANCE WORKS: THE STRATEGIC LOGIC OF NONVIOLENT CONFLICT (2012). In competitive political systems with stable political parties, the potential for alternation of political power in the legislature and executive is higher than less competitive political systems with a dominant political party.

Table 1.2 EACJ Cases Challenging the Legality of Elections to the EACJ

Cases under Article 50 of the Treaty for the Establishment of the EAC	Interim Applications from the Cases
Prof. Peter Anyang' Nyong'o and others vs. The Attorney General of Kenya and others. Reference No. 1 of 2006.	Attorney General of Kenya vs. Prof. Peter Anyang' Nyong'o and Others. Appeal No. 1 of 2009
	George Nangale, Prof. Peter Anyang' Nyong'o & 10 Others vs Attorney General of Kenya and 5 others. Application No. 2 of 2006
	Prof. Anyang' Nyong'o & 10 Others vs Attorney General of Kenya. Application No. 1 of 2010 & No. 2 of 2010
	Prof. Peter Anyang' Nyong'o and 10 Others vs. The Attorney General of Kenya, the Clerk of the EALA and the Secretary General of the East African Community. Taxation Cause No. 6 of 2008
	Prof. Peter Anyang' Nyong'o and Others vs. The Attorney General of the Republic of Kenya. Taxation Cause No. 2 of 2010
	The Attorney General of Kenya vs Prof. Peter Anyang' Nyong'o and 10 others. Application No. 01 of 2010
	The Attorney General of Kenya Vs Professor Peter Anyang Nyong'o and 12 Others. Taxation Cause No. 5 of 2010
	The Attorney General of the Republic of Kenya vs. Prof. Peter Anyang'-Nyong'o and 10 others. Application No. 4 of 2009
	The Clerk of the National Assembly of Kenya Vs Prof. Anyang' Nyong'o and 10 Others. Taxation Cause No. 3 of 2010
	The Attorney General of The Republic of Kenya Vs Prof. Anyang' Nyong'o & 10 Others. Application No. 5 of 2007
	Prof. Anyang' Nyong'o & 10 Others vs The Attorney General of The Republic of Kenya and 5 others. Application No. 1 of 2006
	The Attorney General of Kenya vs Prof. Peter Anyang' Nyong'o and 10 others. Application No. 01 of 2010

Continued

Table 1.2 *Continued*

Cases under Article 50 of the Treaty for the Establishment of the EAC	Interim Applications from the Cases
Mbidde Foundation Ltd & Hon. Margaret Zziwa vs. The Secretary General of the East African Community & the Attorney General of the Republic of Uganda. Reference Nos. 3 and 5 of 2014	Mbidde Foundation Ltd and Rt. Hon. Margaret Zziwa vs. Secretary General of East African Community and Attorney General of Republic of Uganda. Application No. 5 of 2014 & Application No. 10 of 2014
Democratic Party and Mukasa Mbidde vs. The Secretary General of the East African Community and the Attorney General of Uganda. Reference No. 6 of 2011	The Democratic Party & Mukasa Fred Mbidde vs. The Secretary General of the East African Community and the Attorney General of the Republic of Uganda. Application No. 6 of 2011
	Democratic Party and Mukasa Fred Mbidde vs. The Attorney General of the Republic of Uganda. Taxation Cause No. 1 of 2012
Christopher Mtikila vs. The Attorney General of Tanzania and others. Reference No. 2 of 2007	Christopher Mtikila vs. The Attorney General of The United Republic of Tanzania & The Secretary General of the East African Community. Application No. 8 of 2007
Anthony Calist Komu vs. The Attorney General of Tanzania. Reference No. 7 of 2012	Anthony Calist Komu vs. The Attorney General of The Republic of Tanzania. Reference No. 7 of 2012
	The Attorney General of the United Republic of Tanzania vs. Anthony Calist Komu. Appeal No. 2 of 2015
Among A. Anita vs. The Attorney General of Uganda and The Secretary General of the East African Community. Reference No. 6 of 2012	Among A. Anita vs. The Attorney General of the Republic of Uganda. Taxation cause No. 5 of 2013
Abdu Katuntu vs. The Attorney General of Uganda and The Secretary General of the East African Community. Reference No. 5 of 2012	
Legal Brains Trust Limited vs. Attorney General of the Republic of Uganda. Reference No.10 of 2011	Legal Brains Trust Limited vs. Attorney General of the Republic of Uganda. Appeal No. 4 of 2012

Table 1.2 *Continued*

Cases under Article 50 of the Treaty for the Establishment of the EAC	Interim Applications from the Cases
Hon. Margaret Zziwa vs. The Secretary General of the East African Community. Reference No. 17 of 2014.*	The Secretary General, East African Community vs. Rt. Hon. Margaret Zziwa. Application No. 12 of 2015 (Arising from Reference No. 17 of 2014)
	The Secretary General of the East African Community vs. Rt. Hon. Margaret Zziwa. Appeal No. 7 of 2015
	Rt. Hon. Margaret Zziwa vs. The Secretary General, of the East African Community. Reference No. 17 of 2014
	Rt. Hon. Dr. Margaret Zziwa vs. The Secretary General of the East African Community. Application No. 23 of 2014
	Hon. Margaret Zziwa vs. The Secretary General of the East African Community. Reference No. 17 of 2014
	Hon. Dr. Margaret Nantongo Zziwa vs. The Secretary General of the East African Community. Application No.1 of 2016
	Hon. Dr. Margaret Nantongo Zziwa vs. The Secretary General of the East African Community. Application No. 1 of 2016 (Arising from Reference No. 17 of 2014)
	Rt. Hon. Margaret Zziwa vs. The secretary General of the East African Community. Reference No. 17 of 2014

*This case challenged the election of the Speaker of the EALA and is not the subject of this chapter.

By contrast, political opposition parties in Kenya, Uganda, and Tanzania have more wiggle room to challenge the dominant political party both at home and by bringing cases against these dominant parties in the EACJ. This lack of uniformity in resolving coordination problems in East Africa shows that opposition political parties in East African countries that have greater organizational and operational autonomy from the state are more likely to file cases against dominant political parties in the EACJ. National electoral results in more repressive countries like Burundi and Rwanda shows that dominant political party leaders are elected with close to 100 percent of the national vote and the dominant political party holds an overwhelming majority of seats in Parliament. Both Rwanda and Burundi are also good examples of strong personal rule in which the ruling parties have strong party discipline and high level of cohesiveness. Further, as we saw in this chapter, dominant political parties in Rwanda and Burundi favor the existence of opposition parties that operate within the boundaries set by the dominant party.[194] In addition, in both Rwanda and Burundi, civil society groups are subject to more restrictions on their activities than their counterparts in Uganda, Tanzania, and Kenya. For this reason, both opposition parties and civil society groups in Rwanda and Burundi have lower organizational ability than those in Kenya, Uganda, and Tanzania.

In Uganda, Kenya, and Tanzania, the dominant parties have their party leader elected with slightly over 50 percent of the national vote. This latter group of countries therefore feature divided government than Rwanda and Burundi. Two conclusions can be drawn from these observations. First, that the willingness or likelihood of opposition political parties to confront a dominant political party in highly repressive regimes in an international court is very low. Second, that opposition political parties are more likely to confront a dominant political party in an international court in situations of divided politics where the dominant political party does not command an overwhelming proportion of the national vote.[195] Thus a major benefit of examining the extent to which the EACJ acts as a coordination device for opposition parties in East Africa is that it shines a light on the relative power of incumbent parties, on the one hand, and opposition forces and civil society, on the other, and their choices of strategies and tactics in the processes of democratization within each country.

Even though the highly repressive regimes in Burundi and Rwanda have so far preempted judicial challenges to elections to the EALA from those countries, once elected opposition legislators from those countries have used the EALA to coordinate with opposition politicians from other East African countries to demand better respect for human rights. They have done this through resolutions they have passed, hearings they have held or questions posed to the Council of Ministers. The EALA provides these opposition legislators a forum to continue their opposition activity against repression at home in the safety of an international legislative body

---

[194] This is consistent with GEORGE TSEBELIS', VETO PLAYERS: HOW POLITICAL INSTITUTIONS WORK (2002) (noting the power of veto players to prevent changing of the status quo).

[195] This second conclusion is consistent with the likelihood that national courts are likely to be bolder/activist in situations of divided politics. *See* Bill Chavez, Rebecca Ferejohn, John Ferejohn & Barry Weingast, *A Theory of the Politically Independent Judiciary: A Comparative Study of the United States and Argentina, in* COURTS IN LAIN AMERICA (Gretchen Helmke & Julio Rios Figueroa eds., 2011) (arguing that when the executive and legislative branches are united against the courts, the courts have few resources with which to defend an independent course. In contrast, when significant and sustained disagreements arise among elected officials—such as take place under divided government—judges have the ability to challenge the state and sustain an independent course, with little fear of political retribution.).

and with the support of legislators from other East African States. In this sense, both the EALA and the EACJ provide support to mobilize in favor of democratic governance for opposition politicians in ways that are not possible in their home countries that are characterized by relatively less political freedom. In so doing, these international organizations contribute to mobilizing democratic movements in highly repressive environments. Thus rather than seeing the fierce electoral competition to get a seat in the EALA as only motivated by the spoils individual legislators get, the evidence suggests once elected these politicians are also likely to continue their opposition activity against their governments. The foregoing insights are a major insight developed in this book as indicated in its Introduction and in various chapters, particularly the one by Olabisi Akinkugbe and the co-authored chapter by Solomon Ebobrah and Victor Lando.

In short, both the EACJ and the EALA play a role in overcoming the fragmentation that arises from constraints imposed on opposition political activities in each of the six Member States of the EAC. The fact that both of these international institutions are based in Arusha, Tanzania where there is a broad ranging group of human rights and pro-democracy civil society groups has played an important role in catalyzing the mobilization and collective vision that have made it easier to use these international institutions as coordinating devices for opposition parties and politicians. The repressiveness of the governments of Burundi and Rwanda, which spread fear, fragment opposition movements and make it less likely that apathetic individuals would mobilize against them, is partially overcome when opposition politicians learn from each other in sub-regional fora. The example and experience of more vibrant opposition political parties and civil society groups in countries like Kenya and Uganda, become platforms for learning and sharing of experiences with opposition politicians from more repressive countries like Burundi and Rwanda. Sub-regional organizations like the East African Law Society that have membership across all six EAC States institutionalizes the relationships that in turn leverage the EACJ and the EALA as places to advance building and sustaining democratic and human rights movements. They are able to do so even within in the repressive political environment that characterizes governance in these East African countries.

2

Sub-Regional Courts as Transitional Justice Mechanisms

The Case of the East African Court of Justice in Burundi

Introduction

This chapter examines cases in the East African Court of Justice (EACJ) arising from the protracted and systemic abuses of human rights in Burundi. It argues that the EACJ's role in accepting and deciding cases arises in large part from the ongoing conflict and authoritarian governance in Burundi and the absence of transitional justice mechanisms. In so doing, this chapter dovetails with other chapters in this book that show how litigants resort to Africa's sub-regional courts when national institutions perform sub-optimally in addressing their needs. The cases from Burundi are exceptional examples of resorting to Africa's sub-regional courts. The EACJ acts as a powerful transitional justice mechanism by providing a forum for truth and attention to be brought to issues that arise from Burundi's ongoing conflict and authoritarian governance. This chapter also demonstrates how these cases have been used to galvanize resistance outside of Burundi against continued authoritarian rule in Burundi.

This chapter is divided into three parts. After introducing the EACJ, Part One proceeds to make the case that its case-law addressing Burundian matters implicate transitional justice claims. Building on the themes developed in the introduction to this book, it suggests that conventional metrics are not adequate to analyze the EACJ's performance or regional impact; indeed, this analysis requires a multidimensional analysis that encompasses more elements of transitional justice. In Part Two, I show that the cases are best understood primarily in terms of the type of plaintiffs who bring them. I identify three main categories of plaintiffs: repeat players pursuing individual claims, political opposition parties and politicians seeking redress of their political grievances,

* I would like to thank Sara Dezalay for her invaluable discussions and contributions.

Andrew Heinrich, *Sub-Regional Courts as Transitional Justice Mechanisms* In: *The Performance of Africa's International Courts.* Edited by: James Thuo Gathii, Oxford University Press (2020). © The Several Contributors. DOI: 10.1093/oso/9780198868477.003.0003.

and Non-Governmental Organizations (NGOs) pursuing strategic litigation. I then sub-categorize cases brought before the EACJ by each type of plaintiff according to their motives, means, and outcomes. Part Three of the chapter then applies the sociological concept of flow and counter-flow[1] to consider each of the three categories of cases. This sociolegal discussion helps to show the outward flow of cases that would otherwise have been filed in Burundi which are filed in the EACJ and the attendant political activism that flows from Burundi to the EACJ. This chapter also illustrates the counter-flow of transitional justice cases from the EACJ back to the Burundian domestic political context.

Part One: The East African Court of Justice as a Transitional Justice Venue
The Role of the East African Court of Justice

The EACJ serves as the primary judicial organ of the East African Community (EAC).[2] Its role is to ensure adherence to and compliance with the treaties of the EAC.[3] The Court is comprised of a First Instance Division, the trial court, and an Appellate Division, which decides appeals from the First Instance Division.[4] The Court is composed of a maximum of fifteen judges, with a maximum of ten appointed to the First Instance Division and a maximum of five appointed to the Appellate Division. Each EAC Partner State nominates two judges for appointment in the First Instance Division and no more than one Judge for the Appellate Division to ensure balanced representation across Partner States.[5]

Though Partner States' domestic courts can hear issues related to the EAC, EACJ rulings have supremacy over national courts on matters over which it has Article 27(1) jurisdiction.[6] Article 27(2) of the Treaty for the Establishment of the East African Community (EAC Treaty) permits the EAC Council of Ministers to confer jurisdiction to the EACJ. The Council has extended the EACJ's jurisdiction to include trade and investment disputes.[7] Bringing a case to the EACJ does not require the exhaustion of domestic local remedies.[8] As other chapters in this

---

[1] See BONNY IBHAWOH, IMPERIAL JUSTICE. AFRICANS IN EMPIRE'S COURT (1st ed., 2013).
[2] Id.
[3] See id. at arts. 21(1), 27(1).
[4] See id. at arts. 23 (2), (3).
[5] See id. at art. 24(10).
[6] See James Otieno-Odek, Judicial Enforcement and Implementation of EAC Law, in EAST AFRICAN COMMUNITY LAW 2017 468 (Emmanuel Ugirashebuja, John Eudes Ruhangisa, Tom Ottervanger, & Armin Cuyvers eds., 2017).
[7] See Treaty for the Establishment of the East African Community, art. 27(2) (hereinafter "EAC Treaty").
[8] See Venant Masenge v. Attorney Gen. of the Republic of Burundi, EACJ Ref. No 9 at 11 (2012).

book show, the EACJ has decided a large number of cases alleging violations of the EAC's fundamental principles of democracy, the rule of law, social justice, and human rights.[9]

The EACJ's case-law on human rights provided a foothold for litigants from Burundi to bring their cases to the Court. Burundians who have suffered from more than fifteen years of domestic unrest were motivated to bring their cases to the EACJ by transitional justice's promise to mobilize respect for human rights to overcome violence and establish accountability. This chapter adopts the definition of transitional justice that includes "individual prosecutions, reparations, truth-seeking, institutional reform, vetting and dismissals, or an appropriately conceived combination thereof."[10] Although the EACJ was not established as a transitional justice mechanism, nor does it have the jurisdiction to order reparations or institutional reform, scholars have argued in other contexts that international courts nevertheless do sometimes perform the roles of transitional justice institutions.[11] This chapter therefore slightly departs from classic understandings of transitional justice that presume its sole or in fact most important goal is to ensure accountability for past mass atrocities with the aim of contributing to justice, truth, reconciliation, and transformation in the affected communities. This chapter therefore uses to a more expansive understanding of transitional justice. For example, Obiora Okafor and Uchecheukwu Ngwaba have recently argued that the transitional justice mechanisms activated in South Africa, Sierra Leone, Uganda, and Liberia demonstrate that there is no "one single, inexorable transitional justice approach," to transitional justice.[12] Further, as Martti Koskenniemi points out, "studies on the transformation of authoritarian regimes into more or less liberal democracies ... have suggested a much more complex understanding of the role of criminal trials as not merely about punishment or retribution, nor indeed about deterrence, but as an aspect of a larger "transitional justice." '[13] Burundi evokes this more comprehensive understanding of transitional justice. This is not just because human rights norms obtain traction through sub-regional courts in situations where national legal institutions have either been complicit in, or powerless to halt, violations of core rights.[14] Rather, as Ruti Teitel argues, "the purposes and hopes of

---

[9] For the EAC's stipulation of these values, *see* EAC Treaty, *supra* note 7, at art. 7(2).

[10] *See* U.N. Secretary-General, *The Rule of Law and Transitional Justice in Conflict and Post-Conflict Societies*, 9 U.N. Doc. S/2004/616 (Aug. 23, 2004).

[11] *See* ANTOINE C. BUYSE & MICHAEL HAMILTON, TRANSITIONAL JURISPRUDENCE AND THE ECHR. JUSTICE, POLITICS, AND RIGHTS (2011). Conceptualizations of transitional justice have evolved past the traditional "legalistic" view that transitional justice is simply a matter of justice, reconciliation, and domestic rule of law. *See id.* at 2.

[12] Obiora Chinedu Okafor, *Uchechukwu Ngwaba; The International Criminal Court as a "Transitional Justice" Mechanism in Africa: Some Critical Reflections*, 9 INT. J. TRANSITIONAL JUSTICE 9 (2015).

[13] Martti Koskenniemi, *Between Impunity and Show Trials, in* 6 MAX PLANCK YEARBOOK OF UNITED NATIONS LAW 9 (2002).

[14] Buyse, *supra* note 11.

transitional justice are extended beyond state building to advance the promotion and maintenance of human security."[15] Within this account of transitional justice, the role of law takes in the often fraught contexts of transition incorporates that of international courts such as the EACJ as a force for transitional justice.[16]

Scholars have already examined cases which invited international courts to examine rights violations occurring in the course of transition, such as those relating press freedom and election related violations, as well as those directly caused by authoritarian rule, conflict, and the related socio-political and economic fallout. Examples of such cases include land restitution cases in Bulgaria before the European Court of Human Rights.[17] As this chapter shows, citizens of Burundi have brought cases to the EACJ in the same way that cases seeking to authenticate ownership of private property have come before the European Court of Human Rights.

Burundi shares a lot in common with states that joined the Council of Europe after military conflict and authoritarian rule.[18] While Burundi is unique in other respects, most notably the fact that conflict has not ended in Burundi, there are good reasons to analogize the role of the ECHR in these instances with EACJ cases that address past injustices in informing and shaping the contestation victims have with the government of Burundi. These cases have in turn helped to shape the jurisprudence of the EACJ.

For the litigants from Burundi that this chapter examines, the EACJ became a venue to seek remedies unavailable in domestic courts.[19] However, the goal of this chapter is not necessarily to establish if the goals of transitional justice[20] are realized through litigation in the EACJ. Rather, this chapter examines the ways in which EACJ jurisprudence is not simply about punishment or retribution, nor indeed about deterrence, but instead about broader questions that advance the notion of post-conflict transitional justice. This is particularly apt in Burundi, which is still embroiled in conflict notwithstanding many efforts to establish transitional justice mechanisms.[21] Ultimately, this chapter's goal of tracking the cases of the EACJ is consistent with transitional justice literature that links the goals of transitional justice to the role of international courts and institutions.[22] From that perspective,

---

[15] Ruti Teitel, *Foreword, in* MICHAEL HAMILTON & ANTOINE BUYSE, TRANSITIONAL JURISPRUDENCE AND THE ECHR: JUSTICE, POLITICS AND RIGHTS (2011).

[16] *Id.* at 20.

[17] *Id.* at 12.

[18] Buyse, *supra* note 11, at 2.

[19] *See* Rosemary Nagy, *Transitional Justice as Global Project: Critical Reflections*, 29 THIRD WORLD Q. 275, 276–77 (2008).

[20] These goals traditionally include reconciliation, enhancement of the rule of law, and increasing trust in government institutions. *See* Sandra Rubli, *(Re)making the Social World: The Politics of Transitional Justice in Burundi*, 48 AFR. SPECTRUM 3, 4 (2013).

[21] *See* Buyse, *supra* note 11, at 2.

[22] *See* Kieran McEvoy, *Beyond Legalism: Towards a Thicker Understanding of Transitional Justice*, 31 J. L. & SOC'Y 411, 421–23 (2007).

this chapter argues EACJ is one such venue in which transitional justice goals are being pursued, one on which actors are increasingly relying as Burundian civil society continues to be suppressed and the Burundian courts have not proven to be viable options.

Transitional Justice Issues Arising in Burundi

Burundi has been embroiled in violence since its independence in 1962, especially between its Tutsi ethnic minority and the Hutu majority. It has undergone multiple violent changes in government, genocidal violence, political assassination, warfare, and militia warfare. Peace negotiations have often been followed by new outbreaks of war and violence.[23] Though the Civil War ended in 2005 and a comprehensive ceasefire agreement was signed in September 2006, violence between rebel groups and the government of Burundi has continued.[24] Efforts to end the violence and re-build Burundi after a failed transition to democracy in 1993 can also be traced to earlier agreements, including the Arusha Peace and Reconciliation Agreement of 2000. That agreement provided for the appointment of a Truth and Reconciliation Commission which was however not launched until 2016.[25] That slow pace of implementation of the Arusha Accords was compounded by President Pierre Nkurunziza's decision in 2015 to run for a third term, which many critics considered to be inconsistent with the Arusha Accords as read together with Burundi's 2010 Constitution. President Nkurunziza's announcement resulted in a new cycle of violence. In particular, President Nkurunziza brutally responded to what he called a failed coup attempt that came soon after his announcement.[26]

Other transitional justice mechanisms embodied in the Arusha Accords—such as an international judicial commission of inquiry on genocide, crimes against humanity, and war crimes in Burundi and an international criminal tribunal for Burundi, if the commission of inquiry concluded these international crimes had been committed—have not come to fruition.[27] Furthermore, some matters of transitional justice were embraced in the 2010 Constitution and others continue to be debated. For example, a 2006 law gave temporary immunity for rebel leaders in

[23] See Patricia Daley, *The Burundi Peace Negotiations: An African Experience of Peace-Making*, 34 REV. AFR. POL. ECON. 333, 333–34 (2007).

[24] *See id.*

[25] *See* Mark Kersten, *Transitional Justice Battlegrounds: Another Bad Week in Burundi*, JUST. CONFLICT (2016), https://justiceinconflict.org/2016/10/22/transitional-justice-battlegrounds-another-bad-week-in-burundi/.

[26] *See Mind the Coup*, THE ECONOMIST (May 14, 2015), https://www.economist.com/news/2015/05/14/mind-the-coup.

[27] *See* Daley, *supra* note 23, at 340; Stef Vandeginste, *Burundi's Truth and Reconciliation Commission: How to Shed Light on the Past while Standing in the Dark Shadow of Politics?*, 6 INT'L J. TRANSITIONAL JUST. 355–65 (2012), https://academic.oup.com/ijtj/article/6/2/355/2357078.

return for laying down arms, and there has been a process of re-integrating demo-
bilized rebels into national security forces.[28] The questions of whether to pursue
criminal trials and of whether to create a truth and reconciliation process have also
been on this agenda.[29]

The literature on transitional justice in Burundi has primarily focused on how
existing domestic transitional justice initiatives have fared.[30] This chapter focuses
on the manner in which those transitional justice initiatives intersect with the
role of the EACJ. I argue that the EACJ is an important part of transitional justice
initiatives in Burundi. For example, a variety of cases brought to the EACJ– including those seeking to recover reparations for sequestered property in the continuing civil war, and those on free speech and freedom of the press arising from
the authoritarian governance– all intersect with transitional justice themes, such
as enhancing the rule of law and accountability of government institutions. These
examples and other discussed in this chapter show that litigants bring cases to the
EACJ because they are seeking the type of relief transitional justice scholars argue
follows periods of political upheaval, war, and authoritarian governance.[31] Yet, because Burundi's transition from civil war is often marked by the Arusha Accords of
2005, the cases filed at the EACJ relate to both unresolved questions that pre-date
those Accords, as well as to current controversies. Indeed, it is often difficult to distinguish between unresolved questions that arose before the Arusha Accords and
controversies that arose thereafter, as was the case in the highly visible case challenging President Nkurunziza's decision to run for a third term in 2015.[32] Although
the case was filed in 2015, the legal questions it raised pre-date the Arusha Accords.
The case asked the EACJ to interpret whether the Arusha Accords' recognition of
President Nkurunziza's presidency constituted the first term of his presidency in
computing whether or not he had served two terms under the 2005 Constitution.
To account for this continuity of transitional justice questions prior to and after the
Arusha Accords, this chapter applies the sociological concepts of flow and counter-
flow.[33] Originally used to describe the ways in which ideas diffused through
colonial empires,[34] flow and counter-flow are integral to understanding the multi-
directional exchange and transformation of ideas. Rather than the antiquated notion of a one-directional flow of ideas from the metropole to the colonies, flow

---

[28] *See* Pursuit of Power: Political Violence and Repression in Burundi, Hum. Rts. Watch, https://
www.hrw.org/report/2009/06/03/pursuit-power/political-violence-and-repression-burundi   (last
visited July 11, 2019).

[29] Vandeginste, *supra* note 27.

[30] *See, e.g., id.*

[31] Ruti Teitel, *Transitional Justice Globalized*, INT'L J. TRANSITIONAL JUST. 1–4 (2008), https://doi.org/
10.1093/ijtj/ijm041, https://ssrn.com/abstract=2143194.

[32] *See, e.g.*, E. African Civil Soc'y Org. Forum v. Attorney Gen. of the Republic of Burundi and 2
Others, EACJ Ref. No. 2 of 2015.

[33] *See* Ibhawoh, *supra* note 1; *see also* MICHAEL FISHER, COUNTERFLOWS TO COLONIALISM: INDIAN
TRAVELLERS AND SETTLERS IN BRITAIN 1600–1857 (2004).

[34] Seei *e.g.*, Ibhawoh, *supra* note 1, at 13.

and counter-flow emphasize that legal and philosophical traditions in the metro-pole were also impacted by the counter-flow of ideas and people coming from the colonies.[35] These concepts are well suited to improve the understanding the inter-action between a sub-regional court like the EACJ and its Member States' domestic jurisdictions, such as Burundi: there is both a flow of some legal ideas from the EACJ to Burundi, and a corresponding counter-flow of others from Burundi back to the EACJ.

These concepts of flow and counter-flow will help illustrate how jurisdiction that would otherwise be exercised in Burundi is flowing towards the EACJ, and how justice, jurisprudence, rule of law, and reconciliation are returning to Burundi by counter-flow from the EACJ.

Part Two: The Typology of Burundian EACJ Case-law

There are three categories of plaintiffs from Burundi that have brought cases before the EACJ. These are repeat players, political opposition parties, or individuals, and NGOs. Each of them is discussed in turn in this part of the chapter.

Repeat Players

Audace Ngendakumana, a lab technician and a resident of Burundi's capital, Bujumbura, believed himself to be in possession of a valid title to his private resi-dence. He had occupied this property from 1976–2013.[36] To his surprise, when he sold it,[37] the government invalidated the sale and ordered him to surrender the title to the property to the son of the now deceased prior owner.[38] Ngendakumana brought a case before the EACJ seeking to overturn the nullification of his title and the enforcement of his contract of sale.[39]

On its face, it may be hard to understand why this case was filed at the EACJ. It is a simple contract dispute over private property with a local authority. It is hardly, at first glance, a case that raises questions of EAC law. To fit the case within the jur-isdictional ambit of the EACJ, the nullification of the title was framed as a violation of the rule of law, a fundamental tenet in the Treaty for the Establishment of the EACJ.[40] Looking even more closely at the case reveals why it was brought before

---

[35] *See id.*
[36] *See Mr. Audace Ngendakumana v. Attorney Gen. of the Republic of Burundi*, EACJ Ref. No. 11 of 2014 at 8.
[37] *See id.* at 9.
[38] *See id.*
[39] *See id.* at paras. 12(c)–12(d).
[40] *See id.* at 12(a), 12(b).

the EACJ. The applicant's attorney was Horace Ncutiyumuheto, a repeat plaintiff lawyer who has represented over 20 percent of Burundian EACJ applicants who are private citizens.[41] Public records suggest that Ncutiyumuheto funded or secured funding for this case and his other cases.[42] In 2014 alone, Ncutiyumuheto also represented at least one other Burundian citizen with a similar claim[43] and two Burundian citizens as joint applicants challenging the creation of the Burundian Special Court of Land and Other Property.[44] None of the applicants Ncutiyumuheto represented in any of these cases have a legal background, foreign citizenship, or a significant business interest. The unifying factor of these cases is the same lawyer who repeatedly filed cases on behalf of these clients in the EACJ.

I argue that cases are brought by repeat players to the EACJ for at least two primary reasons: to pursue individual justice and, entirely separately, to pursue transitional justice. As previously stated, there is the superficially obvious need to pursue justice for the individual applicant. All individual litigants before the EACJ were represented lawyers who had appeared before the court repeatedly. However, more generally, these cases are united by the theme of advancing transition justice goals for Burundi.

Cases brought by repeat players can be divided into civil cases and constitutional cases, although these categories may not be very distinctive in practice. For example, the contract dispute and property cases brought before the EACJ have both a civil and constitutional aspect. They raise questions of the constitutionality of the Burundian Courts as a basis for the EACJ's jurisdiction to hear the case.[45] In addition, some of the property cases are analogous to constitutional property rights cases, such as the right to just compensation for government takings of property.[46] Pure constitutional challenges, such as right to a fair trial,[47] have also been also been brought to the EACJ.[48]

Though very few cases brought by repeat players are successful, the fact that the cases are not preliminarily dismissed is significant. In each of these cases, the EACJ found that it had subject matter jurisdiction to hear the case even when the government of Burundi opposed the assumption of jurisdiction. I argue that the assumption of jurisdiction in these cases availed an opportunity for the EACJ to shape discussions and considerations of transitional justice in Burundi. These cases centered around classical objectives of transitional justice including reconciliation and dealing with the past and building trust in the rule of law. However, these cases also

---

[41] See id. at Appendix.

[42] See Ngendakumana, *supra* note 36, at 7.

[43] See Georges Ruhara v. Attorney Gen. of the Republic of Burundi, EACJ Ref. No. 4 of 2014.

[44] See Baranzira Raphael v. Attorney Gen. the Republic of Burundi, EACJ Ref. No. 15 of 2014.

[45] See Ngendakumana, *supra* note 36, at 12.

[46] See Masenge , *supra* note 8.

[47] See Hilaire Ndayizamba v. Attorney Gen. for the Republic of Burundi, EACJ Ref. No. 3 of 2012.

[48] For a thorough account of the supranational constitutional elements of EACJ jurisprudence and that of other regional courts in Africa, *see* Chapter 3.

raise questions that go beyond this narrow transitional justice frame. Even those cases pushing the boundaries of the transitional justice frame, such as the seeking of restitution for quartered soldiers on one's property in wartime in *Ruhara*, invariably relate to shining a light on the height of conflict in the past, instead of purely promoting transition to a more peaceful society. Therefore, these cases must find a way to balance dealing with the past while also allowing for transition to occur.

Ngendakumana's claim seeking to recover his property was ultimately unsuccessful. The EACJ found that the claim was time-barred by the two-month time limitation for private litigants before the EACJ, as stipulated in Article 30 (2) of the EAC Treaty.[49] Rather than interpreting the ruling to mean solely that Ngendakumana's property claim failed, the decision signals to Burundi the importance of strengthening the rule of law. The mere fact that litigants were able to air their grievances in a legitimate forum and build coalitions with civil society actors in East Africa contributes to rebuilding the rule of law. As the introduction to this book argues, the value and role of international courts extends far beyond whether or not litigants are successful in their claims.[50] Indeed, one form of success is the opportunity for litigants to be heard under circumstances in which courts in Burundi may have otherwise been unavailable not just to give a remedy, but also for the more fundamental purpose of providing an opportunity for airing of grievances and allowing victims of conflict to be recognized.

Another repeat litigant case is *Georges Ruhara Vs. The Attorney General of the Republic of Burundi*.[51] Represented by the aforementioned repeat player Horace Ncutiyumuheto, applicant Georges Ruhara brought this case before the EACJ to seek damages for unpaid rent from the Burundian government, alleging that soldiers from the Burundian military have been quartered on his property from 2003 to the time when he filed his case in the EACJ.[52] Ruhara sought damages in the

---

[49]   *See* Ngendakumana, *supra* note 36, at 51. For another case in which the EACJ found it had jurisdiction over an economic claim brought by a private litigant only to ultimately rule that the claim was time-barred under Article 30 (2), *see also* Steven Dennis v AG of Burundi & Others, EACJ Ref No. 3 of 2015.

[50]   Some argue that Article 30 (2) is inherently restrictive because it discriminates against private litigants. *See, e.g.*, Ally Possi, *Time-Limitation Clause Against Private Litigants of the East African Court of Justice: A Call for a Purposive Interpretation of Article 30(2) of the East African Community*, International Law Blog (Aug. 7, 2017), https://internationallaw.blog/2017/08/07/time-limitation-clause-against-private-litigants-of-the-east-african-court-of-justice-a-call-for-a-purposive-interpretation-of-article-302-of-the-east-african-community/. In analyzing Steven Dennis, *supra* note 49, Possi argues that Article 30 (2) is "against the maiden spirit of the Treaty" because it deprives private citizens within the EAC of the ability to "have a say in the activities of their economic bloc." *Id.* While it is true that Article 30 (2) applies exclusively to claims brought by private litigants, Possi's critique considers only the formalist understanding of the EACJ. This chapter argues that the EACJ performs important transitional justice functions. The balance the EACJ has struck with respect to Article 30 (2) in *Ngendakumana* and *Steven Dennis* is the ideal of putting transitional justice into practice: it provides the opportunity for victims to be recognized and to have a voice, while also aiding society in moving forward by time-barring past wrongs.

[51]   *See* Ruhara, *supra* note 43.

[52]   *See id.* at 3.

form of unpaid rent, restitution for damaged property, and emotional damages.[53] There was significant press coverage and public discourse regarding the case.[54] The EACJ ultimately found that Ruhara's claim was time-barred and that it therefore would not consider the claims.[55]

I argue that this case created a clear flow to the EACJ of jurisdiction that would otherwise have been exercised in Burundi. A property dispute between a Burundian citizen and the Burundian government should have appeared in a Burundian civil court, yet the plaintiffs chose to have Ruhara appear as an applicant at the EACJ. In so doing, this case brought a flow of Burundi law to the EACJ by enabling it to consider a case that would otherwise appear in Burundian courts. In return, the EACJ also created valuable counter-flows of transitional justice to Burundi. Ruhara was able to bring his claim in a venue, which conferred legitimacy on them and acknowledged that wrongdoings had happened in Burundi.

Political Opposition Litigants

The second category of cases coming from Burundi are those brought by the political opposition to the government of Burundi. Led largely by Isidore Rufyikiri, political opposition litigants bring national political grievances to the EACJ.[56] These cases form a new type of political activism in the context of Burundi's transitional justice process: those who might not be given adequate political voice in the Burundian political process are able to use the EACJ as a platform to air their grievances and as an opportunity to advance their political causes. Whether protecting the rights of those in political opposition or attempting to achieve legislative objectives through the court, political opposition litigants bring their claims to the EACJ as part of a political strategy, not merely as a litigation strategy.

Political opposition litigants bring a variety of political grievances to the EACJ. A first category includes cases brought by opposition political movements in Burundi. For example, in 2014 members of Union pour le Progrès National (Union for National Progress; UPRONA), a minority political party consisting mostly of Tutsi members, brought a case before the EACJ with claims of being

---

[53] See id. at 3–4.

[54] See, e.g., *Burundi Citizen Sues Government over Alleged Forceful Occupation of Property,* IGIHE (May 2, 2015), http://en.igihe.com/news/burundi-citizen-sues-government-over-alleged?fbclid=IwAR3pH-d7lr7BwTB6JSWeqiQzj2GxSOK1ZQSC_Xp3UsQkuZoj2_3m3xXUfa4 (last visited July 9, 2019).

[55] See id. at 19.

[56] See *Burundi Gov't to Attend Next Round of Talks in Tanzania,* XINHUA (PEOPLE's DAILY) (Feb. 9, 2017), http://www.xinhuanet.com/english/2017-02/09/c_136042007.htm?fbclid=IwAR0lIMVYWKbEjO0n-oo90rsc_I-6fwntgqjw1CHP6J36D4nOdZZLKrtaqHk (last visited July 7, 2019) (citing cases brought to the EACJ as part of Burundi's national political process, and demonstrating that both those in power and political opposition cite EACJ cases alongside conventional elements of national politics, such as elections, as a normalized part of the political process.).

harassed by police and not being permitted to exercise its political rights to hold a meeting.[57] Though the EACJ ultimately did not find in favor of the applicants on any of the counts, UPRONA opposition politicians were able to air their political grievances in a way that was perhaps not possible in national courts. Although UPRONA lost on most of its claims in part on the basis of inconclusive evidence,[58] the opposition nevertheless successfully judicialized a question touching on domestic politics. In this case, the EACJ has construed its jurisdiction under Article 27(1) of the EAC Treaty as including questions relating to the rule of law.

Let us now consider *Mr. Bonaventure Gasutwa 2. Mr. Tatien Sibomana 3. Mr. Jean Baptiste Manwangari Vs The Attorney General of the Republic of Burundi*[59] as it relates to the aforementioned flow and counter-flow framework. This case created the flow of political discourse from the Burundian domestic sphere to the EACJ and initiated the flow of jurisdiction that would have otherwise been exercised in Burundi by filing the case in the EACJ. This is particularly important because this was essentially a domestic political dispute between an opposition party and the government. In return, the EACJ created a counter-flow of transitional justice even by simply leaving the door open to consider whether it might have jurisdiction to consider claims regarding domestic political matters in the future. In so doing, the EACJ contributed to the future liberalization and legitimacy of the Burundian domestic political system by giving an opposition party a space in which to air its grievances and potentially find legal recourse in the future.

Another case filed by opposition party litigants challenged the constitutionality of the creation of the Burundian Special Court for Land and Other Property.[60] In this case, the applicants argued that the Burundian Special Court for Land and Other Property violated the separation of powers between the Executive and Judiciary Branches and that this question was within the EACJ's Article 27 (1) jurisdiction. To make the connection between the EACJ's jurisdiction, on the one hand, and the question of separation of powers in Burundi, on the other, the applicants argued that the question involved a violation of the right to fair trial protected under the rule of law clause of the EAC Treaty.[61] The EACJ found the claim to succeed in part and fail in another, most notably finding that the creation of the Burundian Special Court for Land and Other Property violated the separation of powers but that it did not inherently violate the principles of the rule of law and good governance.[62]

---

[57] *See* Bonaventure Gasutwa v. Attorney Gen. of the Republic of Burundi, EACJ Ref. No. 13 of 2014.
[58] *See id.* at 57.
[59] *See id.*
[60] *See* Raphael, *supra* note 44.
[61] *See id.* at 3.
[62] *See id.* at 78–79.

Litigation Brought by NGOs

The final category of cases to the EACJ from Burundi that we discuss are cases filed by NGOs. In general, NGOs bring a high volume of cases before the EACJ, and is certainly true of cases that come before the EACJ from Burundi. NGOs bring a number of cases to the EACJ from Burundi in part because litigation is an important strategy in the tool-kit of NGO strategies. As the Burundian government has stifled domestic civil society and the ability for actors to work within it,[63] NGOs have turned to the EACJ to expose the resulting violations. Chapter 1 in this volume discusses cases relating to elections to the East African Legislative Assembly (EALA) and the limited political space for political opposition parties in Burundi.

One of the most notable cases brought by NGO litigants is a case brought to block President Nkurunziza's bid to run for a third term as president. That case, *East African Civil Society Organization Forum vs. The Attorney General of the Republic of Burundi and 2 Others*, was brought by the East African Civil Society Organization Forum, (EACSOF), an NGO comprised of a broad range of civil society organizations in East Africa. EACSOF filed the case against two agencies of the Burundian government and the EAC, arguing that Nkurunziza's decision to run a third presidential term violated the Burundian Constitution and the Arusha Accords.[64] In effect, EACSOF argued that this constituted a violation of the rule of law clause in the EAC Treaty. By bringing the case, EACSOF also sought to reverse the Constitutional Court of the Republic of Burundi's ruling in Case Number RCCB 303.[65] The EACJ found that it had jurisdiction to consider whether Nkurunziza's seeking of a third term violated the rule of law clause under the EAC Treaty but that it did not have jurisdiction to serve as an appellate court to the Constitutional Court.[66] Though the case ultimately had no legal impact on Nkurunziza's candidacy, it is nevertheless important. By finding that it had jurisdiction to review domestic political events, the EACJ demonstrated its willingness to participate in the upholding of domestic democratic institutions and rule of law, along the lines of the Katabazi cases for which the EACJ is well known, as discussed in the Ebobrah and Lando chapter (Chapter 5) in this book.[67] In so doing, the EACJ's contributions to transitional justice are at least two-fold. First, the EACJ lends legitimacy to democratic processes in Burundi by showing that there is a judiciary, albeit a regional one, that seeks to uphold the rule of law. Second, it provides NGOs a

---

[63] *See, e.g., Burundi Shuts Down Civil Society*, FREEDOM HOUSE (Nov. 23, 2015), https://freedomhouse.org/article/burundi-shuts-down-civil-society.

[64] See E. African Civil Soc'y Org. Forum, *supra* note 32, at 5.

[65] *See id.*

[66] *See id.* at 17–19.

[67] *See also* James Gathii, *Mission Creep or a Search for Relevance: The East African Court of Justice's Human Rights Strategy*, 24 DUKE J. COMP. & INT'L L. 249 (2013).

forum in which to carry out their work and give voice to members of civil society in Burundi.

The very fact that the EACJ accepted it had jurisdiction to decide *East African Civil Society Organization Forum vs. The Attorney General of the Republic of Burundi and 2 Others* is consistent with the flow/counter-flow thesis advanced in this chapter. The litigation created a powerful counter-flow promoting transitional justice in Burundi in at least three respects. First, by applying the EAC Treaty law and the Arusha Accords to an important domestic political question, it made it possible for Burundian civil society to have its grievances heard and to pursue remedies to domestic injustices. This certainly opened the EACJ to receive future similar cases. Second, by allowing an NGO to sue when its own interests in the case were unclear, the EACJ acknowledged that there was systemic harm throughout Burundi, and indeed perhaps throughout the EAC more generally when election law and constitutional law are disregarded. Finally, by enabling an NGO to advocate in the EACJ, the court helped to galvanize civil society groups in Burundi, as well as to embolden them through their solidarity with other civil society groups in East Africa. This theme is further emphasized in James Gathii's chapter (Chapter 1) on elections to the EALA in this book.

Another set of cases brought by NGOs to the EACJ relates to freedom of expression. It is notable that the EACJ has repeatedly acquiesced to NGOs seeking to file *amici curaie* "in the interest of justice" in cases where they sought to strengthen the protections for freedom of expression in Burundi.[68] The EACJ explained that the *amici curaie* were advancing the "interests of justice" because freedom of expression is essential to justice, the rule of law, and the political process.[69] In the EACJ, NGOs seeking to advance individual liberties in Burundi and in other EAC Partner States have found a go-to forum for when there is inadequate opportunity to do so in domestic courts and institutions.

The Typology of the Three Types of Case Summarized

The typology described earlier of cases brought before the EACJ pertaining to Burundi can be best summarized by the type of plaintiff, in terms of the goals they seek to achieve, their means to work towards these goals, the causes of action they bring, and how the cases contribute to transitional justice in Burundi:

---

[68] Forum le Renforcement de la Société Civile (FORSC) v. Burundian Journalists Union, EACJ Ref. No. 7 of 2013.

[69] *See id.* at 22.

Part Three: Flow and Counter-flow between Burundi and the EACJ

The sociological concepts of flow and counter-flow signify the two-way street that is cultural and ideological diffusion in modern times.[70] In place of the antiquated model of through which colonial powers sought to exercise full control of cultural flows from the metropole to the colonies, the joint concept of flow and counter-flow encapsulates that the reality of a two-way movement.[71] Flow and counter-flow are profoundly illustrative of the relationship between the EACJ and the Burundian domestic legal system. There are flows from the Burundian legal system to the EACJ, primarily of cases that would otherwise have been filed in Burundi and of civil society discourse. There are also resulting counter-flows from the EACJ back into the Burundian legal system, namely of transitional justice and jurisprudence.

Flow from Burundi to the EACJ

In more consolidated democracies, each of the three types of plaintiffs bringing cases to the EACJ would be able to advance their aims in domestic courts. Lawyers bringing civil claims would typically seek redress for their clients in a domestic court, as would those bringing election law and constitutional claims. The decision to seek redress for these claims at the EACJ creates a flow of cases that would otherwise have been litigated in Burundi to the EACJ. Though the EACJ has had to establish that it has jurisdiction to hear each of these cases' claims, it is ultimately the plaintiffs' submission of these claims to the EACJ that creates the question of jurisdiction in the first place.

NGOs's presentation of cases on Burundian domestic matters before the EACJ also creates a flow of Burundian civil society efforts to promote, advance, and protect human rights, the rule of law, and good governance out of Burundi and towards the EACJ. As a result of their inability to find space to operate within Burundi, would-be participants of Burundian civil society are creating a flow of civil society towards the EACJ. By hearing their cases, even when their specific injury suffered and individual cause of action might be difficult to discern, the EACJ is creating a venue and platform for Burundians to engage in civil discourse and foster an environment that resembles what domestic Burundian civil society could be. As with the other types of plaintiffs, the NGOs have created the flow that the EACJ then accepted by finding that it has jurisdiction. This flow of Burundian civil society initiatives towards the EACJ signaled to civil society groups to continue bringing future cases, even though prior cases were not successful.

---

[70] See Ibhawoh, *supra* note 1.
[71] *See id.*

Table 2.1 A Typology of EACJ Cases from Burundi

Type of Plaintiff[a]	Goal	Means	Cause(s) of Action	EACJ's Contribution(s) to transitional justice
Repeat players[b]	Individual justice	Representing individuals	Property rights,[c] Contract law[d]	• Providing individuals with a venue to seek remedies for their grievances • A venue for truth telling and legitimation of individuals' experiences during conflict
Political opposition[e]	Political forum	Representing political parties	Election law,[f] political rights[g]	• Lending legitimacy and a forum to political opposition
NGOs[h]	Rule of law and individual liberties	Serving as the applicants	Election law,[i] Constitutional rights[j]	• Lending legitimacy to domestic Rule of law • Providing a forum for Burundian civil society

[a] This table is a visual representation of the preceding section in this chapter. Each type of plaintiff has one representative case in the table; the corresponding "Goals" and "Means" columns correspond to that case. The cause(s) of action each have a representative case as well. Finally, the "EACJ's Contribution(s) to transitional justice" column provides a summary of this section's findings with respect the contributions of each type of case to transitional justice.

[b] *See, e.g.*, Ngendakumana, *supra* note 36.

[c] *See, e.g.*, Ruhara, *supra* note 43.

[d] *See, e.g.*, Manariyo Desire vs The Attorney General of the Republic of Burundi, EACJ Ref. No. 8 of 2015.

[e] *See, e.g.*, Gasutwa, *supra* note 57.

[f] *See, e.g.*, East Africa Law Society Vs. The Attorney General of the Republic of Burundi, Ref. No. 1. of 2014.

[g] *See id.*

[h] *See, e.g.*, Forum le Renforcement de la Société, *supra* note 68.

[i] *See* East Africa Law Society Vs. The Attorney General of the Republic of Burundi, Ref. No. 1. of 2014.

[j] *See, e.g.*, Forum le Renforcement de la Société Civile (FORSC) & 6 Others (NGO's) Vs Burundian Journalists Union and The Attorney General of Burundi, EACJ Ref. No. 7 of 2013.

Though the EACJ is sometimes argued to have an interest in expanding its own jurisdiction in deciding human rights related cases even when it does not have an explicit treaty basis for doing so, these cases illustrate how civil society groups use the EACJ to catalyze this outward flow from Burundi, where it properly belongs, to the EACJ. Without the applicants, the EACJ would be unable to have the impact it seeks to work towards in Burundi.

Counter-flow from the EACJ to Burundi

Once the cases are before the EACJ, they create certain counter-flows back to Burundi. In short, the plaintiffs bring Burundian national jurisdiction and domestic civil society discourse to the EACJ, and the EACJ in turn creates a counter-flow that amplifies issues of human rights, the rule of law, good governance, and transitional justice back towards Burundi. The EACJ's contribution to transitional justice takes three primary forms: its contribution to the rule of law, the legitimacy it gives to those who have suffered wrongs as a truth-telling venue, and the venue it creates for civil discourse and Burundian civil society.

I argue that the EACJ makes meaningful contributions to the rule of law in Burundi in both civil and criminal law. By accepting jurisdiction, but also crucially declining to act as an appellate court of the Burundi Constitutional Court, the EACJ contributes to rule of law in Burundi by providing a judicial venue to those who might not have such a venue at the domestic level. Upholding the rule of law in Burundi, providing a venue for it to be protected, and respecting the ruling of the highest court in Burundi contributes to transitional justice in Burundi by stabilizing the rule of law and fostering public confidence that there is a venue at which it can be litigated.[72]

By repeatedly finding that it has jurisdiction to hear individual claims, particularly everyday tort, property, and contract claims, the EACJ recognized the daily harms suffered in Burundi. Though very few claims are successful, the EACJ's willingness to hear the cases and its findings that its jurisdiction is in part accounted for by the expansive notion of the rule of law is significant. This potentially means that as long as a claim falls within the rubric of the rule of law, it is justiciable. Even when the EACJ declines to award remedies, it advances transitional justice by acknowledging harms and providing an opportunity for grievances to be heard, a crucial element of transitional justice.

Finally, the third form of transitional justice counter-flow the EACJ sends back to Burundi is the opening of discourse within Burundi's civil society. By giving NGOs a forum in which to air their grievances and advocate for their respective causes, the EACJ plays a role in the democratization processes and contestations in Burundi that are highly restricted. Though, as with cases brought by the other plaintiffs, the NGO litigants are largely unsuccessful in their claims, the impact of their cases is hardly confined to the EACJ. By providing the NGOs a forum in which to advocate and have the legitimacy of being able to bring their cases, the EACJ provides a powerful transitional justice counter-flow back to Burundi in the

---

[72] *See* Égide Harerimana, *CAVIB sues Burundi government to EACJ*, IWACU (July 18, 2019), https://www.iwacu-burundi.org/englishnews/cavib-sues-burundi-government-to-eacj/ (last visited July 11, 2019).

form of enabling the gradual growth of the otherwise highly repressed civil society in Burundi.[73]

Conclusion

This chapter has shown that although the EACJ was not established as a transitional justice mechanism and it does not have the jurisdiction to order reparations or institutional reform, it has nevertheless played a role analogous to the roles of transitional justice institutions. In so doing, this chapter follows recent scholarship on the role of international courts as transitional justice institutions. Like that literature, this chapter slightly departs from classic understandings of transitional justice that presume its sole or, in fact, most important goal is to ensure accountability for past mass atrocities with the aim of contributing to justice, truth, reconciliation, and transformation in the affected communities. As such, this chapter shows that in addition to its role in upholding the EAC Treaty, the EACJ has provided a venue for transitional justice claims from three types of plaintiffs: repeat plaintiffs seeking individual justice for their applicants; political opposition parties or politicians seeking recourse for the suppression they experience in the domestic political space; and finally, NGOs carrying out their civil society mandate in a forum that permits them to do so. Thus the EACJ has entertained cases relating to rights violations occurring in the course of protracted conflict in Burundi, such as those relating to press freedom and election related violations, and also rights violations directly caused by authoritarian rule, conflict, and the related sociopolitical and economic fallout, including cases on sequestered property rights. These examples and others discussed in this chapter show that litigants bring cases to the EACJ because they are seeking the type of relief transitional justice scholars argue follows periods of political upheaval, war, and authoritarian governance.

This chapter also argues that these cases create a flow of the issues raised in them, and the attendant political activism that would have otherwise been directed at national courts and the national political space out of Burundi into the EACJ. For example, cases brought by NGOs before the EACJ created a flow of Burundian civil society efforts to promote, advance, and protect human rights, the rule of law, and good governance out of Burundi and towards the EACJ. The EACJ's acceptance of jurisdiction in these cases opens opportunities for the EACJ to participate in shaping the contestations over transitional justice processes in Burundi, as well as

---

[73] For NGOs citing the EACJ as a forum in which to escape the limitations on Burundian civil society, *see* PALO and EACSOF Jointly File a Case at the EACJ Challenging the Constitutional Court of Burundi's Decision Permitting President Nkurunziza's Third Term Re-run for Election—6th July 2015, EACSOF (July 21, 2016), http://eacsof.net/EACSOF/2016/07/21/palu-and-eacsof-jointly-file-a-case-at-the-eacj-challenging-the-constitutional-court-of-burundis-decision-permitting-president-nkurunzizas-third-term-re-run-for-elections-6th-july/, (last visited July 11, 2019).)

those over questions relating to respect for political rights. Far more than resolving disputes, the EACJ bestows legitimacy upon the voices of individuals who believe they were harmed by ongoing conflict in their respective countries It also provides a forum for political opposition parties and politicians to air their grievances and in so doing to keep the government on notice to uphold its commitments under the domestic transitional justice arrangements already in place. Litigation in the EACJ has also enabled sub-regional NGOs to use the EACJ as a fall-back forum to litigate and advance the claims that would otherwise would find no foothold or remedy within Burundi. In this respect, the EACJ plays an important part in emboldening and galvanizing support from outside Burundi for the repressed civil society groups within that country.

3

The ECOWAS Court as a (Promising) Resource for Pro-Poor Activist Forces

Sovereign Hurdles, Brainy Relays, and "Flipped Strategic Social Constructivism"

Obiora C. Okafor* and Okechukwu J. Effoduh

Section One: Introduction

As has been argued elsewhere,[1] in near tandem with scholars like Upendra Baxi and Balakrishnan Rajagopal, the expression "human rights" is capable of accommodating both elite and subaltern politics, both progressives and reactionaries, and both the politics of domination and the politics of liberation/insurrection.[2] As Obiora Okafor also argued in that same article, this point is well illustrated by the fact that:

> For instance, as is well known, both the Egyptian freedom fighters who marched on and massed in Tahrir Square in early 2011 (an admirably progressive and insurrectionary movement) and the Neo-Nazi's who all-too-frequently terrorize racial and other minorities in Europe and North America (a virulently reactionary movement) have laid credible claim to the protection of the human rights to freedom of expression and assembly.[3]

* The authors are grateful to John Mastrangelo of the Osgoode Hall Law School's JD Class of 2017 for his excellent and sustained research assistance on this chapter and the larger project of which it is a part. They are also grateful to him for writing the memo on which Section Two of this chapter is partly based. We also wish to thank all the participants in the authors' workshop held at the Loyola University Chicago School of Law on April 20–23, 2016 for their thoughtful criticism and suggestions which helped strengthen the final product. The Social Sciences and Humanities Research Council deserves our gratitude for the grant that funded the research on which this chapter is based.

[1] *See* Obiora Okafor & Basil Ugochukwu, *Have the Norms and Jurisprudence of the African Human Rights System been Pro-Poor?*, 11 AFR. HUM. RTS. L. J. 396, 397 (2011).

[2] *See* UPENDRA BAXI, THE FUTURE OF HUMAN RIGHTS 6 (1st ed. 2002); Balakrishnan Rajagopal, *Pro-Human Rights but Anti-Poor? A Critical Evaluation of the Indian Supreme Court from a Social Movement Perspective*, 8 HUM. RTS. REV. 157, 158 (2007); *see also* Obiora Chinedu Okafor, *Attainments, Eclipses and Disciplinary Renewal in International Human Rights Law: A Critical Overview*, in ROUTLEDGE HANDBOOK OF INTERNATIONAL LAW 303 (D. Armstrong ed., 1st ed., 2009).

[3] *See* Okafor & Ugochukwu, *supra* note 1; Craig Kanalley, *Egypt Revolution 2011: A Complete Guide to the Unrest*, HUFFINGTON POST (Jan. 30, 2011, 7:21 PM), http://www.huffingtonpost.com/2011/01/30/

Obiora C. Okafor and Okechukwu J. Effoduh, *The ECOWAS Court as a (Promising) Resource for Pro-Poor Activist Forces* In: *The Performance of Africa's International Courts*. Edited by: James Thuo Gathii, Oxford University Press (2020). © The Several Contributors. DOI: 10.1093/oso/9780198868477.003.0004.

As such, as this article also claims, it is fair to say that not every human rights claim, action, set of practices, judicial/administrative decision, or system will—on balance—be pro-poor. While some human rights politics, claims, decisions, or even systems have tended to be more pro-poor than pro-elite, the converse has been true for others. It is therefore imperative that scholars and observers of governance systems and institutions on the African continent as elsewhere not assume that "pro-human rights" necessarily translates to "pro-poor."[4]

It is against this background that this chapter examines the extent to which the re-design, orientation, and action of the Community Court of Justice of the Economic Community of West African States (ECOWAS Court),[5] an increasingly important sub-regional human rights court,[6] functions as a resource for local pro-poor activists more than as a tool in the hands of anti-poor elements. This examination is conducted in the context of simultaneous analysis of efforts by various domestic activist forces in West Africa (such as human rights non-governmental organizations (NGOs) and public interest lawyers) and their foreign allies, to support and build up this Court as a pro-poor judicial actor, as part of a moral (and at the same time self-interested) effort to enhance their own activist leverage and levels of success in respect of local struggles to diminish or overcome certain "sovereign hurdles" and help produce pro-poor social change within the relevant states. Put more pithily, the main question here is "to what extent has the ECOWAS Court been 'arming' these pro-poor activists normatively and procedurally, and to what extent have the activists themselves co-created and co-enhanced this idea, fact and process of arming?" In so doing, this chapter contributes to the goal of this book to examine the utility of Africa's international courts beyond analyzing their impact through compliance and effectiveness analysis.

As such, in order to effectively convey its arguments and conclusions, the chapter is organized into eight main sections, this introduction included. In Section Two, a brief background on the ECOWAS Court is provided. Section Three outlines the conceptual framework that undergirds and shapes the analysis in the chapter, providing working explanations and understandings of the key concepts that frame the analysis, namely: the expressions "the poor," "sovereign hurdles," "brainy relays," and "flipped strategic social constructivism." In Section Four, the extent to which the (re)

---

egypt-revolution-2011_n_816026.html (last visited May 18, 2011); Alex Blasdel, *How the Resurgence of White Supremacy in the US Sparked a War over Free Speech*, THE GUARDIAN (May 31, 2018, 06:00 BST), https://www.theguardian.com/news/2018/may/31/how-the-resurgence-of-white-supremacy-in-the-us-sparked-a-war-over-free-speech-aclu-charlottesville (last visited Dec. 8, 2019).

[4] *See* Rajagopal, *supra* note 2, at 158.

[5] A brief but sufficient background on the Court is provided in Section Two.

[6] See Karen Alter, Lawrence Helfer, & Jacqueline McAllister, *A New International Human Rights Court for West Africa: The ECOWAS Community Court of Justice*, 107 AM. J. INT'L L. 742 (2013); Solomon T. Ebobrah, *A Rights-Protection Goldmine or a Waiting Volcanic Eruption: Competence of, and Access to, the Human Rights Jurisdiction of the ECOWAS Community Court of Justice*, 7 AFR. HUM. RTS. L. J. 307 (2007).

design, orientation, or action of the ECOWAS Court has enhanced the repertoire of pro-poor normative resources available to domestic activist forces (and their foreign allies) in ECOWAS Member States is examined.[7] This question is considered along-side an analysis of the extent to which these activists themselves, acting as brainy relays, have helped in their own interest to co-create and enhance these same norma-tive resources in a process styled in this chapter as "flipped strategic social construct-ivism." It should be noted that here, as in the next section, the concern is not so much to map the (non-)impact of the Court on the poor component of the citizenry of the ECOWAS sub-region, as much as it is to demonstrate the ways in which the Court has been, and can be, a valuable resource to the domestic activist forces who have helped co-produce the Court as we know it, support its judicial action, and struggle to advance the social conditions of the West African poor. And it also does not map and analyze the extent to which the ECOWAS Court's decisions are complied with by ECOWAS States. For its part, Section Five considers similar questions as are analyzed in Section Four, albeit in relation to pro-poor procedural resources. In Section Six, the extent to which the (re)design, orientation, or action of this Court has contrib-uted to the struggle to overcome or diminish certain important domestic socio-legal strictures and obstacles confronted by domestic activist forces in their broader so-cial struggles to help produce pro-poor outcomes is teased out and analyzed. Also examined here is the extent to which such contributions—if any—have also been produced, enhanced, and significantly utilized, in part as a result of the brainy relay work of these activists. Section Seven examines the question of what gaps or deficien-cies, if any, continue to diminish the ability of domestic activist forces to utilize more successfully the (re)design, action, and orientation of the Court in the service of pro-poor ends. It is in this section that the existence or otherwise of a compliance gap in the Court's regime (a matter that is not squarely within the scope of this chapter) is considered in brief since it is related to the general question of significant gaps and deficiencies in the Court's regime that may hinder its utility to pro-poor activists. Following this, the chapter ends with some concluding remarks.

Against this background, it must be noted that an important (if justifiable) limi-tation of the analysis in this chapter of the ECOWAS Court's normative framework and action is its focus largely on economic/social (ES), as opposed to civil/polit-ical (CP), rights. It should of course be made clear that the indivisibility and inter-dependence of all human rights norms has now been well established, and that CP rights jurisprudence or struggles can contribute significantly to the improvement of the social conditions of the poor.[8] Nevertheless, as has been argued elsewhere,[9]

---

[7] Previous joint work by Karen Alter, Lawrence Helfer, and Jacqueline McAllister, as well as a series of papers by Solomon Ebobrah, have laid the foundation for the kind of analysis conducted in Sections Four to Seven of this chapter. *See, e.g.,* Alter et al., *supra* note 6, at 742; Ebobrah, *supra* note 6, at 307.

[8] *See* Siddiqur Rahman Osmani, *Poverty and Human Rights: Building on the Capability Approach*, 6 J. HUM. DEV. 206 (2005).

[9] *See* Okafor & Ugochukwu, *supra* note 1, at 398–99.

other than for reasons of space, this focus—in the main—on ES rights is justified by the fact that the deprivation of this category of human rights is, relatively-speaking, more directly and immediately tied to the production and maintenance of poverty in the ECOWAS sub-region, as elsewhere. What is more, as Thomas Pogge has noted, ES rights are also by far the most violated category of rights, a fact that has also had dire consequences even for the enjoyment of the historically far more favored civil and political rights.[10] It is for these reasons that the portion of our analysis in this chapter that is devoted to a consideration of the ways in which the ECOWAS Court has or has not served as a pro-poor normative resource tends to concentrate on that Court's ES rights framework and action.

Another caveat must also be entered at this juncture. It is that, although almost all the cases decided by the ECOWAS Court to date were read by the authors, only a purposive sample of the total number of cases that have been disposed of to date by the ECOWAS Court are actually analyzed in this chapter. Given the nature of the overarching question with which this chapter is concerned (i.e. the ways in which the court has served, and can serve, as a resource for local pro-poor activists), an analysis of a purposive sample of the cases dealt with by the Court which actually tell the story of the Court's engagement with these activists (and vice versa) suffices for our purposes. For, even if the bulk of the cases decided by the Court have in fact been anti-poor, as long as a *significant* number of pro-poor activist decisions have been rendered by the Court (something that is readily revealed through purposive sampling), this would not have a significant bearing on the specific question whether the Court has served, and can serve, as significant pro-poor activist resource. It could of course shed more light on the relative extent to which decisions have been rendered that are helpful to pro-poor activists vis-à-vis anti-poor forces, but that kind of quantitative comparison is not the main concern of this chapter. In any case, space constraints dictate against the analysis of a larger sample of cases. And the utilization of random sampling would be counter-productive in the circumstances. Nevertheless, effort is made in the penultimate section of this chapter to reflect on many of the gaps/deficiencies that have impeded the ability of the Court to optimize its potential as a resource in the minds/hands of local pro-poor activists in the West African sub-region, and their foreign allies.

A third caveat that must be entered is that the well-known fact that all-too-many (though not all) of the governments of the states which compose the West African sub-region, the geographical area covered by the jurisdiction of the ECOWAS Court do not all-too-often respect the decisions of their own domestic courts. This raises important issues regarding the probability and actuality of their compliance with the ECOWAS Court's decisions, this issue is not within the scope of this chapter. And, in any case, even a low level of state compliance with the Court's

---

[10] *See* Thomas Pogge, *Recognized and Violated by International Law: The Human Rights of the Global Poor*, 18 LEIDEN J. INT'L L. 717, 718 (2005).

decisions does not negate the fact that the Court can serve as a significant resource in favor of local pro-poor activists in West Africa and their allies.

Almost needless to state, there is, of course, no suggestion whatsoever in this chapter that by functioning as a resource in the minds/hands of pro-poor activist forces this Court will somehow directly birth redistributive justice in the ECOWAS sub-region and author the amelioration or elimination of poverty in ECOWAS States. As is well recognized, courts—especially international courts—are not in general well placed to author these kinds of transformations in a direct way. What is rather being suggested is that, in part and in ways consistent with the other chapters in this book, as a result of its engagements with local pro-poor activist forces in the sub-region and their allies, the Court has become not merely a site for the reception and reproduction of international human rights law, but also a site for its production—in ways that provide these activists with significant arms with which to wage their own broader domestic social struggles in favor of the poor. In the result, the Court has also become an important part of the expanded arena within which many of these domestic social struggles are being currently waged.

Section Two: A Brief Background on the ECOWAS Court

On May 25, 1975, the Treaty of the Economic Community of West African States (ECOWAS) was signed—and ratified shortly thereafter—in Lagos, Nigeria, by fifteen West African states.[11] This Treaty and its multitude of protocols, conventions, and subsidiary legal instruments adopted by the authorized ECOWAS authorities, together constitute the legal or normative framework for the socio-economic (and to some extent judicial) integration of the region, and the functioning of the various ECOWAS institutions.[12] The main purpose for the establishment of ECOWAS (as outlined in the Treaty itself) was regional socio-economic integration for the purpose of encouraging development, raising the standards of living of West-Africans, attracting foreign direct investment, and "the unity of the countries of West Africa."[13] These goals were to be achieved through the internal (Pan-West African) opening of borders to ECOWAS citizens, the promotion of intra-regional free-trade, and the internal harmonization of customs regulations and tariffs.[14] It

---

[11] The original fifteen ECOWAS Member States, at its formation in 1975, were as follows: Benin, Burkina Faso, Ivory Coast, the Gambia, Ghana, Guinea, Guinea-Bissau, Liberia, Niger, Nigeria, Mali, Mauritania, Senegal, Sierra Leone, and Togo. Cape Verde acceded to the Treaty in 1978, and Mauritania withdrew its membership in 2000.

[12] See Mousa Leo Kaita v. Republic of Mali, Suit No. ECW/CCJ/APP/05/06, Rul. No. ECW/CCJ/APP/03/07 (ECOWAS Mar. 22, 2007) CCJLR (TP 2) 58.

[13] See the (now defunct) Treaty of the Economic Community of West African States. Treaty of the Economic Community of West African States, 1010 U.N.T.S.18 Treaty No.14843, Preamble (hereinafter "the Original Treaty").

[14] See Alter et al., *supra* note 6, at 740–42; Nneoma Nwogu, *Regional Integration as an Instrument of Human Rights: Reconceptualizing ECOWAS*, 6 J. HUM. RTS. 347, 347–48 (2007).

is important to note that this new Community was part of a larger push within Africa for regional integration, both as a tool to strengthen the then newly independent states, and as a response to economic exploitation from parts of the developed world—especially those countries which had formerly exercised formal colonial authority over most of the continent.[15] It was thus assumed that by looking inwards, the Member States could increase their self-sufficiency and decrease their reliance on foreign economies. Furthermore, as Solomon Ebobrah points out, the ECOWAS was at this point devoid of a significant level of discussion on human rights or security.[16]

New economic and geopolitical developments of the early 1990s—including the fall of Communism and the rise of neoliberalism and humanitarian intervention—sparked a transformation and re-definition of ECOWAS's mandate and function. In addition to a reaffirmation of the commitment to socio-economic integration, the Community became active in the fields of human security, good governance, and human rights—especially after the Liberian civil war.[17] This transformation was also linked to the understanding that economic and developmental objectives could not be met in isolation, and if ECOWAS was to achieve its goals, it would need to actively involve itself in encouraging political and social stability.[18] Additionally, and closely related, was the threat that human rights may be violated in the pursuit of economic objectives, and as such, a regime like ECOWAS would do well to encourage the pursuit of integration policies that respect these rights.[19]

Taking into account these new realities, the ECOWAS Member States revised the original ECOWAS Treaty in 1993, creating a new treaty, a new *grundnorm* so to speak, for the Community,[20] that "embraces social values such as respect for human rights, ecological sustainability, and [improved] labor conditions," which are "deemed fundamental to the economic motivations of the regime."[21] Public participation was also given a higher priority in the Revised ECOWAS Treaty,[22] to give more room for civil society actors—namely NGOs—to shape policy and increase their role in advocacy.[23] In short, ECOWAS was placing a higher priority on

---

[15] KOFI OTENG KUFUOR, THE INSTITUTIONAL TRANSFORMATION OF THE ECONOMIC COMMUNITY OF WEST AFRICAN *States* xii (1st ed., 2006).

[16] Solomon T. Ebobrah, *Critical Issues in the Human Rights Mandate of the ECOWAS Community Court of Justice*, Danish Inst. Hum. Rts.—Research Partnership 10 (Jan. 2008).

[17] *See* Alter et al., *supra* note 6, at 744.

[18] See Nwogu, *supra* note 14, at 348.

[19] *Id.* at 348.

[20] Dr. Emmanuel Akpo & Anor v. G77 South Health Care Delivery Programme & Anor, ECW/CCJ/APP/01/07 (Oct. 16, 2008), http://www.worldcourts.com/ecowasccj/eng/decisions/2008.10.16_Akpo_v_G77_SSHDP.pdf.

[21] *See* Nwogu, *supra* note 14, at 348.

[22] *See* Revised ECOWAS Treaty, vol. 2373, I-42835 (July 24, 1993), http://www.refworld.org/docid/492182d92.html (last visited Mar. 24, 2016) (hereinafter "The Revised Treaty").

[23] *See* Alter et al., *supra* note 6, at 745.

human rights and security, as a response to new realities both within and without its area of the world.

Significantly, Article 15 of the Revised Treaty establishes the ECOWAS Court,[24] and by virtue of Article 15(4), the "judgments of the Court are binding on all [ECOWAS] member states, Community institutions, and on individuals and corporate bodies."[25] All ECOWAS Member States shall, in accordance with its constitutional processes, "take all necessary measures to ensure the enactment and dissemination of such legislative and statutory texts as may be necessary" for the implementation of the provisions of the revised ECOWAS Treaty.[26] Despite these significant textual reforms, the Community still lacked an actually existing court at this point in its historical development.

To address this legal and institutional gap, Protocol No. A/P.1/7/1991 on the Community Court of Justice was adopted.[27] This Treaty laid the foundations and outlined the underpinnings for the creation and physical establishment of a permanent ECOWAS Court. This new Court was created by ECOWAS in order to help settle disputes between Member States inter-se, or between Member States and the Community, or between ECOWAS nationals and either an ECOWAS Member State or an institution of the Community. This Protocol entered into force in November 1996.[28] However, as Alter et al. have correctly noted, the Court it had created only existed on paper until Olusegun Obasanjo, the then President of Nigeria, kick-started the process of its actual physical establishment.[29] Upon assuming office in 2000, he provided the Court with the political support and funding that it needed to begin to function.[30] As per the Protocol and subsequent established procedures, the Court consists of seven independent judges who are of high moral character, and who are selected and shortlisted based on certain parameters, interviewed, and recommended in an independent and transparent process by the fairly new ECOWAS Judicial Council (which is constituted by the chief justices

---

[24] The Community Court of Justice was created pursuant to the provisions of the Revised Treaty of the Economic Community of West African States, arts. 6, 15. Its organizational framework, functioning mechanism, powers, and procedure applicable before it are set out in Protocol A/P1/7/91 of July 6, 1991, Supplementary Protocol A/SP.1/01/05 of January 19, 2005, Supplementary Protocol A/SP.2/06/ 06 of June 14, 2006, Regulation of June 3, 2002, and Supplementary Regulation C/REG.2/06/06 of June 13, 2006.

[25] Article 15, entitled "The Court of Justice: Establishment and Functions," provides: "(1) There is hereby established a Court of Justice of the Community. (2) The status, composition, powers, procedure and other issues concerning the Court of Justice shall be as set out in a Protocol relating thereto. (3) The Court of Justice shall carry out the functions assigned to it independently of the Member States and the institutions of the Community. (4) Judgments of the, Court of Justice shall be binding on the Member States, the Institutions of the Community and on individuals and corporate bodies."

[26] The Revised Treaty, *supra* note 22, at art. 5(2).

[27] *See* Protocol No. A/P.1/7/1991 on the Community Court of Justice (July 6, 1991).

[28] See Alter et al., *supra* note 6, at 747–48.

[29] *Id.*

[30] *Id.*

of all fifteen ECOWAS Member States), then they are formally appointed by the Assembly of Heads of States.[31]

In April 2004, the ECOWAS Court heard and disposed of its first (and arguably most important) case, the landmark *Afolabi v. Nigeria*[32]case. The Court was forced to decline jurisdiction in that case because of its lack of authority at the time to hear matters brought before it by individuals. As Alter et al. and others have recounted, this case prompted a sustained and successful campaign from a range of actors that eventually persuaded both ECOWAS bureaucrats and the responsible ministers and heads of state/governments of the Member States, to afford individuals and organizations direct access to the Court in human rights causes;[33] this was a transformative action for which these sub-regional bureaucrats and domestic state officials ought to have received far more independent credit than they have to date. As such, the first Supplementary Protocol on the ECOWAS Court was adopted in 2005 and subsequently implemented into law.[34] After the passing of this 2005 Protocol, the Court came to be positioned as, among other things, a human rights court, and is now among a number of such regional human rights courts which exist around the world.[35]

The new Article 9(4) of this Protocol thus authorizes the ECOWAS Court to hear and determine "cases of violation of human rights that occur in any Member State," while its new Article 10(d) allows access to the court to "individuals on application for relief for violation of their human rights." The fact that the Court possesses this competence has now been affirmed in a long line of cases, and is not at all controversial. Commendably, the Court has, thus far, heard scores of such cases, with a case load that has in general been on an upward trend.[36]

Section Three: Conceptual Framework—Pro-Poor, Sovereign Hurdles, Brainy Relays, and Flipped Strategic Social Constructivism

It is important at this juncture to offer working understandings of the key concepts that undergird and shape our analysis in this chapter, and pause on their relevance to that analysis. First, what does the term "poor" (within the expression

---

[31] *See* 1991 Protocol on the ECOWAS Court, new art. 3(4), introduced by Supplementary Protocol No. A/Sp.2/06/06 (June 14, 2006).

[32] *See* Olajide Afolabi v. Federal Republic of Nigeria, Suit No. ECW/CCJ/APP/01/03.

[33] *See* Alter et al., *supra* note 6, at 756.

[34] *See* Supplementary Protocol No. A/SP.1/01/05 (Jan. 19, 2005).

[35] *See* Solomon T. Ebobrah, *International Human Rights Courts* in OXFORD HANDBOOK OF INTERNATIONAL ADJUDICATION 225 (C.P.R. Romano, K.J. Alter, & Y. Shany eds., 1st ed., 2014).

[36] *See* the list of all the cases that have been decided by the Court at, http://www.courtecowas.org/site2012/index.php?option=com_content&view=article&id=157&Itemid=27 (last visited Mar. 24, 2016).

"pro-poor") really mean? What notion of poverty animates the use of this term in this chapter? Given the focus of this chapter on interrogating the ECOWAS Court for its normative, procedural, and other kinds of capacity to function as a pro-poor resource in the hands of domestic activist forces, it is important to briefly explain what the expression means. Here again, we rely on previous work,[37] in which it was argued—following others who stated similarly—that the general consensus is now to regard poverty not merely in terms of material deprivation but also in terms of "a very low level of well-being,"[38] or as "the denial of opportunities and choices basic to human development."[39] In this sense is Lanse Minkler correct to note that "income poverty representations may at times belittle the true enormity of human suffering, for even those with higher incomes than the quantitative poverty cut-off may still suffer hardships associated with poor health, housing, and education."[40] What is more, their sources of income may be precarious, they may lack clean water and sanitation, or they may live in a rancid setting. Additionally, as is now widely acknowledged, it should also be kept in mind that poverty tends to disproportionately affect children, women, the disabled, and certain ethno-racial minorities.[41] Thus, in this chapter, the expression "poverty" includes any incidence of the fundamental deprivation, and/or of the serious lack of basic needs (such as food, water, shelter, education, clothing, and essential medicines).[42] Yet, it must be kept in mind that the chapter largely focuses on the latter segment of this definition, i.e. the lack of basic needs.[43] Therefore, as they are used in this chapter, the expression the "poor" refers to those whose lives are characterized by this kind of "lack," and as such the term "pro-poor" refers to any norm, procedure, orientation, action, structure, phenomena, decision, system, etc., that favors, or contributes to, the amelioration or elimination of this kind of condition of poverty.[44] Having said this, it bears emphasis to highlight the fact that that those who fit this definition of poverty also tend to dominate the ranks of those who suffer from the other kinds of fundamental deprivations referred to earlier.

---

[37] *See* Okafor & Ugochukwu, *supra* note 1, at 399.

[38] *See* Osmani, *supra* note 8, at 306.

[39] *See* THE POVERTY OF RIGHTS: HUMAN RIGHTS AND THE ERADICATION OF POVERTY (Willem van Genugten & Camilo Perez-Bustillo eds., 1st ed. 2001).

[40] THE STATE OF ECONOMIC AND SOCIAL HUMAN RIGHTS: A GLOBAL OVERVIEW 1 (Lanse Minkler ed., 1st ed. 2013).

[41] New estimates by the World Bank suggest that "the number of extremely poor people … has fallen from 1.9 billion in 1990 to about 736 million in 2015. However, the number of people living in extreme poverty is on the rise in Sub-Saharan Africa." <<<REF:WBLK>>>Divyanshi Wadhwa, *The Number of Extremely Poor People Continues to Rise in Sub-Saharan Africa*, WORLD BANK BLOGS (Sept. 19, 2018), https://blogs.worldbank.org/opendata/number-extremely-poor-people-continues-rise-sub-saharan-africa<<<REFC>>>. For a comprehensive criticism of how the World Bank calculates its poverty headcount figures and its political and moral implications; *see* FREEDOM FROM POVERTY AS A HUMAN RIGHT: WHO OWES WHAT TO THE POOR? (Thomas Pogge, ed., 1st ed., 2007).

[42] See Okafor & Ugochukwu, *supra* note 1, at 399.

[43] *Id.*

[44] *Id.*

Second, what is meant here by the expression "brainy relays" (or if you like "intelligent transmission-lines") and "flipped strategic social constructivism" and how do these relate to each other and to the analysis in this chapter? As used in this chapter, the expression "brainy relays" is a broad moniker for the role that various kinds of domestic activist forces (including bar associations, public interest lawyers, human rights activists, and other civil society groups) play both in ensuring that a human rights court is designed/oriented, or acts, in a certain manner, and/or in making sure (through their integration of the court's regime into their domestic work) that the design, orientation, or action of international human rights bodies such as the ECOWAS Court matter in fact to the lives of the poor within a particular state.[45] These forces often play this kind of role through their "virtual alliance" with the court on the international plane (e.g. through supporting it sociopolitically and feeding it with cases) and/or via their integration and utilization of such courts (and their design features, actions, and orientations) in on-the-ground, often strategic, broader social engagements.[46] Some of the ways in which activists have supported and helped build up courts like the ECOWAS Court has of course been recognized in the literature.[47]

The ways in which such activists can put international norms and institutions to important domestic uses has also been recognized,[48] none the least in the work of those scholars who have been styled elsewhere as "quasi-constructivists."[49] Martha Finnemore and Kathryn Sikkink's theory of "strategic social constructivism" is one example of this "school of thought."[50] Typically, it has been argued by quasi-constructivists that:

Norm entrepreneurs work to persuade other agents to alter their behavior in accordance with the norm entrepreneur's ideas of appropriate behavior. For constructivists, this means that a norm entrepreneur is attempting to alter other agents' perceptions of the social context—alter what an agent thinks is appropriate

---

[45] Obiora C. Okafor, The African Human Rights System, Activists Forces and International Institutions 94 (1st ed., 2007) (hereinafter "The African Human Rights System").

[46] See Martin Olz, Non-Governmental Organizations in Regional Human Rights Systems, 28 Colum. Hum. Rts. L. Rev. 307 (1997); Dinah Shelton, The Participation of Nongovernmental Organizations in International Judicial Proceedings, 88 Am. J. Int'l L. 611 (1994); Peter J. Spiro, New Global Communities: Nongovernmental Organizations in International Decision Making Institutions, 18 Wash. Q. 45 (1995); Wendy Schoener, Non-Governmental Organizations and Global Activism: Legal and Informal Approaches, 4 Global Legal Stud. J. 536 (1997); Zoe Pearson, Non-Governmental Organizations and the International Criminal Court: Changing Landscapes of International Law, 39 Cornell Int'l L. J. 243 (2006).

[47] See, e.g., Alter et al., supra note 6.

[48] See Okafor, supra note 45.

[49] For an extended analysis of the exercise of the second kind of brainy relay function in the context of the work of another African human rights body, see id. at 28–30, 287–93.

[50] See Martha Finnemore & Kathryn Sikkink, International Norm Dynamics and Political Change, 52 Int'l Org. 887 (1998).

behavior. How this alteration takes place is currently a matter for debate among constructivists.[51]

From this quasi-constructivist perspective, the relevant question here is to what extent have, and can, domestic activist forces in ECOWAS Member States (such as Nigeria), and their allies, acting—in among other ways—as "norm entrepreneurs" effectively utilize the praxis of the ECOWAS Court within the domestic sphere to help produce meaningful pro-poor alterations in the prevalent social, legal, or other conditions? To what extent do these activists fruitfully engage in this kind of *international-to-local* trans-judicial communication, "the brokered transmission of norms, ideas, or knowledge," in this case between the ECOWAS Court (on the one hand) and state and society in ECOWAS Member States (on the other hand), and in the direction of the latter?[52] While we find this specific kind of question and inquiry most interesting and are currently pursuing it squarely in another context, it is not mostly within the scope of the present chapter.

Rather, what is focused on—in the main—here is the extent to which the ECOWAS Court has functioned as a normative or procedural resource for pro-poor activist forces and contributed to the diminishing or overcoming of certain domestic socio-legal obstacles faced by them in their local human rights litigation/campaign efforts. As we have already made clear, the role that these activist forces and their allies have played in co-creating this phenomenon forms a central part of this inquiry. In this last sense, the analysis is concerned with the role of these domestic activist forces and their allies, on the international plane, in working—in part as norm entrepreneurs—to persuade ECOWAS judges, officials of certain political organs of the ECOWAS itself, and other actors who exercise the power to establish, run, and govern ECOWAS and its institutions, to alter their thinking and behavior, and revise prevalent normative and procedural arrangements, in accordance with certain ideas of appropriateness held by these activists. This is a kind of local-to-international trans-judicial communication that differs from that described earlier and which we have therefore chosen to style "flipped strategic social constructivism." This expression thus denotes the process of at once moral and rational, "ends-means calculations" that have led, and can lead, to the production of alterations in the logics of appropriateness prevalent, not really in the local society at issue, but chiefly among international judges and officials. This expression and the idea of rational ends-means calculations is, of course, a play on Finnemore and Sikkink's original variant which rather captures and theorizes a process in which activists act as brainy relays to produce significant changes in domestic states and societies by deploying international human rights norms and institutions to produce alterations in the locally prevalent logics of appropriateness.[53]

---

[51] *Id.*
[52] *See* Okafor, *supra* note 45, at 3, 94.
[53] See Finnemore & Sikkink, *supra* note 50, at 910.

In the kind of flipped strategic social constructivism at issue in this chapter, what rather happens is that activists—acting as flipped norm entrepreneurs—attempt to persuade the authors of a body of laws/procedures, and/or the judges of an international human rights court, to alter their thinking and behavior in accordance with the norm entrepreneurs' ideas of what would be appropriate in the circumstances and the kind of socio-legal regime the latter would like to see in place on the international plane.

Third, it is also as necessary at the outset to explain, albeit briefly, what is meant here by the expression "sovereign hurdles." By this it means the concept, structures, dramatizations, effects, and quotidian life of state sovereignty can, and do, present and position certain types of hurdles which the ECOWAS Court and/or the domestic activist forces which seek to leverage it must scale or at least confront in their efforts to contribute either separately or as a "virtual alliance"[54] to the struggle for domestic social change in the relevant ECOWAS Member States. Thus, some of the analysis in this chapter—especially in Section Seven—also allows us to peer further into some aspects of the real life workings, and the tugs and pulls, of state sovereignty as a living form—even if in only one small dimension of activity in a particular sub-region. To borrow and adapt an expression from Baxi's fecund imagination, this aperture should concomitantly be helpful in observing small slices of evidence regarding "what is living and dead" in state sovereignty,[55] i.e. the very character of the "living" law with respect to the relationship between international (in this case regional) efforts to protect human rights and aspects of the daily life of state sovereignty.[56]

Having offered working understandings of the key concepts used in this chapter and explained their relevance to the analysis conducted therein, what remains at this stage is to consider the contribution or otherwise of the ECOWAS Court to the enhancement of the repertoire of normative and procedural resources available to the domestic activist forces. In addition, we inquire into how these resources are leveraged, or are sought to be leveraged in the socio-economic and political struggles they wage within certain ECOWAS Member States, while integrating in that discussion a sense of the flipped strategic social constructivist role that domestic activist forces and their allies have played in the production of any such realities. Following this discussion, some of those gaps in the Court's design, action, orientation, and consequence that continue to hinder its contribution to these struggles will be examined. In the process, the ways in which domestic activist forces (and their allies) have

---

[54] *Id.* at 94.

[55] *See* UPENDRA BAXI, THE FUTURE OF HUMAN RIGHTS 160–99 (2nd ed., 2006).

[56] *See, e.g.,* Antony Anghie, *Francisco de Vitoria and the Colonial Origins of International Law,* 5 SOC. & LEGAL STUD. 321 (1996); REP. INT'L COMMISSION INTERVENTION & STATE SOVEREIGNTY (2001); Christine M. Wotipka & Kiyoteru Tsutsui, *Global Human Rights and State Sovereignty: State Ratification of International Human Rights Treaties, 1965-2001,* 23 SOC. F. 724 (2008).

co-created whatever contributions that the court has made available to them is also highlighted.

Section Four: Enhancing the Repertoire of Normative Resources Available to Pro-Poor Activists

Writing nearly ten years ago, Ebobrah was of the view that, despite his strong reservations to its very liberal access regime, "the ECOWAS human rights system may well be a gold mine for rights realization."[57] Has the Court met or fallen short of this standard? One way of assessing at least one aspect of this is to, as is done in this section, inquire analytically into the extent to which the (re)design, action, and/or orientation of the ECOWAS Court has enhanced the repertoire of pro-poor normative resources available to the domestic activist forces in ECOWAS Member States who play, and can play, key roles in the on-the-ground production of pro-poor social change. As such, it bears re-emphasis at this point that the concern here is not so much to map the impact or non-impact of the Court on the poor, as much as it is to demonstrate the ways in which the Court has been, and can be, a valuable resource to the activist forces who struggle to advance the social conditions of the poor within the ECOWAS sub-region. It also bears emphasis that the overarching point that is made in this section is not that the normative resources that the Court has helped make available can only possibly benefit pro-poor activists. Rather, the point is that, at the very least, these normative resources have a potential to, in some notable way, significantly aid the work of pro-poor activists.

First, there is hardly any question, as Eghosa Ekhator has partly suggested, that the decisions of the ECOWAS Court have added to the growing jurisprudence on the protection of human rights in countries like Nigeria, as elsewhere; much of which can be deployed toward pro-poor ends.[58] At first glance this may not be as weighty a contribution or set of actions as might be desired; for "adding" to a body of jurisprudence is often seen as a matter of quantity and assessing how much has been in fact added is usually viewed as a question of quantification. But quantity in the human rights field can often mean, or indeed breed, quality. In short, "more" can really mean "more" in this field. This is so because the more human rights jurisprudence has been produced by the court, the more opportunities it has had to do a number of important things (and to also do them in pro-poor ways): clarify human rights texts and provisions (which can too often be vague or conflicting), raise awareness among lawyers and non-lawyers alike of the existence and usefulness of those texts and provisions, and even innovate. The exponential increases in the

---

[57] *See* Ebobrah, *supra* note 6, at 328.
[58] *See* Eghosa Ekhator, *Improving Access to Environmental Justice under the African Charter on Human and Peoples' Rights: The Roles of NGOs in Nigeria*, 22 Afr. J. Int'l & Comp. L. 63, 75 (2014).

utilization within Nigeria, and in pro-poor ways, of the African Charter on Human and Peoples Rights,[59] and the African Commission on Human and Peoples Rights (that monitors state observance of its provisions),[60] aptly illustrates this point.[61] This is because the more that the Treaty and the Commission were utilized by Nigerian activist forces, the more all the useful things outlined earlier occurred.[62] And so this kind of quantity can also lead to the enhancement of the quality of the repertoire of pro-poor normative resources available to domestic activist forces in ECOWAS Member States. As much of the rest of the discussion in this chapter indicates, this can often significantly advantage pro-poor activist forces. As we shall see at the end of this section, domestic activist forces, via playing their flipped strategic social constructivist roles helped co-produce and co-enhance a significant portion of this growing jurisprudence. And they did so in a manner that is telling, howsoever modestly, of the growing routinization in the ECOWAS sub-region of the transgression of more absolutist notions of state sovereignty.

A second way in which the ECOWAS Court has enhanced, and can continue to enhance, the pro-poor normative repertoire available to domestic activists is through its choice to actively apply in its adjudicative praxis the full range of international human rights treaties that have been ratified by the relevant states. By having a full range of treaties it can use, the ECOWAS Court has concomitantly increased to the same degree the opportunities for it to display and act out a kind of pro-poor activist ethic. As such, the Court's normative framework is not limited to any particular human rights treaty. And this is a legally correct and supportable position. Although the legal commitment of the ECOWAS as a whole to respect the "fundamental principles" stated in that organization's Revised Treaty of 1993, including the "recognition, promotion and protection of human and peoples' rights in accordance with the provisions of the African Charter,"[63]clearly suggests that the ECOWAS Court ought to include this particular human rights treaty among its sources of human rights law, nowhere in Revised Treaty or in any of the ECOWAS Court-related Protocols is the Court limited to applying any particular human rights treaty. As importantly, while it is this liberal nature and relative open-endedness of the Court's normative architecture that set the stage for it to assume this progressive interpretive posture, its self-conscious judicial action has consistently made the most of this design model. For example, in one of the *SERAP v. Nigeria* cases that came before it (the one on the rights to a healthy environment, etc), the Court relied on this textual vagueness to boldly fill the concomitant gap in a pro-poor manner.[64] It held that the 2005 Supplementary Protocol had given it expansive authority to hear and determine any cases of human rights violations that arise in any Member State.[65] It fortified this decision in light of the provisions of the ECOWAS Protocol on Democracy and Good Governance in West Africa,[66] and having regard to the provisions of the ECOWAS Revised Treaty, it had the authority to apply any human rights treaty to which a relevant state had ratified.[67] According to the Court:

> Thus, even though ECOWAS may not have adopted a specific instrument recognising human rights, the Court's human rights protection mandate is exercised with regard to all the international instruments, including the African Charter on Human and Peoples' Rights, the International Covenant on Civil and Political Rights, the International Covenant on Economic, Social and Cultural Rights, etc. to which the Member States of ECOWAS are parties.[68]

This was an interpretive choice that the Court made. It could have concluded otherwise, for example, by holding that it was limited to applying the African Charter. In any case, this ability on the part of the Court to apply a range of international human rights treaties has made it possible for activist forces, citizens, judges, etc, within the ECOWAS sub-region to select from among a range of human rights treaties and instruments the texts that best served the interests of human rights in the cases at hand. For pro-poor domestic activist forces, this has allowed them to select from the available texts, the one which best serves the interests of the poor. This has directly led to situations in which otherwise unavailable or weaker arguments have become available to pro-poor domestic activist forces, or strengthened. One good example, to which we will return in more detail later, is the *SERAP v. Nigeria No.1* case mentioned earlier where an eventually victorious Nigerian human rights NGO was able to make arguments before the Court about the justiciability of ES rights in Nigeria which would not have been at all possible, or which would have been far weaker, or which would most likely have been unsuccessful, had that NGO not relied on the African Charter and the International Covenant on Economic, Social and Economic Rights. For, as is well recognized in the Nigerian human rights literature, the rights that belong to this category are not constitutionally justiciable under the Nigerian Constitution.[69] The huge significance of the

---

[64] *See* Registered Trustees of Socio-Economic Rights and Accountability Project (SERAP) v. The Federal Republic of Nigeria, Suit No. ECW/CCJ/APP/08/09, Rul. No. ECW/CCJ/JUD/18/12 (Dec. 14, 2012).
[65] *See* Supplementary Protocol, *supra* note 34.
[66] See the ECOWAS Protocol A/SP1/12/01 (Dec. 21, 2001).
[67] *Id.* at paras. 24–29.
[68] *Id.* at para. 28.
[69] *See, e.g.*, Obiora C. Okafor & Uchechukwu Ngwaba, *Economic and Social Rights: A Century of Constitutional Subordination in Nigeria*, in NIGERIA: A CENTURY OF CONSTITUTIONAL EVOLUTION 1914–2014 688 (Epiphany Azinge & Adejoke Adediran eds., 2013).

enjoyment of such ES rights to the uplifting of the social condition of the poor has already been pointed out in Section One. As such, their importance to the work of any serious pro-poor activist cannot be over-emphasized. Two further points should also be made. The first is a simple one: that the role of a domestic human rights NGO in co-producing the international human rights outcome in the *SERAP* case (via feeding the case to the Court, crafting creative arguments, persuading the Court to buy them, etc), its flipped strategic social constructivism, is noteworthy. The second is that this case is illustrative of the ways in which a supranational judicial arrangement—that, as we have seen, was co-created by a virtual alliance of domestic activists, their foreign allies, ECOWAS Court judges, and the political organs of ECOWAS, in the exercise of sovereign power—is often deployed by local activists in ways designed to jump over or circumvent certain sovereign hurdles. This is one way in which state sovereignty circulates and operates, or lives its quotidian life, especially within a regional integration crucible like the ECOWAS arrangement. This is not to subscribe to the view that state sovereignty is now somehow *passé* (for it is not and is even gaining strength in the immigration area, for example), but to note the character of its manifestation in this context.

A third way in which the ECOWAS Court has enhanced, and can continue to enhance, the repertoire of pro-poor normative resources available to the domestic activist forces in ECOWAS Member States, is through its explication of the details of the general community law in the ECOWAS sub-region. This has, and can have, a direct impact on the enjoyment of the human rights of community citizens, and its offering of an authoritative analysis of aspects of the relationship between such community law and the relevant provisions of the applicable human rights treaties. For example, although the particular plaintiffs in the *Femi Falana v. Benin* case did not succeed on the particular facts alleged,[70] and in spite of the fact that one may or may not agree with the Court's reasoning in this case, the Court was still able to produce useful jurisprudence as to when and how the right of ECOWAS citizens to free movement within the sub-region could be curtailed somewhat, albeit only on reasonable grounds, and how this right interacts with the human rights to freedom of movement in the African Charter. The Plaintiffs (one of them a public interest/human rights lawyer) brought this case to the ECOWAS Court after they claimed to have encountered many roadblocks, tollgates, checkpoints, and closed borders when travelling between Togo, Nigeria, and Benin. The Plaintiffs claimed that this situation prevented them from completing the duties regarding which they had set out on the relevant trip. They thus claimed that their human rights to free movement of persons had been violated. However, the Court found that there was no violation of these rights on the facts, and that neither the ECOWAS Protocol on Free Movement nor the right to freedom of movement under the African Charter

---

[70] *See* Femi Falana v. Republic of Benin, Suit No. ECW/CCJ/APP/10/07, Rul. No. ECW/CCJ/JUD/02/12 (July 24, 2012).

was absolute. In its view, ECOWAS Member States were entitled to close or police their borders in a reasonable way, which the Court felt was the case in this particular dispute. The facts and decision in this case together constitute an example of the ways in which the state sovereignty norm circulates and operates, and lives its quotidian life, in the ECOWAS sub-region, even within the regional integration crucible. It is important, nevertheless, to underline the significance of this decision for the poor in the ECOWAS sub-region, and therefore for pro-poor activist forces, by noting that the roadblocks and other barriers complained of tend to disproportionately affect them. These days, richer or middle-class West Africans tend to fly across the region, but the poor tend not to have this option owing to its relatively very prohibitive cost to them. As such, despite the specific outcome in this case, to the extent that the Court impliedly found as well that such barriers could not be set up by ECOWAS Member States in an unreasonable manner, it was "arming" pro-poor activists in the region with a significant normative resource. The flipped strategic social constructivism role played by a domestic public interest lawyer in co-producing the international human rights outcome in this case should also be highlighted.

A fourth way in which the ECOWAS Court has similarly provided or enhanced normative resourcing to the benefit of pro-poor activists, and can continue to do so, is through the positive example. Thus its broadly pro-poor jurisprudential action and orientation has sometimes set, and can continue to set, for the other international courts and bodies with human rights jurisdiction over the sub-region (as for example the African Court on Human and Peoples Rights), and the domestic courts of ECOWAS Member States.[71] The forward looking and, in general, robustly pro-poor, jurisprudence that it has produced on economic and social rights is one instance of a set of its jurisprudential actions that has set an important example for these other courts.[72] These kinds of normative examples can over time and under the right conditions lead to the kind of alterations within the wider sub-region in the prevalent "logics of appropriateness" that constructivists and quasi-constructivists often map and analyze;[73] alterations which are likely to lead to positive dividends for the poor in the sub-region. The provision of such examples to other bodies around the world by the ECOWAS Court does matter, because pro-poor activists in the sub-region are often at liberty to harness or re-harness the norms set down in these other regimes both in their own domestic legal orders and

[71] See Enyinna S. Nwauche, *Regional Economic Communities and Human Rights in West Africa and the African Arabic Countries, in* HUMAN RIGHTS LAW IN AFRICA: LEGAL PERSPECTIVES ON THEIR PROTECTION AND PROMOTION 319 (Anton Bösl & Joseph Diescho eds., 2009).

[72] See Registered Trustees of Socio-Economic Rights and Accountability Project (SERAP) v. The Federal Republic of Nigeria, Suit No. ECW/CCJ/APP/08/09, Rul. No. ECW/CCJ/JUD/18/12 (Dec. 14, 2012).

[73] See Finnemore & Sikkink, *supra* note 50.

within the ECOWAS Court regime itself (as the Court can apply any treaty ratified by the country that has been sued and can as such rely on the interpretive decisions of such bodies). It would thus be beneficial to pro-poor activists, and eventually to the poor themselves, if these other bodies followed the ECOWAS Court's lead in appropriate cases. The contributions made by, and pro-poor significance of, a number of such exemplary cases are discussed later; while pointing out—as appropriate—the ways in which many of these cases exemplify or illustrate: what is living and what is dead in state sovereignty, or the workings of flipped strategic social constructivism, or both.

Along these lines, it is fair to state that the Court's decision that corporations per se cannot make human rights claims before it can be cited as one such positive example, as an important contribution to the development and advancement of a pro-poor understanding and praxis of international human rights jurisprudence. For example, in *Ocean King Nigeria Limited v. Senegal*,[74] the Plaintiff's ship was awarded to a towing company by a Senegalese court. It then sued Senegal at the ECOWAS Court claiming that it had not been informed of the proceedings that had led to the award, and alleging violations of its rights to own property, to move freely within ECOWAS Member States, and to benefit from a fair trial. The Court held, inter alia, that although it does have jurisdiction to hear human rights cases, it could however not entertain the present case, as corporations, such as the present Plaintiff, not being humans, cannot invoke human rights claims. This decision is a robustly pro-poor and very progressive one because, around the world, the increasing grant of rights to corporations, let alone the grant of human rights to them, has tended to lead to unjust outcomes for the poor, especially in third world states.[75] The decision will therefore help to allay to some degree the kind of justifiable anxiety that, for instance, pervades Baxi's work on the increasing turn from what he styled the paradigm of the Universal Declaration of Human Rights (UDHR) toward a trade-related, market-friendly (i.e. TREMF) paradigm of human rights that tends to devalue human beings and favor the rights of corporations and global capital over the rights of the poor and vulnerable populations (especially of third world states).[76] The decision does not, however, tell us all that

---

[74] *See* Ocean King Nigeria Limited v. The Republic of Senegal, Suit No. ECW/CCJ/APP/05/08, Rul. No. ECW/CCJ/JUD/07/11 (July 8, 2011).

[75] *See, e.g.,* Gus van Harten, *Five Justifications for Investment Treaties: A Critical Discussion,* 2 TRADE L. & DEV. 1, 3–5 (2010); *see also* Gus van Harten, *Harper Moves to Give up More Canadian Sovereignty,* THE TYEE (Nov. 12, 2013), http://thetyee.ca/Opinion/2013/11/12/Harper-Gives-Up-Sovereignty/ (last visited Mar. 30, 2016).

[76] *See* Baxi, *supra* note 2; *see also* O. C. Okafor, *Assessing Baxi's Thesis on the Emergence of a Trade-Related Market-Friendly Human Rights Paradigm: Recent Evidence from Nigerian Labour-led Struggles,* L. SOC. JUST. & GLOBAL DEV. (2007), https://papers.ssrn.com/sol3/papers.cfm?abstract_id=1571291. This article has been re-published as O. C. Okafor, *Is a New "TREMF" Human Rights Paradigm Emerging? Evidence from Nigeria, in* LAW IN TRANSITION: HUMAN RIGHTS, DEVELOPMENT AND TRANSITIONAL JUSTICE 79 (Ruth Buchanan & Peer Zumbansen eds., 1st ed., 2014).

much about either the quotidian life of "modern," twenty-first century, state sovereignty, or the workings of flipped strategic social constructivism, in the ECOWAS sub-region.

Another such significant, albeit modest, contribution is the Court's reasoning in *SERAP v. Nigeria No.2* regarding the status of corruption within that body of law, and its negative effects on the enjoyment of human rights—in this case, the right to education.[77] While the ECOWAS Court is, of course, not the first human rights body in the world to make the latter kind of connection,[78] it interestingly reasoned in this case that, although corruption per se (i.e. isolated instances of that criminal conduct), will not necessarily always amount to violations of human rights, it could lead to such a result if it occurs in a consistent and widespread pattern, since, "admittedly, embezzling, stealing, or even mismanagement of funds meant for the education sector will have a negative impact on education since it reduces the amount of money made available to provide for the education of the people."[79] As such, the decision is a welcome addition to the growing but still inadequate body of jurisprudence on this issue. Its potential benefits to the poor (who tend to suffer the most from the negative effects of corruption on the enjoyment of all human rights (especially economic and social rights) are most obvious. And as with many of cases discussed in this chapter, this decision—one that was co-produced and co-enhanced by a Nigerian human right group's local-to-international brainy relay work—is also instructive about the workings of flipped strategic social constructivism. The decision is also indicative of the increasing acceptance and solidification of judicial supra-nationality in West Africa and of what state sovereignty tends to look like today in the ECOWAS sub-region.

In this same case, the ECOWAS Court also made an even more significant contribution to enhancing the development of a pro-poor orientation and sensibility in international human rights jurisprudence and praxis by affirming and making crystal clear the existence, justiciability, and legal bindingness of the right to basic education in the countries which constitute the ECOWAS sub-region. This decision is especially valuable in the sense of the enhancement of the pro-poor resources available to domestic activist forces in West Africa given the fact that almost nowhere in this sub-region is the human right to education justiciable,[80]

---

[77] *See* Registered Trustees of Socio-Economic Rights and Accountability Project (SERAP) v. The Federal Republic of Nigeria (ECW/CCJ/APP/12/70 & ECW/CCJ/JUD/07/10).

[78] *See, e.g., Negative Impact of Corruption*, U.N. HUMAN RIGHTS COUNCIL, http://www.ohchr.org/EN/HRBodies/HRC/AdvisoryCommittee/Pages/NegativeImpactCorruption.aspx (last visited Mar. 28, 2016) (the work of the U.N. Human Rights Council Advisory Committee on this issue). This committee's final report was submitted to the twenty-eighth session of the UN Human Rights Council in January 2015. *See* A/HRC/28/73 (Jan. 3, 2015).

[79] *See* Registered Trustees of Socio-Economic Rights and Accountability Project (SERAP) v. The Federal Republic of Nigeria, Suit No. ECW/CCJ/APP/08/09, Rul. No. ECW/CCJ/JUD/18/12, para. 19 (Dec. 14, 2012).

[80] Our survey in early 2016 of the legal regimes of all ECOWAS Member States suggests that social and economic rights are in general non-justiciable under the domestic laws of all of these countries.

and in view of the reality in almost every ECOWAS Member State of a widespread lack of access among the poor to (high quality) basic education.[81] The "local-to-international" brainy relay role played by the SERAP, a domestic human rights NGO, in co-producing and co-enhancing this decision is as instructive here about the workings of flipped strategic social constructivism in the West African socio-legal context. As in other cases, the decision is also telling in regard to the workings and solidification of judicial supra-nationality in that sub-region, revealing in the result, glimpses of what State sovereignty-in-action tends to look like today.

A similarly significant contribution is the bolstering of the anti-slavery human rights norm, especially in relation to the less appreciated forms and manifestations of slavery, that the Court was able to accomplish in the now famous *Hadijatou Mani Koraou* case.[82] The Plaintiff in this case, Hadijatou, an ethnic Bouzou woman, was born into slavery in the Republic of Niger.[83] In 1996, she was sold at the age of twelve years for the equivalent of about US$500 by her mother's owner to an ethnic Hausa chief, El Hadj Souleymane Naroua.[84] This transaction was part of the local tradition in which a young girl is sold to a man to be his servant and concubine.[85] She worked as a slave for about nine years, performing domestic and agricultural labour.[86] She was first raped by Naroua around the age of thirteen and continued to be subject to rape, resulting in the birth of four children, but only two survived.[87] In her own words:

> I was beaten so many times I would run to my family [sic]. Then after a day or two I would be brought back. At the time I didn't know what to do but since I learned that slavery has been abolished I told myself that I will no longer be a slave.[88]

These were the experiences and facts that that led her to bring her case to the ECOWAS Court. The basis of her case at the court was that Niger had violated its obligations under the ECOWAS Revised Treaty, the African Charter, and a number of other treaties. The ECOWAS Court held that she was a victim of slavery and that

---

[81] *See* Kevin Watkins, *Too Little Access, Not Enough Learning: Africa's Twin Deficit in Education,* BROOKINGS (Jan. 16, 2013), http://www.brookings.edu/research/opinions/2013/01/16-africa-learning-watkins.

[82] *See* Dame Hadijatou Mani Karaou v. The Republic of Niger, Suit No. ECW/CCJ/APP/08/08, Rul. No. ECW/CCJ/JUD/06/08 (ECOWAS, Oct. 27, 2008). For a critique of the judicial reasoning but not the outcome of this case, *see* Jean Allain, *Hadijatou Mani Koraou v. Republic of Niger Judgment No. ECW/CCJ/JUD/06/08. Economic Community of West Africa States Community Court of Justice, October 27, 2008,* 103 AM. J. INT'L L. 311 (2009).

[83] African *Women's Lives, Contemporary Slavery in Africa, Slavery in Niger,* THE WOYINGI BLOG (Apr. 3, 2011), https://woyingi.wordpress.com/2011/04/03/african-womens-lives-hadijatou-mani-koraou/ (last visited Mar. 9, 2016).

[84] *Id.*

[85] *Id.*

[86] *Id.*

[87] *Id.*

[88] *Id.*

while the Republic of Niger was not the perpetrator of this proven human rights violation, it was nevertheless blameworthy for its failure to fulfil its obligations to protect the human rights of the Plaintiff from violation by others. Hadijatou was granted reparation for the harms she had suffered and an award of CFA10 million (approximately $20,000 USD) as damages for the harms she had suffered. As shall be discussed in Section Seven, this decision was fully and robustly implemented by the government of the Niger Republic. Apart from the benefit of this decision to activists as a resource in their hands, its direct benefits to the poor themselves—to persons in Hadijatou's position—is so obvious that it does not require elaboration here. The decision, which was the result of a suit that was driven by local activists in Niger and their foreign human rights NGO ally (the now defunct INTERIGHTS), is also illustrative of the points made earlier on in this section regarding the role of these activists as brainy relays which sometimes author a kind of flipped strategic social constructivism in the West African context. It is also as revealing about the growing acceptance of judicial supra-nationality and the re-configuration of state sovereignty in that sub-region.

Another way in which the ECOWAS Court has enhanced, and can continue to enhance, the repertoire of pro-poor normative resources available to domestic activist forces in ECOWAS Member States, is its contribution in *SERAP v. Nigeria No. 1*.[89] In this case, the Court added to the normative resourcing of those activists and affected persons who work to improve the socio-economic and political situation in the Niger Delta region of Nigeria; a region that, despite its huge oil wealth, is still among the poorest parts of the country.[90] In affirming the existence, justiciability, and legal bindingness of the rights to a healthy environment, food, water, and so on, in the ECOWAS sub-region, and the obligation of all ECOWAS Member States to effectively implement these rights to the fullest extent practicable, the Court contributed in significant measure to this kind of resource enhancement. In this case, the Plaintiff, SERAP, sued the government of Nigeria and six oil companies over their alleged violations of human rights and associated responsibility for oil pollution in the Niger Delta region of Nigeria. SERAP alleged violations of several economic and social rights in that area, including the rights to a healthy environment, food, and water. It also alleged the failure on the part of Nigeria to enforce its laws and regulations that were designed to protect the environment and prevent pollution. The ECOWAS Court found that, although almost all of these violations had been directly committed by certain oil companies, the Nigerian government was still legally liable for these abuses. In effect, the Court held that, by failing to protect both the people of Niger Delta and their environment from the harmful

---

[89] *See* Registered Trustees of Socio-Economic Rights and Accountability Project (SERAP) v. The Federal Republic of Nigeria, Suit No. ECW/CCJ/APP/08/09, Rul. No. ECW/CCJ/JUD/18/12, (Dec. 14, 2012).
[90] *See* Patrick Oviasuyi & Jim Uwadiae, *The Dilemma of [the] Niger Delta Region as Oil Producing States in Nigeria*, 16 J. PEACE, CONFLICT & DEV. 110, 112–13 (2010).

operations of oil companies in that region of the country, Nigeria had violated the relevant provisions of the African Charter. The court went further to uphold the rights to a healthy environment, food, water, etc, of the people of Niger Delta, and held that these rights had been infringed by virtue of the destruction of the Niger Delta environment through oil pollution. The Court then ordered Nigeria to remedy the environmental damage in the Niger Delta region, to prevent further environmental damage, and to hold the offenders accountable. Needless to say, this decision is of great potential benefit not just to the mass of poor people who populate the Niger Delta area, but to many groups of poor West Africans who face similar violations. The provision of this important jurisprudential resource to the activists who struggle on their behalf can only benefit them ultimately (to the extent that law can help trigger social change in the West African context). There is already evidence that such decisions help make the Nigerian government "more sensitive to the environmental and social responsibilities of the oil companies."[91] And as is shown in Section Seven, there is even some solid evidence that this particular decision is being implemented to an extent by the Nigerian government. This can only enure to the advantage of the (generally poor) people of the Niger Delta. As importantly, the points made above about the ways in which NGOs such as SERAP have functioned as brainy relays in the process of flipped strategic social constructionism that aids the production of these valuable outcomes, and regarding the glimpses into the quotidian life of state sovereignty that an analysis of this process can allow us, also apply here.

It is worth re-emphasizing here that the significance for the poor themselves of the extensive normative repertoire that the ECOWAS Court has made available to the pro-poor domestic activist forces, and which were co-created and co-enhanced by these very activists, was teased out, or at least highlighted, at every stage of the foregoing analysis. As has been noted earlier in this chapter, a discussion of the actual impact that these pro-poor resources have had on the lives of the poor is beyond the scope of this chapter. However, the Court's contribution to the normative resourcing of the domestic activist forces which (along with their allies) operate within the ECOWAS sub-region is on its own a substantial and worthy one.

Also worthy of reiteration here are the important (and some may even say, indispensable) roles that domestic activist forces have played, and can continue to play, in the co-creation or co-enhancement of the very normative resources that can strengthen their own hands and enhance their pro-poor work in the ECOWAS sub-region. In seven of the eight cases discussed in this section (a sample that constitutes some of the most important human rights cases decided by the ECOWAS Court), domestic, i.e. West Africa-based, activist forces (such as human rights

---

[91] *See* O.C. Okafor, *Modest Harvests: On the Significant (but Limited) Impact of Human Rights NGOs on Legislative and Executive Behaviour in Nigeria*, 48 J. Afr. L. 23, 24 (2004); Ekhator, *supra* note 58, at 75.

NGOs and public interest lawyers) played the key role in bringing those cases to the Court, making important (and at times creative) legal arguments, and virtually co-creating or co-enhancing the relevant decisions alongside the Court's judges.[92] The only possible exception is the *CDP v. Burkina Faso* case. This is so because the main drivers of the litigation in this case were political parties. And political parties are not generally considered to be activist forces in the sense in which that expression is used in this chapter. It should nevertheless be acknowledged that some may even be minded to include them in this category. The point though is that, incontrovertibly, in the rest of the cases, "true" activist elements drove the process that generated the relevant decisions at the ECOWAS Court, and that they did so almost always in a direct way. This should not be surprising. After all, was it not, for instance, the expression in legal and social forms of the frustrations felt by domestic activist forces in not being able to litigate at the Court that catalyzed the Court into entering into a kind of virtual alliance with these activists to push hard to secure a human rights jurisdiction from the political organs of the ECOWAS?[93] And this required a measure of alteration in the logic of appropriateness of the judges in this respect. After all, the judges had for years seemed content to live without a human rights jurisdiction until they were confronted by the *Afolabi v. Nigeria* case and the civil society mobilization that ensued after they had been forced by the nature of the then prevailing ECOWAS Court legal framework to decline jurisdiction in that case. This phenomenon, the kind of "flipped strategic social constructivism" that was dramatized in the local-to-international trans-judicial communication of ideas, knowledge, and normative energy that was driven by activist forces who acted as brainy relays, is returned to—howsoever briefly—at the end of each of the next two sections. Additionally, it should be kept in mind that an extensive and richer analysis of the local uses to which domestic activist forces have in fact put the normative resources discussed in this section, i.e. of the international-to-local kind of trans-judicial communication, which is a kind of more widely recognized and therefore more traditional and more Finnemore/Sikkink-type, "strategic social constructivism," is beyond the scope of this chapter.

It also bears emphasis that much of the discussion in this section affords a glimpse into the ways in which the state sovereignty norm circulates and operates, or lives its quotidian life, today, especially in the integrating ECOWAS subregion. State sovereignty is transgressed constantly by the supra-nationality of the ECOWAS Court, even as that norm remains quite alive and well—as is, for instance, manifested by the very need to transgress it at all. More will be said in each

---

[92] Only in one of these cases, Dame Hadijatou Mani Karaou v. The Republic of Niger, Suit No. ECW/CCJ/APP/08/08, Rul. No. ECW/CCJ/JUD/06/08 (Oct. 27, 2008), did the domestic activist group explicitly act in concert with an international/foreign human rights NGO. In this case, the foreign collaborator was the now defunct INTERIGHTS.

[93] *See* Alter et al., *supra* note 6, at 751.

of the remaining sections on this question of the relationship of the analysis done in this chapter to our understanding of what is alive and dead in state sovereignty.

Section Five: Enhancing the Repertoire of Procedural Resources Available to Pro-Poor Activists

Another window through which one can gain insight into the extent to which the ECOWAS Court is functioning or could function, in significant measure, as a pro-poor resource is to inquire analytically into the extent to which the (re)design, action, and/or orientation of the ECOWAS Court has enhanced the repertoire of pro-poor procedural resources. Further, to what extent are those resources available to the domestic activist forces in ECOWAS Member States who play, and can play, key roles in the production of pro-poor social change in those societies. This is what is done in this section. And, once again, it bears re-emphasis that the central concern of this chapter is to demonstrate the various ways in which the ECOWAS Court has been, and can be, a valuable resource in the hands of the domestic activist forces who struggle to improve the social conditions of the poor within the ECOWAS sub-region, and is not to analyze the actual impact or non-impact of this Court on that population.

One major way in which the court has functioned in the aforementioned way is through its remarkably liberal approach to the question of the *locus standi* (or standing to sue) of litigants in human rights cases before it. Despite the apparently narrower language employed in the new Article 10(d) of its constitutive Protocol (as amended), which only explicitly grants standing to sue in human rights cases to "individuals," the ECOWAS Court has allowed human rights NGOs registered under the laws of any ECOWAS Member State to bring public interest law suits before it. Such NGOs may bring human rights matters before the Court even when the group itself was not the victim of the human rights violation complained about, and even when it did not obtain the authorization of those directly victimized by the violation before bringing the suit. For example, in *SERAP v. Nigeria No.1*,[94] the Court held that the Registered Trustees of the Socio-Economic Rights Action Programme (SERAP), a self-described human rights NGO and not-for-profit, that was established in 2014, and which is registered under the laws of Nigeria,[95] could sue the Nigerian government for violations of certain human rights. It overruled a preliminary objection raised by the government of Nigeria to the effect that SERAP lacked the requisite standing to sue "because its Application was filed without

---

[94] *See* Registered Trustees of Socio-Economic Rights and Accountability Project (SERAP) v. The Federal Republic of Nigeria, Suit No. ECW/CCJ/APP/08/09, Rul. No. ECW/CCJ/JUD/18/12 (Dec. 14, 2012). For some observations on this aspect of the decision, *see* Ekhator, *supra* note 58, at 73.

[95] *See* Who We Are, SERAP, http://serap-nigeria.org/who-we-are/ (last visited Mar. 21, 2016).

the prior information, accord and interest of the People of Niger Delta, and that SERAP acts in its own name, with no proof that it is acting on behalf of the people of Niger Delta."[96] A similar preliminary objection which had been raised earlier by other defendants in the suit was similarly dismissed.[97] The Court relied, in part, on "a large consensus in International Law that when the issue at stake is the violation of rights of entire communities, as in the case of the damage to the environment [as was the case here], the [sic] access to justice should be facilitated."[98]The Court also reasoned that given the very liberal "standing to sue" ethos in the law and practice of the African Commission, and given the fact that the claim at issue was brought, in part, for reasons of alleged violations of the African Charter, the court ought to facilitate access to justice by allowing groups like SERAP to bring this kind of case before it.[99] What is more, the Court held that SERAP did not need to obtain the permission of the Niger Delta peoples before bringing this suit as it was not litigating on their behalf, and had instead sued in a public interest capacity.[100]

The Court then concluded that:

> Based on those authorities, and taking into account the need to reinforced [sic] the [sic] access to justice for the protection of human and people [sic] rights in the African context, the Court holds that an NGO duly constituted according to the national law of any ECOWAS Member State, and enjoying observer status before ECOWAS institutions, can file complaints against Human Rights violation [sic] in case that [sic] the victim is not just a single individual, but a large group of individuals or even entire communities.[101]

It should be noted though that the form of *actio popularis* (popular action) authorized by the Court here appears to be restricted to situations in which "the victim is not just a single individual, but a large group of individuals or even entire communities." In other words, there does not seem to be any language in this decision which would allow human rights NGOs to, without prior authorization from an affected person, bring a matter concerning the violation of the rights of a single individual.

Needless to say, the decision (and others to the same effect) still constitutes an exceedingly valuable resource in the hands of the domestic activist forces who

---

[96] See Registered Trustees of Socio-Economic Rights and Accountability Project (SERAP) v. The Federal Republic of Nigeria, Suit No. ECW/CCJ/APP/08/09, Rul. No. ECW/CCJ/JUD/18/12, para. 41 (Dec. 14, 2012).

[97] *Id.*; Registered Trustees of Socio-Economic Rights and Accountability Project (SERAP) v. The Federal Republic of Nigeria, Suit No. ECW/CCJ/APP/08/09, Rul. No. ECW/CCJ/APP/07/10 (Dec. 10, 2010), http://www.worldcourts.com/ecowasccj/eng/decisions/2010.12.10_SERAP_v_Nigeria.htm (last visited Mar. 21, 2016).

[98] *Id.* at paras. 56–59.

[99] *Id.* at paras. 59–60.

[100] *Id.* at para. 62.

[101] *Id.* at para. 61.

struggle for pro-poor social change in the ECOWAS sub-region. The significance and potential of this decision in this connection is aptly illustrated by the situation in countries such as Nigeria in which very narrow standing to sue rules have for several decades impeded the access to justice of the domestic activist forces whose human rights struggles often advance the social status and conditions of the poor.[102] As Tunde Ogowewo did correctly note in the Nigerian context, the:

> Nigerian standing rule has a very narrow concept of personal standing (one that focuses on private legal rights) and no concept of representative standing. Hence, persons with a real interest in an issue of local or national importance invariably will be denied standing; even if what is assailed involves obvious illegality.[103]

As such, despite occasional flashes of liberalism over the years, the Nigerian courts have been mostly consistent in holding that the breach of a public right, constitutional or statutory provision, without any infringement of personal legal rights, does not confer standing on an individual.[104]And in spite of the many pro-poor changes instituted by Nigeria's new Fundamental Rights Enforcement Procedure Rules of 2009 (2009 FREPRs),[105] and the very the lofty words/ethos of that document,[106] which strongly enjoins the courts to encourage public interest litigation; to greatly liberalize the formerly narrow scope of "*locus standi*" (perhaps even to the point of allowing *actio popularis*); and to engage in expansive and purposeful interpretation in human rights litigation,[107] there has—thus far—been little demonstrable change in terms of the attitude of the Nigerian courts in respect of the specific issue of standing to sue. In any case, the Rules' encouragement to the courts to greatly liberalize *locus standi* rules is contained in its Preamble (and not in its operative provisions). And it is—at best—doubtful whether such a change can be wrought merely through a Preamble; for not even the Preamble to a Constitutional

---

[102] *See* O.C. Okafor & B. Ugochukwu, *Raising Legal Giants: The Agency of the Poor in the Human Rights Jurisprudence of the Nigerian Appellate Courts, 1990-2011*, 15 Afr. Hum. Rts. L. J. 397, 407 (2015); *see also* Ekhator, *supra* note 58, at 68.

[103] *See* Tunde I. Ogowewo, *Wrecking the Law: How Article III of the Constitution of the United States Led to the Discovery of the Standing to Sue in Nigeria*, 26 Brook. J. Int'l L. 527, 529 (2000).

[104] *See, e.g.*, Fatayi-Williams' dictum in Adesanya v. President of Nigeria, 2 NCLR 358, 359 (1981); *see also* Fawehinmi v Akilu & Togun: In re Oduneye, 4 NWLR (Pt 67) 797 (1987).

[105] *See Fundamental Rights Enforcement Procedure Rules of Nigeria, 2009*, http://www.refworld.org/pdfid/54f97e064.pdf (hereinafter "2009 FREPRs") (last visited Mar. 21, 2016); *see also* Abiola Sanni, *Fundamental Rights Enforcement Procedure Rules, 2009 as a Tool for the Enforcement of the African Charter on Human and Peoples' Rights in Nigeria: The Need for Far-reaching Reform*, 11 Afr. Hum. Rts. L. J. 511 (2011); Enyinna Nwauche, *The Nigerian Fundamental Rights (Enforcement Procedure) Rules 2009: A Fitting Response to Problems in the Enforcement of Human Rights in Nigeria*, 10 Afr. Hum. Rts. L. J. 502 (2010).

[106] See Dakas C.J. Dakas, *Human Rights Litigation in Nigeria under the Fundamental Rights (Enforcement Procedure) Rules: Novelties and Perplexities* in Judicial Reform and Transformation in Nigeria 334 (Epiphany Azinge & Dakas C.J. Dakas eds., 2012).

[107] *Id.* at 9–11; *see also* 2009 FREPRs, *supra* note 105, at para. 3(e) of the Preamble.

document such as the FREPRs is, on its own, operative hard law.[108] The Nigerian appellate courts may in fact end up authoritatively interpreting the Constitution and other laws in ways that give effect to the liberal orientation of the FREPRs 2009, and this would—in our view—be a good thing, but whether the judiciary will in fact toe this line remains to be seen. This buttresses the point that Nigeria's standing rules in human rights cases remain very restrictive to the point of impeding the access to justice of pro-poor activist forces in such cases. It is against this background that the significant relative advantage (vis-à-vis many domestic legal systems in the ECOWAS sub-region) conferred by the liberal standing rules applicable at the ECOWAS Court in respect of public interest human rights litigation, becomes palpable. For example, SERAP would have had far more difficulty in getting the Nigerian courts to agree to hear the *SERAP v. Nigeria No.1* case, and other such cases.

Clearly, the fact that the ECOWAS standing to sue regime is much more favorable to pro-poor activists increases by a wide margin the chances of them being able to litigate in favor of the poor either at the ECOWAS Court or even at all. Such increased access to litigation at the ECOWAS Court definitely increases the chance of success at the Court. And success at the Court can (as is shown in Section Six) sometimes translate to real improvements in the social conditions of the poor. As importantly, the case calls attention to the role of a Nigerian human right NGO (part of the assemblage of domestic activist forces with which the chapter is concerned in part) in co-generating and co-enhancing the international human rights outcome that was observed (via feeding the case to the Court, crafting creative arguments, persuading the Court to buy them, etc); a kind of local-to-international kind of trans-judicial communication, and a flipped strategic social constructivism, that is noteworthy. The second is that, like others discussed in Section Four, this case offers us a glimpse of the ways in which a supranational judicial arrangement (the ECOWAS Court) that was co-redesigned in part by activists, was deployed by one among that broad group of activist forces to (partially) jump over or circumvent certain sovereign hurdles (in this case the limitations on standing to sue in human rights cases in the national courts of an ECOWAS Member State which themselves were imposed in exercise of sovereign power). This is one way in which today's state sovereignty norm circulates, operates, reconfigures, is impeded, and generally lives its quotidian life; especially within a regional integration crucible like the ECOWAS arrangement.

A second highly significant way in which the procedural (re)design, orientation, or action of the ECOWAS Court has functioned and can function as a pro-poor

---

[108] Eghosa Ekhator believes that the Preamble of the 2009 FREPRs "abolishes the locus standi rule in Nigeria." *See* Ekhator, *supra* note 58, at 78. I am of the view that it is better to state that the 2009 FREPRs aim to abolish that old locus standi requirement. Baring judicial activism on the subject, the actual abolishment of this strict standing requirement will, it would seem, have to be done via an operative provision of one of the following, the Constitution, a statute, or the FREPRs.

resource in the hands of the domestic activist forces is accepting human rights cases without requiring exhaustion all available domestic remedies.[109] This capability was granted to the Court as a result of its (re)design under the Supplementary Protocol of 2005.[110] This Protocol introduced a new Article 10(d) into its original Protocol of 1991 (as amended). This provision achieves this objective by simply omitting any reference to the prior exhaustion of domestic remedies from its rather short list of pre-conditions for the admissibility of human rights cases that are filed at the Court. As such, the prior exhaustion of domestic remedies is not a condition precedent for litigating a human rights case before this Court.[111] This liberal admissibility regime provides a significantly wide aperture for the poor, and many pro-poor activists, who tend not to have the resources and time to expend exhausting local remedies within the notoriously delay-plagued courts of many ECOWAS Member States such as Nigeria, before they can approach the ECOWAS Court to plead their cases. It has thus made the Court much more accessible to pro-poor litigation than it would otherwise have been. For example, had it not been for the non-inclusion in the 2005 Protocol of a prior exhaustion of domestic remedies requirement, key or trend-setting pro-poor cases such as the two SERAP v. Nigeria cases may have either taken more than a decade to get to the Court, or may never even have made it there at all. As such, it is fair to state that this specific procedural (re)design feature and orientation of the ECOWAS Court, and the judicial action that it has taken in affirming this feature/orientation in a multitude of cases (such as in the *Musa Saidykhan v. Gambia* and in the *Professor Etim Moses Essien v. Gambia* cases),[112] has been highly consequential for various struggles for the advancement of the social conditions of the poor in ECOWAS Member States. The specific kind of local-to-international brainy relay role played by West African activists in at least one of these three cases (via feeding the Court the cases and persuading them to staunchly maintain a liberal admissibility regime) also exemplifies the flipped strategic social constructivism process. Here again, the case affords us a glimpse into the real-life dramatization of a re-articulated but still very much alive norm of state sovereignty as it is re-shaped in a regional integration crucible.

A third process-related way in which the ECOWAS Court has functioned, and can continue to function, as a valuable resource in the hands of the pro-poor domestic activists forces who operate within the ECOWAS sub-region is through its attempts (however modest) to make itself more geographically accessible to the litigant. Located as its seat is in Abuja, the Nigerian capital, the Court is in general

---

[109] *See* Ebobrah, *supra* note 6, at 328.

[110] *See* Supplementary Protocol, *supra* note 34.

[111] *See Musa Saidykhan*, Suit. No. ECW/CCJ/APP/11/07, Rul. No. ECW/CCJ/JUD/08/10. For a critique of this position as "starling and unjustifiable," *see* Amos O. Enabuele, *Sailing against the Tide: Exhaustion of Domestic Remedies and the ECOWAS Court of Justice*, 56 J. AFR. STUD. 268 (2012).

[112] *See* Professor Etim Moses Essien v. Gambia, Rul. No. ECW/CCJ/APP/05/05 (ECOWAS, Mar. 14, 2007).

more difficult and expensive to access for those who live and work outside that city. This is even more so for those who reside outside Nigeria, in other West African countries. While the Court does not have circuits or branches in other countries (and budgetary and other constraints may dictate against this), on a minority of occasions (when it has been desirable, possible, and appropriate) it has moved its seat temporarily to other locations both inside and outside Nigeria. It has done so in order to be closer to the parties and witnesses, as well as to make itself more visible to ordinary West Africans. For example, in the *Hajijatou Mani Koraou* case, the Court sat in Niamey, in the Niger Republic, the country in which the violations occurred, therefore making it considerably easier for the plaintiff/victim, the witnesses, the local community, the general public, and even the government of the Niger Republic, to access its proceedings.[113] Similarly, in the *SERAP v. Nigeria No.1* case, the Court moved its seat temporarily to Ibadan, in the South West region of Nigeria and was thus much closer to Lagos, Nigeria, where SERAP's main offices are located.[114] In the *Madame Ameganvi Isabelle Manavi v. Togo* case, the Court sat in Porto Novo, Benin.[115] And in *Mousa Leo Keita v. Mali* (despite eventually declining jurisdiction on the grounds that no specific violations of human rights were identified by the applicant or could be easily identified by the Court) the Court sat in Bamako, the capital of Mali, where both the Plaintiff and the Defendant resided.[116] These are some examples of the modest number of cases in which the Court took itself to the people, so to speak, thereby facilitating access to the justice in the process. In most of these cases, the move to sit in other cities or countries served the interests of the usually much more disadvantaged and vulnerable poor. There is little evidence thus far of the roles, if any, played by activist forces in getting the Court to make these moves. At best it roughly corresponds with the longstanding calls from elements in West African civil society, as well as others, to the ECOWAS as a whole to transform itself from an ECOWAS of the elite to an ECOWAS of the people.[117] In and of themselves, these changes in location, do not also tell us all that much about the workings of the "new" state sovereignty in the regional integration context of the ECOWAS sub-region. At best they suggest that the Court may be taking a bit more seriously, its supranational status, its authority to penetrate deep into the domestic sphere of ECOWAS Member States without the strong mediation of those states. Additionally, the mild local awareness-raising effect of the

---

[113] *See* Dame Hadijatou Mani Karaou v. The Republic of Niger, Suit No. ECW/CCJ/APP/08/08, Rul. No. ECW/CCJ/JUD/06/08 (ECOWAS, Oct. 27, 2008).

[114] *See* Registered Trustees of Socio-Economic Rights and Accountability Project (SERAP) v. The Federal Republic of Nigeria, Suit No. ECW/CCJ/APP/08/09, Rul. No. ECW/CCJ/JUD/18/12 (Dec. 14, 2012).

[115] *See* Madame Ameganvi Isabelle Manavi et autres v. Togo, Suit No. ECW/CCJ/APP/12/10, Rul. No. ECW/CCJ/JUD/09/11 (CEDEAO, Oct. 7, 2011).

[116] *See* Moussa Leo Keita v. Mali, Suit No. ECW/CCJ/APP/05/06, Rul. No. ECW/CCJ/APP/03/07 (ECOWAS, Mar. 22, 2007).

[117] See MORRIS ODHIAMBO AND RUDY CHITIGA, THE CIVIL SOCIETY GUIDE TO REGIONAL ECONOMIC COMMUNITIES IN AFRICA 6 (1st ed. 2016).

Court's rare decisions to sit in other locations in West Africa does accord with the calls of activists and others for the ECOWAS as a whole to be transformed into an ECOWAS of the people.[118]

A fourth, and rather simple/direct, way in which the ECOWAS Court has played, and can continue to play, the kind of pro-poor role that is under discussion in this section is through its free filing fees policy/rules. According to Article 13 of the Court's Instructions to the Registrar, "the lodgment of all applications, pleadings, briefs of argument and addresses in respect of any issued in 2012, proceedings before the Court is free except for copying and certification which shall attract ... [a small fee] per page." While this does not mean that those who bring cases to the Court are now immune from being charged any fees whatsoever, it does reduce the cost of litigation before the Court to an appreciable extent. This reduction, however modest it might seem, still confers a significant benefit to all-too-many citizens in a developing sub-region such as West Africa. Importantly for our purposes in this chapter, it is clearly a welcome contribution to the resourcing of the pro-poor domestic activists forces which operate within the ECOWAS sub-region. The less the poor and their activist allies pay for bringing cases before the Court, the greater their ability to utilize the court in their struggles to reduce poverty in the different countries of the sub-region. Here again, there is little evidence of the roles, if any, played by activist forces in getting the Court to adopt this approach to court fees. And its free filing fees regime suggests little, if anything, about the character and dramatization of the "new" sovereignty in the ECOWAS sub-region.

Overall, the ways in which all the procedural resources co-produced in many cases by activists but which the Court has made available to them to deploy in their work, have functioned and can function in a pro-poor way have been teased out and highlighted at every stage of the analysis. As such, there is no need to repeat that effort here. Additionally, the ways in which the process of the co-creation (and even eventual deployment within states) of the first two procedural resources discussed in this section shed some light on the figure and dramatization of the "new" sovereignty (that lies in-between Westphalian state sovereignty and the kind of contemporary state sovereignty and is being re-articulated and re-configured in the crucible of regional integration) should also be noted. As importantly, it should also be emphasized that the brainy relay role that these domestic activist forces played in co-producing the first two kinds of procedural resources that the court has in turn made available for them to utilize in their own work deserves to be highlighted. These activists played an important role in feeding the Court with many of the cases in which these pro-poor procedural resources were affirmed, strengthened, otherwise enhanced, and helpfully utilized. They also persuaded the court to affirm their arguments and side with them. It is important to remember that this

118 *Id.*

is the kind of phenomenon that we referred to earlier in this chapter as "flipped strategic social constructivism," a process which—it should be reiterated—refers to the process of the production of alterations in the logics of appropriateness that are prevalent, not really in the society as a whole this time, but chiefly among the judges who compose the bodies such as the ECOWAS Court and the officials who design, establish, run, and exercise general governance over, institutions such as the political organs of the ECOWAS. Additionally, it bears repetition here that an analysis of the uses to which domestic activist forces have in fact put these procedural resources within the domestic spheres of the various ECOWAS Member States is beyond the scope of this chapter.

Section Six: Contributions to the Diminishment/Overcoming of Certain Domestic Socio-Legal Strictures or Obstacles Confronted by Pro-Poor Activist Forces

To what extent has the (re)design, orientation, or action of the ECOWAS Court contributed to the struggle to diminish or overcome certain domestic socio-legal strictures or obstacles confronted by pro-poor domestic activist forces as they seek to utilize the law and the courts to advance their causes and effect progressive social change? The main goal of the analysis conducted in this section is to analytically tease out and highlight a number of the ways in which this has occurred. In the process, the important contributions that domestic activist forces (and their foreign allies) have made to the process through which these contributions made by the Court to their own work were generated will be outlined. This is part of the process of flipped strategic social constructivism that has been extensively discussed in the chapter already, and this generally aligns with the kinds of "value-adding" NGO role that others before us have also recognized in some shape or form.[119] In addition, examples of the real life uses within the domestic realm to which certain pro-poor domestic activist forces have put some of the ECOWAS Court's contributions to the facilitation of their work will be discussed, albeit in brief, as a form of more traditional, more Finnemore/Sikkink-type, strategic social constructivism. Although this last discussion is generally beyond the scope of this chapter, it is being included here, in precis, to make the point that the Court's contributions to the enhancement of the work of pro-poor domestic activist forces does not merely promise to yield fruits for the poor themselves, but has already attained that objective, albeit only to a modest extent as yet.

First, the Court's design, orientation, and action has contributed greatly to the diminishment, and even overcoming, of the justiciability deficit that tends to afflict

---

[119] *See* Alter et al., *supra* note 6; Ekhator, *supra* note 58.

almost all economic and social rights (save property rights) within the domestic legal orders of ECOWAS Member States. For sure, the national constitutions of all ECOWAS Member States contain provisions that recognize ES rights. For example, the Constitutions of all the ECOWAS Member States (save that of Guinea-Bissau) recognize the right to education.[120] Guinea-Bissau is also the only ECOWAS Member State that does not recognize a right to property in its Constitution. Other recognized ES rights contained in the constitutions of almost all ECOWAS Member States include the rights to health,[121] housing,[122] food,[123] etc. However, as essential as the robust enjoyment of these ES rights are for the alleviation and even eradication of poverty (especially in the Global South context in which the residents of these ECOWAS Member States tend to find themselves), research strongly suggests that almost all of these rights are not justiciable *in a constitutional form* in the Constitutions of any of ECOWAS Member State. While a detailed discussion of this issue is well beyond the scope of this chapter, the main arguments (all either fallacious or ultimately unconvincing) that have been made against the justiciability of these ES rights have been: that they are more expensive to implement than CP rights (as if restraint from demolishing poor peoples' home is not a cheap way of implementing their right to housing and as if the fair trial right with its requirement of elaborate and costly court institutions and procedures is cheaper to implement?); that they impose positive obligations on the state to do things for citizens (as if the right to fair trial does not?); that their implementation requires unelected judges to make revenue allocation choices that ought to be made by elected political institutions (as if the same does not apply the adjudication of CP rights such as the right to freedom of assembly the implementation of which almost always necessitates the deployment of policing resources); that judicial adjudication of ES rights violates the separation of powers (as if the same does not apply in certain contexts to CP rights); and that they are simply not human rights at all (an argument that has now been discredited). Yet, these ES rights are fully justiciable within the framework of the African Charter, a treaty that the Court is able to apply in

[120] *See* the relevant provisions in the Constitutions of the various ECOWAS Member States: Benin (section 12), Burkina Faso (sections 18 & 27), Cape Verde (sections 49 & 77), Ivory Coast (section 7), Gambia (sections 30 & 217), Ghana (sections 25 & 38), Guinea (section 21), Liberia (section 6), Mali (section 17), Niger (sections 11 & 19), Nigeria (section 18), Senegal (section 22), Sierra Leone (section 9), and Togo (section 35).

[121] For example, see alphabetically, the relevant provisions in the Constitutions of various ECOWAS Member States: Benin (section 8), Burkina Faso (sections 18 & 26), Cape Verde (section 70), Ivory Coast (section 7), Gambia (section 216(4)), Ghana (sections 30 & 36(10)), Guinea (section 15), Liberia (section 8), Mali (section 17), Niger (sections 11 & 49), Nigeria (section 17), Senegal (section 8), Sierra Leone (section 8(3)), and Togo (section 34).

[122] See the relevant provisions in the Constitutions of some ECOWAS Member States: Burkina Faso (Gambia (section 18), Cape Verde (section 71), Mali (section 17), and Nigeria (section 16(2)).

[123] See the relevant provisions in the Constitutions of some ECOWAS Member States: Gambia (section 216(4)), Ghana (section 36(e)), Nigeria (section 16(2)), and Sierra Leone (section 7).

any human rights case brought against any ECOWAS Member State.[124] And despite its explicitly softer language of progressive realization (which in any case has been bolstered by the concept of "a minimum core obligation" that the Committee on Economic, Social and Cultural Rights applies), the International Covenant on Economic, Social and Cultural Rights, with its fuller complement of ultimately justiciable ES rights provisions, is also applicable to cases brought before the Court against almost any such state.[125] The *SERAP v. Nigeria No.1* case (on the right to a healthy environment, and so on), and the *SERAP v. Nigeria No.2* case (on the right to basic education) aptly illustrate the ways in which the Court's design, orientation, and action allowed a Nigerian human rights NGO to jump over the domestic hurdle presented by the constitutional non-justiciability (at least in general) of almost all ES rights in Nigeria. At the very least, the Court's (re)design, orientation, and action in these cases allowed this activist group to diminish the harsher impact of this domestic norm. Briefly put, Chapter II of the Nigerian Constitution contains a number of non-justiciable economic and social rights framed as "fundamental objectives and directive principles of state policy", which may not be litigated in the local law courts as constitutional rights.[126] They may, however, be litigated as statutory rights, but only to the extent that equivalent provisions have been incorporated in a statute in force in Nigeria.[127] It is important to explain at this point that given that Nigeria is a dualist country (although most ECOWAS Member States are in fact not dualist but monist), this means that international human rights and other treaties do not upon ratification by Nigeria automatically apply within that country's domestic legal order. Such treaties first have to be incorporated into the domestic legal order by a statute. And so, as the African Charter has been incorporated into Nigerian domestic law by such a statute (the African Charter on Human and Peoples' Rights (Enforcement and Ratification) Act, 1983), the ES rights provisions contained in that Treaty are in the result clearly justiciable in the Nigerian courts, though only in their statutory (and not their constitutional) forms. The justiciability of these statutory equivalents of otherwise non-justiciable constitutional provisions was affirmed by a Nigerian court in *Odafe and others v. A.G. Nigeria*.[128] However, as others have also recognized, the fact that these rights lack constitutional-level status does pose a problem and can present a legal hurdle if a

---

[124] *See, e.g.*, C.A. Odinkalu, *Analysis by Paralysis or Paralysis by Analysis? Implementing Economic, Social, and Cultural Rights under the African Charter on Human and Peoples' Rights*, 23 Hum. Rts. Q. 327 (2001).
[125] *See International Covenant on Economic, Social and Cultural Rights*, OHCHR (Dec. 16, 1966) http://www.ohchr.org/EN/ProfessionalInterest/Pages/CESCR.aspx (last visited Mar. 29, 2016).
[126] *See* Dakas C.J. Dakas, *Beyond Officialdom: Fallacies and Hypocrisy in Economic, Social and Cultural Rights Discourse and Implementation in Nigeria*, Afr. Yearbook Int'l L. 29 (2007).
[127] *See* Constitution of Nigeria (1999), §6(6)(c); A.G. Ondo State v. A.G. of Nigeria and others, 9 NWLR (Pt 772) 222 (2002); *see also* Ekhator, *supra* note 58, at 70–71.
[128] Odafe and Others v. A.G. and Others, AHRLR 205, 211 (2004).

defendant in a suit relies on a contrary constitutional provision.[129] This is similar to what happened in *Okogie v. A.G. Lagos State*.[130] Thus, the overall point here is that although ES rights are justiciable in their statutory forms in the Nigerian courts, they are not justiciable in those courts in their constitutional forms. As such, their justiciability at the ECOWAS Court is (barring enforcement issues) a way of doing an end-run around this highly consequential and often frustrating domestic stricture/obstacle; one that has for decades put a huge chill on pro-poor ES rights litigation in countries like Nigeria.

Second, the ECOWAS Court's design, orientation, and action has also allowed domestic actors, including activists forces, to circumvent or jump over the domestic courts in circumstances when their confidence in the latter set of courts was even more depressed than it usually is. For example, in the *CDP v. Burkina Faso* case,[131] the Plaintiffs obviously had much more confidence in the supra-national, and therefore much more triadic, ECOWAS Court regime than they had in the geographically more contiguous and therefore more physically accessible domestic courts in Burkina Faso. They could even be said to have had an elevated level of confidence in the ECOWAS Court around the relevant period. This was to be expected, given the general character of the state in the country at issue,[132] and their status as political and other elements perceived by the then new ruling military-backed regime as supportive of the ousted President, and who had been banned as a result from participating in the transitional elections. This was also the case in each of the three cases against the Gambia that were discussed earlier in this chapter, i.e. *Deyda Hydara Jr. v. Gambia*,[133] *Musa Saidykhan v. Gambia*,[134] and *Ebrima Manneh v. Gambia*.[135] In each of these cases, the prevalent social conditions combined with the legal regime in the country to constitute a problematic socio-legal stricture/obstacle for the concerned activist journalists and/or human rights groups that approaching the ECOWAS Court helped diminish or overcome.

Third, it is also important to note in this particular context the way in which the much more liberal and therefore much better "living" law within the ECOWAS Court regime on standing to sue. It has allowed certain domestic activist forces from countries such as Nigeria to overcome, or at least diminish the impact of the much more restricted standing rules which apply within their national legal

---

[129] *See, e.g.,* Amos O. Enabuele & Anthony O. Ewere, *Can the Economic Community of West African States Community Court of Justice Enforce the African Charter Replicas of the Non-Justiciable Chapter II Human Rights Provisions of the Nigerian Constitution against Nigeria?*, 1 INT'L HUM. RTS. L. REV. 312 (2012).

[130] 2 NCLR 337, at 350 (1981); *see* Ekhator, *supra* note 58, at 71.

[131] Congres pour la Democratie et le Progres (CDP), Suit No. ECW/CCJ/APP/19/15, Rul. No. ECW/CCJ/JUG/16/15.

[132] *See* Daniel Eizenga, *Political Uncertainty in Burkina Faso, in* DEMOCRATIC CONTESTATION ON THE MARGINS: REGIMES IN SMALL AFRICAN STATES 74 (Claire Metelits & Stephanie Matti eds., 2015).

[133] Deyda Hydara Jr. et al., Suit No. ECW/CCJ/APP/30/11.

[134] Musa Saidykyam, Suit No. ECW/CCJ/APP/11/07, Rul. No. ECW/CCJ/JUD/08/10.

[135] Chief Ebrima Manneh, Suit No ECW/CCJ/APP/04/07, Rul. No ECW/CCJ/JUD/03/08.

regimes. Since much has already been said on this in Section Five, there is little need to elaborate on this point here. Suffice it to add that the significance of the Court's strong judicial orientation and action in favor of very liberal standing rules for human rights NGOs is increased even more when it is realized that the ena-bling treaty in this regard, i.e. the 2005 Protocol, does not even mention NGOs or civil society actors at all in the relevant provisions (i.e. the new section 10(d)) and, as such, does not explicitly confer standing to sue on these groups. Such standing to sue was in reality introduced by the Court through its strongly progressive and pro-poor interpretive praxis.

It bears reiteration at this juncture that the Court's contributions to: the diminishment or overcoming of ES rights justiciability hurdle within states such as Nigeria; the circumvention of domestic courts in which activists could not be expected to have much confidence given the circumstances. The diminishment or overcoming of the standing to sue hurdle that exists in certain ECOWAS Member States is strongly pro-poor in its presumed intent, tenor, and effect. Without these contributions, pro-poor human rights litigation before the Court would have been at best a hugely more difficult exercise, and would have had little chance of helping to improve the social conditions of the poor in West Africa. And, at worst, it would have been an impracticable and famished undertaking. Without standing to sue, how could pro-poor domestic activist forces approach the Court? Without being able to jump over the justiciability hurdle in domestic ES rights litigation by approaching the ECOWAS Court, how can pro-poor activists utilize the spe-cial and value-adding pressure points afforded by successful litigation in this area? And without the ECOWAS Court allowing them to circumvent domestic courts in which they properly had almost no confidence, to which judicial body (with binding legal force and therefore more power to exert political pressure) could the Plaintiffs in the *CDP* case have as readily turned?[136]

Also, noteworthy here is the fact that that the process of the co-creation (and even eventual deployment within states) of the contributions made by the ECOWAS Court to the ability of activists to diminish or overcome certain do-mestic hurdles or obstacles. This also sheds some light on the ways in which the dramas of the re-articulation and re-configuration of Westphalian state sover-eignty (within the crucible of regional integration) into some kind of 'new sover-eignty' that lies somewhere in-between the polar positions of that more established sovereignty praxis and current illusions about the death of state sovereignty, is being played out. The diminishment or overcoming of the ES rights justiciability hurdle within states like Nigeria, the circumvention of domestic courts in which

---

[136] The plaintiffs in this case could, perhaps, have of course turned to the African Court of Human and Peoples' Rights, since Burkina Faso has made the Declaration allowing NGOs from that country to approach this latter court, but the main plaintiffs were political parties who most likely would not be properly seen as NGOs. *See African Court of Human and Peoples' Rights*, Afr. Commission on Hum. & People's Rts., https://www.achpr.org/afchpr/ (last visited Mar. 29, 2016).

activists could not be expected to have much confidence given the circumstances, and the diminishment or overcoming of the standing to sue hurdle that exists in certain ECOWAS Member States, all exemplify the dramatization of judicial supra-nationality in West Africa in a context in which state sovereignty is nevertheless very much alive and well.

As significantly, as we have seen in the last two sections, domestic activist forces and their allies have, to a significant extent (albeit not always), functioned in a kind of "virtual alliance" with the ECOWAS Court, as brainy relays, in helping to produce these and other such phenomena.[137] These domestic and foreign activist forces have, among others, included, among others, the Nigerian public interest lawyer, Femi Falana; SERAP, Lagos; the Center for Democracy and Development, Abuja; the Centre for the Defense of Human Rights and Democracy, Benin; the Media Foundation for West Africa, Accra; Amnesty International, U.K.; the Open Society Initiative for West Africa, Dakar; and the now defunct INTERIGHTS, London. Other activist lawyers, journalists, and so on have also brought matters before, or worked in virtual alliance with, the ECOWAS Court. And many of these activist forces have been there from the very beginning of the court's international human rights career. For these activists did do a lot of helpful work—in virtual alliance with the court itself—toward persuading an admittedly sympathetic group of ECOWAS bureaucrats, as well as a reasonably amenable set of ECOWAS political organs, to confer human rights jurisdiction on the Court.[138] As Alter, et al explain, NGOs and other civil society actors "lobbied hard for a human rights jurisdiction" to be conferred on the Court, in addition to its function in economic, regional integration-related disputes.[139] Whether or not there was actual coordination between every actor involved, the point here is that the work that these activist forces did supplemented and complemented the work done by the ECOWAS judges themselves. And this total effort, this seed that was sown, met a reasonably fertile international bureaucratic and domestic political soil. Additionally, as was demonstrated earlier in this chapter, once the Court became functional, these domestic activist forces have, among other things, helped feed the Court with many of its most important cases. They have also helped persuade the Court to take a very liberal approach to the issue of standing to sue in human rights causes, one that heavily favored civil society actors such as NGOs and public interest lawyers. And they were able to persuade the Court to do so even though the 2005 Supplementary Protocol that authorizes human rights litigation before the Court is in this respect not quite as liberal on face value. Overall, it is fair to say that these activist forces

---

[137] See Okafor, *supra* note 45.

[138] See Alter et al., *supra* note 6, at 744; Hisene Donli, Paper Presented at a Workshop of the West African Human Rights Forum, Bamako, Mali: *The Law Practice and Procedure of the Community Court of Justice: Meaning and Implication*, at 3 (Dec. 7–9, 2006).

[139] See Alter et al., *supra* note 6, at 744.

have been something like the life-line of the Court. As the Chief Registrar of the Court has himself put it:

> The Civil Society has a crucial role to play in ensuring the survival of a Regional Court. As stakeholders, the Civil Society has a duty to intervene when the pathway to international justice is threatened, or the survival of the Court itself is at stake. The experience of [the] ECOWAS Court of Justice has shown that the Civil Society has been fully engaged in the affairs of the Court. In 2004, Civil Society groups played an active role in the amendment of the Protocol of the Court to grant access to individuals. Again in 2009, Civil Society intervened, when a Member State attempted to amend the Protocol of the Court in order to introduce mandatory provisions for the exhaustion of local remedies.[140]

This is the kind of phenomenon that we referred to at several points in this chapter as "flip strategic social constructivism," the local-to-international, local activist-to-ECOWAS Court, trans-judicial communication that has often resulted in alterations within the court and other ECOWAS bodies in the logic of appropriateness regarding the design, orientation, and action of the court.

In addition to this kind of role, it should be noted that domestic activist forces and their allies have, acting as brainy relays, also helped mobilize the Court's decisions (as resources) within certain ECOWAS Member States in order to catalyze and guide public debate, and shape public and governmental attitudes alike.[141] However, a discussion of this activist-facilitated international-to-local trans-judicial communication, which is more closely in keeping with the core of Finnemore and Sikkink's thesis on strategic social constructivism, lies beyond the scope of the present inquiry. Suffice it to note that, as we will show elsewhere, the Court's contributions to the enhancement of the work of pro-poor domestic activist forces does not merely lie at the point of promise, but has—however modestly—yielded some fruit already for the poor themselves.

Section Seven: Gaps in the Court's "Pro-Poor Activist" Design, Orientation, Action, and Consequence

So far, we have shown the various ways in which the ECOWAS Court has significantly enhanced or can enhance the normative and procedural resources available to pro-poor activist forces in the ECOWAS sub-region. For example, we have

---

[140] *See* Tony Anene-Maidoh, Paper Presented at the Regional Colloquium on the SADC Tribunal, Johannesburg, South Africa: *The Mandate of a Regional Court: Experiences from the ECOWAS Court of Justice* (Mar. 12–13, 2013).
[141] *See* Ekhator, *supra* note 58, at 66, 72.

shown its valuable potential and actual contributions to the struggle to diminish or overcome certain domestic socio-legal strictures or obstacles confronted by these activists. This raises the question what design, orientation, and action gaps or deficiencies, if any, continue to reduce the ability of these activists to utilize the Court more successfully in the service of pro-poor ends? This part considers some of the limitations of litigating in the ECOWAS Court in the service of pro-poor ends.

First, as Enyinna Nwauche has recognized, in the law and practice of the ECOWAS Court, only ECOWAS Member States and its community institutions (such as the ECOWAS Commission or the ECOWAS Parliament) can be sued at this court for alleged human rights violations.[142] This principle is well established in a number of the decisions of the Court, including in the *Peter David v. Ambassador Ralph Uwechue*; *SERAP v. Nigeria No.1*; and *Tandja v. Djibo and another.*[143] As such, the idea and practice of horizontal human rights litigation is totally absent from the legal regime of this Court. One of the things that this means is that individuals cannot be sued at this Court for violating another person's human rights. Although, as Nwauche acknowledges, the Court's decisions in this regard have been well reasoned from a formal legal perspective, we agree with him that this position still reveals an important gap/deficiency in the Court's socio-legal regime.[144] For, as he argues, there are circumstances related to the attainment of integration objectives that may warrant suits at the ECOWAS Court against individual defendants.[145] One such circumstance is the raising of the standards of living of ECOWAS citizens, which cannot be done without adequately protecting the poor from the ravages of rich and powerful individuals in West Africa, including through the important avenue of human rights litigation at the ECOWAS Court. Thus, the complete preclusion of human rights suits at this Court against individuals who are all-too-often almost as powerful as, and may even be more powerful than, ECOWAS States, leaves a significant hole in the repertoire of procedural resources which allow or could allow domestic activist forces to utilize the Court as an integral part of their pro-poor campaigns. This gap is all the more unfortunate given that the domestic legal regimes of some ECOWAS Member States (such as Nigeria) do in fact allow individuals to be sued for committing human rights violations against other persons.[146]

---

[142] *See* Enyinna S. Nwauche, *The ECOWAS Community Court of Justice and the Horizontal Application of Human Rights*, 13 AFR. HUM. RTS. J. 30, 34 (2013) (hereinafter "Horizontal").
[143] *See* Peter David v. Ambassador Ralph Uwechue, Rul. No. ECW/CCJ/RUL/03/10; Mamadou Tandja v. Gen.Salou Djibo & Republic of Niger, Suit No. ECW/CCJ/APP/05/09, Rul. No. ECW/CCJ/JUD/05/10; Registered Trustees of Socio-Economic Rights and Accountability Project (SERAP) v. The Federal Republic of Nigeria, Suit No. ECW/CCJ/APP/08/09, Rul. No. ECW/CCJ/JUD/18/12 para. 71 (Dec. 14, 2012).
[144] See Horizontal, *supra* note 142, at 36.
[145] *Id.*
[146] *See, e.g.*, Abdulhamid v. Akar and another (2006) LPELR-24 at 23.

Similarly, as a result of the Court's admittedly formally well-reasoned decision that only states and community institutions could be sued before it, corporations, including transnational corporations (TNCs), cannot also be sued at the Court. The Court's reasoning in the cases just referred to makes this crystal clear.[147] Given the huge power that such corporations often wield in real life and the trite fact of the many violations they all-too-often commit against residents of the ECOWAS sub-region, however understandable this decision may be from the formal legal standpoint, the socio-legal position it embodies is quite problematic from the perspective of pro-poor activist litigation. This socio-legal position is even more troubling given that a country like Nigeria does allow corporations (including TNCs) to be sued within its domestic legal order for any human rights violations they may be responsible for.[148]

Third, given the wording of the new Article 10(d) of the ECOWAS Court Protocol, it does not explicitly confer a right to groups or communities to litigate human rights causes before the Court. The question that arises here is whether ethnic groups or other communities (such as the Ogoni of Nigeria or the Endorois people of Kenya) can sue at the ECOWAS Court to vindicate their group rights. Such group rights are protected in the African Charter. There are already decisions recognizing such sub-state groups and communities at the African Commission?[149] This question is important given the fact that Article 10(d) confers the right to sue at the ECOWAS Court only to "individuals" (howsoever that term has been interpreted) and because clearly, an individual *qua* individual cannot bring a suit for the redress of a violation of a group/collective right.[150] Of relevance here is the fact that, in *SERAP v. Nigeria No.1*, the Court held that registered human rights NGOs could bring public interest human rights cases before it and do so in their own name, without the need to sue in a representative capacity. Yet, there certainly appears to be a gap in this regard in terms of the explicit wording of the text that confers human rights jurisdiction on the Court; one that would not augur well for the ability of those communities themselves to exercise agency and bring such matters themselves before the ECOWAS Court. This is important as such communities would otherwise have to depend entirely on the goodwill and beneficence of registered human rights NGOs to bring public interest cases that would help

---

[147] *See* Registered Trustees of Socio-Economic Rights and Accountability Project (SERAP) v. The Federal Republic of Nigeria, Suit No. ECW/CCJ/APP/08/09, Rul. No. ECW/CCJ/JUD/18/12, paras. 63–74 (Dec. 14, 2012).

[148] *See, e.g.,* Akwa Savings & Loans Ltd. v. Ime Wilson Udoumana et al., LPELR-8861 (2009) (arising from Nigeria's now revised Fundamental Rights (Enforcement Procedure) Rules, 1979 and which would still be competent under the current 2009 Rules).

[149] *See* Basil Ugochukwu, Opeoluwa Badaru, & Obiora Chinedu Okafor, *Group Rights under the African Charter on Human and Peoples' Rights: Concept, Praxis and Prospects, in* THE AFRICAN REGIONAL HUMAN RIGHTS SYSTEM: 30 YEARS AFTER THE ACHPR AND BEYOND 101 (M. Ssenyongo ed., 2012).

[150] *See, e.g.,* Pinheiro v. Republic of Ghana, Suit No. ECW/CCJ/APP/07/10, Rul. No. ECW/CCJ/JUD/11/12 (ECOWAS, July 6, 2012).

redress the violations of their rights. However, it appears that under the Court's reasoning in the *SERAP v. Nigeria No.1* case, such communities can at least litigate at the Court via the instrumentality of representative causes, i.e. suits in which one or more persons obtain the prior authorization of the relevant community to sue on their behalf. In any case, it must be remembered that although the African Charter does not as well explicitly confer a right on groups/peoples/collectives to bring a communication before the African Commission, the latter body has long interpreted the relevant Article 55 of the African Charter (which only makes reference to "other communications") as entitling such groups and NGOs to do so.[151] This suggests that there might still be room for the Court to fill this hole through its interpretive praxis.

Another important gap/deficiency that has reduced is the ability of activist forces to mobilize effectively following the decisions of the Court in their broader pro-poor struggles within ECOWAS Member States. This is because of the insufficient awareness of the Court's existence and work among the ordinary citizenry of the ECOWAS sub-region,[152] something that has not been helped by the irregularity with which the Court sits (albeit only temporarily) outside its base in Abuja, Nigeria. Here "insufficiency" is not used to imply that little awareness of the Court exists among the population of West Africa. Rather, it denotes a significantly less than optimal situation in that regard. As was discussed in Section Six, while the Court does on occasion sit outside Abuja, it has done so only in a small percentage of cases. The small size of its bench and staff, as well as budgetary constraints, may explain some of this "awareness deficit." However, vastly increasing the level of popular awareness of the existence and work of the Court ought to be a budgetary priority for the Court and the ECOWAS as a whole. For, increased awareness of the existence and value-added of the Court and its work will definitely enhance support for it among the population and lead to the optimization of the ability of domestic activist forces to mobilize state and society alike to implement its human rights decisions; something that will, in many cases, advance pro-poor causes. The fact that the court has not taken steps to ensure that all its decisions are (promptly) published on its website can only have exacerbated this awareness problem and its consequent failure to reap optimally the fruits that will come with greater public awareness of, and access to, its decisions.

There is also an argument that the ECOWAS Court's increasingly consistent demand that all claimants who come before it must adduce evidence of the

---

[151] *See, e.g.*, The Social and Economic Rights Action Centre and another v. Nigeria, Communication No. 155/96 (May 27, 2002), https://www.escr-net.org/caselaw/2006/social-and-economic-rights-action-center-center-economic-and-social-rights-v-nigeria (last visited Mar. 30, 2016) (holding that an NGO was able to bring a communication to the African Commission via Article 55 of the African Charter).

[152] *See* Adewale Banjo, *The ECOWAS Court and the Politics of Access to Justice in West Africa*, 32 AFR. DEV. 69 (2007).

human rights violations that are issue that meets a high standard of proof,[153] can at times mean that the court would not be as friendly and available to pro-poor activists as it ought to be. Given the difficulties often encountered by pro-poor activists in accessing state-held evidence (for example, due to the opacity of all-too-many West African government agencies and operations, the greater ease with which activists and witnesses can be intimidated or even harmed by security forces and other government agents, and the relative lack on the part of pro-poor activists of the often substantial resources required to build up a water-tight case against the government), there is a sense in which this argument is plausible. It must, however, be remembered that there are certain important risks associated with a court—especially an international court that operates in the West African sub-region—requiring a lower standard of proof. For one, the popular legitimacy of any court would become significantly denuded if it con-sistently relies on weak evidence to reach its decisions. And the loss of popular legitimacy could leave it open to an effective backlash from certain (unhappy) ECOWAS states. The resulting situation would be especially risky for a relatively new and therefore fledgling court like the ECOWAS Court. And even more im-portantly, by establishing and conforming to this kind of strict technocratic way of discharging its international judicial functions, the Court aims to insulate itself as much as it possibly can from some of the more common and effective charges against such courts, namely that of a strong and unfair bias in favor of human rights claimants and against ECOWAS Member States. This is re-assuring to ECOWAS Member States which are generally (though clearly not completely) prickly about supranational intrusion into their domestic affairs. Thus, the institution of this "high standard of proof" requirement becomes one way in which the Court has cleverly managed its relationship to the high politics of the ECOWAS regional arrangement and the great political, social, and eco-nomic power relative to it that is projected by ECOWAS Member States. And this, on balance, is a very good thing. For, as we have seen for example from the successful backlash against the SADC Tribunal and other African international courts, and the unsuccessful Gambian-led threat to weaken the ECOWAS Court[154] an international court (especially one such as the ECOWAS Court that must deal intimately with, the generally weaker democracies that constitute the

---

[153] *See* ECOWAS Community Court of Justice, "The Community Court of Justice, ECOWAS: Court Procedure and the Application of Protocols," Abuja, Nigeria, 2014, at 2–3; Registered Trustees of Socio-Economic Rights and Accountability Project (SERAP) v. The Federal Republic of Nigeria, ECW/CCJ/APP/12/70 & ECW/CCJ/JUD/07/10) (bemoaning the absence of "conclusive evidence of the misman-agement of funds"); Musa Saidykyam, Suit No. ECW/CCJ/APP/11/07, Rul. No. ECW/CCJ/JUD/08/10; Daouda Garba v. The Republic of Benin, Suit No. ECW/CCJ/APP/03/09, Rul. No. ECW/CCJ/JUD/01/10 (Feb. 17, 2010); Alter et al., *supra* note 6, at 766.

[154] *See* Karen J. Alter, James T. Gathii, & Laurence R. Helfer, *Backlash against International Courts in West, East and Southern Africa: Causes and Consequences*, DUKE L. SCH. PUBLIC L. & LEGAL THEORY SERIES NO. 2015–19 (2015).

ECOWAS sub-regional grouping, and yet survive), must delicately and carefully manage its relationship to high politics and power.

Lastly, while issues relating to the implementation of the ECOWAS Court's decisions are not within the scope of this chapter, it is important to note that there is a well-acknowledged compliance gap that exists in the ECOWAS Court's socio-legal regime. This can and does hinder the efforts of pro-poor activist forces to utilize the Court effectively in their effort to achieve domestic social change, and will thus also impede—to an extent—the utility of the Court as a resource in the minds/ hands of these activists. Given that this issue falls outside the boundaries of the inquiry in this chapter, it will suffice to simply note this point.

Section Eight: Conclusion

In conclusion, the overarching question explored in this chapter is the extent to which the (re)design, orientation, and action of the ECOWAS Court promises to function, and/or has in fact functioned, as a resource for local pro-poor activists than as an instrument in the hands of anti-poor forces. Put differently, the main question here is to what extent has the ECOWAS Court been normatively and procedurally equipping or "arming" domestic activist forces in West Africa (and their foreign allies), and to what extent have these activists co-created and co-enhanced the very norms and procedures with which they have been armed? As such, in the course of exploring the question of the extent to which the Court has functioned as a valuable resource for pro-poor activists, an analysis is simultaneously conducted regarding the roles played by these activists in support of this Court's efforts to function in aid of their campaigns and struggles. These efforts have been as morally motivated as they have been self-interested (at least in the sense of being designed to enhance their own activist leverage and levels of success in local struggles to diminish or overcome certain sovereign hurdles and help produce their visions of pro-poor social change).

The chapter argues that the ECOWAS Court has indeed served as a valuable normative and procedural resource to many of the domestic activist forces who seek to effect pro-poor social change in the ECOWAS sub-region. The Court has also contributed in as significant a measure to the specific efforts of many of these activists to diminish/overcome certain sovereign hurdles that reduce their ability to litigate effectively in the interest of the poor. This chapter contributes to the themes of this book by showing that the process through which the Court came to provide these resources and make certain contributions to the facilitation of the work of these activists, was itself co-authored or influenced in part by domestic and other activist forces themselves, acting as brainy relays. This process is theorized in this chapter as a kind of local-to-international trans-judicial communication, one that was styled "flipped strategic social constructivism." In addition, the chapter points out that some evidence of the existence of the more traditional, more international-to-local, kind of trans-judicial communication was also deciphered. This was revealed by an analysis of the engagement of these same set of activist forces with the ECOWAS Court's (re)design, orientation, and action, as they sought to deploy these as resources in their domestic social struggles. The chapter also demonstrates that, as significantly useful to pro-poor activist struggles as the Court has been, in terms of its valuable normative and procedural resourcing of domestic activists and its contributions to their effective circumvention of certain sovereign hurdles, significant gaps still exist in this pro-poor repertoire of resources and contributions; deficiencies that continue to reduce the ability of pro-poor activists to optimize their potential to utilize the Court as a resource in their efforts to improve the social conditions of the poor. Overall, however, while it is clearly not yet time to exclaim "uhuru!," and much remains to be done to build up the ECOWAS Court to a point where it can optimize its promise as a resource in the minds/hands of pro-poor activist forces, the promise of the Court in this regard is even now quite palpable.

4

Towards an Analyses of the Mega-Political Jurisprudence of the ECOWAS Community Court of Justice

*Olabisi D. Akinkugbe**

Section One: Introduction

Since the revision of the Economic Community of West African States (ECOWAS) Community Court of Justice Protocol in 2005, cases involving actual or imminent violation of human rights, good governance, and democracy in the region have dominated the Court's docket. Significant academic research has focused on the question whether the ECOWAS Community Court of Justice (ECOWAS Court) has been transformed into a regional human rights court after the order of the European Court of Human Rights or whether the amendment was a mere expansion of the Court's jurisdiction.[1]

The judicialization of mega-political disputes before the ECOWAS Court is understudied. The ECOWAS Court lacks express mandate to adjudicate over political disputes. Despite this limitation, the Court has been innovative in assuming jurisdiction over mega-political disputes where they are intertwined with potential or actual human rights violation. The *Ugokwe* doctrine, enunciated in the case of *Dr. Jerry Ugokwe v. The Federal Republic of Nigeria and Dr. Christian Okeke,*

* An earlier version of this paper was presented at the Africa's International Courts' Authors' Workshop, Loyola University Chicago School of Law, USA: *National Impact and Enforcement of Decisions of Africa's International Courts and African Charter Norms* (April 22–23, 2016). The author acknowledges the gracious support of the Social Sciences and Humanities Research Council of Canada (SSHRC).
[1] *See generally* Karen J. Alter, Laurence R. Helfer, & Jacqueline McAllister, *A New International Human Rights Court for West Africa: The ECOWAS Community Court of Justice*, 108 Am. J. Int'l L. 737 (2013); Karen J. Alter, James T. Gathii, & Laurence R. Helfer, *Backlash Against International Courts in West, East and Southern Africa: Causes and Consequences*, 27 European J. Int'l 293–328 (2016); Horace S. Adjolohoun, *The ECOWAS Court as a Human Rights Promoter? Assessing Five Years' Impact of the Koraou Slavery Judgment*, 31 Neth. Quar. Hum. Rts. 342–71 (2013); Sotonye Godwin-Hart, *Integrating Trade and Human Rights in West Africa: An Analysis of the ECOWAS Experience*, 32 Windsor Rev. Legal & Soc. Issues 57–90 (2012); Solomon T. Ebobrah, *Critical Issues in the Human Rights Mandate of the ECOWAS Court of Justice*, 54 J. Afr. L. 1, 1–25 (2010).

Olabisi D. Akinkugbe, *Towards an Analyses of the Mega-Political Jurisprudence of the ECOWAS Community Court of Justice* In: *The Performance of Africa's International Courts.* Edited by: James Thuo Gathii, Oxford University Press (2020).

provides the precedential "cause of action" for the judicialization of mega-political disputes before the ECOWAS Community Court.[2]

Since the ECOWAS Court articulated the *Ugokwe* doctrine, there has been a rise in the judicialization of mega-political disputes before the Court. Disguised in the language of alleged human rights violation over which the Court has express jurisdiction, the substantive mega-political disputes arise from electoral processes of ECOWAS Member States. The actors that institute these disputes vary. They include individuals, non-governmental organizations (NGOs), political parties, or dissident opposition members.

Mega-political jurisprudence from the ECOWAS Court are unique. Unlike the traditional scholarship that measures effectiveness based on compliance with the decisions of the courts,[3] I contend that the significance of the mega-political disputes judicialized before the ECOWAS Court derives from the instrumental objectives of the litigants. By incorporating the social, political, and economic contexts that gave rise to the disputes, the chapter illuminates the judicialization of mega-political disputes in ways that are not wedded to the traditional analyses of the functions of regional economic courts.

Mega-political disputes refer to high profile cases that arise from national electoral processes and judicial monitoring of electoral procedures. They also include cases relating to good governance and the rule of law, constitutional and electoral law amendments, and regime changes.[4] The common thread between these cases is the level of socio-political attention that they generate at the national level, either through media publications, preliminary contestations before national courts, the national profile of wealthy political elites involved in the dispute or the potential impact of the outcome for the Member State involved. The judicialization of mega-political disputes before ECOWAS Court therefore refers to the instances where the Court is invited to decide on watershed political questions, despite the lack of express jurisdiction. The findings of this chapter on the ECOWAS Court coincide with those in James Gathii's chapter (Chapter 1) in this book on the election cases brought to the East African Legislative Assembly.

In Section Two, I examine the traditional concepts of compliance and effectiveness. In their traditional and mainstream understandings, these concepts are limiting and narrow for illuminating the ECOWAS Court's mega-political jurisprudence. In turn, I contend that by focusing on the motivations of the litigants and the strategic purposes that inform the mega-political disputes, we broaden

---

[2] Discussed in Section Four, "Litigating Mega-Political Disputes before the ECOWAS Community Court".

[3] For an analysis of the differences in these concepts, although in the international environmental law context, *see* Kal Raustiala, *Compliance & Effectiveness in International Regulatory Cooperation*, 32 CASE. W. RES. J. INT'L L. 387–440, 391–99 (2000).

[4] *See* Ran Hirschl, *The Judicialization of Politics, in* THE OXFORD HANDBOOK OF POLITICAL SCIENCE 254, 257 (Robert E. Goodin ed., 2011).

the analyses of these political cases and capture the peculiar social, economic, and political contexts from which the disputes emerge to produce new analysis of the impact of these disputes. In other words, while compliance with judicial decisions is an important aspect of assessing the effectiveness of courts, it should not be the only yardstick as Gathii argues in the Introduction to this book. In Section Three, I examine the ECOWAS "Democracy and Good Governance Protocol" and argue that the Protocol provides an important additional lever for the judicialization of mega-political disputes before the ECOWAS Community Court. Section Four focuses on the empirical analyses of six mega-political disputes from Francophone and Anglophone West African States. To understand the motivations of the actors, the analyses situate the disputes in the national contestations that gave rise to them. In Section Five which concludes this chapter, I reflect on the ECOWAS Court as an alternative forum for opposition or dissident politicians and NGOs to mobilize pressure on national governments. In this context, they access the Court not necessarily for the pursuit of substantive justice, but other strategies. The nuanced and underlying point is that in mega-political disputes, the success of the challenges has been the exception rather than the norm.

Section Two: The Mega-Political Jurisprudence of the ECOWAS Court in Context

Mega-political cases represent a fast-growing aspect of the "trade-plus regimes" in the ECOWAS Court.[5] The role of national, regional, or international courts can be studied from a variety of perspectives that include: law, politics, and sociology.[6] Within each of these fields are also sub-divisions of approaches that one can adopt to illuminate different questions about the functions of courts.[7] Generally speaking, the dominant approach to the study of courts derives from the legal formalist school of thought. The majority of legal and political science "scholarship tends to view [sub-regional courts] in predetermined categories, for example, as transplanted institutions that resemble their national counterparts or other [sub-regional courts], or on the basis of an abstracted hypothesis of institutional behavior or institutional design."[8]

---

[5] See JAMES THUO GATHII, AFRICAN REGIONAL TRADE AGREEMENTS AS FLEXIBLE LEGAL REGIMES (2011).

[6] See Karen J. Alter, Laurence R. Helfer, & Mikael Rask Madsen, Introduction: Why Study International Court Authority? 12 (iCourts Working Paper Series, No. 112 1, 2017), reprinted in INTERNATIONAL COURT AUTHORITY (2018).

[7] MARGARET KECK & KATHRYN SIKKINK, ACTIVISTS BEYOND BORDERS: ADVOCACY NETWORKS IN INTERNATIONAL POLITICS (1998).

[8] Mikael Madsen, Towards a Sociology of International Courts, (iCourts Online Working Paper Series, No. 1, at 7, 2013), reprinted in OXFORD HANDBOOK OF INTERNATIONAL ADJUDICATION (Karen Alter et al. eds., 2014), https://ssrn.com/abstract=2339903.

A legal formalist approach[9] to the study of the ECOWAS Court's mega-political jurisprudence is limiting as it will not capture the motivations and strategies of the actors that instrumentalize the Court. In its different iterations,[10] legal formalists investigate how the decisions of courts are effective, either based on compliance, or their impact or influence on the behaviour of states.[11] An over-emphasis on the causality of compliance and effectiveness "undermines the effectiveness of legal strategies, or how noncompliance can itself be part of a successful regulatory strategy."[12]

Adopting a compliance-centric, effectiveness-oriented, or implementation-focused approach in analyzing the ECOWAS Court's mega-political jurisprudence would only lead to the reproduction of a failure narrative. Such an approach will also not capture the complex historical and contemporary socio-political contexts, domestic politics, and power contestations in the national realm from which these disputes arise. This is the approach adopted by all the chapters in this book.[13] Notably, Solomon Ebobrah and Victor Lando (Chapter 5) come to very similar conclusions in their chapter in this book.

Sub-regional courts in Africa are *reflective* of and embedded in the socio-political contestations of their Member States.[14] Understanding the mega-political disputes therefore require incorporating their peculiar historical, socio-political, and contemporary contexts in the study of the cases.[15] The mega-political decisions of the ECOWAS Court generate varying impacts, mirror different strategies, and reflect a diverse range of strategies deployed by the litigants.[16] To study it in context, the framework of inquiry should be broad enough to illuminate the motivations of the actors before the ECOWAS Court from both the front-end and back-end points.

---

[9] That is, an assessment of the role of a court by the measure of compliance with its decisions.

[10] *See* Alter et al., *supra* note 6.

[11] *See* YUVAL SHANY, ASSESSING THE EFFECTIVENESS OF INTERNATIONAL COURTS (2014).

[12] *See* Kal Raustiala, *Compliance & Effectiveness in International Regulatory Cooperation*, 323 CASE W. RES. J. INT'L L. 387, 412 (2000).

[13] *See* James Thuo Gathii, *Introduction*, *in* THE PERFORMANCE OF AFRICA'S INTERNATIONAL COURTS (2020) ("[A]s many of the chapters in this book show both compliance and effectiveness do not adequately account for the types of impact of Africa's international courts ... this book argues and shows that these courts have broader impacts beyond those that the measures of compliance and effectiveness focus on").

[14] *See* Gathii, *supra* note 13; Mikael R. Madsen, Explaining the Power of International Courts in Their Context: From Legitimacy to Legitimization, *in* RSCAS POLICY PAPER: COURTS, SOCIAL CHANGE AND JUDICIAL INDEPENDENCE 7, 23 (2012).

[15] *See* Akinkugbe D. Olabisi, *Revisiting the Economic Community of West African States: A Socio-Legal Analysis*, (Dec. 20, 2017), https://ssrn.com/abstract=3354070 (forthcoming in print, Routledge Research in International Economic Law series, 2021),

[16] This approach is similar to the work of "interpretive sociology" whose task is "to link habits and motives to action, that is to make action intelligible by corresponding action to the agents in terms of specific form of 'methodological individualism.'" *See* Madsen, *supra* note 8, at 8; *see also* S. Hewa, *The Genesis of Max Weber's "Verstehende Soziologie"*, 31 ACTA SOCIOLOGICA 143 (1988).

A similar, but broader analysis that "assesses how audiences [before international courts] respond to the institutions [rulings]" is the subject of an edited volume by Karen J. Alter, Laurence R. Helfer, and Mikael Rask Madsen.[17] They argue that "the binary of compliance or noncompliance is too rigid a measure of [International Court's] de facto authority."[18] The authors distinguish between "de jure" and "de facto" authority of the international courts while they develop "a five-level metric" that corresponds to different practices and of audiences and the authority of international courts.[19] To the extent that Alter et al.'s framework measures the authority of the international courts based on the practices of key audiences before varying international courts, contending that a court's formal legal powers or its legal rulings cannot be the sole measurement of its authority, there is an overlap conceptually with the analysis in this chapter.[20]

Yet, the focus on the case study of the mega-political jurisprudence of the ECOWAS Court and the analyses of the Court as an alternative forum for the mobilization of opposition politics in the West-African sub-region signifies the originality and contribution of this chapter in extending the boundaries of the scholarship of these courts. The empirical analysis of the mega-political cases in Section Four focuses on the practices, strategies, and motivations of the actors by teasing out their interactions with the sub-regional courts based primarily on the national disputes that gave rise to them.[21] It does not extend to the institutional characteristics, legitimacy, authority, or nature of international courts broadly conceived.[22]

Focusing on selected Francophone and Anglophone election disputes, I explore other unique ways that the political cases before the ECOWAS Court are utilized in contestations arising from the conduct of elections in Member States. While many of the litigants hope to emerge victorious in their claims, they are also aware that implementing the decisions is a challenge. Hence, the importance of the mega-political decisions, will not be found in the black letter of the law. Rather, their value lies in how they are leveraged upon by the litigants in the national context.[23]

---

[17] See Alter et al., supra note 6, at 12.

[18] They argue that most internal courts "possess de facto authority that is partial, variable, and highly dependent on a range of different audiences and contexts." Alter et al., supra note 6, at 5, 16.

[19] The categories of authority are: "no authority"; "narrow authority"; "intermediate authority"; extensive authority; and "popular authority." See Alter et al., supra note 6, at 5.

[20] Alter et al., supra note 6, at 19.

[21] A von Bogdandy & I Venzke, On the Functions of International Courts: An Appraisal in Light of Their Burgeoning Public Authority, 26 LEIDEN J. INT'L L. 49 (2013). See also the very influential work of Y. DEZALAY & B. G. GARTH, DEALING IN VIRTUE. INTERNATIONAL COMMERCIAL ARBITRATION AND THE CONSTRUCTION OF A TRANSNATIONAL LEGAL ORDER (1996).

[22] See generally JOSEPH RAZ, THE AUTHORITY OF LAW: ESSAYS ON LAW AND MORALITY (2009); JUTTA BRUNNÉE & STEPHEN J. TROOPE, LEGITIMACY AND LEGALITY IN INTERNATIONAL LAW: AN INTERACTIONAL ACCOUNT (2010); L. Hooghe, J. Bezuijen, S. Derderyan, & E. Coman, The Rise of Supranational Courts in International Organizations (2014) (unpublished manuscript).

[23] See Karen J. Alter, Laurence R. Helfer, & Mikael Rask Madsen, How Context Shapes the Authority of International Courts, 79 L. & CONTEMP. PROB. 1 (2016).

In this regard, even where they lose the action, some of the litigants have expressed satisfaction in the deterrent capability of such decisions for the future actions of the concerned Member State as exemplified by the *Hope Democratic Party's Case.*

Section Three: The ECOWAS Protocol on Democracy and Good Governance

The aims of this section are two-fold. First, I synthesize relevant provisions of the Democracy and Good Governance Protocol (Democracy Protocol),[24] and second, I link the regionalization of democracy and good governance in the ECOWAS Community to broader events in the sub-regional[25] and national politics of the Member States. The contention is that the rise of mega-political disputes before the ECOWAS Court is in part a reflection of the regional move towards consolidating democratic governance, rule of law, and constitutional democracy in ECOWAS Member States. Litigants before the ECOWAS Court therefore view the Court as an important alternative forum to pursue their mega-political claims. In this regard, the Democracy Protocol provides an important additional lever for the prosecution of mega-political disputes before the ECOWAS Court.

Adopted in 2001, the Democracy Protocol enshrines some of the "best practices" that are expected in a democratic regime. Article 1 mandates all ECOWAS Member States to respect the separation of powers, parliamentary immunity, the independence of the judiciary, freedom of the bar, and accession of power through free, fair, and transparent elections among others. It simultaneously prohibits the formation of political parties along ethnic, religious, or racial considerations; cautions against discrimination in the political process on grounds of ethnicity,

---

[24] *See* ECOWAS Protocol on "Democracy and Good Governance, Supplementary to the Protocol relating to the Mechanism for Conflict Prevention, Management, Resolution, Peacekeeping and Security," Protocol A/SP1/12/01, http://www.internationaldemocracywatch.org/attachments/350_ECOWAS%20 Protocol%20on%20Democracy%20and%20Good%20Governance.pdf   (hereinafter   "Democracy Protocol"). *See generally* Said Adejumobi, *Democracy and Good Governance in Africa: Theoretical and Methodological Issues, in* Breaking Barriers, Creating New Hopes: Democracy, Civil Society and Good Governance in Africa (A. Bujra & S. Adejumobi eds., 2002).

[25] One of the emerging areas where ECOWAS's role is growing is that championed by the ECOWAS Network of Electoral Commissions. Although there is no direct link between the cases that were instituted before the ECOWAS Court and this Commission, as yet the evolving role is examined as part of the wide socio-political context in which ECOWAS is embedded and which has contributed to the rise of the prosecution of mega-political cases before the ECOWAS Court. It is representative of the type of informal norms within the community with significant potential for formality in the future. To advance the Democracy Protocol and ECOWAS' oversight responsibilities for the electoral processes in the West African region, the ECOWAS Network of Electoral Commissions (ECONEC) support national electoral bodies with a view to ensuring the consolidation of democracy and the rule of law as part of the wider involvement of ECOWAS in contemporary political relations of the Member States. *See ECOWAS Commission to Strengthen Regional Electoral Bodies on Democracy*, Elombah.com (July 8, 2017), https://elombah.com/index.php/politics/18263-ecowas-commission-to-strengthen-regional-electoral-bodies-on-democracy?lipi=urn%3Ali%3Apage%3Ad_flagship3_feed%3BDjVjHXmwTBe1 EnNMPOu%2FlA%3 D%3D.

religion, or race; while affirming the freedoms of association and press. To the extent that in reality, ethnic or tribal configurations provide the initial basis for the formation of political parties in many African countries, this provision appears utopian.[26] Indeed, based on a practice referred to as zoning, the recruitment of candidates is conducted in the shadow of ethnic, religious, and tribal representation through the rotational system under which ethnic communities take turns in holding political office.[27] Therefore, zoning serves as a mechanism to mitigate marginalization and enhance peaceful rotation of power among the various ethnic groups. For example, with regard to the 2015 Presidential election in Nigeria, ethnicity and religion were identified as one of the main drivers of Nigeria politics.[28]

Section II (Articles 2–10) of the Democracy Protocol is dedicated to elections. Article 2 prohibits any substantial amendment to electoral laws of Member States in the last six months prior to the elections without the consent of a majority of political actors while Paragraph (2) provides that elections shall be organized on the dates or at periods fixed by the Constitution or the electoral laws of the Member State. All ECOWAS Member States are mandated to take appropriate measures to ensure gender equality in elections, participation in the formulation and implementation of government policies. The provision also guards against discrimination against women holding public offices and in the performance of public functions at all levels of governance. Article 3 provides for the independence and neutrality of electoral bodies of the Member States in order to command the confidence of all their political actors. Whereas Article 5 of the Protocol mandates Member States to prepare a voters' list in a transparent and reliable way that builds on the collaboration of the political parties and citizens who may require access to them whenever needed; Article 6 provides that the conduct of elections as well as the announcement of the results shall be done in a transparent manner.

With respect to the settlement of disputes arising from elections, Article 7 requires ECOWAS Member States to make adequate arrangements to hear and dispose all election petitions.[29] Other than the state, the Protocol recognizes the role

---

[26] See B. Salawu & A.O. Hassan, *Ethnic Politics and its Implications for the Survival of Democracy in Nigeria*, 3 J. PUB. ADMIN. & POL'Y RES. 28–33 (2011); *see also* Brandon Kendhammer, *Talking Ethnic but Hearing Multi-ethnic: The People's Democratic Party (PDP) in Nigeria and Durable Multi-Ethnic Parties in the Midst of Violence*, 48 COMMONWEALTH & COMP. POL. 48–71 (2010); Richard Joseph, *Political Parties and Ideology in Nigeria*, 5 REV. AFR. POL. ECON. 78–90 (1978).

[27] Political zoning is a strategy deployed by politicians to address the marginalization of any particular tribe by ensuring power rotation. *See* Babajide Olusoji Ololajulo, *"Eating with One Spoon": Zoning, Power Rotation and Political Corruption in Nigeria*, 17 J. AFR. STUD. 153–69 (2016).

[28] See Udoka Okafor, *Analysis of the Electoral Data in Nigeria's 2015 Presidential Elections*, HUFFINGTON POST (Apr. 14, 2015), https://www.huffingtonpost.com/udoka-okafor/analysis-of-the-electoral-data-in-nigerias-2015-presidential-elections_b_7038154.html (studying "the electoral data from the Nigerian election in order to understand the factors that best shape our electoral realities and our political landscape").

[29] The provisions of Section III (*Election Monitoring and ECOWAS Assistance*) of the Protocol, in particular, Articles 12–18, complement ECOWAS' earlier Protocol relating to the mechanism for conflict prevention, management, resolution, peace-keeping and security. *See id.* at art. 11; *Protocol relating to the Mechanism for Conflict Prevention, Management, Resolution, Peace-Keeping and Security* (1999)

of civil society organizations in election processes, and therefore, requires Member States to engage them in the education and enlightenment of the public.[30] To guard against autocratic or civilian dictatorship, the Protocol encourages the party that loses an election to concede defeat to the candidate that is declared the winner.[31]

Section VII of the Protocol relates to the rule of law, human rights, and good governance.[32] The Protocol acknowledges that "the rule of law involves not only the promulgation of good laws that are in conformity with the provisions on human rights, but also a good judicial system, a good system of administration, and good management of the State apparatus."[33] Through these provisions, ECOWAS Member States commit to the enforcement of the rule of law, human rights, justice, and good governance. Despite the claim to a democratic system of governance, ethos such as the respect for the rule of law, freedom of speech and association, independence of the judiciary and other fundamental principles, democratic regimes have not taken root in many ECOWAS Member States.[34] Hence, the general claim that the states operate democratic regimes has done little substantively to change the embedded historical and political practices that constrain the conduct of free and fair elections while also clamping down on human rights of political dissidents.[35] Udombana Nsogurua aptly describes the quagmire that African states confront when he argues that "[African states] have remained colonial in their adherence to generally anti-democratic and repressive measures and attitudes."[36] The repressive and anti-democratic practices of the ECOWAS Member States, particularly, as it relates to the political oppositions, as well as the perception that they wield some influence over the national judiciary make the ECOWAS Court an attractive alternative in their search for justice. Curiously, the Democracy Protocol offers Member States an avenue to withdraw from the Protocol upon provision of a one-year notice to ECOWAS. Where an ECOWAS Member State abruptly ends democratic governance in the state or in the event of a massive violation of human rights, ECOWAS is empowered to impose sanctions on the erring state.[37]

HTTP://WWW.ZIF-BERLIN.ORG/FILEADMIN/UPLOADS/ANALYSE/DOKUMENTE/ECOWAS_PROTOCOL_CONFLICTPREVENTION.PDF.

[30]   Democracy Protocol, *supra* note 24, at art. 8.
[31]   *Id.* at art. 9.
[32]   *See* Section VII: Rule of Law, Human Rights and Good Governance, *in* Democracy Protocol, *supra* note 24, arts. 32–39.
[33]   Democracy Protocol, *supra* note 24, at art. 33(1).
[34]   *See generally* Paul Collier & Pedro C. Vicente, *Violence, Bribery, and Fraud: The Political Economy of Elections in Sub-Saharan Africa*, 153 PUB. CHOICE 117–47 (2012); *see also* O'Brien Kaaba, *The Challenges of Adjudicating Presidential Election Disputes in Africa: Exploring the Viability of Establishing an African Supranational Elections Tribunal* (June 2015) (LLD thesis, University of South Africa).
[35]   Said Adejumobi, *Elections in Africa: A Fading Shadow of Democracy?*, 21 INT'L POL. SCI. REV. 59–73 (2000). An example of this case analyzed in the ensuing sections of this paper is the *Dasuki v. Federal Republic of Nigeria*, Suit No. ECW/CCJ/APP/01/16.
[36]   See Nsongurua J. Udombana, *Articulating the Right to Democratic Governance in Africa*, 24 MICH. J. INT'L L. 1210, 1215 (2003).
[37]   *Id.* at art. 45(1).

From the foregoing, the foundational democratic ideals enshrined in the Democracy Protocol are in sharp contrast to the historical and contemporary socio-political practices in which ECOWAS Member States are embedded.[38] Many of these states were governed for many years by military administrations or civilian dictators.[39] As such, the Democracy Protocol should not be read in isolation. Nevertheless, the Democracy Protocol serves an important role for the litigants of mega-political disputes. As will be seen from the ensuing analysis of the case-law, litigants in the political disputes before the ECOWAS Court invoke the provisions of the ECOWAS Democracy Protocol as part of the body of legislation in the cases. The disputes emerge out of a larger phenomenon of allegations of fraudulent and rigged elections, intra-party politics, and disregards of electoral finance provisions to mention a few.[40] With the uncertainty in accessing justice in the national courts, litigants have increasingly turned to the ECOWAS Community Court. However, not being conferred with an express mandate to adjudicate over political disputes strictly has its own drawbacks for the litigants. The challenges faced by these litigants with respect to jurisdiction, as well as the innovative ways by which they overcome them will among other issues are discussed in the empirical section that follows.

Section Four: Litigating Mega-Political Disputes before the ECOWAS Court

The mega-political disputes analyzed in this section are drawn from both anglophone and francophone ECOWAS Member States. The disputes were mostly initiated by opposition politicians or parties based on alleged unconstitutional amendments to the election processes; potential or actual violation of human rights in the election process; complete exclusion from participation; or general dissatisfaction with the election results.

Speaking of the unique trajectory of domestic political conflict in the West African sub-region, Abdoulaye Bathily notes that "apart from the Great Lakes region with the genocide in Rwanda, the democratization process has been more turbulent in West Africa than anywhere else on the African continent. In fact, over

---

[38] *See generally* NIC CHEESEMAN, DEMOCRACY IN AFRICA: SUCCESSES, FAILURES, AND STRUGGLES FOR POLITICAL REFORM (2015).

[39] *See Gambia: Two Decades of Fear and Repression: Disband Paramilitary Groups; Investigative Abuses*, HUMAN RIGHTS WATCH (Sept. 17, 2015), https://www.hrw.org/news/2015/09/17/gambia-two-decades-fear-and-repression; *State of Fear: Arbitrary Arrests, Torture, and Killings*, HUMAN RIGHTS WATCH (Sept. 16, 2015), https://www.hrw.org/report/2015/09/16/state-fear/arbitrary-arrests-torture-and-killings.

[40] André Mbata Mangu, *African Civil Society and the Promotion of the African Charter on Democracy, Elections and Governance*, 12 AFR. HUM. RTS. L. J. 348, 350 (2012) (reflecting "on the African Democracy Charter, its significance and also its shortcomings, as well as on the prospects for its implementation and the particular role that civil society organizations can and should play in promoting the values entrenched therein").

the last twenty years, this sub-region has witnessed the longest and bloodiest con-flicts."[41] As such, it is not uncommon for the victorious political party to celebrate the rule of law, while the losers often point to repressive and oppressive conducts; lack of free and fair elections; restriction or outright denial of fundamental human rights to freedom of association as basis upon which they challenge the outcome of the elections. In other instances, a sitting democratic leader may blatantly seek to amend the Constitution to ensure that they remain in office as long as possible.[42] In other cases, a sitting president's refusal to concede defeat to opposition political parties has been the basis for ECOWAS intervention in national politics.[43] These post-election outcomes and associated contestations provide the primary basis for the majority of the mega-political disputes before the ECOWAS Community Court. With waned confidence in the capability of the national courts to deliver justice, opposition parties, and affected individuals are increasingly turning to the ECOWAS Court as an important alternative for the adjudication of many of these disputes.

Dr. Jerry Ugokwe v. The Federal Republic of Nigeria and Dr. Christian Okeke (Ugokwe Doctrine)

The *Dr. Jerry Ugokwe v. The Federal Republic of Nigeria and Dr. Christian Okeke* case was the first mega-political dispute before the ECOWAS Court. The novel issue be-fore the Court was: whether electoral disputes are subject to the legal order applic-able to the ECOWAS Community? In answering this question, the ECOWAS Court articulated the "cause of action" that provides the precedential basis for many of the other mega-political jurisprudence. I describe the principle that emerges from this dispute as the "*Ugokwe* doctrine". The *Ugokwe* doctrine asserts that although the legal texts applicable to ECOWAS Court confer no general or specific power to adjudicate election disputes or matters arising therefrom, in appropriate cases, the Court will assume jurisdiction where the determination of the human rights of the parties are intertwined with mega-political disputes. The *Ugokwe* doctrine sets an important precedent for the circumstances under which election disputes come

---

[41] Abdoulaye Bathily, *Democracy in West Africa: An Appraisal, in* BUILDING PEACE AND DEMOCRACY IN WEST AFRICA 23, 25 (2005).

[42] These attempts have taken various modes as will be seen from the empirical ana-lysis of the cases. Uganda provides the most recent example of this move by a sitting presi-dent. *See* Elias Biryabarema, *Uganda Lawyers Seek to Quash Museveni "President for Life" Law*, REUTERS (Jan. 15, 2008), https://www.reuters.com/article/us-uganda-politics/ugandan-lawyers-seek-to-quash-museveni-president-for-life-law-idUSKBN1F4280.

[43] *See, e.g.,* Dionne Searcey & Jaime Yay Barry, *Yahya Jammeh, Gambian President, Now Refuses to Accept Election Defeat*, N.Y. TIMES (Dec. 9, 2016), https://www.nytimes.com/2016/12/09/world/africa/yahya-jammeh-gambia-rejects-vote-defeat-adama-barrow.html; *Gbagbo Surrender Stalls Over Refusal to Admit Electoral Defeat*, VOA NEWS (Apr. 5, 2011), https://www.voanews.com/africa/gbagbo-surrender-stalls-over-refusal-admit-electoral-defeat.

under the jurisdiction of the ECOWAS Court. The *Ugokwe* doctrine was reinforced in the case of *Congrès pour la Démocratie et le Progrès (CDP) & others v. The State of Burkina Faso.*

This case originated from the elections conducted to the Nigerian Federal House of Representatives in 2003.[44] Following a declaration of the applicant as the winner by the Nigerian Independent National Electoral Commission (INEC), one Dr. Christian Okeke successfully petitioned against the applicant's victory before the Elections Tribunal.[45] Consequently, the applicant's election was annulled. The applicant's also failed on appeal before the Nigerian Court of Appeal.

Before the ECOWAS Court, the applicant alleged an infringement of his right to fair hearing by the Elections Tribunal and the Nigerian Court of Appeal[46] and prayed for a special interim order restraining INEC from invalidating his certificate of attestation; granting the said certificate to another person; and an order preventing the Federal National Assembly from relieving him of his position as an Assembly Member. The applicant also asked the ECOWAS Court to declare as null and void the procedures and the judgment delivered by the Elections Tribunal and by the Court of Appeal.[47] The applicant relied on the combined provisions of Article 7 of the African Charter on Human and Peoples' Rights, the Universal Declaration of Human Rights, Articles 9(4) and 10(d) of the ECOWAS Court Supplementary Protocol, and Article 36 of the Nigerian Constitution. The Federal Republic of Nigeria filed a preliminary objection arguing that the ECOWAS Court lacks the jurisdiction to entertain election disputes; hence, the Nigerian courts are the appropriate forum with jurisdiction to entertain electoral disputes. Dr. Christian Okeke filed an intervener application seeking to be joined as an interested party as he will be affected by the decision of the Court.

The ECOWAS Court raised the following issue: whether electoral disputes are subject to the legal order applicable to the community? The ECOWAS Court held that the legal texts applicable confers no general or specific power to adjudicate on election disputes or matters arising therefrom. Notwithstanding that a dispute has political dimensions, the determination of the other rights of the parties may be referred to the ECOWAS Court.[48]

---

[44] *See* Ugokwe v. Nigeria, No. ECW/CCJ/JUD/03/05, Judgment, (Oct. 7, 2005), https://ihrda.uwazi.io/fr/document/cvcro182pf4zqv6587z4mwjyvi

[45] *See* Okeke v. Independent National Electoral Commission, No. EPT/AN/NA/6/2003.

[46] *See* C. J. Ubanyionwu, *Election Petition Cases and the Right to Fair Trial within a Reasonable Time in Nigeria*, AFR. JOURNALS 111–23 (2012), https://www.ajol.info/index.php/naujilj/article/viewFile/136349/125840.

[47] Ugokwe v. Nigeria, No. ECW/CCJ/APP/02/05, Appeal, para. 14.

[48] Ugokwe v. Nigeria, No. ECW/CCJ/JUD/03/05, Judgment, para. 19 (Oct. 7, 2005); *see* Statute of the International Court of Justice, art. 38(1)(c); *see generally* Andrew Coleman, *The International Court of Justice and Highly Political Matters*, 4 MELBOURNE J. INT'L L 29 (2003); Marcella David, *Passport to Justice: Internationalizing the Political Question Doctrine for Application in the World Court*, 40 HARV. INT'L L J 81 (1999). For the cases: Case Concerning the Military and Paramilitary Activities in and Against Nicaragua (Nicaragua v. United States of America), Merits, Judgement of June 27, 1986; Case Concerning United States Diplomatic and Consular Staff in Tehran (United States of America v. Iran),

Against this premise, the court proceeded to examine whether the fundamental right of the Applicant to fair hearing was infringed in the course of the hearings before the Election Tribunal and the Court of Appeal.[49] The Court affirmed that it has jurisdiction in cases of alleged denial of fair hearing and asked whether "the fact that the Nigerian Courts invalidated the election of the Applicant constitutes a human right violation?"[50] In declining jurisdiction to entertain mega-political disputes and dismissing the suit, the Court noted:

> Appealing against the decision of the National Court of Member States does not form part of the powers of the Court; the distinctive feature of the Community legal order of ECOWAS is that it sets forth a judicial monism of first and last resort in Community law. And, if the obligation to implement the decision of the Community Court of Justice lies with the national courts of Member States, the kind of relationship existing between the Community Court and these national courts of Member States are not of a vertical nature between the Community and the Member States, but demands an integrated Community legal order. The ECOWAS Court of Justice is not a Court of Appeal or a Court of cassation.[51]

Apart from the precedential value of this case, the decision also illustrates the narrow legal authority of the Court.[52] Following a notification of the existence of this case to the Attorney General of Nigeria, he wrote to the Speaker not to allow Dr. Christian Okeke into the House of Representatives until the determination of the case before the ECOWAS Court.[53] Although an isolated case in the context of mega-political disputes, the authority of the Court is growing. Even if the compliance arose from the fact that the matter was sub judice, the fact that Nigeria was the complying state lens further credence to the intermediate authority of the Court. Simultaneously, the case affirms that litigants in mega-political disputes view the ECOWAS Court as a forum for the mobilization of opposition politics.

Judgement of May 24, 1980, ICJ Reports 3; Case Concerning United States Diplomatic and Consular Staff in Tehran (United States of America v. Iran) (Provisional Measures), Order, 1979 ICJ Reports 7.

[49] " ... besides the electoral problem, there are grounds for us to ponder, in a second instance, on the competence of the Court when the Applicant raises the legal plea on right to fair hearing." Ugokwe v. Nigeria, No. ECW/CCJ/JUD/03/05, Judgment, para. 21 (Oct. 7, 2005).

[50] *Id.* at para. 22.

[51] *Id.* at para. 32.

[52] *See generally*, Alter et al., *supra* note 8; Solomon T. Ebobrah, The ECOWAS Community Court of Justice: A Dual Mandate, *in* Alter et al., *supra* note 8, at 82–102.

[53] Ise-Oluwa Ige, *Nigeria: Olujimi Writes Speaker Not to Accept Man into House*, ALLAFRICA (May 23, 2005), http://allafrica.com/stories/200505230916.html; *see also* Christof Hartmann, *Governance Transfer by the Economic Community of West African States* 34 (ECOWAS, SFB-Governance Working Paper Series, No. 47, Collaborative Research Center, 2013) (investigating how and under which conditions regional organizations prescribe and promote standards for (legitimate) governance (institutions) at the national level).

Hope Democratic Party & Alhaji Haruna Yahaya Shaba v. Federal Republic of Nigeria (FRN) & 5 Others

In *Hope Democratic Party & Alhaji Haruna Yahaya Shaba v. Federal Republic of Nigeria (FRN) & 5 Others*, Hope Democratic Party is a registered political party in Nigeria and Alhaji Haruna Yahaya was the party's Vice-Presidential candidate in the February 14, 2015 Nigerian Presidential election.[54] The plaintiffs contended that the conduct of the third and fourth defendants (respectively Dr. Goodluck Jonathan and the People's Democratic Party) in receiving anonymous monetary donations or gifts in excess of the requirements of the Nigerian electoral laws. They also argued that, in the process leading to the Presidential election, the defendants violated their rights to participate freely and equally on a level playing field in government as guaranteed by the Nigerian Constitution and the African Charter on Human and Peoples' Rights.[55] The plaintiffs sought a declaration that the conduct of the third defendant constituted a form of political intimidation, a violation of the laws and rights of the plaintiffs; damages in the sum of US$300 million and confiscation by the Court of the Presidential campaign fund raised by the defendants.[56]

The defendants denied any wrongdoing that limits the freedom of the plaintiffs to participate in the Presidential election or indeed any violation of the laws of the Federal Republic of Nigeria. They argued that the Court should decline jurisdiction to entertain the matter as none of the claims submitted by the plaintiffs came under Article 9 of the Supplementary Protocol of the Court.[57] In addition, they argued that the plaintiffs failed to exhaust local remedies available under Articles 50 and 56(5) of the African Charter on Human and Peoples' Right.[58]

---

[54] Hope Democratic Party & Alhaji Haruna Yahaya Shaba v. Federal Republic of Nigeria, Attorney-General of the Federation and minister of Justice, Dr. Goodluck Jonathan, People's Democratic Party, Independent National Electoral Commission, & Inspector General of Police; Suit No. ECW/CCJ/APP/04/2015; Judgment No: ECW/CCJ/JUD/19/15.

[55] "In Nigeria, the 1999 constitution (as amended) of the Federal Republic of Nigeria specified in section 225 (1–6) conditions and scrutiny of the sources of funds and expenses of political parties. Section 225 (3)(a) and (b) as well as 225 (4) forbid political parties from foreign funding of any kind. Section 226 (1–3) demands annual reports of account from political parties. By extension, the Electoral Act (2010) stipulates the ceiling of expenses by candidates and political parties for specific elective positions. The maximum limits are pegged at: N1,000,000,000 (naira) for presidential candidates, N200,000,000 for governorship candidates, and N40,000,000 and N20,000,000 respectively for Senate and House of Representatives candidates." See Adebowale Olorunmola, Cost of Politics in Nigeria 1, Background Paper, WESTMINSTER FOUNDATION FOR DEMOCRACY.

[56] In particular, they argued that the actions of the defendants have subjected the plaintiffs and their supporters to "unimaginable political intimidation/exclusion, psychological trauma, victimization and humiliation which affected their participation in the … presidential elections, and right to compete in getting their candidates freely elected at that presidential election on equal and level playing grounds." *Id.* at 9.

[57] *Id.* at 11.

[58] *Id.* at 11–12.

To provide some additional context, since Nigeria's return to the Fourth Republic in 1999, it was ruled by the People's Democratic Party (PDP) (the fourth defendant) for the fourteen years that followed until 2015 when an opposition party overwhelmingly defeated the PDP in what may be described as the most consequential election in Nigeria's turbulent political history.[59] Although the Hope Democratic Party was one of the other thirteen opposition political parties that fielded presidential candidates in the 2015 Presidential election, the main opposition party was the All Progressives Congress (APC). The PDP presidential fundraising angered opposition politicians and their parties.[60] Their dissent arose from the fact that while the presidential candidate of the PDP was limited to only Nigerian N1 billion (approximately US$28 million) campaign funds, it raised over N20 billion (approximately US$55 million).[61] The funds raised may have violated the Nigerian Electoral Act 2010 (as amended) as well as Section 38(2) of the Nigerian Companies and Allied Matters Act.[62]

The ECOWAS Court narrowed the issues to three questions.[63] First, whether or not the Court has *in personam* jurisdiction over *all* the defendants? This question was answered in the negative. While the Court has jurisdiction over Nigeria as an ECOWAS Member State and a proper party against whom a claim for the violation of human rights can be instituted, the second–sixth defendants are not subject to its jurisdiction.[64] Also, the Court did not find that the first defendant

---

[59] "For the first time since the inception of Nigeria's fourth republic, Nigerians had a choice. But more than that, their choices expressed in their electoral votes, actually mattered. In this election, Nigerians and the world were able to see genuine electoral accountability and transparency at play in the country's political process." Udoka Okafor, *Analysis of the Electoral Data in Nigeria's 2015 Presidential Elections*, HUFFINGTON POST (June 14, 2015), https://www.huffpost.com/entry/analysis-of-the-electoral-data-in-nigerias-2015-presidential-elections_b_7038154.

[60] *See, e.g.*, Chikodiri Nwangwu & Olihe Adaeze Ononogbu, *Electoral Laws and Monitoring of Campaign Financing during the 2015 Presidential Election in Nigeria*, 17 JAPANESE J. POL. SCI. 614–34; Clifford Ndujihe, Henry Umoru, Dapo Akinrefon, & Levinus Nwabughiogu, *PDP Presidential Fund-Raising: Presidency, APC bicker over N21BN*, VANGUARD (Dec. 22, 2014), https://www.vanguardngr.com/2014/12/pdp-presidential-fund-raising-presidency-apc-bicker-n21bn/; *see also* Olalekan Adetayo, *Govs, Businessmen, Others Donate N21.27BN to Jonathan*, SAHARA REPORTERS (Dec. 21, 2014), http://saharareporters.com/2014/12/21/govs-businessmen-others-donate-n2127bn-jonathan.

[61] The excessive amount of re-election campaign raised by the incumbent was also the subject of various local news media reports. *See, e.g.*, Ben Agande, *Naira Rain at Jonathan's Re-election Fund Raiser*, VANGUARD (Dec. 21, 2014), https://www.vanguardngr.com/2014/12/naira-rain-jonathans-reelection-fund-raiser/; Adetayo, *supra* note 61.

[62] Section 38(2) of the Companies and Allied Matters Act provides that: "A company shall not have or exercise power either directly or indirectly to make a donation or gift of any of its property or funds to a political party or political association or for any political purpose; and if any company, in breach of this subsection makes any donation or gift of its property to a political party or political association, or for any political purpose, the officers in default and any member who voted for the breach shall be jointly and severally liable to refund to the company the sum or value of the donation or gift and in addition, the company and every such officer or member shall be guilty of an offence and liable to a fine equal to the amount or value of the donation or gift." *See* Yusuf Alli, Adebisi Onanuga, & Bisi Oladele, *N21b Donation Raises Legal Issues for PDP, Jonathan*, THE NATION (Dec 24, 2014), http://thenationonlineng.net/n21b-donation-raises-legal-issues-pdp-jonathan/.

[63] *Id.* at 23–24.

[64] *Id.* at 24–29.

had committed any wrong. Hence, it dismissed the action against Nigeria as being "frivolous, speculative and uncertain, and vague and indistinct."[65] Second, whether or not the ECOWAS Court has jurisdiction to entertain a suit filed by an individual against another individual or against a corporate entity, rather than against a Member State of ECOWAS, the Court declined jurisdiction to entertain Hope Democratic Party (first plaintiff) as it is a political organization. The third question was whether the second plaintiff's (Alhaji Haruna Yahaya Shaba) human rights was violated by the FRN? The Court also found in the negative. Consistent with its previous rulings, the ECOWAS Court noted " ... that it will not interfere with matters of enforcement of domestic laws of member states."[66]

Given that the action had been overtaken by events in Nigeria, the ECOWAS Court judges posed an interesting question to the Plaintiff counsel: whether they would be open to withdrawing the suit—particularly as the PDP and former President Goodluck Jonathan lost the election? Refusing to withdraw the suit, the Counsel said:

> ... wanted [the ECOWAS Community Court] to rule on the issue *so as to* serve as *a deterrent to other would-be violators of the elections law on fairness and equality before the law.*[Emphasis added]

The plaintiff counsel's response is striking and perhaps represents the clearest indication of a motivation of opposition parties in judicializing politics before the ECOWAS Court. This case demonstrates that victory was not the primary reason for the litigation. With victory out of sight, the plaintiff unequivocally wanted a ruling from the Court as a deterrent for future conduct of the Member State. The implication to draw from this case is that it provides a basis to further local activism in various guises while building on the thesis of ECOWAS Court as an alternative forum for the mobilization of opposition politics.[67]

Further, to ensure that the Court was seized of jurisdiction, the plaintiff invoked the *Ugokwe* doctrine, this is, they couched, their grievance in the language of a violation of human rights. Lastly, the ECOWAS Court is very strategic in protecting its jurisdiction as well as the legitimacy of its decisions. It does so, as it did in this case, by accepting rather than declining jurisdiction in what are essentially political disputes as long as they raised a legal issue for determination. Hence, framed as a human rights violation or potential violation of case, litigants adopt human rights as an umbrella term to get the cases heard. The approach of the Court in this context

---

[65] *Id*. at 26.
[66] *Id*. at 30.
[67] I demonstrate this in the context of the analysis of the Burkina Faso case later. *See also* the Introduction chapter in this book.

accords with some general international law scholarship of the International Court of Justice in particular.[68]

Sule Audu & Six Others v. Federal Republic of Nigeria

Sule Audu & Six Others v. Federal Republic of Nigeria is mega-political dispute that arose out of a unique set of facts from a gubernatorial election in Nigeria.[69] Abubakar Audu, then incumbent governor of Kogi State sought re-election on the platform of the APC. His closest challenger was Idris Wada of the People's Democratic Party. Audu was on his way to securing victory, but he died before he could be declared the winner of the elections. The INEC declared the election as inconclusive.[70] His death thrust the state into a constitutional crisis and a path with no legal or political precedent in Nigeria.[71] The question however arose as to which of the candidates should be the governor-elect. The provisions that had the closest relevance to address this scenario was Section 181 of the Nigerian Constitution of 1999.[72] Relying on a combined reading of Section 221 of the Nigerian Constitution and Section 33 of the Nigerian Electoral Act,[73] INEC asked the APC to replace the gubernatorial candidate so that supplementary elections could be held.[74] Audu's

---

[68] *See generally* Andrew Coleman, *The International Court of Justice and Highly Political Matters*, 4 MELBOURNE J. INT'L L 29 (2003). Marcella David, *Passport to Justice: Internationalizing the Political Question Doctrine for Application in the World Court*, 40 HARV. INT'L L J 81 (1999). For the cases: Case Concerning the Military and Paramilitary Activities in and Against Nicaragua (Nicaragua v. United States of America), Merits, Judgement of June, 27, 1986; Case Concerning United States Diplomatic and Consular Staff in Tehran (United States of America v. Iran), Judgement of May 24, 1980, ICJ Reports 3; Case Concerning United States Diplomatic and Consular Staff in Tehran (United States of America v. Iran) (Provisional Measures), Order, 1979 ICJ Reports 7.

[69] *See* Segun Adebowale, *Kogi Governorship Poll: Voters Drag FG to ECOWAS Court*, THE EAGLE (Jan. 12, 2016), http://theeagleonline.com.ng/kogi-governorship-poll-voters-drag-fg-to-ecowas-court/.

[70] The INEC had declared the election inconclusive following the cancellation of the poll in ninety-one units across eighteen local government areas in the state. *See* Hassan Adebayo, *INEC Declares Kogi Governorship Election Inconclusive*, PREMIUM TIMES (Nov. 22, 2015), https://www.premiumtimesng.com/news/193724-inec-declares-kogi-governorship-election-inconclusive.html.

[71] *See* Ibanga Isine & Sani Tukur, *Kogi Election and Abubakar Audu's death: What Lawyers and the Law say*, PREMIUM TIMES (Nov. 23, 2015), https://www.premiumtimesng.com/news/193764-kogi-election-and-abubakar-audus-death-what-lawyers-and-the-law-say.html.

[72] According to Sections 181(1) and (2): "(1) If a person *duly elected* as Governor dies before taking and subscribing the Oath of Allegiance and oath of office or is unable for any reason whatsoever to be sworn in, the person elected with him as Deputy governor shall be sworn in as Governor and he shall nominate a new Deputy-Governor who shall be appointed by the Governor with the approval of a simple majority of the House of Assembly of the State. (2) Where the persons duly elected as Governor and Deputy Governor of a State die or are for any reason unable to assume office before the inauguration of the house of Assembly, the Independent National Electoral Commission shall immediately conduct an election for a Governor and Deputy Governor of the State."

[73] Section 33 (Political Parties changing Candidates) provides that: "A political party shall not be allowed to change or substitute its candidate whose name has been submitted ... except in the case of death or withdrawal by the candidate [emphasis added].".

[74] Hassan Adebayo, *INEC asks APC to Replace Audu, Orders Kogi Election to Continue*, PREMIUM TIMES (Nov. 24, 2015), https://www.premiumtimesng.com/news/headlines/193846-inec-asks-apc-to-replace-audu-orders-kogi-election-to-continue.html.

erstwhile running-mate—Faleke Abiodun[75]—disagreed with INEC's position and asked to be declared the governor-elect ahead of the supplementary elections.[76] Instead of announcing that the deputy-gubernatorial candidate will replace the deceased, the APC notified INEC of their appointment of Prince Yahaya Bello—the first runner-up of its governorship primaries in the state—as the replacement candidate ahead of the supplementary elections.[77] Although the announcement generated internal squabble within the APC in Kogi State,[78] Prince Bello remained the party's candidate with a new deputy-gubernatorial candidate. Following the supplementary elections, APC emerged as the winner of the gubernatorial election in Kogi State.

This case was instituted by seven registered voters in Kogi State to the ECOWAS Court. They contested the propriety of the process for the election of Prince Bello as the governor of Kogi State;[79] challenged the decision of the INEC to declare the candidate of the ruling APC the winner of the gubernatorial supplementary election as his emergence fell "short of the minimum standard of free, fair, transparent, genuine and credible elections which would be the sine qua non for the popular participation of the people in the affairs of governance."[80] The plaintiffs sought an order compelling the defendant to take constitutional, legal, and other necessary measures to "redress the aberrations and fundamental rights violations flowing from the governorship election."[81]

The defendant challenged the jurisdiction of the ECOWAS Court to entertain human rights suit that arose from the 2015 governorship election. They urged the Court to dismiss the suit for lack of cause of action. The plaintiffs' counsel responded that the substantive application before the Court was for the human

---

[75] The opposition party (Peoples' Democratic Party) also asked that their candidate be declared the winner of the elections. *Faleke to INEC: I'm Governor-elect of Kogi*, VANGUARD (Nov. 26, 2015), https://www.vanguardngr.com/2015/11/faleke-to-inec-im-governor-elect-of-kogi/.

[76] Gbade Ogunwale, *PDP to INEC: Declare Wada as Winner of Kogi Elections*, THE NATIONAL (Nov. 26, 2015), http://thenationonlineng.net/pdp-to-inec-declare-wada-as-winner-of-kogi-election/; *see also* Emmanuel Aziken, *PDP Kicks as INEC asks APC to replace Audu*, VANGUARD (Nov. 25, 2015), https://www.vanguardngr.com/2015/11/pdp-kicks-as-inec-asks-apc-to-replace-audu/.

[77] Omeiza Ajayi, *Kogi: INEC receives APC's Yahaya Bello as Audu's Replacement*, VANGUARD (Nov. 30, 2015), https://www.vanguardngr.com/2015/11/kogi-inec-receives-apcs-yahaya-bello-as-audus-replacement/.

[78] In particular, Faleke, the former deputy-gubernatorial refused to continue in this position as Prince Bello's deputy. Eventually, he was replaced by the APC. *See* Ikechukwu Nnochiri, Levinus Nwabughiogu, & Omeiza Ajayi, *Kogi: INEC, APC in Dilemma as Faleke remains Unwilling Running Mate*, VANGUARD (Dec. 2, 2015), https://www.vanguardngr.com/2015/12/kogi-inec-apc-in-dilemma-as-faleke-remains-unwilling-running-mate/.

[79] Audu et al. v. Federal Republic of Nigeria, Suit No. ECW/CCJ/APP/02/16; Court Fixes Date for Ruling on Jurisdiction in Nigeria Election Case, ECOWAS press release (2012).

[80] *Id.*

[81] Court Fixes Date for Ruling on Jurisdiction in Nigeria Election Case, ECOWAS Press Release (Feb. 3, 2017), https://elombah.com/court-fixes-date-for-ruling-on-jurisdiction-in-nigeria-election-case/;*see also* Sunday Ejike, *Kogi Guber Election: ECOWAS Court to Rule on Jurisdiction March 20*, THE NIGERIAN TRIBUNE, http://tribuneonlineng.com/kogi-guber-election-ecowas-court-rule-jurisdiction-march-20/.

right enforcement and as such, the ECOWAS Court pursuant to the provisions of Protocol 2005 has the requisite jurisdiction to adjudicate on complaints of fundamental rights violations that occur in any Member States.

It is not clear whether the ECOWAS Court delivered its judgement. Subsequently, the Supreme Court of Nigerian confirmed Prince Bello as the governor.[82] In short, the plaintiffs' attempt to come within the jurisdictional ambit of the ECOWAS Court by invoking the *Ugokwe* doctrine did not lead to a definitive outcome in this instance.

While there was no none outcome from the ECOWAS Court, it is interesting to note that the plaintiffs commenced their dispute despite the fact that there was another action before the elections tribunal challenging the emergence of Prince Bello as the gubernatorial candidate.[83] Although the case fits more into the category of dissidents within a political party who see the ECOWAS Court as an alternative forum, it nonetheless exemplifies the complexity of the motivations of the parties that appear before the Court and the challenges they confront navigating the national and sub-regional courts.

Congrès pour la Démocratie et le Progrès (CDP) & others v. The State of Burkina Faso

In 2014, Burkina Faso's former President Blaise Compaoré, who had been in power since 1987, and his political party, Congrès pour la Démocratie et le Progrès (CDP), were ousted from power.[84] The dispute arose out of a purported amendment to the electoral laws of Burkina Faso that ousted the Applicants from participation in future electoral processes. The principal question before the ECOWAS Court was whether the amendment of Burkina Faso's electoral law and its application violates the right of certain political parties and citizens to participate and vote in elections? The applicants, a group of opposition political parties and thirteen individuals, alleged the breach of their fundamental human rights by Burkina Faso's Transitional team. President Compaoré's attempt to amend the constitution was met with repeated violent demonstrations which led to the death of many and the destruction of public and private property. The President resigned, and the proposed amendment also failed. The international community and the ECOWAS Community supported a political transition that would eventually lead to democratic and

---

[82] *See Why we Dismissed Faleke, Wada's appeals – Supreme Court*, THE PUNCH NIGERIA (September 20, 2016), https://punchng.com/why-we-dismissed-faleke-wadas-appeals-supreme-court/-/.

[83] *See Faleke Sues INEC, asks Court to Declare him Kogi's Governor-elect*, PREMIUM TIMES (Dec. 1, 2015), https://www.premiumtimesng.com/news/headlines/194238-breaking-faleke-sues-inec-asks-court-to-declare-him-kogis-governor-elect.html.

[84] *See* Daniel Eizenga, *Burkina Faso, in* 12 AFRICA YEARBOOK, POLITICS, ECONOMY AND SOCIETY SOUTH OF THE SAHARA IN 2015, 53–54 (Jon Abbink et al. eds., 2016).

transparent elections in Burkina Faso. The National Forum which brought to-gether the critical interest groups in the Burkinabe nation adopted a Political Transition Charter in November 2004, and also set up a National Transition Council (Council) that was endowed with legislative powers.[85] The Council em-barked on a number of reforms.

Of particular relevance to this case were amendments relating to the electoral law. Those amendments ousted particular persons who supported former President Compaoré from participation in the future electoral processes as ineligible either on the basis of any court decisions or conviction for electoral fraud.[86] In addition, the Council introduced a new category of ineligible persons that included:

> all those who have supported unconstitutional change that undermines the prin-ciple of democratic alternation, including the principle of limiting the number of presidential terms that led to insurgency or any other form of uprising.[87]

At the ECOWAS Community Court, the applicants contended that the new law adopted by the Council violates their right to participate freely in elections in Burkina Faso and several international legal instruments to which Burkina Faso is a signatory.[88] On its part, Burkina Faso built its case on three grounds: that the ECOWAS Court is incompetent to entertain the action; that the applicants' motion is inadmissible; and that it was ill-founded.[89]

On the first issue, Burkina Faso argued that the ECOWAS Court was not seized of jurisdiction as the applicants complaint was premised only on a possible, hypo-thetical, or potential violation of human rights as opposed to one that was concrete, actual, or substantive. Being a potential one, the Court had in the past declared it-self competent to handle such complaints.[90] The ECOWAS Court, however, noted that it can legitimately adjudicate over imminent violations that have not yet been

---

[85] *See Burkina Faso Appoints Transitional Government*, AL JAZEERA (Nov. 23, 2014), http://www.aljazeera.com/news/africa/2014/11/burkina-faso-appoints-transitional-government-20141123225514740864.html.

[86] In this context, on April 7, 2015, the Council adopted Act No. 005-2015 that amended Act No. 014-2001/AN of July 3, 2001 on the electoral code. In respect of ineligible persons, that is, those unable to stand for election a new Section 135 was added, in addition to the following provisions: individ-uals deprived by judicial decision of their eligibility rights under the laws in force; persons with legal advisors; and individuals sentenced for electoral fraud. *See* Congrès pour la Démocratie et le Progrès (CDP) v. The State of Burkina Faso, 3.

[87] *Id.*

[88] They relied on the following international and regional instruments: 1948 Universal Declaration of Human Rights, art. 2, paras. 1, 21; 1966 International Covenant on Civil and Political Rights, art. 26; African Charter on Human and Peoples' Rights, arts. 2 & 13, paras. 1, 2; African Charter on Democracy, Elections and Governance, arts. 3.7, 3.11, 4.2, 8.1, 10.3; and ECOWAS Protocol on Democracy and Good Governance 2001, art. 1(i).

[89] *See* Congrès pour la Démocratie et le Progrès, *supra* note 87, at para. 9.

[90] *See generally* Ministère Public v. Hissein Habré, Extraordinary African Chambers in Senegal, Judgment (May 30, 2016).

carried out, but may that could come to fruition very soon.[91] According to the ECOWAS Court:

> The matter is therefore being referred to the Court urgently. In the present configuration, if it had to wait for applications to be eventually rejected before taking action, if it had to wait for the exhaustion of the effects of a transgression to be expressed in law, its jurisdiction in an emergency context would be meaningless, since the alleged victims of such violations would then find themselves inexorably aggrieved in the electoral competition.[92]

Further, the Court emphasized its previous position that in special circumstances "the risk of a future violation confers on an applicant the status of victim" and in such situations, there are "reasonable and convincing indications of the likelihood of actions" that might violate human rights.[93] The applicants' complaints fell in this category, hence, the Court dismissed Burkina Faso's argument that the Court lacked competence to rule on the matter.

Interestingly, the ECOWAS Court reiterated the *Ugokwe* doctrine in addressing this argument; to wit, although it may lack the jurisdiction to adjudicate over electoral disputes in Member States, "it may be validly seized when it appears that the electoral process is marred by human rights violations, the punishment of which falls within its jurisdiction."[94] In other words, in cases of judicialization of mega-political cases that are intertwined with allegations of breach of human rights, the ECOWAS Court will assume jurisdiction having created the "cause of action" for election disputes in the *Ugokwe* doctrine.

Accordingly, the ECOWAS Court rejected the second submission on inadmissibility of the appeal by Burkina Faso. Although the Court is only seized of jurisdiction over individuals and not political parties—especially where the question of the right to participate in elections and in the management of public affairs are concerned—there is nothing that inherently prevents the Court from knowing about them because such a restriction may have the unintended consequence of harming political formation and participation in the management of public affairs. According to the ECOWAS Court:

> Not only do the texts governing the Court not preclude legal persons from bringing cases before the Court, provided that they are nevertheless victims (Article 10 (d) of the 2005 Protocol), but it would be in a purely artificial and unreasonable way if the Court refused to grant political parties the right to bring

---

[91] Congrès pour la Démocratie et le Progrès, *supra* note 87, at para. 16.
[92] *Id.*
[93] *Id.* at para. 17; *see also* Koraou v. Republic of Niger, No. ECW/CCJ/APP/0808, ECOWAS (Oct. 27, 2008).
[94] Congrès pour la Démocratie et le Progrès, *supra* note 87, at para. 19.

cases before it if rights linked to their vocation as electoral competitors were infringed.[95]

On the third issue, whether the amendment of Burkina Faso's electoral law and its application violates the right to certain political parties and citizens to vote and participate in elections? Reviewing some of its own jurisprudence and governing laws, a number of principles emerge. First, the ECOWAS Court does not adjudicate over any legal issues that are internal or arise from the national constitution of its Member States. The consequences of the first rule for the dispute before the Court were two-fold: first, "... any reference to national law, be it the Constitution of Burkina Faso or any kind of infra-constitutional norms, must be removed from judicial debate."[96] Hence, references by the applicant to the National Constitution and the Transition Charter of Burkina Faso is inappropriate before the ECOWAS Court. Being an "international court, it is intended to penalize only the breach of obligations resulting from international instruments enforceable against [Member] States."[97] Second, given the ambiguity of the new Article 135 of the Electoral Code of Burkina Faso, the Court must resist any temptation to clarify or engage in the exegesis of the text or to orient its interpretation in any particular way.[98] According to the ECOWAS Court:

> its function is not to discover the intention of the national legislator, or to compete with national courts in their own field, which is precisely that of interpreting national texts. However, the Court regains jurisdiction once the interpretation or application of a national text has the object or effect of depriving citizens of rights derived from international instruments to which Burkina Faso is a party.[99]

In the opinion of the Court, there is no doubt that the exclusion of a number of political groups and citizens from the electoral competition that is being prepared constitutes discrimination which is difficult to justify in law. Although, in particular circumstances, a country's legislation may make it impossible for certain citizens to hold elective offices, such restriction of the right of access to public office must nonetheless be justified by the commission of particularly serious offences. According to the Court, the exclusion at issue is neither legal nor necessary to stabilize the democratic order, contrary to the defendant's allegations. Indeed, the restriction imposed by the Electoral Code does not have the sole effect of preventing applicants from standing as candidates, it also significantly limits the choice offered to the electorate, and thus alters the competitive nature of the election. In its final

[95] *Id.* at para. 20.
[96] *Id.* at para. 25.
[97] *Id.*
[98] *Id.* at para. 26.
[99] *Id.* at para. 27.

analysis, the ECOWAS Court held that the political groups and Burkinabe citizens who could stand for election because of the amendment of the electoral law must be reinstated.

Congrès pour la Démocratie et le Progrès (CDP) & others vs. The State of Burkina Faso builds on the *Ugokwe* doctrine as it illustrates circumstances under which the ECOWAS Court has assumed jurisdiction on mega-political jurisprudence. The case thus buttresses the argument in this chapter that the ECOWAS Court is an emerging alternative mobilization forum for opposition political parties or figures who decide to judicialize their disputes. As it is evident from the background socio-political context that challenging the decision of the National Transition Council before the national courts would likely fail, the potential human rights violation lever provided an important strategy for the ECOWAS Court to assume jurisdiction and make pronouncements that not only impacts the human rights of the parties, but also, has implications for their capability to participate in elections in Burkina Faso.

Centre for Democracy and Development, and Another v. Mamadou Tandja & The Republic of Niger

Similar to many of the mega-political cases that have been litigated before the ECOWAS Court, this case arose out of attempts by a sitting president to amend the country's constitution in order to extend his tenure in office for a third term.[100] This complaint was against Mamadou Tandja, former President of the Republic of Niger, and against the Republic of Niger for the violation of the human rights of the people of Niger to freely participate in the conduct of their affairs by the election of a new president in December 2009.

As part of the preparations leading to the 2009 elections, a well-funded movement with the slogan "Tazartche"—translated as "continuity"—called for an extension of the mandate of Tandja beyond 2009. For over three months, the Nigerien civil society, trade unions, and opposition groups protested against President Tandja's attempts to change the Constitution to extend his tenure beyond December 2009.[101] In May 2009, the Constitutional Court of Niger declared that President Tandja's attempt to remain in office after the end of his term was unconstitutional.[102] Following

---

[100] Centre for Democracy and Development, and Center for Defence of Human Rights and Democracy v. Tandja & Republic of Niger, Suit No. ECW/CCJ/APP/07/09; Judgment No. ECW/CCJ/JUD/05/11.

[101] For an account of events from May 2009 to August 2009, *see Niger Opposition groups protest President Tandja's attempts to stay in power, 2009*, GLOBAL NONVIOLENT ACTION DATABASE, https://nvdatabase.swarthmore.edu/content/niger-opposition-groups-protest-president-tandja-s-attempts-stay-power-2009.

[102] *See* Abdoulaye Massalatchi, *Niger's Tandja Dissolves Parliament*, REUTERS (May 26, 2009), https://www.reuters.com/article/ozatp-niger-constitution-20090526-idAFJOE54P0EL20090526.

this declaration, President Tandja dissolved the National Assembly which itself led to other proceedings before the national courts of Niger.[103] The president carried on with the amendment of the constitution by inserting a new clause that removes any limitation on the presidential mandate.[104]

Before the ECOWAS Court, the applicants asked the Court for declarations that President Tandja's decision to remain in power and to organize an illegal constitutional referendum was null and void; and that the violent suppression of protests was illegal and a violation of the human rights of the Nigerien people's freedom of expression, assembly, and association. The applicants also sought orders prohibiting President Tandja from organizing a referendum; remaining in power beyond December 2009; and dispersing the protests against his plan to run for a third term. In response, the defendants, *inter alia*, raised preliminary objections of inadmissibility of the initiation of the proceedings, and also contested the facts presented and legal grounds relied upon by the applicants. They contended that the application was inadmissible. They did so by arguing that applicants were not entitled to act on behalf of the Nigerien people pursuant to a combined reading of the provisions of Article 9 of the ECOWAS Community Court Protocol A/P.1/7/91 (as amended by Supplementary Protocol A/SP.1/01/05, art. 3) and Nigerien Constitution, arts. 5, 6. The former provision only anticipates *persons* as opposed to NGOs, who have been victims of a violation of human rights. They also contended that the ECOWAS Court cannot assess the violation of human rights in abstract or in speculation. In addition, they argued that, should the Court find that it is competent to entertain the matter, it would be assuming jurisdiction over a matter that relates to the internal law of a Member State, contrary to its powers.

First, with regard to jurisdiction of the Court, the ECOWAS Court noted that convening an electoral body for a referendum on the Constitution of the Republic of Niger is an exercise of regulatory power in a sovereign Member State. Consequently, the Court is not competent to adjudicate on the lawfulness or constitutionality of acts complained of or to prohibit the taking of such acts. Hence, it declared itself incompetent to prohibit President Tandja or the agents of the Republic of Niger from organizing the referendum in order to remain in power or to disperse the protest marches against the organization of the referendum. However, in relation to the complaints regarding the violation of human rights, the Court held that it has jurisdiction to examine these complaints.

Second, on the question of inadmissibility of the request on the ground that the applicants are not entitled to act on behalf of the Nigerien people, the Court decided that the applicants have not demonstrated their capacity as victims nor have

---

[103] *Niger Leader Dissolves Parliament*, BBC NEWS (May 26, 2009), http://news.bbc.co.uk/2/hi/africa/8067831.stm.
[104] The applicants argue that the actions of President were a violation of arts. 36 and 136 of the Constitution of Niger and art. 13(1) of the African Charter of Human Rights.

they been justified by standing to act on behalf of victims whose mandates they have received. The fact that both applicants are not registered NGOs in Niger was important to the finding of lack of admissibility by the Court as they cannot be victims of the consequences of the actions of which they complained.

Third, the Court was urged by the defendant to declare the action moot as it had been overtaken by developments in Niger. The applicants however responded with a very interesting argument. According to them, they would maintain their claims on the ground that the ECOWAS Court's decision would help dissuade other officials who intended to manipulate the Constitutions of their country for a longer time while they were in power.[105] Although the Court agreed with the respondent that the orders would be devoid of purpose, the argument of the applicants nevertheless demonstrates that the motivations of the actors before the ECOWAS Court in instituting these mega-political cases. In this respect, the attitude of the applicants was in complete accord with those in the cases discussed earlier insofar as they were not filing the case to get a decision that they seek to enforce.

Valentine Ayika v. Republic of Liberia

Unlike the previous cases, the dispute here does not arise out of a national election of political process. The broad reading of politics for the purpose of this mega-political dispute arises from the national profile of the applicant among Nigeria's wealthy and political elites, and the national implications it has for Liberia and Nigeria.

The plaintiff, a Nigeria businessman, returned to the Republic of Liberia with an undeclared amount of US$508,200 that was confiscated based on an order of the Circuit Court of Liberia.[106] After the confiscation, between 2006 and 2009, investigations were conducted into the source and the purpose of the money. Through a letter dated January 23, 2009, the Liberian Minister of Justice and the Attorney General wrote a letter to the Central Bank of Liberia confirming that the investigations had been concluded in favor of the plaintiff and that the bank should release the money to him, less the penalty for non-declaration of the money. The letter was subsequently withdrawn on the ground that it misrepresented the facts. The Central Bank of Liberia had been directed to continue to hold the money pending further investigations.

The plaintiff sought a declaration before the ECOWAS Court that the confiscation of the money as proceeds of criminal conduct should be declared null and

---

[105] *See* Centre for Democracy and Development, and Center for Defence of Human Rights and Democracy v. Tandja & Republic of Niger, para. 34.

[106] See Valentine Ayika v. Republic of Liberia, Suit No. ECW/CCJ/APP/07/11; Judgment No. ECW/CCJ/JUD/09/12; *see also* George J. Borteh, *West Africa: Ecowas' Court Ruling Not Binding on Liberia—Supreme Court says in Ayika's U.S.$508,200 Case*, AllAfrica (July 25, 2013), http://allafrica.com/stories/201307251585.html.

void; an order directing the release of it with interests, the plaintiff's passport and costs awarded against the defendant. The defendant argued that the investigation into the source and purpose of the funds had not been concluded as at the time the action was instituted, hence, they urged the Court to dismiss the action.

The ECOWAS Court found that the plaintiff did not declare the funds at the airport to any official of the defendant, but, in relation to the confiscation, the "undisputed evidence before the court indicates that the plaintiff was not served with a notice to the hearing of the confiscation proceedings."[107] He was therefore not given the opportunity to be heard and therefore this offended "the letter and spirit of the cardinal confiscation proceedings."[108] However, as the proceedings were only interim and did not dismiss of the matter ad infinitum, "no prejudice resulted from it to the detriment of the plaintiff."[109] In relation to the effect of the investigative reports by the defendant's agents, the Court found that the defendant had over four years to investigate the matter before the plaintiff commenced this action. In the Court's opinion, that was a reasonable time to locate any evidence to support the charge against the plaintiff. The fact that "the defendant [w]as not been able to find evidence to support the charge ... leads the court to the irresistible conclusion that the plaintiff is not indeed guilty of the charge preferred against him. The defendant therefore has no legal justification to withhold the plaintiff's money."[110] The ECOWAS Court ordered the release of the sum with interest to the plaintiff.

The socio-political ramifications of this case indeed demonstrate the rationale for the judicialization of mega-political cases before Africa's international courts. The first point relates to compliance with the order of the Court. The Republic of Liberia complied with the order of the ECOWAS Court to return the sum confiscated from the plaintiff. According to newspaper reports, "the Liberian Government was forced to cough up [US$500,000] it seized from a Nigerian Businessman, Chief Valentine Ayika, who was later elected Senator in Nigeria."[111] In addition to compliance, Chief Ayika was not only a businessman, but also a politician in Nigeria—a regional hegemon in the ECOWAS Community. This gave rise to the possibility of backlash against Liberia in regional politics. The handling of the matter had impacted socio-political relations between Liberia and the Nigeria. For example, shortly after the decision was delivered, there were openings for the appointment of judges to the ECOWAS Court. Liberia planned to put forward some candidates but Nigeria indicated that it will not support the candidature of Liberian judges to the ECOWAS Court.[112] Although a Liberian was eventually

---

[107] *Id.* at 11, para. 27.
[108] *Id.*
[109] *Id.*
[110] *Id.* at 16.
[111] *Disgrace Keeps Hoovering Over Liberia's Judiciary Branch*, Front Page Africa.
[112] *See* Rodney D. Sieh, *West Africa: ECOWAS Court Puts Liberia on Hold over U.S. $500K*, AllAfrica (2014), http://allafrica.com/stories/201401151311.html

appointed as a judge of the Court,[113] the same judge was later withdrawn based on conflict of interest that arose from a case he presided over while at the Supreme Court of Liberia.[114] The implication here is that Nigeria acquiesced to the Liberian judges because Liberia complied with the decision. In the concluding section of this chapter, I ask what implications do we draw from the rising judicialization of mega-political cases in ECOWAS Court.[115]

Section Five: Reimagining the ECOWAS Court as a Forum for the Mobilization and Shaping of Member State Opposition Politics

The intrinsic nature of regional organizations and the courts they create remain a debate. Whereas some scholars have argued that the ECOWAS Court should be re-considered as a human rights court or at least one that promotes human rights[116], others have simply referred to them generically as "trade-plus" regimes.[117] These varying descriptions of the fundamental nature of these organizations, while true, suggest a fragmentation and lack of coherence that may ultimately distract from the significance of the work they do, however modest.

The majority of the mega-political disputes analyzed arise from election processes. Constitutional democracy is still nascent in West Africa. The task of conducting free and fair elections in Africa is a work in progress. I will illustrate briefly with Nigeria—an ECOWAS Community Member State. According to Adigun Agbaje and Said Adejumobi, the institutional weaknesses, normlessness, and lack of civility in electoral politics in Nigeria arises from a "complex interaction of

---

[113] See West Africa: Former Liberia Solicitor General Wilkins Wright Appointed to ECOWAS Court, FRONT PAGE AFRICA (2014), http://allafrica.com/stories/201406200889.html.

[114] Following the suspension of his license by Liberia and recall from the ECOWAS Court where he was the Vice-President, Wilkins Wright has instituted actions against Liberia; see Lenart Dodoo, Supreme Court of Liberia Nails ECOWAS Court Judge Wilkins Wright, FRONT PAGE AFRICA, http://www.frontpageafricaonline.com/politics/supreme-court-of-liberia-nails-ecowas-court-judge-wilkins-wright/; Liberia Fails to File Defense in Wilkins Wright Alleged Rights Violation, FRONT PAGE AFRICA, http://www.frontpageafricaonline.com/news/2016news/liberia-fails-to-file-defense-in-wilkins-wright-alleged-rights-violation/; Bettie K. Johnson Mbayo, ECOWAS Court Calls Off Relationship Building Seminar in Liberia, FRONT PAGE AFRICA, http://www.frontpageafricaonline.com/politics/ecowas-court-calls-off-relationship-building-seminar-in-liberia/.

[115] See Gathii, supra note 13. The Introduction to this book describes sub-regional courts like ECOWAS as one of a number of alternative forums or pressure points opposition political parties turn to in their multi-dimensional struggle against incumbent political parties—this takes away the need to view this as cases filed to be won because the strategy is putting pressure on the incumbent party from many different angles.

[116] Nneoma Nwogu, Regional Integration as an Instrument of Human Rights: Reconceptualizing ECOWAS, 6 J. HUM. RTS. 345; Nani Jansen Reventlow, Strategic Litigation Before the African Regional Courts: Great Potential for Progressive Protection of Human Rights, GRONINGEN J. INT'L L. BLOG (Mar. 12, 2018), https://grojil.org/2018/03/12/strategic-litigation-before-the-african-regional-courts-great-potential-for-progressive-protection-of-human-rights/.

[117] Gathii, supra note 13.

historical and contemporary forces and structures of the Nigerian state system."[118] After many years of military dictatorship, Nigeria, the most economically endowed Community Member within ECOWAS returned to democratic rule in 1999, the country's Fourth Republic. Previous efforts at building sustainable democratic governance were short-lived by military coups.[119] Since 1999, Nigeria has conducted five presidential and gubernatorial elections with meaningful implications for the consolidation and entrenchment of constitutional democracy.[120] For the first time in Nigeria's history, in 2015, an opposition political party won the presidential election and successfully ousted a sitting president.[121] Despite the achievement in transitioning from one civilian regime to another, nagging and important questions remain regarding how institutionalized the cardinal rules of separation of powers is in Nigeria in the context of election disputes.[122]

Many of the opposition parties that loose elective positions challenge the outcomes. They are confronted with the dilemma of litigating their cases before national courts where allegations of " … lack of independence and professionalism, political interference, undemocratic attitude, and lack of respect for the rule of law" are rife.[123]

All around Africa, election disputes are sensitive.[124] The foregoing challenges are not limited to Nigeria. Between 2015 and 2017, The Gambia, Côte d'Ivoire, Burkina Faso, Guinea, Niger, Liberia, and Ghana, among other ECOWAS Community Member States also conducted presidential elections that are embedded in intricate and peculiar socio-political and historical contexts of the individual countries.

---

[118] ADIGUN AGBAJE & SAID ADEJUMOBI, DO VOTES COUNT? THE TRAVAILS OF ELECTORAL POLITICS IN NIGERIA 27 (2006).

[119] The previous republics were: First, 1960–66; Second, 1979–83; Third, 1992–93. *See generally* J. Shola Omotola, *Elections and Democratic Transition in Nigeria under the Fourth Republic* 109 AFR. AFFAIRS 535, 535–36 (2010) (arguing that elections in the Fourth Republic are characterized by ineffective administration at all stages and levels—before, during, and after—resulting in damagingly discredited outcomes.).

[120] Eghosa E. Osaghae, *Democratization in Sub-Saharan Africa: Faltering Prospects, New Hopes*, 17 J. CONTEMP. AFR. STUD. 4–25 (1999).

[121] *See* Associated Press, *Goodluck Jonathan "Concedes Defeat" in Nigerian Election*, NEW YORK POST (Mar. 31, 2015), http://nypost.com/2015/03/31/goodluck-jonathan-concedes-defeat-in-nigerian-election/; *see also* Festus Owete, *Jonathan Concedes Defeat, Congratulates Buhari*, THE PREMIUM TIMES NIGERIA (Mar. 31, 2015), http://www.premiumtimesng.com/news/headlines/180392-jonathan-concedes-defeat-congratulates-buhari.html.

[122] According to Omotola, "allegations of electoral corruption, with the active connivance of INEC and probably the transitional military regime, challenged the administration of the election and raise basic questions regarding INEC's independence, impartiality, and accountability … the elections were rigged in order to avoid a coalition government and the pitfalls of the First Republic, when no party had enough seats to form the government." Omotola, *supra* note 120, at 544. *See also* Severus Ifeanyi Odoziobodo, *INEC and the Conduct of Elections in Nigeria: An Appraisal of the 2007 General Elections*, 11 EUR. SCI. J. 168–88 (2015).

[123] Omotola, *supra* note 120, at 536. *See also* J. Shola Omotola, *From Importer to Exporter: The Changing Role of Nigeria in Promoting Democratic Values in Africa*, in AFRICAN POLITICS: BEYOND THE THIRD WAVE OF DEMOCRATISATION 32–54 (Joelien Pretorius ed., 2008).

[124] *See* Edwin Odhiambo Abuya, *Can African States Conduct Free and Fair Presidential Elections*, 8 Nw. J. INT'L HUM. RTS., 122–64 (2010).

While not all of the elections resulted in the judicialization of the disputes before the ECOWAS Community Court, there is no doubt that the ECOWAS Court is growing in stature as an alternative forum for dissident and opposition politicians who believe they cannot access justice before their domestic courts. Perhaps knowing that the sub-regional courts do not operate under the cloud of national legislative and executive pressures, the plaintiffs in these courts are emboldened by its quick dispensation of justice to seek alternative modes of airing their grievances in an alternative court.

These litigants innovatively and strategically approach the ECOWAS Court to meet its jurisdictional requirements. Litigants do not always go to the Court because they necessarily are seeking compliance of their decisions. In other words, as the cases reveal, litigants who go to the ECOWAS Court are not wedded to the traditional roles of the judicial system as dispute settlers. The plaintiffs are aware that the Court lacks the jurisdiction to entertain these cases, however, to get what is in reality an election dispute before the Court, the litigants couch their claims in the language of potential or actual human rights violation. In turn, the ECOWAS Court has also embraced this opportunity by formulating the *Ugokwe* doctrine. This formulation by the way is similar to the *Katabazi* doctrine in the East African Court of Justice (EACJ) where, because the EACJ does not have explicit jurisdiction to decide human rights cases, it was argued that the Court can decide if the issue at hand involves a question of human rights.[125]

Based on the *Ugokwe* doctrine, while it is still left to the respondent or defendant to challenge the jurisdiction of the Court, the plaintiff will at least have their day in court, even if the Court decides not to rule on the merits of the case. One may ask: how does this differ then from the human rights cases over which the ECOWAS Court has express jurisdiction? The answer to this question lies in large part in the motivations that bring the litigants before the Court in the first place. As the counsel in the *Hope Democratic Party's* case asserted, most litigants want the opportunity for the ECOWAS Court "to rule on [their disputes] so as to *serve as a deterrent to other would-be violators of the elections law on fairness and equality before the law* [emphasis added]." While one is cautious not to over generalize, there is significant weight that must be given to the fact that the motivations of the litigants, outside actual or potential violation of human rights, provide the impetus for the innovative ways that they bring their claims before the ECOWAS Community Court.

On their part, the judges have also been very cautious in entertaining these disputes. While they have stated emphatically that their jurisdiction does not extend to political cases, where a dispute impacts on the fundamental rights of a citizen, the Court has assumed jurisdiction.[126] The precedential value of the "cause of

---

[125] *See* James Thuo Gathii, Mission Creep or a Search for Relevance: The East African Court of Justice's Human Rights Strategy, 24 Duke J. Comp & Int'l L, 249–96 (2013).

[126] On the plausibility of a right to democratic governance, *see* generally Nsongurua J. Udombana, *Articulating the Right to Democratic Governance in Africa*, 24 Mich. J. Int'l Law 1210 (2003).

action" offered by the *Ugokwe* doctrine is an innovative way the Court has addressed this hurdle for litigants. Assuming jurisdiction in this regard accords with the practices of other international courts that accept jurisdiction in judicialization of mega-political disputes. Further, in most cases, where a national court has dealt with a particular matter or where it is still pending before a national court, in the absence of a denial of fair hearing, the ECOWAS Court has been vocal in affirming the validity of those decisions. This affirmation of the boundaries of their power plays a reverse role in strengthening the legitimacy of the ECOWAS Community Court. Similarly, it avoids projecting the perception that they are in competition with the national courts of the Member States of the ECOWAS Community or indeed an appellate court.

Further, it is clear that the litigants before the Court are motivated, not by the success of their action, but by other motivations. For example, it may be because of the instrumental effect it has in pressuring the Member State government to act as a law-abiding member of the international community. As the empirical section (Section Four of this chapter) shows, in most cases, the political event that is the subject of litigation would have ended by the time the decision of the ECOWAS Court is delivered. Hence, it would appear almost irrelevant and a waste of time and resources of the Court to continue to deliver judgments in such situations. However, as the counsel in the *Hope Democratic Party's Case* noted, these cases are instituted at times in order " ... *to serve as a deterrent to other would-be violators of the elections law on fairness and equality before the law*" (emphasis added), even where the offending action they complained of has ceased.

The case for reimagining the ECOWAS Court as an alternative forum for the mobilization of opposition politics should not be interpreted as a case for renaming or fundamentally jettisoning the previous important jurisprudence of the Court mainly in the realm of human rights. Rather, broadening the lens through which we assess the mega-political jurisprudence of the Court offers a new way of understanding the multifaceted nature of the functions and impacts of the ECOWAS Court.[127]

---

[127] Some of the contributions in this volume demonstrate the value of this approach.

5

Africa's Sub-Regional Courts as Back-Up Custodians of Constitutional Justice

Beyond the Compliance Question

Solomon T. Ebobrah and Victor Lando

Introduction

This chapter argues that the protective value of sub-regional courts in Africa lies more in their potential to promote constitutional justice in the long term through direct and indirect impact than in delivering individual justice in the short term. We argue that the litigation processes and the decisions of these sub-regional international courts contribute to constitutional justice in ways that are not obvious when focus is on judgment compliance. By constitutional justice, we refer to the role of international courts acting as back-up mechanisms that support national courts in their role as guardians of constitutional order.[1] International courts play this back-up support role through a variety of mechanisms such as flagging violations within Member States, thus serving as early warning systems; expanding the scope of normative protection; as well as providing doctrinal footholds that domestic courts and litigants can then use at the national level. Furthermore, litigation before these sub-regional courts serve as opportunities for public engagement on pertinent human rights themes within the sub-regions. The litigation in these courts correlates with the creation of platforms and forums for sub-regional cooperation on human rights especially among civil society actors and litigants. This has the effect of influencing the direction of the human rights discourse within a particular sub-region. Our argument is not that these sub-regional courts occupy a hierarchically superior position vis-à-vis national courts, but rather, that both national and sub-regional courts play a role in nudging national political institutions to "increase the commitment to constitutionalism ... by using principled legal ideas to counter political action that is

---

[1] For an insightful analysis of international courts as democracy promoters, *see* Tom Gerald Daly, *The Alchemists: Courts as Democracy-Builders in Contemporary Thought*, 6 GLOBAL CONSTITUTIONALISM 101–30 (2017); *see also* Kim Lane Scheppele, *The Constitutional Role of Transnational Courts: Principled Legal Ideas in Three-Dimensional Political Space*, 28 PENN ST. INT'L L. REV. 451, 452 (2010).

Solomon T. Ebobrah and Victor Lando, *Africa's Sub-Regional Courts as Back-Up Custodians of Constitutional Justice* In: *The Performance of Africa's International Courts.* Edited by: James Thuo Gathii, Oxford University Press (2020). © The Several Contributors. DOI: 10.1093/oso/9780198868477.003.0006.

inconsistent with these principles."[2] In this sense, Africa's sub-regional courts are involved in developing a new supranational constitutionalism anchored outside national constitutions.

A critical challenge international law has faced from its earliest days is the extent to which it compares to the institutions and processes of national law. The comparison has been mobilized to claim that international law is not law in the Austinian sense and that its institutions are at best inelegant caricatures of national institutions of governance. On the basis of such comparison, the "court-ness" or court-quality of international courts is generally questioned, mostly on the grounds that international courts lack the capacity and coercive apparatus to secure compliance with their own judgments. This challenge is greater for international human rights courts because they do not deal with traditional questions of international law like trade, in respect of which states are more likely to trigger compliance by deploying the most effective tools such as retaliatory sanctions. By contrast, international human rights courts deal with matters for which states are very unlikely to compel compliance with retaliatory tools. For international human rights courts in Africa where there is hardly any discernible culture of compliance—as understood in the traditional literature—with court judgments by governments, the challenge is even more acute, throwing open the question whether such courts have any value to warrant their continued existence.[3] This chapter addresses this and related questions from the perspective of sub-regional courts in Africa, particularly the East African Court of Justice (EACJ) and the Economic Community of West Africa (ECOWAS) Community Court of Justice (ECOWAS Court).

The chapter is divided into four parts and it ends with a conclusion. Part One discusses the design of Africa's international courts with regard to compliance. It also discusses how compliance is understood in the traditional literature on international courts and how that relates to our argument in this chapter. Part Two delves into the nature of the human rights jurisdiction of the EACJ and the ECOWAS Court, highlighting the differences and the implications those differences have in the context of debates about compliance. Part Three presents an overview of the state of compliance and the arguably limited scope of the direct impact of the judgments of sub-regional courts. In Part Four, the chapter analyzes the indirect impact of the jurisprudence of sub-regional courts. In so doing, this chapter makes a strong claim using examples from the EACJ and the ECOWAS Court that international law, as produced in the judgments of international courts, can be and are useful even in the absence of clear compliance. In particular, we show that beyond compliance, Africa's sub-regional courts play the following important roles: first, monitoring or flagging violations and acting as early warning systems; second, expanding the normative

---

[2] Scheppele, *supra* note 1, at 452.
[3] For some commentators, international courts in Africa have no real value to warrant their continued existence. For instance, *see* David Abebe, *Does International Human Rights Law in African Courts Make a Difference?*, 56 Va. J. Int'l L. 527, 530 (2017).

and institutional scope and protection of human rights; third, progressing norm de-velopment; and fourth, setting the boundaries of acceptable behavior.

Part One: The Design of Africa's International Courts with Regard to Compliance

Africa's embrace of international law and its processes is probably best exemplified by the proliferation of international courts on the continent within the last few dec-ades. In a clear departure from the post-independence era, when Africa's political leaders resisted any idea of a continental judicial actor overseeing their activities,[4] Africa now has more international courts than any other region.[5] Mostly estab-lished within the framework of Africa's regional economic communities (RECs), these courts originated with their primary mandate being to support the economic objectives of their parent RECs. However, in a dramatic reversal that occurred in the aftermath of the adoption of the Treaty for the Establishment of the African Economic Community (AEC Treaty),[6] some of these sub-regional courts, not-ably the EACJ and the ECOWAS Court have since veered into the field of human rights.[7]

In spite of this proliferation of international "human rights" courts on the con-tinent, Africa is yet to become a beacon of respect for human rights—where claims of violation of human rights are promptly adjudicated and decisions routinely complied. Instead, informed stakeholders claim that the human rights judgments of Africa's international courts mostly remain unimplemented.[8]

---

[4] African leaders were reported to have vehemently opposed the idea of establishing an African Court of Human Rights within the framework of the African Charter on Human and Peoples' Rights. *See*, for instance, Nsongurua J. Udombana, *Towards the African Court on Human and Peoples' Right: Better Late than Never*, 3 Yale Hum R. Develop L. J. 1, 45, 46 (2000).

[5] Statistics of international courts across continents shows that there are more courts located in Africa. The Danish Centre of Excellence for International Courts (iCourts) indicates that there are cur-rently nine international courts operating in Africa. *See* iCourts Finder, Univ. Of Copenhagen: Research Resources, https://jura.ku.dk/icourts/research-resources/ (last visited Nov. 12, 2019) (follow "iCourts Finder" hyperlink).

[6] The AEC Treaty is a continental treaty adopted on the auspices of the Organisation of African Unity. The AEC Treaty refers to the African Charter and apparently served as a model.

[7] Now sharing human rights jurisdiction with the mechanisms of the African Human Rights System (AHRS), particularly the African Court of Human and Peoples' Rights (African Court), the EACJ, and the ECOWAS Community Court have become prominent features in the continental judicial land-scape, jointly exercising compulsory jurisdiction over about nineteen African states. This is better ap-preciated against the background that the African Court currently only has jurisdiction over the eight or so African states that have accepted its jurisdiction involving non-state actors.

[8] In October 2018, the President of the ECOWAS Court lamented that judgments of the ECOWAS Court were not being enforced. *See* Oludare Richards, *ECOWAS Court Lament Poor Enforcement Of Judgements*, THE GUARDIAN (Oct 30, 2018 4.18 AM) https://guardian.ng/features/ecowas-court-laments-poor-enforcement-of-judgments/. For a review of the SADC Tribunal, *see* Karen J. Alter, James T. Gathii, & Laurence R. Helfer, *Backlash Against International Courts in West, East and Southern Africa: Causes and Consequences*, 27 EUROPEAN J. INT'L L. 293 (2016).

From a global perspective, the growth in number and scope of activities of inter-national human rights courts has prompted scholars and policy makers to question the overall utility of these institutions, especially their contribution to the advancement of human rights.[9] For some, the legitimacy of international human rights courts and their entitlement to "our energetic support" depends on whether and to what extent the courts "contribute meaningfully to protection of rights, or at least, promise eventually to do so."[10] For others, not only should it be asked whether human rights (and rights supervisory mechanisms including international courts) are effective in fulfilling their objectives, but that it is useful to determine whether the protection and advancement of human rights can also be pursued and achieved by other more effective means.[11] Specific to Africa's sub-regional courts in their new roles as emerging international human rights courts, direct questions have arisen not only regarding their suitability for this role vis-à-vis the regional human rights court,[12] but also with regards their overall effectiveness as restraints on the rights-violative conduct of African states.[13] If states can ignore the human rights judgments of sub-regional courts, are these courts still useful and do they deserve to enjoy the moral and material support that effective international courts attract?

Compliance versus Effectiveness

For Austinians, international law must be obeyed in order for it to be considered to be effective.[14] This compares to law generally, in respect of which Allot has argued that effectiveness "is measured by the degree of compliance insofar as a law is pre-ventive."[15] Invariably, in relation to courts, effectiveness has become equated with judgment compliance. William M. Reisman therefore contends that "in the final analysis, law is not only … what the courts say, but also what the sheriff does."[16] Yuval Shany is therefore correct when he observes that compliance has become the "dominant proxy" even "a litmus test—for judicial effectiveness" and that "the most

---

[9] See Jillienne Haglund, *The (Conditional) Effectiveness of International Human Rights Courts*, POLITICAL VIOLENCE AT A GLANCE (Apr. 1, 2015), https://politicalviolenceataglance.org/2015/04/01/the-conditional-effectiveness-of-international-human-rights-courts/.

[10] Douglass Cassel, *Does International Human Rights Law Make a Difference?*, 2 CHI. J. INT'L L. 121, 121 (2001).

[11] Sten Schaumburg-Müller, *Pragmatic Challenges to Human Rights*, in IMPLEMENTING HUMAN RIGHTS: ESSAYS IN HONOUR OF MORTEN KJAERUM 14 (Rikke Frank Jørgensen and Klaus Slavensky eds., Danish Institute for Human Rights, 2007).

[12] For instance, L. N. Murungi and J. Gallinetti, *The Role Of Sub-Regional Courts In The African Human Rights System*, 13 SUR INTERNATIONAL JOURNAL ON HUMAN RIGHTS, 119 (2010), who question the role of sub-regional courts as human rights actors.

[13] Abebe, *supra* note 3.

[14] For instance, see Mortimer N. S. Sellers, *The Effectiveness of International Law*, 2 INT'L LEGAL THEORY, 32 (1996).

[15] Anthony Allott, *The Effectiveness of Laws*, 15 VAL. U. L. REV. 229, 234 (1981).

[16] William M. Reisman, *The Enforcement of International Judgments*, 63 AM. J. INT'L L. 1, 1 (1969).

palpable impact" of international courts "on their environment may be ascertained through compliance with their decisions."[17] In Hartian terms, with increased compliance, the legal system comes full circle with "a much more settled and accepted system of secondary rules and institutions."[18]

Yet, there remains the danger of unacceptably low levels of respect for primary rules, resulting in a "high proportion of repeat cases" despite claims of high judgment compliance.[19] Inevitably, there is almost a choice between the pursuit and realization of individual justice, represented by high judgment compliance, and constitutional justice, represented by a focus on securing higher compliance with primary rules at a more general, even abstract level.

In this chapter, we try to show that even in the face of apparently low levels of judgment compliance attracted by international courts such as the sub-regional courts in Africa, the impacts of litigation activities before those courts contribute largely to constitutional justice.

Writing on the extent of state compliance with the recommendations of the African Commission on Human and Peoples' Rights (African Commission), Frans Viljoen and Lirette Louw distinguish between "direct impact" and "indirect impact" of human rights treaties and law.[20] They define "direct impact" as immediately demonstrable results expressed for instance by implementation of a finding of a treaty monitoring body. This is akin to the individual justice secured when the decision of a court is implemented by a respondent state. "Indirect impact" in their view is defined as incremental and occurring over time.[21] A study on the impact of the African Charter on Human and Peoples' Rights (ACHPR or African Charter) and the Protocol to the African Charter on Human and Peoples' Rights on the Rights of Women in Africa (Maputo Protocol) on selected African states by Victor Ayeni defines impact to include "more indirect forms of influence" such as awareness and use by civil society, lawyers, and national human rights institutions, inclusion in law school curricula, as well as reference to the Protocol in academic writings.[22] Jasper Krommendijk's study on domestic impact of state

---

[17] YUVAL SHANY, ASSESSING THE EFFECTIVENESS OF INTERNATIONAL COURTS (2014); see also Lea Shaver, The Inter-American Human Rights System: An Effective Institution for Regional Rights Protection?, 9 WASH. U. GLOB. STUD. L. REV. 639, 665 (2010) (making the point that a court's effectiveness is partly measured by whether the orders it issues are followed); see generally Alexandra Huneeus, Compliance with International Court Judgments and Decisions, in THE OXFORD HANDBOOK OF INTERNATIONAL ADJUDICATION 437 (Cesare P.R. Romano, et al. eds., 2013).

[18] See Mark W. Janis, The Efficacy of Strasbourg Law, 15 CONN. J. INT'L L. 39, 44 (2000).

[19] Shany, supra note 17, at 270.

[20] Frans Viljoen & Lirette Louw, State Compliance With the Recommendations of the African Commission on Human and Peoples' Rights 1994–2004, 101 AM. J. INT'L L. 1–34 (2007).

[21] Id.

[22] VICTOR AYENI, IMPACT OF THE AFRICAN CHARTER AND THE WOMEN'S PROTOCOL IN SELECTED AFRICAN STATES 7 (2012).

reporting under the UN treaty bodies defines impact as the use and discussions of the reporting process and concluding observations at the domestic level by parliament, courts, national human rights institutions, ombudsman institutions, nongovernmental organizations (NGOs), and the media.[23]

Writing on the domestic impact of the African human rights system in Nigeria and South Africa, OBIORA CHINEDU Okafor adopts and advocates for a broader view that evaluates impact beyond the traditional notions of state compliance with the decisions of monitoring regimes.[24] In his view, impact may be incremental in nature through influencing the thinking processes and actions of key domestic actors including national courts, national executive, policy making, and legislative processes and civil society activists.

Applying the foregoing understandings in the context of the decisions of international courts, we align with other scholars who have argued that the utility of these courts lies more in the indirect influence that they are able to assert at the domestic level. Jillienne Haglund, for instance, recognizes the difficulty in establishing the direct impact of international courts on states' domestic human rights practices and contends that an exploration of "the indirect influence of international courts ... allows us to step back from the persistent scepticism that has dogged these ... bodies since their creation." Timothy Meyer similarly argues that "an excessive focus on compliance may understate international law's effectiveness" among other reasons, because "international law can be highly effective at changing state behaviour over time even if compliance remains low."[25] For Shany, beyond the expectation of "changes in the practices of parties to adjudication" international courts can be useful in a variety of other ways, resulting in "long term effects which take place regardless of judgment compliance by immediate parties to the adjudication."[26]

Accordingly, we argue that this long-term incremental impact of international courts is achieved through a variety of mechanisms such as serving as early warning systems by flagging violations within Member States, expanding the scope of normative protection, providing doctrinal footholds that domestic courts and litigants can in turn use at the national level, as well as presenting opportunities for public engagement on pertinent human rights themes within the sub-regions.

---

[23] JASPER KROMMENDIJK, THE DOMESTIC IMPACT AND EFFECTIVENESS OF THE PROCESS OF STATE REPORTING UNDER UN HUMAN RIGHTS TREATIES IN THE NETHERLANDS, NEW ZEALAND AND FINLAND: PAPER PUSHING OR POLICY PROMOTING? 368–75 (2014).

[24] See OBIORA CHINEDU OKAFOR, THE AFRICAN HUMAN RIGHTS SYSTEM, ACTIVIST FORCES AND INTERNATIONAL INSTITUTIONS 3–5 (2007) at 24–26, 91–93.

[25] Timothy Meyer, How Compliance Understates Effectiveness, 108 AM. SOC. INT'L L. PRO. 168 (2014).

[26] Shany, supra note 17, at 132.

Part Two: The Disparate Nature of the Human Rights Jurisdictions of Sub-Regional Courts—the EACJ and ECOWAS Court

Despite their apparent similarity as judicial organs of RECs, the origins and nature of the human rights jurisdictions of the EACJ and the ECOWAS Court are slightly dissimilar. As a result of this dissimilarity, we claim that the EACJ operates a largely declaratory human rights regime while the ECOWAS Court operates a protective (executory) human rights regime.[27] The difference in the decision-making strategy of these courts has consequences about how to frame the compliance question.[28] By a declaratory regime, we mean that litigants largely align their cases with the jurisdiction of the EACJ by requesting a declaratory order that certain conduct is inconsistent with specific treaty clauses. This means that the EACJ is not requested and therefore does not issue mandatory orders that would require states to take some affirmative steps. By contrast, by a protective or executory human rights regime, we mean that the ECOWAS Court exercises its jurisdiction by requiring respondent states to comply with its judgments the same way in which decisions of domestic courts are binding and therefore require compliance.

Article 9 of the 1999 Treaty for the Establishment of the East African Community (hereinafter EAC Treaty) (as amended) established the EACJ as the judicial organ of the East African Community (EAC). Inaugurated in 2001, the EACJ currently consists of a First Instance Division and an Appellate Division.[29] According to Articles 23 and 27(1) of the EAC Treaty, the main role and jurisdiction of the Court is to "ensure adherence to law in the interpretation and application of, and compliance with this Treaty."[30] National courts of the Partner States are vested with limited

---

[27] In recent scholarship, the argument has been made that the EACJ is gradually evolving its judgments away from mere declarations into more executory judgments that require remedial action where necessary. *See* Tomasz Milej, *East African Court of Justice: A Mid-Wife of the Political Federation? The New Case-Law on the Remedies Awarded by the Court*, AFRONOMICS LAW (Oct. 22, 2019), https://www.afronomicslaw.org/2019/10/22/east-african-court-of-justice-a-midwife-of-the-political-federation-the-new-case-law-on-the-remedies-awarded-by-the-court/.

[28] In this chapter, we have used the term *declaratory human rights regime* to mean a regime in which the supervisory organ (e.g. the Court) interprets legal standards vis-à-vis stated facts in order to make a determination whether there has been a violation of standards without any further specific orders or recommendations. A protective human rights regime on the other hand, involves a determination of violation and the authority to make a remedial or compensatory order. The EACJ often times restricts its judgments in human rights cases to declarations. Conversely, the decisions of the ECOWAS Community Court go beyond declarations of violation or non-conformity to include substantive awards including provision of monetary compensation to victims of violations.

[29] The EACJ was originally established as a single-chamber court but was reorganized into a two-chamber court in 2007 with the creation of an appellate division.

[30] It is also empowered to determine disputes between the EAC and its employees with regard to their terms and conditions of employment and arbitrate disputes pursuant to an arbitration clause contained in a contract agreement conferring such jurisdiction to the Court. The EACJ may be seized of a matter through references by natural and juristic persons residing within the Community, EAC Partner States, and the EAC Secretary-General. The EAC Council may also seek advisory opinion from the Court under Article 14 of the EAC Treaty. Detailed provisions on the mandate and functions of the Court are

jurisdiction to adjudicate on issues pertaining to the Community. However, the EACJ's decisions on the interpretation and application of the EAC Treaty take precedence over decisions of national courts.[31]

The EACJ relies on national legal systems to implement its decisions. Article 44 of the EAC Treaty, as read with Rule 74 of the EACJ Rules of Procedure, provides that judgments that impose a pecuniary obligation on a person are executed as per the rules of civil procedure of the Partner State concerned, thus enforcing the EACJ's judgments in the same manner as those of national courts.[32] Judgments that do not impose pecuniary obligations are implemented under the broad framework of Article 38(3), which requires the Council of Ministers or the Partner States to take measures to expeditiously implement the Court's decisions. This means that the national executives in the Partner States are charged with ensuring compliance with these decisions of the Court.

Apart from other roles set out for the EACJ, Article 27(2) of the EAC Treaty declares that "the Court shall have other original, appellate, human rights and other jurisdiction" as the EAC Council of Ministers may determine. The Council was expected to adopt a separate protocol to implement the envisaged additional jurisdiction of the EACJ. As far as competence over human rights is concerned, a so-called Zero Draft Protocol originated from the EAC Secretariat in 2005 to kick-start that process.[33] However, the final version of the Zero Draft Protocol adopted under Article 27(2) of the EAC Treaty excluded human rights jurisdiction from the EACJ based on the argument that all the Partner States had already acceded to the African Charter and thus any human rights claims should be pursued through the African Court.[34] Partner States also argued that they had sufficient national

---

outlined in Articles 23–47 of the EAC Treaty. For the EAC Treaty, *see* Treaty for the Establishment of the East African Community, Nov. 30, 1991, 2144 U.N.T.S. 255 (hereinafter "EAC Treaty").

[31] *See id.* at art. 33. For a discussion on how national courts have engaged with EAC law, *see* James Otieno-Odek, *Judicial Enforcement and Implementation of EAC Law, in* EAST AFRICAN COMMUNITY LAW 467, 468 (Emmanuel Ugirashebuja et al. eds., 2017).

[32] The civil procedure rules regarding execution within the EAC Partner States are fairly similar and would typically involve the extraction of a decree and then execution of the decree through among others, direct payment to the decree holder, payment into court, and attachment and sale of property among others. *See Civil Procedure Act Caps. 21*, THE LAWS OF KENYA (rev. ed., 2010); *Civil Procedure Act Caps. 71*, THE LAWS OF UGANDA (1964); *Civil Procedure Code Caps. 33*, THE LAWS OF TANZANIA (rev. ed., 2002). *See also* Relating to the Civil, Commercial, Labour and Administrative Procedure, Law No. 21/2012 of 14/6/2012 (Rwanda).

[33] Solomy Balungi Bossa, *Towards a Protocol Extending the Jurisdiction of the East African Court of Justice*, 4 E. AFRICAN J. HUM. RTS. & DEMOCRACY 31, 31 (2001).

[34] The final version of the Zero Draft Protocol only extended the EACJ's jurisdiction to cover trade and investment disputes. *See* Report of the 13th Meeting of the Sectoral Council on Legal and Judicial Affairs Ref: EAC/ SCLJA/13/2012; Report of the 16th Meeting of the Sectoral Council on Legal and Judicial Affairs Ref: EACJ/ SCLJA/16/2014. Arguably, this must be seen against the prevailing circumstances at the time—Kenya's President and Deputy President had been indicted at the International Criminal Court (ICC) for crimes against humanity. Kenya then led a spirited onslaught against the ICC, both nationally, sub-regionally, and internationally. We argue that part of this onslaught included political maneuvers against vesting another international court, the EACJ with human rights jurisdiction.

constitutional safeguards for the protection of human rights, thus rendering unnecessary the need to vest the EACJ with express human rights jurisdiction.[35]

Arguably, in the absence of a protocol to operationalize its envisaged human
rights jurisdiction, the EACJ lacks authority over human rights claims. However,
in the 2007 case of *Katabazi & 21 Others v. Secretary General of the EAC & Another*
(*Katabazi* case),[36] the EACJ was confronted with the challenge of interpreting and
applying Articles 6(d) and 7(2) of the EAC Treaty, both of which contain references to human rights. In its judgment in that case, the EACJ famously declared
that while it will not assume jurisdiction to adjudicate on human rights disputes,
"it will not abdicate from exercising its jurisdiction of interpretation under Article
27(1) merely because the reference includes allegation of human rights violation."[37] Perhaps conscious of the limitation imposed by the express suspension in
Article 27(2) of the EAC Treaty, of the human rights jurisdiction of the EACJ, the
applicants in the *Katabazi* case framed their claim as a request for interpretation
of the Treaty, especially as to whether rule of law obligations have been violated.
Following this approach, the EACJ and its users initially had to adopt a strategy
of *avoidance and reclassification*[38] in order to find competence in cases involving
human rights. Avoidance in this context means deliberately steering away from
framing claims brought before the Court as human rights violations as would be
the case in an ordinary human rights court. Reclassification is closely related to
the former. It refers to the repackaging, "disguising," or reclassifying human rights
claims as requests for the interpretation of Treaty provisions such as those providing for good governance and democracy over which the EACJ has express jurisdiction. Avoidance and reclassification have been the practice adopted by litigants
bringing human rights claims before the EACJ in order to circumvent objections
based on the fact that under Article 27(2) of the EAC Treaty, the EACJ lacks explicit
jurisdiction over human rights cases.

Building on the interpretive posture that it adopted in the *Katabazi* case, the
docket of the EACJ (both the First Instance Division and the Appellate Division)
is populated with human rights cases framed as requests for interpretation and

---

[35] *See* Dora Byamukama, Report of the 4th Meeting of the 2nd Session of the East African Legislative
Assembly, Kampala, Uganda: *Question: EALA/PQ/OA/3/34/2013*, (Jan. 19–31, 2014). *See also* Reports
of 13th and 16th Sectoral Council on Legal and Judicial Affairs, *supra* note 34. At the 15th Ordinary
Summit of the EAC Heads of State, the Summit endorsed recommendations by the Council to expand
the Court's jurisdiction to cover trade and investment matters, as well as matters associated with the
East African Monetary Union. *See Communiqué of the 15th Ordinary Summit of the EAC Heads of State*,
at para. 16 (Nov. 30, 2013).
[36] Katabazi v. Secretary-General of the East African Community and Attorney General of Uganda,
Reference No. 1 of 2007, A.H.R.L.R. 119 (EAC 2007), East African Court of Justice (Nov. 1, 2007),
https://www.eacj.org/?cases=james-katabazi-and-21-other-vs-secretary-general-of-the-east-african-
community-and-attorney-general-of-the-republic-of-uganda.
[37] *Id.* at para. 39.
[38] *See* Solomon T. Ebobrah, *Courts of Regional Economic Communities in Africa and Human Rights
Law, in* JUDGING INTERNATIONAL HUMAN RIGHTS 223, 238 (Stefan Kadelbach et al. eds., 2019).

application of the EAC Treaty. In its more recent judgments such as in the case of the *Democratic Party v. The Secretary General of the EAC & 4 Others* (*Democratic Party Appeal* case)[39], the EACJ has become more emboldened in its assumption of human rights jurisdiction, asserting that certain provisions of the EAC Treaty create human rights obligations for EAC Partner States based on the African Charter.

Nonetheless, the EACJ has been careful to restrict its judgments in human rights cases to declarations. This forms the basis of the earlier assertion that the Court operates a largely declaratory regime in human rights cases litigated before it.[40] For instance, in the case of *Plaxeda-Rugumba v Rwanda*,[41] the First Instance Division made a concerted effort to show that the petitioner was not seeking "an enforcement of any human right" but merely sought to establish "whether the subject's arrest and detention was a breach of the Treaty."[42] To buttress the point, the Court went on to underline that the applicant "withdrew her prayer for 'an order that the said Lt Col Seveline Rugigana Ngabo be released' from illegal detention.'" Because the EACJ elects to issue declaratory judgments in human rights cases instead of mandatory judgments, technically, states are not confronted with judgments requiring compliance or implementation. The decisions in the EACJ's human rights cases have to be understood differently from decisions in other cases based on non-human rights claims where the EACJ's jurisdiction is firm under the EAC Treaty which means the EACJ is able to make mandatory orders.[43] It is arguable that the declaratory approach in human rights cases stems from the manner in which claims in those cases are framed before the Court. In most instances, the litigants themselves, perhaps out of an appreciation of the Court's jurisdictional limitations, opt for declaratory remedies as opposed to seeking orders requiring compliance and implementation. It is in the same vein that the EACJ has definitively held that

---

[39] Democratic Party v. The Secretary General of the East African Community, Appeal No. 1 of 2014, East African Court of Justice [E. Afr. Ct. Just.] at para 71 (Aug. 26, 2014), http://eacj.org/?tribe_events=appeal-1-2014-democratic-party-vs-secretary-general-east-african-community-4-others (hereinafter "*Democratic Party Appeal* case"); for instance, where the EACJ asserted itself thus: "nothing can preclude the East African Court of Justice from referring to the relevant provisions of the Charter . . . in order to interpret the Treaty."

[40] *But see* Milej, *supra* note 27 (showing the EACJ is more assertive in some other cases that have to do with advancing economic liberalization, applying EAC law in a constitutional manner that trumps higher (community norms) over lower (often) national norms, and even acts in ways tilting towards the role played by constitutional courts in political federations).

[41] Rugumba v. Secretary General of the East African Community, Reference No. 8 of 2010, East African Court of Justice [E. Afr. Ct. Just.] (Dec. 1, 2011) (hereinafter "*Plaexda-Rugumba* case"), https://eacj.org/wp-content/uploads/2012/11/Plaexda-Rugumba-2010-8-judgment-2011.pdf.

[42] *Id.* at para. 24.

[43] For instance, in the case of African Network for Animal Welfare v. Attorney General of the Republic of Tanzania, Reference No. 9 of 2010, East African Court of Justice [E. Afr. Ct. Just.] (Apr. 25, 2013), https://africanlii.org/ea/judgment/2013/1, the claim was that the actions of the government of Tanzania were unlawful and asserted an infringement of EAC Treaty provisions. Drawing Article 39 of the EAC Treaty that deals with issuing interim orders or issues any directions, the EACJ was able to make a mandatory order of injunction. We argue that this case was not treated as a human rights case and this is why there is no mention of human rights in the entire judgment.

the EAC Treaty is not a human rights treaty, hence the EACJ cannot, in human rights claims litigated before it, render its decisions as a "human rights court." The first instance division of the EACJ observed in the case of *Samuel Mukira Mohochi v. The Attorney General of the Republic of Uganda (Mohochi case)* that:

> ... the Treaty is neither a Human Rights Convention nor a Human Rights Treaty as understood in international law. It is rather a Treaty to govern the widening and deepening of ... cooperation between the Partner States ... we are not aware of a chapter, article or provision in the Treaty, Protocols and Annexes which designates any provisions therein as "the human rights provisions.[44]

By this, the Court was implicitly informing the parties that litigating human rights claims before the EACJ would not be similar to normal human rights litigation based on a human rights treaty as understood in international law. This would then also extend to the remedies and orders issued by the EACJ. Thus, it elects to limit the remedies available in human rights cases to declaratory judgments. In such cases, states are met with the EACJ's authoritative statement of EAC law, which states may or may not ignore. This strategy avoids direct confrontation between the EACJ and its state parties without necessarily removing the burden of the judgment on state parties. However, this is not to say that the EACJ does not issue binding decisions with which states must and do comply. Several cases abound where the EACJ has called out states for non-compliance with Treaty provisions and required them to take steps to comply, including by review of national legislation. For instance, in *Peter Anyang' Nyong'o and 10 others v. The Attorney General of Kenya and 2 others (Nyong'o case)*, the EACJ issued a mandatory injunction to stop Kenya from conducting elections of its representatives to the EALA in a manner that it deemed inconsistent with Article 50(1) of the EAC Treaty.[45] Kenya subsequently complied and amended the relevant national legislation to bring it in line with the EAC Treaty. However, these cases are distinguishable in that the complaints litigated before the Court are not strictly "human rights" claims, but claims of violation of other Treaty provisions over which the EACJ has full and unfettered jurisdiction to issue the relevant applicable orders.[46]

---

[44] Muhochi v. Attorney General of the Republic of Uganda, Reference No. 5 of 2011, East African Court of Justice [E. Afr. Ct. Just.], paras. 28 and 29 (May 24, 2013), https://africanlii.org/ea/judgment/east-african-court-justice/2013/8.

[45] Attorney General of Kenya v. Nyong'o, Reference No. 1 of 2006, East African Court of Justice [E. Afr. Ct. Just.] (Feb. 6, 2007), http://www.worldcourts.com/eacj/eng/decisions/2007.02.06_Attorney_General_Kenya_v_Nyong_o.htm; *see also* Attorney General of Kenya v. Nyong'o, Appeal No. 1 of 2009, East African Court of Justice [E. Afr. Ct. Just.] (Jul. 31, 2010), https://eacj.org/wp-content/uploads/2012/11/Appeal-no-1-of-2009.pdf.

[46] For more information, *see* James Thuo Gathii, *Saving the Serengeti: Africa's New International Judicial Environmentalism*, 16 CHI. J. INT'L L. 386 (2016).

The ECOWAS Court was first conceived as a Community Tribunal in the original 1975 Treaty establishing the ECOWAS. However, when a protocol was adopted in 1991 to operationalize the Community judicial organ, ECOWAS Member States opted for a Community Court of Justice with the usual jurisdiction to "interpret and apply the treaty of the ECOWAS."[47] Despite its inauguration in 2001, the ECOWAS Court was only accessible to state parties and not individuals so that it was not until 2004 that the Court received its first case.[48] In 2005 when a Supplementary Protocol was adopted under the 1993 revised ECOWAS Treaty regime to amend aspects of the functioning of the ECOWAS Court. The Supplementary Protocol made the Court accessible to individuals and gave the Court jurisdiction to receive and determine cases alleging the violation of human rights within the territories of ECOWAS Member States.[49]

Based on the relevant provisions in the 2005 Supplementary Protocol and certain provisions in the revised ECOWAS Treaty[50] and other legal instruments of the ECOWAS Community,[51] the ECOWAS Court affirmed that it was competent to determine and remedy complaints of human rights arising within the territories of ECOWAS Member States. In the cases brought before it since the entry into force of the 2005 Supplementary Protocol, the ECOWAS Court declared that it had a human rights jurisdiction which was not anchored in a specific regime of human rights. The ECOWAS Court has however decided that the African Charter is the main Treaty regime whose rights it would enforce because it is expressly referred to in the legal instruments of the ECOWAS Community.[52]

The revised ECOWAS Treaty and the 1991 Protocol provide that decisions of the Court are binding and immediately enforceable.[53] Article 24 of the 2005 Protocol provides that the execution of any decision of the Court commences by a writ of execution submitted by the Registrar to the relevant Member State to be enforced in accordance with its rules of civil procedure.

---

[47] *See* Protocol A/P/1/7/91 of 6 July 1991 on the Community Court of Justice (1991 ECOWAS Court Protocol) (establishing the ECOWAS Community Court of Justice).

[48] *See generally* Solomon T. Ebobrah, *Critical Issues in the Human Rights Mandate of the ECOWAS Court of Justice*, 54 J. AFR. L. 1–25 (2010); *see also* Karen J. Alter et al., *A New International Human Rights Court for West Africa: The ECOWAS Community Court of Justice*, 107 AM. J. INT'L L. 737–79 (2013).

[49] *See* Supplementary Protocol A/SP.1/01/05 of 2005 (2005 ECOWAS Court Protocol), art. 10(d)(ii); *Id.* at art. 4.

[50] ECOWAS Treaty, art. 4(h), 14 I. L. M. 1200 (May 28, 1975, revised July 24, 1993).

[51] For instance, *see* Protocol A/SP1/12/01 of 2001 on Democracy and Good Governance Supplementary to the Protocol Relating to the Mechanism For Conflict Prevention, Management, Resolution, Peacekeeping and Security.

[52] *See* Obiora C. Okafor & Okechukwu J. Effoduh's chapter (Chapter 3) of this book where they discuss the ECOWAS Court in-depth.

[53] *See also* Rules of the Court of Justice of the Economic Community of West African States (ECOWAS), art. 62 (2002).

Having declared itself to be a Court with human rights jurisdiction, a declaration which was embraced by Court users (mostly individuals and NGOs) and not resisted by ECOWAS Member States, the ECOWAS Court has established itself as a formidable human rights adjudicator.[54] The Court's practice since 2005 has been to receive *mostly* claims of human rights violations, which it considers, makes findings and orders of the affected state to remedy in a variety of ways, including by the payment of monetary compensation.[55] Thus, the ECOWAS Court considers its human rights jurisdiction to be akin to the jurisdiction of national courts—direct and mandatory with obligations that must be immediately implemented within the domestic legal system of ECOWAS Member States. Accordingly, state parties to the ECOWAS Court are faced with real judicial orders from the Court with which the states have to either comply or not comply. Beneficiaries of the Court's judgments legitimately expect that the order(s) in their favor will deliver the individual justice to which they are entitled.

In other words, whereas the EACJ has operated its *assumed* human rights jurisdiction in a restrained manner, considering its findings of violation as "declaratory" in the same manner as the European Court of Human Rights (ECtHR) did originally,[56] the ECOWAS Court considers its *conferred* jurisdiction to be "mandatory." Effectively, the EACJ is a declaratory human rights regime with no immediate and direct compliance consequences either for states or litigants while the ECOWAS Court is a protective regime with direct and immediate consequences for compliance by states.[57] As we show in Part Three, the ECOWAS Court has created this protective regime by interpreting Article 24 of the African Charter as containing both an obligation of attitude (conduct) and an obligation of result where there has been a violation of Charter norms. This distinction notwithstanding, as we shall shortly show, state compliance with the decision of the sub-regional courts has not been radically different from the decisions of the African Court on Human and Peoples' Rights.

---

[54] The ECOWAS Court receives more complaints of human rights violation than the African Court of Human Rights. Not surprisingly, the African Union's Human Rights Strategy document recognizes the ECOWAS Court and the EACJ as regional human rights actors.

[55] Costs awarded by the ECOWAS Court range from CFA10 million (approximately US$18,066 as of Sept. 18, 2020) against Niger in Koraou v. Republic of Niger, ECW/CCJ/APP/08/08, ECOWAS Community Court of Justice [ECOWAS Cmty. Ct. Just.] (Oct. 27, 2008) to US$100,000 and US$200,000 in the cases of Manneh v. Republic of Gambia, ECW/CCJ/APP/04/07, ECOWAS Community Court of Justice [ECOWAS Cmty. Ct. Just.] (June 5, 2008), http://www.worldcourts.com/ecowasccj/eng/decisions/2008.06.05_Manneh_v_Gambia.htm; Saidykhan v. Gambia, ECW/CCJ/APP/11/07, ECOWAS Community Court of Justice [ECOWAS Cmty. Ct. Just.] (Dec. 16, 2010), https://ihrda.uwazi.io/ar/document/froafttgl56tn7350qszzd7vi, respectively.

[56] For instance, *see* Shany, *supra* note 17, at 268 (asserting that the Court (ECHR) long viewed violation in individual cases as "declaratory" in nature).

[57] For the difference between declaratory and protective human rights regimes, *see also* David Forsythe, *Human Rights, The United States and The Organization of American States*, 13 HUM. RTS. Q. 66, 77 (1991).

Part Three: An Overview of Compliance of Judgments of the EACJ and the ECOWAS Community Court of Justice

Against the background of the differences in jurisprudential approach we have high-lighted earlier the question that we interrogate in this section is whether there is a cor-responding difference in how the judgments of the EACJ and the ECOWAS Court deliver on the promise of individual justice through the direct impact that comes with state compliance. We show by representative evidence that the reactions of state parties to both Courts exhibit a similar pattern. Compliance is problematic for both Courts when direct impact and individual justice are in question. In some of the lit-erature, this leads to an erroneous conclusion that these Courts are ineffective and that the protective value of their judgments is questionable. To answer the question whether the rulings of Africa's sub-regional courts influence state behavior,[58] we show in this section that in terms of direct impact or immediate positive state response in the form of behavioral change, action or inaction that can be causally linked to the influence of a judicial decision, neither the EACJ nor the ECOWAS Court can claim a high percentage of compliance or protective value. However, we distinguish direct impact from indirect impact. By indirect impact we mean securing state party compli-ance with the primary rules[59] of the regime (in this case, the provisions of the African Charter) incrementally, by a variety of actions and over a long period of time as a result of a more tenuous causal link with judgments of the Courts.[60]

In *Plaxeda-Rugumba v. Rwanda*,[61] the EACJ declared that the detention of Lieutenant Colonel Rugigana Ngabo by agents of the government of Rwanda was in breach of relevant provisions of the EAC Treaty. No order was made requiring Rwanda to release the victim and there is no evidence that the victim has been re-leased as a result of the judgment. However, there was arguably more information available to the family of Lieutenant Colonel Ngabo after this case was filed in the EACJ than there had been before that.

In *Burundi Journalists Union v. The Attorney General of Burundi*, the EACJ de-clared sections of the Burundi Press Law inconsistent with the EAC Treaty. The Court declined to make any order compelling the government of Burundi to amend its laws notwithstanding the inconsistency.[62] In *Mohochi v. Attorney General of*

---

[58] Laurence R. Helfer, *The Effectiveness of International Adjudicators, in* THE OXFORD HANDBOOK OF INTERNATIONAL ADJUDICATION 464, 465 (Cesare P. R. Romano, et al. eds., 2014) (showing how a ques-tion of this kind has become very common).

[59] On state compliance with primary norms, *see* Helfer, *supra* note 58.

[60] *See also* Viljoen & Louw, *supra* note 20 (for a discussion on the distinction between direct impact and indirect impact).

[61] *See* Rugumba v. Secretary General of the East African Community, Reference No. 8 of 2010, East African Court of Justice [E. Afr. Ct. Just.] (Dec. 1, 2011), https://eacj.org/wp-content/uploads/2012/11/Plaxeda-Rugumba-2010-8-judgment-2011.pdf.

[62] Burundian Journalists Union v. The Attorney General of the Republic of Burundi, Reference No. 7 of 2013, East African Court of Justice [E. Afr. Ct. Just.] (May 15, 2015), https://eacj.org/wp-content/uploads/2015/05/Reference-No.7-of-2013-Final-15th-May-2c-2015-Very-Final.pdf.

Uganda[63] the EACJ came to a conclusion and declared that "the denial of entry into Uganda of the Applicant, a citizen of a Partner State, without according him the due process of law was illegal, unlawful and a breach of Uganda's obligations under Articles 6(d) and 7(2) of the Treaty." The Court did not make any order of damages in favor of the applicant and further ordered each party to bear its own costs. The litigant was successful yet did not enjoy any direct financial or other benefit from the finding that his human rights had been violated. There was no direct impact in favor of the litigant and it is safe to say no individual justice was served. Lastly, in *East African Law Society v. Attorney General of Burundi and the Secretary General of the East African Community*[64] the EACJ held that the disbarment of Gervais Rufyikiri, a Burundian lawyer, was a violation of due process and therefore inconsistent with Articles 6(d) and 7(2) of the EAC Treaty. It nonetheless declined to grant an order quashing and setting aside the Court of Appeal's decision to disbar Rufyikiri, basing its decision on the fact that making such an order was outside its jurisdiction by virtue of the provision to Article 27(1) of the EAC Treaty.

Other cases involving claims of human rights violation follow the same pattern of declaratory judgments.

Thus, within the EAC, it can be safely concluded that the EACJ's human rights decisions have to a large extent not yielded the immediately demonstrable results in the nature of change of law or policy within the Partner States. In short, the EACJ's decision-making strategy makes assessing the direct impact of its decision difficult at best. This is not necessarily the case when the claim is based on alleged violation of non-human rights Treaty provisions. Thus, for instance, the decisions of the EACJ in the *Anyang' Nyong'o* case[65] and *Democratic Party and Mukasa Mbidde v. The Secretary General of the East African Community and the Attorney General of the Republic of Uganda* (*Mukassa Mbidde* case)[66] resulted in the amendment of national legislation in Kenya and Uganda respectively, to make them compliant with Article 50 of the EAC Treaty. These two cases are discussed in James Thuo Gathii's chapter (Chapter 1) on international courts as coordination devices in this book. The decision of the EACJ in *African Network For Animal Welfare (ANAW)*

---

[63] Muhochi v. Attorney General of the Republic of Uganda, Reference No. 5 of 2011, East African Court of Justice [E. Afr. Ct. Just.] (May 24, 2013), https://africanlii.org/ea/judgment/east-african-court-justice/2013/8.

[64] Ruhara v. The Attorney General of the Republic of Burundi, Reference No. 4 of 2014, East African Court of Justice [E. Afr. Ct. Just.] (Aug. 7, 2015), https://africanlii.org/ea/judgment/east-african-court-justice/2015/98.

[65] Attorney General of Kenya v. Nyong'o, Reference No. 1 of 2006, East African Court of Justice [E. Afr. Ct. Just.] (Feb. 6, 2007), http://www.worldcourts.com/eacj/eng/decisions/2007.02.06_Attorney_General_Kenya_v_Nyong_o.htm; *see also* Attorney General of Kenya v. Nyong'o, Appeal No. 1 of 2009, East African Court of Justice [E. Afr. Ct. Just.] (Jul. 31, 2010), https://eacj.org/wp-content/uploads/2012/11/Appeal-no-1-of-2009.pdf.

[66] Democratic Party, et al. v. Attorney General of the Republic of Uganda, Reference No. 6 of 2011, East African Court of Justice [E. Afr. Ct. Just.] (Sept. 13, 2013), http://www.worldcourts.com/eacj/eng/decisions/2013.09.13_Democratic_Party_v_Atty_Gen_Uganda.pdf.

v. The Attorney General of The United Republic of Tanzania (Serengeti case*)* stopped
a major national road project based on the need to protect the environment.[67] As
will be demonstrated in Part Four, a large part of the EACJ's decisions on human
rights cases has invariably yielded more in terms of indirect impact as opposed to
immediately demonstrable changes in law or policy as would be attributed to the
cases already mentioned.

As we already indicated earlier, in the opinion of the ECOWAS Community
Court, only approximately twenty-two out of sixty-four enforceable judgments
of that Court have been implemented or enforced by state parties.[68] The case of
Koraou v. Niger[69] where the Republic of Niger wasted no time in declaring that
it was going to pay the compensation of CFA10 million to the victim is certainly
one of the twenty-two cases where judgment has been implemented.[70] In *SERAP
v. Nigeria*[71] the ECOWAS Court awarded damages in the sum of 11 million Naira
(approximately US$70,000.00) to residents of an informal settlement in Southern
Nigeria who were shot by government forces when they protested against their
forceful eviction from the informal settlement. The NGO involved in the case
(SERAP) acknowledged that the government of Nigeria paid the damages, thus
bringing individual justice to the litigants.

However, in the case of *Manneh v. The Gambia*[72] the ECOWAS Court ordered
the Gambia to pay the victim damages equivalent to US$100,000 after finding that
the state respondent had violated the rights of the plaintiff. Ten years after the judgment of the Court, the Gambia has still not complied with the judgment. This is a
clear case of non-compliance and a lack of direct impact leading to the denial of
individual justice to the plaintiff who has not only suffered violations of his rights
but has also been denied the fruit of his labour of litigation. Similarly, in *Musa
Sadyikhan v. The Gambia*[73] the ECOWAS Court also found the Gambia to have
violated the rights of the plaintiff and awarded damages to the plaintiff in the sum
of US$200,000. As with the *Manneh* case, eight years afterwards, the Gambia has

---

[67] African Network for Animal Welfare v. Attorney General of the Republic of Tanzania, Reference
No. 9 of 2010, East African Court of Justice [E. Afr. Ct. Just.] (Apr. 25, 2013), https://africanlii.org/ea/
judgment/2013/1.
[68] *See* Alter et al., *supra* note 8.
[69] Koraou v. Republic of Niger, ECW/CCJ/APP/08/08, ECOWAS Community Court of Justice
[ECOWAS Cmty. Ct. Just.] (Oct. 27, 2008), http://www.worldcourts.com/ecowasccj/eng/decisions/
2008.10.27_Koraou_v_Niger.htm.
[70] Interview with one of the lawyers who appeared in the case. On file with one of the present authors.
[71] The Registered Trustees of the Socio-Economic Rights & Accountability Project, et al. v. Republic
of Nigeria, ECW/CCJ/APP/10/10, ECOWAS Community Court of Justice [ECOWAS Cmty. Ct. Just.]
(Oct. 29, 2010).
[72] Manneh v. Republic of Gambia, ECW/CCJ/APP/04/07, ECOWAS Community Court of Justice
[ECOWAS Cmty. Ct. Just.] (June 5, 2008), http://www.worldcourts.com/ecowasccj/eng/decisions/
2008.06.05_Manneh_v_Gambia.htm.
[73] Saidykhan v. Republic of Gambia, ECW/CCJ/APP/11/07, ECOWAS Community Court of Justice
[ECOWAS Cmty. Ct. Just.] (Dec. 16, 2010); Saidykhan v. Republic of Gambia, ECW/CCJ/JUD/08/10,
ECOWAS Community Court of Justice [ECOWAS Cmty. Ct. Just.] (Dec. 16, 2010).

failed or refused to implement the judgment of the Court resulting in a denial of individual justice to the litigant. In *Mba v. Ghana*,[74] the ECOWAS Court awarded the plaintiff damages in the sum of US$800,000. Upon failure of the state to comply, the plaintiff approached the national courts in Ghana to try to enforce the judgments but was not able to secure a favorable judgment.[75]

The picture that emerges from the representative evidence supplied earlier is that in spite of a limited number of cases where state parties respond positively to the judgments of the sub-regional courts and deliver immediate direct individual justice to litigants, there are a whole number of other cases in which states simply ignore the judgments. In other words, the Courts struggle with compliance and there is no guarantee of implementation even where a litigant has secured judgment. Does this mean that these Courts have no protective value?

Part Four: Protecting Rights Beyond Judgment Compliance

Notwithstanding the limited demonstrable direct impact of the decisions of REC international courts in human rights cases, we argue that compliance with court orders is not the sole yardstick for evaluating the usefulness of international courts within the context of RECs. In the absence of credible data to the contrary, it cannot reasonably be disputed that Africa's sub-regional courts, like most international courts, have little or no direct impact on the human rights conduct of states. First, even in the face of isolated but celebrated reports of compliance with judgments, there is no evidence that *all* states parties to Africa's sub-regional courts *always* take seriously their obligation to comply with or implement judgments of these courts. Secondly, as some commentators contend, it is difficult to authoritatively assert a cause and effect relationship between judgments and state behavior. This, they argue, is because while "norms may guide behaviour ... inspire behaviour, rationalise or justify behaviour, they may express 'mutual expectations' about behaviour or they may be ignored" they do not "effect cause in the sense that a bullet through the heart may cause death."[76] The Introduction to this book comprehensively discusses the literature on compliance. This chapter, consistent with a major theme of this book, argues that there is utility beyond compliance that accounts for the fact

---

[74] Mba v. Republic of Ghana, ECW/CCJ/APP/01/13, ECOWAS Community Court of Justice [ECOWAS Cmty. Ct. Just.] (Jan. 21, 2013), https://africanlii.org/ecowas/judgment/ecowas-community-court-justice/2019/30.

[75] Unreported, Suit No. HRCM/376/15—In the Matter of Mr. Chude Mba vs. The Republic of Ghana. *See also* Cajetan Osisioma, *Is the ECOWAS Court a Toothless Bulldog that only barks? Issues Arising from the High Court of Ghana in Mr Chuba Mba v The Republic of Ghana*, SPA Ajibade & Co. (Mar. 4, 2016), http://www.spaajibade.com/resources/wp-content/uploads/2016/03/Is-the-ECOWAS-Court-of-Justice-a-Toothless-Bulldog-that-Only-Bark1.pdf.

[76] Robert Howse & Ruti Teitel, *Beyond Compliance: Rethinking Why International Law Really Matters* 10 (N.Y.U. Pub. Law & Legal Theory Research Paper Series, Working Paper No. 10-08, 2010), https://papers.ssrn.com/sol3/papers.cfm?abstract_id=1551923.

that Africa's sub-regional courts remain in active business. One of such reasons, we contend, is the indirect impact that these courts and their judgments bring to bear on the human rights situation in the respective states.

In the rest of this section, we analyze the work and operations of the two sub-regional courts to determine whether such indirect influence or impact can also be associated with Africa's sub-regional courts. In particular, we argue that there are four ways in which the decisions of Africa's international courts matter beyond judgment compliance. These are, first, flagging violations and acting as early warning systems; second, expanding the normative and institutional scope and protection of human rights; third, progressing norm development; and fourth, in setting the boundaries of acceptable behavior for governments. We discuss each of these in turn.

Flagging Violations/Early Warning System

One of the significant indirect impacts of sub-regional courts is that the availability of a forum to file cases that is not controlled by states has opened up opportunities for flagging human rights violations that would likely not have received public attention. From this perspective, filing human rights cases in Africa's sub-regional courts operates as a warning system that flags violations of human rights. Once these cases are filed, these violations are brought to the attention of respondent states, other states in the sub-region as well as non-state actors. Much like the role originally attributed to the European Convention on Human Rights and the ECtHR,[77] the number and nature of cases that come to sub-regional courts from states allow regional policy makers and other heads of state and government to track the human rights situation in each state.[78] As was the case in Europe in the post-World War era, this is an important mechanism for the protection of human rights in weak and emerging democracies as well as in all societies where effective domestic monitoring and protection institutions are either non-existent or are themselves under threat.[79] The chapter in this volume on Burundi by Andrew Heinrich (Chapter 2) also makes this point strongly.

---

[77] Philip Leach, *The European System and Approach*, in THE ROUTLEDGE HANDBOOK ON INTERNATIONAL HUMAN RIGHTS LAW 410 (Scott Sheeran & Nigel Rodley eds., 2013); *see also* Luzius Wildhaber, *European Union, European Convention on Human Rights and Human Rights Protection in Europe*, 26 RITSUMEIKARN L. REV. 155, 156 (2009).

[78] Some scholars have argued that this type of benefit of a human rights treaty regime (i.e. the monitoring or flagging of violations) is "woefully inadequate." *See* Oona A. Hathaway, *Do Human Rights Treaties Make a Difference?*, 111 YALE L. J. 1935, 2008 (2002). *See also* PETER UVIN, HUMAN RIGHTS AND DEVELOPMENT 140 (2004) (arguing that monitoring processes "constitute some of the most powerless, under-funded, formulaic, and politically manipulated institutions of the United Nations." However, it is evident that such conclusions are based on state-driven compliance processes. The analysis employed in this chapter goes beyond state-based processes to include the role of non-state actors.)

[79] *See generally* Leach, *supra* note 77, at 413; *see* Wildhaber, *supra* note 77, at 156.

The case of *Plaxeda-Rugumba v. Rwanda* before the EACJ presents a good example of the utility of the EACJ as a forum for flagging of violations and a warning system. In the aftermath of the 1994 Rwandan genocide and the emergence of President Paul Kagame, Rwanda was widely recognized as an African success story and a model of good governance in sub-Saharan Africa. However, a few human rights organizations, mostly from the global North, and courageous Rwandan opposition figures spoke up in opposition to the authoritarian governance of President Kagame's government. Under President Kagame, genocidal violence ended and the economy prospered. At the same time Rwanda became a police state in which violations of human rights became all too frequent.[80] Yet, there were hardly any cases alleging violations of human rights brought before the Rwandan National Human Rights Commission or the regular national courts. Rwanda had also signed up to the African Charter and therefore falls within the "jurisdiction" of the African Commission on Human and Peoples' Rights (African Commission). Yet again, there were almost no complaints against Rwanda before the Commission alleging violations of rights.[81] In the face of all these, supporters of the Kagame regime were quick to assert that the allegations of the operation of a police state and massive violation of rights were not true but were mere efforts to undermine President Kagame's legacy. It is against this background that the *Plaxeda-Rugumba* matter came before the EACJ.[82]

In the *Plaxeda-Rugumba* case, the applicant who claimed to be the elder sister of a certain Lieutenant Colonel Seveline Rugugana Ngabo of the Rwandan Defence Force complained that her brother (the victim) was arrested in August 2010 by Rwandan authorities and was being held incommunicado without access to his family, lawyer, doctor, or the Red Cross. The applicant argued that "Lieutenant Colonel Ngabo's wife is not in a position to file an application for habeas corpus to cause the release of her husband within Rwanda as the government is hostile to such a process and her attempts to follow up the detention of her husband has led to her being harassed into hiding."[83] In the opinion of the applicant, there was no effective domestic means of finding the whereabouts of the victim, leaving the EACJ as perhaps the only option for a judicial review.[84] The case before the EACJ,

---

[80] *Paul Kagame, Feted and Feared*, THE ECONOMIST (July 15, 2017), https://www.economist.com/briefing/2017/07/15/paul-kagame-feted-and-feared.

[81] At this time, Rwanda had not ratified the Protocol establishing the African Court of Human and Peoples' Rights and had not made the relevant Article 34 § 6 declaration that opens up access to non-state actors.

[82] One exception to the lack of cases challenging Rwanda in international courts is discussed in Gathii and Jacquelene Wangui Mwangi's chapter (Chapter 6) in this book. As a result of that case, the government of Rwanda withdrew the declaration accepting individual petitions to the African Court.

[83] Rugumba v. Secretary General of the East African Community, Reference No. 8 of 2010, East African Court of Justice [E. Afr. Ct. Just.] para. 2 (Dec. 1, 2011), https://eacj.org/wp-content/uploads/2012/11/Plaxeda-Rugumba-2010-8-judgment-2011.pdf.

[84] Rwanda also ratified the Protocol establishing the African Court of Human and Peoples' Rights and made the declaration allowing individuals and NGOs access to the African Court but subsequently withdrew its ratification and declaration.

thus, became one of the rare opportunities by which a sub-regional court and the rest of the international community could peek into the human rights situation in Rwanda. Consequently, the mere filing of the *Plaexda-Rugumba* case could already be described as a victory for the victim's family in a number of ways.

This is particularly true in light of the fact that Rugumba's family had no idea where he was. They were too afraid to even raise question of his whereabouts with the government of Rwanda. Thus the mere filing of the case before the EACJ presented an opportunity for the family to hold the government of Rwanda to account on a relatively level playing field. By filing the case, public attention was brought in the East African Community and the wider international community about the allegation that a police state was being run behind the façade of economic development and order. To add to the string of victories for the victim even before the EACJ reached judgment stage, the military authorities in Rwanda by their own admission hurriedly arraigned the victim before a military court arguably in order to be able to put up a proper defense before the EACJ. Consequently, in their defense to the action, the Rwandan military authorities admitted publicly, probably for the first time, that the victim was in their custody and was being held on suspicions of "crimes against national security."[85] Thus, while the matter was not even close to judgment, the victim family had been able to secure an admission that the victim was in government custody simply by filing the case in the EACJ. The international community was also now aware that the victim and possibly others like him were in the custody of a regime that was receiving accolades around the world for good governance.

It was also significant that while the action before the EACJ was filed in late 2010, Rwandan military authorities confirmed that they brought the victim before the military court in January 2011 to ask for an order of preventive detention.[86] Thus the filing of this case in the EACJ signaled that similar violations were likely taking place. This in turn brought to broader international attention what was going on in Rwanda where the opportunity to seek judicial relief had probably shrunken to near non-existence. The EACJ process thus, could be seen as an early warning system for interested stakeholders that all was not well in Rwanda under an administration that was consistently receiving accolades from the international community for its free market reforms. In other words, notwithstanding the eventual judgment of the EACJ which was declaratory and did not necessarily require (and may not have received) a compliance decision from Rwanda, the EACJ had contributed to the protection of human rights in the sub-region by creating opportunities that were rare or non-existent at the national level.

---

[85] Rugumba v. Secretary General of the East African Community, Reference No. 8 of 2010, East African Court of Justice [E. Afr. Ct. Just.], para. 15 (Dec. 1, 2011), https://eacj.org/wp-content/uploads/2012/11/Plaexda-Rugumba-2010-8-judgment-2011.pdf.

[86] *Id.*

In *East African Law Society v. Attorney General of Burundi and the Secretary General of the East African Community,*[87] the EACJ had the occasion to adjudicate over a claim filed by the East African Law Society on behalf of Isidore Rufyikiri, who was at the time the President of the Burundi Bar Association. The reference arose from his un-procedural disbarment from the Roll of Advocates in 2014 and his subsequent arrest and prosecution for corruption as well as the imposition of a travel ban prohibiting him from leaving Burundi after he allegedly called a press conference and made statements against state security and public peace. In essence, Rufyikiri's troubles were as a result of having spoken out against the government of Burundi.

Thus, unable to personally file his case at the EACJ in Arusha, Tanzania,. Rufyikiri approached the East African Law Society (EALS) to pursue a reference at the EACJ on his behalf. His complaint against the authoritarian government of Burundi was that his prosecution for corruption, his disbarment from the Roll of Advocates, as well as the travel ban imposed on him were in breach of the rule of law, good governance, and freedom of movement, inconsistent with Articles 6(d) and 7(2) of the EAC Treaty.

In the case, a declaration was sought that his prosecution, disbarment and travel restriction was a violation of the EAC Treaty; a declaration that the EAC Secretariat had breached his obligations under Article 71 of the Treaty, and an order by the Court quashing his disbarment by the Court of Appeal and reinstating his name to the Roll of Advocates.

On the allegations of malicious prosecution for corruption, the Court, upon examining Burundi's anti-corruption legislation and Penal Code, concluded that the relevant laws empowered the Prosecutor General to initiate investigations and prosecutions against any person suspected of corruption and thus there was no violation of the EAC Treaty. With reference to Rufyikiri's disbarment, the Court concluded that the flawed procedure followed by the Prosecutor General to disbar him was a violation of due process and therefore inconsistent with Articles 6(d) and 7(2) of the Treaty.[88] On the alleged failures by the Secretary General, the Court ordered the Secretary General to operationalize a task force to investigate the situation in Burundi, and directed the government of Burundi to take measures to implement its judgment, including allowing the Secretary General to conduct its investigative mission.

---

[87]   Ruhara v. The Attorney General of the Republic of Burundi, Reference No. 4 of 2014, East African Court of Justice [E. Afr. Ct. Just.] (Aug. 7, 2015), https://africanlii.org/ea/judgment/east-african-court-justice/2015/98.

[88]   Whereas the Court made a declaration that the failure of due process by the Court of Appeal was a Treaty violation, it declined to grant an order quashing and setting aside the Court of Appeal's decision to disbar Rufyikiri, basing its decision on the fact that making such an order was outside its jurisdiction by virtue of the provision to Article 27(1) of the EAC Treaty.

A useful outcome of the decision of the EACJ in this case was the action taken by the Court, on its own motion, to red-flag the governance situation in Burundi and require the Secretary General to make operational the task force to investigate the human rights and governance situation in Burundi. As such, the decision of the EACJ, although not far reaching in terms of individual justice, served a higher, longer-term constitutional function of flagging a deteriorating human rights and governance situation in Burundi, and calling upon the EAC's organs to take steps to address the spiraling events. It is important to note that almost at the same time, there were ongoing efforts at the East African Legislative Assembly (EALA) through its Committee on Regional Affairs and Conflict Resolution, which conducted public hearings on the human rights situation in Burundi in 2016. The Committee issued a preliminary report strongly recommending an independent inquiry into alleged human rights violations by the Burundi regime.[89] As a result, the Assembly recommended to the Council of Ministers to request the EAC Summit of Heads of State and Government, to facilitate the establishment of a credible panel of inquiry to investigate all human rights violations in Burundi.

In West Africa, two cases brought against the Gambia on behalf of two journalists represent how the ECOWAS Court constitutes a forum for flagging violations and warning governments on the state of violations within an authoritarian state. In 2007, in the case of *Manneh v. The Gambia*,[90] Nigerian lawyers approached the ECOWAS Court on behalf of Gambian journalist, Chief Ebrimah Manneh alleging that he was a victim of illegal arrest and detention by Gambian secret police. According to his lawyers, the victim was arrested and held incommunicado, with no access to his family, friends, and lawyers.[91] Possibly as a result of the notoriety of the Gambian secret police and the alleged weakness of the Gambian judiciary, other than a letter demanding his release, no real effort could be made to secure justice within the domestic legal system. Thus, an action could only be brought before the ECOWAS Court, which in any case did not require prior exhaustion of domestic legal remedies. Before the ECOWAS Court, the application sought a declaration that Ebrimah Manneh's arrest by the National Intelligence Agency and his continued detention was a violation of rights. Hence, the application asked for an order mandating his release from detention and requiring the state to pay him compensation of US$5 million.[92] Following the refusal and failure of the Gambian authorities to make an appearance before the ECOWAS Court, the Court found in favor of the victim after hearing witnesses on his behalf. Three witnesses, two

---

[89] *See* Adam Ihucha, *EALA: Probe Burundi Human Rights Violations*, THE EAST AFRICAN NEWSPAPER (Feb. 20, 2016), http://www.theeastafrican.co.ke/news/EALA-Probe-Burundi-human-rights-violations-/-/2558/3065054/-/ljnmvsz/-/index.html.
[90] Manneh v. Republic of Gambia, ECW/CCJ/APP/04/07, ECOWAS Community Court of Justice [ECOWAS Cmty. Ct. Just.] (June 5, 2008), http://www.worldcourts.com/ecowasccj/eng/decisions/2008.06.05_Manneh_v_Gambia.htm.
[91] *See id.* at para. 5.
[92] *Id.* at 2–3.

of whom were Gambian-based journalists freely testified to the facts of Manneh's arrest and detention. It also came out in evidence by a third witness that Gambian lawyers advised that "they could not obtain justice in the Gambia."[93] It was against this rather bleak background that the *Manneh* case was filed before the ECOWAS Court, providing a fairly level playing field for the victim's family and representatives to confront a dreaded regime to challenge violations of rights. After hearing the applicant's case, the ECOWAS Court concluded that the actions of the Gambia were in violation of the African Charter on Human and Peoples' Rights and ordered the Gambia to release Chief Manneh and pay him damages in the sum of US$100,000.[94]

From the outset, the notoriety of the Yayah Jammeh regime in the Gambia and the state's refusal to take part in the proceedings or even cooperate with the ECOWAS Court would have signaled that the state would eventually refuse or fail to implement any adverse decision. Notwithstanding, the applicants continued with the presentation of their case, calling witnesses to prove their case on the merits of their fear of possible reprisal against potential witnesses by the Gambian government.[95] One effect of this strategy was that the family of the victim and the victim's lawyers were able to publicly denounce the regime in the Gambia whilst putting out their story in the public and international domain.[96] The publicity that the *Manneh* case received in the sub-region, particularly in the Gambia, Ghana, and Nigeria ensured that the allegations of the suppression of journalists and the violation of their rights could no longer be considered as speculations nor be ignored.[97] The apparent silence of the ECOWAS Authority of Heads of State and Government contrasted sharply with the public trial the case received before the ECOWAS Court, just as the refusal to participate and the failure to comply showcased at the international level, the Gambian regime's disregard for the rule of law within its domestic legal system. If ECOWAS states pretended that the violating conduct of the Gambian regime was a domestic affair, the *Manneh* case sent a warning to ECOWAS states and the international community that the regime's disregard for human rights and the rule of law was total and unequivocal. Thus, the filing of the *Manneh* case before the ECOWAS Court also resulted in small victories with potential for improving constitutional justice even if the individual

---

[93] *Id.* at para. 9.

[94] *Id.* at para. 44.

[95] *ECOWAS Court Defers Judgment in Case Against Gambia Government*, VOA NEWS: ARCHIVE (Nov. 1, 2009, 4:21 PM), https://www.voanews.com/archive/ecowas-court-defers-judgment-case-against-gambia-government (stating "We know we have witnesses but cannot produce them because of fear of reprisal by the Gambian government.").

[96] Apart from the local media attention that the case attracted in Nigeria and to an extent in the Gambia, international attention was also drawn with the regional body of journalists mounting an advocacy campaign around the *Ebrimah Manneh* case. *See id.*

[97] For instance, *see ECOWAS Court Rules Gambia Failed to Investigate Journalist Murder*, THE PREMIUM TIMES NIGERIA (June 11, 2014), https://www.premiumtimesng.com/news/162565-ecowas-court-rules-gambia-failed-investigate-journalist-murder.html.

justice that would have resulted if the Gambia complied with the judgment was not realized. Indirectly, the proceedings at the ECOWAS Court had consequences for human rights in the Gambia even when the judgment of the Court has remained unenforced. However, since the change of regime in the Gambia and the departure of former President Jammeh, the Gambia has taken a different approach to its judgment obligations.[98]

Following closely on the heels of the *Manneh* case was the case of *Saidykhan v. the Gambia*[99] in which the state was again called out in the judicial setting of the ECOWAS Court for its violation of the rights of journalists. The victim/plaintiff, Musa Saidykhan, who was the editor of a local newspaper in the Gambia alleged that the Jammeh regime had violated his right to personal liberty, dignity, and fair hearing by arresting and detaining him incommunicado for twenty-two days and subjecting him to torture and inhumane treatment during his detention. Although he was released on bail and escaped to a neighboring country while on bail, Saidykhan had approached the ECOWAS Court for declarations that his rights had been violated, an order restraining further harassment and intimidation of his family members still based in the Gambia, and for damages amounting to US$2 million.[100]

Unlike its approach to the *Manneh* case, the Gambia had legal representation in the *Saidykhan* case, creating a better opportunity for engagement which the victim and his family may never have had in the national legal system.[101] In fact, the state tried unsuccessfully to present a thinly disguised justification for its treatment of the victim.[102] Despite its denial of the allegation and the attempt to justify the treatment that its agents may have given to the victim, the state was put in a position where it had to open itself to scrutiny before an independent judicial body at the prompt of the victim who would not have been similarly empowered within the domestic legal system. More importantly from the perspective of the flagging of violations by the state and serving as a warning system to the regional and wider international community, the litigation presented an opportunity for the Court to judicially affirm the claims of the victim. According to the ECOWAS Court, it

---

[98] As of January 2018, the new regime which defeated and replaced the Jammeh administration in general elections had publicly pledged to pay the judgment debt, consequently guaranteeing individual justice as well.

[99] Saidykhan v. Republic of Gambia, ECW/CCJ/APP/11/07, ECOWAS Community Court of Justice [ECOWAS Cmty. Ct. Just.] (Dec. 16, 2010), https://ihrda.uwazi.io/ar/document/froafttgl56tn7350qszzd7vi; Saidykhan v. Republic of Gambia, ECW/CCJ/JUD/08/10, ECOWAS Community Court of Justice [ECOWAS Cmty. Ct. Just.] (Dec. 16, 2010), https://ihrda.uwazi.io/ar/document/froafttgl56tn7350qszzd7vi.

[100] Saidykhan v. Republic of Gambia, ECW/CCJ/APP/11/07, *supra* note 99, at para. 8.

[101] *Id.* at para. 9 (stating the ECOWAS Court records that the Gambia was represented by counsel and that the defence "consisted largely of a complete denial of all the averments contained in the initiating application").

[102] *Id.* at para. 32 (stating in the judgment that the Counsel for Gambia suggested the "confrontational and unpatriotic acts" of the plaintiff would justify the treatment he received if indeed such treatment was given, which the state denied).

"considers that the evidence of the plaintiff is consistent and credible and stands largely uncontroverted so we accept it that he was arrested and detained by the security agents of the defendant."[103] The Court equally gave judicial affirmation to the claim by the victim that he was tortured and suffered injury as a result of the treatment meted to him.[104] This judicial affirmation of his claims which contrasted sharply with the fact that the state generally ignored the mandatory orders in his favor did little to deny the victim small victories that arguably were unattainable within the national legal system. There was thus a flagging of the specific violations and a reinforcement of the warning that the Gambian regime was authoritarian. Similar to the *Manneh* case, the victim's story was out in the public and international domain just as opportunity was created for the victim and his family to denounce the government without reprisal, which was impossible within the domestic context of the Gambia. The fact that the ECOWAS Parliament became engaged in the Gambian situation is also reflected in East Africa. As Heinrich's chapter (Chapter 2) in this book shows, the EALA took up the debate on massive violations of human rights following an attempted coup in 2015.

With the adverse judgments in these two cases and the Gambia's negative and uncompromising attitude to compliance, attention was drawn to the situation in that state and the international community, particularly ECOWAS Member States became alerted to the need for intervention. For instance, in the ECOWAS Parliament's consideration of reports on the human rights situation in ECOWAS Member States, representatives of the Gambia were called out by their colleagues from other states with demands for explanations.[105] Thus, even though the ECOWAS Authority of Heads of State and Government—the Community's highest policy-making organ populated by heads of the executive branches of national government—failed to take punitive steps against the Gambia, the human rights situation in that state could no longer be ignored or swept under the carpet. Litigation before the ECOWAS Court, even though it had not led to individual justices for any of the two victims, effectively created opportunity for flagging the violations of rights and gave early or reinforced warning to the international community that all was not well in the Gambia.

In both the EAC and ECOWAS, integration has apparently been hinged on certain principles, including on the principle of respect, promotion, and protection of human rights.[106] In fact, in the case of the EAC, the human rights situation within a prospective Partner State is considered as a criteria for admittance into the REC.[107] In these contexts, litigation before the sub-regional courts provides some

---

[103] *Id.* at para. 36.

[104] *Id.* at para. 38–39.

[105] Personal observation of parliamentary session by one of the authors in 2012.

[106] *See* EAC Treaty, *supra* note 30, at arts. 6 & 7; ECOWAS Treaty, *supra* note 50, at art. 4.

[107] EAC Treaty, *supra* note 30, at art. 3(3)(b) (requiring the state's observance of human rights into account in considering an application to join). This condition was recently applied to applications from Somalia and South Sudan.

of the clearest information that the RECs may require. Thus, even in the face of a failure of individual justice arising from a direct impact of court judgments, sub-regional courts are able to indirectly advance human rights by drawing attention to the state of constitutional justice within Member States of sub-regional communities. Ultimately, bringing litigation in an international court can lead to exposing human rights violations in forms that extremely authoritarian governments do not control.

Expansion of Normative and Institutional Scope of Protection

Another indirect manner in which sub-regional courts in Africa shape domestic human rights outcomes irrespective of the judgment-compliance situation is that these courts expand the normative and institutional scope of protection beyond the restrictions of/in national legal systems. This generally occurs not in the specific case in which the expanding decision is made, but is useful for shaping future litigation. Sub-regional courts generally extend the reach of regional human rights norms into the domestic sphere of Member States; increase the categories of actors with access to justice; expand access to judicial relief for human rights violations; and narrowly construe limitations imposed by states on potential litigants in the form of pre-action requirements. Very often, this occurs independent of and in spite of unfavorable or unfavorably interpreted provisions in national constitutional or against the apparent express intention of the states being sued.[108]

The cases of *Democratic Party v. the Secretary General, East African Community and Four Others* (*Democratic Party* cases)[109] probably represent the best examples of the EACJ's intervention in this regard. Notwithstanding the EACJ's decision in the *Katabazi* case, the suspension of the EACJ's human rights jurisdiction in Article 27(2) of the EAC Treaty remains intact and restricts (or ought to restrict) the submission of human rights claims before that Court. In other words, the institutional restriction that Article 27(2) of the EAC Treaty imposes on the EACJ narrows the subject-matter jurisdiction of the EACJ by removing human rights from its jurisdiction. Against this background, the applicant in the *Democratic Party* case subtly invited the EACJ to stretch the boundaries of its assumed human rights jurisdiction when it challenged the failure by EAC Partner States to make country declarations accepting the competence of the African Human Rights

---

[108] Commentators on the European Human Rights system have equally recorded that part of the effectiveness of the ECtHR is in the area of "periodic addition of new substantive rights" to Convention rights. *See* Leach, *supra* note 77, at 410.

[109] Democratic Party v. The Secretary General of the East African Community, Reference No. 2 of 2012, East African Court of Justice [E. Afr. Ct. Just.] (Nov. 29, 2013) (hereinafter "*Democratic Party* case"), http://eacj.org/wp-content/uploads/2014/02/REFERENCE-NO-2-of-2012-Democratic-party-VS-SG-and-4-Others.pdf (for the judgment level of the case). *See also Democratic Party Appeal* case, *supra* note 39 (the appeal of the case).

Court to receive cases from non-state actors.[110] Significantly, in their respective responses to the action, EAC Partner States challenged the EACJ's competence over the African Charter and any of its protocols[111] effectively triggering the question whether that Court was a proper forum for the adjudication of claims based on the African Charter. Declaring that Articles 23, 27(1), and 30 of the EAC Treaty were the basis of its interpretative jurisdiction,[112] the First Instance Division of the EACJ admitted that it could not "properly delve into obligations created on the Respondents by other international instruments."[113] Explaining that its invocation of the African Charter in the *Rugumba* case must be understood in the context of "specific violations of Article 6(d) of the Treaty for the Establishment of the EAC and not the Charter per se,"[114] the First Instance Division held that the EACJ could not hold states to their obligation under the African Charter. The EACJ lacked competence and the African Charter was not applicable under the EAC regime.

In sharp contrast to the First Instance Division's judgment, the Appellate Division of the EACJ considered the same question and came to a different conclusion. It held that in view of Article 6(d) of the EAC Treaty, which "obligates the Partner States to adhere to ... recognition, promotion and protection of ... rights in accordance with the provisions of the African Charter." EAC states must act in accordance with the Charter such that failure to do so was an infringement of the EAC Treaty that could "legally be challenged before the EACJ."[115] In this important judgment, the Appellate Division expanded the jurisdictional competence of the EACJ, claiming jurisdiction over the African Charter while also expanding the EAC Treaty obligations to include obligations under the Charter. In so doing, the Appellate Division of the EACJ silently lowered some of the conditions for invoking the Charter at a transnational level by excluding the requirement to exhaust local remedies.[116] Thus, notwithstanding whether or not individual justice was delivered in the form of a positive judgment and compliance thereto, the case had resulted in an expansion of the protective coverage of an instrument beyond its original scope.

Although the ECOWAS Court enjoys an express human rights jurisdiction, the indeterminacies in the definition of conditions for the exercise of the jurisdiction represented potential obstacles for the positive application of the

---

[110] Democratic *Party* case, *supra* note 109, at para. 3.
[111] See *Id.* at paras. 15, 16, 20, & 25.
[112] *Id.* at para. 26–29.
[113] *Id.* at para. 55.
[114] *Id.* at para. 34.
[115] Democratic Party Appeal case, *supra* note 39, at para. 63–64.
[116] This follows the footsteps of the ECOWAS Court which also takes the view that the requirement to exhaust local remedies in the African Charter does not apply to claims before it even where such claims are based on the Charter.

granted jurisdiction. Apart from the fact that the 2005 Supplementary Protocol of the ECOWAS Court which authorized the exercise of human rights jurisdiction did not state the applicable catalogue of rights, the Protocol was also silent on the categories of potential litigants that could come before the Court. In a line of cases submitted by the Socio-Economic Rights Accountability Project (SERAP), the ECOWAS Court confronted the question whether NGOs could submit claims when they have not suffered any direct harm. In the case of *SERAP v. Federal Republic of Nigeria & the Universal Basic Education Commission* (*SERAP Education* case),[117] the Court faced challenges to its jurisdiction (based on the contention that socio-economic rights are aspirational in the Nigerian Constitution) and the competence of SERAP to bring the case.

In response to the action, Nigeria as respondent argued that "the Court does not have the competence to adjudicate on the subject matters outside a treaty, convention or protocol of the Community,"[118] that the right to education was not justiciable under the Nigerian Constitution[119] and that the "plaintiff lacks *locus standi* to initiate or bring the action."[120] In its ruling, the ECOWAS Court declared that it "has jurisdiction over human rights enshrined in the African Charter" and the domestication of some of those rights in municipal law did not take away its jurisdiction.[121] The ECOWAS Court went further to assert that human rights litigation has moved progressively toward allowing public interest litigation and "this court must lend weight to it in order to satisfy the aspirations of the citizens of the sub-region in their quest for a pervasive human rights regime."[122] Despite the debate that has raged regarding the judgment compliance status in this case, the ECOWAS Court was able to apply the judgment to reaffirm its institutional authority to supervise implementation of the Charter in ECOWAS Member States; overrule the national constitutional principle of non-justiciability of socio-economic rights; and grant NGOs access to the Court in public interest cases. These advancements have become useful in the sense that this judgment constituted judicial precedent upon which the Court based subsequent adjudication of socio-economic rights and access to NGOs.

---

[117] Socio-Economic Rights And Accountability Project v. Federal Republic of Nigeria & Universal Basic Education Commission, ECW/CCJ/APP/12/07, ECOWAS Community Court of Justice [ECOWAS Cmty. Ct. Just.] (Nov. 30, 2010); Socio-Economic Rights And Accountability Project v. Federal Republic of Nigeria & Universal Basic Education Commission, ECW/CCJ/JUD/07/10, ECOWAS Community Court of Justice [ECOWAS Cmty. Ct. Just.] (June 7, 2016) (hereinafter "SERAP Education Ruling"), http://www.worldcourts.com/ecowasccj/eng/decisions/2010.11.30_SERAP_v_Nigeria.htm.

[118] SERAP Education Ruling, *id.* at para. 4.

[119] *Id.* at para. 13.

[120] *Id.* at para. 20.

[121] *Id.* at para. 13.

[122] *See id.* at para. 33.

Norm Development

With all the value of the international human rights protection system, its capacity to accommodate and resolve disputes arising from states is relatively limited. While reliable statistics are currently unavailable, it can safely be argued that the number of cases that actually get to trial before an international court or other quasi-judicial system represents a very small fraction of the overall complaints of human rights violation that take place within the domestic spaces.[123] In Africa, apart from the challenge of the requirement of prior exhaustion of local remedies (in some regimes), lack of awareness and resource constraints combine to ensure that the majority of complaints do not get to international trial. Further, a general feature of international treaty-making, as compared to domestic legislative practices is that treaty-making usually involves compromises that sometimes result in provisions and or treaties that are vague and ambiguous. In other cases, treaty provisions may have no ambiguity but the interpretation given to such provisions may vary from state to state, usually to suit the interest of the powerful political interests in the given state. In all of these situations, sub-regional courts play an important rights protecting role when they develop norms through authoritative pronouncements that lead to the creation of a "common understanding" of community human rights law.[124] As the ECtHR held in its judgment in *Karner v. Austria*, "judgments in fact serve not only to decide those cases brought before the Court but, more generally, to elucidate, safeguard and develop the rules instituted by the Convention, thereby contributing to the observance by the States of the engagements undertaken by them as Contracting Parties."[125]

Given the cautionary approach with which the EACJ has had to engage with norms in the African Charter, there is currently no experience of elaborate norm development in that regime. Nonetheless, the Court in the *Democratic Party Appeal* case affirmed that it has jurisdiction to entertain disputes based on among others, the provisions of the African Charter.[126] Furthermore, the EACJ has been instrumental in developing a sub-regional normative framework which has been useful to civil society networks, individual litigants, and public interest lawyers in terms of framing and litigating their cases before the Court. Thus for instance, in the *Anyang' Nyong'o* case, the Court clarified that exhaustion of local remedies was not a pre-condition to instituting a suit before the EACJ. The famous *Katabazi Case*

---

[123] For a similar argument in the European context, *see* Janis, *supra* note 18, at 42 (contending that the most meaningful enforcement of Strasbourg law has to be taking place before national courts since only a small number of cases make it to the Strasbourg Court).

[124] *See also* ANDREW T. GUZMAN, HOW INTERNATIONAL LAW WORKS: A RATIONAL CHOICE THEORY 180 (2008).

[125] Karner v. Austria, 38 E.H.R.R. 528 (2003).

[126] *See* Democratic Party v. The Secretary General of the East African Community, Appeal No. 1 of 2014, East African Court of Justice [E. Afr. Ct. Just.] (Aug. 26, 2014), http://eacj.org/?tribe_events=appeal-1-2014-democratic-party-vs-secretary-general-east-african-community-4-others.

established the Court's jurisdiction over human rights disputes. In the *Mohochi* case, the Court reaffirmed the precedence of Community law over national law on matters pertaining to integration. And, in *East African Law Society and 4 Others v. Attorney General of Kenya and 3 others*,[127] the Court was categorical that any amendment to the EAC Treaty must be preceded by public participation and consultation. Lastly, in *Omar Awadh and 6 Others v. Attorney General of Uganda*[128] and in *Independent Medical Unit v. Attorney General of Kenya*,[129] the Court engaged with the doctrine of continuing violation with respect to the sixty-day period under the treaty for filing petitions. All these are normative tools that activists and lawyers may take advantage of, and in particular, apply in terms of framing their cases, presenting their arguments and devising their overall legal strategies when litigating before the EACJ. These sub-regional normative tools have also be utilized, where applicable, in litigation before national courts. Most notably, the *Anyang' Nyong'o* case has been relied on in several cases before the Uganda High Court, in *Oulanyah v. Republic*, in *Akidi Margaret v. Adong Lilly and the Electoral Commission*[130] as well as in *Toolit Simon Akesha v. Oulanyah Jacob L'Okori and Electoral Commission*.[131]

For the ECOWAS Court, which regularly adjudicates on claims based on the Africa Charter, its norm development role is best appreciated when it entertains claims on Charter provisions which have not been frequently adjudicated upon by mechanisms of the African human rights system. One such claim is the oil pollution claim brought by SERAP against Nigeria alleging a violation of the right to a satisfactory environment as guaranteed under the African Charter. In *Social and Economic Rights Action Centre (SERAC) and Another v. Nigeria*,[132] a communication brought before the African Commission, the applicants acting on behalf of the Ogoni people of the Niger Delta in Nigeria claimed a violation of the right to a satisfactory environment as guaranteed under Article 24 of the Charter. In its interpretation of the said Article 24 of the African Charter, the African Commission declared

---

[127] East African Law Society v. Attorney General of the Republic of Kenya, Reference No. 3 of 2007, East African Court of Justice [E. Afr. Ct. Just.] (Sept. 1, 2008), http://www.saflii.org/ea/cases/EACJ/2008/1.html.

[128] Awadh v. Attorney General of the Republic of Uganda, Appeal No. 2 of 2012, East African Court of Justice [E. Afr. Ct. Just.] (June 27, 2012), https://eacj.org/wp-content/uploads/2014/06/Application-No.-1-of-2012-Appellate-Division-Omar-Awadh-Omar-6-Others-Vs-The-Attorney-General-of-the-Repubic-of-Uganda.pdf.

[129] Independent Medical Unit v. Attorney General of Kenya, Reference No. 3 of 2010, East African Court of Justice [E. Afr. Ct. Just.] (June 29, 2011), http://www.worldcourts.com/eacj/eng/decisions/2011.06.29_Independent_Medical_Unit_v_Attorney_General.pdf.

[130] Akidi v. Adong and the Electoral Commission, Election Petition No. 0004 of 2011, High Court of Uganda (July 21, 2011), https://ulii.org/ug/judgment/election-petitions/2011/8.

[131] Toolit Simon Akecha v. Jacob Oulanyah L'okori and the Electoral Commission, Election Petition No. 001 of 2011, High Court of Uganda (July 21, 2011), https://ulii.org/ug/judgment/high-court-uganda/2011/97.

[132] Social and Economic Rights Action Center and the Center for Economic and Social Rights v. Nigeria, A.H.R.L.R. 60, African Commission on Human and Peoples' Rights [Afr. Comm'n H.P.R.] (Oct. 27, 2001) (hereinafter "SERAC Decision"), https://africanlii.org/afu/judgment/african-commission-human-and-peoples-rights/2001/34.

that "the right ... imposes clear obligations upon a government. It required the state to take reasonable and other measures to prevent pollution and ecological degradation, to promote conservation and to secure an ecologically sustainable development and use of natural resources."[133] The Commission added that "compliance with ... Article 24 ... must also include ordering or at least permitting independent scientific monitoring of threatened environments, requiring and publicising environmental and social impact studies prior to any major industrial development." It added that "undertaking appropriate monitoring and providing information to those communities exposed to hazardous materials and activities and providing meaningful opportunities for individuals to be heard and to participate in the development decisions affecting their communities."[134] This was the understanding of the scope of the Article 24 right to a satisfactory environment under the African Charter when the *SERAP Education* case came before the ECOWAS Court.

Developing the right further, the ECOWAS Court held that "Article 24 of the Charter ... requires every state to take every measure to maintain the quality of the environment understood as an integrated whole, such that the state of the environment may satisfy the human beings who live there and enhance their sustainable development."[135] Emphasizing that Article 24 contained both an obligation of attitude (conduct) and an obligation of result, the ECOWAS Court held that it was also a state duty under Article 24 to take "concrete measures aimed at preventing the occurrence of damage and ensuring accountability, with effective reparation of the environmental damage suffered."[136] Thus, notwithstanding the state of compliance with the judgment in this case, the ECOWAS Court managed to push the parameters of understanding of Article 24 of the Charter, creating precedent for future use by courts and litigants.

The discussion by Obiora C. Okafor and Okechukwu J. Effoduh in Chapter 3 of this book is also instructive in this context, where they argue that the ECOWAS Court of Justice has added to the body of jurisprudence on the protection of human rights through its explication of the details of the general community law and its interpretive choice to actively apply the full range of international human rights treaties that have been ratified by the relevant states.

Setting the Boundaries of Acceptable Behavior

Like other international courts, sub-regional courts in Africa also indirectly contribute to the protection of human rights in the national legal systems by assisting

---

[133] SERAC Decision, *supra* note 130, para. 52.
[134] *Id.* at para. 53.
[135] *See* SERAP Education Ruling, *supra* note 117, at para. 101.
[136] *See* SERAP Education Ruling, *supra* note 117, at para. 105.

their parent international organizations to set the boundaries of acceptable behavior for states. As some commentators argue, although fear plays a role in
influencing the behavior of states, it is fear of "appearing unjust in one's own eyes or
in the eyes of one's friends" rather than fear of force or coercion.[137] In regimes with
judicial organs, unbiased third-party evaluation of evidence and law leading up to
the apportionment of blame is delegated to such judicial organs so that respondents in cases before such organs and other states look to the outcome of litigation to
shape their future conduct even if past conduct does not meet accepted standard.
In some regimes such as the EAC, membership is also tied to compliance with pre-
agreed standards.[138] The findings of sub-regional courts in cases involving states
then become important parameters for adjudging qualification for membership.
Thus, even where a state fails or neglects to implement or comply with the judgment in a given case, "praise and blame" by the courts are important indicators of
what constitutes acceptable behavior in the Community.[139]

Rwanda's response to the *Rugumba* case, particularly the effort made to bring
the victim in that case before a competent court in order to avoid condemnation by
the EACJ exemplifies this aspect to the impact of sub-regional courts. Similarly, the
reaction of the ECOWAS Parliament to the Gambia's human rights record as exposed by the ECOWAS Court is indicative of that Court's role in setting the parameters of acceptable behavior.

Conclusion

In this chapter, we have argued that the protective value of international courts,
and more particularly, sub-regional "human rights courts," such as the EACJ and
the ECOWAS Court cannot be determined solely on the basis of a consideration
of the rate of compliance with the judgments that emanate from the Courts. While
compliance with judgments assures the litigant of individual justice in his case, the
wider impact of their human rights judgments is more indirect and windy. We have
argued that such indirect impacts are not altogether worthless as they very often result in constitutional justice that potentially benefits a larger class of people. Using
the EACJ and the ECOWAS Court as case studies, the chapter has shown, through
a review of systematically selected court decisions, that by rethinking the approach
to evaluation of international courts, greater value can be found in these courts. The
litigation processes and the decisions of these sub-regional international courts act
as back-up mechanisms that support national courts in their role as guardians of
constitutional order. This is achieved through flagging violations within Member

[137] Sellers, *supra* note 14, at 32.
[138] *See also* Howse & Teitel, *supra* note 76, at 12.
[139] *See also* Sellers, *supra* note 14, at 33.

States thus serving as early warning systems, expanding the scope of normative protection, as well as providing doctrinal footholds that domestic courts and litigants can in turn use at the national level.

This chapter shows that the EACJ and the ECOWAS Court have developed a new supranational constitutionalism anchored outside of national constitutions. We have demonstrated that litigation in these Courts generally flag violations in ways that may not have been possible within national jurisdictions. In that sense, those proceedings serve as early warning in the monitoring of human rights. We have also shown how the Courts have expanded the normative and institutional scope of human rights protection in the sub-regions. We have further shown how norm development occurs in the proceedings, enabling the sub-regional courts to set the boundaries of acceptable behavior for states within the sub-regional communities. For these reasons, we believe that what these Courts are doing is not merely or simply rhetorical flourishes of activism.

6

The African Court of Human and Peoples' Rights as an Opportunity Structure

James Thuo Gathii and Jacquelene Wangui Mwangi

Introduction

Of the thirty African states that have ratified the Protocol to the African Charter on Human and Peoples' Rights (African Charter), only six have made the optional declaration under Article 34(6) of the Protocol to the African Charter on the Establishment of the African Court on Human and Peoples' Rights, (African Court). That declaration allows individuals and states to bring cases to the Court.[1] Tanzania, Rwanda, Benin and Côte d'Ivoire have recently withdrawn their optional declarations.[2] Between 2006 and 2016, the Court decided seven out of eighty-seven cases submitted under the optional declarations filed under Article 34(6).[3] The cases filed and decided by this court have been subject to sustained scholarly inquiry. This chapter adds to this scholarship by examining how the African Court embodies an attractive legal opportunity structure that has provided a forum for filing cases often by high profile opposition politicians and political parties against

---

[1] *The Gambia Becomes the Ninth Country to Allow NGOs and Individuals to Access the African Court Directly*, African Court on Human and Peoples' Rights (Nov. 23, 2018, 10:56 AM), http://www.african-court.org/en/index.php/news/press-releases/item/257-the-gambia-becomes-the-ninth-country-to-allow-ngos-and-individuals-to-access-the-african-court-directly (stating that "[t]he Republic of The Gambia has made the declaration required under Article 34(6) of the Protocol to allow NGOs and individuals to access the African Court directly"). Note that in November 2019, Tanzania withdrew the right of individuals and NGOs to file cases before the African Court, leaving eight countries with a declaration under Article 34(6). Benin and Cote d'Ivoire also withdrew in April 2020, leaving six countries with a declaration.
[2] See Nicole De Silva, *Individual and NGO Access to the African Court on Human and Peoples' Rights: The Latest Blow from Tanzania*, EJIL Talk! Blog (Dec. 16, 2019), https://www.ejiltalk.org/individual-and-ngo-access-to-the-african-court-on-human-and-peoples-rights-the-latest-blow-from-tanzania/#more-17746.
[3] For an excellent analysis, *see* Frans Viljoen, *Understanding and Overcoming Challenges in Accessing the African Court on Human and Peoples' Rights*, 67 Int'l & Comp. L.Q. 63–98 (2018) (hereinafter "Viljoen, Understanding and Overcoming Challenges") (arguing that very few cases are filed before African international courts because people do not perceive harms to them in legal terms (i.e. they do not judicialize their cases). The prisoners who have filed cases before the African Court are not the typically highly mobilized litigants such as political parties. The cases filed by these prisoners may largely be accounted for by the proximity of the Court to them since all these cases arise from Tanzania.

James Thuo Gathii and Jacquelene Wangui Mwangi, *The African Court of Human and Peoples' Rights as an Opportunity Structure* In: *The Performance of Africa's International Courts*. Edited by: James Thuo Gathii, Oxford University Press (2020). © The Several Contributors. DOI: 10.1093/oso/9780198868477.003.0007.

their repressive governments, but also by litigants such as criminal defendants with fair trial claims. The chapters in this book have shown how the filing of cases in Africa's sub-regional courts have helped to mobilize opposition politicians and parties as well as social movements. This chapter adds to that theme by showing how politicians and political parties closed off from pursuing their goals of political reform under national law and through national institutions resort to the African Court. It also shows how this Court serves as a further judicial forum for prisoners who have grievances over the conduct of their criminal trials in national courts. In this sense, the prisoners frame their grievances as fair trial violations that can be entertained at the African Court, rather than as appeals on the basis of criminal law and evidence. The high number of fair trial cases from Tanzania is largely due to the close proximity of the Court to the prisoners.[4]

In addition to the fair trial cases, three additional cases form the subject of this chapter. The first is a case filed against Rwanda by an opposition politician, Ingabire Victoire Umuhoza (Ingabire). The second is a case filed by a Tanzanian politician, the late Christopher Mtikila. The third is a case filed by a human rights non-governmental organization (NGO), Actions Pour La Protection Des Droits De L'Homme (APDH), in Ivory Coast (Côte d'Ivoire). These three cases originated in countries that are particularly repressive and where the opportunity structures for pursuing their goals at the national level are constrained. For example, when Tanzania introduced multi-party politics in 1992, Mtikila unsuccessfully sought to register his political party after he was locked out of the elections since the law did not allow independent candidates to run for office. He successfully petitioned the High Court and Court of Appeal to allow him to run as an independent candidate. However, Parliament changed the Constitution withdrawing the amendment that had initially permitted independent candidates to run for office. Without any further options, he filed a case before the African Court.

On her part, Ingabire, an opposition politician, brought a case in the African Court challenging a variety of criminal offenses brought against her by the Rwandese government. These offenses were spreading the ideology of genocide; undermining the internal security of the state; spreading rumors meant to incite the population against the political authorities, and attempted recourse to terrorism, as in violation of her rights under the African Charter. She argued these politically motivated charges violated her rights.

In the third case, APDH filed a case against the government of the Ivory Coast challenging a newly adopted law establishing the country's electoral body. APDH argued that the government had violated its obligation to establish an independent and impartial body, by granting itself eight seats in comparison to the oppositions

---

[4] *See* Ally Possy, "It is Better that Ten Guilty Persons Escape than that One Innocent Suffer": The African Court on Human and Peoples' Rights and Fair Trial Rights in Tanzania, 1 African Human Rights Yearbook 311–36, 316 (ACHPR, ACtHPR, & ACERWC ed., 2017).

four seats in the electoral body. Civil society groups filed all the three cases in the African Court on behalf of those alleging violations. In both the *Mtikila* and *Ingabire* cases, the civil society groups that filed the cases had experience litigating before the African Court. Once these cases were filed, they provided additional opportunities to engage with the respective governments on issues that domestic courts and institutions had closed off. It was precisely because domestic institutional spaces were shut down that made it necessary to look for opportunity structures elsewhere.

This chapter proceeds as follows. Part One discusses the legal opportunity structure literature. Part Two then discusses the foundational cases that helped the African Court develop a favorable opportunity structure, setting the pace for future cases. Part Three discusses how the African Court serves as a legal opportunity structure that opens up opportunities to directly engage the governments not only in the courtroom but also in the media and in international organizations as well. This part also reflects on what the analysis of the three cases discussed in the chapter say about the African Court as an opportunity structure for politicians and political parties.

Part One: The Legal Opportunity Structure Literature

This chapter discusses the manner in which the African Court has created a political opening for new types of advocacy for litigants with grievances against their governments. The cases that are explored in this chapter were brought by individuals and groups who used litigation as an additional point of leverage vis-à-vis their government. In this sense, the African Court becomes a fulcrum through which grassroots movements and individuals can collectively mobilize, organize, promote, and advance their causes. Without this collective organization, the openings provided by international courts would come to naught.

The legal opportunity structures literature seeks to explain why some groups resort to courts to advance their causes, while others do not. This scholarship decenters the focus on courts and instead centers analysis on the actors who go to these courts and their strategies for doing so. This grassroots perspective makes it possible to focus on how social movements mobilize[5] or how they frame their claims before these courts.[6] From the legal opportunity structures perspective, filing cases before international courts is often a strategic decision by individuals

---

[5] Lisa Vanhala, *Social Movements Lashing Back: Law, Social Change and Socio-Legal Backlash in Canada*, 54 STUD. IN L., POL., AND SOC'Y 113–40 (2011).

[6] Nicholas Pedriana, *From Protective to Equal Treatment: Legal Framing Processes and Transformation of the Women's Movement in the 1960s*, 111 AM. J. SOCIOLOGY 1718–61 (2006); Anna-Maria Marshall, *Injustice Frames, Legality, and the Everyday Construction of Sexual Harassment*, 28 L. & SOC. INQUIRY 659–89 (2003).

and non-state actors as their way of organizing discontent with the hope that it in turn spurs mobilization for corrective action so that the grievances that underlie such discontent can be addressed. This chapter uses the legal opportunity structure because litigants and social movements who choose to litigate in Africa's international courts face particular constraints in getting redress for their grievances in domestic courts. This is because domestic courts and political forums are unwilling to provide a remedy because they are under the control of repressive governments that are often hostile to such claims. Additional barriers such as the cost of litigation in domestic courts make international courts a preferable alternative venue.

Although there are debates about what falls within and without a legal opportunity structure,[7] there is common ground that there are three factors that account for some groups resorting to advance their causes in court while others do not. First, the existing body of law and the manner in which it creates openings for social movements to "articulate their claims" is considered an important prerequisite. Second, the rules governing access to courts such as those relating to standing, jurisdiction, and admissibility, especially where they are permissive or interpreted as such, are also important. Third, the rules regarding who bears the cost of the litigation determines whether groups and individuals will resort to litigation or not. In general, where the rules are quite permissive and the costs are low, it is more likely that social movements will file cases and vice versa.[8] The next section of the chapter discusses each of the three foregoing factors.

Existing Body of Law Creates Openings for Social Movements

Since social movements are not passive actors, they actively participate in creating their own legal opportunities by participating in the creation of a body of law that creates openings for them to continue coming to the court.[9] In the East African Court of Justice (EACJ), for example, civil society groups actively worked together with the judges through a series of workshops and informal meetings to set the stage for the first case ever filed before the court by an individual. Among the preparatory work these civil society groups helped to put together were the procedural rules for litigating before the court.[10] The interaction between judges and civil

---

[7] Lisa Vanhala, *Legal Opportunity Structures and the Paradox of Legal Mobilization by the Environmental Movement in the UK*, 46 L. & Soc'y Rev. 523, 525 (2012) (hereinafter "Vanhala, Legal Opportunity"). *See also* Doug McAdam, Political Process and the Development of Black Insurgency, 1930–1970 (2nd ed., 1999); David S. Meyer, *Protest and Political Opportunities*, 30 Ann. Rev. Sociology 125–45 (2004).

[8] Lisa Vanhala, *Shaping the Structure of Legal Opportunities: Environmental NGOs Bringing International Environmental Procedural Rights Back Home*, 40 L. & Pol'y 110, 112 (2018) (hereinafter "Vanhala, Shaping the Structure").

[9] Vanhala, Legal Opportunity, *supra* note 7, at 525.

[10] James Gathii, *Mission Creep or a Search for Relevance: The East African Court of Justice's Human Rights Strategy*, 24 Duke J. Comp. & Int'l L. 249–96 (2013) (hereinafter "Gathii, Mission Creep").

society groups in opening up access to the EACJ at a time when East African States were not formally supporting the Court to entertain any cases against them demonstrates the dynamic nature of legal opportunities. Beyond such interactions, the legal rulings made by an international court can create openings for social movements. For example, the EACJ in a case brought by a Ugandan opposition party announced, quite significantly, that it had jurisdiction to interpret the African Charter.[11] The fact that the Court found that East African Member States could be sued for violations under the African Charter was a significant legal opening for at least two reasons. First, it is notable because the African Charter is only mentioned in a preambular paragraph of the Treaty for the Establishment of the East African Community (EAC Treaty), and the First Instance Division of that Court had held that it had no jurisdiction to interpret international instruments like the African Charter. In essence, this was an expansionist reading of the Court's jurisdiction. Second, it is significant because it confirmed that the Court could as a result receive a whole swath of cases under the African Charter. The EACJ did this at the urging of civil society groups who filed *amicus* briefs in the case and with resistance from the Secretariat of the East African Community. In essence, legal opportunities are not necessarily shut because there are no permissive rules allowing access to a court, or vice versa, but rather that the agency of civil society actors and judges of international courts can forge relationships that help to open access to international courts.[12]

In this chapter, we show how the African Court referred cases from indigent litigants to the Pan African Lawyers Union (PALU) so that they could provide legal assistance. These cases, from indigent defendants facing lengthy imprisonment terms, were the initial set of cases to be litigated at the African Court. Because the African Court referred these litigants to lawyer groups to provide legal assistance, these cases provided the Court with an opportunity to begin exercising its jurisdiction. These cases were not only low-hanging fruit in the sense that they were unlikely to provoke political resistance, but also significant because they helped the Court create a body of law that enabled access for future litigants. For example, in these initial set of cases, the African Court established that its acceptance of cases should not be construed as appeals from national courts. This principle lowered the barriers to filing cases because as long as a case raised a potential violation of the African Charter, the Court could exercise jurisdiction.

[11] Democratic Party v. Secretary General of the EAC and Others, Appeal No. 1 of 2014, Decision of the Appellate Division, East African Court of Justice [E. Afr. Ct. Just.], para. 73 (July 28, 2015), https://www.eacj.org/?cases=democratic-party-vs-1-the-secretary-general-of-the-eastafrican-community-2-the-attorney-general-of-the-republic-of-uganda-3-the-attorney-general-of-the-republic-of-kenya-4-the-attorney-general-of.

[12] ELLEN ANN ANDERSON, OUT OF THE CLOSETS AND INTO THE COURTS: LEGAL OPPORTUNITY STRUCTURE AND GAY RIGHTS LITIGATION 7–8 (2005).

Another example is the permissive interpretation of the requirement to exhaust local remedies. By permissively interpreting the exhaustion requirement, the Court declined to shut the door to new cases where it was still possible for the litigants to pursue remedies at the national level. The African Court required applicants to exhaust only what they termed "ordinary remedies." Under its definition of ordinary remedies, appeals of criminal convictions had to be exhausted. By contrast, remedies such as constitutional petitions and applications for review were deemed "extra-ordinary" i.e. uncommon and exceptional. The African Court allowed cases to be filed where applicants had not pursued these "extra-ordinary" remedies. Additionally, the African Court will deem all remedies exhausted in situations where national laws do not provide any remedies to be exhausted. This interpretation has enabled the Court to entertain fresh disputes on non-justiciable matters under national law. In *Jebra Kambole v. United Republic of Tanzania*,[13] the Court considered the Tanzanian Constitution, which bars courts from inquiring into the election of a Presidential candidate. Given that such a matter would not be entertained in Tanzanian courts for want of jurisdiction, the Court held that the applicant had fulfilled the exhaustion of remedies requirement.

Lawyers in West Africa worked together with officials of the Secretariat of the Economic Community of West African States (ECOWAS) as well as with lawyers advising their governments in their capitals to lobby for a treaty that allowed individual access to file cases in the ECOWAS Community Court of Justice (ECOWAS Court).[14] The Protocol that created individual access for human rights cases in ECOWAS Court did not contain an exhaustion requirement and the Court has not found that litigants must have exhausted remedies under customary international law prior to filing cases.[15] By contrast, business interests did not pursue a similar strategy and therefore, to date that Court does not have jurisdiction over cases filed by individuals or businesses for violation of the ECOWAS trading rules. In another African international court, the Common Market for Eastern and Southern Africa (COMESA) Court of Justice, the Treaty Establishing COMESA has an exhaustion rule (specifically Article 26) requiring exhaustion of domestic remedies before cases can be filed before it. Thus although the COMESA Court of Justice has jurisdiction to entertain cases from individuals, the exhaustion rule has been interpreted so strictly that the Court has experienced a dearth of cases.[16] For this

---

[13] Jebra Kambole v. United Republic of Tanzania, Application No. 018/2018, Judgment, African Court on Human and Peoples' Rights [Afr. Ct. H.P.R.] (July, 15 2020).

[14] Karen J. Alter et al., *A New International Human Rights Court for West Africa: The ECOWAS Community Court of Justice*, 107 AM. J. INT'L L. 737–79 (2013).

[15] Solomon T. Ebobrah, *A Rights-Protection Goldmine or a Waiting Volcanic Eruption? Competence of, and Access to, the Human Rights Jurisdiction of the ECOWAS Community Court of Justice*, 7 AFR. HUM. RTS. L.J. 307–29 (2007).

[16] James Thuo Gathii, *The COMESA Court of Justice, in* THE LEGITIMACY OF INTERNATIONAL TRADE COURTS AND TRIBUNALS 314–48 (Robert Howse, Helene Ruiz Fabri, & Geir Ulfstein eds., 2018).

reason, the COMESA Court of Justice has not developed the kind of case-law we see in the ECOWAS Court or in the EACJ.

Rules Governing Access, Standing, Jurisdiction, and Admissibility

Rules governing access, standing, jurisdiction, and admissibility are a crucial condition for the existence of a favorable legal opportunity structure because they determine who can file a legal claim. The lower the barriers to access, particularly for individuals and groups to file claims, the more favorable the legal opportunity structure. Lower barriers give access to courts to those with limited resources including money and even legal expertise.[17] For example, the Organization of American States (OAS) allowed Member States as well as all OAS organs to request advisory opinions from the Inter-American Court of Human Rights.[18] This broad access to request advisory opinions was critical to invigorating it. Even though the African Court has added NGOs to the list of those who can request advisory opinions, in practice it has not received many such requests, perhaps because it does not have express jurisdiction to issue advisory opinions "about the compatibility of a State's domestic laws with the treaties within the Court's jurisdiction."[19] Nevertheless, the absence of express jurisdiction to issue advisory opinions has not stopped the African Court from making pronouncements on the compatibility of States' Constitutions with the African Charter. Using rights-based approaches based on provisions of the African Charter and Protocol, public interest litigants have evoked the Court's subject-matter jurisdiction, enabling it to determine whether States' Constitutions violate rights enshrined in the African Charter. In a recent decision, *Jebra Kambole v. United Republic of Tanzania*, the African Court considered Article 41(7) of the Tanzanian Constitution that bars any court from inquiring into the election of a Presidential candidate after the Electoral Commission has declared a winner. The Petitioner claimed that this provision was a violation of the Charter's provisions on non-discrimination and right to a fair hearing. Using a rights-based approach, the African Court found that the provision violated a litigant's right of access to a court of adjudication of one's grievances, which is one of the fundamental elements of the right to a fair hearing. It ordered the government of Tanzania to take all necessary constitutional and legislative measures,

---

[17] Bruce M. Wilson & Juan Carlos Rodríguez Cordero, *Legal Opportunity Structures and Social Movements: The Effects of Institutional Change on Costa Rican Politics*, 39 COMP. POL. STUD. 325–51 (2006).

[18] J.M. Pasqualucci, *Advisory Practice and the Procedure of the Inter-American Court of Human Rights: Contributing to the Evolution of International Human Rights Law*, 38 STAN. J. INT'L L. 241–88 (2002).

[19] Viljoen, Understanding and Overcoming Challenges, *supra* note 3, at 93.

within a reasonable time, to ensure that Article 41(7) of its Constitution is aligned with the provisions of the African Charter.[20]

By contrast to the constraints imposed on accepting advisory opinions in the African Court, the EACJ has construed its jurisdiction expansively to receive cases from individuals. In a 2007 case, the Court announced a new cause of action to enforce human rights.[21] Now known as the *Katabazi* doctrine, that cause of action was a bold and expansionist interpretation of that Court's jurisdiction. This is because the EAC Treaty establishing that court does not give it jurisdiction over human rights. In fact, it explicitly provides that such jurisdiction will be conferred to it at a future date.[22] This notwithstanding, under the *Katabazi* doctrine, the EACJ held that it had jurisdiction to interpret and apply any provision of the Treaty, whether or not it was concerned with human rights. Because the Court was enmeshed in an informal network of very supportive civil society groups, particularly the East African Law Society which has membership in the bar societies in East Africa, the Court was protected from a potential backlash for such an expansionist reading of its jurisdiction.[23] To date, the *Katabazi* doctrine and the cause of action created in 2007 is the route through which a large majority of cases are filed before the court. In short, seen from a legal opportunity perspective, rules governing access, standing, jurisdiction and admissibility are not static, but rather in a dynamic relationship with the agency of social movements.[24]

In the African Court, Frans Viljoen has recently shown that although the Court has received a rather low number of cases because only six states have filed a declaration allowing direct access by individuals and NGOs, the Court has interpreted its rules in a way that has permitted broad access. Between 2006 and 2016, the first decade of its existence, the African Court has received the following direct access cases: seventy-one cases from Tanzania, six from Rwanda, four from Mali, three from the Ivory Coast, two from Burkina Faso, and one from Malawi.[25] Other avenues of filing cases before the Court such as through referrals from the African Commission on Human and Peoples' Rights has not been a source of many cases.[26]

---

[20] Jebra Kambole v. United Republic of Tanzania, Application No. 018/2018, Judgment, African Court on Human and Peoples' Rights [Afr. Ct. H.P.R.] (July, 15 2020).

[21] Katabazi and 21 Others v. Secretary General of the East African Community and Attorney General of Uganda, Reference No. 1 of 2007, Merits, East African Court of Justice [E. Afr. Ct. Just.] (Nov. 1, 2007), https://www.eacj.org/?cases=james-katabazi-and-21-other-vs-secretary-general-of-the-east-african-community-and-attorney-general-of-the-republic-of-uganda.

[22] Treaty for the Establishment of the East African Community, Nov. 30, 1991, 2144 U.N.T.S. 255 at art. 27(2).

[23] *See* Gathii, Mission Creep, *supra* note 10.

[24] Vanhala, Legal Opportunity, *supra* note 7, at 528.

[25] Viljoen, Understanding and Overcoming Challenges, *supra* note 3, at 69. *See also* Oliver Windridge, *Necessary Check Points or Immovable Roadblocks? Accessing the African Court on Human and Peoples' Rights*, 35 WIS. INT'L L.J. 458, 483 (2018).

[26] Such other routes to bringing cases before the Court include requests for advisory opinions, amendments of the rules permitting the African Children's Rights Committee. For a detailed discussion, *see* Viljoen, Understanding and Overcoming Challenges, *supra* note 3, at 75–86.

In addition, Viljoen argues that there are structural constraints to accessing the Court such as "long delays in finalizing cases [and] other institutional inefficiencies, and corruption."[27] Summarizing these limitations of accessing the African Court, Oliver Windridge argues that for the Court to review applications from individuals and NGOs concerning a Member State, the Member State must have ratified or signed three instruments: the African Charter, the African Court Protocol, and Articles 5(1) and 34(6) of the African Court Protocol (Additional Declaration).[28] Only six countries have signed the Additional Declaration, effectively meaning that only citizens of these six African countries can directly petition the African Court alleging violations of their rights.[29] NGOs must also have "observer status" in order to directly petition the Court, a separate standing granted by the African Commission.[30]

The foregoing barriers are compounded by additional challenges. First, there is a lack of widespread knowledge about the African Court and other international courts within Africa. Second, there has been a minimal judicialization of grievances that can then be filed in the African Court.[31] This has made the African Court much less accessible than its counterparts in Europe and the Americas.[32] In fact, it has decided less cases than the EACJ and the ECOWAS Court.

The foregoing factors explain why notwithstanding the limited number of countries that have filed declarations accepting the African Court's jurisdiction to receive cases from individuals and NGOs, there have nevertheless been cases from the very mobilized civil society groups in the countries that have filed those declarations. These civil society groups use the Court as one among several strategies in their engagement with their governments. Thus, when Rwanda made a declaration allowing individuals to file cases before the African Court, six cases were quickly filed against it. Political opponents of the Rwandese government brought these cases arguing that the government had violated their rights. In the *Ingabire* case discussed later in this chapter, the alleged rights violations stemmed from what she termed politically instigated charges against her for spreading genocide ideology, abetting terrorism, and undermining state security. In *Kennedy Gihana & others v. Rwanda*, the applicant contested the cancellation of their passport. *Laurent Munyandilikirwa v. Rwanda* involved the illegal removal of the president of an NGO critical of the Rwandese government. *Kayumba Nyamwasa & others*

---

[27] *Id.* at 74.
[28] Windridge, *supra* note 25, at 467.
[29] *Id.* at 470.
[30] *Id.* at 468–69.
[31] Viljoen, Understanding and Overcoming Challenges, *supra* note 3, at 96 (noting that there is a "small number of cases finding their way to the Court ... [because] only a small percentage of sociological 'problems,' are in most of these States, ever conceptualized as 'legal disputes ....' ").
[32] Françoise Hampson, et al., *Inaccessible Apexes: Comparing Access to Regional Human Rights Courts and Commissions in Europe, the Americas, and Africa*, 16 INT'L J. CONST. L. 161–86 (2018).

v. Rwanda involved the amendment of the Rwandese Constitution that removed Presidential term limits.

Rwanda decided to withdraw its declaration allowing individuals to file cases before the African Court after this spate of cases. This shows that individual access can be withdrawn when international court judges overstep their boundaries leaving governments unhappy. In its withdrawal, Rwanda alleged that the African Court had provided "genocide fugitives" a right to be heard "in the guise of defending the rights of Rwandese peoples."[33] Thus Viljoen concludes that declarations to allow citizens to bring cases before the African Court are a "necessary but not a sufficient condition for access" to the Court.[34] As he concludes, these declarations should be thought of as a basis on which domestic groups can mobilize "to overcome legal, political and institutional hurdles restricting domestic and regional access" to the Court.[35] Once those cases reach the Court, its Practice Directions allow *amicus curiae* to participate in filing papers and in oral proceedings.[36] A minority opinion of four judges of the African Court have recognized the importance of access to its jurisdiction by holding that the fact that countries have the discretion whether or not to sign a declaration permitting their citizens to file cases before the Court constitutes a deprivation of the right of access to justice.[37] The African Court has also held that withdrawal of a declaration accepting the jurisdiction of the Court does not take effect until one year after the filing of the declaration. As a consequence, cases filed before the African Court prior to the filing of a withdrawal declaration can continue to be litigated.[38]

In a similar turn of events, Benin and Côte d'Ivoire withdrew their declarations after significant decisions touching on elections. In April 2020, the government of Benin released a statement[39] on the withdrawal of its declaration, citing that the African Court's decision in a commercial dispute had caused disarray within Benin's business community. Commentators, however, suggest that this withdrawal was triggered by the African Court's order to postpone elections in Benin following an application by a prominent opposition

---

[33] *Clarification*, REPUBLIC OF RWANDA MINISTRY OF JUSTICE (Aug. 3, 2016), http://www.minijust. gov.rw/fileadmin/Documents/Photo_News_2016/Clarification2.pdf (stating that Rwanda did not withdraw from the African Court on Human and Peoples' Rights).

[34] Viljoen, Understanding and Overcoming Challenges, *supra* note 3, at 97.

[35] *Id.*

[36] *Id.* at 94–95.

[37] Falana v. African Union, App. No. 1 of 2011, Dissenting Opinion of Vice President Akuffo, Judge Ngoepe, & Judge Thompson, African Court on Human and Peoples' Rights [Afr. Ct. H.P.R.] (June 26, 2012), http://www.worldcourts.com/acthpr/eng/decisions/2012.06.26_Falana_v_African_Union.pdf.

[38] Kennedy Gihana and Others v. Republic of Rwanda, Application No. 017/2015, Order, African Court on Human and Peoples' Rights [Afr. Ct. H.P.R.] (June 3, 2018), http://www.african-court.org/en/ images/Cases/Orders/Order_Appl.017-2015_.pdf.

[39] Withdrawal of Benin from the ACHPR—Statement by the Minister of Justice and Legislation, The Republic of Benin (Apr. 28, 2020), https://www.gouv.bj/actualite/635/retrait-benin-cadhp--- declaration-ministre-justice-legislation/.

leader.[40] The Ivorian government issued its statement also in April 2020, citing that the African Court was making political decisions and undermining its sovereignty. This came after the Court had ordered suspension of an arrest warrant of Guillaume Soro, a former rebel leader running for president.[41]

It is notable that the African Court has received seventy-one cases from Tanzania. As noted in this chapter, many of these cases were filed by prisoners challenging the failure of their trial to meet the African Charter protections on the right to fair trial. Like Viljoen, we believe the first set of these cases played an important "trigger effect" of inspiring "the opening of the 'floodgates' by others" raising similar fair trial issues.[42] In turn, the favorable jurisprudence developed from these sets of cases helped create a favorable legal opportunity structure that remained useful for future litigation in similar fair trial cases and in other unrelated cases such as those involving opposition politicians. In addition, location does matter. The fact that the African Court is located in Arusha, Tanzania, where there is a constellation of very active groups and individuals that litigate in Africa's international courts partially explains the large number of cases from Tanzania.[43] The government of Tanzania withdrew its declaration that had allowed individuals and NGOs to file cases before the African Court. On Nov. 21, 2019, the government submitted its notice of withdrawal arguing that access to the Court had been conducted inconsistently with "the reservations submitted by the United Republic of Tanzania when making its Declaration."[44] This came at a time when Tanzania was defending a fair trial violation case brought against it by indigent prisoners, *Ally Rajabu and Others v. United Republic of Tanzania (Ally Rajabu)*.[45] A key difference between *Ally Rajabu* and other fair trial violation cases before the African Court is that all previous cases had dealt with claims from prisoners facing lengthy imprisonment terms, whereas in *Ally Rajabu*, the applicants were facing the death penalty.[46] Notably, the applicants challenged not only the imposition of the death sentence upon them, but also the provision of the Penal Code of Tanzania for the mandatory imposition of the death penalty in murder cases.[47] Thus, for the first time Tanzania had to defend the

---

[40] *Benin and Côte d'Ivoire to Withdraw Individual Access To African Court*, INTERNATIONAL JUSTICE RESOURCE CENTER (May 6, 2020), https://ijrcenter.org/2020/05/06/benin-and-cote-divoire-to-withdraw-individual-access-to-african-court/.

[41] *Id.*

[42] Viljoen, Understanding and Overcoming Challenges, *supra* note 3, at 69.

[43] *Id.* at 94–95. The only other piece of scholarship we are aware of that discusses the fair trial rights cases of the African Court is in Possy, *supra* note 4.

[44] Notice of Withdrawal of the Declaration Made Under Article 34(6) of the Protocol to the African Charter, United Republic of Tanzania (Nov. 14, 2019), https://www.southernafricalitigationcentre.org/wp-content/uploads/2019/12/Tanzania-Withdrawal-Article-36-4-African-Court.pdf.

[45] Ally Rajabu & others v. United Republic of Tanzania, App. No. 007/2015, Judgment, African Court on Human and Peoples' Rights [Afr. Ct. H.P.R.] (Nov. 28, 2019), http://www.african-court.org/en/images/Cases/Judgment/Judgment_Summary_Application_007-2015-Ally_Rajabu_and_Others_v_Tanzania_Final.pdf.

[46] *Id.* at para. 1.

[47] *Id.* at para. 2.

death penalty before an international court. Indeed, the African Court had already issued provisional measures enjoining Tanzania not to implement the death sentence and when the case was concluded, made consequential orders for the government of Tanzania to take measures to repeal the relevant section of its Penal Code.[48] While some argue that this decision could have triggered Tanzania's withdrawal,[49] others opine that Tanzania's withdrawal was a long time coming given the myriad of cases that have been decided against it since the African Court's inception.[50] We surmise that Tanzania's withdrawal at this time is consistent with the authoritarian regime of the country's current President, John Magufuli, whose tenure has been marked with wanton abuse of human rights, including the enforcement of laws that inhibit independent journalism and restrict the work of NGOs.[51] In a joint statement, twenty human rights organizations with a presence in Africa have expressed concern over the regressive nature of Tanzania's withdrawal and have urged the country to reconsider. They note with concern that "the Tanzania government has refused to implement several East African Court of Justice judgments against it"[52] and that it has also participated in the withdrawal of individuals' access to the South Africa Development Community (SADC) Tribunal.

Tanzania's withdrawal of its Article 34(6) declaration is significant because most of the cases in the African Court are from Tanzania. Tanzania, Rwanda, Benin and Côte d'Ivoire's withdrawal of the optional declarations allowing individuals' access to the African Court are in part the result of the effectiveness with which litigants brought pressure and unwelcome scrutiny to bear on their governments. In this sense, these withdrawals very well indicate that the African Court is a victim of its success.

Rules Regarding Who Bears the Cost of Litigation

The lower the costs of litigation, the more open a legal opportunity structure is and vice versa. This means the risks are much greater where the rules for who bears the cost of litigation fall on the loser such as in the United Kingdom.[53] By contrast, in the United States where each party bears their own litigation costs, the risks and potential costs of losing are not as high.[54] In both the African Court and the EACJ,

---

[48]   *Id.* at paras. 3, 30.
[49]   Joint Statement Condemning Tanzania's Withdrawal of Individuals Access to the African Court, AMNESTY INTERNATIONAL, https://www.amnesty.org/download/Documents/AFR5615422019ENGLISH.PDF. /
[50]   De Silva, supra note 2.
[51]   *See generally, Tanzania: The Price We Pay: Targeted for Dissent by the Tanzanian State,* AMNESTY INTERNATIONAL (Oct. 28, 2019), https://www.amnesty.org/en/documents/afr56/0301/2019/en/
[52]   Joint Statement, *supra* note 49.
[53]   Vanhala, Shaping the Structure, *supra* note 8, at 112.
[54]   *Id.*

the procedural rules are very favorable to losing parties. First, the costs of filing cases are quite low. Second, in the African Court, the general practice is for each party to bear its own costs unless determined otherwise, whereas in the EACJ, the court explicitly declines from making orders on costs in cases that it designates as being of significant public interest. For example, in the case referred to above when it held it had jurisdiction to decide cases raising questions of compliance with the African Charter, the court declined to make orders on costs. It argued that it would have been "inappropriate to order any Party to pay the costs of the other" because the case was of "great public interest."[55]

Part Two: A Case Study of Fair Trial Rights Cases to Illustrate the African Court as an Opportunity Structure

In this part of the chapter, we discuss the inaugural set of eight cases that came to the African Court from convicts alleging violations of their fair trial rights under the African Charter. All these cases came from Tanzania and we use them to demonstrate how these otherwise inconspicuous cases helped the African Court develop a very favorable opportunity structure for litigants.

Fair Trial Violation Cases Before the African Court

One of the most prevalent legal issues that the African Court has dealt with to date concerns fair trial rights in the conduct of criminal trials in national courts. Having decided close to twenty fair trial rights cases, the African Court has developed a jurisprudence that has created legal openings for a continuous flow of new cases. These cases are typically brought by or on behalf of indigent applicants convicted and sentenced for long prison terms for armed robbery. Their cases follow a similar pattern. They all invited the African Court to determine whether their trials were conducted in accordance with the right to fair trial under African Charter and other human rights instruments. In all these cases, the African Court has overruled the objections of states, that in entertaining these cases, it was acting as an appellate court over decisions of national courts. The African Court held that it exercises its jurisdiction appropriately when it examines whether the procedures followed by national courts are consistent with the rights guaranteed under the African Charter and other instruments ratified by a respondent state. Our basic argument is that the African Court's very permissive approach to jurisdiction, admissibility,

---

[55] Democratic Party v. Secretary General of the EAC and Others, App. No. 1 of 2014, Judgment, East African Court of Justice [E. Afr. Ct. Just.], para. 78 (July 28, 2015), https://www.eacj.org//wp-content/uploads/2015/08/Democratic-Party-vs-2c-SG-REVISED-Draft-2-FINAL-31-07-2015.pdf.

legal standing, and rules on who bears the costs of litigation has created a body of law that provides more opportunity for filing of other similar cases.[56]

How Eight Fair Trial Cases Illustrate that the Existing Body of Law Creates Openings for Potential Litigants

The African Court has developed very permissive rules for filing of cases by indigent persons who have very little or no knowledge of the law. It is striking that these permissive rules are not in the Court's formal rules. Rather, the judges have applied their wide-ranging discretion under the written rules to lower barriers for filing cases at the Court. For instance, through its interpretation of Rule 31 of the Rules of the African Court on Human and Peoples' Rights (the Rules), which grants the Court the power to offer free legal assistance in appropriate cases, the African Court invited the Pan African Lawyers Union (PALU), an Arusha based regional bar association, to provide free legal representation to indigent persons. The Court first did this in *Peter Chacha v. United Republic of Tanzania (Chacha)* and then consistently applied this principle in seven subsequent cases. In so doing, the African Court encouraged more applications from indigent persons who would otherwise have been unable to procure legal counsel because of the small number of legal practitioners in Tanzania. Most of these lawyers are mostly based in urban areas and the cost of their legal services is quite high.[57] PALU's presence in Arusha therefore makes up for the difficulty of obtaining lawyers to litigate in the African Court.

This permissive interpretation of its rules allowed PALU to develop the expertise to litigate these cases. In essence, the costs of litigating subsequent similar cases was much lower once the basic principles had been tested and litigated in the initial set of cases. By opening legal representation to a civil society group to represent indigent litigants, the African Court opened its doors to other civil society

---

[56] The focus of this section is on eight cases: Christopher Jonas v. United Republic of Tanzania, App. No. 011/2015, Judgment, African Court on Human and Peoples' Rights [Afr. Ct. H.P.R.] (Sept. 28, 2015); Thobias Mango & Another v. United Republic of Tanzania, App. No. 005/2015, Judgment, African Court on Human and Peoples' Rights [Afr. Ct. H.P.R.] (May 11, 2018); Wilfred Onyango & 9 others v. United Republic of Tanzania, App. No. 006/2013, Judgment, African Court on Human and Peoples' Rights [Afr. Ct. H.P.R.] (Mar. 18, 2016); Peter Joseph Chacha v. United Republic of Tanzania, App. No. 003/2012, Judgment, African Court on Human and Peoples' Rights [Afr. Ct. H.P.R.] (Mar. 28, 2014); Mohamed Abubakari v. United Republic of Tanzania, App. No. 007/2013, Judgment, African Court on Human and Peoples' Rights [Afr. Ct. H.P.R.] (June 3, 2016); Kennedy Owino Onyachi & Others v. United Republic of Tanzania, App. No. 003/2015, Judgment, African Court on Human and Peoples' Rights [Afr. Ct. H.P.R.] (Sept. 28, 2017); Alex Thomas v. United Republic of Tanzania, App. No. 005/2013, Judgment, African Court on Human and Peoples' Rights [Afr. Ct. H.P.R.] (Nov. 20, 2015); and Minani Evarist v. United Republic of Tanzania, App. No. 027/2015, Judgment, African Court on Human and Peoples' Rights [Afr. Ct. H.P.R.] (Sept. 21, 2018).

[57] Robert Makaramba, *Unearthing Key Challenges and Solutions in Advancing Justice in Tanzania* 12–13 (Paper Presented at the Tanganyika Law Society Annual Conference and General Meeting, Feb. 20, 2015).

organizations to bring cases before the Court. These civil society groups in turn participated in shaping answers to complex questions on jurisdiction and admissibility when they arose before the African Court. The choice of PALU to represent indigent litigants was important in another respect. First, it has a Memorandum of Understanding for Cooperation with the African Union and has extensive experience working with the African Court.[58] Second, its lawyers have extensive knowledge on the human rights system through litigation at the Court, and it has a strategic litigation agenda that aims to positively impact democracy, rule of law, human rights, and governance in Africa.[59]

Another mechanism that the Court has employed to facilitate access is the adoption of procedurally lenient rules for drafting of applications to the Court. While national courts generally apply stringent drafting rules that require a litigant to follow a fixed drafting format and articulate their claims through complex legal language, the African Court registry generally accepts pleadings that would easily be rejected in national courts. A cursory examination of applications published on the Court's website reveals plain/basic drafting that articulates claims in what is effectively layperson's terms. This contrasts sharply with the practice within national courts. For example, in Kenya, allegations of violations of the Bill of Rights must be pleaded with specificity so that adequate notice of the violated right is given— vaguely drafted pleadings alleging violations of the Bill of Rights would therefore fail to give such notice.[60] By contrast, the experience so far in the African Court is that there are no similar rules that would preclude the filings of pleadings that would not meet the thresholds set under domestic law for national courts. Given that the applicants before the African Court in the fair trial cases discussed in this

---

[58] Under the Memorandum of Understanding with the African Union, PALU and the AU agreed to cooperate in a variety of areas including: promoting regional and international jurisdictions, strengthening the rule of law, improving systems for legal aid to the public, and advancing the science of law and jurisprudence. In furtherance of this, PALU often engages in activities with the African Court, the Office of Legal Affairs, and the Department of Political Affairs, among other AU institutions. *See What PALU Does*, PAN AFRICAN LAWYERS UNION, https://lawyersofafrica.org/what-palu-does/ (last visited Dec. 15, 2019). Memorandum of Understanding Establishing the Framework for Cooperation and Collaboration Between the African Union and the Pan African Lawyers Union, Pan African Lawyers Union (May 5, 2006).

[59] What Palu Does?, *supra* note 58.

[60] *See* Trusted Society of Human Rights Alliance v. Attorney General & 2 others (2013) K.L.R. (The Court of Appeal) (Kenya), where a three-bench judge of the High Court held:

> [t]he proper test under the new Constitution is whether a Petition as stated raises issues which are so insubstantial and so attenuated that a Court of law properly directing itself to the issue cannot fashion an appropriate remedy due to the inability to concretely fathom the constitutional violation alleged. The test does not demand mathematical precision in drawing constitutional petitions. Neither does it demand talismanic formalism in identifying the specific constitutional provisions which are alleged to have been violated. The test is a substantive one and inquires whether the complaints against Respondents in a constitutional petition are fashioned in a way that gives proper notice to the Respondents about the nature of the claims being made so that they can adequately prepare their case.

Id. at para. 43.

section are prisoners, the Court's permissive approach further lowers the barriers to filing of cases.

One crucial way in which the African Court employs procedurally lenient drafting rules is in its finding that pleadings need not mention the provisions of the African Charter that are claimed to be violated. In *Chacha,* the Court held that failure to cite specific articles of the African Charter or other ratified human right instruments is no reason to oust the jurisdiction of the Court over the matter.[61] The Court explained that the facts of the application would be enough to demonstrate a *prima facie* violation of rights.[62] Further, where an applicant cites national law only, the Court may look for corresponding articles in the African Charter or other human rights instruments in order to satisfy the claim.[63] The Court set a precedent that was applied in the subsequent cases such as in *Mohamed Abubakari v. United Republic of Tanzania (Abubakari)*,[64] and *Onyango Nganyi v. United Republic of Tanzania (Nganyi)*.[65] In these cases, the government of Tanzania unsuccessfully challenged the Court's jurisdiction by arguing that the applicants had not invoked both the provisions of the Charter that were violated and provisions of the Protocol that grant jurisdiction to the Court.

The African Court's pre-trial procedures are also relatively expedient and relatable to ordinary litigants. Notably, and unlike the procedure in domestic systems, the African Court registry facilitates pre-trial stages, regularly communicating with parties to the case to set mutually convenient hearing dates, and effecting service of pleadings on behalf of the parties.[66] Further, parties can regularly communicate with the registry through email thus cutting significant costs on travel and mail charges, as well as time that would have been taken to complete pre-trial stages in court. Compared to national courts, the African Court also sets higher time limits for response to pleadings. For example, while a respondent would have sixty days[67] to respond to an application filed at the African Court, a respondent would be required to file a defense within fourteen days of service of an application filed in a Kenyan court. Further, the African Court is often willing to indulge a party who is

---

[61] Peter Joseph Chacha v. United Republic of Tanzania, App. No. 003/2012, Judgment, African Court on Human and Peoples' Rights [Afr. Ct. H.P.R.], para. 122 (Mar. 28, 2014), http://en.african-court.org/index.php/55-finalised-cases-details/850-app-no-003-2012-peter-joseph-chacha-v-united-republic-of-tanzania-details.

[62] *Id*. at para. 123.

[63] *Id*. at para. 113.

[64] Mohamed Abubakari v. United Republic of Tanzania, App. No. 007/2013, Judgment, African Court on Human and Peoples' Rights [Afr. Ct. H.P.R.], paras. 48–50 (June 3, 2016), http://en.african-court.org/images/Cases/Judgment/Judgment%20Appl%20%20007%20-%202013%20Mohamed%20Abubakari%20v%20Tanzania.pdf.

[65] Wilfred Onyango & 9 others v. United Republic of Tanzania, App. No. 006/2013, Judgment, African Court on Human and Peoples' Rights [Afr. Ct. H.P.R.], paras. 54, 57, 78 (Mar. 18, 2016), http://en.african-court.org/images/Cases/Judgment/Onyango_Judgment.pdf.

[66] See African Court on Human and Peoples' Rights, R. 34(6), 35(1), 35(2), 36.

[67] *Id*. at 37.

Table 6.1 Comparison of Procedures between the African Court and the Tanzanian Court of Appeal

lll[a]	African Court	Tanzanian Court of Appeal
Filing requirements	No superfluous requirements on the form of pleadings.	Strict requirements on the form court documents should take.
	An application should specify the alleged violation; evidence of exhaustion of local remedies; contain the particulars of the applicant and the party against whom the application is brought; and be written in one of the official languages of the Court.[a]	Documents should be on paper of durable quality; appellate documents be bound in book form with stout paper; all pages must be numbered consecutively, with an indication of every tenth line on each page.[b] The Registrar may refuse to accept documents that do not comply.[c]
CService of Court documents	Registry facilitates service.[d]	Parties are responsible for serving their pleadings on the other party in the manner prescribed in the Rules. They are then required to provide proof of service to the Court.[e]
Form of applications	No specific requirements as to the form applications should take.	Applications must be made by Notice of Motion in the provided form, and supported by an Affidavit. However, the Court may sometimes allow informal applications where the same are made in the course of a hearing.[f]

[a] African Court on Human and Peoples' Rights, R. 34.
[b] Tanzania Court of Appeal, R. 12.
[c] *Id.* at 14(4).
[d] African Court on Human and Peoples' Rights, R. 34(6); *id.* at 35(1), 35(2), 36.
[e] Tanzania Court of Appeal, R. 22.
[f] *Id.* at 48.

late in filing their response without the party having to necessarily apply for an extension of time, even when such a litigant has received a reminder to file a response to an application from the Registrar of the Court. Despite this reminder, in *Alex Thomas*, the Tanzanian government was once again late in filing a response, but the African Court was willing to accept the pleadings and serve them on the applicant with no penalties to the government.[68] In contrast, national courts operate under very strict time limits: a party must file for extension of time in the event that they are late in filing their defense. Even more stringently, an aggrieved party can seek judgment in default of court appearance or filing of a defense in national judicial

[68] Alex Thomas v. United Republic of Tanzania, App. No. 005/2013, Judgment, African Court on Human and Peoples' Rights [Afr. Ct. H.P.R.], para. 9 (Nov. 20, 2015), http://en.african-court.org/index.php/55-finalised-cases-details/858-app-no-005-2013-alex-thomas-v-united-republic-of-tanzania-details.

proceedings. While the African Court has dismissed cases that have not been dili-gently pursued by those that brought them, it is a more forgiving venue than na-tional courts when parties fail to show up at the hearings. In addition, the fact that the Court actively seeks lawyers[69] to represent litigants before the African Court is indicative of how its convenient procedures are designed to facilitate the filing and hearing of cases before it. Table 6.1 below contrasts procedures at the African Court and those of the Tanzanian Appellate Court, demonstrating the ease with which litigants can file cases at the African Court as compared to a domestic court.

Collectively, these factors have built a body of law that facilitates access to the Court. They epitomize a user-friendly institution where all, regardless of their status, can approach and seek justice for human rights violations. Given the similar set of cases that are continuously being filed by indigent prisoners alleging viola-tion of the right to a fair trial, we surmise that the African Court embodies a legal opportunity structure that makes it favorable to filing of such cases.

Rules Governing Access to the African Court: Jurisdiction and Admissibility

The rules governing jurisdiction and admissibility of cases at the African Court largely account for the influx of human rights violation claims emanating from criminal trials. These permissive rules constitute a favorable legal opportunity structure, which facilitate the filing of broad claims to the Court. As earlier men-tioned, the only limitation/qualification here is that an individual applicant must belong to one of the six states that have signed the declaration allowing individuals and NGOs with observer status at the African Commission, to file claims before the Court. Like in the analysis earlier, this favorable opportunity structure does not result from a standard set of rules but rather has been built by the African Court through its interpretation of the African Charter, and the Court Protocol and its Rules. The Court is in part aided by Rule 39(1) of its Rules of Procedure which re-quires it to conduct a preliminary investigation of its jurisdiction and admissibility of the application.

Jurisdiction relates to the powers of the Court/the extent of the powers of the Court. Pursuant to Article 3(1) of the Protocol and Rule 26 (1) (a) of the Rules of the Court, the African Court's material jurisdiction extends to "all cases and dis-putes submitted to it concerning the interpretation and application of the Charter, the Protocol and other relevant human rights instruments ratified by the State con-cerned." Construed in the context of cases challenging fair trial violations arising from national criminal convictions, the main argument against the African Court's material jurisdiction has been that hearing these cases effectively makes the Court

---

[69] *See* African Court on Human and Peoples' Rights, R. 37.

act as an appellate/Supreme Court with respect to decisions rendered by national courts. The African Court often examines the substantive evidence presented in the national court in a bid to determine whether a national courts' finding is/was consistent with the provisions of the African Charter. Like other international courts presented with this question, the African Court has determined that it has jurisdiction to examine the procedure followed by national courts and the evidence presented to it so that it can ascertain whether or not there was a violation of any rights in the African Charter or other human rights instrument ratified by the respondent state. In other words, litigating whether or not there was a violation of the African Charter or of another international treaty before the international court, was a matter separate and apart from determinations made by a domestic court. In effect, the jurisdiction of the African Court, it has held, is not in exercise of an appeal over the jurisdiction of a national court. This principle, first established in *Alex Thomas v. United Republic of Tanzania (2015)*, has been followed in subsequent cases including *Abubakari (2016) Christopher Jonas v. United Republic of Tanzania (Jonas) (2017)*[70] and *Thobias Mango & Others v. United Republic of Tanzania (Mango) (2018) and Minani Evarist v. United Republic of Tanzania (2018)*. In *Alex Thomas,* the Court noted that although the African Court "is not an appellate court with respect to decisions of national courts, this does not preclude it from examining relevant proceedings in the national courts."[71] Examining national court proceedings the African Court held, was "appropriate in order to determine whether they are in accordance with the standards set out in the Charter or other human rights instruments ratified by the State concerned."[72]

Regarding admissibility, the African Court has adopted a very generous interpretation of the requirements for exhaustion of local remedies, and filing of applications within a reasonable time from the date on which local remedies were exhausted. The Rules of the Court expressly require that all applications to the Court "be filed only after exhausting local remedies, if any, unless it is obvious that this procedure is unduly prolonged."[73]While this is an express requirement, it is not followed rigorously; rather, the Court has set a considerably low threshold for the exhaustion requirement.

The Court's approach has been to distinguish between "ordinary" and "extra-ordinary" remedies in a given legal system, finding that ordinary remedies are the usual or "normally thought about" remedies while extra-ordinary remedies

---

[70] Christopher Jonas v. United Republic of Tanzania, App. No. 011/2015, Judgment, African Court on Human and Peoples' Rights [Afr. Ct. H.P.R.], para. 28 (Sept. 28, 2015), http://en.african-court.org/images/Cases/Judgment/011-2015-Christopher%20Jonas%20V.%20United%20Republic%20of%20Tanzania-Judgment-28%20September%202017.pdf.

[71] Alex Thomas v. United Republic of Tanzania, App. No. 005/2013, Judgment, African Court on Human and Peoples' Rights [Afr. Ct. H.P.R.], para. 130 (Nov. 20, 2015), http://en.african-court.org/index.php/55-finalised-cases-details/858-app-no-005-2013-alex-thomas-v-united-republic-of-tanzania-details.

[72] *Id.*

[73] African Court on Human and Peoples' Rights, R. 40(5).

are the uncommon and those usually exercised in exceptional circumstances.[74] For instance, in a case involving an allegation of rights violations in criminal proceedings in Tanzania, the Court would analyze the type of remedies that would normally be conceived as ordinary in criminal proceedings in Tanzania, and hold that these are the only remedies that must be exhausted before filing a case at the African Court.

In effect, this creates a very pro-litigant rule where a litigant is only required to exhaust ordinary judicial remedies in their jurisdiction. In the case of Tanzania where most of these fair trial violation cases emanate, the Court has observed that trial proceedings in the High Court, and appeals at the Court of Appeal are ordinary remedies in Tanzania. By contrast, Constitutional Petitions and Applications for Review are extra-ordinary remedies that are neither necessary nor mandatory. The latter are deemed extra-ordinary because they are resorted to exceptionally in accordance with a set of standard rules. By contrast, the typical remedy of an appeal to the Tanzanian Court of Appeal is available as of right. In Tanzania, a Constitutional Petition for the redress of human rights violations cannot be entertained by a court of law as of right. The Court must be satisfied that there are no other adequate means of redress available to the litigant.[75] Similarly, reviews at the Tanzanian Court of Appeal can only be entertained in exceptional circumstances. These include where there is a manifest error on the record of proceedings; where a person's right to be heard was denied; where the Court's decision was a nullity; where the decision was procured by fraud, illegality, or perjury; and where the Court had no jurisdiction to entertain the case. This principle was first established in the African Court decision of Alex Thomas.[76] It was subsequently followed in *Abubakari*,[77] *Owino Onyachi & Another v. United Republic of Tanzania (Onyachi)*,[78]

---

[74] Mohamed Abubakari v. United Republic of Tanzania, App. No. 007/2013, Judgment, African Court on Human and Peoples' Rights [Afr. Ct. H.P.R.], paras. 68–71 (June 3, 2016), http://en.african-court.org/images/Cases/Judgment/Judgment%20Appl%20%20007%20-%202013%20Mohamed%20Abubakari%20v%20Tanzania.pdf.

[75] Basic Rights & Duties Enforcement Act of Tanzania, Section 8(2) states "The High Court shall not exercise its powers under this section if it is satisfied that adequate means of redress for the contravention alleged are or have been available to the person concerned under any other law, or that the application is merely frivolous or vexatious."

[76] Alex Thomas v. United Republic of Tanzania, App. No. 005/2013, Judgment, African Court on Human and Peoples' Rights [Afr. Ct. H.P.R.], para. 63 (Nov. 20, 2015), http://en.african-court.org/index.php/55-finalised-cases-details/858-app-no-005-2013-alex-thomas-v-united-republic-of-tanzania-details.

[77] Mohamed Abubakari v. United Republic of Tanzania, App. No. 007/2013, Judgment, African Court on Human and Peoples' Rights [Afr. Ct. H.P.R.], para. 72 (June 3, 2016), http://en.african-court.org/images/Cases/Judgment/Judgment%20Appl%20%20007%20-%202013%20Mohamed%20Abubakari%20v%20Tanzania.pdf.

[78] Kennedy Owino Onyachi & Others v. United Republic of Tanzania, App. No. 003/2015, Judgment, African Court on Human and Peoples' Rights [Afr. Ct. H.P.R.], para. 54 (Sept. 28, 2017), http://en.african-court.org/images/Cases/Judgment/003-2015-%20EN-Kennedy%20Owino%20Onyachi%20and%20Charles%20John%20Mwanini%20Njoka%20v.%20United%20Republic%20of%20Tanzania-Judgment-28%20September%202017%20-%20Optimized.pdf.

Nganyi,[79] *Jonas*,[80]and *Minani*.[81] Thus, the African Court would entertain a case even where there are "extra-ordinary remedies" available to the litigants, and where unnecessary delays hamper ordinary judiciary proceedings (trial and appeal procedures) as was found in *Nganyi*.[82]

Substantively, the African Court can only entertain claims that have been raised in national courts, as a precondition to fulfilling its exhaustion requirement. However, the African Court has in addition entertained new claims with the understanding that these claims fall within the bundle of fair trial rights, and thus no remedies need to have been exhausted in respect of the claims. In *Mango*, for instance, the Court held that it could admit certain new claims with regard to denial of legal assistance, prolonged detention, and illegality of sentence, even though they had not been raised at the domestic level as they "constituted part of the bundle of rights and guarantees relating to fair trial."[83] In *Ababukari*, the Court clarified this reasoning, holding that as long as a litigant has alleged a fair trial violation in the domestic court, they do not need to specifically spell out all the aspects of such violation, and thus new claims within the realm of fair trial rights would still be admissible at the African Court.[84] Possy has also extensively analyzed these cases in light of the Court's substantive interpretation of the right to a fair trial.[85] He shows how the African Court broadly interpreted Article 7 of the African Charter that guarantees the right to be heard, which he notes is not as expansive as Article 14 of the International Covenant on Civil and Political Rights (ICCPR).[86] As a result, the Court's expansive approach consolidated the essential elements of fair trial safeguards, and nurtured fair trial norms in Tanzania.[87] The application of these norms, he argues, could have positive effects for criminal justice reform

---

[79] Wilfred Onyango & 9 others v. United Republic of Tanzania, App. No. 006/2013, Judgment, African Court on Human and Peoples' Rights [Afr. Ct. H.P.R.], para. 95 (Mar. 18, 2016), http://en.african-court.org/images/Cases/Judgment/Onyango_Judgment.pdf.

[80] Christopher Jonas v. United Republic of Tanzania, App. No. 011/2015, Judgment, African Court on Human and Peoples' Rights [Afr. Ct. H.P.R.], para. 44 (Sept. 28, 2015), http://en.african-court.org/images/Cases/Judgment/011-2015-Christopher%20Jonas%20V.%20United%20Republic%20of%20Tanzania-Judgment-28%20September%202017.pdf.

[81] Minani Evarist v. United Republic of Tanzania, App. No. 027/2015, Judgment, African Court on Human and Peoples' Rights [Afr. Ct. H.P.R.], para. 34 (Sept. 21, 2018), http://en.african-court.org/images/Cases/Judgment/Judgement%20MINANI%20Vs%20URT%20-%20Optimized.pdf.

[82] Possy, *supra* note 4, at 328.

[83] Thobias Mango & Another v. United Republic of Tanzania, App. No. 005/2015, Judgment, African Court on Human and Peoples' Rights [Afr. Ct. H.P.R.], para. 46 (May 11, 2018), http://en.african-court.org/images/Cases/Judgment/005%20-%202015%20-Thobias%20Mango%20and%20Others%20Vs.%20Tanzania%20-%20Judgement%2011%20May%202018%20-%20Optimized.pdf.

[84] Mohamed Abubakari v. United Republic of Tanzania, App. No. 007/2013, Judgment, African Court on Human and Peoples' Rights [Afr. Ct. H.P.R.], para. 76 (June 3, 2016), http://en.african-court.org/images/Cases/Judgment/Judgment%20Appl%20%20007%20-%202013%20Mohamed%20Abubakari%20v%20Tanzania.pdf.

[85] Possy, supra note 4.

[86] *Id.* at 318.

[87] *Id.* at 321.

in Tanzania.[88] Possy sets out these safeguards to include: the equality of arms of principle that guarantees accused persons the right to be heard and tried before an independent and impartial court, and the right to a defense; the right to free legal aid; the right to trials without inordinate delay; the presumption of innocence; the right to an appeal or review; the right to be informed of the nature and context of the charges in a language an accused person understands; and the right to an effective remedy.[89]

Another procedural innovation that the African Court has adopted is a generous application of the requirement that cases before it must be filed within a reasonable period from the time local remedies were exhausted.[90] While six months is widely considered to be a "reasonable period," a fact that the African Court acknowledges, the Court has deemed admissible applications that were filed as late as seven years from the date local remedies were exhausted (*Abubakari*). Other long time periods include five years in *Jonas*, and four years, eight months, thirty days in *Mango*. The Court's jurisprudence is clear that that computation of time depends on the particular circumstances of each case.[91] The Court has been very consistent in interpreting this rule in favor of indigent applicants who may lack prior knowledge of the Court or how to approach it, are illiterate, lack legal representation, and are further constrained by virtue of being incarcerated. Once again, this permissive approach has created a very favorable legal opportunity structure for litigants.

Rules on Party that Bears the Costs of Litigation

As we noted earlier, a legal opportunity structure is considered more open where the costs of litigation are low—particularly where each party bears its own litigation costs. The Procedural Rules of the African Court provide that "unless otherwise decided by the Court, each party shall bear its own costs."[92] Although this requirement is not mandatory, it presumes that the norm shall be for each party to bear its own costs unless there are exceptional circumstances to warrant otherwise. Without explaining itself much, the Court has consistently held that each party

---

[88] *Id.* at 335.
[89] *Id.* at 321–34.
[90] African Court on Human and Peoples' Rights, R. 40(6).
[91] Minani Evarist v. United Republic of Tanzania, App. No. 027/2015, Judgment, African Court on Human and Peoples' Rights [Afr. Ct. H.P.R.], paras. 45 & 54 (Sept. 21, 2018); Christopher Jonas v. United Republic of Tanzania, App. No. 011/2015, Judgment, African Court on Human and Peoples' Rights [Afr. Ct. H.P.R.], paras. 53 & 54 (Sept. 28, 2015); Mohamed Abubakari v. United Republic of Tanzania, App. No. 007/2013, Judgment, African Court on Human and Peoples' Rights [Afr. Ct. H.P.R.], para. 92 (June 3, 2016); Wilfred Onyango & 9 others v. United Republic of Tanzania, App. No. 006/2013, Judgment, African Court on Human and Peoples' Rights [Afr. Ct. H.P.R.], para. 68 (Mar. 18, 2016); Alex Thomas v. United Republic of Tanzania, App. No. 005/2013, Judgment, African Court on Human and Peoples' Rights [Afr. Ct. H.P.R.], para. 74 (Nov. 20, 2015).
[92] African Court on Human Rights and Peoples' Rights, R. 30.

bears its own costs in seven of the eight cases examined in this section. For the one remaining,[93] the Court has deferred this decision to when it considers prayers for reparation. The decision is still pending at the time of this writing.

This section has discussed the development of a favorable legal opportunity structure through fair trial rights violations in criminal prosecutions. A testament to this favorable structure, individual litigants in civil disputes have also filed cases alleging similar violations of the right to a fair trial. In *Ramadhani Issa Malengo v. United Republic of Tanzania*,[94] the African Court asserted its subject-matter jurisdiction by applying the same principles in the aforementioned criminal cases—a lengthy trial of nine years and with only three witnesses was deemed to be directly related to "the right to be tried within a reasonable time by an impartial court/tribunal."[95] Although the African Court eventually denied admissibility of the matter for failure to exhaust local remedies, it provided guidance for exhaustion of remedies in civil disputes. The Court suggested that litigants in civil disputes cannot rely on civil appeals alone to satisfy the exhaustion requirement. They should also translate these disputes into human rights violations and seek redress of those claims.[96]

Part Three: Additional Cases Illustrating How the African Court Provides a Legal Opportunity Structure for Civil Society Groups and Opposition Parties

This part of the chapter discusses three cases: *Ingabire v Rwanda*, *Mtikila v. Tanzania*, and *ADPH v. Ivory Coast*. These three cases brought by opposition politicians or civil society groups involved in democratization processes in the respective countries. We use these cases to further buttress our claim that litigants use the African Court as one of many fora to advance their pro-democratization agenda in national political contexts that are particularly inhospitable to expansive political space for organizing against incumbent and often very repressive and authoritarian governments.

Victoire Ingabire v. Rwanda

Victoire Ingabire Umuhoza, the leader of the opposition political party FDU Inkingi that the government has refused to register, was charged under a Rwandese

---

[93] Kennedy Owino Onyachi & Others v. United Republic of Tanzania, App. No. 003/2015, Judgment, African Court on Human and Peoples' Rights [Afr. Ct. H.P.R.] (Sept. 28, 2017)

[94] Ramadhani Issa Malengo v. United Republic of Tanzania, App. No. 030/2015, Judgment, African Court on Human and Peoples's Rights [Afr. Ct. H.P.R.] (July 4, 2019).

[95] Article 7(1)(d) of the African Charter.

[96] Ramadhani Issa Malengo v. United Republic of Tanzania, App. No. 030/2015, Judgment, African Court on Human and Peoples' Rights [Afr. Ct. H.P.R.], paras. 40–42 (July 4, 2019).

statute for the offense of minimalization of genocide referred to as genocide denial in October 2010. Ingabire is the daughter of an opposition politician believed to have died under mysterious circumstances. She is a vocal critic of the government. She argued that the charges preferred were designed to silence her outspoken opposition against political repression of those opposed to President Kagame and his ruling party. Ingabire was critical of the inequitable sharing of national resources and politicization of the administration of justice against regime opponents. Before Rwanda's courts, she argued that the charges against her constituted a violation of her freedom of expression. Her political party used its website calling upon Rwanda's donors to freeze any budgetary aid to "a judicial system controlled by a government which has no respect for justice."[97]

In September 2018, Ingabire was released from custody after her case became a *cause celebre* highlighting the use of Rwandese courts to prosecute political opponents of President Kagame's government that has been in power since 1986. Since the case had provided critics of the Rwandese government a rallying point inside and outside Rwanda, a case was filed in the African Court challenging the prosecution as a violation of her right to a fair trial under the African Charter.

There were a number of advantages of filing the case in the African Court. First it created an opportunity for Ingabire and her supporters to have the government of Rwanda defend her prosecution in a forum that it did not control. Ingabire's lawyers prevailed in convincing the Court that it had jurisdiction contrary to the objections of the Rwandese government. The government of Rwanda unsuccessfully argued that the African Court was being used as an appeals court over criminal convictions of a national court. As scholars of the African Court have argued, the *Ingabire* case did not inaugurate any new significant jurisprudential development on its jurisdiction and admissibility decision.[98] As important as the decision of the African Court to the effect that Rwanda had failed to protect Ingabire's right to a fair trial, a right that had been firmly established in the Court's jurisprudence in the cases from Tanzania discussed earlier, the value of litigating in the African Court lies elsewhere, not in its jurisprudence.

The fact that Ingabire was able to file the case in the first place was the crucial point. By filing the case, she brought international attention not only to her persecution, but also forced the government of Rwanda to defend its conduct in the Court and other international fora. In short, the case became a *cause celebre* for

[97] Innocent Biruka, *The Rwandan State Has Boycotted the African Court on Human and Peoples' Rights in Case No. 003/2014, Which Opposes It to Ms. Victoire Ingabire Umuhoza, President of the FDU-Inkingi*, FDU RWANDA (Mar. 19, 2017), http://www.fdu-rwanda.com/en/english-the-rwandan-state-has-boycotted-the-african-court-on-human-and-peoples-rights-in-case-no-0032014-which-opposes-it-to-ms-victoire-ingabire-umuhoza-president-of-the-fdu-inkingi/.

[98] Oliver Windridge, *Treading a Fine Line: the Ingabire Victoire Umuhoza v. Rwanda Judgement (Part Two)*, THE ACtHPR MONITOR (Feb. 19, 2018), http://www.acthprmonitor.org/treading-a-fine-line-the-lngabire-victoire-umuhoza-v-rwanda-judgement-part-two/.

giving wider exposure to Rwanda's repression. Human rights groups both inside and outside Rwanda used the case to publicize the government's repression and monopolization of political power. These groups galvanized support to pressurize the Rwandese government to re-consider its political repression in resolutions in international organizations; from members of the European Parliament, and in press coverage including in magazines like *The Economist* that have a global reach. Similarly,

> a letter written in support of Ms. Ingabire by 64 Members of the European Parliament[99] denounced weeks of police harassment, intimidation and media lynching in Rwanda. They said that charges of genocide ideology, genocide denial, and conspiracy were "commonly used to silence any opposition in a country where freedom of expression is severely curtailed."[100] In their view, what had led her to file a case in the African Court was a loss of "all confidence in the justice of her country led by an authoritarian regime."[101]

The case before the African Court also helped to bring together opposition parties in Rwanda, in a not too frequent moment of unity. The Rwandan political opposition platform composed of the following political organizations: Amahoro PC, FDU—Inkingi; PDP—Imanzi; PS—Imberakuri; and Rwanda National Congress—RNC. These organizations, apparently emboldened following the arrest of Ingabire and the attention it galvanized, responded to Ingabire's prosecution as a group. They denounced the "harassment of critics as a common practice of the Rwandan regime to punish anyone who poses a serious threat to President Kagame's tight grip on power and to silence critics."[102] They also noted that the charges of denying, minimizing genocide, or divisionism or incitement to ethnic violence were intended to silence the critics of the government.

Citing the arrest and prosecution of Ingabire, the UN Special Rapporteur on the rights to Freedom of Association and Peaceful Assembly in Rwanda (2014), Maina Kiai, noted: "*a society without room for critical voices to speak freely and peacefully is unsustainable.*" For its part, Amnesty International condemned the speech-related charges that were brought against Ingabire, stating that these "should not have been brought before a court in the first place."[103]

---

[99] Letter of Support From 64 MEPs to Ms. Victoire Ingabire Umuhoza to High Representative (Dec. 18, 2015), http://l-hora.org/?p=3629&lang=en.

[100] *Id.*

[101] *Id.*

[102] Justin Bahunga, *Rwanda: Opposition Platform Strongly Condemns The Police Harassment of Miss Diane Rwigara and Her Family*, FDU RWANDA (Aug. 31, 2017), http://www.fdu-rwanda.com/en/english-rwanda-opposition-platform-strongly-condemns-the-police-harassment-of-miss-diane-rwigara-and-her-family/.

[103] *Rwanda: Ensure Appeal After Unfair Ingabire Trial*, AMNESTY INTERNATIONAL (Oct. 30. 2012), https://www.amnesty.org/en/press-releases/2012/10/rwanda-ensure-appeal-after-unfair-ingabire-trial/.

In August 2017, after the final judgment of the African Court was issued a coalition of opposition political parties called upon the UN Security Council "to take
up its responsibility and rein on President to release all political prisoners, open the
political space and to accept a highly inclusive national dialogue to agree on constitutional and legal instruments that reassure every Rwandan."[104]

The impact of the pressure put on the government of Rwanda from the different
pressure points from the African Court, to the media, and to international organizations, is difficult to measure. However, it is quite clear that the Rwandese government recognized that its decision to allow individuals to file cases to the African
Court was the opening that in turn multiplied the variety of venues in which it had
to defend its repression. As a result, the Rwandese government withdrew its declaration allowing its citizens to file cases before the African Court before it could
reach a final decision in the *Ingabire* case.[105] This withdrawal demonstrates that the
government wanted to close off the availability of the African Court as an avenue
through which its citizens could in turn open up multiple fronts which it did not
control and in which to defend itself.

This withdrawal is also consistent with Rwanda's initial hesitation in appearing
before the African Court when Ingabire filed the case.[106] The withdrawal of the
declaration was filed a few days before the hearing of the case on the merits was
scheduled to begin.[107] Rwanda not only failed to appear before the Court, but also
prevented Ingabire from traveling from Rwanda to Tanzania where the African
Court is based for the hearing of her case.[108]

The Involvement of International Leaders in the *Ingabire* Case: Shedding
Light on Detention Conditions

On January 24, 2012, the UK High Commissioner to Rwanda and the Embassy
Political Counselor visited Ingabire in her prison cell to discuss the conditions of

---

[104] Etienne Masozera, *Rwanda: The Entrenchment of President Kagame in Power Is a Threat to Peace
and Security in the Great Lakes Region—P5 Open Letter to Chair UNSC: Open Letter to Chair Security
Council*, THE RWANDAN (Aug. 6, 2017), http://www.therwandan.com/rwanda-the-entrenchment-of-
president-kagame-in-power-is-a-threat-to-peace-and-security-in-the-great-lakes-region-p5-open-
letter-to-chair-unsc/.

[105] Rwanda notified the African Court of its withdrawal of the optional declaration under Article
34(6) of the African Court Protocol a few days prior to a scheduled hearing in the *Ingabire* case. Rwanda
unsuccessfully argued that the effect of the withdrawal of its declaration was the suspension of the
case before the Court. *See* In the Matter of Ingabire Victoire Umuhoza v. Republic of Rwanda, Order
(Ruling) on Application 003/2014, African Court on Human and Peoples' Rights (Mar. 18, 2016).

[106] Biruka, *supra* note 97.

[107] Oliver Windridge, *The Folly of Being Comforted: Rwanda Withdraws Its Article 34(6) Declaration*,
THE ACtHPR MONITOR (Mar. 7, 2016), http://www.acthprmonitor.org/the-folly-of-being-comforted-
rwanda-withdraws-its-article-346-declaration/.

[108] Justin Bahunga, *Rwanda: The Hearing of the Appeal of "Mrs. Victoire Ingabire Umuhoza Against the
Rwandan Government" Before the African Court of Human and Peoples' Rights, Due on 22/03/2017*, FDU
RWANDA (Mar. 15, 2017), http://www.fdu-rwanda.com/en/english-the-hearing-of-the-appeal-of-mrs-
victoire-ingabire-umuhoza-against-the-rwandan-government-before-the-african-court-of-human-
and-peoples-rights-due-on-22032017/.

her detention.[109] This visit created an international platform on which Ingabire and her political opposition party could shed light on Rwandese detention conditions. Ingabire asked the Ambassador to intercede on her behalf so that President Kagame could order that she gets more humane detention conditions. "You can see it by yourself, there is little or no fresh air in this cell and no natural light at all," Ingabire stated. In response to this visit, the FDU-INKINGI (FDU) (a coalition of opposition groups) immediately posted an online article on its blog for its followers stating that the "political party FDU-INKINGI welcomes the visit and trusts the UK will continue to engage the government of Rwanda on crucial issues of human rights, political prisoners and political space, freedoms and legal reforms." Furthermore, the FDU used this same platform to recall that the British Foreign Secretary, William Hague on January 5, 2012, on his visit to Burma, called for the release of political prisoners.[110] The FDU argued that "the time has arrived to discuss openly those issues with the Rwandan leadership as well and to condition aid to the government of Rwanda on political reforms and freedoms."[111]

Caroline Buisman, Ingabire's Attorney, and Her Media Presence

Caroline Buisman, Ingabire's criminal defense attorney, was part of the legal team that successfully defended another Rwandese prisoner, Gen Kabirgi, who was acquitted of crimes of genocide against the Tutsis. Since the beginning of the trial, Buisman has had an active online presence, conducting interviews with the Rwandan press.

In 2017, Buisman held a press conference with the newspaper, *The Rwandan*, to expose the Rwandan government and to denounce the violations of Ingabire's human rights.[112] In discussing jurisdiction, she discussed Rwanda's withdrawal of its optional declaration accepting the African Court's jurisdiction to receive cases from individuals just a few days before the Court could hear arguments on jurisdiction..[113] The government claimed that this was a complete coincidence and had nothing to do with the *Ingabire* case, but Buisman claimed that Rwanda did not want two political prisoners facing similar charges to use the African Courts as a

---

[109] Boniface Twagirimana, *UK High Commissioner to Rwanda Pay a Visit to Victoire Ingabire in Her Prison Cell*, VICTOIRE-INGABIRE.COM (Jan. 26, 2012), https://www.victoire-ingabire.com/Eng/uk-high-commissioner-to-rwanda-pay-a-visit-to-victoire-ingabire-in-her-prison-cell/ (The author of this article, Boniface Twagirimana, was the interim vice president of the FDU-INKINGI at the time of this press release).

[110] *Id.* Hague called on political prisoners to be released and said: "I made clear that the British Government stands ready to respond positively to evidence of further progress towards that lasting improvement in human rights and political freedom that people of Burma seek."

[111] *Id.*

[112] Caroline *Buisman, Victoire Ingabire's Lawyer Explains How They Won Against the Rwandan Government*, THE RWANDAN (Dec. 2, 2017), http://www.therwandan.com/caroline-buisman-victoire-ingabires-lawyer-explains-how-they-won-against-the-rwandan-government/(hereinafter "Buisman 2017 Interview").

[113] *Id.*

platform against the government of Rwanda.[114] She used the media to denounce the lack of cooperation she had received from the Rwandese government in her defense of Ingabire, pointing to Rwanda's absence when the Court issued its decision as well as for any part of the proceedings.[115] Since the Rwandese government had not shown any signs of immediately releasing her Buisman resorted to lobbying other governments to nudge Rwanda to release her.[116] She argued that because there was a violation of Ingabire's rights, the only proper remedy was her release. She argued if Rwanda did not release Ingabire, she would turn to donor states such as the European Union, who had already made statements critical of Ingabire's deplorable prison conditions. She promised to look for states who would then take up this matter and try to convince Rwanda that they could not just ignore it.[117]

In a 2018 interview following the release of Ingabire, Buisman once again agreed to an online interview with *The Rwandan*. In her interview, she expressed her joy that her client was being released, however, the interviewer remained skeptical as to whether this release was actually a promise of her freedom.[118] Buisman agreed that this was not the avenue through which the attorneys believed Ingabire would be released (i.e. by Presidential clemency).[119] She argued that there was no need for a pardon since the judgment of the African Court required the Rwandan government to rectify its violations and a pardon went against that message, instead resulting in Ingabire being perceived as a criminal.[120] However, Buisman remained optimistic about the release, admitting that there were many motives behind the release. Buisman speculated that it was more probable that the Presidential pardon was not out of free will but due to international pressure.[121] Moreover, Buisman pointed out that Ingabire had not asked for a pardon, but merely for her freedom—and that this was an important distinction.[122]

Buisman was also critical of the conditions of Ingabire's release following the pardon. She was required to remain in Rwanda and check in with government authorities monthly.[123] Buisman stated that the conditions imposed were not the usual procedures for clemency, and that the Rwandese government did so to silence her from engaging in her opposition activities.[124] She also emphasized that

---

[114] *Id.*
[115] *Id.*
[116] *Id.*
[117] *Id.*
[118] The Release *of Victoire Ingabire: Views of Her Lawyer Caroline Buisman*, THE RWANDAN (Sept. 22, 2018),   http://www.therwandan.com/the-release-of-victoire-ingabire-views-of-her-lawyer-caroline-buisman/ (hereinafter "Buisman 2018 Interview").
[119] *Id.*
[120] *Id.*
[121] *Id.*
[122] *Id.* This was in response to the interviewer's question as to why Ingabire had refused to answer the media on the question of whether she had asked the President for clemency.
[123] *Id.*
[124] *Id.*

the Presidential clemency in no way rendered Rwanda a legitimate government.[125] In addressing whether the government would be aggravated if Ingabire were to continue voicing her views, Buisman emphasized that this was not one of the conditions of the clemency—so she was free to do so. In fact, Buisman expressed her joy at having finally been able—for the first time—to speak to her client over the phone. She further stated that the government would be naïve to think that being imprisoned had changed Ingabire from the opposition politician she was prior to her imprisonment.

Implications of Ingabire's Clemency and Release

Multiple press reports indicate it was widely believed that President Kagame chose to free Ingabire in an attempt to deceive the international community into believing that Rwanda was engaging in political reform. The Chairman of the Rwandan Political Platform P5, Jerome Nayigiziki, denounced the Rwandan government for its attempt to use the release of Ingabire to blind the international community from recognizing that unlawful detentions of other political prisoners and arbitrary arrests were still going on unabated.[126] "It is our very considered view that, like in all dictatorships, the release is a political ploy to ease diplomatic and economic pressure and score a political point."[127] Nayigiziki argued real reforms required that President Kagame scrap the laws that have made Rwanda a *de facto* one-party state and put citizens at risk of being arrested for expressing their views and voicing an opinion critical of government.[128]

Several critics pointed to the Presidential Order Number 131/01, which granted mercy to Ingabire on September 14, 2018 and released her from prison, as evidence that her freedom was deceptive.[129] President Kagame's critics argued that the decree was designed to hoodwink that Ingabire had been freed.[130] A journalist for *The Rwandan* reminded his readers that prior to her release, Ingabire had been made to plead for mercy from the government.[131] After her release, she was put

---

[125] *Id.*

[126] Jérôme Nayigiziki, *P5 Welcomes The Release of Political Prisoner Mrs. Ingabire Victoire Umuhoza*, THE RWANDAN (Sept. 17, 2018), http://www.therwandan.com/p5-welcomes-the-release-of-political-prisoner-mrs-ingabire-victoire-umuhoza/.

[127] *Id.*

[128] He argued that "The government should adapt laws that create room for critical voices to speak freely and peacefully. It is the political space and atmosphere that need to change in Rwanda, and not a political calculation done to blind the international community." *Id.*

[129] David Himbara, *How Kagame Deceived The World That He Freed Victoire Ingabire Umuhoza*, THE RWANDAN (Sept. 17, 2018), http://www.therwandan.com/how-kagame-deceived-the-world-that-he-freed-victoire-ingabire-umuhoza/.

[130] *Id.*

[131] As the Presidential Order puts it, "The beneficiary of the presidential mercy, herself, requests for the lifting of the imprisonment conditions. 'She addresses a written reasoned request to the President of the Republic.'" *See Presidential Order Number 131/01*, OFFICIAL GAZETTE NO. 21 OF 22/05/2017 (Mar. 22, 2017), http://primature.gov.rw/index.php?id=2&no_cache=1&tx_drblob_pi1%5BdownloadUid%5D=196.

under 24/7 surveillance by the village, cell, sector, and district levels.[132] She was required to appear before the prosecutor once a month;[133] further, she was not allowed to travel freely outside of Rwanda.[134]

The Associated Press newsagency also discussed Ingabire's release, but in the context of past criticisms of the Rwandese government.[135] The article raised doubt as to the circumstances surrounding the release, especially since it was unusual for President Kagame to pardon potential challengers.[136] The Associated Press interviewed a prison official who stated that "when prisoners are filing forms requesting a presidential pardon, prisoners charged with genocide denial and conspiracy against the government are not allowed to fill such forms."[137] Specifically, critics argue that the unusual timing of the release may be an effort to ease the pressure surrounding the arrest of Diane Rwigara, another prominent opposition politician in Rwanda.[138] Rwigara's sister argued that Ingabire's release should not blind those who have advocated for free speech and rights for every Rwandan and that "the momentum to fight for rights for every citizen must continue."[139] In late November 2018, Rwigara, who had been charged in what was believed to be another politically instigated trial of an enemy of President Kagame, and her mother were acquitted by a Rwandese court. The Court held that the government had been unable to prove the charges against her and her mother. It is widely believed that these acquittals are the result of the enormous pressure put on the Rwandese government by civil society groups in a variety of venues. As recent events indicate, the Rwandese government is more likely to succumb to this type of pressure whenever a case rises to prominence and attracts attention in both local and international fora. It is therefore unclear Rwanda has entered a new era in which open political dissent is allowed. To the contrary, arbitrary arrests, mysterious deaths, and disappearances of Ingabire's aides and other members of her opposition party continue.[140] In fact, before Ingabire was released, all nine members of her party's executive committee were arrested and

---

[132] *See id.* Upon receiving mercy from President Kagame, Ingabire had "to report to the Primary Level Prosecutor of her place of residence, at the prosecution office and notify the Prosecutor of the Village, Cell, Sector and District of her residence, within fifteen days."

[133] *See id.* Further, Ingabire has to "appear before the Primary Level Prosecutor of her place of residence, at the prosecution office, once a month, on a day determined by the Primary Level Prosecutor."

[134] *See id.* In order to do so, she "shall seek authorization from the Minister in charge of justice every time she wishes to go out of the country."

[135] Ignatius Ssuna, *Rwanda Free Opposition Leader, 2,100 Others From Prison*, THE ASSOCIATED PRESS: NEWS (Sept. 15, 2018), https://apnews.com/ecca19e0ccfd4b4dad18b808eccaf0e2.

[136] *Id.*

[137] *Id.*

[138] *Id.* (stating Rwigara is currently in detention in Rwanda for challenging President Kagame in last year's election but was disqualified over allegations that she forged some signatures on her nomination papers. She was later charged with inciting insurrection).

[139] *Id.*

[140] Silja Fröhlich, *Rwanda's Disappearing Opposition*, DEUTSCHE WELLE (Aug. 5, 2019), https://www.dw.com/en/rwandas-disappearing-opposition/a-49887045.

imprisoned.[141] Numerous reports have also been made of opposition members found dead, brutally strangled, disappearing from high security prisons, and sometimes tortured to death.[142]

Christopher Mtikila v. Tanzania

In *Christopher Mtikila v. Tanzania*,[143] a popular opposition politician in Tanzania, the late Reverend Christopher Mtikila, brought an application against the Republic of Tanzania for refusing him the right to run as an independent candidate in Tanzania's Presidential, parliamentary, and local government elections. Mtikila filed this case at the African Court after failing to get favorable orders in three cases in Tanzanian national courts. His case was joined by two NGOs—the Tanganyika Law Society and the Legal and Human Rights Centre—who, with him, argued that the constitutional prohibition of independent candidature in elections in Tanzania was a violation of his rights to participate in elections contrary to Articles 2 and 13(1) of the African Charter. By agreeing with him, the Court held that the proscription of independent candidates in Tanzania violates the right to non-discrimination, the right to participate in public affairs, and the freedom of association under the African Charter.

The African Court Provided Mtikila an Avenue to Overcome Legislative and Judicial Barriers in Tanzania

This case was particularly significant given the contextual history of Tanzanian politics. One party, Chama cha Mapinduzi (CCM) (Party of the Revolution) has dominated Tanzanian politics and governance since its formation in 1977 and has maintained its dominance notwithstanding the reintroduction of multi-party politics in 1992.[144] Following the move to multi-party politics, CCM and the

---

[141] Ann Garrison, *Rwanda's Victoire Ingabire: I will not Live in Fear of Prison or Assassination*, SAN FRANCISCO BAY VIEW (Aug. 22, 2019), https://sfbayview.com/2019/08/rwandas-victoire-ingabire-i-will-not-live-in-fear-of-prison-or-assassination/.

[142] Fröhlich, *supra* note 140. *See also* Aanu Adeoye, *Aide to Leading Rwandan Opposition Politician Found Dead*, CNN (Mar. 11, 2019), https://www.cnn.com/2019/03/11/africa/rwanda-opposition-leader-aide-killed-intl/index.html; Ida Sawyer, *One Month Since Rwandan Opposition Leader "Disappeared"*, HUMAN RIGHTS WATCH (Nov. 8, 2018), https://www.hrw.org/news/2018/11/08/one-month-rwandan-opposition-leader-disappeared.

[143] Tanganyika Law Society & Legal and Human Rights Centre & Reverend Christopher Mtikila v. United Republic of Tanzania, App. Nos. 9/2011 & 11/2011, Judgment, African Court on Human and Peoples' Rights [Afr. Ct. H.P.R.] (June 14, 2013), http://www.african-court.org/en/images/Cases/Judgment/Judgment%20Application%20009-011-2011%20Rev%20Christopher%20Mtikila%20v.%20Tanzania-1.pdf.

[144] *See* Barak Hoffman & Lindsay Robinson, *Tanzania's Missing Opposition*, 20 J. DEMOCRACY 123–36 (2009) (discussing the dominance of CCM and the strategies it has employed to silence/wipe out its competitors i.e. "regulating political competition, the media, and civil society; blurring the boundary between the party and state; and the targeted use of blatantly coercive illegal actions.").

Tanzanian government opposed independent candidacy on the grounds that it would promote individualism, and disrupt peace, order, and security.[145] Thus, the Constitution was amended in 1992 to require that all candidates for elective positions belong to and be sponsored by a political party.[146] Mtikila first attempted to register a political party in 1992 but his application was denied for failure to get membership from Zanzibar, as required by the Tanzanian Political Parties Act of 1992.[147] He therefore commenced his long struggle for independent candidature. In 2002, he was finally able to successfully register his party.

He first challenged the Constitutional amendment in 1993 at the High Court of Tanzania and alleged that the bar against independent candidacy unfairly limited his right to political participation and to free association.[148] The High Court unprecedentedly found in his favor, holding that the amendment was null and void.[149] Rather than follow on with an appeal, the government, through Parliament, amended the Constitution again to prohibit independent candidates from contesting elections.[150] The effect of this amendment was to nullify the 1994 High Court decision that had allowed independent candidates. Mtikila, challenged this in the High Court once again. The High Court held in his favor and confirmed the earlier finding in 1994.[151] The government thereafter appealed to the Court of Appeal, the highest court in Tanzania. The Court of Appeal held that the independent candidacy issue was a political question to be determined by Parliament.[152] The Court of Appeal also held that since the requirement of membership to a political party was now embedded in the Constitution pursuant to a constitutional amendment, the courts had no power to amend the Constitution, as this was a Parliamentary function.[153] Having no domestic recourse available, Mtikila decided to file a case in the African Court.

The African Court Enabled Mtikila to Mobilize Political Support against the Ruling Party

His reasons for approaching the African Court are illustrative of our argument that the African Court serves as a forum where opposition politicians can advance

---

[145] Frank Matengé, *Protesting the Independent Candidacy in Tanzania's Elections: A Bona Fide Cause?*, 5 J. POL. & L. 18–32 (2012).

[146] Alexander Makulilo, *"Join a Party or I Cannot Elect You": The Independent Candidate Question in Tanzania*, 6 CENT. EUR. U. POL. SCI. J. 6–7 (2011) (hereinafter "Makulilo, Join a Party").

[147] *Rev. Christopher Mtikila, National Chairman, Democratic Party of Tanzania, Pastor, Full Salvation Church*, HEAVEN ON EARTH, Interviews, http://www.heavenonearthdocumentary.com/interviews_mtikila.html (last visited Dec. 17, 2019).

[148] Makulilo, Join a Party, *supra* note 146, at 9.

[149] *Id.* at 10; Matengé, *supra* note 145, at 3–4.

[150] Matengé, *supra* note 145, at 4; Makulilo, Join a Party, *supra* note 146, at 11.

[151] Makulilo, Join a Party, *supra* note 146, at 11–12.

[152] The Attorney General v. Reverend Christopher Mtikila, Civil App. No. 45 of 2009, Judgment, 49 (Ct. of App. of Tanz.) (May 5, 2006), http://www.kituochakatiba.org/sites/default/files/legal-resources/The%20Attorney%20General%20versus%20Reverend%20Christopher%20Mtikila%20Civil%20Appeal%20No.%2045%20Of%202009.pdf.

[153] *Id.* at 48–49.

their causes and mobilize political support for their causes. In the words of his counsel at the African Court, Mtikila wanted to create a different political dynamic; to present his case in a forum that was non-politicized and that was not biased in favor of the ruling party.[154] To summarize, the African Court presented Mtikila with a number of advantages. As already alluded to earlier, it provided an opportunity for him to overcome the legislative and judicial obstacles, as well as the political barriers put in his way to run as an independent candidate in Tanzanian elections. This was because Parliament had amended the Constitution to effectively render the 1994 High Court ruling inconsequential and effectively precluding any possibility of being ordered to amend its electoral law in future. The Court of Appeal's holding that independent candidacy was a political question and that the courts had no power to overturn a constitutional amendment was another significant barrier. In fact, scholars of democracy and political practice in Tanzania observe that although the country is a multiparty state by law, the dominance of the CCM party and its style of governance has resulted in a "de facto one-party state" where the government and the ruling party operate as a single entity.[155] Mtikila argued that due to this fusion, the ruling party is often able to safeguard its interests through state machinery such as the use of parliamentary and judicial influence to prevent independent candidates from running.[156] The African Court not only enabled Mtikila to sidestep these barriers but also availed another forum for Mtikila to continue his fight for independent candidature in Tanzanian elections.

The African Court as a Neutral Arbiter for the Opposition and the Government

The African Court is also a neutral forum for opposition candidates to engage the government in a venue that it does not control. This is particularly vital for emerging democracies in African states. At the time, the three cases that were decided against him in Tanzania reflected the Tanzanian government's control of the judiciary. For instance, in the 1994 case, the government successfully blocked a popular pro-human rights judge from presiding the case to preempt the likelihood that the judge would side with the opposition.[157] Further, while the two High Court cases were successful, the gains made were shortly handicapped by constitutional amendments. As for the Court of Appeal case, it has been argued by many that the court failed to exercise its mandate of administering justice due to the "fear by the justices from the ruling party and its government, which are reluctant to endorse

---

[154] Interview with Roland Adjovi, counsel for Mtikila at the African Court (Nov. 5, 2018).

[155] Makulilo, Join a Party, *supra* note 146, at 24.

[156] Alexander B. Makulilo, *The Fallacy of De Facto Independent Candidacy in Tanzania: A Rejoinder*, 6 Cent. Eur. U. Pol. Sci. J. 111–37 (2012).

[157] J.T. Mwaikusa, *The Limits of Judicial Enterprise: Judicial Powers in the Process of Political Change in Tanzania*, 40 J. Afr. L. 243, 4–5 (1996).

independent candidates."[158] Thus, when all else fails nationally, the African Court stands as a neutral arbiter for the opposition and the government, especially by allowing individuals to file cases at the Court. In fact, Mtikila believed that the Tanzanian Judiciary was politicized and wanted the African Court, as an unbiased forum, to explicitly affirm that independent candidates were permissible under Tanzanian law.[159] This is also the view among popular media in East Africa. One such media outlet editorialized after the Mtikila decision that if "you can't beat the establishment the first three times? There's always Arusha."[160] The African Court is based in Arusha, Tanzania.

The African Court as an Opportunity Structure for NGOs and the Opposition

As an international court, the African Court is guided by progressive international principles found in international treaties. These principles are enshrined in its constitutive charter, thus enabling the Court to impart these progressive principles to growing democracies in Africa through its decisions. This role is recognized by NGOs who support the Court's work by bringing strategic cases to it. Following the decision of the African Court, the International Federation of Human Rights (FIDH), an affiliate of Tanzania's Legal & Human Rights Centre, remarked:

> this decision demonstrates two fundamental things. First of all, it clearly shows that the African Court has a significant role to play in the interpretation of the human rights instruments freely adopted and ratified by our governments. Besides, it is another illustration of the positive role that can be played by NGOs and individuals in guaranteeing the effectiveness of the Court.[161]

Opposition politicians likewise use the Court to force their governments to abide by their international obligations especially regarding civil and political rights. In the *Mtikila* case, the applicants invited the Court to impart progressive democratic principles to Tanzania as provided in the ICCPR, the African Charter, and the Universal Declaration of Human Rights (UDHR). It should be noted that one of

---

[158] Makulilo, Join a Party, *supra* note 146, at 2.

[159] Adjovi, *supra* note 154.

[160] Elsie Eyakuze, *If You Can't Beat Govt the First Three Times, Do Not Despair, There's Always Arusha*, THE EAST AFRICAN (Aug. 3, 2013), http://www.theeastafrican.co.ke/oped/comment/If-you-cant-beat-govt-the-first-3-times-there-is-always-Arusha-/434750-1935612-70q1jn/index.html.

[161] *African Court Orders Tanzania to Guarantee Civil and Political Rights. A Victory for Democracy!*, INTERNATIONAL FEDERATION FOR HUMAN RIGHTS (June 18, 2013), https://www.fidh.org/en/region/Africa/tanzania/13488-african-court-orders-tanzania-to-guarantee-civil-and-political-rights-a.

the government's grounds for appeal at the Tanzanian Court of Appeal was that the High Court erred by subjecting the Constitution to international instruments.[162] Although the Court of Appeal dismissed this ground, it did so because the High Court considered the international instruments in addition to the Constitution and the laws of Tanzania—that the international instruments were not the conclusive factor in the High Court decision.[163] The implication here is that the Tanzanian Constitution prevails over domestic law.

Before the African Court, Mtikila argued that the rule of law was a principle of customary international law and that by initiating a constitutional amendment to settle a legal dispute pending before a domestic court which nullified the Court's judgment, Tanzania abused the process of constitutional amendment and, therefore, the principle of the rule of law. Although this argument did not succeed, it shows the underlying goal of Mtikila to apply international law was one of his strategies in challenging the prohibition of independent candidates in Tanzania.

Although the Mtikila case was decided in 2013, the Tanzanian government is yet to implement the Court's recommendations to take constitutional, legislative, and all necessary measures to remedy its violations. The government's main contention has been that the case was wrongly decided and was inconsistent with Tanzania's Constitution.[164]

Actions Pour La Protection Des Droits De L'Homme (APDH) v. Ivory Coast

In July 2014, a human rights NGO in Ivory Coast, APDH filed a case against its government in the African Court.[165] APDH argued that a newly adopted law establishing the Ivory Coast's Independent Electoral Commission (IEC) violated the government's constitutional obligation to establish an independent, impartial electoral body, and further that this was in violation of the African Charter on Democracy, Elections and Governance.[166] APDH claimed that IEC's membership reservations for the President's representatives as well as the President of the National Assembly, granting them eight seats in comparison to the opposition's

---

[162] The Attorney General v. Reverend Christopher Mtikila, Civil App. No. 45 of 2009, Judgment, 13 (Ct. of App. of Tanz.) (May 5, 2006), http://www.kituochakatiba.org/sites/default/files/legal-resources/The%20Attorney%20General%20versus%20Reverend%20Christopher%20Mtikila%20Civil%20Appeal%20No.%2045%20Of%202009.pdf.

[163] *Id.* at 14.

[164] Oliver Windridge, *Mtikila v. Tanzania: Ruling on Reparations*, THE ACtHPR MONITOR (July 15, 2014), http://www.acthprmonitor.org/mtikila-v-tanzania-ruling-on-reparations/.

[165] Marie Joseph Ayissi, *Introductory Note to Actions Pour La Protection Des Droits De L'Homme (APDH) v. Republic of Côte D'Ivoire*, 56 INT'L LEGAL MATERIALS 574, 574 (2016).

[166] *Id.*

four, constituted a breach of the principle of candidate equality between the majority and opposition.[167]

The African Court found that the Ivory Coast not only violated its obligation to establish an independent and impartial electoral body, but also its obligation to protect the right of citizens to participate in the management of public affairs and the right to equal protection before the law.[168] This was the first such case before the African Court. APDH leveraged this victory and the opportunity to litigate the case before the African Court in a variety of ways. First, APDH used the case to publicize the repressiveness of the government and in so doing to mobilize international support for its goals. Second, it used the opportunity to litigate the case to increase domestic support for opposition political parties in Ivory Coast. Third, APDH used the case as an avenue to force the government to defend its repressive conduct in an international court. Each of these strategies is discussed in turn.

Publicity on the Repressiveness of the Government and Mobilized International Support

Litigating *APDH v. Ivory Coast* in the African Court provided APDH with a platform to publicize the repressiveness of the Ivorian government. The case gave the APDH a very high profile in the media and in Ivory Coast's civil society. APDH became recognized as one of the Ivory Coast's top human-rights NGOs. Prior to the Court announcing the decision in November 2016, Peace Insight, one of the leading resources for peace-building efforts in conflict zones, contacted APDH and interviewed its President.[169] In the interview, the President of the APDH outlined the various repressive measures the Ivorian government was engaging in against its people and its efforts to hold the government accountable.[170] The President of the APDH cited its advocacy which showed that in the 2015 electoral year, at least 99 percent of opposition party meetings were violently repressed under the pretext that they were not authorized.[171] APDH's President was also interviewed by Germany's public international broadcaster, Deutsche Welle, in a broadcast focusing on how the Ivory Coast was still experiencing turmoil from its 2010–2011

---

[167] The Matter of Actions Pour La Protection des Droits de L'Homme v. The Republic of Côte D'Ivoire, App. No. 001/2014, Judgment, African Court on Human and Peoples' Rights [Afr. Ct. H.P.R.], art. 15 (Nov. 18, 2016), http://en.african-court.org/images/Cases/Judgment/JUDGMENT_APPLICATION%20001%202014%20_%20APDH%20V.%20THE%20REPUBLIC%20OF%20COTE%20DIVOIRE.pdf.

[168] *African Court: Côte d'Ivoire's Partisan Electoral Body Violated International Norms*, INTERNATIONAL JUSTICE RESOURCE CENTER (Dec. 7, 2016), https://ijrcenter.org/2016/12/07/african-court-cote-divoires-partisan-electoral-body-violated-international-norms/.

[169] Daniel Ozoukou, *Human Rights in Ivory Coast: A Progress Check*, PEACE INSIGHT (Sept. 29, 2016), https://www.peaceinsight.org/blog/2016/09/human-rights-in-ivory-coast/.

[170] *Id.*

[171] *Id.*

political crisis.[172] In the article, APDH's President noted that "there is no dialogue between the government and the opposition" and that APDH was working on how to bring about reconciliation.[173] Although neither article directly mentioned *APDH v. Ivory Coast*, it is very likely that both media organizations reached out to APDH due to its prominence in working on domestic Ivorian human rights issues. More importantly for purposes of this chapter, the activism of APDH in a variety of forums is consistent with our argument that filing cases before international courts, such as the African Court, is only one dimension of a multidimensional strategy engaged in by those who bring cases before Africa's international courts.

APDH received recognition for its pro-democracy efforts by Ivorian civil society. APDH received the second National Commission of Human Rights of Côte d'Ivoire's Prize for the Rights of Man in December 2016.[174] Although there was no information on why it was received, the timing of the award makes it seem likely that it was related to APDH's successful litigation in the case before the African Court.

ADPH used its website to publish a series of articles about the case. The first article, published before the Court's decision, gave an overview of APDH's analysis of the IEC's shortcomings and its inability to provide independent election oversight.[175] The next article was a press statement released after the Court's decision celebrating the APDH's success at the African Court.[176] The third article published in conjunction with a press conference discussed why the APDH's brought the case and what the decision of the African Court now required of the IEC.[177] Next, APDH published an article noting that it held an advocacy workshop for the peaceful reform of the IEC.[178] The last article APDH published covering *APDH v. Ivory Coast* was a brief statement noting that the Court

[172] Katrin Gänsler, *Ivory Coast: A Country Still Deeply Divided*, DEUTSCHE WELLE (Feb. 2, 2018), https://www.dw.com/en/ivory-coast-a-country-still-deeply-divided/a-42549922.
[173] *Id.*
[174] Adou Judicael, *The APDH Wins the 2nd Human Rights Prize 2016 of the CNDHCI*, ACTIONS POUR LA PROTECTION DES DROITS DE L'HOMME, http://www.apdhci.org/index.php/13-activites/105-l-apdh-remporte-le-2e-prix-des-droits-de-l-homme-2016-de-la-cndhci.html (Apr. 3, 2019, 8:16 PM) (Fr.).
[175] Abraham Denis Yaurobat, *Is The Creditability of Elections Threatened?*, ACTIONS POUR LA PROTECTION DES DROITS DE L'HOMME, http://www.apdhci.org/index.php/2-non-categorise/92-la-credibilite-des-elections-est-elle-menacee.html (May 11, 2019, 11:18 AM) (Fr.).
[176] *APDH-CI Press Release On the Judgment of the African Court on Human and Peoples' Rights (ACHPR) On the CEI*, ACTIONS POUR LA PROTECTION DES DROITS DE L'HOMME, http://www.apdhci.org/index.php/13-activites/103-communique-de-presse-de-l-apdh-ci-relatif-a-l-arret-de-la-cour-africaine-des-droits-de-l-homme-et-des-peuples-cadhp-sur-la-cei.html (Apr. 5, 2019, 9:08 PM) (Fr.).
[177] *Press Conference of the APDH on the Execution of the Judgment of the African Court of Human Rights and Peoples Relating to the Reform of the Law Establishing the CIS*, ACTIONS POUR LA PROTECTION DES DROITS DE L'HOMME, http://www.apdhci.org/index.php/publications/112-conference-de-presse-de-l-apdh-sur-l-execution-de-l-arret-de-la-cour-africaine-des-droits-de-l-homme-et-des-peuples-relative-a-la-reforme-de-la-loi-portant-creation-de-la-cei.html (Apr. 5, 2019, 9:16 PM) (Fr.).
[178] Adou Judicael, *Advocacy Workshop for Peaceful Electoral Reform in Côte d'Ivoire*, ACTIONS POUR LA PROTECTION DES DROITS DE L'HOMME, http://www.apdhci.org/index.php/13-activites/113-atelier-de-plaidoyer-pour-une-reforme-electorale-apaisee-en-cote-d-ivoire.html (Apr. 3, 2019, 8.19 PM) (Fr.).

refused the Ivorian government's request for an interpretation of the Court's decision.[179]

While we cannot draw direct connections between political mobilization to reform Ivorian electoral law and the ADPH's case in the African Court, it is quite clear that ADPH used the victory in the African Court to continue to lobby and advocate for electoral reform. This advocacy and lobbying activity coincided with the presence of a United Nations peacekeeping force present in the Ivory Coast from 2004 until 2017.[180] The United Nations released periodic progress reports detailing the Ivory Coast's political and human rights situation. In the final report, there was an entire section devoted to the progress and issues surrounding human rights in the Ivory Coast.[181] The report also noted that the Special Representative for the Ivory Coast met with various opposition and government politicians leading up to a constitutional referendum in October 2016, leading to the resumption of dialogue between the two sides.[182] In addition, the report covered the government's efforts of shutting down opposition.[183]

Efforts to Increase Support for Opposition Political Parties
In April 2017, five months after the African Court handed down the ADPH decision, Ivorian opposition political parties formed a coalition to challenge the ruling parties in the upcoming 2020 Presidential election.[184] The coalition, Together for Democracy and Sovereignty (EDS), is comprised of four political parties and several political civil society organizations such as the Pan-African Youth and National Agricultural Trade Union for Progress.[185] While there is no direct link between litigating in the African Court and the decision of the opposition to come together to challenge the incumbent government, the premise of this chapter is that litigating in the African Court is one of the several venues civil society groups and opposition parties use in their struggle against incumbent governments.

Further, civil society groups and opposition political parties do not bring these cases because they expect incumbent governments will readily comply. Indeed, as of March 2018, the Ivorian government had not taken any practical measures to

---

[179] Adou Judicael, *Exclusive!!! The State of Côte d'Ivoire Declared Inadmissible Before the African Court of Human Rights (ACHPR)*, ACTIONS POUR LA PROTECTION DES DROITS DE L'HOMME, http://www.apdhci.org/index.php/2-non-categorise/117-exclusif-l-etat-de-cote-d-ivoire-declare-irrecevable-en-sa-demande-en-interpretation-dans-l-affaire-apdh-contre-l-etat-de-cote-d-ivoire-sur-l-independance-de-la-cei.html (Apr. 3, 2019, 8.20 PM) (Fr.).

[180] Feature: *Mission Accomplished—UN Operation in Côte d'Ivoire*, UN NEWS (May 1, 2017), https://news.un.org/en/story/2017/05/556382-feature-mission-accomplished-un-operation-cote-divoire.

[181] *Id.* at arts. 31–36.

[182] U.N. Security Council, *Final Progress Report of the Secretary-General on the U.N. Operation in Côte d'Ivoire*, art. 6, U.N. Doc. S/2017/89 (Jan. 31, 2017).

[183] *Id.*

[184] Ivorian *Political Parties Form A New Opposition Coalition*, AFRICA NEWS (Apr. 21, 2017), http://www.africanews.com/2017/04/21/ivorian-political-parties-form-a-new-opposition-coalition//.

[185] *Id.*

reform the composition of the IEC as ordered by the Court.[186] In response to questions about its failure to comply, the Ivorian government stated that the membership of the IEC was created through a broad consensus of leading political actors and that the international community was satisfied with how the IEC had previously organized elections.[187] The government's inaction, however, emboldened opposition political figures. In response to the government's reluctance to reform the IEC, the leader of the opposition alliance coalition, EDS, called for a "democratic march" or demonstration calling for free and fair polls ahead of senatorial, municipal, and regional elections.[188] Abdoudramane Sangare, the leader of the Ivorian Popular Front, a member of the EDS coalition, was also quoted saying that "we are asking for the electoral commission to be re-organized."[189] Sangare also noted that electoral list accuracy and security issues were matters of concern for the upcoming elections.[190] In response to the protest organized by the opposition alliance, the police shut down the demonstration.[191] Several hundred people reassembled to demonstrate against the government before they were violently scuttled by the police.[192] There was national and international press coverage of the government's violent repression of the demonstration.[193] Arguably, *ADPH v. Ivory Coast* in the African Court was one among many of the strategies civil society groups and opposition politicians in the Ivory Coast were using to mobilize their supporters. Our argument in this chapter is to emphasize that cases before Africa's international courts must be seen in the larger context of mobilization against repressive governance. Such a perspective de-emphasizes looking at these cases to determine whether or not there was compliance in isolation of the broader context within which they arise in the first place.

In late 2018, Ivory Coast held municipal elections in which the Ivorian government's ruling coalition overwhelmingly won.[194] Sixty-six members from

---

[186] Abidjan Wassimagnon, *Côte d'Ivoire: Malgré la Décision de l'APDH, le Pouvoir Dit Non à la Reforme de la Composition de la CEI, Tensions en Vue*, PRESS AFRIK (Mar. 12, 2018), https://www.pressafrik.com/Cote-d-Ivoire-Malgre-la-decision-de-l-APDH-le-pouvoir-dit-non-a-la-reforme-de-la-composition-de-la-CEI-tensions-en-vue_a179590.html.

[187] *Id.*

[188] Ivory *Coast Opposition to Launch Protest*, eNEWS CHANNEL AFRICA (Mar 17, 2018, 9:38 PM), https://www.enca.com/africa/ivory-coast-opposition-to-launch-protest.

[189] *Id.*

[190] *Id.*

[191] Security *forces in Ivory Coast Avert Planned Opposition Protests*, AFRICA NEWS (Mar. 22, 2018), http://www.africanews.com/2018/03/22/security-forces-in-ivory-coast-s-capital-avert-planned-protest-by-opposition/.

[192] *Id.*

[193] *See Ivory Coast's Security Forces Stop Opposition March*, CHANNELS TELEVISION (Mar. 22, 2018), https://www.channelstv.com/2018/03/22/ivory-coasts-security-forces-stop-opposition-march/ (noting Agence France Press journalists were at the scene to document police using tear gas and arresting a dozen demonstrators).

[194] Loucoumane Coulibaly, *Ivory Coast Inaugurates New Senate Amid Opposition Criticism*, REUTERS (Apr. 12, 2018), https://www.reuters.com/article/us-ivorycoast-politics/ivory-coast-inaugurates-new-senate-amid-opposition-criticism-idUSKBN1HJ2V4.

President Alassane Ouattara's Rally of the Republicans and its coalition partner, the Democratic Party of Ivory Coast, were elected to the ninety-nine-seat Senate after opposition groups boycotted the polls.[195] Local and international media covered the election. Reuters directly quoted Boubakar Kone, one of the leaders of the EDS coalition, who stated that the election was "the worst of democratic retreats. It's abhorrent."[196] Various media outlets quoted Ivorian opposition politicians critical of the Ivorian government as "bloated" after President Ouattara expanded his cabinet from thirty-four to forty-one ministers.[197] In effect, although the filing of a case in an international court had not helped to blunt the authoritarian regime from its excesses against the opposition, the case forced the government to be answerable for its conduct in a forum that they do not control. We now turn to that theme.

Cases in International Courts Compel Authoritarian Governments to be Answerable for their Conduct

By bringing a case against the government of the Ivory Coast, APDH secured an opportunity that forced the government to defend its repressive conduct in a forum that it did not control. During the proceedings of the case, the Ivorian government objected to the admissibility of APDH's written briefs stating that they contained "insulting language" toward the government and its institutions.[198] In response, the African Court found that the government did not produce evidence showing that APDH's language was insulting and rejected the government's claims.[199] Further, the Ivorian government argued that APDH did not exhaust domestic remedies, a requirement to bring a case before the Court, and that APDH could have had the Constitutional Council or an administrative body review the law's constitutionality.[200] APDH countered that there were procedural limitations allowing the Council to review laws only prior to their enactment.[201] The African Court sided with APDH and even noted that in a separate proceeding that the Council had already concluded that the law in question was constitutional.[202] These examples show two things. First, that the Ivorian government was unprepared to defend its control of the electoral process on the merits hence it efforts to defeat the case on procedural technicalities. Second, it was quite clear that there were really no good arguments on the merits that made the challenged conduct, particularly the fact that it had twice as many IEC seats as the opposition, defensible.

---

[195] *Id.*
[196] *Id.*
[197] *Ivory Coast Opposition Says New Government is "Bloated"*, NEWS24 (July 12, 2018, 6:06 AM), https://www.news24.com/Africa/News/ivory-coast-opposition-says-new-government-is-bloated-20180711
[198] Ayissi, *supra* note 165, at 20.
[199] *Id.* at 21.
[200] *Id.* at 72.
[201] *Id.* at 85–88.
[202] *Id.* at 93–102.

In a follow-up case, *Suy Bi Gohore Emile & Others v. Republic of Côte d'Ivoire*,[203] the applicants again challenged the impartiality of the IEC on the basis of its recomposition in 2019. The Ivorian government once again attempted to challenge the case on technicalities. It alleged the Court's adoption of the matter would be unlawful as the African Court did not have jurisdiction to monitor the execution of its judgments. This single objection opened up an opportunity for the Court to assert itself on the matter on execution of its judgments. The Court held that States had an obligation to comply with its judgments pursuant to Article 30 of the Charter, and that failure to do was tantamount to "a violation of human or peoples' rights"[204] and therefore the Court had jurisdiction to determine the case. This powerful pronouncement will serve as another opening for civil rights groups and individuals to bring cases to the court in instances where States do not comply with judgments, a very common phenomenon in the history of the African Court.

The African Court's careful vetting of the arguments of the Ivorian governments, such as those relating to "insulting language" may not have been possible in Ivorian courts since the government controls the judiciary. In effect, the Africa Court forced the government's hand so that it had to argue the case on the merits, and through their submissions, the ADPH had succeeded in making it answerable for its conduct.

Conclusions

This chapter has used the legal opportunity structure to explain why litigants take cases to the African Court. The advantage of the legal opportunity structures scholarship is that it decenters the focus on courts and instead centers analysis on the actors who go to these courts and their strategies for doing so. This grassroots perspective makes it possible to focus on how social movements mobilize or how they frame their claims before these courts. The three main elements of the legal opportunity structure are: first, the law has to provide legal openings for cases to be filed; second, rules governing standing, jurisdiction and admissibility are interpreted permissively; and third, the rules relating to costs must not burden potential litigants.

Using these elements of the legal opportunity structure, the chapter has shown how the inaugural set of cases to the African Court from Tanzania were possible. The African Court made itself very accessible by permitting very lenient rules in the drafting of petitions that came before it. Handwritten petitions were accepted

---

[203] Suy Bi Gohore Emile & Others v. Republic of Côte d'Ivoire, App. No. 044/2019, African Court on Human and Peoples' Rights [Afr. Ct. H.P.R.] (July 15, 2019), https://en.african-court.org/images/Cases/Judgment/Appl.%20044%20-2019%20-%20Suy%20be%20Gohore-%20English.pdf.

[204] Suy Bi Gohore Emile & Others v. Republic of Côte d'Ivoire, App. No. 044/2019, African Court on Human and Peoples' Rights [Afr. Ct. H.P.R.] (July 15, 2019), para. 59.

from prisoners alleging violation of fair trial rights. The Court also referred those cases to the PALU to take up the cases *pro-bono* thereby assuring itself of the initial caseload that it handled. The Court used these initial set of cases to develop a robust case-law on fair trial rights.

Thus when more politically sensitive cases like the *Ingabire* case involving a political prisoner in Rwanda came before the Court, there was already a fairly well developed case-law upon which to draw in finding in her favor. As this chapter has shown, when Ingabire's case was being litigated in the African Court, her supporters were mobilizing in several other forums exposing the unfairness of her trial and the fact that she was being prosecuted for her political views. While her release did not happen immediately after the case, it is very unlikely that she would ever have been released had it not been for the case and the enormous mileage that those who supported her got out of keeping her story in the news and in international organizations like the United Nations.

The *Mtikila* case from Tanzania involving a politician who had been denied the opportunity to run for elections as an independent candidate did not result in compliance. By contrast, in the *Ingabire* case, the Rwandese President extended clemency to Ingabire after her victory in the African Court and a lot of public pressure and discussion of the case. But just like in the *Ingabire* case, the groups that supported Mtikila against the incumbent ruling party in Tanzania used many venues to bring publicity to his political frustrations. Like Ingabire's case, Mtikila's case shows how filing before international courts is often a strategic decision by individuals and non-state actors as their way of organizing discontent with the hope that it in turn spurs mobilization for corrective action so that the grievances that underlie such discontent can be addressed. This is particularly the case where domestic courts and political forums are unwilling to provide a remedy because they are controlled by a government hostile to the claims of such litigants and movements, or because there are other barriers to successfully being able to advance their claims in domestic courts such as the cost of litigation. This was the case with the third case discussed in Section Three of the chapter involving the NGO, APDH, in the Ivory Coast. The African Court provided an opportunity for APDH to seek the government's justification for this restriction. APDH prevailed before the African Court.

Ultimately, this chapter shows how international courts become a go-to venue because of the difficult political environments that opposition politicians and their supporters face. This is particularly the case because often a dominant party controls the political space available for their political activity. Going to an international court is a strategy to keep pressure on such incumbent regimes answerable in a forum that they do not control. This is because in the national context, such incumbent regimes control electoral competition using constitutional and legal rules to undermine the impartiality and independence of election bodies. In so doing, they tilt electoral processes including how electoral boundaries are drawn, the registration of voters, which parties and candidates are allowed to compete, how campaigns are regulated, as well as how ballots get counted after they are cast on election day. As has been argued by James Gathii in Chapter 1, these structural advantages incumbents enjoy in many of Africa's authoritarian regimes illustrate the difficulties opposition political parties and civil society movements involved in democratization processes face.[205] Notwithstanding these limitations facing opposition political parties and civil society movements and the fact that the design of the Court of Justice of the African Union is quite protective of the sovereign prerogatives of African states,[206] the Court has nevertheless provided an important avenue for litigants to engage African states in ways that they did not anticipate. Therefore, although the African Court was designed in a manner protective of the sovereignty of African states, the manner in which litigants have used it indicates that the constraints the states designed may not always work in the ways they anticipated.

---

[205] James Gathii, *Term Limits and Three Types of Constitutional Crisis in Sub-Saharan Africa*, in CONSTITUTIONAL DEMOCRACY IN CRISIS? 313 (Mark A. Graber, Sanford Levinson, & Mark Tushnet eds., 2018).

[206] *See, e.g.*, Gina Bekker, *The African Court on Human and Peoples' Rights: Safeguarding the Interests of African States*, 51 J. AFRICAN L. 151–72 (2007) (noting how the design of both the African Court and Commission as well as the refusal to merge the African Court on Human and Peoples' Rights and the African Court of Justice indicates a continuation of the reluctance of African states to "compromise their position of power and privilege," *id.* at 177).

7

Backlash Against International Courts in West, East, and Southern Africa

Causes and Consequences

Karen J. Alter, James Thuo Gathii, and Laurence R. Helfer

Part One: Introduction

Many scholars, journalists, and attorneys express concern about backlashes against international courts (ICs). Upon investigation, most supposed examples of backlash turn out to be little more than piqued criticisms, impassioned speeches, or policy suggestions that are never seriously pursued. In fact, the vast majority of state-approved revisions of IC founding treaties have expanded the courts' jurisdiction and access rules rather than overturning disfavored decisions or sanctioning judges.

This chapter provides new evidence at odds with this sanguine account. In doing so, this chapter contributes to one of the objectives of this book—to show what happens when international court judges overstep their boundaries. We explore credible backlash threats against three similarly-situated ICs in Africa over the last decade. In all three instances, an African government responded to a politically controversial adverse ruling by a sub-regional court with a formal sanction proposal—to eliminate the court, narrow its jurisdiction and access provisions, or augment the rules for disciplining its judges.

The outcomes of these proposals were strikingly different, however. In West Africa, Member States rejected the Gambia's effort to curb the Economic Community of West African States (ECOWAS) Court's broad access to private complainants in human rights cases. In East Africa, while Kenya failed to persuade neighboring countries to eliminate the East African Court of Justice (EACJ) or oust its Kenyan judges, it achieved other meaningful reforms—creating an appellate division, adding strict time limits for filing complaints, and providing rules for removing judges accused of corruption at home. In Southern Africa, Zimbabwe maneuvered to suspend the Southern African Development Community (SADC) Tribunal and its judges, and later reconstitute it without the power to review complaints from private litigants.

Karen J. Alter, James Thuo Gathii, and Laurence R. Helfer, *Backlash Against International Courts in West, East, and Southern Africa* In: *The Performance of Africa's International Courts*. Edited by: James Thuo Gathii, Oxford University Press (2020). © The Several Contributors. DOI: 10.1093/oso/9780198868477.003.0008.

This chapter provides the first ever comparative documentation and analysis of these three IC backlashes and their varied outcomes. We draw heavily on field research in West Africa in 2011, and in East and Southern Africa in 2013 and 2014, including over fifty interviews and a workshop with government officials, human rights lawyers, bar associations, international and national judges, and the staff of the secretariats of the sub-regional communities. A review of the courts' case-law, non-governmental organization (NGO) press releases, and news media reports provides additional context for our analysis.

Our findings provide new evidence to explore a range of theoretical debates relating to ICs, including whether international judges are independent of states and the extent to which international adjudication is bounded by political constraints. Rationalist theories expect judges to anticipate and avoid negative political responses. The judges on all three recently established ICs could readily anticipate that their rulings would provoke a heated governmental reaction. Yet they issued their controversial rulings even when it was clear that governments stood ready to respond with court-curbing plans. What explains this audacious behavior? Our answer emphasizes the judges' awareness that non-state actors in the sub-regions—officials with regional Community secretariats and lawyers associations in particular—were likely to back the courts, at least tacitly and often openly, in post-litigation mobilization in support of the rulings. Variations in the extent and political influence of this mobilization and in the independence and political power of civil society groups on the one hand, and regional secretariats and parliaments on the other, helps explain the divergent outcomes in each sub-region.

Part Two tells the stories of the backlash attempts against the ECOWAS, East African Community (EAC), and SADC Courts. Part Three explains the different outcomes of these attempts, focusing on the extent to which Community Secretariats, civil society groups, and sub-regional parliaments supported each court. The formal structures of the Secretariats and the opportunities for civil society input are similar in all three communities. However, the institutional culture and political influence of these actors varies. In all three backlash attempts, governments attempted to circumvent procedural rules that give these non-state actors a say in Community decision-making. Where Secretariats and NGOs blocked these circumventions, the backlash campaigns failed or were slowed down. Part Four concludes by briefly identifying other theoretical implications of our findings for the study of ICs.

Part Two: Backlashes Against Three
Sub-Regional Courts in Africa

This section explains the causes and consequences of the three IC backlashes. The three situations we examine are like and hard cases that produced divergent outcomes.[1] The three courts are alike in several respects. Each is associated with a sub-regional integration Community in which the primary goal of economic liberalization is supplemented by a softer commitment to human rights and good governance—a commitment that has generated most of the cases decided by all three ICs. These Communities include several common institutional features: the adoption of legally binding rules and collective decisions by consensus; a requirement to consult with civil society groups; and, in principle at least, a commitment to put common state and societal interests above the preferences of any one government. Another similarity concerns the political and legal features of each Community's Member States. ECOWAS, EAC, and SADC are each comprised of a mix of emerging or fragile democracies and authoritarian regimes. And all three include national legal systems with little tradition of judicial independence and at least some countries where the rule of law is fragile or illusory. Yet another commonality relates to the design features of each IC, in particular the ability of individuals and NGOs to file suits directly with the courts against Member States alleging violations of international law.

The three sub-regional courts are also hard cases. As compared to Europe, the relatively small size of each Community should facilitate coordination to sanction judges or restrict a court's jurisdiction and access rules. Moreover, many African nations have a tradition of strong executive branches, weak judiciaries, citizens who share a deep post-colonial distrust of external interference, and relatedly, a reluctance on the part of political leaders to openly challenge the actions of other African governments.

Since very little is known about these courts or the backlashes against them, our account is fairly detailed. We begin with a summary of each Community's origins and institutions, identifying key similarities and differences across the three systems. We then describe the IC rulings that precipitated the backlash in each sub-region, including the government proposals to eliminate ICs or narrow their jurisdiction. We conclude by analyzing the extent to which Community Secretariats, civil society groups, and the judges themselves mobilized to defend the courts and their rulings.

The ECOWAS Court of Justice: A Failed Backlash

Like the other two sub-regional tribunals discussed in this chapter, the ECOWAS Court of Justice (ECOWAS Court) has adjudicated cases filed by individuals

---

[1] *See also* Mikael Rask Madsen, Pola Cebulak, & Micha Wiebusch, *Backlash Against International Courts: Explaining the Forms and Patterns of Resistance to International Courts*, 14 INT'L J. L. CONTEXT 197–220 (2018) (also finding that there is unevenness in backlash efforts against ICs and in their outcomes).

and NGOs alleging violations of human rights. Unlike those tribunals, however, ECOWAS judges have an express mandate to hear such cases—a 2005 Protocol that expanded the Court's delegated powers by granting it "jurisdiction to determine cases of violation of human rights that occur in any Member State" in response to complaints by private litigants.[2]

The 2009 backlash stemmed from a suit against the Gambia that fell squarely within the Court's human rights authority. We first explain several unusual features of the Protocol that are essential for understanding these events. We then describe the cases that triggered the backlash, the proposals that the Gambia introduced in response, and the events that ultimately led to the proposal's defeat.

The Protocol was approved by all fifteen ECOWAS Member States, but unlike most treaties it entered into effect provisionally on the day it was signed. This enabled the Court to begin hearing human rights cases immediately, something that ECOWAS officials and national political leaders alike supported to give the then recently appointed judges something to do.[3] But this decision also meant that the Court's new powers would remain tentative—and therefore potentially subject to revision—until the Protocol had been ratified by the Member States.[4]

The Protocol gives the ECOWAS Court broad jurisdiction over human rights complaints. Private litigants from all fifteen West African nations have direct access to the court without the need to exhaust domestic remedies. This design feature is highly unusual. In other global and regional human rights systems, including the African Court on Human and Peoples' Rights (African Court), multiple filtering mechanisms—a commission to vet complaints, optional jurisdiction, an exhaustion requirement, and a restriction on which actors can refer cases—create multiple hurdles that protect states against unwanted judicial scrutiny.

Among the first human rights suits to reach the ECOWAS Court were two complaints filed in 2007 by an NGO, the Media Foundation for West Africa, on behalf of Gambian journalists who had been arrested, detained, and allegedly tortured for publishing news articles critical of the government.[5] The Gambia was long ruled by one of the most repressive executives in West Africa. Supporters of former President Yahya Jammeh regularly harassed and intimidated critics and are especially intolerant of independent and opposition media. The country's judiciary was

---

[2] 2005 Supplementary Protocol, arts. 3, 4.

[3] The 1991 ECOWAS Court Protocol authorized the adjudication of cases filed only by Member States or by Community institutions. However, no such cases were filed in the first few years of the Court's existence. Karen J. Alter, Laurence R. Helfer, & Jacqueline R. McAllister, *A New International Human Rights Court for West Africa: The ECOWAS Community Court of Justice*, 108 AM. J. INT'L L. 737 (2013).

[4] 2005 Supplementary Protocol, art. 11 (providing that the Protocol "shall definitively enter into force upon the ratification by at least nine (9) signatory States").

[5] Manneh v. The Gambia, Case No. ECW/CCJ/JUD/03/08, Judgment, Economic Community of West African States Court of Justice (June 5, 2008); Saidykhan v. The Gambia, Case No. ECW/CCJ/RUL/05/09, Judgment, Economic Community of West African States Court of Justice (June 30, 2009).

also politically cowed. Judges risk being fired if they rule against the government and so rarely do.[6]

Given this climate of repression, the two complaints to the ECOWAS Court provoked an openly hostile reaction. As one West African human rights lawyer explained, President Jammeh had already "conquered his own judiciary," and he "refused to be bound by a court in Abuja"[7] (the seat of the ECOWAS Court). In response to the first suit by Chief Ebrima Manneh, the Gambia flatly ignored multiple requests to file documents or appear in court. The stonewalling strategy backfired. In June 2008, the ECOWAS judges issued a carefully reasoned and evidence-rich decision finding the Gambia responsible for torture and other human rights abuses and ordering the government to release Manneh from detention and to pay him US$100,000.[8]

The ECOWAS Court's judgment and damage award in the *Manneh* case sent shock waves across West Africa. As the same human rights lawyer noted, "with a $100,000 fine, the embarrassment was huge."[9] The case—and the repression of journalists that it faithfully represented—also received widespread negative publicity. As one NGO press release explained, "[t]he Gambian media environment has long been hostile and dangerous, but the government's flagrant disregard for the ECOWAS legal proceedings represents a low point."[10] Nor was pressure limited to civil society. Foreign governments and international organizations were equally condemning, demanding that the Gambia fully comply with the ECOWAS Court's judgment.[11]

The second suit, concerning the detention and torture of Musa Saidykhan, was harder to ignore because the journalist was alive, exhibited clear signs of torture, and pursued the case from the safety of exile.[12] The government had also learned from the *Manneh* case the costs of remaining mute in the face of credible allegations of human rights abuses. It responded to Saidykhan's complaint with a broadside of legal and political arguments, including a jurisdictional challenge and a claim that

---

[6] U.S. Dep't of State, *Country Reports on Human Rights Practices for 2013, The Gambia: Executive Summary*, HUMANRIGHTS.GOV, http://www.state.gov/j/drl/rls/hrrpt/humanrightsreport/index.htm?year=2013&dlid=220116#wrapper.

[7] Interview with Human Rights Advocate C.

[8] *Manneh, supra* note 5, at 4, 28, 44.

[9] Interview with Human Rights Advocate C.

[10] International Press Institute, *IPI Calls on the Gambian Government to Cooperate with ECOWAS Legal Proceedings*, SENEGAMBIA NEWS (Mar. 13, 2008), https://ipi.media/ipi-calls-on-the-gambian-government-to-cooperate-with-ecowas-legal-proceedings/.

[11] *See, e.g., U.S. Senators Call for Release of Journalist*, FOROYAA NEWSPAPER (SERREKUNDA) (Apr. 28, 2009), https://allafrica.com/stories/200904280913.html; *Durbin, Other Senators Press Commonwealth Nations on Case of Missing Journalist*, STATES NEWS SERVICE (Mar. 18, 2010), https://www.durbin.senate.gov/newsroom/press-releases/durbin-other-senators-press-commonwealth-nations-on-case-of-missing-journalist; Linda Akrasi Kotey, *Ghana: Akoto Ampaw, Two Others in Gambia*, GHANAIAN CHRONICLE (July 17, 2009), http://allafrica.com/stories/200907171086.html.

[12] *ECOWAS Torture Case against the Gambia Nears an End*, AFROL NEWS (Sept. 22, 2010), http://www.afrol.com/articles/36623.

the suit was "an affront to [Gambian] sovereignty."[13] The ECOWAS judges stood their ground. In June 2009, the Court published an interim ruling that carefully considered and rejected each of the Gambia's objections.[14]

Having failed to defeat Saidykhan's suit with procedural objections, and with the prospect of another embarrassing decision looming, President Jammeh adopted a different strategy—working within ECOWAS to challenge the Court's jurisdiction and thwart the judgments against the Gambia. The government's attack began, ironically, in the news media. Officials announced that the Gambia was "aggrieved" by the *Manneh* judgment and would "set the political process in motion to take the matter to the next level and get the decision set aside."[15]

In late September 2009, the Gambia submitted to the ECOWAS Commission, the sub-regional Secretariat, an official request to revise the 2005 Protocol. The request was accompanied by the text of a "draft Supplementary Act," revealing the seriousness of the government's intentions. The Act consisted of five specific amendments to the ECOWAS Court's jurisdiction and access rules:

(a) that with respect to human rights cases, the Court should only have jurisdiction in respect of international instruments ratified by the respondent country;

(b) also in human rights cases, the ECOWAS Court's jurisdiction should be made subject to the exhaustion of domestic remedies;

(c) cases should only be admissible if instituted not later than twelve months after the exhaustion of local remedies;

(d) cases should not be anonymous; and

(e) the Court should not hear cases that are before other international mechanisms of settlement.[16]

In addition, the Gambia sought an amendment to the Revised ECOWAS Treaty "to create an appeals procedure for all decisions of the Community Court," a proposal that the Council of Ministers had previously asked the ECOWAS Commission and the judges themselves to consider and that was still under review.[17]

On the face it, these proposals appear relatively modest and uncontroversial, particularly when considered in light of the expansiveness of the ECOWAS Court's

[13] Saidykhan v. The Gambia, Case No. ECW/CCJ/RUL/05/09, Judgment, Economic Community of West African States Court of Justice, para. 11 (June 30, 2009).

[14] *Id*. para. 37.

[15] *Gambian Attorney-General Denies Holding Missing Journalist*, AGENCE FRANCE PRESSE (Apr. 7, 2009).

[16] *West Africa: Country Submits Proposals to Amend ECOWAS Protocol*, FOROYAA NEWSPAPER (SERREKUNDA) (Sept. 25, 2009) ; *see also* Nana Adu Ampofo, *Gambian Authorities Seek to Limit Reach of Regional Human Rights Court*, GLOBAL INSIGHT (Sept. 28, 2009).

[17] A. Jallow, *Rights Groups Sue Gambia over Access to ECOWAS Court*, INFORMATION CENTER FOR ONLINE RESOURCES AND SERVICES, INC. (Sept. 30, 2009), https://web.archive.org/web/20160617181533/ http://listserv.icors.org/scripts/wa-ICORS.exe?A2=ind0909e&L=gambia-l&F=&S=&P=11181.

delegated human rights powers described earlier. For the Media Foundation for West Africa and other rights groups in the region, however, the true motivation for the proposals and their harmful consequences were immediately apparent. In a press release issued just three days after the ECOWAS Commission called for a meeting of experts to consider the Gambia's proposals, a consortium of eleven NGO civil society organizations denounced the amendments in no uncertain terms.[18]

According to the joint press release, the "Gambian government propose[d] these amendments so that the Court will be weakened in its capacity to deal effectively with tyrannical governments trampling on citizens' rights." In the NGOs' view, the proposal to require exhaustion of local remedies aimed to "depriv[e] citizens of free access" to an "independent judicial instrument that is not usually available in many countries" in a region "where the judiciary is an arm of the executive." And the attempt to limit the ECOWAS Court's jurisdiction to ratified human rights treaties was a ploy "to prevent the Court from adjudicating on the [Saidykhan] case against the Gambia"—one of "the rare African countries which have not ratified the United Nations Convention Against Torture."[19] The press release concluded with a plea to the ECOWAS Commission to "invite civil society organizations in the region ... to the proposed experts' meeting," or to postpone the meeting "until there are broad consultations with representatives of civil society organizations as well."[20] Although the joint press release suggests that civil society had been excluded from the process for reviewing the Gambian proposals, in fact officials in the ECOWAS Commission's Legal Affairs Directorate had already reached out to key lawyers and rights groups in the region to vet the proposals and attend the experts' meeting.[21] To turn up the heat in advance of the meeting, two leading human rights organizations—the Registered Trustees of the Socio-Economic Rights and Accountability Project (SERAP) and the Centre for Defence of Human Rights and Democracy in Africa (CDHRDA)—represented by the influential head of the West African Bar Association, Femi Falana, filed a lawsuit and *ex parte* motion with the ECOWAS Court seeking an emergency order "to stop

---

[18] *Four IFEX Members, Civil Society Groups fear Gambia Proposal will Prevent ECOWAS Court from Ruling in Saidykhan Case*, INTERNATIONAL FREEDOM OF EXPRESSION EXCHANGE (Sept. 28 2009), http://www.ifex.org/west_africa/2009/09/28/ecowas_court_jurisdiction/ (hereinafter "Four IFEX Members") (listing the eleven NGOs that signed the press release). Global human rights NGOs issued similar statements denouncing the amendments. *See, e.g., Proposed Amendment to ECOWAS Court Jurisdiction is a Step Backward*, AMNESTY INTERNATIONAL, WEST AFRICA (Sept. 28 2009), https://www.amnesty.org/download/Documents/44000/afr050052009en.pdf.

[19] Four IFEX Members, *supra* note 18.

[20] *Id.*

[21] Interviews with Human Rights Advocates B and C; Interview with ECOWAS Legal Affairs Directorate A. One interviewee suggested that the ECOWAS officials had initially leaked information about the Gambian proposals to human rights lawyers. Interview with ECOWAS Legal Affairs Directorate A.

the Government of Gambia and the ECOWAS Commission from amending the laws concerning the jurisdiction and access to" the Court.[22]

The suit, publicized in press releases and in the news media, challenged the legality of the Gambian proposals on multiple grounds.[23] The NGOs lambasted the revisions of the 2005 Protocol as an attempt to "limit access of the Community citizens to the Court with respect to the protection of human rights and weaken the ability of the Court … to effectively exercise its jurisdiction and to advance the objectives and fundamental principles of the Community."[24] The NGOs attacked the appeals proposal as an effort to undermine the authority of the ECOWAS Council of Ministers, which, as noted earlier, had previously commissioned a study of this issue. Finally, the complainants tied the proposals to the Gambia's ongoing bad faith refusal to comply with the Court's judgment and damage award in the *Manneh* case.[25]

Two days later, legal experts from across West Africa gathered in the Nigerian capital to consider the proposals. Although accounts of the meeting differ on some details, all sources agree that an ECOWAS Committee of Legal Experts decisively recommended against narrowing the Court's human rights powers.[26] One week later, the Council of Justice Ministers endorsed the legal experts' recommendation. Their decision effectively shelved the proposals.[27] The Gambia could have sought a further review before the Council of Ministers, but interviews confirm that the government at this point abandoned its campaign to sanction the Court.[28]

The Gambia's proposals provided a clear opportunity for West African governments to reconsider the ECOWAS Court's expansive human rights jurisdiction and access rules. Their decision to decisively reject the Gambian challenge is striking. One explanation was the widely shared perception of the Gambia as a bad actor with limited political clout in ECOWAS.[29] But the defeat would not have occurred without the extensive mobilization efforts of the region's human rights NGOs and attorneys. By issuing press releases, filing an emergency suit, and demanding access

---

[22] Jallow, *supra* note 17; the complaint was apparently withdrawn after the defeat of the Gambia's proposals.

[23] Innocent Anaba, *SERAP, CHRDA Challenge Plans to Amend ECOWAS' Court Powers*, VANGUARD, NIGERIA (June 26, 2008).

[24] Jallow, *supra* note 17.

[25] *Id.*

[26] Interview with Human Rights Advocate C; Telephone interview with Human Rights Advocate A; Modou Nyang, *Amendment [sic] to ECOWAS Court Mandate: Gambia Isolated By State Parties*, INFORMATION CENTER FOR ONLINE RESOURCES AND SERVICES, INC. (2009), https://web.archive.org/web/20160621134105/http://listserv.icors.org/scripts/wa-ICORS. exe?A2=ind0910a&L=gambia-l&F=&S=&P=810.

[27] Sources disagree as to whether the justice ministers rejected the Gambian proposal unanimously, defeated it by a nine to six vote, or whether the government withdrew the proposal. *See Justice Ministers Endorse Experts' Decision*, Media Foundation for West Africa (Oct. 14, 2009), https://www.ifex.org/ west_africa/2009/10/14/gambian_proposal_defeated/; Telephone interview with Human Rights Advocate A; Interview with Human Rights Advocate C.

[28] Interview with ECOWAS Legal Affairs Directorate A; Interview with Human Rights Advocate C.

[29] Interview with ECOWAS Legal Affairs Directorate A.

to a key meeting, these actors ensured that the government's backlash campaign was well publicized, that procedures were followed, and that their voices would be heard when experts convened to discuss the proposals.[30]

Equally essential was the overt and tacit support of individuals within the ECOWAS Commission. Just a few years earlier, the Commission had blessed the Member States' decision to provisionally delegate capacious human rights authority to the then-inactive ECOWAS Court. The judges had only recently begun to exercise this authority, and one of their judgments—against Niger for condoning modern forms of slavery—had received widespread recognition and praise, including in the foreign media.[31] In addition, West African governments had doubled down on their support of the Court in 2006 by creating a Judicial Council[32] to screen applications for open judgeships and recommend a slate of the best qualified candidates to the Member States. To impose additional hurdles to private litigants suits just when the court was beginning to hear cases and develop its jurisprudence would have undercut these political and institutional investments in the Community's fledgling judicial body—an outcome that Commission officials disfavored.[33]

Since the rejection of its proposals, the Gambia has continued to flout the ECOWAS Court's 2007 decision in the *Manneh* case and its 2010 judgment in favor of the second journalist, Saidykhan.[34] However, the defeat of the government's campaign had the opposite of its intended goal—it effectively ended debate over the Protocol's provisional status.[35]

---

[30] *Id.* (noting the importance of "civil society engagement and pressure," including the ECOWAS law suit in the defeat of the Gambian proposals).

[31] Hadijatou Mani Koraou v. Niger, Case No. ECW/CCJ/APP/08/07, Judgment, Economic Community of West African States Court of Justice (Oct. 27, 2008); *see* Lydia Polgreen, *Court Rules Niger Failed by Allowing Girl's Slavery*, N.Y. TIMES, Oct. 28, 2008, at A6.

[32] *Decision A/Dec.2/06/06 Establishing the Judicial Council of the Community*, 46 ECOWAS Official J. (adopted June 14, 2006). The Council comprises the chief justices from Member States that were not then represented on the seven-member Court.

[33] Interview with legal advisor at the ECOWAS Legal Affairs Directorate (Mar. 7, 2011) (discussing the Secretariat's desire for the ECOWAS Court to "pay its way" from being given cases to adjudicate).

[34] In 2010, the ECOWAS Court issued a judgment holding the Gambia responsible for illegally detaining and torturing Saidykhan and awarding him damages of US$200,000. Saidykhan v. The Gambia, Case No. ECW/CCJ/APP/11/07, Judgment, Economic Community of West African States Court of Justice, para. 47 (Dec. 16. 2010). In 2011, the Gambia denied responsibility for Manneh's death and asked the Court to set aside both judgments on the ground that the judges failed to properly assess the evidence. In 2012, the Court rejected the Gambia's arguments and reaffirmed the judgments. Saidykhan v. The Gambia, Case No. ECW/CCJ/APP/11/07, App. for Review, Economic Community of West African States Court of Justice (Feb. 7, 2012). Pressure for compliance with the judgments continues, as evidenced by human rights reports from the United States, the United Kingdom, and the United Nations.

[35] ECOWAS Secretariat and Court officials and human rights attorneys view the 2005 Protocol's provisional status as a non-issue politically. *See* Interview ECOWAS Legal Affairs Directorate A; Interview with Human Rights Advocate C; Interview with ECOWAS Court Official C. In 2013, the Court resoundingly rejected a challenge to its human rights jurisdiction based on the Protocol's provisional status. Ayika v. Liberia, Case No. ECW/CCJ/APP/07/11/REV, Judgment, Economic Community of West African States Court of Justice (July 2, 2013).

In subsequent cases, the ECOWAS Court has continued to develop its human rights jurisprudence, albeit in manner suggesting that it is aware of the political limits of its authority and the serious challenges of securing compliance with its judgments. The judges have condemned clear human rights abuses—including in high-profile cases—while rejecting litigant pleas to construe its jurisdiction expansively, and using public speeches and meetings to urge governments to comply with its judgments.[36] The Court has pursued these actions notwithstanding a multi-year delay in judicial appointments, during which time the existing judges remained in office and continued to hear cases.[37] With the swearing in of a new slate of judges recommended by the Judicial Council in 2014,[38] the ECOWAS Court's human rights authority now rests on a more solid legal and political foundation.

The EACJ: A Backlash Redirected

The current EAC, launched in 1999, is a revival of an earlier EAC that operated from 1967–1977 and consolidated colonial-era cooperation and regional institutions dating back to 1917. The reestablishment of the EAC in 1999 reflected a renewed commitment to sub-regional integration and cooperation that, unlike the old EAC, involved not only the states but also the private sector and peoples of East Africa.

The EAC's judicial arm, the EACJ, has a similar historical legacy. The EACJ replaced the East African Court of Appeal, which was established in 1902 and closed down in 1977 with the collapse of the earlier EAC. The Court of Appeal served as the apex tribunal of the region's national legal systems and is still remembered by judges and lawyers for high-quality rulings that continue to influence legal practice across the region. While the EACJ, launched in 2001, is sometimes confused with its historical precursor, it is an IC with a different and narrower jurisdiction—to interpret and apply EAC treaties and other legal texts.[39]

The most controversial aspect of the EACJ's jurisdiction concerns human rights.[40] Unlike the ECOWAS Court, which has an express mandate to hear human

---

[36] *See* Alter, Helfer, & McAllister, *supra* note 3 at 766–68; *see also* Laurence R. Helfer & Karen J. Alter, *Legitimacy and Lawmaking: A Tale of Three International Courts*, 14 THEORETICAL INQUIRIES L. 479, 498–501 (2013).

[37] Article 4(3) of the 1991 Protocol provides: "At the expiration of the term of a member of the Court, the said member shall remain in office until the appointment and assumption of office of his successor."

[38] Judicial Council Endorses Recruitment of 7 Judges for ECOWAS Court of Justice, ECOWAS, Press Release No. 051/2014 (Mar. 21, 2014). The delay is likely the result of disagreements over which Member States were eligible to appoint a judge to the Court.

[39] Treaty for the Establishment of the East African Community, art. 27(1) (hereinafter "EAC Establishment Treaty"). There were two other judicial organs under the defunct EAC, the East African Common Market Tribunal and the East African Industrial Court. The functions of these two defunct organs were also folded into the jurisdiction of the EACJ.

[40] For a detailed analysis, *see* James Gathii, *Mission Creep or a Search for Relevance: The East African Court of Justice's Human Rights Strategy*, 24 DUKE J. COMP. & INT'L L. 249 (2014).

rights suits, and the SADC Tribunal, which interprets a sub-regional treaty that arguably includes human rights commitments, the EAC Treaty explicitly states that the EACJ shall have a human rights jurisdiction "as will be determined by the [EAC] Council at a suitable subsequent date" once Member States "conclude a protocol to operationalise the extended jurisdiction."[41] Although EAC Member States have yet to adopt such a protocol, human rights cases comprise most of EACJ's docket.[42]

This seeming paradox is the result of sustained advocacy by human rights lawyers in East Africa, who have successfully urged the Court to interpret references to the rule of law, social justice, and human rights in the objectives and fundamental principles clauses of the EAC Treaty as justiciable commitments to protect individual rights even in the absence of the Protocol's adoption.[43] EAC Member States have repeatedly contested the EACJ's jurisdiction to entertain these human rights suits. Yet the Court, while acknowledging that it is not a human rights tribunal as such, has just as frequently reasserted its power to interpret every provision in EAC legal instruments, including those relating to human rights.

The case that provoked a backlash did not, however, involve human rights. Rather, Kenya was upset because the EACJ, in its first ruling in a contentious case, ordered Community officials to reject the slate of candidates chosen by the Kenyan government to sit in the East African Legislative Assembly (EALA). The case concerned Article 50 of the EAC Treaty, which, according the complainants, required holding an election for seats in the EALA.[44] Instead of an election, the Kenyan government had divided up the EALA seats among the country's political parties in proportion to their strength in the Parliament.[45] The opposition party viewed this as part of a broader procedural maneuver to control the domestic legislative agenda and renege on promises to share power.

Opposition politicians turned to the EACJ, hoping to inflict an embarrassing loss on the governing party in the lead up to national elections. The key event triggering the backlash against the Court was an interim ruling in *Anyang Nyong'o v. Attorney General of Kenya* (hereinafter *Nyong'o*) that barred Community officials

---

[41]   EAC Establishment Treaty, *supra* note 39, at art. 27(2).

[42]   East African Court of Justice—Decisions, http://eacj.org/?page_id=2414. Many complainants to the EACJ seek preliminary injunctive relief; thus, a majority of EACJ rulings are interim decisions. The EACJ's website indicates that the Court has issued forty-three final judgments. If all final judgments and rulings such as interlocutory appeals, tax, and cost rulings are counted, there are 106 decisions in all since the EACJ's creation.

[43]   EAC Establishment Treaty, *supra* note 39, at art. 6(d) (fundamental principles); *id.* at art. 7(2) (operational principles).

[44]   Article 50 "stipulates that the elected members shall, as much as feasible, be representative of specified groups, and sets out the qualifications for election." Although the slate was arguably representative, the litigants emphasized that Article 50 required an "election." Nyong'o v. Attorney Gen. of Kenya, Reference No. 1 of 2006, Ruling, at 3, 5, East African Court of Justice (Nov. 26, 2006), http://www.saflii.org/ea/cases/EACJ/2006/3.pdf (hereinafter "Nyong'o, Reference No. 1 of 2006").

[45]   *Id.* at 2–5.

from recognizing Kenya's slate of EALA nominees until the Court had decided the case on the merits.[46] As we explain later, the ruling incensed Kenya's government, triggering a campaign to kill the sub-regional court or bring its judges under greater Member State control. The EACJ survived the backlash in no small part due to efforts of the East African Law Society (EALS), which swiftly came to the Court's defense. When Kenya's plans to retaliate against the EACJ became public, the Society published editorials in the press and sent letters to the Presidents of the three EAC Member States.[47]

A blow-by-blow account of the legally and procedurally complex *Nyong'o* litigation is beyond the scope of this chapter.[48] Instead, we highlight those aspects of the case that are relevant to Kenya's backlash against the EACJ and the responses to the case by the other EAC Member States, civil society groups, the EAC Secretariat, and the sub-regional Parliament.

An initial contestation concerned the appropriate venue for adjudicating the dispute. On its face, a challenge to the process of EALA elections fell squarely within the EACJ's jurisdiction. Kenya argued, however, that the case could only be heard in the Kenyan High Court in a suit brought by the Attorney General. For the government, the high stakes political implications of the case overshadowed the EAC Treaty's unequivocal delegation of authority to the sub-regional tribunal. For the East African judges, however, the *Nyong'o* case presented their first opportunity to interpret and apply Community law and to develop their remedial powers.

The EACJ's ruling of November 27, 2006 is noteworthy for its unvarnished conclusion that Kenya had breached the EAC Treaty by holding a "fictitious election in lieu of a real election," and for the issuance of an interim injunction in favor of the opposition politicians that the delayed the EALA's second session by more than six months.[49] Two aspects of the Court's ruling especially vexed the government. First, Kenya viewed the decision as unwelcome external interference in a sensitive domestic political dispute and, even worse, as taking the opposition's side. Kenya's President went so far as to label the EACJ ruling as undermining the country's sovereignty.[50] Second, Kenya objected to the Court's conclusions that its

---

[46] *Id.* at 9.

[47] *See, e.g., No Integration Without The Rule of Law*, Press Release, East African Law Society (Dec. 4, 2006).

[48] For a comprehensive analysis, *see* Gathii, *supra* note 40, at 268–71.

[49] Nyong'o v. Attorney Gen. of Kenya, Reference No. 1 of 2006, Judgment, at 43, East African Court of Justice (Mar. 30, 2007), https://www.eacj.org/wp-content/uploads/2012/11/EACJ_Reference_No_1_20061.pdf (hereinafter "Nyong'o, Judgment of 2007"). Interview with Judge C of the EACJ First Instance Division, Nairobi, Kenya (Aug. 2, 2013) (asserting that the EACJ was aware that its decision would delay the EALA's opening).

[50] *Speech Delivered by Kenyan President Mwai Kibaki*, JALUO.COM, 8th EAC Summit, Arusha, Tanzania (Nov. 30, 2006), http://www.jaluo.com/wangwach/1206/Leo_Odera_Omolo120106a.html (noting that the "ruling of the Court poses serious challenges to the East African Community. The Council of Ministers is well seized of these challenges and their grave implications" and has "made appropriate proposals to the Summit for consideration and direction").

interpretation of the EAC Treaty binds national courts and that standing and exhaustion of domestic remedies doctrines did not bar the Court from hearing suits
from private litigants.[51]

Kenya's reaction to the *Nyong'o* ruling was swift and furious. The government
was dogged in its determination to retaliate against the EACJ judges. Officials
pursued several lines of attack more or less simultaneously. When one avenue
was thwarted, the government pushed ahead with other strategies, ultimately suc-
ceeding in rushing through amendments to the EAC Treaty that curbed the EACJ's
authority.

Kenya's first move was a behind-the-scenes campaign to kill the fledgling sub-
regional court. Individuals with first-hand knowledge of these events described
the government's plans in off-the-record interviews.[52] They told us that the campaign was led by Kenya's Attorney General, Amos Wako, that it began just days
after the Court's interim injunction, and that the proposal was not sympathet-
ically received by Uganda and Tanzania,[53] which resisted regionalizing Kenya's
domestic political squabbles.[54] Both countries were committed to reviving the
fledgling East African integration project and did not want another collapse of
the EAC. Tanzanian officials viewed killing the Court as "too extreme,"[55] while
President Yoweri Museveni of Uganda supported EAC institutions with the hope
of becoming the Community's President if the EAC were to later become a political federation.

Blocked in its efforts to kill the court, Kenya turned to a strategy that it could
implement without the agreement of the other Member States—threatening
to oust the EACJ's two Kenyan judges, one of whom was the Court's President.
By removing the judges from the *Nyong'o* case, the government hoped to avoid
an adverse ruling on the merits that would solidify the opposition's influence in
the EALA.

An opportunity to implement this strategy arose during a status conference at
the Court's seat in Arusha, Tanzania. A high level legal team led by Kenya's Solicitor
General visited the chambers of the EACJ President. During this unscheduled *ex
parte* meeting, the attorneys urged the President and his Kenyan colleague to recuse
themselves from the *Nyong'o* case. If they did not, the Solicitor General threatened
to file a formal recusal motion asserting that the two jurists had engaged in "corruption, unethical practice, and absence of integrity" in the performance of their

---

[51] Nyong'o, Judgment of 2007, *supra* note 49, at 20.
[52] Interview with EACJ Appellate Judges A and B in Arusha, Tanzania (July 30, 2013). *See also*
Interview with Human Rights Advocate L, Arusha, Tanzania (July 30, 2013).
[53] Tanzania and Uganda were the only other Member States of the EAC at the time. Rwanda and
Burundi did not join the EAC until several years later, after an amendment to the EAC Treaty.
[54] Gitau Warigi, *Our Free Wheeling Politics May Frustrate Regional Unity*, DAILY NATION (Dec. 3,
2006), http://allafrica.com/stories/200612040362.html.
[55] Interview with Human Rights Advocate L, Arusha, Tanzania (July 30, 2013).

judicial offices in Kenya.[56] (Many EACJ judges continue to serve as national judges while appointed to the sub-regional court, which is not a full-time judicial body.)

Refusing to accede to pressure tactics the EACJ later described as "akin to intimidation,"[57] and an "ambush,"[58] the Kenyan jurists sought the advice of their colleagues. The judges unanimously backed their Kenyan colleagues and scheduled the recusal motion for a public hearing. At the hearing, the government made good on its threat to "wash the dirty laundry" of the Kenyan judges.[59] It argued that because the judges had been suspended from their duties on Kenyan courts due to allegations of corruption, they could not render a fair judgment in the *Nyong'o* case.[60]

In the end, it was the government that was embarrassed. Kenya withdrew its complaint against one of the judges who, by the time the recusal motion was heard, had voluntarily resigned from the Kenyan judiciary after the government commended him for his service and wished him a "prosperous time in the EACJ."[61] Caught in its own inconsistency, the government apologized.[62] As for the second judge, the EACJ found no basis to question his impartiality and dismissed the government's motion. A Kenyan court later found that the corruption investigation violated the judge's "natural justice rights," leading to his reinstatement in the national judiciary.[63]

Undaunted by its inability to oust the Kenyan judges, the government pursued a third approach—amending the EAC Treaty. Kenya's treaty proposal had several goals: to pressure the judges to refrain from further adverse rulings in the *Nyong'o* litigation; to restrict the Court's ability to hear cases from private litigants; to create an appellate chamber staffed by pro-government jurists; and to create a procedure to remove judges for misconduct.[64] The EALS perceived the amendments not

---

[56] Attorney Gen. of Kenya v. Nyong'o, Appl. No. 5 of 2007, at 19 (Feb. 6, 2007), https://www.eacj.org//wp-content/uploads/2007/02/EACJ_application_No5_2007.pdf (hereinafter "Nyong'o, Appl. No. 5") ; *see Kibaki Rails at EAC Court as Rwanda, Burundi Join Up*, THE EAST AFRICAN (Dec. 4, 2006), http://www.theeastafrican.co.ke/news/-/2558/252342/-/t6awg5z/-/index.html.

[57] Nyong'o, Appl. No. 5, *supra* note 56, at 11.

[58] *Id.* at 8–9; *see* Interview with EACJ Appellate Judges A and B, Arusha, Tanzania (July 30, 2013) (describing the support of the other EACJ judges in a meeting following the recusal request to the Kenyan judges).

[59] Interview with EACJ Appellate Judge A and President, Arusha, Tanzania (July 30, 2013).

[60] Nyong'o, Appl. No. 5, *supra* note 56.

[61] *Id.* at 11. On the withdrawal, *see* at 14.

[62] *Id.* at 12.

[63] Republic v. Chief Justice of Kenya and Others Ex Parte Moijo Ole Keiwua (2010) eKLR. On the reinstatement, *see* Patricia Kameri Mbote & Migai Aketch, KENYA: JUSTICE SECTOR AND THE RULE OF LAW: A REVIEW BY AFRIMAP AND THE OPEN SOCIETY INITIATIVE FOR EASTERN AFRICA 111 (Mar. 2011) (noting that in 2010 "[t]he tribunal for the Court of Appeal clears Justice Moijo Ole Keiwa of corruption charges. President Kibaki reinstates him into office"); Mwalimu Mati, *Kenya is Guilty of Judicial Interference*, E. AFR. (Feb. 26, 2007), http://www.theeastafrican.co.ke/opOrEd/-/434748/253402/-/rbk891z/-/index.html.

[64] Henry Onoria, *Botched-Up Elections, Treaty Amendments and Judicial Independence in the East African Community*, 54 J. AFR. L. 84 (2010).

as a good faith court reform initiative, but rather as a brazen and illegal ploy "to threaten and cow down the Court"[65] and intimidate its judges.[66]

The amendments were proposed, drafted, and adopted with exceptional haste. This swiftness suggests the depth of Kenya's desire to limit the EACJ's review powers and to circumvent EAC institutional processes that might have blocked or weakened its proposals. On November 28, 2006—the very next day after the *Nyong'o* injunction—the EAC Council of Ministers called for a study of the Court's jurisdiction. Two days later, the three EAC Presidents endorsed the Council's re-commendations to reconstitute the EACJ as a two-level court with a First Instance and Appellate Divisions, to review "the procedure for removal of Judges from of-fice" to expand the grounds for removal, and to convene a special Summit to adopt these changes as amendments to the EAC Treaty.[67]

On December 7, 2006, Kenyan Attorney General Wako chaired a meeting of EAC Attorneys General at which they considered and finalized draft amend-ments to the EAC Treaty that Wako himself had prepared.[68] The very next day, the Council of Ministers approved the draft amendments at an extraordinary meeting and submitted them to the Member States for comments.[69] Uganda approved the amendments on December 11, 2006, Tanzania the next day and Kenya the day after. The Summit endorsed the amendments on December 14, 2006 on the side-lines of a non-EAC meeting,[70] and they entered into force in May 2007 after all three Member States had ratified them.[71]

As adopted, the amendments made substantial changes to the EACJ's struc-ture, jurisdiction, and access rules. They split the Court into two divisions; pro-vided rules for appeals to the Appellate Division; added new grounds for removing or suspending EACJ judges due to allegations of "misconduct" in their respective home countries; clarified that the Court had no power to review cases for which "jurisdiction [is] conferred by the Treaty on organs of Partner States;" and added a

---

[65]   East African Law Society and 4 others v. Attorney General of Kenya and 3 others, Reference No.3 of 2007, East African Court of Justice, at 32 (Aug. 2008), http://eacj.org/wp-content/uploads/2012/11/ Ref-3-of-2007.pdf (hereinafter "Reference No.3") (quoting EALS pleadings stated that "the impugned amendments were undertaken with a view to threaten and cow down the Court"); *see No Integration Without the Rule of Law*, Press Release, East African Law Society 2 (Dec. 4, 2006) (describing attempts "to intimidate and bully the Court").

[66]   )*East Africa: Why Undermining EA Court is Sheer Folly*, THE EAST AFRICAN (Dec. 12, 2006), https:// allafrica.com/stories/200612120533.html; *see also Wagging Tongues Over EALA Ruling is Contempt of Court*, ARUSHA TIMES (Dec. 10–15, 2006), https://allafrica.com/stories/200612110956.html.

[67]   Communiqué of the EAC Summit (Nov. 30, 2006).

[68]   See EAC, *Report of the Extraordinary Meeting of the Attorneys General on the Proposed Amendment of the Treaty for the Establishment of the East African Community*, Ref. EAC/AG/EX/2006, para. 2 (Dec. 7, 2006) (noting that "[t]he Attorneys General considered a draft proposal for the amendment of the Treaty prepared by the Hon. Attorney General of Kenya which is attached hereto as Annex II").

[69]   EAC, *Report of the Extraordinary Meeting of the Council of EAC Ministers* (Dec. 7–8, 2006).

[70]   *East Africa: Irate Kibaki Clips the Wings of EACJ Judges*, THE EAST AFRICAN (Dec. 19, 2006), http:// allafrica.com/stories/200612190758.html.

[71]   Onoria, *supra* note 64, at 82, n. 49.

two-month time limit for legal and natural persons to file complaints challenging national actions or decisions as contrary to the Treaty.[72]

Critics argued that the amendments were designed to weaken the Court in multiple ways.[73] The creation of an Appellate Division provided a safety-valve to reverse decisions of the First Instance Division that governments found objectionable. Our review of the EACJ case-law and interviews with key actors reveals that the Member States have often exercised this safety-valve by appointing more government-friendly judges to the Appellate Division and by frequently appealing orders and rulings of the First Instance Division.[74]

The addition of corruption charges against judges in their home countries as a basis for suspension or removal from the EACJ was directly aimed at the two Kenyan judges who, as described earlier, were facing or had faced corruption allegations at the time of the *Nyong'o* litigation. On the face of it, the suspension clause seemingly threatens judicial independence, since it gives Member States the power to temporarily remove and replace a judge who is merely "subject to investigation" for alleged corruption in his or her home country, until "a tribunal or other relevant authority" in that country—institutions that may be closely controlled by the executive branch—recommends against the judge's removal from the office.[75] We found no evidence, however, that this provision has been used by governments to threaten or influence judges. Indeed, our interviews suggest that EACJ judges do not worry about governments carrying out this threat.

The two other revisions limited the EACJ's review powers. The amendment denying the Court the ability to hear matters delegated to another Member State organ—appended to a provision authorizing the Court to interpret and apply the entire EAC Treaty—allowed governments to strip the Court of jurisdiction by choosing a domestic institution as an alternative forum. The rule requiring private litigants to challenge national decisions or policies within two months of their adoption provided a very narrow window to file suits with the EACJ.

The adoption of the amendments triggered a vociferous reaction from civil society groups, opposition politicians, and the plaintiffs in the *Nyong'o* case, all of whom focused on the circumvention of EAC and national procedures. The EALS led NGOs in protesting their exclusion from discussions leading up to the

---

[72] Treaty for the Establishment of the East African Community, arts. 26(1), 26(2), 27(1), 30(2), as amended Dec. 14, 2006, and Aug. 20, 2007, WIPO Lex, https://wipolex.wipo.int/en/text/173330.

[73] Onoria, *supra* note 64, at 84; *see* Anne Pieter van der Mei, *The East African Community: The Bumpy Road to Supranationalism: Some Reflections on the Judgments of the Court of Justice of the East African Community in Anyang' Nyong'o and others and East African Law Society and others* 12 (Maastricht Faculty of Law, Working Paper, 2009–07).

[74] Interview with Human Rights Advocate L, Arusha, Tanzania (July 30, 2013) (noting that the EACJ's First Instance Division "is more accepting of human rights cases"); *see* Ben Batros & Haben Fecadu, *Case Watch: Narrowing the Door for Human Rights in East Africa*, OPEN SOCIETY JUSTICE INITIATIVES (July 30, 2013).

[75] Revised EAC Treaty, *supra* note 72, arts. 26(2)(b), 26(2)(2B).

EAC-level amendment process.[76] Kenyan legislators protested the adoption of the amendments by executive decree.[77] The *Nyong'o* plaintiffs challenged the amendments in a domestic suit, but the High Court of Kenya ruled that it could not restrain the executive branch from exercising its power to enter into treaties.[78]

These contestations soon reached the EACJ when the EALS challenged the amendment's adoption as a violation of the EAC Treaty.[79] In a July 2008 decision, the EACJ reaffirmed that any East African can bring a suit challenging Member State infringements of the Treaty.[80] The judges agreed with the Law Society that the amendments were procedurally defective because the Member States had not allowed the private sector and civil society to participate in their drafting.[81] The EACJ also categorically rejected as a "veiled intimidation" the unsubstantiated allegation that "the hurried process [of adopting the amendment] was necessitated by the loss of public confidence in the Court."[82] Yet, in a clear indication of judicial caution, the Court refrained from invalidating the amendments because the "infringement was not a conscious one," the violation was "not likely to recur," and "not all the resultant amendments are incompatible with Treaty objectives."[83] The decision can thus be viewed as a rhetorical pushback but a substantive acquiescence to the amendments.

Kenya's efforts to overturn the EACJ's edicts in the *Nyong'o* case were less successful, however. In a March 2007 decision, the Court confirmed its interim injunction against swearing in the Kenyan EALA members and ordered Kenya to undertake fresh elections consistent with EAC Treaty.[84] The government sought to evade the judgment by lobbying Uganda and Tanzania, but the two states stood behind the EACJ.[85] President Museveni of Uganda even sent emissaries to persuade Kenyan leaders to put their political house to avoid impeding the EAC integration agenda.[86] Lacking the support of the other governments, Kenya finally

---

[76] *See East African Lawyers Rap Leaders for Signing Amendments without Consultations*, Xɪɴʜᴜᴀ Nᴇᴡꜱᴀɢᴇɴᴄʏ (Pᴇᴏᴘʟᴇ'ꜱ Dᴀɪʟʏ Oɴʟɪɴᴇ) (Dec.16, 2006), http://english.people.com.cn/200612/16/print20061216_333151.html.

[77] *Kenya Parliamentary Debates, National Assembly, Official Report*, Mᴢᴀʟᴇɴᴅᴏ 1339–429 (May 16, 2007), http://info.mzalendo.com/hansard/sitting/national_assembly/2007-05-16-09-00-00.

[78] Anyang Nyong'o and 10 Others v. AG, Nairobi High Court Civil Case No. 49 (2006), http://kenyalaw.org/caselaw/cases/view/37525.

[79] Reference No. 3, *supra* note 65.

[80] East Africa Law Society v Attorney General of Kenya, Application No. 9 (2007) *arising from* Reference No. 3 of 2007 at 13–14 (July 11, 2007), https://www.eacj.org/wp-content/uploads/2013/10/EACJ_application_No9_2007.pdf.

[81] Reference No. 3, *supra* note 65, at 14.

[82] Nyong'o, Appl. No. 5, *supra* note 56, at 11.

[83] Reference No. 3, *supra* note 65, at 43–44.

[84] Nyong'o v. Attorney Gen. of Kenya, Ref. No. 1 of 2006, at 36 (Mar. 30, 2007). The EALS praised the decision. *East African Court of Justice Ruling: An Embarrassment for Kenya*, Aʀᴜꜱʜᴀ Tɪᴍᴇꜱ (Apr. 7–13, 2007), https://allafrica.com/stories/200704120900.html.

[85] Nyakundi Nyamboga, *Partners Decline to Support Kenya's Plea*, Aʟʟ Aꜰʀɪᴄᴀ (May 9, 2007), http://allafrica.com.proxy.lib.duke.edu/stories/200705081068.html.

[86] *Uganda Advises Kenya on Nominations to Regional Assembly*, BBC Mᴏɴɪᴛᴏʀɪɴɢ Iɴᴛᴇʀɴᴀᴛɪᴏɴᴀʟ Rᴇᴘᴏʀᴛꜱ, (Apr. 5, 2007), http://docs.newsbank.com/s/InfoWeb/aggdocs/AWNB/11853697CFB6F300/0E6DA1973A0A75D5?p_multi=BBAB&s_lang=en-US.

capitulated. In May 2007, the Parliament revised the rules for EALA membership and conducted fresh elections conforming to the Court's interpretation of the EAC Treaty.[87]

The EACJ survived Kenya's backlash campaign, but the Court reform amendments to the EAC Treaty have indelibly altered its subsequent evolution. The two-month time window for filing cases has presented challenges for lawyers, and the Appellate Division has reversed some of First Instance Division's more expansive rulings. Yet both the First Instance and Appellate judges have asserted jurisdiction over a broad range of legal issues covered by the EAC Treaty, including in particular suits alleging human rights violations.

By far the most important post-*Nyong'o* development has been the Court's embrace of human rights cases. In *Katabazi v. Secretary General of the EAC*, decided less than a year after the interim injunction in *Nyong'o*, the EACJ held that it would not "abdicate" jurisdiction over human rights complaints framed as breaches of the EAC Treaty's fundamental principles.[88] This was a strikingly bold conclusion given the Treaty's explicit statement that the Member States would confer such jurisdiction via a yet-to-be-adopted protocol.[89]

A series of human rights suits have flowed from *Katabazi*, many of which have been filed by or with the support of the EALS. These cases have engendered a split between the EACJ's more expansive First Instance Division and the more pro-government Appellate Division, the two chambers established by the post-*Nyong'o* treaty amendments. Both divisions have endorsed *Katazabi*'s core holding, but the First Instance Division has been more forgiving to private litigants, applying a continuing violations doctrine to circumvent the amendment's very short two-month window for challenging national policies and decisions as contrary to the EAC Treaty.[90] In contrast, the Appellate Division has strictly construed this provision, which it views as a embodying "principle of legal certainty" that forbids East African judges from adopting the "liberal and purposive interpretation" of international human rights courts.[91]

---

[87] East African Community (Election of Members of Assembly) Rules 2007 adopted by the Parliament of Kenya on May 23, 2007. Elections under these rules were held on May 29, 2007. Election of Members of the EALA, Kenya Gazetter Notice No. 4873, vol. CIX No. 37 (May 31, 2007). In subsequent disputes involving elections to the sub-regional Parliament, the EACJ has continued to issue injunctions against election procedures that violate the EAC Treaty. *See, e.g.,* Democratic Party v. EAC Sec'y Gen., Ref. No. 6 of 2011, Judgment, 1st Inst. Div. (May 10, 2012), https://www.eacj.org//wp-content/uploads/2012/10/REF-NO.-6-OF-2011.pdf.

[88] Katabazi v. Sec'y Gen. of the E. African Cmty., Ref. No. 1 of 2007, at 1–2 (Nov. 1, 2007). The case involved the re-arrest by paramilitary personnel of Ugandans who had been freed on bail on the premises of the High Court in Kampala.

[89] EAC Establishment Treaty, *supra* note 39, art. 27(2).

[90] *See, e.g.,* Indep. Medical Unit v. Attorney Gen. of Kenya, Ref. No. 3 of 2010, 1st Inst. Div. (June 29, 2011).

[91] Omar Awadh and 6 Others v. Attorney General of Uganda, Appeal No. 2 of 2012, at 15, East African Court of Justice, App. Div. (Apr. 15, 2013), https://www.eacj.org//wp-content/uploads/2013/09/AG_Uganda_v_Omar_Awadh_and_6_Others.pdf.

Subsequently, in a case challenging the construction of a road through the Serengeti national park, the Appellate Division adopted a *Katabazi*-style approach to environmental protection suits. The judges held that the Treaty binds Member States "to observe a variety of express undertakings and obligations concerning the promotion, preservation, conservation and protection of the environment" that are "clearly and emphatically" within the Court's purview.[92] The First Instance Division later ruled against Tanzania on the merits, permanently enjoining the government from building the road—an injunction that attracted significant news media attention and that Tanzania has now appealed.[93]

The SADC Tribunal: A Successful Backlash

Unlike its sub-regional cousins, whose integration projects have roots in the immediate post-independence period, the SADC is a more recent institution. When governments launched the SADC in the early 1990s, they solicited financial support from European governments. Political leaders in the region, worried that European aid might be diverted to other priorities, decided to "visibly emulate" the supranational "EC-style common market model" without much debate "on the advantages and disadvantages of each arrangement."[94] That emulation, however, existed alongside and often in tension with the Member States' strong desire to "retain a more sovereignty-preserving institution 'in practice.'"[95]

The 1992 SADC Treaty envisioned a tribunal but required the adoption of a separate protocol before it could be established. After SADC's membership expanded to include five more countries, including South Africa,[96] this larger group discussed the Protocol in the late 1990s. Several governments voiced a preference for arbitration and mediation, but European donors expressed doubt that SADC could enhance its commitment to sub-regional integration without a more "effective and credible" dispute settlement mechanism.[97] Partly in response to this

---

[92] Attorney General of the United Republic of Tanzania v. African Network for Animal Welfare (ANAW), Appeal No. 3 of 2011, at 11 (Apr. 26, 2012), https://www.eacj.org//wp-content/uploads/2012/10/Appeal-Ref-No.-3-of-20112.pdf.

[93] African Network for Animal Welfare (ANAW) v. Attorney General of the United Republic of Tanzania, Ref. No. 9 of 2010, East African Court of Justice (June 20, 2014), https://www.eacj.org//wp-content/uploads/2014/06/Judgement-Ref.-No.9-of-2010-Final.pdf; *see* Adam Ihucha, *Dar Files Appeal on Serengeti Ruling*, THE EAST AFRICAN (Oct. 11, 2014), https://web.archive.org/web/20141015011534/https://www.theeastafrican.co.ke/news/Dar-files-appeal-on-Serengeti-ruling--/-/2558/2483138/-/lpa0fdz/-/index.html.

[94] Tobias Lenz, *Spurred Emulation: The EU and Regional Integration in Mercosur and SADC*, W. EUR. POL. 155, 163 (2011).

[95] *Id.* at 166; *see* Laurie Nathan, *The Disbanding of the SADC Tribunal: A Cautionary Tale*, 35 HUM. RTS. Q. 870, 876–77 (2013).

[96] At its launch, the SADC was comprised of Angola, Botswana, Lesotho, Malawi, Mozambique, Namibia, Swaziland, Tanzania, Zambia, and Zimbabwe. Mauritius, the Democratic Republic of the Congo, the Seychelles, South Africa, and Madagascar joined between 1995 and 2006.

[97] Lenz, *supra* note 94, at 166.

external pressure, the Protocol's drafters—who included a British judge funded by the European Community—created a European Court of Justice-style court with direct access for private litigants (after exhausting domestic remedies) and a preliminary ruling mechanism for national judges to refer cases involving the interpretation of SADC agreements.[98]

Two technical aspects of the Tribunal Protocol, adopted in 2000, are essential to understand the political backlash that began almost a decade later—the procedures for the Protocol's entry into force, and provisions authorizing private litigants to file suits challenging Member State violations of SADC rules.

The first issue raises a complex question later debated by attorneys on both sides of the Tribunal suspension controversy: did the 2000 Protocol enter into force when it was adopted by three-quarters of the heads of state of SADC, as provided for in the 1992 Treaty of the Southern African Development Community?[99] Or did the Protocol require domestic ratification by two-thirds of the Member States, as specified in the Protocol itself?[100] If the former interpretation prevailed, the Tribunal was legally constituted as of August 7, 2000, the date when the leaders of thirteen countries—including Zimbabwean President Robert Mugabe himself—signed the Protocol. Zimbabwe later championed the latter view, claiming a lack of consent to the SADC Tribunal's jurisdiction because its Parliament had not ratified the Protocol.[101]

This debate over legal technicalities masks a more fundamental political question. Is the SADC, like many other regional integration pacts, a supranational entity whose Member States have delegated powers to community institutions? Or is it an inter-governmental body whose actions were closely controlled by those states?

The second set of design features that later created controversy for the Tribunal was its far-reaching provisions on jurisdiction, access, and legal sources. The 2000 Protocol authorized SADC judges to interpret and apply the SADC Treaty, its Protocols, and subsidiary Community acts.[102] The Tribunal's jurisdiction over suits alleging violations of these legal instruments extended to "disputes . . . between natural or legal persons and Member States," even if the government did not give its consent to the suit.[103] In addition, the Protocol contained an expansive directive

---

[98]   Protocol on the Tribunal and Rules thereof (2000), arts. 15, 16, http://www.sadc.int/files/1413/5292/8369/Protocol_on_the_Tribunal_and_Rules_thereof2000.pdf (hereinafter "2000 Protocol").

[99]   Treaty of the Southern African Development Community (SADC Treaty), art. 36(1).

[100]   2000 Protocol, *supra* note 98, art. 38; *see also* Derek Matyszak, *The Dissolution of the SADC Tribunal*, RESEARCH AND ADVOCACY UNIT (Aug. 19, 2011), http://archive.kubatana.net/docs/demgg/rau_dissolution_sadc_tribunal_110905.pdf. For a broader discussion of the complexities of treaty ratification practice in Africa, *see* Tiyanjana Maluwa, *Beyond Rhetoric: Commitment to and Ratification of African Human Rights and Human Rights-Related Treaties, in* LAW, POLITICS AND RIGHTS: ESSAYS IN MEMORY OF KADER ASMAL 58 (Tiyanjana Maluwa ed., 2013).

[101]   For an argument that the 2000 Tribunal Protocol had been implicitly amended by the 2001 SADC Treaty Revisions, *see* Nathan, *supra* note 95, at 876–77.

[102]   2000 Protocol, *supra* note 98, art. 14.

[103]   *Id.* at art. 15, paras. 1, 3.

to the Tribunal to "develop its own Community jurisprudence having regard to applicable treaties, general principles, and rules of public international law …."[104]

The SADC Tribunal's first major case was filed in 2007 by Michael Campbell, a white landowner from Zimbabwe.[105] The Tribunal's fate became inextricably intertwined with the *Campbell* litigation. The legal and political issues in the case were highly controversial, Campbell was a tenacious litigant, his attorneys were creative and aggressive, and the suit challenged the signature land redistribution program of Zimbabwe's President Mugabe—a former rebel leader lionized across the region for his role in overthrowing white minority rule, but who was also one of the region's most autocratic rulers.

In post-independence Zimbabwe, the best land ended up in the hands of a relatively small number of white farmers. The government initially followed a "willing seller, willing buyer" approach to land reform that was part of the settlement ending Rhodesian civil war and white minority rule. However, because relatively few white farmers agreed to sell, Zimbabwe later adopted a policy of forced land expropriations, many of which involved violent occupations, limited compensation, and redistribution of land to Mugabe's political loyalists.[106]

The government's land policies took a sharp turn in the late 1990s when President Mugabe made a political bargain with civil war veterans to shore up his waning political support.[107] Mugabe used his control over the Parliament and the Supreme Court to close legal loopholes that white farmers had previously used to challenge the forced expropriations. He pushed through a statute and a constitutional amendment authorizing automatic land seizures without compensation,[108]

In 2006, the government notified Campbell that it intended to seize his farm. Campbell challenged the decision before the Zimbabwean Supreme Court.[109] He also filed an application with the SADC Tribunal, alleging violations of three human rights: discrimination on the basis of race, lack of due process in the deprivation of property, and lack of access to the courts.[110] Over the next several years, escalating legal confrontations with Campbell and other white landowners, the Mugabe government, land reform supporters, and the SADC Tribunal played out

---

[104] *Id.* at art. 21(b).

[105] Campbell v. Zimbabwe (Merits), Case No. SADC(T) 2/2007, at 4 (Nov. 28, 2008) (complaint filed Oct. 11, 2007) (*Campbell* judgment).

[106] Sam Moyo, *Land Reform and Redistribution in Zimbabwe Since 1980*, *in* LAND AND AGRARIAN REFORM IN ZIMBABWE: BEYOND WHITE-SETTLER CAPITALISM (Sam Moyo & Walter Chambati eds., 2013) (hereinafter "Moyo, Land Reform and Redistribution").

[107] Zvakanyorwa Wilbert Sadomba, *A Decade of Zimbabwe's Land Revolution: The Politics of the War Veteran Vangard*, *in* LAND AND AGRARIAN REFORM IN ZIMBABWE: BEYOND WHITE-SETTLER CAPITALISM (Sam Moyo & Walter Chambati eds., 2013).

[108] *Id.* at 85–95 (discussing the struggle over land reform through the 2001 revision of the Land Reform Act); *see also Campbell* Judgment, *supra* note 105, at 9–11.

[109] Minister of National Security Responsible for Land, Land Reform and Resettlement, Constitutional App. No. 124/06, Judgment No. SC 49/07, at 2 (Jan. 22, 2008), https://jsc.org.zw/jscbackend/upload/Judgements/Supreme%20Court/Harare/2007/SC%2049%20-07.pdf.

[110] *See Campbell* Judgment, *supra* note 105, at 16–17.

against a backdrop of contested elections in Zimbabwe and futile efforts at mediation by the region's political leaders. As we now explain, SADC judges issued a series of interim rulings, judgments, and contempt orders that broadly interpreted both their jurisdiction and the SADC Treaty, setting the stage for Mugabe's backlash.

In November 2007, the Tribunal issued a preliminary injunction against evicting Campbell or interfering with his use of the land.[111] After the Zimbabwe Supreme Court rejected Campbell's suit, the SADC judges decided that Campbell—and the seventy-seven other white farmers whose suits were joined to his case—had exhausted domestic remedies.[112] Mugabe's supporters responded to this interim ruling by kidnapping and roughing up Campbell and his son-in-law and extracting promises to drop the suit. Once released, however, Campbell and his lawyers continued the case, notwithstanding the burning of their farm and Campbell's subsequent death, which newspaper accounts attributed to his injuries during the kidnapping.[113]

The Tribunal ruled on the merits of Campbell's claims in November 2008. The judgment was legally bold in multiple respects. First, with regard to jurisdiction, the judges unanimously claimed the authority to hear suits alleging human rights violations by SADC Member States. Zimbabwe argued that the references to human rights in the "Principles" and "General Undertakings" clauses of the SADC Treaty[114] were too vague to be judicially enforced and could only be adjudicated after the adoption of a separate protocol on human rights and land reform.[115] Since the Member States had adopted other protocols clarifying the issues to be referred to the Tribunal or handled in other ways,[116] the judges could reasonably have declined jurisdiction over human rights cases until the adoption of such a protocol. Instead, they summarily rejected Zimbabwe's argument, citing the Principles and

---

[111] Campbell v. Zimbabwe (Interim Relief Ruling), Case No. SACD(T) 2/2007, at 8 (Dec. 13, 2007).

[112] *See, e.g.*, Theron v. Republic of Zimbabwe, Case No. SADC(T) 02/08 (Mar. 28, 2008); Taylor-Freeme v. Republic of Zimbabwe, Case No. SADC(T) 03/08 (Mar. 28, 2008); Stidolph v. Republic of Zimbabwe, Case No. SADC(T) 04/08 (Mar. 28, 2008); Anglesea Farm (Pvt) Ltd. v. Republic of Zimbabwe, Case No. SADC(T) 06/08 (Mar. 28, 2008) (allowing interventions and ordering injunctive relief); Mike Campbell (Pty) Ltd v. Minister of National Security Responsible for Land, Land Reform and Resettlement, Case No. SC 49/07 (Feb. 22, 2008) (finding domestic remedies exhausted); *see* Admark Moyo, *Defending Human Rights and the Rule of Law by the SADC Tribunal: Campbell and Beyond*, 9 AFR. HUM. RIGHTS L. J. 590 (2009) (hereinafter "Moyo, Campbell and Beyond").

[113] Denis Herbstein, *Mike Campbell Obituary*, THE GUARDIAN (Apr. 24, 2011), http://www.theguardian.com/world/2011/apr/24/mike-campbell-obituary.

[114] SADC Treaty, *supra* note 99, art. 4(c) ("human rights, democracy, and the rule of law") & art. 6(2) (non-discrimination on multiple grounds, including race).

[115] *Campbell* Judgment, *supra* note 105, at 23. During the drafting of the 2000 Protocol, an expert panel considered but ultimately rejected the "inclusion of human rights in the mandate of the SADC Tribunal." However, the panel also noted that the SADC already had "a more general human rights mandate." FRANS VILJOEN, INTERNATIONAL HUMAN RIGHTS LAW IN AFRICA 492 (2012).

[116] SADC Overview: Protocols, SADC, http://www.sadc.int/about-sadc/overview/sa-protocols/. For example, the SADC Trade Protocol envisions a World Trade Organization-style dispute settlement procedure administered by the Tribunal's Registrar but involving ad hoc panels rather than adjudication by the Tribunal. SADC Consolidated Protocol on Trade, Annex VI.

Applicable Law provisions of the SADC Treaty but providing little explanation or analysis.[117]

Turning to the merits, the Tribunal ruled that Zimbabwe had violated the land-owners' human rights in three respects—denying access to justice, failing to provide fair compensation, and discriminating on the basis of race. The first of these holdings was the least controversial. Had the Tribunal confined its decision to the access to justice issue, the judgment would likely have been a mostly symbolic victory for the plaintiffs. But the two additional violations struck at the heart of Mugabe's land redistribution program.

The Tribunal first concluded that Zimbabwe had violated the SADC Treaty's equality clause. The government defended the program as a way to correct inequities persisting from colonialism. That most owners of large agricultural landowners happened to be white could not, therefore, "be attributed to racism but [rather to] circumstances brought about by colonial history."[118] The judges disagreed. Invoking other human rights treaties and case-law, the Tribunal found that the land reform program had a disparate impact on white farmers that was "unjustifiable and disproportionate" as well as "arbitrary and ... based primarily on considerations of race."[119] Redistribution might be legitimate, the judges reasoned, if "the lands under the program were distributed to poor, landless, and other disadvantaged and marginalized groups." On the facts presented, however, "there can be no doubt that it is unfair discrimination ... to award the spoils of expropriation primarily to ruling party adherents."[120] The Tribunal next ruled that international law required the government to "to protect the possession, occupation and ownership of" the white farmers still on their land, and to compensate those whose lands it had already seized. Moreover, Zimbabwe could not rely on its Constitution to avoid these obligations.[121]

The political fallout of the *Campbell* judgment was immediate. Mugabe showed nothing but contempt for the decision and the Tribunal. His statement to supporters a few months after the judgment is illustrative: "Some farmers went to the SADC [T]ribunal in Namibia, but that's nonsense, absolute nonsense, no one will follow that .... We have courts here in this country, that can

---

[117] *Campbell* Judgment, *supra* note 105, at 24 ("we do not consider that there should first be a Protocol on human rights in order to give effect to the principles set out in the Treaty, in the light of the express provision of Article 4(c) of the Treaty" which requires SADC Member States "to act in accordance with human rights, democracy and the rule of law"); *id.* (asserting that Article 21(b) "settles the question whether the Tribunal can look elsewhere to find answers where it appears that the Treaty is silent").

[118] *Id.* at 44.

[119] *Id.* at 53. The racial discrimination finding was disputed by Judge Onkemetse Tshosa, who concluded that whites controlled most of the country's agricultural land and were thus more significantly affected by the land redistribution policy.

[120] *Id.* at 53–54.

[121] *Id.* at 58.

determine the rights of people. Our land issues are not subject to the SADC [T]ribunal."[122]

Faced with government intransigence, the white farmers returned to Court in June 2009. Although Zimbabwe did not participate in the proceedings, the SADC judges found sufficient evidence to hold the state "in breach, and contempt" of the *Campbell* judgment and reported that finding to the SADC Summit— the Community's highest political body—for further action.[123] The contempt ruling—and the prospect that the case would soon land on the Summit's agenda— galvanized Mugabe into action.

Events unfolded with lightning speed over the next few weeks. Mugabe tasked Patrick Chinamasa, Zimbabwe's Minister of Justice and Legal Affairs, to develop a legal strategy to challenge the *Campbell* case and discredit the Tribunal. Chinamasa drafted a memorandum presented at a meeting of the SADC Ministers of Justice and Attorneys General in July 2009. His opinion capitalized on the ambiguity, dis- cussed earlier, in the entry into force rules of the 2000 Tribunal Protocol. Adopting the pro-sovereignty interpretation, Chinamasa argued that the Court was never properly established because two-thirds of the Member States—including Zimbabwe—had never ratified the Protocol. As a result, all SADC Tribunal rul- ings were null and void and Member States were under no obligation to comply with them.[124] A week later, Chinamasa took the next logical step, informing the Registrar that Zimbabwe "would not appear before [the Tribunal] anymore, and neither would Government be bound by any decisions already made or future ones emanating from there."[125]

The Zimbabwean Justice Minister's memorandum was made public on the last day of August 2009. The Tribunal's defenders rushed to refute Chinamasa's legal analysis. The attorneys for the white farmers were the first to publish a response.[126] Similar legal opinions soon followed from the Tribunal's NGO supporters, in- cluding the South African Litigation Centre, Zimbabwe Lawyers For Human Rights, and the Zimbabwe Human Rights NGO Forum.[127]

---

[122] Cris Chinaka, *Mugabe Says Zimbabwe Land Seizures will Continue*, REUTERS (Feb. 28, 2009), https://www.reuters.com/article/us-zimbabwe-crisis-mugabe/ mugabe-says-zimbabwe-land-seizures-will-continue-idUSTRE51R0VS20090228.

[123] Campbell and Another v. Republic of Zimbabwe, SADC(T) 03/2009, Southern African Development Community Tribunal, at 1 (June 5, 2009), http://www.saflii.org/sa/cases/SADCT/2009/ 1.html.

[124] Derek Matyszak, *The Dissolution of the SADC Tribunal*, RESEARCH AND ADVOCACY UNIT (Aug. 19, 2011) (citing Execution and Enforcement of Judgments of the SADC Tribunal, Opinion of the Government of the Republic of Zimbabwe on issues relating to International Law Raised at the Meeting of Ministers of Justice/Attorneys-General, Pretoria, South Africa (July 30–31, 2009)), http://archive. kubatana.net/docs/demgg/rau_dissolution_sadc_tribunal_110905.pdf.

[125] Mabasa Sasa, *Zim Pulls out of SADC Tribunal*, HERALD (ZIMBABWE), quoting letter dated Aug. 7, 2009, (Sept. 2, 2009), http://www.zimbabwesituation.com/sep3_2009.html.

[126] *A Reply to the Chinamasa Response, from the CFU's Lawyers*, THE ZIMBABWE SITUATION (Sept. 18, 2010), http://www.zimbabwesituation.com/sep20_2009.html.

[127] *See, e.g.*, The Southern Africa Litigation Centre, *SALC Legal Position on SADC Tribunal* (Sept. 22, 2009), https://nehandaradio.com/2009/10/07/salc-legal-position-on-sadc-tribunal/.

With the competing legal arguments now out in the open, the other Member States now had to decide how to respond to Zimbabwe's attack. While "Chinamasa travelled to the regional capitals" to lobby other governments to support Zimbabwe's position,[128] the SADC Council of Ministers "was tasked with responding to Zimbabwe's objections and presenting a draft answering opinion" at the next SADC Summit scheduled for August 2010.[129] A month before that meeting, the Tribunal upped the political stakes by issuing another contempt ruling against Zimbabwe and again referring the country's treaty violations to the Summit for action.[130]

We interviewed a former SADC judge about these contempt orders, asking whether the Tribunal members in fact expected the Summit to enforce the *Campbell* judgment. At the time, Mugabe was brazenly ignoring a power-sharing deal that SADC had brokered. If the sub-region's political leaders had not sanctioned the President for violating an accord that they had publicly endorsed, it seems unimaginable that they would demand that Mugabe respect a ruling that sounded the death knell of his signature land redistribution policy. For the judges, however, the law provided a simple answer—"the applicant was given a remedy; it needed to be enforced."[131] The Tribunal deliberated about the issue and unanimously agreed to refer the case, as permitted by SADC law. They also decided that the Tribunal's President should attend the Summit and make the case for sanctioning Zimbabwe for non-compliance.[132]

At the August 2010 Summit, Mugabe "threatened to block any discussion of Zimbabwe and its human rights record."[133] There is no public record of the Summit proceedings. As best as we can determine, however, several Member States opposed Zimbabwe's actions. Officially, a compromise was reached whereby the Summit "decided that a review of the role, functions and terms of reference of the SADC Tribunal should be undertaken and concluded within six months."[134]

On its own, this was a plausible way to address the Tribunal's unsettled legal status. Yet the compromise must be understood in light of decisions that the

---

[128] Laurie Nathan, *Solidarity Triumphs over Democracy: The Dissolution of the SADC Tribunal*, 57 DEVELOPMENT DIALOGUE 123, 130 (2011), http://repository.up.ac.za/handle/2263/19451?show=full.

[129] SALC & Ditshwanelo, Implications of the Decision to Review the Role, Functions and Terms of Reference of the SADC Tribunal: An Opinion, para. 2 (undated, but likely early 2011), https://africancourtcoalition.org/wp-content/uploads/2015/12/SADC-Opinion-final.pdf (hereinafter "SALC Opinion") (We have not been able to find this study, and it appears not to have been completed in time for the Summit.)

[130] Fick and Another v. Republic of Zimbabwe, SADC(T) 01/2010, Southern African Development Community Tribunal (July 16, 2010), http://www.saflii.org/sa/cases/SADCT/2010/8.html.

[131] Interview with former Judge of the SADC Tribunal, Gaborone, Botswana (Aug. 9, 2013) (hereinafter "Interview with former SADC Judge").

[132] *Id.*

[133] Frederick Cowell, *The Death of the Southern African Development Community Tribunal's Human Rights Jurisdiction*, 131 HUM. RTS. L. REV. 153, 161 (2013).

[134] Final Communiqué of the 30th Summit of SADC Heads of State and Government, para. 32 (Aug. 19, 2010).

Summit did *not* take—the renewal of five SADC judges whose terms were about to expire, and the replacement of the Zimbabwean judge whom Mugabe had withdrawn in 2009. The SADC Secretariat had placed these issues on the Summit's agenda. By taking no action, the heads of state left the Tribunal with only four judges—below the minimum required to accept new complaints.[135]

The failure to reappoint the judges was part of a deliberate strategy by Mugabe to exploit a legal ambiguity in the SADC Tribunal Protocol—its silence regarding what happens if Member States fail to renew the terms of sitting judges or select jurists to replace them.[136] Mugabe took advantage of this silence to slowly starve the Tribunal of the judges and staff it needed to function. The strategy provided a crucial back-up plan; by refusing agree to renew or reappoint judges—acts that required the agreement of all Member States—Mugabe could guarantee that the Tribunal would eventually cease to function even if its formal mandate remained unchanged.

For the time being, however, the outcome of the 2010 Summit was only a partial victory for Zimbabwe, since the remaining SADC judges were still in office and were pressing for compliance with the *Campbell* judgment. To counter this threat, Justice Minister Chinamasa spun the Summit's decision in the press as a formal suspension of the Tribunal.[137] The SADC Executive Secretary Tomaz Salomão sought to thwart this disinformation campaign by reiterating the Summit's official position that SADC "judges don't entertain any new cases but they can deal with those they have at hand."[138] Mugabe soon joined the fray, issuing a vitriolic broadside that labeled the Tribunal as a "monster" created at the behest of foreign powers—a claim repeated by Zimbabwean legal elites.[139]

With charges and countercharges spinning in the press, the next act in the backlash drama began to unfold—the Summit-mandated review of the Tribunal's powers and terms of reference. This review resulted in legal analyses that supported

---

[135] SALC Opinion, *supra* note 129, at paras. 4, 22–23. Several sources also assert that the Summit instruct[ed] the Tribunal not to take on any new cases. We found no official documentation of this instruction, but as a practical matter the result was the same—the Tribunal was unable to hear new cases pending the completion of the review. SALC Opinion, *supra* note 129, at para. 5.

[136] Article 4(6) of the SADC Tribunal Protocol provides that judicial vacancies shall be filled "within three (3) months of the vacancy occurring," but is silent on what happens if a judge's term expires and the vacancy is unfilled. The EAC Treaty also does not address this issue, leaving the issue to "be determined by the Summit on the recommendation of the Council." EAC Treaty, arts. 25(3), 25(5). By contrast, as noted earlier, the ECOWAS Court Protocol expressly provides that a judge shall remain in office until a successor is appointed.

[137] Caesar Zvayi, *Southern African Development Community Tribunal Suspended*, THE HERALD (Aug. 17, 2010).

[138] *SADC Tribunal was Never Suspended, Executive Reveals*, ZIMEYE (Aug. 19, 2010), https://web. archive.org/web/20100829004736/http://www.zimeye.org/?p=21010.

[139] *Mugabe Insists SADC Tribunal "Has Been Suspended"*, ZIMEYE (Aug. 23, 2010), https://web. archive.org/web/20130609035733/www.zimeye.org/?p=21146; *see Southern Africa: Call for Inquiry into SADC Tribunal*, THE HERALD (June 2, 2011), https://www.herald.co.zw/call-for-inquiry-into-sadc-tribunal/ (a former High Court Judge and Minister of Justice, Legal and Parliamentary Affairs labeled the SADC Tribunal as a "judicial charade," a "kangaroo court," and an "illegitimate monster").

the *Campbell* cases, but that Mugabe and other political leaders repeatedly re-jected. The review originated with a request by the SADC Attorneys General and Ministers of Justice for an external evaluation of Zimbabwe's complaints against the Tribunal. The Secretariat issued a tender for the review and later awarded the contract to Lorand Bartels.[140] Bartels' report to the Ministers of Justice and Attorneys General categorically rejected Zimbabwe's legal arguments, concluding that the Tribunal was validly constituted and authorized to review human rights complaints from private litigants.[141] Bartels also recommended a series of amend-ments to clarify ambiguities and resolve conflicts across SADC legal instruments while maintaining the Tribunal's broad jurisdiction and access rules.[142]

When the Secretariat declined to release the report, the Tribunal's backers posted it on the internet. Contemporaneous accounts suggest that government ministers were divided over how to proceed. During an Extraordinary Summit in May 2011, Zimbabwe reiterated its opposition to any outcome of the review pro-cess that would affirm the status quo. The Summit's final communiqué thus dir-ected the Justice Ministers to prepare a fresh report proposing "amend[ments to] the relevant SADC legal instruments" by August 2012. The communiqué also pur-ported to "reiterate[] the moratorium on receiving any new cases or hearings of any cases by the Tribunal," and declined to reappoint or replace any SADC judges.[143] These decisions officially suspended the Tribunal, although some scholars and NGOs continued to challenge the suspension's legality.[144]

During the next fifteen months, human rights attorneys, civil society groups, and SADC judges themselves—all of whom had previously been shut out of the review process[145]—mobilized to save the Tribunal. They faced an uphill battle. The supporters' natural ally—the SADC Secretariat—was suspicious about transpar-ency and civil society participation in SADC activities. Indeed, one source reports that, when asked whether the Justice Ministers' proposal to revise the Tribunal Protocol would be made public, SADC Executive Secretary Salomão responded

---

[140] Authors' email correspondence with Lorand Bartels (Apr. 14, 2015).
[141] Lorand Bartels, *Review of the Role, Responsibility and Terms of Reference of the SADC Tribunal—Final Report* 6 (2011), http://www.scribd.com/doc/115660010/WTIA-Review-of-the-Role-Responsibilities-and-Terms-of-Reference-of-the-SADC-Tribunal-Final-Report.
[142] *Id.* at 82–87.
[143] Communiqué of the Extraordinary Summit of SADC Heads of State and Government, paras. 7–8 (May 20, 2011).
[144] *See, e.g.,* Daniel Steinmann, *Summit Assigns itself Jurisdictional Powers it does not have,* NAMIBIA ECONOMIST (Aug. 17, 2012), https://economist.com.na/2548/editors-desk/summit-assigns-itself-jurisdictional-powers-it-does-not-have/.
[145] *See, e.g., Letter Submitted to Honorable Ministers of Justice and Attorneys General re: Amendments to the Protocol Establishing the SADC Tribunal,* SADC 4 (June 1, 2012), http://www.africancourtcoalition.org/images/docs/subregionalcourts/sadctribunal/NGOs%20Letter%20to%20SADC%20Ministers%20of%20Justice%20and%20Attorneys%20General.pdf (complaining that "it has been virtually impossible for us as SADC NGOs even to attend the SADC Summit or Ministers of Justice meetings on the sidelines").

that "neither the media nor SADC citizens needed to know what was in the report."[146]

To highlight the ill effects of emasculating the Tribunal, SADC judges gave speeches and NGOs held conferences and drafted resolutions and press statements. They also prepared legal briefs outlining their objections to the suspension and proffering recommendations for a redesigned tribunal that would preserve direct access for private litigants and review of human rights violations.[147] Partly in response to this "heavily lobbying," the Ministers of Justice and Attorneys General adopted a revised Tribunal Protocol that offered a compromise.[148] The draft preserved private litigant suits challenging violations of SADC rules, but it narrowed the Tribunal's standing requirements and made its human rights jurisdiction contingent on the adoption of a new protocol.[149] On the crucial issue of the *Campbell* case, however, the draft Protocol was unequivocal: "All actions, decisions, judgments and other administrative acts undertaken pursuant to the 2000 Protocol ... shall remain valid and in force."[150]

Once again, Mugabe used the Summit to defeat a more legally nuanced compromise. Zimbabwe could have insisted upon giving the Tribunal an extremely limited human rights jurisdiction, or appointing a new set of politically timid judges. Instead, Mugabe lambasted the Justice Ministers' compromise proposal, renewing his claim that the SADC review process was being stage-managed to target the country's land redistribution policies.[151] Although the Summit proceedings are not public, our interviews reveal that South Africa's President Jacob Zuma left the meeting early to tend to a domestic matter, undermining the leverage and voice of moderate countries. The result was an unequivocal victory for Mugabe—a Summit

---

[146] Henning Melber, *Promoting the Rule of Law: Challenges for South Africa's Policy*, SAFPI Commentary No. 5, 9 (Aug. 13, 2012), https://www.researchgate.net/publication/282440295_Promoting_the_Rule_of_Law_Challenges_for_South_Africa%27s_Policy.

[147] *See, e.g., Resolutions of SADC Lawyers, Judges and Rule of Law Advocates adopted at the 2nd Regional Legal Consultative Conference on The Review of the SADC Tribunal*, SADC (July 28, 2011), http://www.africancourtcoalition.org/images/docs/subregionalcourts/sadctribunal/2nd%20Consultative%20conference%20on%20the%20review%20of%20SADC%20Tribunal%20-%20Resolutions.pdf; Ariranga Pillay et al., *Letter to the Executive Secretary of SADC: Three Illegal and Arbitrary Decisions Taken in Bad Faith by the SADC Council of Ministers and Summit of Heads of State and Government*, POLITICSWEB (June 13, 2011), http://www.politicsweb.co.za/politicsweb/view/politicsweb/en/page71656?oid=242579&sn=Detail&pid=71616; Ariranga Pillay, Former President of SADC Tribunal, Speech: SADC Tribunal Dissolved by Unanimous Decision of SADC Leaders (July 11, 2011), http://www.africancourtcoalition.org/images/docs/subregionalcourts/sadctribunal/SADC%20Tribunal%20Dissolved%2020110718.pdf (hereinafter "Pillay Speech"); *Submission Regarding Amendments to the SADC Tribunal Protocol: Relating to Access Provisions, The Relationship with Superior National Courts and its Human Rights Mandate*, SADC (undated, but likely June 1, 2012), http://www.africancourtcoalition.org/images/docs/subregionalcourts/sadctribunal/NGOs%20Submission%20-%20Access%20and%20jurisdiction%20issues%20at%20SADC%20Tribunal.pdf.

[148] Felix Nijini, *Zimbabwe wins Key Battle at Maputo Summit*, SOUTHERN TIMES (Aug. 20, 2012) (copy on file with authors).

[149] Draft Protocol on Tribunal in the Southern African Development Community 2000 as Amended, SADC/MJ/2/2012/4 (June 19, 2012) (copy on file with authors).

[150] *Id.* at art. 58.

[151] Nijini, *supra* note 148.

official communiqué directing that "a new Protocol on the Tribunal should be ne-gotiated and that its mandate should be confined to interpretation of the SADC Treaty and Protocols relating to disputes between Member States."[152]

Moreover, it would not be long before Mugabe's continued refusal to appoint judges or Tribunal staff would, on its own, effectively kill the sub-regional court. By the mid 2013, the Tribunal had no serving judges, and the terms of other court em-ployees, including the Registrar who processes complaints from litigants, was set to expire. As a government official in Botswana explained, the contracts of the judges and staff had run out, "[s]o now there is no SADC Tribunal."[153] This *fait accompli* gave Zimbabwe the upper hand in the negotiations to reconstitute the Tribunal.

The Summit's official communiqué devastated civil society groups, who la-mented that SADC leaders had "destroyed" the Tribunal. [154] Advocates challenged the Tribunal's suspension before the African Commission on Human and Peoples' Rights, but the Commission rejected the complaint, leaving the way clear for the SADC Summit, in August 2014, to adopt a protocol confining the Tribunal's juris-diction to interstate disputes. Several African leaders—including Mugabe—signed the new instrument at the Summit, while civil society groups, Campbell's lawyers, and a former SADC judge decried the creation of a "toothless and useless" sub-regional court that is unlikely to hear any cases.[155] Meanwhile, lawyers for the white farmers sought to enforce the Tribunal's rulings in South African courts, eventually collecting some damages from Zimbabwe.[156]

Part Three: Comparing the Three Backlashes— Similarities and Differences

Before turning to our own explanation of the divergent outcomes of the three backlash campaigns, we first recap key aspects of the narratives described in the previous sections. We also identify institutional and power-based similarities and differences among the three cases, seeking to eliminate alternative explanations.

---

[152] Final Communiqué of 32nd Summit of SADC Heads of State and Government, para. 24 (Aug. 18, 2012).

[153] Interview with Official of the Botswana Trade Ministry, Gaborone, Botswana (Aug. 8, 2013).

[154] Richard Lee, *SADC Leaders Destroy SADC Tribunal*, OPEN SOCIETY INITIATIVE FOR SOUTHERN AFRICA (Aug. 20, 2012), https://web.archive.org/web/20150630040730/http://osisa.org/law/regional/sadc-leaders-destroy-sadc-tribunal.

[155] Interview with former SADC Judge, *supra* note 131; *see* Ray Ndlovu, *SADC Tribunal back with Mandate Reduced to Interstate Cases*, BUSINESS DAY (Aug. 20, 2014), https://web.archive.org/web/20140821175336/http://www.bdlive.co.za/africa/africannews/2014/08/20/sadc-tribunal-back-with-mandate-reduced-to-interstate-cases.

[156] The lawyers secured a favorable ruling from the South African Constitutional Court that forced the Zimbabwe to make a US$20,000 payment to avoid execution on property it owned in South Africa. David Smith, *Zimbabwe Government's U-Turn on White Farmers*, MAIL & GUARDIAN (Sept. 20, 2013), http://mg.co.za/article/2013-09-20-00-zimbabwe-governments-u-turn-on-white-farmers/.

Our focus on like and hard cases allow us to hold constant a number of plausible explanatory factors. For all three courts, membership in the sub-regional community brings with it the compulsory jurisdiction of the sub-regional court. Unilateral withdrawal from the court's jurisdiction is not a legally viable option. All three courts emulate the European Court of Justice, including direct access by private litigants alleging state violations of community treaties. All three ICs are also young institutions that began to function in the 2000s, and all three backlashes occurred in response to adverse rulings of each court issued it its first few years of operation.

Also similar is that consensus is required to modify each court's jurisdiction and access rules. The give and take required to reach consensus surely affects whether court-curbing campaigns succeed and to what extent. In East Africa, for example, the opposition of Tanzania and Uganda to Kenya's initial desire to eliminate the EACJ was crucial to moderating the backlash. The need for consensus may also explain why the Gambia touted its campaign against the ECOWAS Court as a relatively modest judicial reform proposal. It is also possible, however, for one state to repeatedly block consensus proposals to change the status quo, transforming the decision-making rule into a *de facto* unanimity requirement. Zimbabwe's repeated refusals to acquiesce in reforms that fell short of suspending and removing private party access to the SADC Tribunal demonstrate how, in practice, a single hold-out state can block consensus to achieve its strategic goals.

Table 7.1 recaps the essential similarities across cases, listing backlash proposals according to whether they succeeded or failed in whole or in part.

The table reinforces a key finding that emerges from the three narratives—the governments leading the backlash campaign had to work hard to achieve their objectives, and even then they did not succeed immediately or in full. For example, the aggrieved governments failed to pressure sub-regional judges to revise or withdraw their decisions, and they failed to convince other Member States to eliminate the tribunal or void its contested legal rulings.

The swiftness of the EAC backlash stands out by comparison. Kenya's partial success in restructuring the Court was aided by the small number of geographically close states in the EAC whose leaders meet regularly and discuss sub-regional integration issues outside of official decision-making venues. Whether a government could again push judicial reforms through using unofficial channels is unclear.

The time required for Zimbabwe to strip the right of private access to the SADC Tribunal is also striking. Repeatedly, the consensus rule required to revise the Tribunal's mandate yielded compromise proposals that Zimbabwean officials thwarted by lobbying and obfuscation. Equally as important, Mugabe's "plan B"— starving the Tribunal by blocking judicial renewals and appointments—was necessarily a multi-year strategy. Thwarting compromise proved easier than building support for moderate structural reforms. But once the sub-regional court was

Table 7.1 Three Sanctioning Efforts Compared

	ECOWAS	EACJ	SADC
Number of Member States	15	5 (3 at time of backlash)	15
Year operational/ year of first ruling	2001/2004	2001/2006	2005/2007
Decision rule to revise the Court's founding legal instrument	Consensus	Consensus	Consensus in principle Unanimity in practice
Date of IC ruling triggering backlash	June 5, 2008	November 27, 2006	November 28, 2007
Collective decision on sanctioning proposal	October 7, 2009	December 14, 2006	August 18, 2012
Time between first adverse ruling and final backlash decision	~16 months	~1 month	~45 months
Failed backlash proposals	• Require exhaustion of local remedies • Narrow human rights jurisdiction • Add time restrictions for filing complaints • Create an appeals mechanism	• Eliminate the EACJ • Fire the Kenyan judges	• Declare the Tribunal illegally constituted • Nullify the contested rulings
Successful backlash proposals	• None	• Create an Appellate Division with more conservative judges • Add short time limits for filing complaints • Retain national jurisdiction over designated issues • Corruption in appointing country added as a ground for judge removal	• Remove private litigant access to the Tribunal
Compliance with the contested ruling(s)?	No	Yes	Generally no, but partial enforcement of one damages award in South Africa

no longer operational, Zimbabwe could dictate the terms of its resurrection by insisting on stripping private party access as a condition of reviving the Tribunal.

One factor we have not yet discussed is the economic and political power of the country orchestrating the backlash. Kenya and Nigeria are the undisputed economic and political hegemons in East and West Africa, respectively. Zimbabwe's economy is in disarray, but its political influence in SADC was elevated by Mugabe's prominence as one of Africa's longest-serving leaders and his unquestioned anti-colonial bona fides. The clear outlier among the three countries is the Gambia, which is small in size, population, and economic clout.

Might the failure of the ECOWAS Court backlash be attributable to the Gambia's relatively weak status in West Africa? Opposing President Jammeh was arguably less costly than challenging leaders of more powerful West African nations.[157] The lack of popular support for the Gambian government in the region also facilitated opposition to its proposals. We do not see these factors as decisive, however. Prior to issuing the two judgments that enraged the Gambia, ECOWAS judges had found other West African governments in violation of their citizens' human rights and had affirmed the lack of an exhaustion of local remedies rule. Moreover, many of the cases then pending before the ECOWAS Court were against Nigeria, which had previously objected to the Court's attempt to intervene in a contested election in that country.[158] Moreover, the Gambia's reforms were the most modest of the three backlash proposals, and some of them were recently revived in the guise of improvements to the Court.[159] For all of these reasons, it would have been relatively uncontroversial for the other fourteen ECOWAS Member States to accede to the Gambia's proposals, either as drafted or with modest amendments.

During presentations, we were often queried about whether the process for appointing judges to the sub-regional courts mattered in explaining the backlashes. The rules governing appointments might, in theory, explain the extent to which IC judges are bold or timid, but they cannot explain whether court-curbing campaigns succeed or fail. Stacking an IC with pro-government judges following a disfavored ruling might, however, be another way to clip a court's wings. Yet none of the three governments pursued this strategy. A possible exception is Kenya, which, together with the other EAC Member States, appointed somewhat more conservative judges to the newly created Appellate Division. We observe, however, that the

---

[157] See Viljoen, *supra* note 115, at 499 (referring to the Gambia's status as "one of the smallest and least powerful states in ECOWAS" as helping to defeat its proposal).

[158] For a discussion of the case and Nigeria's response, *see* Alter, Helfer, & McAllister, *supra* note 3, at 758–60.

[159] ECOWAS Retreat Adopts Recommendation For Setting Up an ECOWAS Court Appellate Body and Sub-Registries, Press Release, ECOWAS COMMUNITY COURT OF JUSTICE, https://web.archive.org/web/20131020102708/http://www.courtecowas.org/site2012/index.php?option=com_content&view=article&id=214:ecowas-retreat-adopts-recommendation-for-setting-up-an-ecowas-court-appellate-body-and-sub-registries.

appointments have not appreciably constrained the EACJ's subsequent foray into human rights.

A final difference pertains to the subject matter of the contested rulings. The decisions against the Gambia—disappearance and torture of dissident journalists—were unequivocal human rights abuses that no government would openly defend. The EALA elections case, in contrast, involved a jurisdictional dispute over the boundary between Community and domestic law, a technical legal issue where good faith disagreement could exist. Campbell's challenge to Zimbabwe's land rights regime was by far the most incendiary of the three suits. All post-colonial societies struggle with the fraught legacy of highly concentrated property ownership, an extremely sensitive topic for judges and politicians alike. There was thus much sympathy among regional heads of state when Mugabe argued that "if it happens to us, it happens to you next."[160] Moreover, while Mugabe's strong-arm tactics were distasteful to many, within Southern Africa his land reforms enjoyed significant popular support.[161]

On its own, however, these subject matter differences cannot explain why Kenya's and Zimbabwe's backlash succeeded in part. Land rights may well be a third rail of post-colonial politics, but without Mugabe's intransigence one of the many compromise proposals could well have succeeded. In fact, NGOs repeatedly convinced national attorneys general and justice ministers to endorse reform proposals that retained private access to the Tribunal. Mugabe's strategy of blocking these proposals while running out the clock—to the point that the SADC Tribunal ceased to exist in practice—eventually forced other Member States to accept the inevitable. Removing the right of private access became the price to be paid for resurrecting the Tribunal.

Part Four: Explaining the Divergence in Backlash Outcomes— The Role of Community Secretariats, Civil Societies, and Sub-Regional Parliaments

The three backlash attempts we analyze highlight the difficulty of collectively sanctioning ICs for politically embarrassing rulings, even for governments that are weakly committed to judicial independence. The barriers to carrying out backlash proposals are political and institutional. Politically, governments that share

---

[160] Interview with a former official of the SADC Lawyers Association, Gaborone, Botswana (Aug. 9, 2013).

[161] Sam Moyo, *Land Reform and Redistribution in Zimbabwe Since 1980, in* LAND AND AGRARIAN REFORM IN ZIMBABWE: BEYOND WHITE-SETTLER CAPITALISM 42, 50 (Sam Moyo & Walter Chambati eds., 2013). *See also* Achiume Tendayi, *The SADC Tribunal: Socio-Political Dissonance and the Authority of International Courts, in* INTERNATIONAL COURT AUTHORITY (Karen Alter, Laurence Helfer, & Michael Rask Madsen eds., 2018).

concerns about politically controversial adverse IC rulings may be reluctant to openly support political leaders who carry out human rights abuses or use strong-arm tactics against their own citizens. Institutionally, inertia is on the side of ICs; blocking change is easier than reaching a consensus in favor of altering the status quo.

The difficulty of a successful backlash suggests a clear strategy for IC supporters. Delaying and publicizing sanctioning campaigns allows tempers to cool, ex-poses the ulterior motives of seemingly benign proposals, and shames other governments away from tacitly supporting court-curbing efforts. Also, by insisting that states follow formal rules and decision-making procedures, Community Secretariats, civil society groups, and regional parliaments can slow down sanctioning initiatives, enhance transparency, and create opportunities to rally against backlash proposals.

This section examines the varying ability of these actors to mobilize to defeat the three backlash campaigns. We focus on the political and institutional culture within the Community Secretariats and their relationships to civil society groups, as well as the groups' organizational capacity and resources. In East Africa, the EALA also provided an additional source of support for the Court, something that was lacking in the other two sub-regions.

Sub-Regional Secretariats as Brokers in Managing IC Backlash

The Secretariats in each sub-region are comprised of a chief executive, a political appointee, supported by a professional and legal staff whom Member States consult on most policy matters within the Community's purview. Secretariats organize meetings of Member State officials, set agendas, coordinate logistics, and prepare official documents such as draft legislation, reports about meetings, and records of official decisions. The Secretariat legal staff advises policy-makers on draft legislation and helps to coordinate reviews of Community adjudicatory mechanisms. On paper, these decisions are matters of public record. In reality, Community websites are often out of date. Knowledge of these decisions—and opportunities for input by civil society groups—thus depend on how forthcoming Secretariat officials are in disseminating the decisions to interested stakeholders.

The political culture and level of professionalization within the Secretariats determine how effectively these bodies exert independent influence within an over-arching structure of state power. In particular, these factors affect the willingness and ability of Secretariat officials and staff to openly and regularly engage civil society actors, and thus the extent to which Secretariat officials serve as meaningful defenders of Community interests. This culture is instilled by political appointees and the expectations of Member States. Where governments expect Secretariats to be concierges or helpmeets, Community officials and staff become less transparent, excluding civil society groups and acquiescing to extra-legal pressures to ignore Community decision-making rules.

In West Africa, the professional staff of the ECOWAS Secretariat has earned the Member States' trust and thus has considerable autonomy to carry out its activities. For example, the Legal Affairs Department spearheaded the initiative to give the ECOWAS Court a human rights jurisdiction. When governments expressed concern about some early Court decisions, the Secretariat facilitated the creation of an ECOWAS Judicial Council that uses a merit-based process for selecting ECOWAS judges. Perhaps most importantly, the Secretariat coordinated the various meetings at which the Gambia's reform proposals were discussed.

To be sure, the ECOWAS Secretariat pays close attention to the Member States' views on Community initiatives. It would be unthinkable for the Secretariat to openly oppose a proposal that governments collectively favored. But Secretariat staff often know more about the views of individual governments than do political leaders in other Member States. Thus, even acting within the scope of its limited authority, the ECOWAS Secretariat can influence the fate of proposals through information sharing and coalition building.

With regard to the Gambian backlash, Secretariat officials followed procedural rules that require informing ECOWAS judges about initiatives relating to the Court, a disclosure that enabled the judges to reach out to allies to oppose the proposals.[162] In addition, the Secretariat scheduled and announced meetings in advance, enabling civil society groups to attend key meetings and present their views. The presence of civil society actors at these meetings signaled to government officials that their actions were being scrutinized by networked groups who would quickly disseminate decisions to a wider audience.

The situation in the EAC was quite different. The Secretariat either did not or could not object when Kenya scheduled a series of rushed extraordinary meetings at which national political leaders discussed the EACJ's fate. In fairness, the Secretariat faced immense pressure from Kenya, whose top officials—incensed at the EACJ's injunction in the *Nyong'o* case—were highly motivated, called meetings on their own, and themselves drafted treaty amendments to accomplish their objectives. Moreover, Uganda and Tanzania—although unwilling to kill the Court— seemed happy to go along with Kenya's court reform proposals, likely limiting any maneuvering room Secretariat officials may have had to slow down the EACJ reform initiative.

Yet the EAC Secretariat refrained from following mandatory procedures that could have bolstered support for the sub-regional court.[163] In particular, we

---

[162] ECOWAS Legal Affairs Directorate, Legal Advisor, Abuja, Nigeria (Mar. 7, 2011).

[163] For the variety of provisions in EAC Treaties providing for the participation of civil society groups and how these have been operationalized and the challenges that have emerged, *see* Don Deya, The Place of Civil Society in the Eastern African Community, outline to Kitua Cha Katiba Intensive

found no evidence that Secretariat officials informed or sought the input of civil society actors regarding Kenya's backlash proposal, notwithstanding express Community rules requiring such consultation. On the contrary, we were told that the Secretariat—and in particular its Office of Legal Counsel—generally avoided or put off interactions with civil society groups agitating to strengthen the Community legal order.[164]

That EAC Secretariat officials tend to view their mandate through the prism of Member State interests is not surprising. Until recently, EAC professional staff were recruited in response to heavy government lobbying rather via a competitive process focusing on individual merit.[165] Further, the Secretariat reports to the Council of Ministers—the Community's top political body that represents Member State interests—which has a preeminent role in EAC policy-making. The control exercised by the Council has deterred the Secretariat from expanding its autonomy or even from exercising the authority conferred on it by the EAC Treaty.[166]

In sum, the EAC Secretariat apparently chose to distance itself from civil society groups that promote human rights and the rule of law in East Africa. As a result, its officials did not attempt to leverage these groups as a counterweight to Kenya's proposal to narrow the EACJ's jurisdiction and access rules. Perhaps ironically, the Court itself has done a much better job of mobilizing support from civil society actors in the face of pushback from governments upset with its rulings.[167]

In the SADC, the Secretariat initially attempted to protect the Tribunal from Mugabe's wrath. For example, Executive Secretary Salomão countered early attempts by Zimbabwean officials to spin a modest Summit decision as a vindication of the country's more radical position. We are unsure whether the Secretariat or national political leaders drafted the many compromise proposals that would have preserved the Tribunal's human rights jurisdiction, at least in part. Nor do we know who proposed hiring an outside consultant to review Zimbabwe's legal challenges to the Tribunal's mandate. What is certain, however, is that justice ministers

---

Seminar: The East African Community: Organs, Institutions and Procedures, Kampala, Uganda (Sept. 12–14, 2012) (on file with authors).

[164] Interview with Human Rights Advocate M, Nairobi, Kenya (Aug. 1, 2013).
[165] *See* Alan Odhiambo, *Five Kenyans Short-Listed for Top EAC Jobs*, BUSINESS DAILY AFRICA (Jan. 18, 2015), http://www.businessdailyafrica.com/Five-Kenyans-shortlisted-for-top-EAC-jobs/-/539546/2593728/-/14rpt43/-/index.html.
[166] Article 71(1) of the EAC Establishment Treaty provides: "In the performance of their functions, the staff of the Community shall not seek or receive instructions from any Partner State .... They shall refrain from any actions which may adversely reflect on their position as international civil servants and shall be responsible only to the Community."
[167] According to the first EACJ Registrar, the judges "boldly went around the region meeting its stakeholders including bar associations, business communities, civil societies, law reform commissions and Attorneys General." John Ruhusinga, *Litigation in the East African Court of Justice*, Paper Presented to the EALS, African Executive (July 12–19, 2006), https://web.archive.org/web/20060821170259/http://www.africanexecutive.com/modules/magazine/articles.php?article=794.

and attorneys general supported proposals for moderate reforms to the Tribunal's jurisdiction.

After Mugabe blocked these proposals, the Secretariat became less forthcoming in sharing information with Tribunal supporters and more closely aligned with Zimbabwe's backlash campaign. The Secretariat also circumvented formal procedures for notifying stakeholders about the content and timing of upcoming decisions. For example, the Tribunal's President complained bitterly about his exclusion from key meetings, which he attributed to Secretariat officials notifying him only days before a Summit scheduled months earlier.[168] And in contrast to the Executive Secretary's early resistance to Zimbabwe's political spin, one source asserted that high-level Secretariat officials later colluded with Zimbabwe in preparing public statements that misrepresented official Summit decisions.

By this point, civil society complaints of exclusion from SADC meetings fell on deaf ears. This may well have reflected political reality—the unbending will of Mugabe, the de facto withering of the Tribunal due to blocked judicial appointments, and the continued acquiescence of SADC leaders. By August 2013 when Mugabe was elected to the rotating chairmanship of SADC,[169] any astute Community official could see the writing on the wall.

Civil Society Mobilization to Oppose IC Backlash

Civil society participation is a common and distinctive feature of European-style economic communities. To implement their espoused objectives, the West, East, and Southern Africa integration projects include procedures for soliciting the views of civil society actors as part of collective decision-making processes. All three sub-regions require that civil society group register with Community institutions. Registered groups are granted various opportunities to consult with officials and attend key meetings as observers and sometimes as participants. To be eligible for registration, civil society groups must demonstrate that their membership extends across each sub-region. Partly to meet this requirement, many bar associations, law societies, and human rights NGOs in Africa have organized themselves transnationally.

In all three cases in our study, sub-regionally organized civil society groups were aware of the government's backlash efforts and actively mobilized to oppose them. What, then, explains the groups' varied influence in thwarting the backlash campaigns? Part of the answer is how organized, cohesive, and well-resourced the groups were in each sub-region, and how close a relationship they developed with

---

[168] Pillay Speech, *supra* note 147, at 4–5.
[169] Mugabe to Become Next SADC Leader, News 24 (Aug. 20, 2013), http://www.news24.com/Africa/Zimbabwe/Mugabe-to-become-next-SADC-leader-20130820.

Community Secretariats. These relationships, in conjunction with the Secretariat's political culture, determined whether Community officials served as helpful and timely conduits for information about court reform proposals.

In West Africa, human rights organizations and law societies have been working with the ECOWAS Secretariat for many years. Human rights appeared on the ECOWAS agenda in the early 1990s in response to credible evidence of atrocities committed by military forces involved in an ECOWAS-sanctioned humanitarian intervention in Liberia.[170] When Member States revamped the sub-region's collective security institutions in the mid-1990s, they also added a sub-regional court and restructured Community institutions and decision-making procedures so as to included broad participation rules for civil society actors.[171]

Capitalizing on these participation rules, human rights groups organized transnationally beginning in 2001, the same year the ECOWAS Court was created. The West African Bar Association followed in 2004, resolving to "supplement the work of [ECOWAS] by promoting [the] rule of law, fundamental human rights and democracy in the sub-region."[172] Human rights groups and the regional bar association partnered with the Secretariat to strengthen the Community legal order. The Legal Affairs Directorate actively consulted the groups regarding the 2005 Protocol giving the ECOWAS Court a human rights jurisdiction. And, as described in detail earlier in Part Two in "The ECOWAS Court of Justice: A Failed Backlash," the Directorate followed the Community's civil society participation rules to ensure that the Bar Association and human rights activists attended key meetings at which the Gambia's challenge to the Court was debated.

In East Africa, the EALS and the Pan-African Lawyers Union (PALU) are highly organized and maintain a permanent presence in Arusha (the home of the EAC), the EACJ, and other ICs. Founded in 1995 and based in Arusha, the EALS has built personal connections with Secretariat officials and sub-regional judges. PALU is a more recent creation, founded in 2010 to better coordinate Africa's anglophone and francophone lawyers' associations. These organizations operate with a lean but highly capable staff. They are well supported financially by mandatory dues collected from individual attorneys who pay these dues when they renew their practicing certificates with their national bar association.

As a formal matter, the EALS has observer status with the EAC and the right to participate in Council meetings.[173] Yet the Society's influence has been stymied by a lack of close alignment between the Society's objectives and those of the EAC's

---

[170] Alter, Helfer, & McAllister, *supra* note 3, at 744.

[171] KOFI OTENG KUFUOR, THE INSTITUTIONAL TRANSFORMATION OF THE ECONOMIC COMMUNITY OF WEST AFRICAN STATES 49–50 (2006) (citing Decision A/DEC.9/8/94 Establishing Regulations for the Grant to Non-governmental Organisations (NGOs) the Status of Observer Within the Institutions of the Community (Aug. 6, 1994)).

[172] *West African Bar Association Inaugurated*, General News Association (Aug. 24, 2004), http://www.ghanaweb.com/GhanaHomePage/economy/artikel.php?ID=64712.

[173] Gathii, *supra* note 40, at 282.

Office of Legal Counsel.[174] Human rights attorneys told us that meetings between EALS and PALU officials on the one hand, and EAC Legal Counsel officials on the other, are often canceled at the last minute, and lawyers' requests for documents are often lost or greatly delayed. Other EAC practices, either by design or happenstance, also minimize participation. "Council meetings are often planned at the last minute, and there is often little prior notice given to EALS so that it can secure attendance of one of its officers."[175]

As explained earlier, EAC officials are focused on carrying out the objectives of Member States, whose human rights records are the primary target of EALA and PALU litigation. Consultations with civil society groups do occur, but mainly when the Secretariat's interests overlap with those groups. The East African Business Council frequently meets with the Secretariat and was regularly consulted regarding drafts of sub-regional economic legislation.[176] NGOs working on issues such as Community development, gender, youth, children, and business issues are also involved in EAC Secretariat activities.[177]

For human rights groups, however, EAC Legal Counsel officials are more wary. One lawyer told us that after Member States found a Secretariat report on a legal issue to be insufficient, the Legal Council staff informally consulted with PALU lawyers.[178] The Secretariat also met with EALS and PALU to discuss government proposals to give the EACJ jurisdiction over international crimes, while, at the same time, sidelining the EALS's priority of adopting a protocol giving the Court an express human rights mandate.[179] These examples suggest that such consultations occur only when Member States are unlikely view them as objectionable.

Seen in this light, it is not surprising that the EALS and PALU were not consulted about Kenya's plans to weaken the EACJ following the *Nyong'o* ruling. The EALS later challenged the lack of civil society participation in the treaty amendment process, and the judges validated their complaint:

> We think that construing the Treaty as if it permits sporadic amendments at the whims of officials without any form of consultation with stakeholders would be a recipe for regression to the situation lamented in the preamble of "*lack of strong participation of the private sector and civil society*" that led to the collapse of the previous Community.[180]

---

[174] EAC Treaty establishes the EAC Office of Legal Counsel as a Body within the EAC Secretariat, art. 69.

[175] Gathii, *supra* note 40, at 214.

[176] Interview at East African Business Council (EABC), Arusha, Tanzania (July 30, 2013).

[177] Deya, *supra* note 163.

[178] Interview with Human Rights Advocate L, Arusha, Tanzania (July 30, 2013).

[179] Interview at the Pan African Lawyer's Association, Arusha, Tanzania (July 30, 2013).

[180] East Afr. Law Soc'y v. Attorney Gen. of Kenya, Ref. No. 3 of 2007, Judgment, at 30 (2008) (emphasis in original).

The EACJ held that the lack of civil society participation violated the EAC Treaty, and that such violations could lead to the annulment of the amendments. Yet the Court declined to exercise this power on prudential grounds, declaring that "the requirement of involvement of people in the Treaty amendment process shall have prospective application."[181] This cautious holding may reflect the judges' recognition that, although the Secretariat had circumvented rules requiring civil society participation in EAC decision-making, the amendments were a *fait accompli* that Member States would not reverse.

In Southern Africa, the SADC Lawyers Association was mostly excluded from Community consultations regarding the Tribunal and the Community legal order. Even before Zimbabwe's backlash campaign, the SADC Secretariat and the Association had a stand-offish relationship. According to a former member of the Association's leadership, the Secretariat viewed the lawyers group as "too noisy" and tended to avoid informal contact. In addition, the group's observer status in SADC has remained in a "gray area." The group does not want to formalize its status because, according to a former association official, registered NGOs are pressured to "toe the line" of the Member States and the Secretariat.[182]

The lack of a close relationship with the Secretariat is one reason why the SADC Lawyers' Association has moved twice since it was established in 1999—first, in 2003, from its initial home in Pretoria, South Africa to Gaborone, Botswana, and again in 2011 from Gaborone back to Pretoria.[183] The first move was in hopes of working more closely with the Secretariat. The second reflected the difficulty of partnering with SADC officials and the reality that more businesses, law firms, and NGOs are based in Pretoria.

Capacity constraints also undermine the influence of the SADC Lawyers Association. Unlike the EALS, which is funded by mandatory dues from individual lawyers, the Association is dependent on dues collected by national bar associations. National associations often fail to pay or are late in forwarding dues.[184] The lack of a stable funding forces the Association to rely on volunteers, making it more difficult to file complaints or *amicus* briefs with the Tribunal.[185]

---

[181] *Id.* at 44.

[182] Interview with a former official of the SADC Lawyers' Association, Gaborone, Botswana (Aug. 9, 2013).

[183] History and Structure, SADC Lawyers Association, https://web.archive.org/web/20140929212144/http://www.sadcla.org/new1/history_and_legal_structure.

[184] Interview with Officials of the Law Society of Botswana, Gaborone, Botswana (Aug. 8, 2013).

[185] *See Whither the SADC Tribunal: Report of Regional Colloquium on the SADC Tribunal, Johannesburg*, SADC Lawyers Association, 19–20 (Mar. 2013), https://lawsdocbox.com/Politics/82501569-Whither-the-sadc-tribunal.html (hereinafter "Whither the SADC"). At its 2013 Annual Conference, the Association condemned the decision to strip private litigant access to the Tribunal. Statement on SADC Tribunal: Regional Governance *Issues*, SADC Lawyers Association (Aug. 16, 2013), https://web.archive.org/web/20130819101224/http://www.safpi.org/news/article/2013/sadc-lawyers-association-statement-sadc-tribunal-regional-governance-issues (hereinafter "Statement on SADC").

Dispersed geography is also a factor. The SADC Lawyers' Association and most regional NGOS are based in Pretoria, the SADC Secretariat is based in Botswana, and the Tribunal's seat is in Windhoek, Namibia. Summit meetings rotate around major cities in the fifteen Member States. This dispersion makes it more difficult for lawyers and NGOS to develop informal and formal contacts and relationships with SADC judges and officials.

The lack of a strong and cohesive bar association in SADC created space for the civil society stage to be occupied by foreign-funded NGOs like the Open Society Initiative of Southern Africa (supported by the Soros Foundation) and the Southern Africa Litigation Center (jointly funded by Soros and the International Bar Association). While these NGOs hire and support skilled human rights lawyers, they make easy targets for political leaders like Mugabe, who discredited them as thinly-veiled efforts by Western nations to interfere with the internal political processes of African nations.[186] The location of these foreign-funded NGOs in the much more constitutionally liberal South Africa adds to this perception.

For all these reasons, the SADC Secretariat mostly sidelined the civil society groups that rallied to save the Tribunal. As noted earlier, foreign-funded NGOs repeatedly protested their exclusion from SADC meetings at which political leaders debated the Tribunal's fate. The SADC Lawyers' Association fared little better. Instead, it focused on public pronouncements and lobbying government officials.[187] These tactics helped to secure the support of the Ministers of Justice, who endorsed a compromise proposal that Mugabe and the other the heads of state later rejected.

Sub-Regional Parliaments as Potential Venues for Opposition Politics

Parliamentary bodies associated with regional and sub-regional integration projects may provide another venue for resisting attempts by national executives to circumvent Community procedures, including those protecting ICs against political backlashes. This has in fact occurred in East Africa, where the EALA has supported the nascent sub-regional court in disputes with EAC Member States.

Many will find this claim surprising. Conventional wisdom holds that regional legislatures are, with the possible exception of the European Parliament, little more than talk shops. This is largely true for the ECOWAS Parliament, which lacked any legislative powers or budgetary approval authority until a 2014 institutional

---

[186] See, e.g., Permanent Mission of the Republic of Zimbabwe to the United Nations, Statement of Patrick A. Chinamasa (MP), UN Human Rights Council (June 2006), https://www.ohchr.org/Documents/HRBodies/HRCouncil/RegularSession/Session1/HLS/zimbabwe.pdf.

[187] See Whither the SADC, supra note 185. At its 2013 Annual Conference, the Association condemned the decision to strip private litigant access to the Tribunal. Statement on SADC, supra note 185.

overhaul.[188] The SADC Parliamentary Forum is even weaker. It is not formally recognized as a SADC institution and does not coordinate its activities with other
Community initiatives.[189]

The situation in East African is different. The members of the EALA are elected
from their respective national parliaments in proportion to the strength of each
country's political parties. The sub-regional legislature is also financially and politically independent from the Member States. As the *Nyong'o* litigation aptly demonstrates, these attributes make the EALA an attractive venue for opposition
politicians. They also provide opportunities for parliamentarians to support IC
judges against attacks by national executives.

The EALA was an early supporter of the EACJ in at least three important ways.
First, the Assembly passed resolutions pressing the EAC Summit to appoint the inaugural group of EAC judges and to upgrade the position of Registrar of the Court
to an executive level.[190] Second, after the Court was constituted, the three members of EALA brought the very first case before the EACJ challenging the ability of
the Council of Ministers to supervise the legislative agenda of the EALA. Notably,
the entire Assembly supported the EACJ's intervention over the objections of the
EAC Legal Secretariat.[191] The EACJ overruled the EAC Ministerial Council's assertion of authority to control the EALA's agenda—a decision lauded by civil society groups as a milestone in spreading the rule of law in East Africa.[192] Third, the
EALA has lobbied for increased funding for the EACJ to ensure that the Court can
effectively discharge its human rights mandate.[193] By supporting the activation of

---

[188] In 2014, the Member States expanded the Parliament's powers to include approval of the
Community budget, certain oversight responsibilities for ECOWAS organs, and the appointment
of Community officials. *See Finally ECOWAS Enhances Power of ECOWAS Parliament*, AFRICAN
EXAMINER (Dec. 15, 2014), http://www.africanexaminer.com/finally-ecowas-enhances-the-powers-of-
the-ecowas-parliament/.

[189] Article 9(1) of the SADC Treaty, which establishes SADC institutions, does not mention the
Forum. *Contra* Bookie Monica Kethusegile v. SADC Parliamentary Forum, SADC Tribunal Case No.
SADC 02 (2009) (asserting that a SADC Summit decision elevated the Forum to a SADC institution);
see Stephen Kingah, *EU's Engagement with African Sub-Regional Parliaments of ECOWAS, SADC, EAC
and AU* (UNU-Cris Working Papers W-2012/8, 9, 2012), available at https://web.archive.org/web/
20140719081440/http://www.cris.unu.edu/fileadmin/workingpapers/W-2012-8.pdf.

[190] *See* Eight Years of EALA: 2001–2009, EALA 9 (Sept. 2009) (noting that the EALA passed a resolution urging the Council of Ministers to appoint EACJ judges and a registrar to establish their terms of
service).

[191] Mwatela v. EAC, Appl. No. 1 of 2005, Ruling, East African Court of Justice, at 15 (Oct. 1, 2006),
http://www.eala.org/documents/view/59th-sitting-first-assembly-fifth-session-first-meeting   (hereinafter "Mwatela v. EAC"). On the objections of the EAC Legal Counsel, *see Official Report of the
Proceedings of EALA, 59th Sitting—First Assembly: First Meeting-Fifth Session, Tuesday*, EALA (Dec. 6
2005), http://www.eala.org/key-documents/doc_details/70-6-december-2005.html.

[192] Mwatela v. EAC, *supra* note 191. The Court also allowed civil society groups to file *amicus curiae*
submissions, a precedent that opened the door for civil society participation in its future cases.

[193] Hon. Shem Bageine, EAC Budget Speech, Financial Year 2013/2014, at the EALA (May 30,
2013) (on file with authors); Roundtable on Strengthening the Implementation of Human Rights in
the EAC Region, *Arusha, Tanzania: The Role of the East African Legislative Assembly* (May 27, 2011),
https://web.archive.org/web/20110709121916/http://www.wfd.org/upload/docs/Communique%20-
%20Launch%20of%20Human%20Rights%20Handbook%20in%20EALA.pdf.

the EACJ, bringing its first case, which in turn provided the Court an opportunity inaugurate a place for civil society actors in litigation, and publicly supporting the inclusion of a human rights mandate, the EALA provided an additional venue to defend the judges against the wrath of national executives.

Part Five: Conclusion

This chapter has described three credible attempts to sanction sub-regional ICs in Africa for rulings that criticized the behavior of governments. In ECOWAS, the Secretariat and ECOWAS judges brought in civil society supporters to ensure that Member States did not collude behind closed doors to hobble the sub-regional court. Even though the Gambia's proposals were the most modest of all three court-curbing campaigns, they failed to secure the support among the other Member States.

In the EAC, Kenya's government used rushed, unofficial meetings to circumvent Community decision-making processes. The speed of Kenya's actions, facilitated by the reality that at the time the EAC contained only three member countries, made it difficult for civil society groups to mobilize to thwart these extra-legal efforts. Still, Kenya's Attorney General failed to accomplish the government's more radical goal—the EACJ was not disbanded; its Kenyan judges were not removed; and the offensive EACJ ruling retained enough support that the government reluctantly complied with the injunction and the ruling on the merits.

Since SADC officials and national political leaders ultimately acquiesced to Mugabe's demands, it may seem that the Tribunal's demise is vastly different. But for many years the SADC Secretariat and sympathetic government officials thwarted Mugabe. His Minister of Justice failed to persuade the Member States that Zimbabwe could unilaterally withdraw from the Tribunal's jurisdiction, that the Tribunal was illegally constituted, or that the Tribunal's land rights rulings should be nullified. In the end, Mugabe's persistence, tenacity, and wily political tactics won out.

We have argued that the success of governments' backlash efforts depended upon whether formal decision rules and procedures were followed or circumvented. In ECOWAS, Secretariat officials ensured the civil society consultation and decision-making procedures were adhered to. The Gambia garnered some sympathy for its court-curbing initiatives, but the majority of West African governments would not publicly back its self-interested reaction to court rulings that exposed the country's abysmal human rights record. In the EAC, Kenya rapidly convened unofficial meetings to circumvent more deliberative consultation procedures, creating a *fait accompli* of reforms that, while less than what the government wanted, have nonetheless affected the EACJ's future trajectory. In SADC,

Zimbabwe's President Mugabe relied on public spin, misinformation, and closed-door Summit meetings to force his will through.

The three backlash cases also raise other theoretically interesting questions. Why did the sub-regional judges rule against governments when they could readily anticipate a negative response? Why are sub-regional Secretariats easier for governments to control than regional courts? And were the different procedural rules regarding the failure to appoint judges part of the Member States' rational plans to cabin these ICs? We briefly address each question in turn.

Why didn't judges rationally anticipate, and thus avoid, provoking a backlash? When we asked sub-regional judges about their unyielding behavior in the face of government threats, they cited their obligation to follow the requirements of the law. While this answer is not surprising, we also see the judges' reliance on legal arguments as both strategic and rational. If judges are seen as caving into political demands and ignoring legal rules, their authority will be questioned and their *raison d'etre* will be undermined. On the other hand, overly expansive rulings create easy targets for rebuke. We thus see further evidence of strategic judicial behavior in the ECOWAS Court and EACJ's post-backlash caution in fashioning remedies.

Yet this still does not explain why the SADC Tribunal was so confrontational, condemning Mugabe's signature land reforms, demanding that he compensate white farmers, and referring Zimbabwe to the Summit for sanctions? One possible explanation is that the judges were frustrated that SADC political bodies seemed unwilling to name and shame Mugabe for his numerous violations of the law. With little chance of political backing, perhaps judges decided to "go big or go home"—that is, to use their power to the full and hope that civil society and public opinion would tip the balance in favor of meaningful action against Zimbabwe.

Why are sub-regional judges willing to act independently of governments, especially as compared to sub-regional Secretariats? The EACJ and ECOWAS Court are clearly aware of the limits of their power. They display, however, a greater willingness to act independently of governments than do regional Secretariats. This difference is unsurprising for a few reasons. First, Secretariats exist to facilitate Member State cooperation and to promote community objectives. This can be done only by close collaboration with governments. Second, Secretariat officials tend to be diplomats or individuals with national government experience or aspirations. Third, Secretariats are not expected to follow legal rules and procedures in the same way that judges are expected to do as they render decisions. Although unsurprising, the difference between ICs and Secretariats is worth underscoring since scholars and politicians often expect regional judges to be easily influenced as other regional officials.

Was the ECOWAS Court designed to be more independent, and the EACJ and SADC Tribunal designed to be more vulnerable to political rebuke, such that governments got exactly what they wanted? The ECOWAS Court is structurally different than its sub-regional counterparts. The Court has an explicit human rights jurisdiction, and the majority of ECOWAS Member States have repeatedly supported the Court's power to adjudicate human rights complaints. The addition of a sub-regional Judicial Council, the professional independence of the Secretariat, and the rejection of the Gambia's backlash effort are further indications of a deeper commitment to Community policy-making in ECOWAS.

This does not mean, however, that the SADC or EAC outcomes reflect the rational design of sovereignty-jealous states. Governments in East Africa have refrained from conferring human rights jurisdiction on the EACJ and regularly contest the EACJ's backdoor adjudication of human rights claims. The addition of the Appellate Division has provided a mechanism to reverse more expansive First Instance rulings. Yet, as the *Serengeti* case illustrates, both chambers of the EACJ remain stubbornly independent. The SADC Tribunal also did not appear to fit a rational design story. Everyone we interviewed was aware that the Tribunal's first case involved perhaps the most contested issue in Southern Africa—the rights of minority white landowners. Moreover, it is doubtful that Mugabe anticipated that the Tribunal would adjudicate human rights cases. And the appointments rule that Mugabe exploited to kill the Tribunal appears to be more of an oversight than part of a rational design strategy.

Overall, we find that Africa's sub-regional ICs remain surprisingly resistant to Member State tampering. Although authoritarian African governments seem to have no qualms about radically revising the jurisdiction and procedures of Community courts, employing the same strategies used to cow domestic judiciaries, more democratic governments were more reluctant to alter the ICs' mandates. Yet those governments also struggle with the competing desire of African leaders not to have their prerogatives judicially reversed.[194]

This struggle means that aggrieved governments avoid full-frontal attacks on sub-regional courts. Instead, they impose restrictions on access and time limits on the filing of cases and attempt to shift to venues that they can more easily control. Wily politics, rather than rational design and institutional checks and

---

[194] Another strategy adopted by African governments angered by decisions of the African Court on Human and Peoples' Rights is their withdrawal of the optional declaration under Article 34(6) of the Protocol to the African Charter on the Establishment of the African Court on Human and Peoples' Rights allowing individuals and NGOs direct access to the Court. Rwanda withdrew its declaration in 2018, and Tanzania followed suit in 2019. Neither of these actions was accompanied by the kind of sustained politics of backlash directed against the three sub-regional courts discussed in this article. For further discussion of the two withdrawals, *see* James Gathii and Jacquelene Mwangi's chapter (Chapter 6) in this book titled, "The African Court on Human and Peoples' Rights as a Legal Opportunity Structure." *See also* Nicole De Silva, Individual and NGO *Access to the African Court on Human and Peoples' Rights: The Latest Blow from Tanzania*, EJIL TALK (December 9, 2019) https://www.ejiltalk.org/individual-and-ngo-access-to-the-african-court-on-human-and-peoples-rights-the-latest-blow-from-tanzania/#more-17746.

balances, thus seem to be the preferred means of influencing ICs.[195] In responding to backlash attempts, civil society groups and Secretariats can act as buffers to protect IC judges. But persistent authoritarian leaders can prevail in their court curbing campaigns if their more democratic leaning counterparts acquiesce to their antics.

---

[195] *See also* Karen J. Alter and Michael Zurn, *Theorizing Backlash Politics*, BRI J INT'L RELS (forthcoming 2020) (arguing that backlash politics movements and politics that meet three necessary conditions: (i) a retrograde objective; (ii) extraordinary goals, tactics, and means; and (iii) has reached the threshold of entering public discourse).

8

Reference Guide to Africa's International Courts

An Introduction

James Thuo Gathii and Harrison Otieno Mbori

Introduction

This reference guide introduces the eight active international courts in Africa.[1] Also included is a ninth inactive court, the Arab Maghreb Union's Judicial Organ. The discussion of the Arab Maghreb Union's Judicial Organ in this reference guide examines why there has been less judicialization in North Africa relative to other parts of Africa. All of Africa's active international courts came into existence in the last two and half decades.[2] At the end of the Cold War, only a single quasi-judicial adjudicative body, the African Commission on Human and Peoples' Rights (ACHRP or the Commission) was in existence. These international courts stem from two sources: sub-regional economic integration arrangements and the regional human rights system of the African Union (AU). The African Court on Human and Peoples' Rights (ACtHPR or African Court), formed in 2006, is the regional human rights court in Africa.[3] It complements the human rights

---

[1] In this Reference Guide, we have focused only on judicial institutions (except the African Commission on Human and Peoples' Rights) and operational institutions (except the AMU Judicial Organ). There are present in Africa other quasi-judicial institutions such as the African Committee of Experts on the Rights and Welfare of the Child (ACERWC), High Commission of Appeal of the African Intellectual Property Organization (AIPO), and the Board of Appeal of the African Regional Industrial Property Organization (ARIPO), which this chapter does not cover. Additionally, the following are other non-operationalized international courts in Africa that the chapter does not address: the African Economic Community Court of Justice (AECCJ), the Arbitration Tribunal of the Economic Community of West African States, and the Economic Community of Central African States (ECCAS) Court of Justice.

[2] KAREN ALTER, THE NEW TERRAIN OF INTERNATIONAL LAW: COURTS, POLITICS, RIGHTS 68 (2014) (affirming that when the Cold War ended in 1989, there were six permanent international courts plus the non-compulsory dispute settlement system of the General Agreement on Tariffs and Trade (GATT)).

[3] The yet to be constituted ACJHPR will replace the ACtHPR when its Protocol (the Malabo Protocol) receives its requisite number of ratifications to enter into force. The ACJHPR, if it comes to fruition, will introduce inter-state dispute resolution mandate similar to that of the International

James Thuo Gathii and Harrison Otieno Mbori, *Reference Guide to Africa's International Courts* In: *The Performance of Africa's International Courts.* Edited by: James Thuo Gathii, Oxford University Press (2020). © The Several Contributors. DOI: 10.1093/oso/9780198868477.003.0009.

promotional mandate of the ACHRP formed in 1986. The ACHRP is a quasi-judicial body. The other international courts in Africa are as follows:

1. East Africa Court of Justice (EACJ) (established in 2001)
2. Economic Community for West African States (ECOWAS) Court of Justice (ECCJ) (established in 2001)
3. South Africa Development Community (SADC) Tribunal (established in 2005)
4. West African Economic and Monetary Union (WAEMU) Court of Justice (established in 1995)
5. Organization for the Harmonization of Business Law in Africa Common Court Justice and Arbitration (OHADA CCJA) (established in 1997)
6. Common Market for Eastern and South Africa (COMESA) Court of Justice (established in 1998)
7. Court of Justice of the Central African Economic and Monetary Community (CEMAC) (established in 2000)
8. Arab Maghreb Union (AMU) Judicial Organ.

This reference guide proceeds as follows. Part One provides an overview of the general characteristics of Africa's international courts. Part Two then proceeds to discuss each of these international courts individually. The guide starts with the human rights-oriented courts: the EACJ, ECCJ, and SADC Tribunal, as well as the African Court and Commission. It then proceeds to discuss the COMESA Court of Justice. It goes on to discuss the courts that focus more on economic disputes. These are the OHADA CCJA and the CEMAC Court of Justice and, to some extent, the WAEMU Court of Justice. The last court is the least active of them, the AMU Judicial Organ.

For each court, the guide discusses when and by whom it was established, its jurisdiction, its rules relating to access for litigants, and its composition and organization. The overall aim of this guide is to introduce these courts to the reader unfamiliar with them. In this sense, this guide is an important reference tool that provides the context for understanding these international courts. This guide therefore serves the important goal of making the analytical nature of the chapters in the rest of the book more accessible to readers unfamiliar with these courts. The guide ends with a table summarizing the subject matter jurisdiction of each court, the year it was created, the year it made its first ruling, the number of Member States subject to its jurisdiction, and how many binding rulings it has made.

Court of Justice (ICJ) and the international crimes mandate akin to that of the International Criminal Court (ICC).

Part One: The General Characteristics of Africa's International Courts

All these international courts share the following three distinctive features. First, with the exception of the AMU Judicial Organ, they all allow, or at some point in the past, entertained cases from individuals and non-governmental organizations (NGOs), in addition to suits by states against states. Second, with the exception of the African Court for cases instituted by individuals or NGOs they have compulsory jurisdiction, meaning that the cases filed can continue even without the defendant's state consent.[4] The fact that they allow individuals to file cases is a large part of the reason why some of them have become very active. Third, although all these courts without exception allow states to file cases against each other, with the exception of a case between Ethiopia and Eritrea in the COMESA Court of Justice, there have been no cases between states filed in these courts.

Courts Specializing in International Human Rights

One of the distinctive characteristics of Africa's international courts is that although three of them were established as sub-regional economic/trade courts, they have primarily decided human rights cases. These are the EACJ, the SADC Tribunal, and the ECCJ. Yet, only the ECCJ has an explicit jurisdictional mandate to decide human rights cases. By contrast, the EACJ and the SADC Tribunal, until it was suspended in 2010, have pursued a broad interpretive strategy to justify assuming jurisdiction over human rights. Thus, a major feature of these courts is the manner in which they have re-purposed their original mandate over trade disputes to become bold adjudicators of human rights cases and disputes of a political nature. The repurposing of their mandates is evidence that these courts are enmeshed within regional movements that are aimed at advancing human rights at the national level and that are increasing spreading at the regional and sub-regional level.

There is a vast difference between the jurisprudence of these sub-regional courts, on the one hand, and the jurisprudence produced by the regional body established to receive complaints under the African Charter on Human and Peoples' Rights (the Banjul Charter), the ACHRP, on the other. Although the Commission argues that its decisions are binding on states, it has taken an extremely deferential remedial approach towards states when complaints are brought. It has

---

[4] *See* KAREN ALTER, THE NEW TERRAIN OF INTERNATIONAL LAW: COURTS, POLITICS, RIGHTS 42–44 (2014).

often sought amicable resolutions and failed to quantify and award damages notwithstanding receiving cases involving serious and massive violations of human rights.[5]

Decision-making over human rights cases has been politically consequential especially where these decisions have been consistent with the strongly held preferences of states found to be in violation. The SADC Tribunal's jurisdiction to receive individual complaints was formally removed in 2014 after it decided against the Zimbabwean government's land reform program constituted discrimination based on race and that it was conducted without due process. In East Africa, the jurisdictional structure and rules of the EACJ were changed after it decided a politically sensitive case from Kenya. In West Africa, Gambia unsuccessfully attempted to persuade ECOWAS states to review the jurisdiction of the ECCJ by denying it the right to receive individual petitions after the court decided it had violated the rights of journalists. Karen Alter, James Gathii, and Laurence Helfer discuss these backlashes more fully in Chapter 7 in this book.

By contrast, to the broad interpretive strategy of the courts in East, West, and Southern Africa, the COMESA Court of Justice has undertaken a more restrictive interpretive strategy. Further, the COMESA Court of Justice has largely remained an industrial tribunal. Its case-law has primarily arisen from employees of the regional integration organization within which the Court is nestled. It is notable, however, that the WAEMU and CEMAC Courts of Justice have a sizeable share of employment disputes on their docket.

The COMESA Court of Justice, unlike the EACJ, the SADC Tribunal and the ECOWAS Court of Justice, has not decided human rights cases. A large part of the explanation for the COMESA Court's unique trajectory in redeploying to become an industrial as opposed to a trade integration court has to do with the lack of civil society interlocutors to bring cases to the Court, to defend the Court, and to lobby for court reform. This together with its restrictive interpretive mandate and its location, first in Lusaka, Zambia and currently in Khartoum, Sudan, strongly suggests why the Court has been unable to build a broader jurisdictional reach and constituencies to bring cases and to defend it as the other sub-regional courts have been able to do. In addition, even though it shares similarities in its individual access and jurisdictional rules to other sub-regional courts, it is also limited by an exhaustion of domestic remedies rule, which together with its restrictive interpretive strategy has effectively left it to become an industrial tribunal.[6]

---

[5] RACHEL MURRAY, THE AFRICAN COMMISSION ON HUMAN AND PEOPLES' RIGHTS AND INTERNATIONAL LAW 176–78 (2000); Rachel Murray & Elizabeth Mottershaw, *Mechanisms for the Implementation of Decisions of the African Commission on Human and Peoples' Rights*, 36 HUMAN RTS. Q. 349–72 (2014).

[6] For more, *see* James T. Gathii, *The COMESA Court of Justice, in* THE LEGITIMACY OF INTERNATIONAL TRADE COURTS AND TRIBUNALS 314 (Robert Howse, Helene Ruiz Fabri, & Geir Ulfstein eds., 2018).

Sub-Regional Courts Specializing in Sub-Regional
Economic Law

Another set of Africa's international courts have focused relatively more on economic than other issues such as human rights. These set of courts have therefore begun to challenge, and in some respects, are breaking down the previously closed-off national legal regimes and their presumed hierarchical superiority over sub-regional, regional, and international legal rules. The best example of supranational economic regulation in Africa, the supra-national corporate, commercial, and business laws of the OHADA region. The OHADA Court of Justice is the highest judicial body charged with the enforcement and monitoring of compliance with OHADA law. The Member States of the OHADA region have accepted the authority of the OHADA Court of Justice.

Another court that has done that is the WAEMU Court of Justice. In 2002, this Court declared the supremacy of WAEMU competition law over national law of Member States. This has meant that Senegal as a WAEMU Member State has had to give up its ability to enforce competition law at the national level to the WAEMU Commission. The fact that Senegal unsuccessfully contested what it saw as a "power-grab" by WAEMU, and eventually relented after losing the case in the WAEMU Court of Justice, demonstrates the efficacy of this Court with regard to a supra-national economic issue. It is notable though, as noted earlier, the WAEMU Court of Justice has decided more employment related disputes arising between WAEMU institutions and its employees.

Another example of a court that deal with economic comes from the CEMAC region. Here, the Member States have surrendered to CEMAC sub-regional law jurisdiction over banking regulation. A powerful sub-regional banking institution, Banque des États de l'Afrique Centrale (BEAC), has emerged. BEAC has asserted and successfully defended its competence to govern sub-regional banking law through the CEMAC Court of Justice.

Although African sub-regional courts have generally not been invited to decide more trade cases, the experience in the WAEMU, CEMAC, and OHADA sub-regional regimes demonstrates the emerging transnational regulation of economic activities. In addition, both the EACJ and the COMESA Court of Justice have decided their first purely trade cases.[7] These cases may herald a new phase of litigation on trade issues to add to the already large number of human rights cases for those courts.

---

[7] For the EACJ case, *see* James Gathii, *The East African Court of Justice: Human Rights and Business Actors Compared,* in INTERNATIONAL COURT AUTHORITY (Karen Alter, Laurence Helfer, & Mikael Madsen eds., 2018). For the COMESA case, *see* James Gathii, *The Court of Justice, in* THE LEGITIMACY OF INTERNATIONAL TRADE COURTS AND TRIBUNALS 314–48 (R. Howse, H. Ruiz-Fabri, G. Ulfstein, & M. Zang eds., 2018).

Why is there No Judicialization in North Africa?

The AMU Judicial Organ is the least active of Africa's international courts. Why has judicialization been so difficult in North Africa? We offer four plausible explanations. First, North African countries in the immediate period of decolonization placed more emphasis on developing national cohesion than developing a pan-Arab sub-regional identity.[8] Each of these countries faced irredentist movements within them that made building national cohesion an imperative. In addition, threats posed to Arab regimes with the rise of Islamic movements including the Muslim Brotherhood and Al Qaeda has required these regimes to bolster their internal order from domestic and international threats in a manner that partly explains the lip service paid to the pan-Arab project.[9] Second, the development of a sub-regional institutional framework within the AMU was hindered by territorial conflicts among these states as well as deep divisions between them.[10] Most significantly is the dispute between Algeria and Morocco over Western Sahara over which a war between 1975 and 1991 culminated in closing the border between the two in 1994. That dispute spilled over into the International Court of Justice (ICJ) and in the AU and to date remains unresolved. In addition, disputes between Libya and Mauritania weakened the possibilities of regional integration in the AMU.[11] Third, the Maghreb area countries have individually negotiated trade and other agreements with the European Union (EU) which remains their most important trading partner. So much so that Morocco had attempted in 1987 to join the EU and had their bid rejected. In the words of William Zartman, "[r]egional unity has made little headway in northern Africa. National rivalries and the Algerian war have kept pan-Maghrebism from solidifying; national consciousness and national ideologies have kept Nilotic unity, or even foreign policy cooperation with Egypt, from crystallizing in northeast Africa."[12]

Finally, some scholars have argued that judicialization is not highly favored as a dispute settlement mechanism among states that share an Islamic background. According to Emilia Justyna Powell countries to the north of Africa, which are largely Islamic, prefer mediation and negotiation as opposed to the kind of dispute settlement through international courts.[13] This view dovetails well with Makane

---

[8] Cesare P.R. Romano, *Mirage in the Desert: Regional Judicialization in the Arab World, in* EXPERIMENTS IN INTERNATIONAL ADJUDICATION: HISTORICAL ACCOUNTS 186 (Ignacio de la Rasilla & Jorge E. Vinuales eds., 2019) (noting that "pan-Arabism has been used by Arab Maghreb countries to buttress their legitimacy and sovereignty, externally vis-à-vis non-Arab states and internally vis-à-vis each other … but at the same time [feared that] proactive Arab unity would threaten their sovereignty"). *Id.* at 186.

[9] *Id.* at 182.

[10] *Id.* at 184.

[11] Cesare P.R. Romano, *Trial and Error in International Judicialization, in* THE OXFORD HANDBOOK OF INTERNATIONAL ADJUDICATION 117 (Cesare PR Romano, Karen J. Alter, & Yuval Shany eds., 2014).

[12] WILLIAM ZARTMAN, GOVERNMENT AND POLITICS IN NORTHERN AFRICA 184 (1964).

[13] EMILIA JUSTYNA POWELL, ISLAMIC LAW AND INTERNATIONAL LAW: PEACEFUL RESOLUTION OF DISPUTES (2019).

Mbengue's view that inter-state dispute settlement in Africa indicates a preference for solitary diplomacy.[14] However, Powell and Mbengue's views are contradicted by the fact that Islamic states in North Africa have litigated in inter-state disputes before the ICJ.[15] In our view, the combination of all these factors compounded by the relatively weak to the non-existence of the AMU as a sub-regional body makes cooperation around any set of issues including dispute settlement through an international court next to impossible. Some scholars have, however, argued that it is the weakness in the rule of law in the Maghreb region, which is a precondition for international adjudication, that partly explains why this Court was "nipped in the bud."[16]

Part Two: Individual Reference Guide to Africa's International Courts
The African Court on Human and Peoples' Rights (ACtHPR)

Establishment
The Member States of the now defunct Organization of African Unity (OAU) adopted the Banjul Charter on 27 June 1981 in Nairobi, Kenya.[17] The Banjul Charter entered into force on 21 October 1986. In an effort to achieve the objectives set out in the Banjul Charter, Member States adopted the Protocol to the African Charter on Human and Peoples' Rights on the Establishment of an African Court on Human and Peoples' Rights on 9 June 1998 which entered into force on January 25, 2004 (the Protocol). Previously, the African human rights system only had a quasi-judicial[18] and promotional[19] institution in the form of the Commission.[20] Article 1 of the Protocol establishes the ACtHPR. The Court, which is also discussed in Chapter 6 of this book, is set up to complement the protective mandate of the ACHPR.[21] The Court started functioning officially in 2006 when its first set of eleven judges were

---

[14] Makane Mbengue, *African Perspectives on Inter-State Litigation, in* INTERNATIONAL LAW DISPUTES: WEIGHING THE OPTIONS 182 (Natalie Klein ed., Cambridge Univ. Press 2014).

[15] *See also* Cesare P.R. Romano, *Mirage in the Desert: Regional Judicialization in the Arab World, in* EXPERIMENTS IN INTERNATIONAL ADJUDICATION: HISTORICAL ACCOUNTS 182 (Ignacio de la Rasilla & Jorge E. Vinuales eds., 2019) (arguing that existing international adjudicative courts have been the "fora of choice for many Arab disputes").

[16] Cesare P.R. Romano, *Trial and Error in International Judicialization, in* THE OXFORD HANDBOOK OF INTERNATIONAL ADJUDICATION 118 (Cesare PR Romano, Karen J. Alter & Yuval Shany eds., 2014).

[17] The Charter is referred to as the Banjul Charter to celebrate Sir Dawda Jawara, a former head of the State of Gambia who played a pioneering role towards its adoption.

[18] Frans Viljoen, *Understanding and Overcoming Challenges in Accessing the African Court on Human and Peoples' Rights*, 67 INT'L & COMP. L. Q. 64 (2018).

[19] African Charter on Human and Peoples' Rights (hereinafter "Banjul Charter"), art. 30.

[20] Victor Dankwa, *The Promotional Role of the African Commission on Human and Peoples' Rights, in* THE AFRICAN CHARTER ON HUMAN AND PEOPLES' RIGHTS: THE SYSTEM OF PRACTICE 1986–2000, at 335 (Malcolm Evans & Rachel Murray eds., 2002).

[21] The Protocol, art. 2.

elected. Unlike the ACHPR which could arguably only deliver non-binding views or recommendations on communications or petitions, the ACtHPR issues judgments that are legally binding on the state parties to the Protocol.[22]

Jurisdiction

The Court has broad jurisdiction over both contentious cases[23] and advisory opinions. Jurisdiction over contentious cases presented by individuals and NGOs is subject to the state sued in the Court having accepted the jurisdiction of the Court by signing a declaration to that effect as required under Article 34(6) of the Protocol. The Court has jurisdiction over all cases and disputes submitted to it on the interpretation and application of the Charter, Protocol, and other human rights instruments ratified by Member States.[24] The Court may also give an advisory opinion on any legal matter relating to the Banjul Charter or any other relevant human rights instrument. The Court is limited from giving an advisory opinion on a matter being examined before the Commission.[25] In exercising its function, the Court applies the provisions of the Charter as well as any other human rights instruments ratified by the states concerned.[26] A minimum number of seven judges is required for quorum.[27] A party to a case is to be represented by a legal representative of their choice.[28] The Court delivers judgment ninety days after the completion of deliberations.[29] The judgment is read in open court and is considered final. A judgment of the Court represents the unanimous or majority decision with judges being entitled to deliver dissenting opinions.[30]

Access to the Court

The access to the African court is bifurcated into direct access and indirect. Direct access to the Court is granted to the following entities: the Commission; a state party which has lodged a complaint to the Commission; a state party against which the complaint is lodged at the Commission; a state party whose citizen is a victim of human rights violation; and African Intergovernmental Organizations.[31] Additionally, the Court may entitle NGOs with observer status before the Commission, and individuals to institute cases directly before it but only subject to Article 34(6) of the Protocol.[32] This provision then requires that at the time

---

[22] Joseph M. Isanga, *The Constitutive Act of the African Union, African Courts and the Protection of Human Rights: New Dispensation?*, 11 SANTA CLARA J. INT'L L. 269, 284 (2013).
[23] KAREN ALTER, THE NEW TERRAIN OF INTERNATIONAL LAW (2014).
[24] The Protocol, art. 3.
[25] *Id.* art. 4.
[26] *Id.* art. 7.
[27] *Id.* art. 23.
[28] *Id.* art. 10(2).
[29] *Id.* art. 28(1).
[30] *Id.* art. 28.
[31] *Id.* arts. 5(1)(a)–(e).
[32] *Id.* art. 5(3).

of ratification or any time after ratification, the state ratifying the Protocol can make a declaration accepting the competence of the Court to receive cases under Article 5(3) of the Protocol from NGOs and individuals. The Court shall not receive any petition under Article 5(3) involving a state party which has not made such declaration (the Article 34(6) declaration).[33] There are therefore four cumulative criteria for access in cases involving NGOs and individuals: first, the state involved must have ratified the Banjul Charter; second, the state must have ratified the Court's Protocol; third, (in cases of NGOs) it must have observer status before the Commission; and finally, the state must have made a declaration under Article 34(6).

The indirect access to the Court is set out in Rules 118 and 119 of the Commission's Rules of Procedure. What this means is that the indirect access route is *only* possible through the Commission. Leading African human rights scholar Frans Viljoen has argued that indirect access should also be possible through referral by the African Committee on the Rights and Welfare of the Child if the access provisions of the Protocol are interpreted with a purposive and non-textualist approach.[34] Viljoen offered this as a critique of the Advisory Opinion rendered by the Court barring the possibility of a referral by the African Committee on the Rights and Welfare of the Child.[35] The possibility of such indirect access through the Commission would have carved a path to file cases in the Court by NGOs and individuals in the absence of the requirements on ratification of the Protocol and the Article 34(6) optional declaration that are perquisites to filing cases in the Court.

Under the current rules of the Court, indirect access route has four sub-routes. First, the Commission can refer its non-compliance merits findings to the Court.[36] Second, the Commission can refer its non-compliance interim measures to the Court.[37] Third, the Commission can refer serious or massive human rights violations at any stage of the examination of a communication when it deems it necessary.[38] Finally, pursuant to Article 6 of the African Court Protocol, the Court can request the Commission to give its opinion on admissibility of a communication pending before the Court or the Court can transfer a communication to the Commission.[39]

---

[33] *Id.* art. 34(6); Michelot Yogogombaye v. Senegal, Appl. No. 1/2008, ACtHPR, Judgment (Dec. 15, 2009).

[34] Viljoen, *supra* note 18, at 85.

[35] Advisory Opinion 2/2013, The African Committee of Experts on the Rights and Welfare of the Child on the Standing of the African Committee of Experts on the Rights and Welfare of the Child before the African Court and Human and Peoples' Rights (Dec. 5, 2014).

[36] Rule 118(1) of the Rules of Procedure of the African Commission on Human and Peoples' Rights.

[37] Rule 118(2) of the Rules of Procedure of the African Commission on Human and Peoples' Rights; The Protocol, art. 6(3).

[38] Rule 118(3), Rules of Procedure of the African Commission on Human and Peoples' Rights.

[39] Rule 119(1), Rules of Procedure of the African Commission on Human and Peoples' Rights.

Composition and Organization

The Court is composed of eleven judges.[40] To be elected as a judge, one must be a jurist of high moral character, and of recognized practical, judicial, or academic competence.[41] One must also possess experience in the field of human and peoples' rights. Judges are nominated by state parties, who can nominate up to three candidates, two of whom must be nationals of the state. The Secretary-General then prepares a list of nominees to be transmitted to the state parties thirty days prior to the next session of the Assembly. The judges are elected by secret ballot by the Assembly. In doing so, the Assembly should ensure that there is representation of the main regions of Africa as well as gender representation.[42] Judges are appointed for a period of six years and may be re-elected only once.[43] The Court elects a president and vice president for a period of two years and they also may be re-elected once.[44] The President is employed on a full-time basis to perform judicial functions, thus resides at the seat of the Court (currently in Arusha).[45] A judge cannot be suspended or removed from office unless found to be no longer fulfilling the conditions required to be a judge.[46] A judge who is elected to replace another judge whose term has not expired will serve until the end of his predecessor's term.[47]

The Economic Community for West African States (ECOWAS) Court of Justice

Establishment

The heads of state and government of the West African states formed ECOWAS when they signed the Treaty of the Economic Community of West African States in Lagos Nigeria on May 28, 1975 (Treaty of Lagos). Article 4 of the Treaty established institutions to achieve the aims set out in the Treaty. Among the institutions created was the Tribunal for the community.[48] In 1991, the Member States revised the Treaty and through Articles 6 and 15 of the Revised Treaty of the Economic Community of West African States (ECOWAS Treaty), established the Community Court of Justice. In pursuance with Article 6(2) of the ECOWAS Treaty, the Member States adopted the Protocol on the Community Court of Justice.[49]

---

[40] The Protocol, art. 11.
[41] Id.
[42] Id. art. 14(2) & (3).
[43] Id. art. 15.
[44] Id. art. 21(1).
[45] Id. art. 21(2).
[46] The Protocol, art. 19(1).
[47] Id. art. 15(3).
[48] Article 1(d) of the Treaty of the Economic Community of West African States.
[49] Protocol A/P.I/7/91 on the Community Court of Justice.

Jurisdiction

The Court has jurisdiction to hear and determine disputes referred to it on the interpretation and application of the provisions of the Treaty.[50] Disputes regarding the Treaty or its application can only to be settled by the Court.[51] The Court may also give advisory opinions on questions arising from the Treaty.[52] A request for an advisory opinion is to be made by a Member State, the ECOWAS Authority (the highest ECOWAS decision-making body), the Council, the Executive Secretary, and institutions of the community.[53] The Court has personal jurisdiction over disputes between Member States; and disputes between one or more Member States and institutions of the community.[54] In 2004, in *Olajide Afolabi v Nigeria*, the ECOWAS Court declined to adjudicate over a human rights claim arguing that the Protocol did not confer jurisdiction over human rights.[55] In 2005, Member States adopted the Supplementary Protocol A/SP.1/01/05 which expressly provides that ECOWAS Court has the power to hear cases relating to the violation of human rights.[56] This was done in pursuance of the fundamental principles of ECOWAS in which Member States undertake to recognize, promote, and protect human and peoples' rights in accordance with the Banjul Charter.[57]

A Member State may institute proceedings against another Member State or institution of the community on behalf of its nationals.[58] Efforts to have the dispute resolved amicably must have first been attempted and failed.[59] This is not the case for human rights disputes. Private litigants (natural and legal persons) from ECOWAS Member States may approach the Court without exhausting local remedies.[60] In *Hadijatou Mani Koraou v Republic of Niger* the Court held that an application of a human rights violation before the Court must not be anonymous or pending before another international court.[61] A party to a dispute is to be represented by one or two agents nominated by that party. These agents may request assistance of one or more Advocates or Counsels who are recognized to practice law by the laws and regulations of Member States.[62] Proceedings of the Court are in

---

[50] Article 9(2) of the Protocol on the Community Court of Justice (hereinafter "Protocol on the CCJ").

[51] Protocol on the CCJ, art. 22(1).

[52] Protocol on the CCJ, art. 10(1).

[53] *Id.*

[54] Protocol on the CCJ, art. 9(2).

[55] Lucyline Nkatha Murungi & Jacqui Gallinetti, *The Role of Sub-Regional Courts in the African Human Rights System*, 7 SUR—INT'L J. HUMAN RTS. 119, 133 (2010).

[56] Supplementary Protocol A/SP1/01/05 on the Community Court of Justice.

[57] Solomon Ebobrah, *Human Rights Developments in African Sub-regional Economic Communities during 2010*, 11 AFR. HUMAN RTS. L. J. 216, 228 (2011).

[58] Protocol on the CCJ, art. 9(3).

[59] *Id.*

[60] Karen Alter, James Gathii, & Laurence Helfer, *Backlash against International Courts in West, East and Southern Africa: Causes and Consequences*, 27 EUR. J. INT'L L. 292, 296 (2016).

[61] Hadijatou Mani Koraou v. Republic of Niger, ECW/CCJ/JUD/06/08 (Oct. 27, 2008).

[62] Protocol on the CCJ, art. 12.

two parts: written and oral.[63] The President and two other judges are required for a sitting of the Court to be valid.[64] More judges may sit but the number of judges sitting must be an uneven number.[65]

The Court determines disputes in accordance with the Treaty and the Rules of Procedure of the Court.[66] It may also apply the body of laws contained in Article 38 of the Statute of the International Court of Justice.[67] The Banjul Charter has also been used by the Court as a rights catalogue.[68] Decisions are read in open court with reasons for the decision being stated.[69] The decisions are final.[70] That means that they can only be reviewed where there is discovery of a fact that would have a decisive factor on the decision that was unknown to the Court or the party.[71] Under the Treaty, such ignorance should not be due to negligence.[72] An application for revision must be made within five years.[73]

Composition and Organization

The seat of the Court is determined by the Authority which is the highest ECOWAS decision-making body. However, the Court may decide to sit in the territory of another Member State where the facts of the case demand.[74] Currently, the Court sits in Abuja, Nigeria. The official languages of the Court are English and French.[75] The Court is composed of seven independent judges selected and appointed by the Authority from nationals of Member States of the community.[76] The appointees must possess the qualifications of appointment to the highest judicial office in their countries.[77] The seven judges of the Court elect a president and vice president from among themselves. The President and Vice President serve for a term of three years.[78] Judges are appointed from a list of persons nominated by Member States.[79] Nominees must be between forty and sixty years of age.[80] A judge of the Court is not eligible for re-appointment after they attain sixty-five years of age.[81] Judges of the Court are appointed for a period of five years which is only renewable

---

[63] *Id.* art. 13.
[64] *Id.* art. 14.
[65] *Id.* art. 13.
[66] *Id.* art. 19(1).
[67] *Id.* art. 19(1).
[68] Murungi & Gallinetti, *supra* note 55, at 119, 130.
[69] Protocol on the CCJ, art. 19(2).
[70] *Id.*
[71] *Id.* art. 25.
[72] *Id.* art. 25.
[73] *Id.* art. 25(4).
[74] *Id.* art. 26.
[75] *Id.* art. 31.
[76] *Id.* art. 3(2).
[77] *Id.* art. 3(1).
[78] *Id.* art. 3(2).
[79] *Id.* art. 3(4).
[80] *Id.* art. 3(7).
[81] *Id.* art. 3(7).

once.[82] A judge whose term has expired shall remain in office until his successor has been appointed.[83] The Protocol requires a judge whose term has expired to continue hearing the cases which he had begun.[84] A judge may resign at any time by writing a letter of resignation.[85] Where a judge is unable to perform his functions, has a physical or mental disability, or is involved in gross misconduct, the Court draws a report which is transmitted to the Authority which may relieve the judge in question of his post.[86] Article 4(11) of the Protocol prohibits judges from exercising any political or administrative functions, or engaging in other professional occupations.

East Africa Court of Justice (EACJ)

Establishment of the Court

The establishment and history of the establishment of the EACJ can be traced to the Treaty for the Establishment of the East African Community (EAC Treaty) signed on November 30, 1999 by the heads of state and governments of East African States. That Treaty entered into force on July 7, 2000. It was subsequently amended on December 14, 2006 and again on August 20, 2007. Article 9(1)(e) of the EAC Treaty establishes the EACJ. The Court is mandated to ensure the adherence to law in the interpretation, application, and compliance of the EAC Treaty.[87] The EACJ became operational on November 30, 2001.

Jurisdiction

The EACJ has a contentious and advisory jurisdiction.[88] In both instances, its primary role is that of the interpretation and application of East African Community (EAC) treaties.[89] In its original structure, the Court had one chamber.[90] However, amendments to the Treaty for the Establishment of the EAC (EAC Establishment Treaty) that came into effect in March 2007 created an Appellate Division, making the Court a two-chamber court.[91] The First Division is comprised of ten

---

[82] *Id.* art. 4(1).
[83] *Id.* art. 4(3).
[84] *Id.* art. 4(3).
[85] *Id.* art. 7.
[86] *Id.* art. 4(7).
[87] Article 23 of the Treaty for the Establishment of the East African Community, 2144 U.N.T.S. 255 (Nov. 30, 1999) (hereinafter "EAC Treaty").
[88] EAC Treaty, art. 27–36.
[89] EAC Treaty, art. 27(1).
[90] *User Guide*, EACJ 11 (2013), https://www.eacj.org//wp-content/uploads/2013/11/EACJ-Court-Users-Guide-September-2013.pdf.
[91] EAC Treaty, art. 24. The EAC Treaty provides that the Court "shall consist of a First Division and an Appellate Division." *Id.* art. 23(2). These amendments were made following a decision of the EACJ that was strongly objected to by the government of Kenya. For more on the circumstances leading to the amendments, *see* Chapter 7 in this book.

judges,[92] two from each of the five EAC Member States.[93] The Appellate Division is comprised of five judges,[94] one from each of the five Member States.[95] The current location of the Court is Arusha, Tanzania. This location is deemed to be temporary; a permanent seat for the Court has not yet been determined by the Summit,[96] the highest organ in the EAC.[97] The Summit also appoints judges to the Court.[98] Other than the President of the Court, who also heads the Appellate Division, and the Principal Judge of the First Instance Division,[99] the judges do not reside in Arusha.[100] They come to Arusha when there is a prescheduled convening of Court business.[101] Judges hold office for a seven-year period[102] and must retire at seventy years of age.[103] As further evidence of the novelty of this Court, the salaries, conditions of service, and other terms of EACJ judges are yet to be determined.[104]

As noted earlier, the EACJ has jurisdiction "over the interpretation and application" of the EAC Establishment Treaty.[105] The Treaty that established the EACJ also provides that it "shall have such other original, appellate, human rights and other jurisdiction *as will be determined* by the Council at a suitable subsequent date."[106]

---

[92] EAC Treaty, art. 24(2) (providing that the First Instance Division shall not be comprised of more than ten judges).

[93] *Id.* art. 24(1)(a) (providing that no more than two judges can be appointed from the same EAC Partner State).

[94] *Id.* art. 24(2) (providing that the Appellate Division shall not be comprised of more than five judges).

[95] *Id.* art. 24(1)(b).

[96] *Id.* art. 47 (providing that the "[s]eat of the Court shall be determined by the Summit").

[97] *Id.* art. 10 (stating that the Summit comprises the heads of government of the five East African Partner States).

[98] *Id.* art. 24.

[99] Under the EAC Treaty, the President "shall direct the work of the Court, represent it, regulate the disposition of matters before the Court, and preside over its sessions." *Id.* art. 24(10). Under art. 24(8), the "Principal Judge shall direct the work of the First Instance Division, represent it, regulate the disposition of the matters brought before the Court and preside over its sessions." *Id.* art. 24(8). The EAC Treaty provides that '[t]he President and Vice-President ... shall not be nationals of the same Partner State.' *Id.* art. 24(6).

[100] *EACJ Judge President, Principal Judge Now Full-Time in Arusha*, EACJ (July 2, 2012), https://www.eacj.org/?p=397.

[101] Since 2013, both divisions of the Court have held longer quarterly sessions every year as the number of cases has increased. For example, the First Division continued to meet between February 4 and 28. See *EACJ 5th Quarter Sessions Resume Today*, EACJ (Jan. 27, 2014), http://eacj.org/?p=1756.

[102] EAC Treaty, *supra* note 87, at art. 25(1).

[103] *Id.* art. 25(2). As a matter of practice, judicial appointments are staggered to prevent all the judges' terms coming to an end at the same time. In the first appointment round, judges are appointed for seven years. In the second appointment round, judges are appointed for five years. The cycle is then repeated with each subsequent appointment round. Interview with Justice Butasi, Principal Judge of the EACJ First Division, in Arusha, Tanzania (June 25, 2014).

[104] See EACJ, Strategic Plan: 2010–2015, at v (Apr. 2010), http://eacj.org/wp-content/uploads/2013/09/EACJ_StrategicPlan_2010-2015.pdf. The EAC Treaty provides that the Summit, which consists of the heads of government of EAC states, shall determine the salary, terms, and conditions upon recommendation of the EAC Council of Ministers. EAC Treaty, *supra* note 87, at art. 25(5).

[105] EAC Treaty, *supra* note 87, at art. 27(1). In addition, the EAC Treaty provides that the role of the Court shall be to "ensure the adherence to law in the interpretation and application of and compliance with this Treaty." *Id.* art. 23(1).

[106] *Id.* art. 27(2) (emphasis added).

At the 15th Ordinary Summit of the EAC's heads of state, a decision was made to defer giving the EACJ jurisdiction over human rights and to instead consult with the AU on the matter.[107] The Summit, however, extended the Court's jurisdiction over trade and investment cases as well as cases arising under the EAC's Monetary Union treaty.[108] The Court also has jurisdiction over disputes between the EAC and its employees;[109] arbitral disputes arising from commercial contracts between private parties; and agreements to which the EAC, any of its institutions, or EAC Member States are parties if an arbitration clause in such a contract or agreement confers such jurisdiction.[110]

For the parties with direct access, the jurisdiction of the Court, subject to the limitation of Article 27(1) of the EAC Treaty that provides that the Court shall be granted jurisdiction over human rights at a future date,[111] is compulsory once the relevant state has ratified the EAC Treaty. However, under its *Katabazi* doctrine, the Court has assumed jurisdiction over human rights cases based on the argument that in doing so, the Court is simply exercising its jurisdiction to interpret and apply treaty provisions.[112]

Access to the Court

The access to the EACJ can only be made through direct access as stipulated in Articles 28, 29, and 30 of the EAC Treaty. This means that unlike the ACtHPR, the EACJ does not have any means of indirect access. Any person residing in the EAC can bring cases to the EACJ.[113] Such suit can only be filed against one of the EAC Member States or an institution of the EAC for a declaration that its conduct is inconsistent with the EAC Treaty.[114] Employees of the EAC may sue regarding

[107] *See* EAC IRC Repository, Communiqué the 15th Ordinary Summit of the EAC Heads of State, para. 16 (Nov. 30, 2013), http://repository.eac.int/bitstream/handle/11671/546/Annex%20VI-COMMUNIQUE%20OF%20THE%2015TH%20ORDINARY%20SUMMIT%20OF%20HEADS%20OF%20STATE.pdf?sequence=1&isAllowed=y (extending the jurisdiction of the EACJ to include commercial, investment, and monetary matters, but deciding to work with the AU (rather than the EACJ) on matters relating to human rights and crimes against humanity).
[108] EAC IRC Repository, Communiqué of the 16th Ordinary Summit of the East African Community Heads of State, para. 9 (Feb. 20, 2015), http://repository.eac.int/bitstream/handle/11671/547/COMMUNIQUE%2016TH%20ORDINARY%20EAC%20HEADS%20OF%20STATE%20SUMMIT%2018TH%20FEB%202015-1.pdf?sequence=1&isAllowed=y. *See also* EAC, EACJ Gets New Judges and Deputy Principal Judge (Jan. 27, 2015), http://eacj.org/?p=1754 (noting that "[t]he summit approved the Council recommendation to extend the jurisdiction of the [EACJ] to cover trade and investment as well as matters associated with the East African Monetary Union. On Human Rights matters as well as crimes against humanity, the Summit directed the Council of Ministers to work with the African Union on this matter.")
[109] EAC Treaty, *supra* note 87, at art. 31.
[110] *Id.* art. 32.
[111] *Id.* art. 27(1).
[112] Katabazi and 21 others v. Secretary General of the East African Community and Another, Ref. No. 1 of 2007, EACJ 3 (Nov. 1, 2007).
[113] EAC Treaty, supra note 87, art. 30(1).
[114] *Id.* art. 30 (providing that in such a case the Court could be asked to determine "the legality of any Act, regulation, directive, decision or action of Partner State or an institution of the EAC on grounds that such Act, regulation, directive, decision or action is unlawful or is an infringement of the provisions

the terms and conditions of their service to the EAC.[115] The Court's arbitral juris-diction can be invoked pursuant to an agreement or contract between commercial actors, the EAC, or EAC Member States.[116] A matter may be referred to the Court first by a Partner State.[117] Second, by the Secretary General (SG) of the Community possesses a power of ensuring the enforcement of the Court's decision. The SG can do so by submitting a reference to the Court in cases where the SG considers that a Partner State has failed to fulfil an obligation under the Treaty or has infringed a provision of the Treaty.[118] Before reference to the Court, the SG is required to submit a report with observations and findings of the infringement or violation to the Partner State.[119] The Appellate Division of the EACJ has affirmed the holding in the *Katabazi* case that there is nothing in the EAC Treaty preventing the SG from conducting an investigation into treaty violations on his or her own initiative.[120] Further, the Appellate Division has held that failure to submit a report under Article 29(1) may constitute a contravention of the Treaty.[121]

If the Partner State does not submit any responses to a report by the SG under Article 29(1) within four months, its observations are unsatisfactory, the SG is re-quired to submit the matter to the Council.[122] The Council then decides whether the SG can refer the matter to the Court or the matter is resolved by the Council.[123] In addition, the Council is empowered to direct the SG to refer the matter to the Court if it fails to resolve the matter.[124] In all the proceedings before the Court, every party to a dispute must be represented by an advocate entitled to appear in the Court of any of the Partner States.[125]

Finally, the third entities that have direct access to the Court are legal and nat-ural persons who are resident in a Partner State.[126] These entities include resident companies, NGOs, and individuals in the six Partner States in the EAC. They are granted access to the Court to make any reference to the Court to determine the legality of an Act, regulation, directive, decision, or action of a Partner State, or an institution of the Community on the grounds that such Act, regulation, directive,

---

of this Treaty"). A carve-out in art. 30(3) provides that the Court shall have no jurisdiction "where an Act, regulation, directive, decision or action has been reserved under this Treaty to an institution of a Partner state." *Id*. art. 30(3).

[115] *Id*. art. 31.
[116] *Id*. art. 32.
[117] *Id*. art. 28.
[118] *Id*, art. 29(1).
[119] *Id*.
[120] Democratic Party v. The Secretary General of the East African Community and Others, Appeal No. 1 of 2014, paras. 76 and 77 (July 28, 2015).
[121] *Id*. at para. 79(v).
[122] EAC Treaty, *supra* note 87, art. 29(2).
[123] *Id*.
[124] *Id*. art. 29(3).
[125] *Id*. art. 37(1).
[126] *Id*. art. 30 .

decision, or action is unlawful or in an infringement of the provisions of the Treaty.[127] This access provision makes it possible for a non-citizens of the EAC Partner State to make a reference to the Court since the requirement for access is for residency and not citizenship. This widens the doors of access to many more entities than would have access to the Court were the provision to be only for citizens in the Partner States.

Composition and Organization

As noted earlier, the EACJ has two divisions: a First Instance Division and an Appellate Division. The Court is composed of a maximum of fifteen judges. Ten of the fifteen judges sit at the First Instance Division while five sit at the Appellate Division.[128] Judges are appointed by the Summit from a list of persons nominated by the Partner States,[129] and serve for a term of seven years.[130] The Summit also appoints, from the Appellate Division, two judges to serve as the President and Vice President of the Court.[131] A principal judge and a deputy principal judge are also appointed from the First Instance Division to direct the work of the division. Before the 2006/7 amendments, the EACJ consisted of no more than six judges, with no more than two from each of the original three Partner States. This structure was based on the fact that the EAC then had five members who would appoint two First Instance Judges (for a maximum of ten) and one Appellate Division Judge (up to a maximum of five as provided by the EAC Treaty). When South Sudan joined the EAC in 2016, the membership rose to six but the EAC Treaty was not amended to accommodate the appointment of more judges in equal numbers from the expanded membership of the EAC. The Court has now implemented a rotational system of appointments to accommodate the expanded membership.

A judge may resign at any time by giving a three months' written notice to the Chairman of the Summit.[132] Misconduct, bankruptcy, conviction of a criminal offence, or the inability to perform functions may result in the removal of a judge from office.[133] Removal from office is only done by the Summit. A judge may be suspended pending determination from a tribunal concerning the removal from office.[134] In such a case, a temporary judge is appointed for the duration of the suspension.[135]

Disputes in which the Community is a party are not excluded from national jurisdiction solely on this basis.[136] The official language of the Court is English. The

---

[127] *Id.* art. 30.
[128] *Id.* art. 24(2).
[129] *Id.* art. 24(1).
[130] *Id.* art. 25.
[131] *Id.* art. 24(2).
[132] EAC Treaty, *supra* note 87, art. 24(5).
[133] *Id.* art. 26(1).
[134] *Id.* art. 26(2).
[135] *Id.* art. 26(2A).
[136] *Id.* art. 33.

seat of the Court is determined by the Summit.[137] Decisions of the Court are delivered in open court.[138] Only one judgment is delivered, which is the majority decision. A judge, however, has the option of delivering a dissenting opinion.[139] An application of review is only permitted where there is discovery of a fact that would have had a decisive influence on the judgment that was unknown to the Court and the parties before the decision was made.[140] Article 35A of the Treaty provides for the right of appeal which may only be done on points of law, grounds of lack of jurisdiction, or procedural irregularity.

South Africa Development Community (SADC) Tribunal

Establishment of the Tribunal

On August 17, 1992, in Windhoek, Namibia, the heads of state or government of the Southern African states signed the Declaration and Treaty establishing the SADC.[141] Through Article 9(1)(g) of the Treaty a Tribunal was established. To give effect to the goals set out in the Treaty, Article 22 made provision for Member States to conclude a series of Protocols. On August 7, 2000 at the SADC Summit in Windhoek, the Member States adopted the Protocol on the Tribunal of the Southern African Development Community.[142] The Protocol makes provisions on the functioning of the Tribunal including organization, jurisdiction, and procedure of the Tribunal. The Tribunal also functions in accordance with the Rules of Procedure of the Southern African Development Community Tribunal. The first Protocol of the Tribunal and the Rules of Procedure (Tribunal Protocol) was adopted by the SADC Summit on August 7, 2000 and was subsequently amended on October 3, 2002. As we note later, the SADC Tribunal established in 2000 was disbanded and a 2014 Protocol was introduced to re-establish it, this time without individual access to the Tribunal, but it has yet to come into force.[143]

Jurisdiction

The Tribunal as constituted by the 2000 Protocol had jurisdiction over all cases relating to the interpretation and application of the Treaty; interpretation, application, and validity of the Protocols, all subsidiary instruments adopted with the framework of the Community and acts of the institution of the Community. It

---

[137] *Id.* art. 47.
[138] *Id.* art. 35(2).
[139] *Id.*
[140] *Id.* art. 35(3).
[141] Declaration and Treaty establishing the Southern African Development Community (hereinafter "Declaration and Treaty").
[142] Preamble, Agreement Amending the Protocol on the Tribunal, Southern African Development Community 2000.
[143] For the full account of how this happened, *see* Chapter 7 in this book.

also had jurisdiction over all matters specifically provided in any agreements that Member States may conclude among themselves or within the Community and which confer jurisdiction on the Tribunal.[144] The Tribunal also had jurisdiction over disputes between Member States, and between natural or legal persons and Member States.[145] The claims by natural persons could only be accepted after the exhaustion of domestic remedies, and the Protocol also explicitly confers compulsory jurisdiction on the Tribunal.[146] The Protocol empowered the Tribunal to give preliminary rulings in proceedings of any kind and between any parties before the courts or tribunals of the states. However, it did not have original jurisdiction.[147] The Tribunal also had exclusive jurisdiction on disputes between the Member States and the Community[148] over disputes between natural or legal persons and the Community,[149] and over disputes between the Community and staff.[150] Finally, the Tribunal had advisory jurisdiction which could have been requested by the Summit or by the Council in terms of Article 16(4) of the SADC Treaty.[151]

The Tribunal had no express mention of jurisdiction over human rights.[152] Inclusion of a specific human rights mandate for the SADC Tribunal was debated and rejected.[153] While there is no express human rights mandate before the removal of its jurisdiction to receive cases from individuals in the 2014 Protocol the Tribunal decided several human rights cases. One of the most well-known cases is *Mike Campbell (PVT) Ltd and 78 others v The Republic of Zimbabwe* (the *Campbell* case). In that case Zimbabwe challenged the jurisdiction of the Court arguing that the Tribunal had no jurisdiction over human rights issues. In response, the Tribunal held that the fact that the SADC Treaty included references to human rights, democracy, and rule of law as principles of SADC sufficed to grant it jurisdiction over these matters.[154]

The jurisdiction of the Tribunal extended to Member States, the Community, and, prior to 2014, natural or legal persons who could bring cases before the Tribunal.[155] A dispute could have been referred to the Tribunal either by the Member States, or by the competent institution or organ of the Community and, prior to 2014, by natural or legal persons. Representation of states and institutions of the Community was possible through an appointed agent.[156]

---

[144] Protocol on the Tribunal in the Southern African Development Community 2000, art. 14 (hereinafter "Protocol on the Tribunal 2000").

[145] *Id.* art. 15(1).

[146] *Id.* arts. 15(2) & (3).

[147] *Id.* art. 16.

[148] *Id.* art. 17.

[149] *Id.* art. 18.

[150] *Id.* art. 19.

[151] *Id.* art. 20.

[152] Murungi & Gallinetti, *supra* note 55, at 123.

[153] *Id.* at 132.

[154] *Id.* at 133.

[155] Declaration and Treaty, *supra* note 141, arts. 17, 18.

[156] Protocol on the Tribunal 2000, *supra* note 144, at art. 27.

Decisions of the Tribunal were to be considered final and binding.[157] The decision were required to be in writing and delivered in open court stating reasons for decision. Decision were required to be taken by majority.[158] An application for a review of a decision could have been made where there is discovery of a fact which might have had decisive influence on the decision of the Tribunal.[159] Enforcement of a judgment was governed by the civil procedure rules in the territory of the state in which the judgment was to be enforced.[160] A party concerned was entitled to refer non-compliance of a decision by a state to the Tribunal.[161] Where the Tribunal found that there has been non-compliance, it reports its finding to the Summit for appropriate action.[162]

As alluded to earlier, the SADC Tribunal has been suspended since 2010 after it made a ruling against Zimbabwe in the *Campbell* case and is discussed more extensively in Chapter 7 of this book.[163] Zimbabwe failed to comply with the decision of the Tribunal. The Tribunal referred the non-compliance of Zimbabwe to the Summit in accordance with Article 32(4) of the Protocol on the Tribunal of the SADC.[164] Zimbabwe submitted a legal opinion challenging the legality of the SADC Tribunal on the grounds that the Protocol never entered into force.[165] In April 2010, Zimbabwe's non-compliance was discussed by SADC Ministers of Justice and Attorneys Generals. They then submitted their advice to the Summit.[166] At the same time, the Tribunal made another ruling of non-compliance. In August 2010, the Summit decided not to reappoint judges to the Tribunal.[167] The judges of the Tribunal at the time were to hear and determine the pending cases before them but did not take any new cases.[168] In 2014, a new protocol on the Tribunal was adopted but it has not entered into force. The new Protocol establishes a new judicial organ with limited jurisdiction.[169] Under the new Protocol, the Tribunal does not hear and determine complaints from private litigants.[170]

---

[157] Declaration and Treaty, *supra* note 141, at art. 16.

[158] Protocol on the Tribunal 2000, *supra* note 144, at art. 24.

[159] *Id.* art. 26.

[160] *Id.* art. 32(1).

[161] *Id.* art. 32(4).

[162] *Id.* art. 32(5).

[163] Henok Asmelash, *Southern African Development Community (SADC) Tribunal, in* MAX PLANCK ENCYCLOPEDIA OF INTERNATIONAL PROCEDURAL LAW (June 1, 2017), https://papers.ssrn.com/sol3/papers.cfm?abstract_id=2991562.

[164] Solomon Ebobrah, *Human Rights Developments in African Sub-regional Economic Communities during 2010*, 11 AFR. HUMAN RTS. L. J. 216, 247 (2011).

[165] *Id.*

[166] *Id.*

[167] *Id.* at 228.

[168] *Id.*

[169] Gino Naldi & Konstantinos Magliveras, *The New SADC Tribunal: Or the Emasculation of an International Tribunal*, 63 NETHERLANDS INT'L L. R. 133–59 (2016).

[170] Karen Alter, James Gathii, & Laurence Helfer, *Backlash Against International Courts in West, East and Southern Africa: Causes and Consequences*, 27 EUR. J. INT'L L. 292, 294 (2016).

Composition and Organization

Under the Agreement Amending the Protocol on the Tribunal, Southern African Development Community 2000, the Tribunal consisted of a minimum of ten members, appointed from nationals of Member States. The appointees were required to possess qualifications required for appointment to the highest judicial position in their states or are jurists of recognized competence.[171] Each Member State was entitled to nominate one candidate. From the list of nominated candidates, the Council recommended ten nominees to the Summit for appointment as Members of the Tribunal.[172] Members of the Tribunal were appointed for a term of five years, renewable only once for a period of five years.[173] Of the ten members to the Tribunal, there were five regular members and five additional members. Regular members were designated to sit regularly on the Tribunal. The additional members could be invited to sit on the Tribunal by the President when a regular member was temporarily absent or unable to perform his or her function.[174]

The President of the Tribunal was elected by the Tribunal for a term of three years.[175] The 2000 Protocol was silent on whether this term was renewable. Where the President was temporarily absent or unable to perform their functions, other Members could elect an acting president.[176] Members of the Tribunal could resign at any time by a letter to the Council through the Executive Secretary.[177] Dismissal of Members could only be done in accordance with the Rules.

Constitution of the Tribunal required three members whereas a full bench is constituted of five members.[178] However, no two or more members shall be nationals of the same state.[179] Members were not appointed on a full-time basis as the Tribunal only sat when it is required to consider a case submitted to it.[180] The Council could decide, following the recommendation of the President, that the workload of the Tribunal requires members to serve on a full-time basis. In such cases, the members elected or subsequently appointed to serve on full-time basis could not hold any other office or employment.[181] A member was required to continue to hear and complete cases partly heard by that member regardless of expiration of his term of office.[182] A registrar, appointed by the Tribunal, was charged with the responsibility for the day-to-day administration of the Tribunal.[183] The

---

[171] Protocol on the Tribunal 2000, *supra* note 144, at art. 3(1).
[172] *Id.* art. 4. The Council is an institution consisting of one Minister from each Member State.
[173] *Id.* art. 6.
[174] *Id.* art. 3(2).
[175] *Id.* art. 7(1).
[176] *Id.* art. 7(2).
[177] *Id.* arts. 8(1) & (2).
[178] *Id.* art. 3(3).
[179] *Id.* art. 3(3).
[180] *Id.* art. 6(2).
[181] *Id.* art. 6(3).
[182] *Id.* art. 8(4).
[183] *Id.* art. 12.

Tribunal had a seat at a place designated by the Council.[184] This did not, however, limit it from sitting anywhere within the Community for a particular case, if this is considered desirable.[185] The working languages of the Tribunal were English, Portuguese, and French.[186]

The 2014 SADC Tribunal Protocol removed individual access for individuals when the Tribunal is eventually reconstituted.[187] The 2014 Protocol also provides that the law to be applied by the Tribunal is now limited to the SADC Treaty and applicable to SADC Protocols.[188] This is a significant reduction from the "old" Tribunal which could interpret the SADC Treaty, the SADC Protocols, all subsidiary instruments adopted by the Summit, the Committee of Ministers (CoM), or by any other institution or organ of the Community pursuant to the SADC Treaty.[189] Another significant change is that under the 2014 Protocol the President of the Tribunal will be elected by the Summit[190] and not by the other judges as was previously.[191]

African Commission on Human and Peoples' Rights (ACHPR)

Establishment
The Organization of African Unity (OAU), the forerunner to the AU, adopted the Banjul Charter in 1981 which entered into force in 1986. The Banjul Charter establishes an African commission to promote, protect, and interpret the rights in the Charter.[192] The Commission shares this role with the ACtHPR. The OAU inaugurated the Commission in 1987. The Banjul Charter mandates the Commissioners to act in their personal capacity and to be impartial.[193] This requirement of impartiality and independence explains why the Commission's headquarters is located in Banjul, the Gambia, away from the OAU headquarters in Addis Ababa.[194] The Commission is a human rights "monitoring body" or a "supervisory institution."[195]

---

[184] *Id.* art. 13.
[185] *Id.*
[186] *Id.* art. 22.
[187] Protocol on the Tribunal in the Southern African Development Community 2014, art. 33 (hereinafter "Protocol on the Tribunal 2014").
[188] *Id.* art. 35.
[189] Protocol on the Tribunal 2000, *supra* note 144, art. 21.
[190] Protocol on the Tribunal 2014, *supra* note 187, art. 5(1).
[191] Protocol on the Tribunal 2000, *supra* note 144, art. 7.
[192] OAU, *African Charter on Human and Peoples' Rights (Banjul Charter)* 21 INT'L LEG. MATERIALS 58, arts. 30, 45 (1982).
[193] *Id.* art. 31.
[194] M. L. Balanda, *African Charter on Human and Peoples' Rights, in* NEW PERSPECTIVES AND CONCEPTIONS OF INTERNATIONAL LAW: AN AFRO-EUROPEAN DIALOGUE 134 (K. Ginther & W. Benedek eds., 1984).
[195] Gino J. Naldi, *The African Union and the Regional Human Rights System, in* THE AFRICAN CHARTER ON HUMAN AND PEOPLES' RIGHTS: THE SYSTEM PRACTICE 1986–2006, at 35 (Malcolm Evans & Rachel Murray eds., 2008).

It is important to note that the Commission is not a court or tribunal with compulsory jurisdiction. The Commission can be compared with such bodies as the United Nations Human Rights Committee, and is thus best described as a "quasi-judicial" organ with jurisdiction to receive inter-state communications and "other" communications.[196]

Jurisdiction

The Commission's mandate is to promote human and peoples' rights through documentation, research, and formulation of rules and principles. It also charged with ensuring the protection of human and peoples' rights, interpretation of the provisions of the Charter, and any other tasks entrusted to it.[197] The Commission has three missions:

1. The promotion of human and peoples' rights;
2. The protection of human and peoples' rights; and
3. The interpretation of the Banjul Charter.[198]

In exercising its protective mandate, the Commission receives two types of communications: communications from states[199] and other communications other than those of state parties.[200] The Rules of Procedures of the Commission allows natural (individuals) or legal persons to present communications to the Commission under Article 55 of the Banjul Charter.[201] The Commission has allowed applicants other than the harmed victims, especially NGOs, to present communications on behalf of human rights violation victims through the system of *actio popul009aris*.[202] Through these communications, petitioners inform the Commission that they believe another state has violated the provisions of the Charter.[203] States have seldom initiated petitions.[204] The provision for other communications other than those of

---

[196] *Id.*

[197] Banjul Charter, *supra* note 19, art. 45.

[198] *Id.*

[199] *Id.* arts. 47, 54.

[200] *Id.* arts. 55–59.

[201] African Commission on Human and Peoples' Rights Rules of Procedure, rule 93 (hereinafter "ACHPR Rules").

[202] Article 19 v. Eritrea, Communication 275/2003, AHRLR 73, African Commission on Human and Peoples' Rights [ACHPR] (May 2007); Malawi African Association and Others v. Mauritania, No. 54/91, AHRLR 149, ACHPR (May 11, 2000); Constitutional Rights Project (in respect of Lekwot and Others) v. Nigeria, No. 87/93, AHRLR 183, ACHPR (Mar. 22, 1995).

[203] Banjul Charter, *supra* note 19, art. 47.

[204] RACHEL MURRAY, THE AFRICAN COMMISSION ON HUMAN AND PEOPLES' RIGHTS AND INTERNATIONAL LAW 65 (2000) (according to Murray, "a complaint was received from Sudan alleging human rights violations by Ethiopian troops in Sudanese territory during the alleged Ethiopian invasion of the Kurmuk and Gissan regions in Sudan on 12ᵗʰ January 1997. The Commission referred the matter to the OAU Secretariat and advised Sudan to do likewise because Ethiopia is not a party to the Charter and thus not subject to the Commission's jurisdiction," *Id.* In March 1999 an African radio station, Gabon's African Number One, noted that the Democratic Republic of Congo had submitted a complaint against Rwanda, Uganda, and Burundi, although there is no official record of this from the

states has made it possible for individuals and NGOs to have direct access to the Commission (ICJ Press Communiqué 99/34, 23 June 1999; at the 25th Session (see 25th Session Transcripts, 12).

Seizure and Admissibility of Individual Communications
Any natural or legal person can submit a communication to the Commission through the Chairperson of the Commission pursuant to Article 55 of the Banjul Charter.[205] The Commission has never decided not to be seized of a matter submitted through this procedure. The main aim of admissibility is to serve a screening or filtering mechanism between national and international institutions.[206] The question of admissibility is normally determined separately from the substantive questions. The principle of exhaustion of local remedies applies when referring a matter to the Commission.[207] Article 56 of the Banjul Charter set out the grounds for admissibility. They are as follows: all communications should identify their author; the communication must be compatible with the AU Constitutive Act and the Banjul Charter; communications must not be written in disparaging language; communication must not be based solely on media information; and all communications must be sent after exhaustion of domestic remedies. The Commission prepares a report of facts and findings after it has gathered all information deemed necessary in relation to a particular communication.[208] The report is sent to the states concerned and communicated to the Assembly. The report transmitted to the Assembly may contain recommendations the Commission deems useful.[209] The Commission submits a report to the Assembly at each ordinary session of the Assembly of heads of state and heads of government.[210]

Composition and Organization
The Commission consists of eleven members (Commissioners), who must be nationals from different African states.[211] The AU Assembly of heads of state and government elects the eleven Commissioners for a renewable period of six years. They

---

Commission. A case has subsequently been submitted to the ICJ by the same state although it is not clear whether the facts are the same: Democratic Republic of Congo v. Burundi, Uganda and Rwanda, ICJ Press Communiqué 99/34 (June 23, 1999). In addition, at the 25th Session (*see* 25th Session Transcripts, 12), Ethiopia made a statement alleging violations by Eritrea. The Commission mentioned Article 47 of the Charter and stated that it would be willing to consider a case. It is not known if any has been submitted.).

[205] ACHPR Rules, *supra* note 201, rule 93.
[206] *See* Frans Viljoen, *Communications under the African Charter: Procedure and Admissibility, in* THE AFRICAN CHARTER ON HUMAN AND PEOPLES' RIGHTS: THE SYSTEM PRACTICE 1986-2006, at 88 (Malcolm Evans & Rachel Murray eds., 2008).
[207] Banjul Charter, *supra* note 19, art. 50.
[208] *Id.* art. 52.
[209] *Id.* art. 53.
[210] *Id.* art. 54.
[211] *Id.* art. 32.

are eligible for re-election.[212] The members should be persons of high morality, integrity, impartiality, and competence in matters of human and peoples' rights.[213] The members of the Commission also serve in their personal capacity. State parties to the Charter nominate persons to serve as members of the Commission.[214] The members elect from themselves a chairperson and a deputy who serve for a period of two years and are eligible for re-election.[215] Seven members are required for a sitting to have quorum.[216]

Common Market for Eastern and South Africa (COMESA) Court of Justice

Establishment

The states party to the Preferential Trade Area for Eastern and Southern African States signed the Treaty For the Establishment of the Common Market for Eastern and Southern Africa (COMESA Treaty) on November 5, 1993 in Kampala, Uganda. The Treaty was ratified on December 8, 1994. The Common Market replaced the Preferential Trade Area which had existed since the Agreement for the Establishment of the Preferential Trade Area (PTA) was signed on December 21, 1981. Article 7(1) (c) of the COMESA Treaty established the Court of Justice as one of the organs of the Common Market.[217] The COMESA Court of Justice is mandated to ensure adherence to law in the interpretation and application of the COMESA Treaty.[218] The Court is also governed by its Rules of Procedure.[219]

Jurisdiction

According to Article 23(1) of the Treaty, the Court has jurisdiction to adjudicate all matters referred to it pursuant to the Treaty. Matters are first heard and determined by the First Instance Division. A matter may be appealed to the Appellate Division on the following grounds if they relate to: (i) a point of law; (ii) lack of jurisdiction; and (iii) procedural integrity.[220] The Court also has jurisdiction over claims by employees of the Common Market related to their terms and conditions of employment.[221] It may also determine claims against the Common Market by third parties

---

[212] *Id.* arts. 32, 34.
[213] *Id.* art. 31.
[214] *Id.* art. 36.
[215] *Id.* art. 42.
[216] *Id.* art. 42(3).
[217] Treaty Establishing the Common Market for Eastern and Southern Africa, art. 7(1)(c) (hereinafter "COMESA Treaty").
[218] *Id.* art. 19(1).
[219] Rules of the Court of Justice of the Common Market for Eastern and Southern Africa 2016.
[220] COMESA Treaty, *supra* note 217, art. 23(3).
[221] *Id.* art. 27(1).

over acts performed by its employees in the exercise of their duties.[222] The Court has jurisdiction to hear matters arising out of a contract which confers jurisdiction to the Court through an arbitration clause. It also has jurisdiction over disputes arising out a special agreement between Member States regarding the Treaty.[223] Disputes to which the Common Market is a party are not excluded from national jurisdiction solely on this basis.[224] Article 32 of the COMESA Treaty makes provision for the Court to give advisory opinions on questions of law arising from the Treaty. An advisory opinion may be requested by the Authority (COMESA's highest decision-making body), the Council, or by Member States.[225] The Court has jurisdiction to issue interim orders in any case in which it considers it necessary.[226] The first case received by the COMESA Court was between Ethiopia and Eritrea concerning dispute over goods in transit.[227] The proceedings in this case were suspended so that the parties could settle it out of Court.[228] This dispute that was not decided by the Court, is the only recorded dispute between two states in an African international court.

A matter may be referred to the Court by a Member States,[229] the Secretary-General,[230] as well as by natural and legal persons resident in the country of a Member State.[231] A party to a matter before the Court must be represented by Counsel.[232] The treaty allows for a Member State, the Secretary-General, or a resident of a Member State, who is not party to a case, to intervene in the case by providing evidence to support or oppose arguments of a party.[233]

The seat of the Court determined by the Authority[234]was in March 2003 located in Khartoum, Sudan.[235] The official languages of the Court is English, French, and Portuguese.[236] The Treaty requires that judgments of the Court to be delivered in public.[237] A judgment may be delivered privately between the parties in special circumstances where the Court determines it is undesirable to deliver the judgment in public.[238] The decision of the Court is considered final and conclusive. Decisions

---

[222] *Id.* art. 27(2).
[223] *Id.* art. 28.
[224] *Id.* art. 29.
[225] *Id.* art. 32.
[226] *Id.* art. 35.
[227] Desire Kayihura, *Parallel Jurisdiction of Courts and Tribunals: The COMESA Court of Justice Perspective*, 36 COMMONWEALTH L. BULL. 588 (2010).
[228] *Id.*
[229] COMESA Treaty, *supra* note 217, art. 24.
[230] *Id.* art. 25.
[231] *Id.* art. 26.
[232] *Id.* art. 33.
[233] *Id.* art. 36.
[234] *Id.* art. 44.
[235] James Gathii, *The Under-Appreciated Jurisprudence of African Regional Trade Judiciaries,* 12 OR. REV. INT'L L. 245, 247 (2010).
[236] COMESA Treaty, *supra* note 217, art. 43.
[237] *Id.* art. 31(1).
[238] *Id.*

of the Court are not open to appeal.[239] A party may apply for a review of a judgment where there is discovery of a fact that could have had a decisive influence on the judgment that was unknown at the time of making the application.[240] The execution of judgments imposing a pecuniary obligation on a person are governed by the civil procedure rules of the Member State in which its execution is to take place.[241]

Composition and Organization

The Court of Justice is divided into two divisions: (i) the First Instance Division and; (ii) the Appellate Division.[242] The First Instance Division is composed of seven judges whereas the Appellate Division is composed of five judges.[243] One of the judges of the Appellate Division shall be designated as the President of the Court. A judge from the First Instance Division shall be designated as the Principle Judge. A person appointed as a judge must fulfil the conditions required for holding high judicial office in their country or must be a jurist of recognized competence.[244] No two or more judges may be nationals of the same Member State.[245]

Judges hold office for a period of five years and may be re-appointed for another term of five years.[246] The judges of the Court were first appointed by the Authority on June 30, 1998.[247] Where the term of a judge comes to an end before delivering a decision or opinion with respect to a matter the judge was hearing, the judge shall continue to sit as a judge only for the purpose of completing that particular matter.[248] The President may resign his office by giving one year's written notice to the Chairman of the Authority. This resignation is not effective until a successor is appointed.[249] Removal from judicial office is only permissible for misbehavior or the inability to perform the functions of the office.[250] If a judge is appointed to replace the President or other judge before expiry of their term, the appointed judge shall serve in office for the remainder of the term of the replaced President or judge.[251] A temporary judge may be appointed where one of the judges is absent or unable to perform his function for a period that could cause significant delay in the work of the Court.[252]

---

[239] *Id.*
[240] *Id.*
[241] *Id.* art. 40.
[242] *Id.* art. 19(2).
[243] *Id.* art. 20(1).
[244] *Id.* art. 20.
[245] *Id.* art. 20(2).
[246] *Id.* art. 21(1).
[247] Gathii, *supra* note 235.
[248] COMESA Treaty, *supra* note 217, art. 21(3).
[249] *Id.* art. 21(4).
[250] *Id.* art. 22(1).
[251] *Id.* art. 22(2).
[252] *Id.* art. 22(3).

West African Economic and Monetary Union
(WAEMU) Court of Justice

The WAEMU was created through the Treaty on the West African Economic and Monetary Union (WAEMU Treaty).[253] The Treaty was signed on the January 10, 1994 in Dakar, Senegal.[254] The Treaty was signed by Benin, Burkina Faso, Ivory Coast (Cote d'Ivoire), Mali, Niger, Senegal, and Togo. Guinea-Bissau joined the Union on May 2, 1997, bringing the number of states in the Union to eight.[255] The Union was created with the aim of promoting economic integration between its members.[256]

WAEMU Member States all share a common currency, the CFA Franc.[257] The CFA Franc will be replaced by the Eco in 2020. The Eco is a new currency which will remain pegged to the euro like the CFA Franc. However, France will no longer have a representative on WAEMU's currency board and WAEMU Member States will not be required to keep 50 percent of their foreign reserves in the French Treasury.

Establishment

In an effort to achieve its functions, WAEMU established various bodies, among them the WAEMU Court of Justice.[258] Article 39 of the Treaty establishes the WAEMU Court of Justice. The Court of Justice is mandated to ensure the observance of the law of the Union by Member States in interpretation and implementation.[259] The Court was officially set up on January 27, 1995.[260] The Court has rendered thirty-seven decisions since its inception until 2018.[261] More than three-quarters of these cases have been cases between the Union and its staff, and advisory opinions.[262] As a result the Court has acted more as administrative tribunal as opposed to supporting the integration process through ensuring observance of the law.[263]

---

[253] *Treaty on the West African Economic and Monetary Union,* https://investmentpolicy.unctad.org/international-investment-agreements/treaty-files/2426/download.

[254] Illy Ousseni, *The WAEMU Court of Justice, in* THE LEGITIMACY OF INTERNATIONAL TRADE COURTS AND TRIBUNALS 349 (R. Howse, H. Ruiz-Fabri, G. Ulfstein, & M. Zang eds., 2018).

[255] *Id.*

[256] Ousseni, *supra* note 254.

[257] *Voluntary Peer Review of Competition Policy: West African Economic and Monetary Union, Benin and Senegal,* United Nations Conference on Trade and Development, UNCTAD/DITC/CLP/2007, 1, 2 (2007).

[258] *Id.* at 1, 3.

[259] Ousseni, *supra* note 254, at 350.

[260] *Id.*

[261] *Id.*

[262] *Id.* at 351.

[263] *Id.*

Jurisdiction

The jurisdiction of the Court falls into two categories: contentious jurisdiction and advisory jurisdiction. Under its contentious jurisdiction there are seven types of proceedings possible.[264] These are actions for infringements; actions for annulment of the Union Acts; actions relating to competition matters; disputes between the Union and its staff; actions relating to non-contractual liability and compensation; and reference for preliminary ruling and arbitration.[265] The arbitration jurisdiction of the Court is neither automatic nor compulsory. Instead, parties involved must agree on arbitration through a submission agreement notified to the Court.[266]

An advisory opinion may be sought on the Union texts; on international agreements and their compliance with the WAEMU Treaty; and opinion on any difficulty regarding the application or interpretation of union law.[267] The right to seek an advisory opinion from the Court is limited to the Commission, the Council of Ministers, the Authority of heads of state and government, Member States, Union bodies, and institutions.[268] The decisions of the Court are final and binding but an application for revision may be made.[269]

Composition and Organization

The Court is composed of eight judges, one from each Member State.[270] The judges are appointed by the WAEMU Authority (the highest decision-making body in WAEMU), from nationals of Member States who possess the qualifications required for appointment to the highest judicial officers in their states.[271] The judges are appointed for a period of six years which can be renewed.[272] Once appointed, a judge cannot be dismissed or his/her salary or pension suspended unless s/he is no longer able to fulfil the conditions and obligations required to be a judge.[273] A registrar is appointed by the Court to govern the administrative matters of the Court. The register is appointed for a renewable six-year term.[274] A case may be brought before the Court by Union bodies, institutions and agencies, Member States, national courts, and natural and legal persons.[275]

---

[264] *Id.* at 354.
[265] *Id.* at 354–58.
[266] *Id.* at 358.
[267] *Id.* at 359.
[268] *Id.* at 349.
[269] *Id.* at 361.
[270] *Id.* at 353.
[271] *Id.*
[272] *Id.*
[273] *Id.* art. 12; Additional Act No.10/96 Regarding the Status of the Court of Justice of WAEMU.
[274] Ousseni, *supra* note 254, at 353.
[275] *Id.* at 360.

Organization for the Harmonization of Business Law in Africa Common Court Justice and Arbitration (OHADA CCJA)

Establishment

Sixteen mainly francophone West African states signed the Treaty on the Harmonization in Africa of Business Law (OHADA Treaty) on October 17, 1993 in Port Louis, Mauritius.[276] The acronym OHADA translates to its French title, *Organisation pour l'Harmonisation en Afrique du Droit des Affaires*. The organization currently has seventeen members after the Democratic Republic of Congo became a member in 2012.[277] This means that OHADA currently has seventeen members mainly within the CFA Franc zone[278] and are thus largely civil law-based francophone countries.[279] The OHADA Treaty is, however, open to membership by any state of the African Union (AU).[280] OHADA connects countries in both the WAEMU, which mainly covers the West African CFA Franc zone and the Central African Economic and Monetary Community (CEMAC) covering the Central African CFA Franc zone. The first sixteen members revised the OHADA Treaty in Quebec, Canada on October 17, 2008. One of the amendments increased the official languages of OHADA from one, French, to four, French, English, Spanish, and Portuguese.[281] The OHADA Treaty establishes the OHADA.[282] The OHADA's objective is to harmonize business law in state parties by developing and adopting simple, modern, and common rules, adapted to their economies, setting up appropriate judicial procedures, and encouraging recourse to arbitration for the settlement of contractual disputes.[283]

OHADA also aims to promote African unity as well as the gradual economic integration for countries in the CFA Franc zone in order to improve company business, ensuring legal security of economic activities, promoting development and investment, and the promotion of arbitration and mutual efforts to improve professional justices and judicial officers.[284] To achieve these aims, the OHADA

---

[276] *Preamble, Treaty on the Harmonization of Business Law in Africa*, OHADA (Official Bulletin) (Nov. 24, 2016), http://www.ohada.com/content/newsletters/3247/jo-ohada-se-nov2016-official-translation.pdf (the sixteen members were Benin, Burkina Faso, Cameroon, Central African Republic, Comoros, Congo (Brazzaville), Ivory Coast, Gabon, Guinea, Guinea Bissau, Equatorial Guinea, Mali, Niger, Senegal, Chad, and Togo) (hereinafter "Treaty on the Harmonization in Africa of Business Law, Official Translation").

[277] OHADA, *OHADA History: Table of Ratifications*, https://www.ohada.org/index.php/fr/ohada-en-bref/presentation-ohada-historique (last visited on Feb 12, 2020) (Fr).

[278] These countries use the CFA Franc as their currency and are former French colonies within a colonially established monetary cooperation policy created in the late 1930s.

[279] All members are francophone except Cameroon (bilingual English-French and English common law applies), Equatorial Guinea (Spanish), and Guinea-Bissau (Portuguese).

[280] Treaty on the Harmonization in Africa of Business Law, Official Translation, *supra* note 276, art. 53.

[281] *Id.* art. 42.

[282] *Id.* art. 3.

[283] *Id.* art. 1.

[284] *Id.* at Preamble.

Treaty establishes four organs: the Conference of Heads of State and Government, the Council of Ministers, the Common Court of Justice and Arbitration (OHADA CCJA), and the Permanent Secretariat.[285] The Treaty also declares the head-quarters or official seat of OHADA to be Yaoundé, Cameroon, and that this location is transferable by the decision of the Conference of Heads of State.[286] The OHADA harmonizes business laws among its state parties through the enactment and adoption of Uniform Acts.[287] The OHADA currently has nine Uniform Acts that override national legislation in areas including general commercial law, law of commercial companies and of economic interest grouping, law of sureties, law of cooperative societies, and arbitration and mediation.[288] The OHADA CCJA is thus established as an organ of this *de-novo* and innovative supranational regionally binding law-making system.[289]

Jurisdiction

The OHADA CCJA has jurisdiction over verifying OHADA draft Uniform Acts (UAs) and issuing opinions to other OHADA organs.[290] Before getting to the OHADA CCJA, the Permanent Secretariat (PS) forwards the draft UAs to the governments of state parties, who submit their written observations to the PS within ninety days.[291] The PS may double the ninety-day timeline depending on the circumstances and the nature of the draft UA.[292] It is after this timeline that the draft UAs are submitted to the OHADA CCJA for verification. The OHADA CCJA exercises its power of verification by issuing an opinion. After receiving the opinion of the CCJA, the PS prepares the final text of the draft UA and proposes its inclusion in the agenda of the next Council of Ministers meeting.[293] The OHADA CCJA, also has the jurisdiction to interpret and uniformly apply the OHADA Treaty, its promulgated regulations, and the UAs.[294]

In addition, the OHADA CCJA has advisory jurisdiction over consultations or questions presented by any state party or the Council of Ministers on any questions within the scope of the OHADA Treaty, regulations, UAs, or other decisions.[295] The national courts of state parties may also request advisory opinions from the

---

[285] *Id.* art.3.
[286] *Id.* art.3.
[287] *Id.* art.4.
[288] OHADA, *OHADA Uniform Acts*, https://www.ohada.org/index.php/fr/ohada-en-bref/presentation-ohada-historique (last visited Feb. 12, 2020) (Fr.).
[289] *See* Regis Y. Simo, *Regional Integration in Africa through Harmonization of Laws*, *in* REGIONAL INTEGRATION AND POLICY CHALLENGES IN AFRICA 118 (Adam B. Elharaika, Allan C.K Mukungu, & Wanjiku Nyoike eds., 2015).
[290] Treaty on the Harmonization in Africa of Business Law, Official Translation, *supra* note 276, art. 7.
[291] *Id.*
[292] *Id.*
[293] *Id.*
[294] *Id.* art.14.
[295] *Id.*

OHADA CCJA.[296] Finally, the OHADA CCJA has appellate jurisdiction to receive appeals from the national appellate courts of state parties on all matters over the application of the UAs, regulations, except those decisions administering criminal sanctions. The OHADA CCJA can also exercise its appellate jurisdiction on decisions from national courts, which are not appealable to their national court of appeal.[297] In exercising its appellate mandate, the Treaty empowers the OHADA CCJA to quash decisions of national courts and to hear this cases afresh on their merits.[298]

The OHADA CCJA thus has three types of jurisdiction: interpretive and dispute settlement jurisdiction in contentious cases; advisory jurisdiction, and appellate jurisdiction from national courts. The Court has compulsory jurisdiction and acts as the apex judicial entity on OHADA law. The subject matter jurisdiction of the OHADA CCJA is limited to purely economic disputes that spring directly from OHADA UAs, regulations, and decisions. These UAs, regulations, and decisions are limited to business and commercial codes.

Appellate Jurisdiction

The OHADA CCJA exercises its appellate jurisdiction when appeals are referred either directly by the parties to a dispute or by the highest appellate national court of a state party.[299] This means that two private actors can have a dispute adjudicated in the Court without a state party involved. The access to the OHADA CCJA is thus broad enough to allow private individuals and companies to present their disputes before it. The OHADA Treaty also allows preliminary rulings from the OHADA CCJA when referrals are done by the state party's national courts. This is a good example of the preliminary ruling mechanism present in some supranational courts. The lodging of an appeal before the OHADA CCJA has the effect of staying any proceedings pending before the highest appellate national court.[300] This rule, however, does not affect the enforcement of the decision under appeal.[301] The national court may only relist such a case once the OHADA CCJA declares that it lacks jurisdiction.[302] The OHADA CCJA has jurisdiction to declare it manifestly lacks jurisdiction on its own motion or in *limine litis* (before a review on the merits) by any party to the proceedings.[303] The Court has a thirty-day limit to make a ruling after receipt of the observations of lack of jurisdiction or on expiry of time limit for the presentation of the said observations.[304] Additionally, the OHADA Treaty

---

[296] *Id.*
[297] *Id.*
[298] *Id.*
[299] *Id.* art. 15.
[300] *Id.* art. 16.
[301] *Id.*
[302] *Id.*
[303] *Id.*
[304] *Id.* art. 17.

empowers the OHADA CCJA to receive appeals from any party challenging the rulings on jurisdiction of a national appellate court as long as such appeal is lodged within two months of the notification of the national court's decision.[305]

In cases where the OHADA CCJA overrules the jurisdictional finding of the national court, the finding is deemed final and the national court decision is nullified.[306] Thus unlike other African international courts, the OHADA CCJA hears appeals in cases where both parties are private natural or artificial persons.

Finality of decisions

The OHADA Treaty declares that the judgments of the OHADA CCJA are final and enforceable. These decisions are enforceable in the state parties in the same manner as decisions of national courts.[307] This makes the OHADA CCJA and the OHADA system a supranational system that allows its apex judicial entity to make final determinations on OHADA law. The OHADA Treaty strengthens this by providing that any decisions delivered by a national court that are contrary to a judgment of the OHADA CCJA in respect to the same matter shall not be enforceable in the territory of a state party.[308] The hearings of the OHADA CCJA are required to be in public and the presence of all the parties.[309] The assistance of counsel in these cases is also a mandatory requirement.[310]

Arbitration

The OHADA CCJA has supervisory jurisdiction over arbitrations administered by the OHADA CCJA Arbitration rules.[311] It is important to note that this supervisory jurisdiction covers the two main types of arbitrations under OHADA: a OHADA CCJA administered arbitration and a Uniform Act arbitration. Under a OHADA CCJA administered arbitration, the CCJA operates as the administering body and is subject to OHADA CCJA Arbitration rules.[312] In such cases, the CCJA has a dual role, where it functions both as an arbitral institution and as a supervising court.[313] Its role as an arbitral institution entails stipulation of the applicable procedural rules and playing an administrative role.[314] As a supervisory court, it has authority to hear and deal with applications to annul an award rendered under a CCJA arbitration.[315] In a Uniform Act arbitration, the court can assume arbitral jurisdiction where any of the parties is domiciled or has their usual place of residence in the

---

[305] *Id.* art. 18.
[306] *Id.* art.18.
[307] *Id.* art. 20.
[308] *Id.* art. 20.
[309] *Id.* art. 19.
[310] *Id.* art. 19.
[311] *Id.* art. 21.
[312] Arbitration Rules of the Common Court of Justice and Arbitration (1999), arts. 1, 2.
[313] *Id.*
[314] *Id.*
[315] *Id.* arts. 29–34.

territory of a State Party, or where the contact is performed or will be performed wholly or partly in the territory of one or more State Parties.[316] Additionally, it is important to note that the arbitration mandate of OHADA CCJA administered arbitrations includes inter-state arbitration and investor-state disputes.[317]

The OHADA CCJA's arbitral jurisdiction can be invoked pursuant to an arbitration clause in a contract or by agreement. As explained above, for both types of arbitrations, it is not the OHADA CCJA itself that hears the arbitration but rather the court appoints or confirms arbitrators who then keep the Court informed of the progress of the proceedings and submit the draft award to the Court for approval in conformity with Article 24 of the Treaty.[318] The Court acts as an appointing authority where the parties fail to agree on a slate of arbitrators within a period of thirty days, or where the parties fail to agree on a sole arbitrator.[319] The Treaty mandates also empowers the Court to approve the arbitrators the parties choose.[320] The Court selects arbitrators from a list of arbitrators updated annually and also finally decides any challenge of appointment of arbitrator made by a party to a dispute.[321] The treaty also empowers the Court to verify the form of arbitral awards before the arbitral panel issues them as final awards.[322]

Mediation

The OHADA Council of Ministers adopted the Uniform Act on mediation in November 2017. The OHADA CCJA supervisory role over mediation is not part of the revised OHADA Treaty but is established under the OHADA Uniform Act on Mediation (UAM). The UMA defines mediation as including any process where the parties to dispute request a third person to assist them in their attempt to reach an amicable settlement of their dispute, adversarial relationship or disagreement arising out of a legal or contractual relationship or related to such relationship, involving natural persons or legal entities, including public bodies or states.[323] This means that the OHADA CCJA can supervise mediations involving individuals, companies, or states. The OHADA UAM allows mediations to be implemented by the parties (conventional mediation), at the request or invitation of a state court (judicial mediation), an arbitral tribunal, or a competent public entity.[324] Mediations under the UAM can also be *ad hoc* or institutional.[325] This

---

[316] Treaty on the Harmonization in Africa of Business Law, art. 21 (Official Translation).
[317] OHADA Uniform Act on Arbitration (2017), arts. 2, 3. *See* GETMA International v. Republic of Guinea (I), Case No. 001/2011/ARB, paras. 1–2, Award, Common Court of Justice and Arbitration of OHADA [CCJA] (Apr. 29, 2014).
[318] *Id.* art. 21.
[319] *Id.* art. 22.
[320] *Id.* art. 22.
[321] *Id.* art. 22.
[322] *Id.* art. 24.
[323] OHADA Uniform Act on Mediation 2017, art. 1(a).
[324] *Id.* art. 1(b).
[325] *Id.*

means that the OHADA CCJA does not have to act the only institution that administers mediation since most of these will be conducted at the domestic state level. The UAM has rules on the conduct of mediations, status of mediator, guiding principles of mediation, correspondence between the mediator and the parties, confidentiality of mediations, admissibility of evidence in mediations, termination of mediation procedure, mediation costs, recourse to arbitral or judicial procedure, and implementation settlement agreements.[326] The OHADA CCJA will thus only interact with mediation cases as an administrative institution or when cases form state courts or arbitral tribunals involving mediation are referred to it.

Composition and Organization

The OHADA CCJA is composed of nine judges. The Council of Ministers may, depending on the needs of the service and the financial means, also fix a higher number of judges than the nine required above.[327] The judges are elected for a seven-year non-renewable term.[328] These judges must be selected from among nationals of the state parties and the Court shall not consist of more than one judge from the same state party.[329] This rule ensures that no single state party dominates the appointees and thus creating any legitimacy deficits. The judges must be selected from a list of individuals who fulfil any of the following three conditions. First, they must be judicial officers with at least fifteen years of professional experience, having held high judicial or legal office. They must be lawyers who are members of the bar of one of the state parties with at least fifteen years of professional experience. They must be lecturers of law with at least fifteen years of professional experience.[330] The Treaty, however, limits the numbers of practicing lawyers and academics to only two members of the Court.[331] This means that the other five members or more of the Court must always be judges or former judges with at least fifteen years' experience. The terms of one seventh of the members of the Court are renewed each year.[332]

The Court meets in plenary session. However, since 2005, the Court has been formed into two sections in order to better manage the cases brought before it.[333] Each section has three judges each and is presided by the two vice-presidents.[334] Documents are first published in French and should there be divergence between different translations, the French version prevails.[335] While OHADA

---

[326] *Id.* arts. 2–16.
[327] *Id.* art. 31.
[328] *Id.*
[329] *Id.*
[330] *Id.*
[331] *Id.*
[332] *Id.*
[333] Salvatore Mancuso, *OHADA Report*, 20 Eur. Rev. Priv. L. 179 (2012).
[334] *Id.*
[335] *Id.*

is headquartered in Yaounde, Cameroon, the OHADA Court of Justice and Arbitration sits in Abidjan, Ivory Coast.[336]

Court of Justice of the Central African Economic and Monetary Community (CEMAC)

The Central African Economic and Monetary Community commonly known by its French acronym CEMAC (*Communauté Économique et Monétaire de l'Afrique Centrale*) was established by the signing of the Treaty establishing the Economic and Monetary Community of Central African States in N'Djamena, Chad on March 16, 1994.[337] CEMAC replaced the Customs Union, *Union Douanière des Etats de l'Afrique Centrale,* that previously existed between the members post-independence.[338] The CEMAC Treaty became operational in 1999 after its ratification and was later revised in Yaounde, Cameroon on June 25, 2008.[339] The Member States of CEMAC are Cameroon, Central African Republic, Congo, Gabon, Equatorial Guinea, and Chad.[340]

Establishment

The Court of Justice was agreed in the *Traité Constitutif* of CEMAC, in Article 2. The Court has two chambers: one for judicial matters, the other for budgets and accounts.[341] The Judicial Chamber assures compliance with CEMAC treaties and conventions with regard to their interpretation and application.[342] The Accounts Chamber assures the management of CEMAC's accounts.[343] The Court of Justice was established on June 25, 1999 and became operational on December 14, 2000. As of 2006, the Court had issued twenty-two decisions and five advisory opinions.

---

[336] OHADA, *Organization for Harmonization in Africa Business Law,* https://www.ohada.org/index.php/fr/notre-organisation/presentation-ohada-organisation (last visited on Jan. 19, 2020) (Fr.).

[337] Victor Essien, *UPDATE: Regional Trade Agreements in Africa—A Historical and Bibliographic Account of ECOWAS and CEMAC,* NYU GlobaLex, https://www.nyulawglobal.org/globalex/CEMAC_ECOWAS1.html#CEMAC (last visited on Jan. 18, 2020).

[338] Angela Meyer, *Central African Economic and Monetary Union, in* THE DEMOCRATIZATION OF INTERNATIONAL ORGANIZATIONS, FIRST INTERNATIONAL DEMOCRACY REPORT 2011, at 3 (G. Finizio, L. Levi, & N. Vallinoto eds., 2011).

[339] Victor Essien, *UPDATE: Regional Trade Agreements in Africa—A Historical and Bibliographic Account of ECOWAS and CEMAC,* NYU GlobaLex, https://www.nyulawglobal.org/globalex/CEMAC_ECOWAS1.html#CEMAC (last visited on Jan. 18, 2020).

[340] CEMAC Member States, *Economic and Monetary Community of Central Africa,* http://www.cemac.int/etats_membres (accessed on Jan. 19, 2020) (Fr.).

[341] *Traité Constitutif CEMAC,* DROIT AFRIQUE, art. 2 http://www.Droit-Afrique.com (Fr.).

[342] *Id.* art. 5.

[343] *Id.*

Jurisdiction

According to the *Traité Revisé* of CEMAC, the Court of Justice has the power to issue sanctions against Member States who do not abide by the Treaty.[344] Prior to a Court of Justice ruling, the issue must first go to the Council of Ministers, and if they decide not to act, the Court of Justice may be called upon.[345] The Court of Justice, on referral by the Council of Ministers, also has the power to determine whether Commission members can continue in their positions after gross misconduct or incapacity.[346] Furthermore, the Court of Justice may suspend enforcement of CEMAC laws.[347]

The Convention Governing the Court of Justice provides that the role of the Court is two-fold—adjudicative and advisory.[348] In its adjudicative function, the Court of Justice makes the final judgments on the cases alleging violation of CEMAC treaties and subsequent conventions. It makes final judgments on litigation interpreting treaties, conventions, and other CEMAC rules, regulations, and enactments. It decides appeals and makes final judgments on disputes between the Banking Commission of Central Africa (COBAC) and credit institutions. It makes initial and final judgments regarding disputes arising between CEMAC and the agents of the Community institutions, except those governed by contracts under local law.[349]

In its advisory role, the Court of Justice advises Member States or CEMAC bodies on compliance with CEMAC legal standards, legal acts, or draft acts initiated by a Member State or CEMAC body under the relevant treaties.[350] The Judicial Chamber gives preliminary rulings on the interpretation of the CEMAC Treaty and subsequent texts when a national court or legal organization is called upon to hear during a dispute.[351] In addition, whenever a national court faces a CEMAC legal question, it is required that it must first notify the Judiciary Chamber for an advisory opinion before issuing a final decision. This advisory opinion is discretionary if the national court's ruling is subject to appeal.[352]

The Judicial Chamber has jurisdiction to issue final judgments in disputes relating to the compensation for damages caused by the bodies and Institutions of the Community or their agents in the exercise of their functions.[353] The Court of Justice also has jurisdiction over disputes arising between the Community and its

---

[344] *Traité Revisé*, CEMAC, art. 4, http://www.cemac.int/sites/default/files/ueditor/55/upload/file/20190718/1563448018616342.pdf (Fr.).

[345] *Id.* art. 35.

[346] *Id.* arts. 29, 30.

[347] *Id.* art. 45.

[348] *Convention Regissant la Court de Justice de la CEMAC*, art. 3, https://www.ceja.ch/images/CEJA/DOCS/Bibliotheque/Legislation/Africaine/Textes%20Regionaux/DE/DE2.pdf (Fr.).

[349] *Id.* art. 4.

[350] *Id.* art. 6.

[351] *Id.* art. 17.

[352] *Id.* art. 17.

[353] *Id.* art. 20.

agents.[354] Moreover, the Court has jurisdiction over disputes between Member States where there is a link with the Treaty and subsequent texts if these disputes are submitted to it.[355]

The Additional Acts regarding the Judicial Chamber and Account Chamber of the Court of Justice set the rules of the Court's operation, organization, responsibilities, and jurisdiction. The Court's session begins on October 1 and ends on September 30 each year with a hiatus from July 1 through September 30.[356] The judges are nominated by the Member States, with two judges nominated from each state. the conference of heads of states then appoints the judges for a non-renewable term of six years.[357] The judges may be removed from the Court under four circumstances including: the end of a term, death, dismissal, and where a judge decides to give up his/her position in which case s/he sits on the Court until a suitable replacement is appointed.[358] A judge may only be relieved of his duties in the case that the General Assembly, at the request of the *Premier Président* or the Executive Secretary of CEMAC, has determined that s/he no longer meets the requirements of a judge or is no longer able to satisfactorily perform his duties. The judge will have an opportunity to defend him/herself orally or in writing, and may request counsel.[359]

The members of the Court are required to refrain from any activity that is incompatible with their office, or which would compromise the independence, impartiality, and ability of the Court to perform its functions. If there is disagreement over whether a Court member's outside activities are inconsistent with preserving the Court's neutrality, the Court makes the final determination on the issue.[360]

The Court—including both the Accounts and Judicial Chambers—is comprised of thirteen judges led by a judge elected by his peers as *Premier Président*, as well as two other judges elected *Présidents de Chambre*.[361] The *Premier Président* represents the Court, coordinates the judicial and administrative functions of the Court, administers the services of the Court, manages the personnel, and approves the budget of the Court.[362] The Judicial Chamber is composed of six judges who elect, by a majority vote, the President of the Chamber.[363]

---

[354] *Id.* art. 21.
[355] *Id.* art. 22.
[356] Acte Additionnel Numero 06/00/CEMAC-041-CCE-CJ-02 Portant Statut de la Chambre Judiciaire de la Cour de Justice de la CEMAC (Dec. 14, 2000), arts. 7–8, https://www3.nd.edu/~ggoertz/rei/rei080/rei080.34tt1.pdf (Fr.).
[357] *Id.* art. 10.
[358] *Id.* arts. 21–21.
[359] *Id.* art. 22.
[360] *Id.* art. 17.
[361] *Id.* art. 26.
[362] *Id.* art. 28.
[363] *Id.* arts. 33–34.

The Judicial Chamber of the CEMAC Court of Justice

The jurisdiction of the Judicial Chamber is outlined in Articles 48 and 49 of the Additional Act. The Court has final appellate and initial jurisdiction in the following types of cases. First, differing opinions between states regarding language in the CEMAC Treaty and subsequent texts as long as the issue is presented to the Judicial Chamber for resolution. Second, cases arising between CEMAC and its agents. Third, judicial review of the legality of legal acts referred for its censure.[364] The Judicial Chamber also has final appellate jurisdiction over the following types of cases. First, interlocutory or direct appeals regarding the interpretation of judicial acts, treaties, conventions, and other subsequent texts of CEMAC. Second, cases related to determination of damages caused by the bodies and institutions of the Community or its agents in the exercise of their functions. Third, cases arising between COBAC and credit-granting establishments.[365] The Chamber also has jurisdiction as an arbitrator over disputes submitted to it by states, institutions, bodies, and organs of CEMAC, as well as any case submitted to it as a result of a contractual arbitration clause.[366]

The Accounts Chamber of the CEMAC Court of Justice

There is also an Additional Act which outlines the functioning of the Accounts Chamber. The Accounts Chamber is responsible for verifying the accounts of CEMAC and ensuring that CEMAC is financially well managed.[367] Like the Judicial Chamber, the Accounts Chamber is comprised of six judges who elect, by majority vote, the President of the Chamber.[368] The Accounts Chamber performs its functions through three means including: 1) judicial opinions; 2) through its general assembly; and 3) through its *Chambre du Conseil* or advisory chamber.[369] The general assembly includes all of the members and personnel of the Chamber and meets to deliberate on the functioning of the Chamber itself.[370] The *Chambre du Conseil* is comprised only of the Chamber judges and is responsible for the following: requests for opinion, procedural or case-law questions related to the Chamber's jurisdiction, drafting the budget report for CEMAC and its institutions, drafting the annual report, and drafting of specific reports related to the jurisdiction of the Chamber.[371]

The writing of an opinion recognizing the legitimacy of the audit reports is done following the examination of the reports. This examination is done in by the President of the Chamber, two to four judges, the court clerk, and an attorney

---

[364] *Id.* art. 48.
[365] *Id.* art. 48.
[366] *Id.* art. 49.
[367] *Id.* art. 47.
[368] *Id.* arts. 33–34.
[369] *Id.* art. 43.
[370] *Id.* art. 45.
[371] *Id.* art. 45.

where one is needed. The Chamber then makes a ruling based on a majority vote of the parties and the decision is signed by the President of the Chamber, the judges, and the court clerk.[372]

In the exercise of its judicial functions, the Chamber spot-checks the legality and regularity of revenue and expenses, takes precautionary measures when it finds serious failings capable of affecting the interests of CEMAC, judges the accounts, sanctions the management, pronounces the sentences in terms of fines, and rules on appeals.[373] The Accounts Chamber receives feedback from the National Courts of Accounts regarding the results of its audits, and may also provide these National Courts with additional support upon request from the Member State.[374] The Presidents of the National Courts of Accounts meet to evaluate the auditing system and results of completed audits. From this meeting, called by the *Premier Président* of the Court of Justice, a report is compiled with suggestions for the improvement of the auditing system and in order to harmonize the auditing systems of the Member States. This report also provides information as to the whether the accounts meet the established requirements and evaluates the weaknesses of the accounts discovered through the audits.[375]

Sanctions imposed by the Accounts Chamber

The Chamber may impose a fine on public accountants in the following cases: first, for delay in production of the accounts, if it does not present its accounts for examination on time. The fine is set at 100,000 francs CFA for the first month and 200,000 francs CFA from the second to sixth months. It is liquidated at the end of the sixth months. Second, For a delay in responding to the injunctions pronounced against it in the time allowed by decision of the Chamber or if it has produced no valid excuse for the delay. In the latter case, the fine is between 10,000 and 50,000 francs CFA.[376] Anyone who interferes in revenue or expenses operations or in the handling of funds and who is not by profession a Public Accountant or has not acted under the control or on behalf of a Public Accountant, is declared the *de facto* Accountant. The Public Account's management is subject to the judgment of the Chamber and is subject to the same obligations and responsibilities as other officials. They can be fined based on the size and duration of the delay or mishandling of funds. The amount of the fine can exceed the amounts unduly detained or handled.[377]

The Chamber sanctions any management inconsistencies committed by authorizing officers, officials, and other agents of the Community if they: (1) infringe the

---

[372] *Id.* art. 46.
[373] *Id.* art. 48.
[374] *Id.* arts. 49–50.
[375] *Id.* art. 51.
[376] *Id.* art. 52.
[377] *Id.* art. 54.

rules on the implementation of revenue and expenditure or interfere with the management of Community goods; (2) incur expenses without having the authority; (3) engage in over-spending irregular expenditures; (4) they have, in the exercise of their duties, knowingly failed to document that which they must knowingly document or have provided inaccurate or incomplete documentation; and (5) have provided to others or themselves or attempted to procure an unjustified advantage, financial, or in kind, resulting in damage to the Community.[378] The perpetrators referred to here may incur fines of between 100,000 and 1 million francs CFA. However, they will incur no penalty if they show a written order to commit the act previously given by their supervisor or by the person legally authorized to give such an order. In this case, the supervisor will then be held liable, in place of the original perpetrators.[379]

The Chamber may check the management of financial assistance granted by the Community to the states or to any community organization. It may also check the use of financial assistance paid to the Community by any third state or any national or international organization, as well as all donations.[380]

Arab Maghreb Union (AMU) Judicial Organ

On June 10, 1988, the heads of states of Algeria, Libya, Morocco, Mauritania, and Tunisia met in Zeralda, Algeria, where they decided to set up a commission responsible for defining the ways and means of realizing a union between the states.[381] On February 17, 1989 in Marrakech, Morocco, the Member States founded the union by signing the Treaty Establishing the Arab Maghreb Union.[382] Member States also adopted the Solemn Declaration on the establishment of the Arab Maghreb Union.[383] The AMU is an economic and political organization formed by five states; Algeria, Libya, Mauritania, Morocco, and Tunisia.[384] The aim of the union is to coordinate, harmonize, and rationalize policies and strategies among Member States to achieve sustainable development in all sectors of human activities.[385] Since the AMU was founded, it has adopted thirty-six Maghreb conventions on various sectors.[386]

Among the institutions established within the Union is the AMU Judicial Organ, established under Article 13 of the AMU Treaty.[387] The AMU Judicial Authority

---

[378] *Id.* art. 55.
[379] *Id.* art. 56.
[380] *Id.* art. 57.
[381] United Nations Economic Commission for Africa (UNECA), 'AMU-Arab Maghreb Union' https://www.uneca.org/oria/pages/amu-arab-maghreb-union (last visited on Jul. 26, 2020).
[382] United Nations Economic Commission for Africa, *AMU*, https://www.uneca.org/oria/pages/amu-arab-maghreb-union (last visited on Jan. 13, 2020).
[383] *Id.*
[384] Arab Maghreb Union, *supra* note 381.
[385] United Nations Economic Commission for Africa, *supra* note 382.
[386] Arab Maghreb Union, *supra* note 381.
[387] *See also* Murray Carole, *Treaty Creating the Arab Union of the Maghreb*, 7 ARAB L. Q. 207 (1992).

Table 8.1 Summary of Preliminary Information from International Courts in Africa

International courts	Subject matter jurisdiction	Year created	First ruling	Member States	Binding rulings
African Court on Human and Peoples' Rights	– Contentious jurisdiction – Advisory jurisdiction – Constitutional review – Human rights – Dispute settlement – Administrative review – Enforcement	2006	2009 App. No. 001/2008: *Michelot Yogogombaye v Republic of Senegal*	30	62 as of Sept. 2019
Economic Community for West African States (ECOWAS) Court of Justice	– Dispute settlement – Advisory jurisdiction – Human rights	2001	February 8, 2011 *Aboubacar v Central Bank of West Africa and Anor.* (01/11) [2018] ECOWASCJ 79	15 Benin, Burkina Faso, Cape Verde, Ivory Coast, Gambia, Ghana, Guinea, Guinea-Bissau, Liberia, Mali, Niger, Nigeria, Senegal, Sierra Leone, and Togo	131 as of Feb. 6, 2020
East Africa Court of Justice (EACJ)	– Dispute settlement – Administrative review – Enforcement – Constitutional review – Human rights – Appellate jurisdiction	2001	October 1, 2006 *Mwatela & Ors v East African Community* (Application No. 1 of 2005) [2006] EACJ 1	6 Burundi, Kenya, Rwanda, South Sudan, Tanzania, and Uganda	189 as of Feb. 6, 2020

Continued

Table 8.1 *Continued*

International courts	Subject matter jurisdiction	Year created	First ruling	Member States	Binding rulings
South Africa Development Community (SADC) Tribunal	– Disputes relating to application of SADC Treaties – Advisory opinions	2005	November 28, 2007 *Campbell & Ors v Republic of Zimbabwe* (SADCT: 2/07) [2007] SADCT 10	16 Angola, Botswana, Comoros, Democratic Republic of Congo, Eswatini, Lesotho, Madagascar, Malawi, Mauritius, Mozambique, Namibia, Seychelles, South Africa, Tanzania, Zambia, and Zimbabwe	25 as of Feb. 6, 2020
Common Market For Eastern And South Africa (COMESA) Court of Justice	– Dispute settlement – Appellate jurisdiction – Arbitration	1998	March 29, 2001 *Eastern and Southern African Trade and Development Bank & Anor v Ogang* (Reference 1B/2000) [2018] COMESACJ	21 Burundi, Comoros, Democratic Republic of Congo, Djibouti, Egypt, Eswatini, Eritrea, Ethiopia, Kenya, Libya, Madagascar, Mauritius, Rwanda, Seychelles, Somalia, Sudan, Tunisia, Uganda, Zambia, and Zimbabwe	23 as of Feb. 6, 2020
Arab Maghreb Union (AMU) Judicial Organ	– Disputes relating to the application of treaties and agreements concluded by the Union – Advisory jurisdiction	Non-operative	Inoperative	5 Algeria, Libya, Mauritania, Morocco, and Tunisia	Inoperative

Institution	Jurisdiction / Functions	Year	First Case / Decision	Members	Cases
West African Economic and Monetary Union (WAEMU) Court of Justice	– Contentious jurisdiction over WAEMU Treaties and Agreements – Advisory jurisdiction on WAEMU Treaties and agreements – Arbitration			8 Benin, Burkina Faso, Guinea-Bissau, Mali, Niger, Ivory Coast, Senegal, and Togo	37 as of 2018
Organization for the Harmonization of Business Law in Africa Common Court Justice and Arbitration (OHADA CCJA)	– Business-related disputes – Business law – International arbitration	1997	October 11, 2001 *Etablissements Thiam Baboye "ETB" v Compagnie Française Commerciale et Financiere "CFCF"* (Judgment 001/2001)	17 Benin, Burkina Faso, Cameroon, Central African Republic, Chad, Comoros, Ivory Coast, Congo, Democratic Republic of Congo, Equatorial Guinea, Guinea, Gabon, Guinea-Bissau, Mali, Niger, Senegal, and Togo	Approx. 1,452 as at 2020
Court of Justice of the Central African Economic and Monetary Community (CEMAC)	– Contentious jurisdiction over disputes relating to CEMAC Treaties and agreements – Advisory jurisdiction – Disputes between CEMAC and its employees	2000		6 Cameroon, Chad, Central African Republic, Congo, Equatorial Guinea, and Gabon,	22 as of 2006 and 5 advisory opinions.
African Commission on Human And Peoples' Rights (ACHPR)	– Promotion of Human and Peoples' Rights – Protection of Human and Peoples' Rights – Interpretation of the African Charter	1987	October 8, 1988 *Alphonse v DRC*	54	238 as of Feb. 6, 2020. Most recent decision Nov. 15, 2018

has the jurisdiction to examine disputes that might relating to the interpretation of the AMU Treaty. The Presidential Council or a Member State involved in a dispute are empowered to petition the court pursuant to the Judicial Authority's Principal Regulations.[388]

Under the Treaty Creating the AMU (AMU Treaty), the AMU Judicial Organ should be composed of two judges from each state appointed by the state concerned for a period of six years.[389] Half of the members of the Tribunal are renewed every three years.[390] A president should be elected from the appointed judges.[391] The President serves for a period of one year.[392] The role of the judicial authority ought to be to examine disputes relating to the interpretation and application of treaties and agreements concluded within the framework of the Union.[393] It also ought to have the jurisdiction to offer advisory opinions on legal matters as may be requested by the Presidency Council.[394] Matters could also be referred to the Judiciary by Presidency Council or one of the state parties to the conflict.[395] Even if it was operational, there would be no access for natural or legal persons.[396] Finally, its decisions would considered final and binding.[397] The seat of the Judicial Authority was designated to be in Nouakchott, Mauritania.[398]

As noted at the beginning of this chapter, the Judicial Organ is one of the most, if not the most inactive, international courts in Africa.

---

[388] Robert W. McKeon Jr., *The Arab Maghreb Union: Possibilities of Maghrebine Political and Economic Unity, and Enhanced Trade in the World Community*, 4 DICKINSON J. INT'L L. 288 (1992).
[389] Murray Carole, *Treaty Creating the Arab Union of the Maghreb*, 7 ARAB L. Q. 207 (1992).
[390] *Id.*
[391] *Id.*
[392] *Id.*
[393] Arab Maghreb Union, *supra* note 381.
[394] Murray Carole, *Treaty Creating the Arab Union of the Maghreb*, 7 ARAB L. Q. 207 (1992).
[395] *Id.*
[396] *Id.*
[397] *Id.*
[398] Arab Maghreb Union, *supra* note 381.

Index

For the benefit of digital users, indexed terms that span two pages (e.g., 52–53) may, on occasion, appear on only one of those pages.

Tables and figures are indicated by *t* and *f* following the page number.